# THE ZOHAR

LAITMAN
KABBALAH PUBLISHERS

Rav Michael Laitman, PhD

# THE ZOHAR

Copyright © 2007 by MICHAEL LAITMAN

All rights reserved
Published by Laitman Kabbalah Publishers
www.kabbalah.info info@kabbalah.info
1057 Steeles Avenue West, Suite 532, Toronto, ON, M2R 3X1, Canada
Bnei Baruch USA, 2009 85th street, #51, Brooklyn, NY 11214, USA
Printed in Canada

Library of Congress Cataloging-in-Publication Data

Laitman, Michael.

  The Zohar: annotations to the Ashlag commentary / Michael Laitman. ~ 1st ed.

     p. cm.

  ISBN 978-1-897448-09-0

1.  Ashlag, Yehudah. Perush ha-sulam. 2.  Zohar. 3.  Cabala.  I. Title.

  BM525.A59A7755 2009

  296.1>62~dc22

                              2008015080

Translation: David Brushin, Keren Applebaum
Copy Editors: Michael R. Kellogg, Mark Berelekhis
Editorial Assistance: Leah Goldberg
Proofreading: Lily Solopov, Natasha Sigmund, Sarah Talal
Layout: Luba Visotzki
Diagrams: Baruch Khovov, Luba Visotzki
Cover Design: Bat Sheva Brosh
Printing: Doron Goldin
Post Production: Uri Laitman
Executive Editor: Chaim Ratz

FIRST EDITION: FEBRUARY 2009
Second printing

# Table of Contents

# PROLOGUE

## ABOUT RABBI SHIMON BAR-YOCHAI[1]

In the second century CE, a single man was granted the spiritual knowledge that Kabbalists had accumulated for 3,000 years before his time. Rabbi Shimon Bar-Yochai (Rashbi) put it all on paper and then hid it, as humanity was not ready for it. Today, we are ready for the revelation of *The Book of Zohar*.

Rabbi Shimon Bar-Yochai (Rashbi), author of *The Book of Zohar* (*The Book of Radiance*) was a Tana—a great sage in the early Common Era centuries. Rashbi's name is tied to numerous legends, and he is mentioned constantly in the Talmud and in the Midrash, the sacred Hebrew texts of his time. He lived in Sidon and in Meron, and established a seminary in the Western Galilee.

Rashbi was born and raised in the Galilee (a mountainous region in today's Northern Israel). Even as a child, he was not like other children his age. Questions such as, "What is the purpose of my life?" "Who am I?" and "How is the world built?" plagued him and demanded answers.

In those days, life in Galilee was very harsh: the Romans persecuted Jews and continually invented new laws to make their lives more difficult. Among these laws was a decree that prohibited Jews from studying the Torah (then synonymous with Kabbalah).

1   The articles, "About Rabbi Shimon Bar-Yochai" and "About The Book of Zohar" are presented here courtesy of the paper *Kabbalah Today*.

However, despite the Romans' prohibition, Rashbi immersed himself in the Kabbalah and tried to understand its subtle teachings. He felt that beneath the Biblical stories was a profound and hidden truth, which held the answers to his persistent questions.

Gradually, Rabbi Shimon came to realize that he had to find a teacher who had already been through the spiritual path, gained experience, and could guide others up the spiritual ladder. He decided to join the group of the greatest Kabbalist of the time—Rabbi Akiva—a decision that turned out to be the turning point in Rashbi's life.

## STUDYING WITH RABBI AKIVA

Rabbi Shimon was an avid, devoted student, burning with desire to discover the Higher realms of reality. Before long, he was one of Rabbi Akiva's prime students. He studied with Rabbi Akiva for thirteen years, and achieved the highest levels on the spiritual ladder.

The Bar-Kokheva revolt abruptly ended the great days of Rabbi Akiva's seminary. Almost all of his 24,000 students died in plagues, and in fierce battles against the Romans. Of the 24,000 students, only five survived, and Rashbi was among them.

Rashbi was among the leaders of the Bar-Kokheva revolt against the Roman rule in the land of Israel. His resistance became even more fierce and unyielding when he'd learned how his teacher, Rabbi Akiva, had been ruthlessly executed.

The Talmud writes that once, when Rashbi spoke against the Roman rule, a fellow Jew heard him and alerted the Roman authorities. In consequence, Rashbi was tried in absentia and was sentenced to death. The Roman emperor sent men in search of him, but to their disappointment, Rashbi seemed to have vanished into thin air.

## THE CAVE AT PEQI'IN

Legends have it that Rashbi and his son fled to the Galilee, hid in a cave at Peqi'in, a village in the north of Israel, and remained there for thirteen years. During that time, they delved in the secrets of the wisdom of the hidden. Their efforts succeeded, and they discovered the entire system of creation.

After thirteen years in a cave, Rashbi heard that the Roman emperor had died. He could finally heave a sigh of relief. After leaving the cave, Rashbi gathered nine students and went with them to a small cave in Meron, known as

The Idra Raba (Great Assembly). With their help, he wrote *The Book of Zohar*, the most important book of Kabbalah.

Baal HaSulam described Rashbi and his students as the only beings who achieved perfection, the 125 spiritual degrees that complete the correction of one's soul. When he finished his commentary on *The Book of Zohar*, Baal HaSulam held a festive meal to celebrate its completion. At that celebration, he stated that "...prior to the days of the Messiah, it is impossible to be awarded all 125 degrees... except the Rashbi and his contemporaries, meaning the authors of *The Book of Zohar*. They were awarded all 125 degrees in completeness, even though they lived prior to the days of the Messiah. Hence, we often find in *The Zohar* that there will not be a generation such as the Rashbi's until the generation of the Messiah King. This is why his composition made such a strong impression in the world, since the secrets of the Torah in it occupy the level of all 125 degrees. This is also why it is said in *The Zohar* that *The Book of Zohar* will not be revealed except at the end of days, meaning in the days of the Messiah."

## THE IDRA RABA (GREAT ASSEMBLY) AND *THE BOOK OF ZOHAR*

Idra Raba is a cave located in the north of Israel, between Meron and Zephath. Rashbi took his students to this cave, and there he wrote *The Book of Zohar*. It is almost impossible to understand how great Rabbi Shimon Bar-Yochai really was. He belongs, as Baal HaSulam puts it, to the highest Inner Light. This is why he had to use Rabbi Abba to put his words into writing. In *The Book of Zohar*, the Rashbi tells his students: "I am arranging you as follows: Rabbi Abba will write, Rabbi Elazar, my son, will study orally, and the rest of the friends will converse in their hearts" (*Zohar*, Haazinu).

*The Book of Zohar* was written in the second century CE, not long after the ruin of the Second Temple and the beginning of the last exile of the people of Israel from its land. But even prior to the exile, Rashbi predicted that *The Book of Zohar* would only be revealed at the end of the exile. He stated that its appearance to the masses would symbolize the end of the spiritual exile: "...in it, they will come out of the exile with mercy" (*Zohar*, Naso).

It is also written in *The Book of Zohar* that its wisdom would be revealed to all toward the end of the six thousand years, the period allotted to the correction of humanity: "And when it is near the days of the Messiah, even infants in the world are destined to find the secrets of the wisdom, and know in them the ends and the calculations of redemption, and at that time it will be revealed to all" (*Zohar*, VaYera).

## THE REINCARNATION OF A UNIQUE SOUL

Rashbi is an incarnation of a unique soul, which coordinates and connects the Upper Force to every creation. This soul comes down into our world and incarnates in the patriarchs of Kabbalah. This is the order of its appearance: Abraham, Moses, Rabbi Shimon Bar-Yochai, the ARI (Rabbi Isaac Luria), and Rabbi Yehuda Ashlag (Baal HaSulam). Each incarnation of this soul promotes humanity to a new spiritual degree and leaves its mark in Kabbalah books, which serve the generations that follow.

An example of this process can be found in special sections of *The Zohar* called *Raia Meheimna* (The Loyal Shepherd). In these parts, Rashbi speaks from a state of clothing in Moses' soul. Another example of this is the book, *Shaar HaGilgulim* (*Gate of Reincarnations*), where Rashbi speaks from a state of clothing in the soul of the ARI.

*The Book of Zohar* is undoubtedly unique and one of the world's most renowned compositions. Since its writing, thousands of stories have been linked to *The Zohar*, and the book is still shrouded in mystery today. The fascination around it is so great that even though the book is completely incomprehensible to our generation without proper interpretation, millions of people diligently read it.

## RASHBI'S DEPARTURE

According to tradition, Rabbi Shimon Bar-Yochai passed away in the presence of his friends on *Lag BaOmer* (the 33rd day of the *Omer* count, which starts on the first day of Passover) of the year 160 CE, and was buried in Meron. With his death, the soul of a giant Kabbalist completed its task in our world.

Rashbi fulfilled his destination. Hundreds of thousands visit his gravesite yearly, trying to sense some of the Light that he had brought to the world. The greatest Kabbalists praise his composition and repeatedly claim that *The Book of Zohar* is destined to bring redemption to the world.

Rav Kook, the first Chief Rabbi of Israel, writes about the *Zohar* (*Ohr Yakar*): "This composition, called *The Book of Zohar*, is like Noah's Ark, where there were many kinds, but those kinds and families could not exist unless by entering the ark. ...**Thus the righteous will enter the secret of the Light of this composition to persist, and thus is the virtue of the composition, that immediately when engaging, with his desire for the love of God, it will draw him as a magnet draws the iron. And he will enter it to save his** soul and spirit and his correction. And even if he is wicked, there is no fear should he enter."

We are living in a historic time. The soul of Rashbi is completing its mission in our generation, and thanks to this spiritual giant, who lived nearly 2,000 years ago, the wisdom of Kabbalah is emerging so we may all ascend to a life of eternity and wholeness.

# ABOUT *THE BOOK OF ZOHAR*

*The Book of Zohar* is the most mysterious, and at the same time the most significant book of Kabbalah. In recent years, it has become increasingly clear that although *The Book of Zohar* was written eighteen centuries ago, it was actually written for our time. Rabbi Yehuda Ashlag (Baal HaSulam) opened it to us and rekindled what has long been forgotten from our hearts.

*The depth of the wisdom in The Book of Zohar is locked behind a thousand doors.*

–Rabbi Yehuda Ashlag (Baal HaSulam), "Preface to the Book of Zohar"

Since the dawn of humanity, unique individuals climbed the spiritual ladder and achieved the highest level of bonding with the Upper Force, the Creator. We call those people "Kabbalists."

Through this bonding, they came to understand that the whole of reality, from the highest spiritual worlds down to our world, is founded on love and bestowal. They realized that there is nothing in the world except for this Force, and that everything that happens in reality was made only to bring humanity to permanent existence with this sensation.

Kabbalists have searched and found the answers to every question they asked—the purpose of our lives, the structure of the world, and how we can determine our destiny. They wrote about what they discovered in books such as *Raziel Hamalaach (The Angel Raziel)*, *Sefer Yetzira (The Book of Creation)*, *Etz Chaim (The Tree of Life)*, and others.

Of all the books, the most seminal, mysterious, and profound is *The Book of Zohar (The Book of Radiance)*. *The Book of Zohar* describes the hidden system of the Upper Guidance. It depicts the worlds, the great powers that govern them, and how one who chooses to study Kabbalah affects his or her own fate and that of humanity.

*The Zohar* also explains how every event cascades from the Upper World to ours, and the dressings it acquires here. But what makes *The Zohar* unique is the fact that it was not written for its contemporaries; it was rather intended for a generation that would live two millennia later—our generation.

## REMOVING THE COVERS

*Our generation stands at the very threshold of redemption, if we only know how to spread the wisdom of the hidden in the masses.*

                         –Baal HaSulam, "Messiah's Horn"

The twentieth century has brought unprecedented changes. These opened the door to a whole new phase, which the greatest Kabbalists have been describing for centuries in their writings. The greatest change of all is that in this century, Kabbalists state that studying Kabbalah is not only permitted, it is a must!

It is written in *The Book of Zohar* itself that the wisdom of Kabbalah would begin its spreading from the year 1840. The great 18th century Kabbalist, The Vilna Gaon (GRA), wrote in his book *Kol HaTor* (*Voice of the Turtledove*) that the process of the revelation of the Kabbalah would begin in 1990. In his book, *Even Shlemah* (*A Perfect and Just Weight*), Chapter 11, he even stated that redemption *depends primarily* on the study of Kabbalah.

Rav Kook explained that "the great spiritual questions that were once resolved only for the great and the excellent, must now be resolved to various degrees within the entire nation" (*Eder HaYaker ve Ikvey HaTzon*, p. 144).

But it was Baal HaSulam who turned the words of the Kabbalists from a vision to a tangible reality. He clearly saw that the time had come to allow everyone to study *The Book of Zohar*. He claimed that by studying *The Zohar*, the whole of humanity would rise and attain the spiritual world.

With this vision in mind, Baal HaSulam devoted himself to composing a comprehensive, accurate, and systematic interpretation of *The Book of Zohar*. His goal was to unveil the book to the public and make it suitable for the souls of our generation.

In the introduction to his commentary on *The Zohar*, he explained why he wrote it: "I have named the commentary *HaSulam* (The Ladder) to indicate that the function of my commentary is as the function of any ladder. If you have an attic filled with abundance, you need only a ladder to climb it, and all the bounty in the world will be in your hands."

## ACCELERATING THE SPREAD OF THE WISDOM

All the Kabbalists dreamed of our generation, when the whole of humanity could discover the wondrous things they already had. They prayed that through reading the authentic sources they had left for us, we, too, would achieve bonding with the Upper Force, as did they. In his commentary on *The Book of Zohar*, Baal HaSulam threw us a rope, "a life buoy." In doing so, he paved our way to a future of abundance and prosperity.

Baal HaSulam called upon us to give greater weight to engagement in the wisdom of Kabbalah, and accelerate the spreading of the wisdom. He knew that only the wisdom of Kabbalah could elevate the world to the spiritual realm and into the eternity that Kabbalists had been experiencing throughout the generations.

Webster's Dictionary defines a generation as "a group of individuals born and living contemporaneously (at the same time)." In Kabbalah, however, a generation is a *spiritual* phase. According to great Kabbalists such as the Holy ARI, our generation—our spiritual phase—began in the sixteenth century.

The longer we wait with the spiritual ascension our generation is meant to achieve, the greater will be our discomfort. The spiritual realm, which determines what happens in our world, will increase its pressure on us until we decide to achieve this realm for ourselves.

In the words of the great Kabbalist Rabbi Avraham Azulai (in his introduction to the book, *Ohr ha Chama* (*Light of the Sun*)), "I have found it written that the above decree to not openly engage in the wisdom of truth was only for a time—until the end of the 1490. From then on ... the sentence has been lifted, and permission was given to engage in *The Book of Zohar*. And from the year 1540 it has become praiseworthy to engage in great numbers since it is by virtue of this the Messiah King will come, and not by another virtue. It is inappropriate to be negligent."

"But the wise shall understand that their elevation comes from the Creator, the Tree of Life. And they who are righteous shall shine like the brightness of the firmament" (Daniel, 12:3).[2]

"By virtue of Rabbi Shimon's composition, *The Book of Zohar*, from the Supernal Force that brings all things back to the Creator, at the end of days, the children of Israel will taste from the Tree of Life, which is *The Book of Zohar*; and they will be redeemed from exile by the Creator's mercy" (Naso, 90).

---

2   To facilitate comprehension of the spiritual meaning of ancient Hebrew sources, quotes are not direct translations, but rather reflect the Kabbalistic meaning of the texts.

# INTRODUCTION

*The Book of Zohar* narrates that Rabbi Shimon Bar-Yochai (Rashbi) and his son, Rabbi Aba, attained the level of Prophet Eliyahu (Elijah). Hence, it is said that Eliyahu himself visited their cave and taught them the Torah. (Incidentally, the cave in the village of Peqi'in still exists today.)

The author of *Divrey Yoel (The Words of Yoel)* wrote the following in the book *The Torah of Rashbi*: "Before Rabbi Shimon studied the secrets of the Torah, there was a rule in the cave—to settle disputes according to the opinion of Rabbi Yehuda, the author of the Talmud. However, after Rabbi Shimon left the cave, everything that he had written in *The Zohar* was considered to have exceeded all human attainments." Rashbi himself received the name *Butzina Kadisha* (Holy Candle), as he had attained the soul of Moshe (Moses).

Verdicts on legislative and procedural matters are rendered in accordance with the Talmud or *The Book of Zohar*, depending on where this matter is examined more strictly. If the matter is mentioned neither in the Talmud nor in *The Zohar*, then the decision is based on the source that best elucidates this matter. If the disputed matter is between the Talmud and the legislators, the decision is based on the assertion from *The Book of Zohar*. If the legislators themselves cannot come to an agreement on the matter in dispute, the decision is based on the opinion of *The Zohar* (*Mishna Brura*, 25, 42).

The great follower of Rashbi, an heir (next receiver) to his soul, Rabbi Isaac Luria (The Holy ARI) wrote that his soul was a return of the soul of Rabbi Shimon, and the soul of Rabbi Shimon was a return of the soul of Moshe (*Shaar HaGilgulim*, item 64). He also wrote that the soul of Moshe clothed in Rashbi to correct the soul of *Achiya HaShiloni* (Ahijah the Shilonite), who "corrupted" *Malchut* on account of the sin of King Yerav'am (Jeroboam), which prompted the transgression of all Israel. Hence, the soul of Rashbi appeared

15

to correct Israel's sins. The part of *The Zohar* titled *Raya Meheimna* (Loyal Shepherd) relates how Rashbi attained the soul of Moshe, merged with it, and attained the supernal wisdom.

In his works *Maranan ve Rabanan* and *Kli Yakar* (*Melachim*, 2, 12), the great HaChida also says that Rashbi's entire work lay in correction of the sin of *Achiya HaShiloni*.

As Rashbi says in the Talmud (*Sukkah*, 45, 2): "I can redeem the entire world from judgment from the day of my birth to the present day. And if my son is with me, from the day the world was created to the present day. And if Yotam Ben Uziyahu is with us, from the day the world was created to its end." The book of *Melachim* narrates about Yotam Ben Uziyahu (20, 15).

After the verdict was lifted, Rashbi founded his seminary in the settlement of Tekoa and in the village of Meron. There he taught his disciples Kabbalah and wrote *The Book of Zohar*, thereby revealing what was forbidden to reveal from the time of Israel's reception of the Torah (*Tikuney Zohar*, *Hakdamah*, p. 17).

However, to write down all the secrets of the Torah, Rabbi Shimon had to express them in a secret form. Rashbi's disciple, Rabbi Aba, had a unique quality to his soul. This quality enabled him to convey spiritual knowledge in a secret, concealed form. Hence, Rabbi Shimon asked his disciple to express his thoughts for him, that is, to commit Rashbi's thoughts to paper. The ARI explained it in the following way: "*The Book of Zohar* must remain concealed until the generation of the coming of the *Mashiach* (Messiah), as through the study of this book will humankind return from its spiritual exile" (The ARI, *Shaar HaHakdamot*, *Hakdamah*, p. 3). That is why Rabbi Aba wrote the teachings of Rabbi Shimon in Aramaic, as it is the reverse side of Hebrew.

The ARI wrote (*Maamarey Rashbi* (Articles of Rashbi), p. 100) that the writing of *The Zohar* in a secret form was possible because the soul of Rabbi Aba originated from the Surrounding Light, and not from the Inner Light. For this reason, the ARI explained, he could express the most supernal wisdom in a secret form as simple stories.

(Rabbi Shimon lived approximately to the age of eighty and passed away on the holiday of *Lag BaOmer*, the eighteenth day in the month *Iyar*, surrounded by his disciples, and recognized by the entire nation. This day is celebrated as the holiday of Light. Rabbi Shimon's body was buried in a cave off Mount Meron, and the body of his son, Rabbi Elazar, is buried a few meters from him.)

Like the subsequent compositions of the ARI and other Kabbalists (evidently, such is the lot of all true spiritual books), *The Book of Zohar* was concealed for some 1,100 years in a cave near Meron, since the day it was written, until an Arab man found it and sold it in the market as wrapping cloth.

Part of the torn sheets fell into the hands of a sage, who recognized and appreciated the value of the writings. After a long search, he recovered many sheets from refuse bins or bought them from spice vendors, who were selling their merchandise wrapped in the sheets of *The Zohar*. It was out of these recovered sheets that the book (as we know it today) was compiled.

For many centuries, since that time until today, *The Book of Zohar* has been the subject of controversy. Philosophers, scientists, and other "sages," still debate it today. Yet, the fact remains that only a Kabbalist, one who ascends to a particular spiritual degree, attains what this book conveys. To all other people, it seems like a collection of narratives, stories, and ancient philosophy. Only those who do not comprehend this book argue over it; but Kabbalists know for certain that Rashbi's book is the greatest source of spiritual attainment that the Creator imparted upon the people in this world.

Although *The Book of Zohar* was written in the second century, only Rabbi Yehuda Ashlag was able to provide a full commentary on it in the 1930s-40s. The reason for the concealment of *The Zohar* from the second century to thirteenth century and the lack of a complete commentary on it for eighteen centuries is explained in the "Introduction to the Book of Zohar."

Rabbi Ashlag called his commentary *HaSulam* (The Ladder) because by studying it, one can ascend the spiritual degrees of attainment of the Upper Worlds as one would climb a ladder in our world. Following the publishing of the *Sulam* commentary, Rabbi Ashlag received the epithet *Baal HaSulam* (Owner of the Ladder), as it is customary among sages of the Torah to call a person not by his name, but according to his highest attainment.

## THE BOOK OF ZOHAR CONTAINS:

**1. *Hakdamat Sefer HaZohar*** (*The Introduction of the Book of Zohar*)—containing several articles that fully reveal the inner meaning of the Torah.

**2. *Sefer HaZohar*** (*The Book of Zohar*)—divided into parts and chapters that correspond to the weekly portions of the Torah:

The Book of **Beresheet** (*Genesis*): *Beresheet, Noach, Lech Lecha, Vayera, Chaiey Sarah, Toldot, Vayetze, Vayishlach, Vayeshev, Miketz, Vayigash, Vayichi.*

The Book of **Shemot** (*Exodus*): *Shemot, Vayera, Bo, Beshalach, Yitro, Mishpatim, Terumah (Safra de Tzniuta), Tetzaveh, Ki Tissa, Veyikahel, Pekudey.*

**The Book of Vayikra** (Leviticus): Vayikra, Tzav, Shmini, Tazria, Metzura, Acharey, Kedushim, Emor, BaHar, Vechukotay.

**The Book of Bamidbar** (Numbers): Bamidbar, Naso (Idra Raba), Baalotcha, Shlach Lecha, Korach, Chukat, Balak, Pinchas, Matot.

**The Book of Devarim** (Deuteronomy): VeEtchanen, Ekev, Shoftim, Titze, Vayelech, Haazinu (Idra Zuta).

**3. Zohar Hadash** (The New Zohar): additions to the weekly chapters:

Beresheet, Noach, Lech Lecha, Vayera, Vayetze, Vayeshev, Bashalach, Yitro, Terumah, Ki Titze, Tzav, Acharey, BaHar, Naso, Chukat, Balak, Matot, VeEtchanen, Ki Titze, Ki Tavo.

**4. Additional books in The Book of Zohar** that are not a direct commentary on the Torah:

Idra Raba, Idra Zuta, Safra de Tzniuta, Raza de Razin, Tosefta, Raya Mi'emna, Ashmatot, Sitrey Torah, Sitrey Otiot, and Tikuney Zohar.

**5. Midrash HaNe'elam** (The Commentary on the Writings): Song of Songs, Ruth, Eicha (Lamentations)—and on the Torah (Pentateuch).

Baal HaSulam wrote the commentary on the portions of The Zohar that are known to us. His main commentaries in the "Introduction to the Book of Zohar" and the chapter "Beresheet" are expressed in terms of man's spiritual work. The most valuable articles of The Zohar for the science of Kabbalah are Idra Raba, Idra Zuta, and Safra de Tzniuta. All of them are expressed in the language of Kabbalah. Besides these articles, the rest of The Zohar is written in the language of Midrash.

In its original form, The Book of Zohar—written by Rabbi Aba sixteen centuries ago—was not divided into weekly chapters. Its volume was several times larger than the text that reached us; it expounded not only the Torah, but also twenty-four other books of the Bible (Pentateuch, Prophets, and Writings).

Besides The Book of Zohar itself, Rabbi Shimon's book of Tikkunim (corrections) had reached us, as well. It comprises seventy commentaries on the first word of the Torah, Beresheet (in the beginning), since it includes everything.

This book offers a semantic translation of The Zohar itself, Rabbi Yehuda Ashlag's The Sulam commentary, and my own explanations. The book also contains the first part of The Book of Zohar—Hakdamat Sefer HaZohar (Introduction of The Book of Zohar).

At the beginning of the text, the semantic translation is given in bold script. *The Sulam* commentary and my explanations are in regular script or *italics* because it turned out to be extremely difficult to separate my explanations from Rabbi Ashlag's holy texts. The numbers at the beginning of the items correspond to the numbers of the items in *The Book of Zohar* with *The Sulam* commentary, vol. 1.

The reason for the interlacing of texts is the need to explain the meaning of *The Zohar* in several languages simultaneously: a) the language of Kabbalah (*Sefirot, Partzufim, Gematria,* and worlds), b) the language of spiritual work (emotions), c) the language of the Torah (narrative), and d) the language of the Talmud (judicial).

To comprehend the style of *The Book of Zohar*, I recommend the reader to return to the translation of the original text after reading and mastering the commentary.

*The Book of Zohar*, like the whole of the Torah, speaks exclusively of man (creation) and his relationship with the Creator. The Torah attaches worldly appellations to all of man's inner properties. Thus, the aspiration to the Creator is called "Israel," and the aspiration to selfish reception of pleasures is called "nations of the world." However, there is no connection whatsoever between these names in the Torah and the Jews and other nations in our world. Kabbalah appeals to *man*, to creation!

The book contains articles commented upon in the language of Kabbalah, and others commented upon in the language of emotions, which is easier to understand for the beginner. The reader can begin the study of the book with such articles as "Night of the Bride," and "Who rejoices on holidays." Nevertheless, a complete study of *The Zohar* entails systematic learning of the material. The more accustomed we are to Kabbalah, the more it permeates our hearts, and it can only be mastered by repeatedly reviewing the studied material.

*Rav Michael Laitman*

# List of Abbreviations and Explanations

**AA**—Arich Anpin—the *Partzuf* of *Hochma*, the central, initial *Partzuf* in the world of *Atzilut*, from which all the other *Partzufim* originate.

**Aba**—Father —the *Partzuf* of *Hochma*.

**Ima**—Mother—the *Partzuf* of *Bina*.

**ZA**—*Zeir Anpin*—Son (with regard to AVI).

**ZON**—ZA and *Nukva*—*Malchut*.

**Nukva, Malchut**—a *Sefira* (singular for *Sefirot*) or *Partzuf* that receives from all the preceding *Partzufim* (plural for *Partzuf*). *Malchut* of the world of *Atzilut* is the sum of all the creatures, all human souls. For this reason it is called *Knesset Israel* (The Assembly of Israel).

**Israel**—the property of "bestowal," altruism. This is the property of the Creator, the property of *Bina*. *Israel* derives from the Hebrew words *Yashar*—straight, and *El*—the Creator. Thus, *Israel* is the property of aspiring to attain equivalence of form with the Creator. The "nations of the world" are the aspiration to selfish reception of pleasure. Naturally, these two properties are present in everyone, and Kabbalah is the method for the development of the property of Israel within man, with the purpose of attaining the Creator in this life.

**Kli** (vessel) egoistic desires and aspirations are not considered a *Kli*. A *Kli* is the corrected desires, suitable for reception of Light. These are altruistic desires with a screen that has transformed them from egoism into altruism.

The human heart that receives all sensations is called the *Kli* (vessel) of reception of sensations. The spiritual vessel, the only vessel that *The Zohar* speaks of, is the desire to bestow upon the Creator: to hand over all of man's desires to the Creator, as though saying that he agrees with all his heart to relinquish all of himself for His sake. Such a complete and true intention is called "*Lishma*" (for the Creator's sake).

| SEFIROT | THE CREATOR'S NAMES |
|---------|---------------------|
| KETER | EKYEH=Aleph-Hey-Yod-Hey |
| HOCHMA | YAH= Yod-Hey |
| BINA | HaVaYaH with Nikud Elokim |
| HESED | EL=Aleph-Lamed |
| GEVURA | ELOKIM= Aleph-Lamed-Hey-Yod-Mem |
| TIFFERET | HaVaYaH with Nikud of Shvah-Holam-Kamatz |
| NETZAH and HOD | TZEVAOT |
| YESOD | SHADDAY=Shin-Dalet-Yod or EL=Aleph-Lamed CHAI=Chet-Yod |
| MALCHUT | ADNI=Aleph-Dalet-Nun-Yod |

**Mittuk** (sweetening/mitigation) of a restriction law. Restriction is a ban for *Malchut* to receive Light. This ban is lifted when *Malchut* is corrected by the properties of *Bina*.

**Zivug**—coupling—is translated as a sexual union between a man and a woman in this world. Since spiritual actions are *absolutely detached* from the way we would normally perceive them, I have chosen to use the Hebrew term *Zivug*, as it is more abstractedly perceived by people with no knowledge of Hebrew. This will help prevent confusions based on previously existing conceptions. The spiritual *Zivug* is an aspiration of the Upper One (ZA—male part) to pass the Light (pleasure) to the lower one (*Malchut*—female part). In doing so, both desires are completely selfless, as in the example of the guest and the host.

**PBP**—*Panim be Panim* (face to face). This state occurs when a *Zachar* (male *Sefira*), or *Aba* (father), passes *Ohr Hochma* (Light of Wisdom) to the female *Sefira*, or *Ima* (mother), for the subsequent transfer to the children (ZON). The same relationships of *ABA* (see below) and *PBP* also transpire between their children, ZON (ZA and *Malchut*).

**ABA** – *Achor be Achor*, back to back (pronounced *Ach be Ach*). If *Partzuf Aba* (*Hochma*) has *Ohr Hochma*, but is unwilling to pass it on to *Partzuf Ima* (*Bina*), and if *Ima* also does not want to receive it, such a relationship between them is called back to back. The same relationship can exist between ZA and *Malchut*.

**Hesed**—mercy, compassion, altruism, *Ohr Hassadim* (the Light of Mercy, compassion, and altruism). It appears only within a *Kli* (desire) that wishes to give selflessly and be similar to the Creator. This is the property of the *Sefira* or *Partzuf* of *Bina*. *Bina* of the world of *AK* (*Adam Kadmon*) is called *SAG*. *Bina* of the world of *Atzilut* is called *Ima*, the Supernal Mother, *YESHSUT*, and *AVI*. The Light of *Bina* is the pleasure of being similar to the Creator's properties; hence, this Light (sensation) is the most reliable protection from the impure forces. And the *Kli* that possesses the properties of *Bina* is unable to transgress, as its desire is solely to bestow.

**KHB**—*Keter-Hochma-Bina* (pronounced *Kahab*). These are the first three *Sefirot* that form the *Rosh* (head) of the *Partzuf*. The *Rosh* decides how much pleasure the *Partzuf* can accept not for its own sake but for the sake of the Creator. This Light descends from the *Rosh* to the *Guf* (body).

**HBD**—*Hochma-Bina-Daat* (pronounced *Habad*). This is the same as *Keter-Hochma-Bina* (the *Rosh* of the *Partzuf*). *Sefira Daat* is not a *Sefira*, but the request (also known as *MAN*) of *ZON* (*Zeir Anpin* and *Nukva*). *Daat* is the appeal of *ZON* to *Bina* regarding their desire to receive *Ohr Hochma* from her. This prayer of *ZON* is called *MAN*, for it ascends to *Bina* and evokes in *Bina* (*Ima*—their mother) the desire to bestow upon her children—*ZON*. *MAN* in *Bina* is called *Sefira Daat*. This is not a *Sefira* like the other ten *Sefirot*; it is rather a request. However, to stress this state, we use the name *HBD* instead of *KHB*.

**HGT**—*Hesed-Gevura-Tifferet* (pronounced *Hagat*). These are the *Sefirot* of the *Guf* (body), similar to the *Sefirot* of the *Rosh*: *Hesed* is tantamount to *Keter*, *Gevura* is tantamount to *Hochma*, and *Tifferet* is tantamount to *Bina*. They are called *GE* (see below) of the body.

**NHYM**—*Netzah-Hod-Yesod-Malchut* (pronounced *Nehim*). These *Sefirot* receive from the *Sefirot HGT* (*GE*). Since they receive and have the will to receive, they are called *AHP* of the body.

**GE**—*Galgalta-Eynaim* (skull and eyes). *Sefirot Keter-Hochma*-and *GAR* of *Bina*. These *Sefirot* do not have the will to receive and wish only to bestow. Hence, they cannot become egoistic.

**NRN**—*Nefesh-Ruach-Neshama* (pronounced *Naran*). This is the Light that fills the small *Partzuf*. *Katnut* (small state) is when the *Partzuf* has the strength (a screen) only to bestow, but is unable to receive for the Creator's sake, despite its desire to do so. In this case, the *Partzuf* has only *Ohr Hassadim* (Light of Mercy), but not *Ohr Hochma* (Light of Wisdom). This is why it is considered a small *Partzuf*, without strength and reason, similar to a child in our world.

**AHP**—*Awzen-Hotem-Peh* (ear-nose-mouth), pronounced *Ahap*. These are *Sefirot* *ZAT* of *Bina-ZA-Malchut*, which possess a will to receive. Therefore, in the absence of a proper screen (resistance to that desire), they become egoistic. A *Partzuf* without a screen on its *AHP* is called *Katan* (small) and its state is called *Katnut* (smallness, incompleteness). It is like a child in our world, as this *Partzuf*, too, has no strength (screen), and can therefore have only *Ohr Hassadim* without *Ohr Hochma*).

**Gadlut**—big state. A *Partzuf* with a screen (strength to resist its egoistic nature) to not only refrain from receiving for its own sake, but to receive not for its own sake (as in the example of the guest and the host. In this case, the *Partzuf* fills all of its desires (all ten *Sefirot*) with the Lights of *Hassadim* and *Hochma*.

**First Big State**—*Gadlut Aleph*, the attainment of the Light of *Neshama*.

**Second Big State**—*Gadlut Bet*, the attainment of the Light of *Haya*.

**Ohr Hochma**—Light of Wisdom. This Light fills the *Kelim* (vessels/desires) of reception. It comes only if there is a screen on altruistic reception.

**Ateret Yesod**—literally "foreskin," the place of union between Israel and the Creator. After the second restriction, it is forbidden to make a *Zivug* (spiritual coupling) on *Malchut* herself due to the absence of the screen. However, a *Zivug* can be made on the properties that *Malchut* received from ZA, called *Ateret Yesod*. Just as the desires of *Malchut* herself are cut off, the foreskin is circumcised, and the desires that remain within her are those received from ZA, called *Ateret Yesod*. On these desires, *Malchut* can make a *Zivug* with ZA, and receive the Light of *Hochma*. Naturally, this is not the same Light of *Hochma* that *Malchut* would receive if she were able to make a *Zivug* on her desires, that is, on herself, on her own properties, called "the central point of creation," the truly egoistic desires. *Malchut* will be able to do that only after 6,000 years, at the end of correction. But before that happens, these desires are called the mark of union with the Creator, since a *Zivug* on *Ateret Yesod* brings her closer to the Creator.

Ateret Yesod is also *Malchut de Malchut* that remains after the circumcision, the removal of the *Orla* (foreskin). This is the corrected part of *Malchut*, her unification with *Sefira Yesod*, upon which a *Zivug* can be made while still during the 6,000 years, thus bringing *Malchut* to the end of correction.

**NRNHY**—*Nefesh-Ruach-Neshama-Haya-Yechida* (pronounced **Naranhay**). This Light fills the big *Partzuf*, consisting of GE and AHP.

**Ohr** (Light)—pleasure, the sensation of the Creator. *Ohr* should always be interpreted as the same concept, for although the term is used in general, all of its synonyms are implied!

**Kli** (vessel)—desire, creature. Like *Ohr*, the word *Kli* is used in general, but all of its synonyms are implied!

**Gematria**—numerical value of a letter, or a combination of letters and words. This is a special way of recording spiritual information.

**Parsa**—firmament, the division between the world of *Atzilut* and the worlds BYA. The *Parsa* divides the ten *Sefirot* into two parts: the altruistic *Kelim* of bestowal (GAR, KHB, and GE) and the *Kelim* of reception (ZON or *Bina-ZA-Malchut*), for *Bina* deliberately fell into ZA (AHP) with the purpose of correcting him. *Malchut*, which ascends above *Bina* and stands below *Hochma*, is called *Parsa* or "firmament," and separates GE from AHP.

**ZAT, ZAK**—the seven *Sefirot Hesed, Gevura, Tifferet, Netzah, Hod, Yesod, Malchut* (HGT NHYM).

**VAT, VAK**—the six *Sefirot Hesed, Gevura, Tifferet, Netzah, Hod, Yesod* (HGT NHY, pronounced *Hagat Nehy*).

**De** – the preposition 'of' in a possessive meaning. For example, *Malchut* **de** *Atzilut* means *Malchut* **of** the world of *Atzilut*.

**English translation**—Whenever it says so in parenthesis, this refers to the books of the Torah (Pentateuch), *Nevi'im* (Prophets), and *Ketuvim* (Writings/Hagiographa), published by Mosad HaRav Kook, in Hebrew with English translation. For example, (*Yeshayahu*, 11:9; English translation p. XXX, 9) means that if you open page XXX in the book of Prophets, what you are looking for will be in sentence number nine. When the original source is indicated, it is recommended to refer to it there and then to read at least the passage that the quoted saying is ascribed to. This will help you to see even more clearly that the Torah, using an allegorical, figurative language, speaks only of the spiritual world and man's ascension to it, and not at all about history or about our world.

**Garments**—attributes, desires, *Kelim*. Generally, the garments in question are those that *Malchut* receives from *Bina*.

**Huppah**—a wedding baldachin, a canopy under which a marriage ceremony takes place.

**Nartik**—the covering of ZA; same as the *Huppah*.

**Adornments**—the Light of *Hassadim*, Light of *Bina*, which she passes into *Malchut*. This corrects *Malchut*, and enables her to receive the Light of *Hochma* in the Light of *Hassadim*.

**Orla**—foreskin on the *Sefira Yesod*, the place of the *Zivug* between ZA and *Malchut*. The *Orla* must be removed, for during the 6,000 years, it is impossible to make a *Zivug* (intention) on *Malchut* herself and receive for the Creator's sake. Only a *Zivug* on the union of *Malchut* with ZA can be made. This is called *Ateret Yesod*, the part of the *Sefira Yesod* that remains after the cutting off of the *Orla*. *Orla* is also *Malchut de Malchut*, or the impure forces.

**Ima**—Mother—*Bina* with regard to *Malchut*, who is the daughter.

**Daughter**—*Malchut* with regard to *Bina*, mother.

**Kodesh ha Kodashim**—Holy of Holies—the Light of GAR—*Neshama-Haya-Yechida*.

**Question**—the sensation of lack of the Light of *Hochma* in *Malchut*.

**Sela**—rock or truth. The name of *Malchut*.

**Shechina**—Divinity—the sensation (appearance, vision) of the Creator to those who attain Him. *Malchut* in the state of reception of the Light (the Creator) is called *Shechina*. The sensation of the Creator, the place where one experiences the Creator is called *Shechina*.

**Techum**—zone—the distance beyond the bounds of which one is forbidden to go on *Shabbat* (the Sabbath). *Techum Shabbat* constitutes the maximal distance within which one can move about during Sabbath.

**Sigim**—dross—impure desires that exist within pure desires. Man's work is to separate the two, and to gradually correct the *Sigim*. The term *Sigim* comes from SAG, for they appeared as a result of the breaking of the *Kelim* of the world of *Nekudim*, which refer to the system of the *Partzufim* of *Partzuf* SAG. The term *Sigim* found its way from Kabbalah into spoken Hebrew.

**SHACH**—*Shin-Chaf*—300 + 20 = 320 fragments of the broken vessel.

**RAPACH**—*Reish-Peh-Chet*—200 + 80 + 8 = 288 fragments of the broken vessel, which one can and must be corrected during the 6,000 years, by climbing the 6,000 steps of the spiritual ladder.

**Lev ha Even**—Stony Heart—*Lev* = *Lamed-Bet* = 30 + 2 = 32 fragments into which *Malchut* had broken. These fragments of *Malchut* cannot be corrected and made altruistic; one can only refrain from using these desires. *Lev ha Even* is corrected only after the 6,000 years, that is, after the Creator Himself corrects the 288 fragments within man. It becomes completely altruistic and receives the name *Lev Basar* (heart of flesh).

**Lo Lishma**—not for the sake of the Creator. Since nothing exists in creation but the Creator and man, if something is not done "for the sake of the Creator," it is done "for one's own sake." Thus, *Lo Lishma* denotes man's egoistic intention.

**Lishma**—for the Creator's sake. Man's selfless intention to act only to please and bring joy to the Creator.

**Four angels that participate in the creation of man**—the four basic properties of nature: mercy—*Hesed*, justice—*Tzedek*, truth—*Emet*, and peace—*Shalom*.

**Eretz Israel**—Land of Israel—*Yetzira* of this world. *Yerushalaim* (Jerusalem) is *Ateret Yesod* in *Malchut*.

## ORIGINAL NAMES AND THEIR EQUIVALENTS ACCEPTED IN THE ENGLISH TRANSLATION

**Aaron** – Aaron
**Amon** – Ammon
**Ana'el** – Anahel
**Anafiel** – Anafiel
**Ariel** – Ariel
**Avraham** – Abraham
**Bat Sheva** – Bathsheba
**Benayahu** – Benaiah
**Betzalel** – Betzalel
**Bil'am** – Balaam
**Chagai** – Haggai
**Chava** – Eve
**Eden** – Eden
**Eicha** – Eichah
**Elisha** – Elisha
**Eliyahu** – Elijah
**Esav** – Esau
**Ester** – Esther
**Ezra** – Ezra
**Gavri'el** – Gabriel
**Gazaria** – Gazardiel
**Hanoch** – Eunuch
**Havakuk** – Habakkuk
**Iyov** – Job
**Korach** – Korach

**Leah** – Leah
**Lilit** – Lilith
**Machaniel** – Manhiel
**Matat** – Metatron
**Micha** – Micah
**Moav** – Moab
**Moshe** – Moses
**Nachum** – Nahum
**Navuchadnetzar** – Nebuchadnezzar
**Nechemia** – Nehemiah
**Noach** – Noah
**Ovadia** – Obadiah
**Petachia** – Petahyah
**Pinchas** – Pinchas
**Pisgania** – Pesagniyah
**Rahel** – Rachel
**Rivka** – Rebecca
**Rut** – Ruth
**Sandalphon** – Sandalphon
**Shet** – Seth
**Shimon** – Simeon
**Shlomo** – Solomon
**Shmuel** – Samuel
**Tamar** – Tamar
**Tzefania** – Zephaniah

Tzur – Tyre
Yaakov – Jacob
Yehoyada – Jehoiada
Yechezkel – Ezekiel
Yehoshua – Joshua
Yehudah – Judah
Yerushalaim – Jerusalem

Yeshayahu – Isaiah
Yirmiyahu – Jeremiah
Yishmael – Ishmael
Yitzchak – Isaac
Yosef – Joseph
Zachariah – Zechariah
Zvuliel – Zebuliel

# ORIGINAL TITLES AND THEIR EQUIVALENTS ACCEPTED IN THE ENGLISH TRANSLATION

Beresheet – Genesis
Shemot – Exodus
Vayikra – Leviticus
Bamidbar – Numbers
Devarim – Deuteronomy
Kohelet – Ecclesiastes
Shmuel 1 and 2 – Samuel 1 and 2
Melachim 1 and 2 – Kings 1 and 2
Divrey HaYamim – Chronicles
Mishley – Proverbs
Tehilim – Psalms
Shir HaShirim – Song of Songs
Shoftim – Judges

# An Example of the Original Text of The Zohar

א) רבי חזקיה פתחת כתיב, כשושנה בין החוחים. מאן שושנה, דא כנסת ישראל. בגין דאית שושנה ואית שושנה, מה שושנה דאיהי בין החוחים אית בה סומק וחוור, אוף כנסת ישראל אית בה דין ורחמי. מה שושנה אית בה תליסר עלין אוף כנסת ישראל אית בה תליסר מכילן דרחמי דסחרין לה מכל סטרהא.אוף אלקים דהכא, משעתא דאדכר, אפיק תליסר תיבין לסחרא לכנסת ישראל ולנטרא לה.

ב) ולבתר אדכר זמנא אחרא. אמאי אדכר זמנא אחרא, בגין לאפקא חמש עלין תקיפין דסחרין לשושנה. ואינון חמש, אקרון ישועות.ואינון חמש תרעין.ועל רזא דא כתיב, כוס ישועות אשא , דא כוס של ברכה. כוס של ברכה אצטריך למהוי על חמש אצבען ולא יתיר, כגוונא דשושנה דיתבא על חמש עלין תקיפין דוגמא דחמש אצבען. ושושנה, דא איהו כוס של ברכה, מאלקים תנינא עד אלקים תליתאה חמש תיבין. מכאן ולהלאה, אור דאתברי ואתגניז , ואתכליל בברית ההוא דעאל בשושנה ואפיק בה זרעא. ודא אקרי עץ קיימא באות ברית ממש.

ג) וכמה דדיוקנא דברית אזדרע בארבעין ותרין זווגין ההואזרעא. כך אזדרע שמא גליפא מפרש, בארבעין ותרין אתוון דעובדא דבראשית.

ד) בראשית. רבי שמעון פתח הנצנים נראו בארץ, הנצנים דא עובדא דבראשית. נראו בארץ, אימתי, ביום השלישי, דכתיב ותוצא הארץ, כדין נראו בארץ. עת הזמיר הגיע, דא יום רביעי, דהוה ביה זמיר עריצים, מארת חסר. וקול התור, דא יום חמישי, דכתיב ישרצו המים וגו', למעבד תולדות. נשמע דא יום ששי, דכתיב נעשה אדם, דהוה עתיד למקדם עשיה לשמיעה דכתיב הכא נעשה אדם, וכתיב התם נעשה ונשמע. בארצנו, דא יום שבת, דאיהו דוגמת ארץ החיים.

ה) ר"א הנצנים אלין אינון אבהן,דעאלו במחשבה, ועאלו בעלמא דאתי ,ואתגניזו תמן. ומתן נפקו בגניזו ואטמירו גו נביאי קשוט, אתיליד יוסף, ואטמרו ביה. עאל יוסף בארעא קדישא ונציב לון תמן, וכדין נראו בארץ ואתגלו תמן. ואימתי אתחזן. בשעתא דאתגלי קשת

בעלמא, דהא בשעתא דקשת אתחזי כדין אתגליין אינון, ובההיא שעתא עת הזמיר הגיע עדן לקצץ חייבין מעלמא. אמאי אשתזיבו. בגין דהנצבים נראו בארץ, ואלמלא דנראו לא אשתארון בעלמא , ועלמא לא אתקיים.

ו) ומאן מקיים עלמא וגרים לאבהן דאתגליין, קל ינוקי דלעאן באורייתא, ובגין אינון רביין דעלמא, עלמא אשתזיב. לקבליהון, תורי זהב נעשה לך, אלין אינון ינוקי רביין עולמין, דכתיב ועשית שנים כרובים זהב.

ז) בראשית. ר' אלעזר פתח, שאו מרום עיניכם וראו מי ברא אלה. שאו מרום עיניכם. לאן אתר. לאתר דכל עיינין תליאן ליה, ומאן איהו. פתח עינים. ותמן תנדעון, דהאי סתים עתיקא דקיימא לשאלה, ברא אלה. ומאן איהו, מ"י. ההוא דאקרי מקצה השמים לעילא, דכלא קיימא ברשותיה. ועל דקיימא לשאלה, ואיהו בארח סתים ולא

אתגליא, אקרי מ"י דהא לעילא לית תמן שאלה. והאי קצה השמים אקרי מ"י.

ח) ואית אחרא לתתא ואקרי מ"ה, מה בין האי להאי, אלא קדמאה סתימאה דאקרי מ"י קיימא לשאלה, כיון דשאל בר נש ומפשפש לאסתכלא ולמנדע מדרגא לדרגא עד סוף כל דרגין, כיון דמטי תמן מ"ה, מה ידעת, מה אסתכלתא, מה פשפשתא, הא כלא סתים כדקדמיתא.

ט) ועל רזא דנא כתיב, מה אעידך מה אדמה לך. כד אתחריב בי מקדשא, נפיק קלא ואמר, מה אעידך ומה אדמה

לך, בההוא מ"ה אעידך, בכל יומא ויומא אסהידת בך  מיומין
קדמאין. דכתיב העדותי בכם היום את השמים ואת הארץ.
ומה אדמה לך, בההוא גוונא  ממש, עתרית לך בעטרין
קדישין, עבדית לך שלטנו על עלמא, דכתיב הזאת העיר
שיאמרו כלילת יפי וגו'. קרינא לך ירושלם הבנויה כעיר
שחברה לה.  מה אשוה לך,  כגוונא דאנת יתבה, הכי הוא
כביכול לעילא,  כגוונא דלא עאלין השתא בך עמא קדישא
בסדרא קדישין, הכי אומינא לך דלא איעול אנא לעילא עד
דיעלון בך אוכלסך  לתתא.    ודא איהו נחמה דילך, הואיל
דדרגא דא אשוה לך בכלא.  והשתא דאנת הכא, גדול  כים
שברך. ואי תימא דלית לך קיימא ואסוותא,  מ"י ירפא לך,
ודאי ההוא דרגא סתימאה  עלאה, דכלא קיימא ביה, ירפא
לך וייוקים לך.

י) מ"י קצה השמים לעילא, מ"ה קצה  השמים לתתא, ודא
ירית יעקב דאיהו מבריח מן הקצה אל הקצה,  מן  הקצה
קדמאה דאיהו מ"י, אל הקצה בתראה דאיהו מ"ה, בגין
דקאים באמצעיתא. ועל דא, מי  ברא אלה.

יא) אמר ר"ש אלעזר בני פסוק מילך, ויתגלי סתימא דרזא
עלאה דבני עלמא לא  ידעין. שתיק רבי אלעזר. בכה רבי
שמעון, וקאים רגעא חדא. א"ר שמעון,  אלעזר, מאי אלה. אי
תימא כבכיא ומזלי, הא אתחזן תמן תדיר.  ובמ"ה אתבריאו,
כד"א  בדבר ה' שמים נעשו. אי על מלין סתימין, לא לכתוב
אלה דהא אתגלייא איהו.

יב) אלא  רזא דא לא אתגליא, בר יומא חד דהוינא על כיף
ימא, ואתא אליהו ואמר לי, ר' ידעת  מה הוא  מי ברא אלה.
אמינא ליה, אלין שמיא וחיליהון, עובדא דקב"ה דאית ליה
לבר  נש לאסתכלא בהו, ולברכא ליה, דכתיב כי אראה

שמיך מעשה אצבעותיך וגו׳ ה׳ אדונינו מה אדיר שמך בכל
הארץ.

יג) א״ל, ר׳: מלה סתימה הוה קמי קב״ה, וגלי במתיבתא
עלאה, ודא הוא. בשעתא דסתימא דכל סתימין בעא
לאתגלייא, עבד ברישא נקודה חדא, ודא סליק למהוי
מחשבה. צייר בה כל ציורין חקק בה כל
גליפין.

יד) ואגליף גו בוצינא קדישא סתימא גליפו דחד ציורא
סתימאה קדש קדישין בניינא עמיקא דנפיק מגו מחשבה,
ואקרי מ״י שירותא לבניינא קיימא ולא קיימא. עמיק וסתים
בשמא. לא אקרי אלא מ״י. בעא לאתגלייא ולאתקרי בשמא
דא, ואתלבש בלבוש יקר דנהיר, וברא אל״ה, וסליק אל״ה
בשמא. אתחברון אתוון אלין באלין ואשתלים בשמא אלהים.
ועד לא ברא אלה לא סליק בשמא אלהים. ואינון דחבו
בעגלא. על רזא דנא אמרו אלה אלהיך ישראל.

טו) וכמה דאשתתף מ״י באלה, הכי הוא שמא דאשתתף
תדיר,

ברזא דא אתקיים עלמא. ופרח אליהו ולא חמינא ליה. ומניה
ידענא מלה דאוקימנא על רזא וסתרא דילה. אתא רבי אלעזר
וכלהו חברייא ואשתטחו קמיה, בכו ואמרו, אלמלא לא
אתינא לעלמא אלא למשמע דא די.

א

## רבי חזקיה

**נ"א רבי אלעזר**

בזהרי חמה ובנוסחת א"י

### מאמר השושנה

**א) פתח, כתיב** א) א) א) כשושנה בין החוחים. מאן שושנה, דא ב) ב) כנסת ישראל. ב בגין דאית שושנה ואית שושנה, ג מה שושנה דאיהי בין ג) החוחים

**מסורת הזהר**

א) (שיר ב) ב"א אות רצח תולדות יח ויחי רלד שמות שסד כי תשא לא שמיני לט אמור שלג חקת יח פנחס סח שצג שצח ואתחנן סו האזינו י יב ת"ז תכ"ה דף עא. תכ"ו שם תל"ח דף עח : ז"ח יתרו יב. ב) יתרו שסה.

**דרך אמת** א) רחל. ב) לאח כלת משה מלגאו. ג) רחל.

**חלופי גרסאות**

א נ"א כשושנה בין החוחים מה שושנה דא דאיהי בין החוחים וכו' (אור הלבנה). ב נ"א בגין דאית שושנה ואית שושנה דאיהו בין החוחים. ג ג נ"א ד"א מה שושנה דאיהו בין החוחים וכו' (אה"ל).

### מאמר

**א) ר' חזקיה פתח וכו':** ר' חזקיה פתח. כתוב. כשושנה בין החוחים. שואל מהי שושנה. ומשיב, זו היא כנסת ישראל. שהיא מלכות. משום שיש שושנה ויש שושנה. מה שושנה בין החוחים יש בה אדום ולבן אף כנסת ישראל יש בה דין ורחמים. מה שושנה יש בה י"ג עלים, כך כנסת ישראל יש בה י"ג מדות הרחמים המסבבות אותה מכל צדדיה. אף אלקים, שבמקרא שבכאן דהיינו בראשית ברא **אלקים**, משעה שנזכר, הוציא י"ג מלים לסבב את כנסת ישראל ולשמרה. שהן : את, השמים, ואת, הארץ, והארץ, היתה, תהו, ובהו, וחשך, על, פני, תהום, ורוח. דהיינו עד אלקים מרחפת וגו'.

ביאור הדברים, עשר ספירות הן, כתר, חכמה, בינה, חסד, גבורה, תפארת, נצח, הוד, יסוד ומלכות. ועיקרן הוא רק חמש, כתר, (דפי"י דף א' ע"א)

### הסולם

### השושנה

חכמה, בינה, תפארת ומלכות, משום שספירת התפארת כוללת בתוכה שש ספירות חג"ת נה"י. והן נעשו חמש פרצופין : א"א. וא"רא. וזו"ן. הכתר נק' בשם אריך אנפין. חכמה ובינה נק' בשם אבא ואמא. ת"ת ומלכות, נק' בשם זעיר אנפין ונוקבא. (ביאורן של עשר הספירות עי' בפתיחה לחכמת הקבלה אות ה').

ודע, שסוד ז' ימי בראשית ה"ס ב' הפרצופין ז"א ונוקבא דאצילות, שיש בהם ז' ספירות חג"ת נה"י ומלכות, כנ"ל. אשר באלו הכתובים דמעשה בראשית מתבאר, איך אבא ואמא, שהם חו"ב, האצילו אותם מתחילת התהוותם עד סוף הגדלות, שנוהג בהם בהמשך שתא אלפי שני. וענין זה מתבאר והולך כאן בזוהר בראשית.

ור' חזקיה פתח בביאור הנוקבא ־דד"א, לבאר סדר אצילותה מאמא, שהיא הבינה הנק' בשם

## ב       הקדמת ספר הזהר

אית בה (ג) סומק וחוור, אוף כנסת (ד) ישראל אית בה (ד) דין (ה) ורחמי. מה שושנה
אית בה (ו) (ה) תליסר עלין, אוף כנסת ישראל אית בה (ו) תליסר מכילין דרחמי

### מסורת הזהר

(ג) ב"א ע תולדות טו וישלח יא ויחי תקח ויקרא רכג אמור שלג האזינו קסב ת"ז תל"ו דף עז :
עשה ולא תעשה תק"ח דף קא : (ד) ויחי רלו אמור שלג האזינו קעז. (ה) פנחס שצד ת"ז תכ"ה דף
עא. תכ"ו שם. (ו) ב"א קיב קכו ויצא שטו יתרו תקיב תצוה כ ויקהל קנה אחרי קפד נשא צו שם קכא קסד
שמא פנחס רפו שסז שצד תרמו כי תצא יז ת"ז תכ"ב דף סז. ז"ח בראשית מו תק"ח דף ק. קא. קיג.

**דרך אמת** (ד) לאה. (ה) ולא גוון. (ו) י"ב דידיה וי"ב דידה והכוללים.

---

### השושנה        הסולם        מאמר

בשם אלהים. וזהו שפתח בביאור השושנה, שהיא הנוקבא דז"א. והנוקבא דז"א בעת גדלותה נקראת בשם כנסת ישראל, כמ"ש להלן, וזהו שאומר, **מאן שושנה, דא כנסת ישראל.**

ויש בשושנה זו ב' מצבים: מצב של קטנות, דהיינו של תחלת התהוותה, שאז אין בה אלא ספי' אחת כתר, שבתוכה מלובש אור הנפש שלה, וט' הספירות התחתונות שלה נבחנות כנפולות לבר מאצילות. והן בעולם הבריאה. ועוד בה מצב של גדלות, שאז מתעלות ט' התחתונות שלה מן עולם הבריאה אל עולם האצילות. והיא נבנית עמהן לפרצוף שלם בעשר ספירות. ואז עולה עם ז"א בעלה לקומה שוה עם אור"א דאצילות ומלבישים אותם. ואז נק' ז"א, בשם ישראל. שהוא אותיות לי ראש, והנוקבא נק' בשם כנסת ישראל, על שם שכונסת בתוכה כל האורות של ישראל בעלה שהיא משפעת אותם אל התחתונים.

והמצב של הקטנות נק' בשם שושנה בין החוחים, משום שט"ס התחתונות שלה נתרוקנו מאור האצילות, ונשארו כחוחים. והמצב של הגדלות נק' בשם שושנה סתם, או כנסת ישראל. וזה אמרו **אית שושנה ואית שושנה.**

והנה גוון סומק סומק מורה שם שיש אחיזה לחיצונים ולקליפות לינק ממנה, וזהו בזמן המצב של הקטנות, שט"ס התחתונות שלה הן בבריאה, ויש בה ג"כ בחינת חוור, דהיינו בכלי דכתר שלה, שאין שם אחיזה לחיצונים. וז"ש **מה שושנה דאיהי בין החוחים אית בה סומק וחוור, אוף כנסת ישראל אית בה דין ורחמי** להורות כי גם בגדלותה בעת שנקראת כנסת ישראל, אע"פ שעולה אז ומלבישה את הבינה במצב גדלותה כנ"ל, מ"מ
(דפוי"י דף א' ע"א)

---

נשארת בה בחינת דין, כי היא נצרכת לסוד המסך המתוקן בה לצורך הזווג דהכאה, שמסבת הדין שבמסך, הוא מכה על האור העליון ומחזירו לאחוריו, ומעלה עי"ז ע"ס דאור חוזר הנקרא אור של דין, וממשיך בתוכן ע"ס דאור ישר, הנקרא אור של רחמים. (עי' בפתיחה לחכמת הקבלה אות י"ד) וע"כ גם בכנסת ישראל אית בה דין ורחמי כנגד הסומק והחוור שיש לשושנה בין החוחים.

וז"ס הים שעשה שלמה, העומד על שני עשר בקר. כי אלו טה"ס התחתונות שלה שנפלו לבריאה, כנ"ל, נתתקנו שם בסוד שני עשר בקר, ונקודת הכתר שנשארה באצילות ה"ס הים העומד עליהם מלמעלה, וכללותם יחד נק' **תליסר עלין** דשושנה. וענין ההתחלקות הזו של עה"ס שלה לסוד י"ג מתבאר להלן במראות הסולם.

והנה המוחין דגדלות של הנוקבא, שיש בהם מהארת החכמה, הם נמשכים מסוד י"ג השמות הנק' י"ג מדות הרחמים. וז"ש **אוף כ"י אית בה י"ג מכילין דרחמי.** והעיקר מה שבא ר' חזקיה להורות בהשואה הזו משושנה דבין החוחים לכנסת ישראל, הוא ללמדנו, שכל שיש לנוקבא במצב גדלותה צריך להמצא בה כנגדן בחי' הכנה והכשר עוד בתחילת הויתה דהיינו במצב הקטנות, וז"ש, שכנגד חוור וסומק דקטנות יוצא בה דין ורחמי בגדלות, וכנגד י"ג עלין דקטנות יוצא בה י"ג מדות הרחמים בגדלות, והוא מביא זאת כאן, בכדי ללמדנו איך הכתובים שלפנינו מבארים אותם ב' הסדרים דקטנות וגדלות, הנוהגים באצילות הנוקבא, כמו שממשיך והולך, אוף אלהים דהכא וכו'.

וז"ש, **אוף אלהים וכו' אפיק י"ג תיבין:** מורה, שאלהים שבמקרא דהכא בראשית

## הקדמת ספר הזהר　　ג

דסחרין לה מכל סטרהא. אוף אלהים ז) דהכא, משעתא דאדכר, אפיק ז) תליסר תיבין לסחרא לכנסת ח) ישראל ד ולנטרא לה.

ב) ולבתר אדכר זמנא אחרא, אמאי אדכר זמנא אחרא, בגין ט) לאפקא ח) חמש עלין תקיפין דסחרין לשושנה. ואינון חמש, אקרון ישועות. ואינון

| חלופי גרסאות | מסורת הזהר |
|---|---|
| ד ולנטלא (אה״ל). | ז) פנחס שצו ת״ז תכ״ו דף עא. ח) פנחס שצז ת״ז תכ״ו דף עא. תל״ח דף עח. תק״ח קיז : |

**דרך אמת** ז) פי׳ אימא. ח) לאה. ט) אימא אפיק ה׳ גבורות מנצפ״ך להושיעם מן הקליפות.

---

### מאמר　　הסולם　　השושנה

**מאמר**

בראשית ברא אלהים, שה״ס הבינה המאצלת לנוקבא דז״א, אפיק י״ג מלים שהן : את השמים ואת הארץ והארץ היתה תהו ובהו וחושך על פני תהום ורוח, דהיינו עד אלהים תנינא, שאלו י״ג תיבין רומזים על אותם י״ג עלין של שושנה בין החוחים בסוד הים העומד על שני עשר בקר, כנ״ל, שהם הכנה והכשר לכנסת ישראל שתקבל י״ג מכילן דרחמי. וז״ש, לסחרא לכנסת ישראל ולנטרא לה, כי י״ג מדות הרחמים, שהן המוחין השלמים דנוקבא, נבחנות שהן מסבבות ומאירות אליה מכל הצדדים סביב סביב, ונשמרת על ידיהן ממגע החיצונים, כי כל זמן שאין בה המוחין הגדולים בהארת החכמה מי״ג מדות, יש בה יניקה לחיצונים.

ב) **ולבתר אדכר** וכו׳ : ואח״כ נזכר שם אלקים פעם אחרת, דהיינו **אלקים** מרחפת וגו׳. ולמה נזכר פעם אחרת. הוא כדי להוציא חמשה עלים קשים המסבבים את השושנה. ואלו חמשת העלים נקראים ישועות, והם חמשה שערים, ועל סוד זה כתוב, כוס ישועות אשא. זו היא כוס של ברכה. כוס של ברכה צריכה להיות על חמש אצבעות ולא יותר, כמו השושנה היושבת על חמשה עלים קשים, שהם כנגד חמש אצבעות. ושושנה זו היא כוס של ברכה. מהשם אלקים השני עד שם אלקים השלישי חמש מלים. שהן : מרחפת על פני המים ויאמר. שהן כנגד ה׳ עלים הנ״ל מכאן ולהלאה, שנאמר, אלקים יהי אור וגו׳, הוא האור שנברא ונגנז ונכלל בברית ההוא שנכנס בשושנה והוציא בה זרע, וזה נקרא עץ עושה פרי אשר זרעו בו. והזרע ההוא נמצא באות ברית ממש.

(דפו״י דף א׳ ע״א)

---

**השושנה**

ביאור הדברים, **חמש עלין תקיפין** : ה״ס ה״ג של הנוקבא, שהן ע״ס דאו״ח, שהנוקבא מעלה על ידי זווג דהכאה באור העליון, הנק׳ אור של דין, (כנ״ל ד״ה סומק) כי עה״ס דאור ישר נק׳ ה׳ חסדים חג״ת נ״ה, והן מתלבשות בה׳ גבורות חג״ת נ״ה דאו״ח, ואלו חמש עלין תקיפין הן, כחות הדין שבמסך המעכב את האור העליון מהתלבש ממטה ולמטה. וע״כ נק׳ עתה רק ה׳ עלין תקיפין, כי עוד אינה ראויה לזווג עליהם. ובזמן הגדלות כשהמסך בא בזווג עם האור העליון הם נק׳ ה׳ גבורות. כנ״ל.

ואלו ה׳ עלין תקיפין ה״ס ה׳ תיבות שיש מאלקים תנינא עד אלהים תליתאה, שהן : מרחפת על פני המים ויאמר. וז״ש **אמאי אדכר זמנא אחרא**, שמשמע שיש כאן פעולה חדשה, ואומר, שהוא כדי להוציא מהנוקבא ה׳ עלין תקיפין אלו, שהם הכנה לזווג בזמן הגדלות.

ומה שאלו ע״ס דאו״ח נקראות ה״ג שהן חג״ת נ״ה ואינן נקראות כח״ב תו״מ, כנ״ל. הענין הוא, מפני שאינן ממשיכות אלא אור חסדים לבד, ולכן ירדו כח״ב ממעלתם ונקראים חג״ת, ות״ת ומלכות נק׳ בשם נו״ה.

וז״ש, **חמש תרעין וכו׳ כוס ישועות** : היינו בעת הגדלות, שה׳ עלין תקיפין נעשו לה׳ גבורות, אז הם נבחנים לחמש תרעין, שהם שערים פתוחים לקבל ה׳ החסדים דאור ישר. וכן הם נקראים ישועות מטעם זה. ואז נק׳ הנוקבא **כוס ישועות או כוס של ברכה**, כי בסגולתן נעשית הנוקבא כלי מחזיק הברכה, שהיא ה״ח ה״ג הנ״ל.

**הנה**

# LITERAL TRANSLATION OF THE AFORECITED TEXT FROM ARAMAIC INTO ENGLISH[3]

1. Rabbi Hizkiyah opened, "It is written, as a rose among thorns." That a rose is the Assembly of Israel. Because there is a rose and there is a rose, just as a rose among thorns is tinged with red and white, the Assembly of Israel consists of judgment and mercy. Just as a rose has thirteen petals, the Assembly of Israel is surrounded on all sides by the thirteen attributes of mercy. However, *Elokim*, that is here, thought to bring out the thirteen words that surround the Assembly of Israel and guard it.

2. Afterwards, this is mentioned another time. The reason it is mentioned another time is to bring out the five rigid leaves that surround the rose. And these five stand for salvation. These are also the five gates.

It is written of this secret, "I will raise the cup of salvation, it is the cup of blessing." The cup of blessing must rest on five fingers, and no more, just as a rose rests on five rigid leaves that correspond to the five fingers. And this rose is the cup of blessing. From the second to the third mention of the name *Elokim*, there are five words. From here on, the Light was created and concealed, enclosed within that covenant, and entered the rose and fructified it. And this is referred to as a fructiferous tree, wherein is the seed thereof. And this seed truly exists in the letter of the covenant.

3. And just as the form of the covenant is sown in forty-two conceptions from that seed, so is the legislative, special name of creation sown.

4. In the beginning, Rabbi Shimon opened, the flower buds appeared on the earth. "The flower buds" refer to the act of creation. They appeared on the earth when, on the third day, as it is said, "And the earth shall pullulate." That was when they appeared on the earth. The time of singing has come, and this is the fourth day, when there was a reduction from the Light of *Hassadim*. The voice of the turtle dove refers to the fifth day, where it is written, "Let the waters swarm," so as to produce offspring. "It is heard" refers to the sixth day, where it is written, "Let us stand and create man," and there it is said, "We will do and we will hear." "In our land" refers to the day of *Shabbat*, which represents the Land of Life.

5. Another meaning is that these flower buds are the Patriarchs who entered the thoughts of the future world, and there they are concealed. They emerged from

---

3    The translation in the book is semantic and not literal

there in concealment, and concealed themselves in the true prophets. Yosef was born and they concealed themselves in him. When Yosef entered the Holy Land and founded them there, they appeared in the land (earth) and were revealed there. When are they seen? When a rainbow is seen in the world. It is when the rainbow is seen that they are revealed. As the time of pruning has come. The time has come to eradicate the wicked from the world. Why were the wicked saved? Because the flower buds can be seen in the earth. And if they could not be seen, they would not have remained in the world, and the world would not be able to exist.

6. Who animates the world and causes the Fathers to appear? It is the voice of the children, who study the Torah, meaning that these children of the world save the world. In deference to them, "We will make you pendants of gold." Those are the children, children of the world, as is it said, "You shall make two Cherubs of gold."

7. In the beginning, Rabbi Elazar opened, "Raise your eyes above and see who has created this." Raise your eyes. To what place? To the place where all eyes depend on Him. And who is He? He is one who opens eyes. And you will know this. It is the concealed *Atik*, wherein lies the question, who has created this. And who is He? *MI* = who. He is called from the edge of Divine Heaven, where everything belongs to Him. As there is a question, He is along a concealed path, and does not reveal Himself. He is called *MI*, as there is no question Above, this edge of Heaven is called *MI*.

8. And there is another below, called MA. What is between this and that? The first one, called *MI*, is concealed. There is a question in him, because man asks, searches and looks, and beholds from degree to degree until the end of all the degrees. And after he arrives there, he is asked: MA? (What?). What have you learned? What have you seen? What have you investigated, since everything is still concealed, just as it was before.

9. It is written of this secret, "Who can I point out to you? Who can I compare you to?" After all, the Temple was destroyed, and a voice came forth and said, "What can I point out to you, and what can I compare you to?" The word MA = what, testimony, each day and the day of testimony to you from the days of past, as it is written: "I call to witness Heaven and earth," which is like unto you.

According to the same type, "I adorned you with holy ornaments," made you ruler over the world, as it is written: "Is this the city that was called the quintessence of beauty?" and so forth. I have called you, "Jerusalem, a city built by me." "What could be compared to you?" Just as you sit, so he is like Above, just as now the holy nation does not enter into you to perform holy work, so I swear to you that I will not enter Above until I dwell down below. This is your consolation, as this degree is equal to you in all things. And now that I am here, "Your misery is great, like the sea." And if you claim that there is no existence or remedy for you, then *MI* (who) shall heal you? It shall be precisely that concealed Supernal Degree, which animates all things; it shall heal you, and exist within you.

10. *MI* is the upper edge of Heaven, *MA* is the lower edge of Heaven. This was inherited by Yaakov, that he shines from edge to edge, from the first edge, which is *MI*, until the last edge, which is *MA*, for he stands in the middle. Therefore, who has created this?

11. Rabbi Shimon said: Elazar, my son, stop talking and reveal to us the supernal secret, which the people of the world know nothing of. Rabbi Elazar was silent. Rabbi Shimon wept and said: One minute. Rabbi Shimon said: Elazar, what is *ELEH* (these)? If you say the stars and the signs of the zodiac, have they not always been seen? However, *MA* (what) were created, as it is said, by the word of the Creator were the Heavens made. If it is about concealed things, then it is not written *ELEH*, because they are revealed.

12. But this secret was never revealed, until one day when I was at the seashore, Eliyahu came and told me: "Rabbi, do you know what this is, WHO HAS CREATED THIS?" I told him: "These are the Heavens and their hosts, the works of the Creator, that man can look at them and bless them, as is written, 'When I behold Your Heavens, the work of Your hands, our Master, how glorious Your name is throughout all the earth'!"

13. He told me: "Rabbi, there was one thing concealed before the Creator, which He revealed to the Supernal Assembly, and it is this. When the concealed of all the concealed desired to reveal Himself, He first made one single point, and this point ascended and became a Thought. With it, He drew all the forms and with it engraved all the images."

14. He engraved inside a concealed, sacred candle an image of a concealed image of the holy of holies. A profound structure emerged from the depth of that thought, and it is called *MI* – who, which is the inception of the structure both standing and not standing, which is hidden deep inside the name. It is not called, but only *MI* – who. He desired to reveal Himself and to be called this name, so He clothed Himself in a precious, radiant garment and created *ELEH*, and *ELEH* ascended in name. These letters combined with these, and the name *Elokim* was completed. And until He created *ELEH* – this, *Elokim* did not ascend

to form the name *Elokim*. And these sinned in worshipping the golden calf. Of this secret it is said, *ELEH* is your Lord, Israel.

15. Just as the letters *MI* joined the letters *ELEH*, so does this name remain forever united, and on this secret stands the world. Eliyahu then flew away, and I could not see him. It is from him that I knew this, which stands on the secret, and its explanation. Rabbi Elazar has come, and all the disciples, too, and they bowed down before him, wept and said, if we had (not) come into this world but only to hear this secret, it would have been enough.

16. Rabbi Shimon said, "Onto these Heavens and their hosts were created in MA, as it is said, 'When I behold the Heavens, the works of Your hands,' and it is said, 'MA, how glorious Your name is throughout all the earth, which You set Above the Heavens, it ascends in name.' That is why it created Light for Light, clothed this into this, and elevated in the Supernal Name, this the Creator created in the beginning. This is the Supernal Creator, for MA is not such and was not created."

# THE ROSE

1. Rabbi Hizkiyah opened (began): "It is said, as a rose among thorns" (*Shir HaShirim*, 2:2). He asks, "What does a rose represent?" He answers, "It is the Assembly of Israel, meaning *Malchut*. For there is a rose, and there is a rose. Just as a rose among thorns is tinged with red and white, so does the Assembly of Israel (*Malchut*) consist of judgment and mercy. Just as a rose has thirteen petals, so the Assembly of Israel consists of thirteen properties of mercy, surrounding it on all sides. After all, *Elokim* (the name of the Creator that alludes to His attitude towards the lower ones by the force of judgment), as it is said, 'In the beginning, *Elokim* created' (the first sentence in the Torah), In the beginning (initially) when He thought it, He created thirteen words to surround the Assembly of Israel and to protect it, and here they are: THE, HEAVEN, AND-THE, EARTH, AND-THE EARTH, WAS, EMPTY, AND-CHAOTIC, AND-THE DARKNESS, OVER, THE FACE, OF THE ABYSS, AND-THE SPIRIT, up to the word *Elokim*" (In Hebrew, "and" is written in conjunction with the word following it. Hence, it is considered as one word).

As its object of study, Kabbalah takes the only creation, the only thing that exists besides the Creator—man's self, or "I," and researches it. This science breaks down the self into parts, explains the structure and properties of each part, and the purpose of its creation. Kabbalah explains how every part of man's self, called "the soul," can be changed so that one would reach the goal of creation, the state desired by both the Creator and man himself, provided he realizes it.

There is not a science in the world that can describe, either graphically or analytically, through use of formulas, our sensations and desires, and how diverse and multifaceted they are. That is how fickle, unpredictable, and absolutely distinct they are in everyone. This is because our desires surface in our mind and sensations in a gradual order, in a certain sequence, so we may acknowledge and correct them.

Our self is our essence, the only thing that characterizes an individual. However, it is ever-changing, and what remains is merely an external, animate shell. This is why it is said that every moment man is born anew. Yet, if this is so, how should we regard one another, and how should we perceive ourselves? How can we possibly "stabilize" anything within and outside of us if we are constantly changing, and all that we perceive is a function of our inner state?

The Creator is the source of Light (pleasure). Those who draw near Him sense Him as such. Such people, who draw near the Creator and thereby sense Him, are called Kabbalists (from the word *Lekabel*—to receive the Creator's Light). One can draw near the Creator only through equivalence of desires. The Creator is incorporeal, and can only be sensed with our heart. Naturally, what is meant by "heart" is not the pump that mobilizes blood through our veins, but the center of man's every sensation.

However, one cannot sense the Creator with just his heart, but only with a small point in it. And to feel this point, man must develop it himself. When one develops and expands this point, the sensation of the Creator, His Light, can enter it.

Our heart is the sum of our egoistic desires, and the small point within it is part of the spiritual, altruistic desire implanted from Above by the Creator Himself. It is our task to nurture this embryo of a spiritual desire to such an extent that it (and not our egoistic nature) will determine all of our aspirations. At the same time, the egoistic desire of the heart will surrender, contract, wither, and diminish.

After being born in our world, one is obliged to change his heart from egoistic to altruistic, while living in this world. This is the purpose of his life, the reason behind his appearance in this world, and it is the goal of all creation. A complete replacement of egoistic desires with altruistic ones is called "the End of Correction." Every individual and all of humanity must attain it in this world together. Until one achieves this, he will continue to be born into this world. The Torah and all the prophets speak exclusively of this. The method of correction is called "Kabbalah."

One can change his desires only if one wishes to change them. Man is created an absolute egoist; he can neither adopt different desires from other people or from the surrounding world—as his surroundings are just like him—nor does he have any link to the spiritual worlds, since such a link is possible only through mutual properties. The spiritual can only be perceived in altruistic desires.

Hence, an individual in our world has no chance of transcending the boundaries of this world on his own. That is why we were given the Torah and its most effective part, Kabbalah—to help man acquire the desires of the spiritual worlds.

In order to create man in remoteness to Himself, so that man would realize his insignificance and would come independently to the desire to ascend, the Creator created all creation as degrees descending from Him. The Creator's Light descended along these degrees, and at the lowest degree, created our world and man in it. Having realized his insignificance and wishing to ascend to the Creator, man (to the extent that he wishes to approach the Creator) ascends along the same degrees by which his initial descent took place.

In all, there are ten degrees, called "ten *Sefirot*": *Keter, Hochma, Bina, Hesed, Gevura, Tifferet, Netzah, Hod, Yesod,* and *Malchut.* Like ten screens or curtains, these ten *Sefirot* conceal the Creator's Light from us or the Creator Himself (which is the same thing). These ten screens constitute the ten degrees of our remoteness from the Creator.

Therefore, in order to draw near the Creator by one degree, the lowest one above our own properties, we must acquire the properties of that (lowest) degree. This means that our properties become similar to the properties of that degree, rather than remaining inferior to it. To acquire similar properties means to have the same desires. As soon as our desires coincide with the desires of that degree, its concealment fades, and we seemingly exist on it, and only nine degrees separate us from the Creator.

However, the last, lowest degree differs from all the others: as soon as one ascends out of our world and onto the first degree, he already begins to see (sense) the Creator. And all the subsequent degrees are degrees of drawing closer to the Creator. Only the very last degree, at which we presently exist, conceals the Creator completely, whereas all of the Higher Degrees only distance Him.

Although we count ten degrees, there are in fact only five of them. This is because six degrees: *Hesed, Gevura, Tifferet, Netzah, Hod,* and *Yesod* combine into one *Sefira,* called *Zeir Anpin* (ZA). ZA itself is sometimes referred to as *Tifferet,* for this *Sefira* reflects the common attributes of all of its six *Sefirot.*

So, there are five degrees of concealment from the Creator down to our world: *Keter, Hochma, Bina,* ZA, and *Malchut.* Every degree is alternatively called *Olam* (world), from the word *Haalamah* (concealment). Every degree has its sub-degrees, called *Partzufim* (plural for *Partzuf*), and every sub-degree has its own sub-degrees, called *Sefirot* (plural for *Sefira*). Thus, in all, 5 x 5 x 5 = 125 degrees-*Sefirot* exist between us and the Creator.

Below is a table of the degrees from the Creator down to our world:

The Creator: an absolutely altruistic desire to create a soul (man) in order to fill it with delight.

The world of Infinity: the existence of souls in the ultimate, perfect state.

| WORLDS | SEFIROT | PARTZUFIM | |
|---|---|---|---|
| 1st World Adam Kadmon (AK) | Keter | Galgalta | ( * ) |
| | Hochma | AB | ( * ) |
| | Bina | SAG | ( * ) |
| | ZA | MA | ( * ) |
| | Malchut | BON | ( * ) |
| 2nd World Atzilut | Keter | Arich Anpin (AA) | ( * ) |
| | Hochma | Aba ve Ima (AVI) | ( * ) |
| | Bina | Israel Saba ve Tvuna (YESHSUT) | ( * ) |
| | ZA | MA (ZA and Malchut are called ZON) | ( * ) |
| | Malchut | BON, Nukva | ( * ) |
| 3rd World Beria | Keter | Arich Anpin (AA) | ( * ) |
| | Hochma | Aba ve Ima (AVI) | ( * ) |
| | Bina | Israel Saba ve Tvuna (YESHSUT) | ( * ) |
| | ZA | MA (ZA and Malchut are called ZON) | ( * ) |
| | Malchut | BON, Nukva | ( * ) |
| 4th World Yetzira | Keter | Arich Anpin (AA) | ( * ) |
| | Hochma | Aba ve Ima (AVI) | ( * ) |
| | Bina | Israel Saba ve Tvuna (YESHSUT) | ( * ) |
| | ZA | MA (ZA and Malchut are called ZON) | ( * ) |
| | Malchut | BON, Nukva | ( * ) |
| 5th World Assiya | Keter | Arich Anpin (AA) | ( * ) |
| | Hochma | Aba ve Ima (AVI) | ( * ) |
| | Bina | Israel Saba ve Tvuna (YESHSUT) | ( * ) |
| | ZA | MA (ZA and Malchut are called ZON) | ( * ) |
| | Malchut | BON, Nukva | ( * ) |

Our world: the five egoistic desires felt in the heart.

(*) – Consists of five *Sefirot*– *Keter, Hochma, Bina, ZA,* and *Malchut.*

In all, there are 125 degrees from the Creator to our world.

## THE GOAL OF CREATION

Since there is no notion of time in the spiritual, we already exist in our ultimate, perfect state in the world of Infinity (*Ein Sof*). Because desire in the spiritual designates action, desire itself acts, without a body. Therefore, when the desire to create souls (the will to enjoy) appeared in the Creator, when He wished to fill them with the most perfect delight—to sense Him and to delight in His perfection—to make creatures just as He is, His desire was immediately realized. Thus appeared the World of *Ein Sof*, in which we already exist in our final state.

However, we still need to attain this state in our sensations. This is reminiscent of a sleeping person: even though he is sleeping somewhere, he does not understand where he is until he wakes up. However, in order to achieve this perfect state, we must go through a gradual process of transformation of our inner properties (desires), which corresponds to the spiritual ascension from our world through all the worlds, to the World of *Ein Sof*.

To lead us to the final state, the Creator governs us from Above through all the worlds. Thus, there is nothing in our world that does not originate in the World of *Ein Sof*, where the final state of every soul determines the path that it is destined to travel **in general** and the changes that it has to undergo **in particular** at every moment (state) of its spiritual advancement towards the World of Infinity.

There is no way back: everything that happens is dictated by the necessity to bring every soul to its final state. Only this goal determines the state of our world at every second, what happens to it in general and to each of us in particular. The Creator created nothing for naught. Rather, everything serves His purpose.

However, the will that stems from Above does not exclude our active participation in our own advancement. Instead of being slaves that move under the compulsion of a beating stick called suffering, we can turn our path of suffering into the path of Torah—to actively and quickly travel this path from below upwards on our own by realizing that the Creator's purpose is indeed desirable.

This is possible via a request for spiritual elevation—raising MAN, a prayer. In response, we will receive spiritual strength from Above that will help us improve our qualities, i.e., to ascend. The entire Torah speaks only of this, and Kabbalah goes further still and provides a detailed explanation of the path itself. As if on a map, it depicts what we go through and where (in what state and at which degree) we are now.

Kabbalah studies the structure of the spiritual worlds. The purpose of these worlds is to weaken the Creator's signals (desires) so that we could understand them with our egoism and realize them with our mind. In Hebrew, the word for "world" is *Olam* (from the word *Haalamah*—meaning concealment), for these worlds conceal and weaken the Creator's Light to such an extent that we can feel it.

Depending on everyone's spiritual qualities, on the degree of one's attainment (complete egoism = our world, partial altruism = spiritual worlds), we perceive the Creator or His Light differently at each of the 125 degrees. These 125 degrees amount to just ten, called "the ten *Sefirot* between the Creator and us," where every lower *Sefira* transmits less of the Creator's Light, as perceived by those at that degree. The lower the *Sefira*, the less of the Creator's Light it lets through to those that are below it.

## SEFIROT

These are the names of the *Sefirot*: *Keter*, *Hochma*, *Bina*, *Hesed*, *Gevura*, *Tifferet*, *Netzah*, *Hod*, *Yesod*, and *Malchut*. However, six of them are combined into one *Sefira*, called *Zeir Anpin*, so in all there are five *Sefirot*: *Keter*, *Hochma*, *Bina*, ZA, and *Malchut*. Also, ZA himself (ZA is usually considered a male *Sefira*) is sometimes called *Tifferet*, since *Tifferet* is his main *Sefira*, absorbing within itself the properties of all six *Sefirot* of ZA. Thus, the Creator created only five *Sefirot*:

*Keter*—the Creator's desire to bestow delight upon us, *Malchut*;

*Hochma*—the pleasure itself, which the Creator wishes to bestow upon us;

*Bina*—passes the pleasure from *Hochma* to ZA;

ZA—accepts the pleasure from *Bina* and passes it to *Malchut*;

*Malchut*—receives the pleasure.

*Bina* consists of two parts: her upper part, called GAR or AVI, is unwilling to receive the Light from *Hochma*. However, since the Creator wishes to impart this Light to the lower ones, the lower part of *Bina*, called ZAT or YESHSUT, receives the Light from *Hochma* and passes it to ZA. ZA does not want to receive the Light, but *Malchut* (to the extent of her correction) evokes ZA to receive the Light from *Bina* and pass it on to her. Hence, we sometimes speak of the general reception of the Light by ZA and *Malchut*, which are together called ZON (ZA and *Nukva*).

The process is such that *Malchut*—to the extent that her desires are corrected from egoism to altruism—asks ZA to receive the Light "for the Creator's sake."

To this extent, ZA requests the Light from *Bina*. Subsequently, *Bina* turns to and receives the requested amount of Light from *Hochma*, then passes it to ZA. *Malchut* (to the extent of her corrected properties) merges with ZA via equivalence of form (desires), and receives this Light.

*Keter*, *Hochma*, and GAR of *Bina* do not want to receive the Light, but starting with ZAT of *Bina* (*YESHSUT*), the desire to receive the Light so as to pass it to the lower ones appears in the *Sefirot*.

| Keter | | Galgalta or Metzah - forehead | "bestowal" |
|-------|---|-------------------------------|------------|
| Hochma | | Eynaim -                        eyes | GE |
| Bina | GAR of Bina | Nikvey Eynaim -               pupils | |
|      | ZAT of Bina | Awzen -                         ear | |
| ZA | | Hotem -                         nose | AHP |
| Malchut | | Peh -                         mouth | "reception" |

*Malchut* herself is the creature—the egoistic will to receive pleasure, to enjoy the Creator's Light. This desire is to enjoy the Creator's Light or the Creator (which is the same thing) is the essence of *Malchut*. We are parts of *Malchut*. However, if we have only egoistic desires, we feel the Creator's Light as pleasures in our world. This is a micro dose of His Light. By correcting our desires (properties), we can ascend the spiritual degrees of the Upper Worlds, and there experience the Creator's true delight.

According to the Thought of Creation, *Malchut* must receive the Light from the four previous *Sefirot*, and delight in it. Hence, *Malchut* herself consists of five parts: she receives the Light from the preceding *Sefirot* in four parts, and senses it in the fifth.

All the *Sefirot* that precede *Malchut* (excluding *Malchut*) are similar to our sensory organs, and *Malchut* is like the heart that receives from all organs: brain, sight, hearing, smell, taste, and touch. The heart is *Malchut*, and the sensory organs are the first nine *Sefirot* that precede *Malchut*. All of these parts of *Malchut* are egoistic—they wish to receive the Light (pleasure) so as to enjoy it. With such properties, *Malchut* cannot receive more than a micro dose of the Light of our world, sensing the Creator in a manner called "this world."

However, if *Malchut*, i.e., every one of us, were to receive desires (aspirations) from Above to *bestow* delight upon the Creator to the same extent that we feel the Creator bestowing upon us, with this property (desire), man would ascend spiritually to a degree above our world. He would sense the Creator as spiritual Light, altruistic pleasure and great knowledge, attainment of supernal thoughts and the essence of existence.

## SCREEN

*Malchut* (man) can receive the Light only in anti-egoistic desires. If such desires appear in *Malchut* as a result of the realization that egoism is her enemy (with the help of Kabbalah), to the extent of her hatred for it, *Malchut* can repel the egoistic pleasures for the sake of spiritual perfection, i.e., similarity to the Creator in her desire to please Him and act for His sake.

This ability to repel selfish reception of pleasure is called "a screen," and the repelled pleasure is called "Reflected Light," and the pleasure that comes to *Malchut* is called "Direct Light." It is precisely in the repelled pleasure, meaning in the desire to bestow whole-heartedly, selflessly, that man can sense the Creator's Light and Supreme Knowledge.

Since *Malchut* (man's egoism) has to repel pleasure from the five parts of her egoism, the reflecting screen must also consist of five parts. Hence, it creates five parts of the Reflected Light. The five parts in *Malchut* are called by the names of the *Sefirot* from which they receive. The five kinds of Direct Light are called NRNHY: *Nefesh, Ruach, Neshama, Haya* and *Yechida*. The Light that emanates from the Creator descends in the following order:

**Yechida**

**Haya**

**Neshama**

**Ruach**

**Nefesh**

## PARTZUF

After *Malchut* reflects the Light (pleasure), she decides to receive it in order to delight the Creator, because He wants *Malchut* to receive pleasure and feel Him. The reflection of all the incoming pleasure is called *Rosh* (head). The partial reception of the Light to the extent of one's anti-egoistic powers is called *Toch* (interior). The unfulfilled desires (due to the absence of a screen on them) are called *Sof* (end) (see below diagram).

This is the structure of the soul (*Kli*, vessel, corrected altruistic desire, *Partzuf* or spiritual body). We call the parts of the spiritual structure by the names of our physiological body: head, body, and limbs. There are five parts in the *Rosh* (head): skull—*Galgalta*, eyes—*Eynaim*, ears—*Awznaim*, nose—*Hotem*, and mouth—*Peh*. There are five parts in the *Guf* (body) from the mouth—*Peh* to the navel—*Tabur*. In the limbs, there are five parts from the navel to the toes (see below diagram).

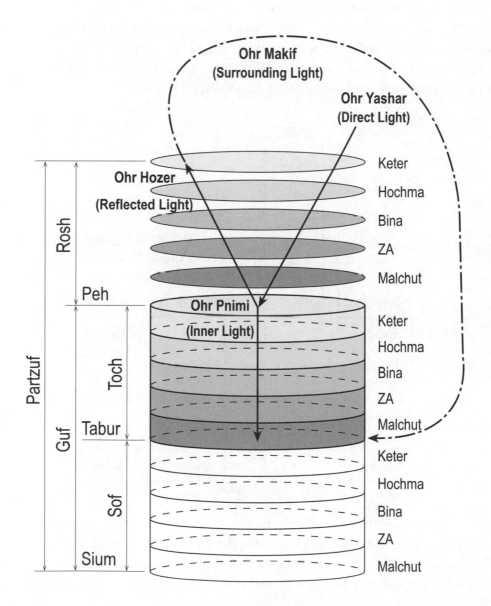

## THE INVERSE PROPORTION BETWEEN THE VESSEL AND THE LIGHT

The more strength *Malchut* has to oppose egoism, the greater the Light that enters her. However, although one works on the correction of the vessel's coarser part, he receives the Light from his efforts in his subtler desires. In other words, there is an inverse proportion between the vessel and the Light: the coarser the desire (*Kli*) that is corrected, the greater the Light that enters *Malchut* (vessel); however, it enters her Upper *Kli* (desire).

Since *Malchut* (i.e., all that exists apart from the Creator) is absolutely egoistic, she can only be corrected by imparting onto herself the properties of *Bina*, the Creator—bestowal without reception. This is the property of absolute altruism, of selfless bestowal. To receive such a property (desire) is tantamount to ascending from the level of *Malchut* to the level of *Bina*.

| LIGHT |
|-------|
| Yechida |
| Haya |
| Neshama |
| Ruach |
| Nefesh |

If all parts of the *Kli* can receive the Light, then all the outside Light enters the *Sefirot*:

| SEFIRA | |
|--------|---|
| Keter | - |
| Hochma | - |
| Bina | - |
| ZA | - |
| Malchut | - |

| SEFIRA | LIGHT |
|--------|-------|
| Keter | Yechida |
| Hochma | Haya |
| Bina | Neshama |
| ZA | Ruach |
| Malchut | Nefesh |

*Malchut* herself is the will to receive pleasure. The ban imposed on the reception of pleasure for oneself is called the **First Restriction** (*Tzimtzum Aleph*). Restriction is a ban on the reception of pleasure; however, if the receiver aspires to please the Creator and not himself, he is allowed to receive the pleasure.

Whether *Malchut* wants it or not, if she (soul, man) has egoistic desires, the Light will not enter her (be felt within her). Hence, we are utterly unable to feel the spiritual (the Creator).

## THE STATE OF *KATNUT* (SMALLNESS)

Yet, *Malchut* is not the only *Sefira* that cannot receive the Light: from the world of *Atzilut* and below, *Sefirot Bina* and ZA cannot receive the Light either. This ban is called the **Second Restriction** (*Tzimtzum Bet*). In this restriction, *Malchut* seemingly ascends in her desires to *Sefira Bina*. Her desires of "reception" dominate three *Sefirot*: *Bina*, ZA, and *Malchut*, as *Sefirot Bina* and ZA also fall under the rule (desire) of the elevated *Malchut*.

If a *Partzuf* has no strength to oppose its egoistic desires of reception in *Sefirot Bina*, ZA and *Malchut* (AHP), its lower part is not entitled to receive the Creator's Light, as it will receive it selfishly, thereby causing great harm to itself. To avoid this, the upper part of the *Partzuf*—*Sefirot Keter* and *Hochma* (GE)—separates from the lower part by *Parsa* (partition), through which the Light cannot pass downwards. Therefore, as a result of *Malchut's* ascent to *Bina*, each degree was divided into two parts:

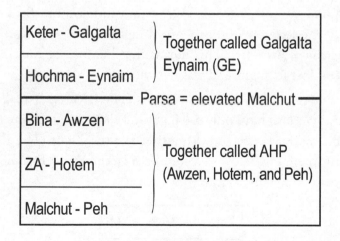

Keter - Galgalta / Hochma - Eynaim — Together called Galgalta Eynaim (GE)

Parsa = elevated Malchut

Bina - Awzen / ZA - Hotem / Malchut - Peh — Together called AHP (Awzen, Hotem, and Peh)

*Malchut* restricted the spreading of Light inside the *Partzuf*, and two parts were formed in her: GE receives the Light, i.e., *Sefirot Keter* and *Hochma* receive the Lights *Nefesh* and *Ruach*, while the other part of the *Partzuf* (*Sefirot Bina*, ZA, and *Malchut*) is below the *Parsa*, and therefore does not receive the Light. Their corresponding Lights—*Neshama*, *Haya* and *Yechida*—also remain outside of the *Partzuf*.

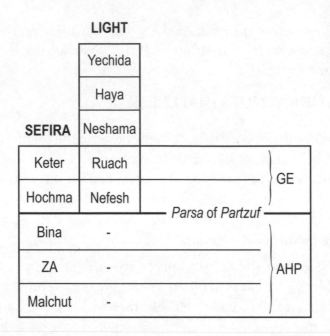

This degree (*Partzuf*) is deprived of the Light *Neshama-Haya-Yechida* and is left with just the Light *Nefesh-Ruach*, called "air." This is designated by the entry of the letter *Yod* into the word Light (*Ohr* = *Aleph-Vav-Reish*). Thus, the word Light (*Ohr*) turns into air (*Avir* = *Aleph-Vav-Yod-Reish*). This state of the vessel is called *Katnut* (small state). In other words, the ascent of *Malchut* to *Bina* is designated by the entry of the letter *Yod* into the word Light (*Ohr* = *Aleph-Vav-Reish* +*Yod* = *Aleph-Vav-Yod-Reish* = *Avir*—air). This means that because of *Malchut's* ascent to *Bina*, the *Partzuf* lost its Light and was left with air.

In such a state, the degree or *Partzuf* is called *Katnut* (smallness), where *Sefirot Keter* and *Hochma* have only the Light *Nefesh-Ruach*, as *Sefirot Bina, ZA* and *Malchut* are below the *Parsa*, and do not receive the Light. The *Parsa* prevents the Light from spreading below it. *Sefirot Keter-Hochma* and *Bina-ZA-Malchut* are designated by the following letters:

| | | |
|---|---|---|
| Keter | - Mem | - M |
| Hochma | - Yod | - I |
| Bina | - Hey | - H |
| ZA | - Lamed | - LO |
| Malchut | - Aleph | - E |

In the reverse order, these letters form the Creator's name *Elokim*, where *GE* = letters *Mem* + *Yod* = *IM* (pronounced as *MI*), and *AHP* = letters *Aleph* + *Lamed* + *Hey* = *ELEH*. Since man attains the Creator from below upwards, the Creator's name *ELOKIM* is read from below upwards.

After the birth of all the worlds and the descent of the entire Creation to our world, all the *Partzufim* of the world of *Atzilut* and the worlds of *BYA* passed into the state of *Katnut*. Thus, the Light is present in *GE*, but absent in *AHP*. *AHP* of the Upper Degree fell into *GE* of the lower degree, thus forming the spiritual ladder between the Creator and man in our world, and the lowest part of the last spiritual degree of the world of *Assiya* fell into a point in man's heart. Consequently, all the intermediate degrees now exist one inside the other: *AHP* of the Upper Degree is inside *GE* of the lower one:

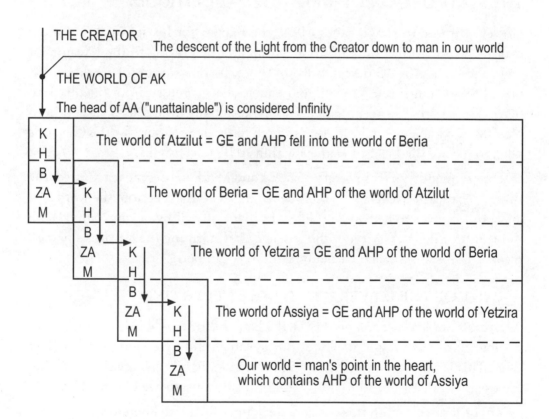

The sum of man's desires is referred to as his heart. Since the nature with which we are born is absolute egoism, man does not feel the spiritual point in his heart. However, at some point in one of his reincarnations, man begins to gradually strive towards attainment of the causes of life, its evaluation; he

yearns to attain himself, his source, just as you do right now. Man's aspiration
to the Creator is precisely this aspiration to attain his origin. Man's discontent
in life often helps him in this search, when there's nothing that appeals to him
in his surroundings. Such circumstances are sent from Above in order for man
to start feeling an empty point in his heart, and to stimulate in him the desire
to fulfill it.

The Creator manifests as the altruistic property to bestow pleasure without
any benefit for Himself. From this, we can understand the property of *Sefirot
Keter*, *Hochma*, and *Bina* that share the Creator's property of bestowal. The only
Creation is *Malchut*, the will to receive the Light (pleasure). All of us and our
entire world are the lowest part of this egoistic *Malchut*.

## THE STATE OF *GADLUT* (GREATNESS/ADULTHOOD)

However, if one (*Malchut*) raises *MAN*, the request for his spiritual ascent, by
making efforts to free himself from egoism and by praying to the Creator for
help, the Light *AB-SAG* descends from Above. It comes from the world of *AK*,
brings *Malchut* altruistic strength and enables her to return from *Bina* back to
her place. In other words, *Malchut*'s ability to refrain from selfish reception of
pleasure is complemented with the strength to receive pleasure for the Creator's
sake, to receive the Light of *Hochma* within *AHP*, for His sake.

Subsequently, *AHP*, or *Sefirot Bina*, *ZA* and *Malchut*, become reactivated, the
*Partzuf* regains all five *Kelim* (parts), the letter *Yod* disappears from the word *Avir*
(air), and it turns to being *Ohr* (Light). In that state, all five Lights *NRNHY* fill
the *Partzuf*, the letters *MI* join the letters *ELEH*, forming the Creator's name—
*Elokim*. This state is called *Gadlut* (greatness/adulthood).

## ASCENT OF THE LOWER ONE TO THE UPPER ONE

As a result of *Malchut*'s ascent to *Bina*, the Upper *Partzuf* establishes contact with
the lower one. As a result, the lower *Partzuf* can ascend to the level of the Upper
One. This is the reason for the second restriction: to give the lower ones (man)
the opportunity to ascend to the World of Infinity, up to the Creator Himself.

In order to establish this contact, the Upper *Partzuf* deliberately diminishes
itself, descends to the level of the lower *Partzuf*, and becomes similar to the lower
one in its properties. *AHP* of the Upper *Partzuf* willingly falls into *GE* of the
lower one, as though it has no strength to receive the Light, and they become
a single whole. This is similar to a scenario when a strong individual joins a
society of criminals, imitating their behavior, so that after being admitted into

their circle and establishing contact with them, he will gradually influence and correct them.

How? The Upper Light (the so-called Light of *AB-SAG*) comes and provides *AHP* of the Upper *Partzuf* with the strength to ascend to their *GE*. And *GE* of the lower *Partzuf* ascend together with them: because they were a single whole and equivalent in their properties below, they receive the same strength to ascend.

Upon receiving the Light of *AB-SAG*, *GE* of the lower *Partzuf* become like Upper One. Therefore, we should not regard the second restriction as negative, but as help from the Upper *Partzuf*. It descends to the lower *Partzuf* by corrupting its own properties in order to equalize itself with the lower one, so as to subsequently ascend together with it to its previous level. This way, the lowest degree can ascend not only to the next Higher One, but also to the Highest Degree of the spiritual ladder.

## THE LIGHT OF ZON IS THE LIGHT OF THE WORLDS BYA

*Partzuf YESHSUT* is *AHP* of *Partzuf Bina* of the world of *Atzilut*, and all that it receives and passes to *ZON* of the world of *Atzilut* subsequently descends to the worlds of *BYA* and then to us.

In the small state (*Katnut*), *AHP* of *YESHSUT* falls into *ZON*. Then *YESHSUT* receives strength, and by elevating its *AHP*, it elevates *ZON*, too. By ascending to *YESHSUT*, *ZON* become similar to it and receive the Light at the level of *YESHSUT*. *ZON* can never receive the Light of *Hochma* in their own level; they can only receive the Light of *Hassadim*, the Light essential to their existence.

*ZON* of the world of *Atzilut* are called *Olam* (world), just as our world is also called *Olam*, for all that *ZON de Atzilut* receive can be received by man in this world. And vice versa—all that *ZON de Atzilut* cannot receive is unattainable to man, for we attain only up to the level of *ZON*, and not higher.

And since *ZON* cannot receive the Light of *Hochma* in their place, the Creator purposely initiated the second restriction, thereby lowering the *Sefirot* of *AHP* of *Partzuf YESHSUT* down to *ZON*, so that *ZON* would be able to ascend to *YESHSUT* and higher, up to the Highest Degree. Hence, it is said in the Torah (*Beresheet Barah*): "In the beginning the Creator created all in judgment (restriction), but after seeing that the world (*ZON*) cannot exist (receive all of the Light of *Hochma* prepared for it), added to judgment the property of mercy."

In the beginning, He elevated *Malchut* (the restriction of *YESHSUT*, for *Malchut* is restricted from receiving Light) to *Bina* (mercy of *YESHSUT*). As a result, *AHP* of *YESHSUT* fell into *ZON* and merged with them. However, the world (*ZON*) still cannot exist in this way. Hence, the Creator added mercy to judgment: He gave *YESHSUT* the strength to elevate its *AHP* together with *ZON* to the degree of *YESHSUT*. There, *ZON* receive the Light of *YESHSUT* and pass it down to all the worlds of *BYA* and to our world.

## CORRECTION IN THREE LINES

Each of the ten *Sefirot* in turn consists of ten individual sub-*Sefirot*. *Malchut* ascends to *Bina* in each individual *Sefira*, i.e., to the full height of the ten *Sefirot*; in each particular *Sefira*, *Malchut* moves up from its place to the place of *Bina* in that *Sefira*:

$$(M - ZA - | B - H - K) - K$$
$$(M - ZA - | B - H - K) - H$$
$$(M - ZA - | B - H - K) - B$$
$$(M - ZA - | B - H - K) - ZA$$
$$(M - ZA - | B - H - K) - M$$

The sign | signifies a particular *Parsa* in a *Sefira*, the restriction imposed on the spreading of Light. *GE* that remain in each *Sefira* above the *Parsa* are called the **"right line,"** for there is Light in them. *Malchut* that ascends to *Bina* in each *Sefira* creates the **"left line"** with her restriction on the reception of Light. A *Zivug* made on the elevated *Malchut* (only on the free, unrestricted *Kelim KHB*) allows the Light of *Hassadim* to shine in *GE*, and this reception of the Light of *Hassadim* in *GE* is called the **"middle line."**

Now let us clarify what is written in *The Zohar*: There are ten *Sefirot*: *Keter* (K), *Hochma* (H), *Bina* (B), *Hesed* (H), *Gevura* (G), *Tifferet* (T), *Netzah* (N), *Hod* (H), *Yesod* (Y), and *Malchut* (M). However, there are actually only five of them: *Keter* (K), *Hochma* (H), *Bina* (B), *Tifferet* (T), and *Malchut* (M). This is because *Tifferet* (alternatively called *Zeir Anpin*—ZA) consists of six *Sefirot*, from *Hesed* to *Yesod*. Five *Sefirot* KHB-ZA-M created five *Partzufim* in each world. In the world of *Atzilut*, these *Partzufim* are *Arich Anpin* (AA), *Aba ve Ima* (AVI), and *Zeir Anpin* and *Nukva* (ZON). *Keter* is called AA; correspondingly, *Hochma* and *Bina* are called AVI; and ZA (*Tifferet*) and *Malchut* are called ZON.

The essence of the seven days of creation lies in *Partzufim* ZA and *Nukva* of the world of *Atzilut*, which consist of seven *Sefirot*: HGT-NHYM. And from the description of creation it transpires how *AVI* (*Hochma* and *Bina*) beget *ZON* (all of creation, including us) and elevate them to their final state during the 6,000 years. This is what *The Book of Zohar* tells us.

Rabbi Hizkiyah began his explanation of *Nukva* of the world of *Atzilut* by clarifying the birth of *ZON* from *Ima* (*Bina*), called *Elokim*. That is why he began his explanation with a rose, *Nukva* of *ZA*. At the utmost completion of its development, *Nukva* of *ZA* is called *Knesset Israel*, the Assembly of Israel. For *Nukva* consists of all the souls called *Israel*; hence, it is said that a rose is *Knesset Israel*.

There are two states in a rose (*Malchut*). The lowest, initial, small state (*Katnut*) is when *Malchut* consists only of *Sefira Keter* filled with the Light *Nefesh*, while her other nine *Sefirot* are those that fell from the world of *Atzilut* to the world of *Beria*. The other state of *Nukva* is mature, big, complete (*Gadlut*), when her nine *Sefirot* ascend from the world of *Beria* back to the world of *Atzilut*, and complete the full ten *Sefirot* of her *Partzuf*. Then, being equal to her husband, *Malchut* ascends together with him to *AVI* and clothes them, i.e., receives their Light.

The clothing of the lower, outer *Partzuf* onto the Upper, Inner One means that the lower *Partzuf* attains a part of the Upper One, ascends to a Higher spiritual level, and becomes in some way similar to the Upper *Partzuf*.

In that state, *ZA* is called Israel, from the letters *LI* (to me) and *ROSH* (head), which signifies the state of *Gadlut*, while *Nukva* is called "the Assembly of Israel," for she accumulates all of the Light of her husband, *ZA*, and passes it to the lower ones—the souls in the worlds *BYA*.

*Nukva's* state of *Katnut* is called "a rose among thorns," for nine of her lower *Sefirot* in the *Katnut* state fell under the *Parsa* of the world of *Atzilut*, thereby losing the Light of the world of *Atzilut*, and becoming as dry as thorns. And in her *Gadlut* state, *Nukva* is simply called "a rose" or "the Assembly of Israel." This is why it is written, "there is a rose, and there is a rose."

The color red designates the rose's connection with the outer, impure forces, which, because of this connection, can suck the strength (Light) from it. This is because nine of her *Sefirot* are in exile below the world of *Atzilut*, in the world of *Beria*, which may already contain impure forces. And the rose also has a color white in its *Sefira Keter*, for her *Sefira Keter* is in the world of *Atzilut*, above the *Parsa*, where there is no contact with the lower, impure forces. In other words, there are two opposite states: perfection and its absence, Light and darkness. They are felt by him who merits it.

It is therefore written that just as a rose among thorns is tinged with red and white, so does the Assembly of Israel consist of judgment and mercy. This shows that in *Gadlut*, when *Malchut* is called *Knesset Israel*, even though she ascended to *Bina* and clothed her, she still retains the property of judgment, of restriction—an attitude that's tough and just, rather than compassionate. This is so because she needs a screen (a force of resistance to her egoistic desires), which, if available, enables *Malchut* to receive the Upper Light.

The law, judgment, or restriction does not allow for the reception of Light in egoistic desires. The screen, the aspiration to oppose one's egoistic desires, repels the Upper Light (pleasure) back to its source, the Creator. The Light that man sends back is called "Reflected Light" or the "Light of Judgment." To the extent of the intensity of the reflective force (i.e., the force of resistance to one's will to receive), man is allowed to receive the ten *Sefirot* of the Upper Light (called the Direct Light or the Light of Mercy) for the Creator's sake, in precisely these altruistic desires. And that is why, even in its complete state, the Assembly of Israel consists of judgment and mercy, which corresponds to the red and white colors of a rose among thorns.

And this is the pool made by King Shlomo (Solomon). It is built on twelve bulls, for the nine lower *Sefirot* of *Malchut* that fell to the world of *Beria* were corrected there from twelve heads of bulls. One of their *Sefirot*, *Keter*, which remained in the world of *Atzilut*, is called the "pool" that is built on these bulls. Together, they are called thirteen rose petals. (The reason why the ten *Sefirot* of *Malchut* are divided by ten-*Hassadim* or thirteen-*Hochma* will be clarified later).

The Light of a complete *Nukva* is called *Hochma*, as it contains the Light of Wisdom, and originates from the thirteen names called "the thirteen attributes of mercy." However, the main thing that Rabbi Hizkiyah wants to tell us is that a rose among thorns is above the Assembly of Israel, because, as is well known, all that is present in *Nukva's* complete state must exist in her small state as well, albeit in diminished similarity.

Therefore, it is said that the properties of white and red in the small state correspond to the properties of mercy and judgment in the big state. And the thirteen petals of the small state, when corrected, create in *Nukva* the thirteen attributes of mercy in her big state. Later on, we will see how these thirteen attributes of *Malchut* of the world of *Atzilut* change her in both the small and big states.

It is written that, in the process of creation, "in the beginning *Elokim* (*Bina de Atzilut*) created" *Nukva* of ZA with thirteen words: *ET, SHAMAIM, VE'ET,*

*ARETZ, VEARETZ, HAITA, TOHU, VABOHU, VECHOSHECH, AL, PNEI, TEHOM, VERUACH* (from the word *Elokim* to the word *Elokim*). And these thirteen words signify the thirteen petals of a rose among thorns (her small state), like the pool built by the King Shlomo, which stands on thirteen bulls (nine lower *Sefirot* of *Malchut* without Light, as they are in the world of *Beria*, below the *Parsa* of the world of *Atzilut*). These words are the preparation for the purification and correction of the Assembly of Israel in order to receive the thirteen attributes of mercy.

These thirteen attributes of mercy (the Light of a complete *Nukva*) surround her and shine upon her from all sides, and guard her from the touch of foreign (egoistic) desires. After all, until she is filled with all the Light of *Hochma* in her complete, big state, there's a potential for foreign, egoistic desires to cling to and feed off her.

**2. Afterwards, the name *Elokim* is mentioned once more, "*Elokim* soars." Why is it mentioned in this sense? So as to bring out the five rigid leaves that surround the rose, which are called "salvation." And these are the five gates. And it is said of this secret, I will raise the "cup of salvation" (Psalms, 116:13). It is the cup of blessing. The cup of blessing must rest on five fingers, just as a rose rests on five rigid leaves that correspond to the five fingers. And this rose is the cup of blessing, from the second to the third mention of the name *Elokim* (*Beresheet*, 1:2-3), there are five words: "soars," "over," "the surface," "of the waters," "and said"—in all, five words parallel the five leaves. And further, "The Creator said, 'Let there be Light'"—this Light was created. However, it was concealed and enclosed within that covenant that entered the rose and fructified it. And it is referred to as "A fructiferous tree, wherein is the seed thereof" (*Beresheet*, 1:12). And this seed exists in the mark of the covenant.**

The five leaves are the five *Sefirot* of the Light reflected from *Malchut*, which she raises from the *Zivug de Hakaa*. The direct incoming Light is called five *Hassadim HGT-NH*, and it clothes into five parts (types of restrictions) of the Reflected Light *HGT-NH*, called the five rigid leaves of a rose, which correspond to the text from the second (the spirit of God soared over the waters) to the third (and said) mention of the word *Elokim* in the Torah.

These words explain how the five rigid leaves (attributes) can be extracted from *Malchut* so that she will be fit for a *Zivug* and achieve the big state. And during the big state, when the five rigid leaves become five restrictions, they are defined as the five gates of reception of the Light of *Hassadim* of the Direct Light, and they are called salvation, and *Malchut* is called the cup of salvation or the cup of blessing and good fortune, for, thanks to these leaves (restrictions), *Malchut* can receive the Light of *Hassadim*—a blessing.

The cup of blessing must rest on five fingers, for *Malchut* can receive the Light of *Hochma* only if she is clothed in the Light of *Hassadim* beforehand. Therefore, first she has to make a blessing, which means to receive the five parts (*NRNHY*) of the Light of *Hassadim* with the help of five fingers (five restrictions), and only then to receive in them (i.e., in the corrected intentions) the Light of *Hochma*.

Hence, a cup of wine must be raised with two hands, as five fingers of the right hand symbolize mercy—*Hassadim*, and five fingers of the left hand symbolize restrictions. However, having started the blessing, the cup must only be held with the five fingers of the right hand (*Hassadim*, bestowing). Otherwise, the impure forces that take from the left (receiving) side become active, as such forces cling only to a place where there is reception of Light.

What follows is the big state of *Malchut*, which corresponds to the words of the Torah: "Let there be Light." These are the five lights, in which Adam saw the world from end to end, as it is written in the Talmud (*Hagigah*, 12). But the Creator saw that there would be transgressions in the generations of the Flood and the Tower of Babel, and concealed this Light. And the following generations will then need to attain it on their own.

Previously, these five *Hassadim* were in *Yesod* of ZA, and *Malchut* received from it, and not from *Bina*, called *Elokim*, as she does now. *Yesod de* ZA is called the mark of the covenant with the Creator (after the corrections, called circumcision, are made), and five *Hassadim* received on the five restrictions are called "seed." The main force of restrictions and the impact forces of the screen, with which it repels the Light, are in *Ateret Yesod* (the end of the *Sefira Yesod*). There occurs *Zivug de Hakaa*, from which *Malchut* receives the Light. Only at the end of correction will this *Zivug* pass on to *Malchut* herself.

Therefore, during the 6,000 years, the screen that is in *Yesod*, strikes at the incoming Light (pleasure) with its five restrictions (the forces that oppose egoistic reception of pleasure), thus creating five parts of the Reflected Light, and receiving in them the five parts of the Light of *Hassadim*. Subsequently, ZA passes these five Lights of *Hassadim* from his *Yesod* to *Nukva*. And these five Lights of *Hassadim* are called "seed."

**3. Just as the covenant is conceived from that seed in forty-two *Zivugim*, so the secret name fills and inseminates all forty-two letters of the initial act of creation.**

The name "forty-two" = MB = *Mem* + *Bet* = 40 + 2 is composed of *HaVaYaH* (four letters), filled *HaVaYaH* (ten letters), and doubly filled *HaVaYaH* (twenty-eight letters). In all, 4 + 10 + 28 = 42, signifying the seed that exists in the mark of the covenant that is enclosed in five *Hassadim* and five *Gevurot*.

There are two aspects to *Nukva*: her body (*Partzuf*), which emerges from *Bina*, and her *Zivug*, called the secret of unity with ZA. *Nukva* can be in two states: small or big (*Katnut* or *Gadlut* respectively). The small state is an incomplete, insufficient state of *Malchut*, but it is necessary as preparation for the big state, called the revelation of the secret, of the concealed.

And since the big state reveals the small, and all that is concealed in the small state becomes clear in the big, he who is in a state of spiritual descent does not see the reasons for his state, but it all becomes clear to him when he attains the big state that follows.

As a result of the ascent of *Malchut* of AVI to their *Bina*, *Partzuf* of *Bina* (AVI) was divided into two parts: the upper part, GE, acquired the name AVI, while the lower part, AHP, became known as YESHSUT. AVI are filled with the Light of *Hassadim*, since they wish for no other, and YESHSUT receives it from them, for, although it desires the Light of *Hochma*, it cannot receive it in view of the fact that *Malchut* of AVI ascended above it.

However, although there is no Light of *Hochma* in AVI, they do not suffer without it whatsoever, and therefore exist in perfection called GAR, even in the absence of the Light of *Hochma*. And even when one raises MAN requesting strength (i.e., the Light of *Hochma*) so as to overcome his impure desires, AVI do not receive the Light of *Hochma*. YESHSUT receives this Light and passes it to ZA. Hence, although AVI are below the *Rosh* of AA, and there is no Light of *Hochma* in them, they do not suffer from it.

However, YESHSUT suffers from the absence of the Light of *Hochma*, wishing to pass it to ZA, so it waits for MAN from ZA in order to ascend to AVI in the form of *Sefira Daat*. For when the lower ones raise MAN, the whole of *Bina* ascends to the *Rosh* of AA; YESHSUT receives the Light of *Hochma* from AA and passes it to ZON. This corresponds to the disappearance of the letter *Yod* from the word *Avir* (air), and *Avir* turns into *Ohr*—Light (*Hochma*) once more.

However, for all that, even in the *Rosh* of AA, AVI remain only with the Light of *Hassadim* (air). Hence, the heads of both AA and AVI are called "Supreme Waters" or "Heaven." This is considering the fact that AVI can be beneath the *Rosh* of AA; however, since it does not affect their independence and perfection, it is as if they are in the *Rosh* of AA.

Under *AVI* there is a firmament (*Parsa*) of the world of *Atzilut*, which separates the *Kelim* of bestowal from the *Kelim* of reception of the world of *Atzilut*. *YESHSUT* and *ZON* (inferior waters) that need the Light of *Hochma* stand below the *Parsa*, which is in the chest of *AA*. It is therefore said that the inferior waters weep (i.e., their state is small), for they feel the lack of *Ohr Hochma* and wish to ascend to the *Rosh* of *AA*. In no way should one confuse the *Parsa* of the world of *Atzilut* (located within the world of *Atzilut*) that divides it into *GE* and *AHP* with the *Parsa* below the world *Atzilut* that separates it from the worlds of *BYA*.

The Light that is received above the *Parsa* of the world of *Atzilut* is called the Light of *Mem-Bet* (*MB*). However, the seven *Sefirot* of *ZON* (six *Sefirot* of *ZA* and one *Sefira* of *Malchut*) that designate the seven days of creation cannot receive this Light of *MB*, as they are located below the *Parsa* and receive only the Light of *Hassadim* (minimal sustenance) from *YESHSUT*.

However, when the lower ones (man) raise *MAN*, and *MAD* descends from *AB-SAG* (the Light that brings *Bina* back to the *Rosh* of *AA*), *YESHSUT* receives the Light of *Hochma* and passes it to *ZON*, allowing *ZON* to ascend above the *Parsa* that stands in the *Chazeh* (chest) of *AA*, and receive the Light of *MB*.

That is why the Light of *MB* in *ZON* is manifested in thirty-two *Elokim* and ten sayings, where thirty-two *Elokim* represent *YESHSUT* in the state of ascent, when *YESHSUT* receives thirty-two streams of wisdom (*Hochma*) that create in it the thirty-two names of *Elokim*, mentioned in the act of creation: "In the beginning the Creator created," and so on.

The ten sayings are five *Hassadim*. After *ZON* have already received the Light of *Hochma* from thirty-two *Elokim*, the five Lights of *Hassadim* that were received from *AVI* (signifying *MB*) are called "Supreme Waters." We see that the five *Hassadim* in *ZON* do not turn into the name *MB* before they receive from thirty-two *Elokim*. It is therefore said that thirty-two *Elokim* and ten sayings form the name *MB*, i.e., in the state of ascent.

Hence, Rabbi Hizkiyah said that the five Lights in the saying "Let there be Light" (signifying the five *Hassadim*) are called "seed" (abundance), which *Yesod* of *ZA* passes to *Malchut*. And it is called *MB*, although essentially it is merely five *Hassadim*; however, since it has the Light of *Hochma* that was received from thirty-two *Elokim* of *YESHSUT*, it refers to *MB*.

# FLOWER BUDS

**4. In the Beginning, Rabbi Shimon opened, "The flower buds have appeared on the earth"** (In Hebrew the words "land" and "earth" are designated by the same word, *Eretz*; Song of Songs, 2:12). **"The flower buds" refer to the act of creation; "appeared on the earth." When? On the third day, as it is said, "And the earth brought forth grass"** (*Beresheet*, 1:12). **"The time of singing has come" refers to the fourth day, the time of strictness, judgment, restriction. Therefore, on the fourth day, the word "lights" is written with a missing letter, which hints at the strictness of judgment and a curse. "And the voice of the turtle dove is heard" refers to the fifth day, on which it is said, "Let the waters swarm," so that they can produce offspring. However, the words "is heard" already refer to the sixth day, on which it is said, "Let us make man," who, in the future, shall put action before understanding (we shall do and we shall hear, *Naaseh ve Nishmah*). For here it is said, "Let us make man," and there it is said, "We shall do and we shall hear." "In our land" refers to the day of Shabbat, which is like the Land of Life, the world to come.**

It is completely incomprehensible to us how *The Zohar* compares the words from *Shir HaShirim* (Song of Songs, 2:12) with what is written in the Torah about the first days of creation. The six days of creation symbolize the six *Sefirot HGT-NHY* of ZA, onto which all ten *Sefirot* of *Nukva* are built. This is because *Nukva* is only the will to receive (pleasure), while her entire spiritual body (desires of bestowal) consists of her husband's *Sefirot*, ZA, the altruistic properties that ZA passes to *Nukva*.

*Nukva* herself (the created desire to receive pleasure) is an empty place unfilled with Light (the Creator). This is because the Light can only enter a desire (*Kli*) with similar properties to itself. Therefore, to the extent of her similarity to ZA, the properties that *Malchut* receives from ZA, those corrected properties of *Malchut* turn into a *Partzuf* and become filled with the Light that corresponds to their correction.

Thus, the greater the correction that is made in a particular part, the greater the Light (of the five Lights *NRNHY*) that enters that part. The corrected and fulfilled part of *Malchut* is referred to as a "world." Here and henceforth, *The Zohar* explains how *Nukva* is built out of ZA, i.e., how the world is created.

*Nukva* is called "earth." Flower buds are *Sefirot*—the properties of ZA that appear and grow within *Malchut* on the third day of creation, which corresponds to *Sefira Tifferet* (*Hesed-1, Gevura-2, Tifferet-3*). In the beginning, *Malchut* was created as ZA in height; two equally great celestial bodies, the Sun—ZA and the Moon—*Malchut*. This is why we see them as being equal in size when the Moon is full. After all, all that is said with regard to man. In the initial state following her creation, *Malchut* is a point at the feet of ZA, and subsequently grows along him.

That is to say, on the third day of creation, *Malchut* was equal in height (had the same properties) to *Tifferet* of ZA. However, *Malchut* was not able to receive the Light in such a state. Hence, it is said, STRICTNESS (judgment) APPEARED ON THE EARTH (in *Malchut*); the flower buds merely appeared.

And after that, THE TIME OF SINGING HAS COME already refers to the fourth day of creation, when *Malchut* was diminished, because she complained to the Creator: "Two angels cannot wear one crown"—if *Malchut* is equal to ZA in height, she cannot receive the Light of *Hochma* from him.

The reason for that being—not having received the Light of *Hassadim* from ZA beforehand, *Malchut* cannot receive the Light of *Hochma*, as the Light of *Hochma* can only be received within the Light of *Hassadim*, by clothing the Light of *Hochma* (pleasure) into the Light of *Hassadim* (the intention to enjoy "for the Creator's sake").

And the Creator answered *Malchut*: "Go and diminish yourself." In other words: if, owing to your egoistic properties, you cannot receive the Light independently, but only from ZA, then diminish your own properties, accept His, and gradually correct yourself. Then you will be able to receive all of the Light and be like Him (ZA—the Creator). All of this is described in the Talmud (*Hullin*, 60:2), but only with the explanation provided in *The Zohar* do we stop perceiving it as a fairytale.

Then *Malchut* descended below *Yesod* of ZA, and her nine lower *Sefirot* fell below *Parsa* into the worlds of BYA. And only her *Sefira Keter* remained in *Atzilut* as a point standing below *Yesod* of ZA. And from here on, *Malchut* is built not of her own *Sefirot* (properties) that exist in BYA, but of *Sefirot* (properties) *Netzah* and *Hod* of ZA.

Although *Malchut* was previously bigger, she was not able to receive the Light for lack of the Light of *Hassadim*; now she will be smaller, but she will have the Light of *Hassadim*, in which she will be able to receive the Light of *Hochma*. Even though *Malchut* will be at a lower degree, she will be able to utilize it, for the Light of *Hassadim* repels the impure forces that cling to *Nukva*. That is the meaning of the word *Zamir* (singing/pruning). However, there is another meaning to this word that is at use here—cutting off, or pruning the impure forces from *Malchut* (rose bud).

THE VOICE OF THE TURTLE DOVE: The turtle dove is a *Sefira*, the property of *Netzah de ZA*, and the voice of the turtle dove represents *Sefira Hod* of ZA, the fifth day of creation. And since *Malchut* receives from *Yesod* (which receives from *Hod* that is joined with *Netzah*), such reception by *Malchut* is referred to as "the voice of the turtle dove."

Therefore, the words "is heard" refer to the sixth day, since the voice of the turtle dove (*Malchut*) is heard only with the help of the sixth day, *Yesod* of ZA, which includes both *Netzah* and *Hod*, and passes their Light to *Malchut*. Hence, it is said that this voice is heard in *Malchut* only from *Yesod*, on the sixth day.

The reason for this is that *Malchut* can receive the Light only from the middle line of ZA: either from *Yesod* of ZA (she receives the degree called NHY, *Ibur* – embryo) or from *Tifferet* of ZA (she receives the degree called HGT = VAK, *Yenika* – nursing or *Katnut* – smallness) or from *Daat* of ZA (she receives the degree called HBD = GAR, *Mochin* - brain or *Gadlut* - big).

| LINES<br>Left Middle Right | NAME<br>OF DEGREE | THE LIGHT<br>IN THE DEGREE |
|---|---|---|
| Bina — Hochma<br>Daat | HBD (*HaBaD*) | The Light of Neshama<br>= The light of HBD |
| Gevura — Hesed<br>Tifferet | HGT (*HaGaT*) | The Light of Ruach<br>= The light of HGT |
| Hod — Netzah<br>Yesod | NHY (*NeHY*) | The Light of Nefesh<br>= The light of NHY |

LET US MAKE MAN, FOR IN THE FUTURE HE SHALL PUT ACTION BEFORE LISTENING: sight refers to *Sefira Hochma*, hearing refers to *Sefira Bina*. Action or deed is a property of *Malchut*. In order to correct *Malchut*, the Creator's only creation (other *Sefirot* are properties of the Creator Himself, with which He gradually created *Malchut*), a second restriction was made—*Malchut* ascended to *Bina* so as to combine her egoistic properties of reception with *Bina*'s altruistic properties of bestowal; *Malchut* ascended to *Aba-Hochma*, and *Ima-Bina* found herself below *Malchut* (*Parsa*), where she became similar in her properties to *Malchut*.

Eyes refer to *Sefira Hochma* or *Aba*. *Malchut* ascended to the level of eyes and stands at the level of pupils. *Malchut* is called *Nukva*; and *Malchut* that stands at the level of eyes is called *Nikvey Eynaim* (pupils) or *NE*. That is why there are only *Keter* and *Hochma* in the *Rosh* (head) of AA: *Bina* fell from the *Rosh* to the *Guf* (body) and *Malchut* is above *Bina*, that is, *Malchut* represents an action that is Above, i.e., precedes perception and understanding. This is what is meant by "we will do, and we will hear"—the act of the second restriction, limiting reception only to GE. Such a state is called the "return" (in one's properties to the Creator). The "complete return" occurs when *AHP* of *Malchut* gets corrected and joins GE at this degree.

As a result of *Malchut*'s ascent to *NE*, she changes her properties (every one of us needs only this—to ascend to the level of the Creator's properties, so that we can receive them and become like Him), and is now ready to ascend to *AVI* and receive the Light of *Haya*. The constant Light of this level is called the First Temple. That is why when receiving the Torah, Israel elected to act first and hear after. And for this reason they merited reception of the Torah (Talmud, *Shabbat*, 85:1), as the action (*Malchut*) ascended and clothed *AVI*, and thus the secret of the fifty gates of *Bina* was revealed.

Construction of the Temple does not pertain to it being built in this world, but rather to the attainment of the degree of the Temple, the degree of *AVI de Atzilut*, the Light of *Haya* (the First Temple) or the degree of *YESHSUT de Atzilut*, the Light of *Neshama* (the Second Temple).

Here *The Zohar* tells us: "it is heard" on the sixth day, for on this day (in this state) *Malchut* was corrected by means of her ascent above *Bina*, referred to as "placing action before listening," to do and to hear as during the reception of the Torah. *Malchut* in the state of ascension to *Bina* is called the Eternal Land or the Land of Life, for she inherits life from *Bina*.

"IN OUR LAND" REFERS TO *SHABBAT*, WHICH IS LIKE THE ETERNAL LAND OF LIFE: *Ima-Bina* is called the Land of Life or the Eternal Land. As a result of the act on the sixth day, meaning the Creator's action from Above (the factor of time is designated by an action of the Creator Himself, which has no causes in our world), *Malchut* ascended to *Ima* on the seventh day of creation (*Shabbat*) and became like *Ima*, for when the lower one ascends to the degree of the Upper One, they become equal (in properties). Hence, upon ascending to *Bina* and there receiving the Light of *Haya*, *Malchut* is called the Land of Eternal Life.

5. Another explanation: flower buds are the Patriarchs, who entered the mind and entered into the world to come, **Bina**, where they remain concealed. From there they emerge in concealment and conceal themselves in the true prophets. Yosef was born and they concealed themselves within him. When Yosef entered the Holy Land, he erected them there, and then "they appeared on the earth" and were revealed there. When did they appear? When a rainbow can be seen, they become revealed. At that moment, "the time of singing has come," meaning the time to eradicate all the wicked in the world. Why did they survive? Because the flower buds have appeared on (from) the earth. And if they were to be seen beforehand, they could not have remained in the world, and the world would not have been able to exist.

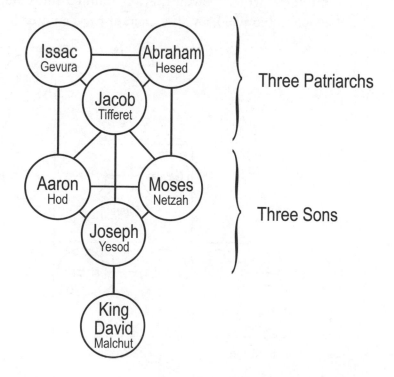

Here *The Zohar* explains the attainment of the Light of *Haya* by ZA. NHY of ZA are called "sons" and HGT of ZA are called "patriarchs," as well as the "turtle dove." ZA himself (seemingly) consists of two parts: above his *Chazeh*, his *Sefirot* HGT are called the big ZON; below his *Chazeh*, *Sefirot* NHY are called the small ZON. *Sefirot* HGT correspond to Avraham, Yitzchak and Yaakov, while NHY correspond to Moshe, Aaron and Yosef. *Malchut* corresponds to King David.

*Sefirot* NHY are called "prophets," and *Yesod* is called "the righteous one." Here *The Zohar* speaks of the buds that gradually grow from the small state to the big state of ZON: first ZON were small, consisting of *Sefirot* NHY with the Light of *Nefesh* and called *Ubar* (embryo). Then, with the help of *Yenika* (nursing), i.e., receiving Light from *Ima*, ZON grew. Accordingly, the properties of *Sefirot* NHY grew to equalize those of *Sefirot* HGT, and *Sefirot* NHY received the Light of *Ruach*.

Thus, the *Partzuf* now consists of parts of HGT and NHY with the Lights *Ruach* and *Nefesh*. Subsequently, by further reception of strength from the Upper One, and further growth, they've attained the state of *Gadlut Aleph*, the first big state. Accordingly, *Sefirot* HGT became HBD with the Light of *Neshama*, *Sefirot* NHY became *Sefirot* HGT, and received new *Sefirot* NHY.

Thus, the *Partzuf* grew to include three parts: HBD, HGT, and NHY with the Lights *Nefesh*, *Ruach*, and *Neshama*. And it is called *Gadol* (big—the first big state). Then, through further growth, they've attainted the state of maturity (*Gadlut Bet*, the second big state), and the Light of *Haya* entered *Sefirot* HBD.

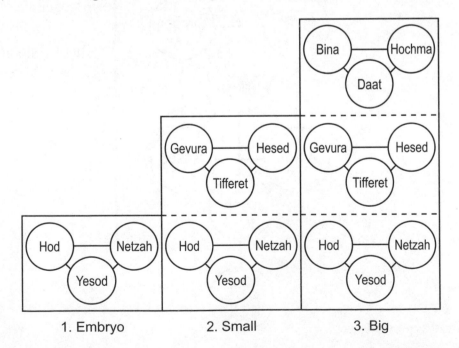

1. Embryo             2. Small             3. Big

The word "growth" refers to the growth of a screen, of man's inner anti-egoistic forces and desires. This is the only difference between a big vessel and a small one, the only difference between the *Partzufim*. Their inner properties change depending on the change in the magnitude of the screen.

THESE FATHERS ENTERED THE SUPERNAL MIND AND ASCENDED INTO THE WORLD TO COME: this sentence speaks of the prenatal development of *ZA*, when he ascends to *AVI* (called "Supernal Mind" or "Supernal Thought"). *Aba-Hochma* is called "mind" or "thought," and *Ima-Bina* is called "the world to come." And together they are called "parents"—father and mother, *AVI*. It is there that creation begins—conception of *ZA* in the initial state of a spiritual embryo.

Just as an embryo in our world is completely dependent on the mother, having absolutely no desires or life of its own, and developing only thanks to her, so can every man become a spiritual embryo; if he completely relinquishes all of his desires and actions, and submits entirely to the will of the Upper *Partzuf*, he will turn himself into a spiritual embryo, just like a physiological one. The difference between a physiological embryo and a spiritual one lies in the fact that becoming a spiritual embryo requires tremendous personal desire and effort, whereas the conception of a physiological embryo depends on the parents.

As a result of its prenatal development within *Bina* (which means that one completely extinguishes all of his personal desires and thoughts, and, like an embryo, is ready to accept all that the mother gives: all of her thoughts and properties, regardless of how incomprehensible or unnatural they may seem to his essence), this embryo achieves the state of its spiritual birth.

However, this is a state of an even greater concealment of the Upper Light with regard to the embryo, for it does not yet have a screen for the reception of this Light. Hence, this state is called *Katnut*, CONCEALED IN THE TRUE PROPHETS, i.e., in *Sefirot Netzah* and *Hod*, which *ZA* attains as a result of the process of nursing, reception of milk, the Light of *Hassadim* from *Ima* (mother) *Bina*.

The Light of nursing comes to the *NHY* of *ZA*, and *ZA* attains *VAK* (Light of *Nefesh-Ruach*), the state of *Katnut*. During nursing, *ZA* attains the *Sefira Yesod*, which is why it is said that Yosef is born. After the nursing period is over, *ZA* ascends to *AVI* so as to receive from them the Light of *Neshama*, and this constitutes the state of *Gadlut*, called "Yosef."

ZA consists of three parts: *HBD*, *HGT*, and *NHY*. The process of *Zeir Anpin's* growth, of acquiring a screen on his desires, begins with the purest, least egoistic part—*Sefirot HBD*, in which he first receives the Light of *Nefesh*.

Afterwards, ZA acquires a screen on coarser egoistic desires—*Sefirot HGT*; the Light of *Nefesh* passes from *HBD* to *HGT*, and the Light of *Ruach* enters the empty *HBD*.

Finally, ZA acquires a screen on the most egoistic *Kelim—Sefirot NHY*; the Light of *Nefesh* passes from *HGT* to *NHY*, the Light of *Ruach* moves from *HBD* to the empty *HGT*, and the Light of *Neshama* enters the empty *HBD*.

The attainment of the big state by ZA is called the birth of Yosef, for there emerge *Sefirot NHY*, of which the last *Sefira*, *Yesod*, is called "Yosef." However, since the Light of *Haya* is not yet present, this state is called "concealment." WHEN YOSEF ENTERED THE HOLY LAND AND ERECTED THEM THERE: that is, after the attainment of the first big state, the reception of the Light of *Neshama*, ZA continues to grow, cultivating his screen until the Light of *Haya* enters it.

In such a state, *Malchut* of ZA separates from him into an independent *Partzuf*, called THE HOLY LAND, as the Light of *Haya* is called holiness. It is therefore said that Yosef entered or, rather, ASCENDED TO THE HOLY LAND in the *Gadlut* state of ZA. ZA and *Nukva* became equally big in the state of *PBP* (*Panim be Panim*, face to face), which is the state that determines the *Zivug* between ZON.

AND YOSEF ERECTED THEM THERE: the Light of *Haya* or *Hochma* fills the *Partzuf* only during a *Zivug*, when ZON (ZA and *Nukva*) make a *Zivug* together. And this Light remains in *Malchut*, for only she (her screen) can reveal it. Just as *AVI* are *GAR de Bina*, *YESHSUT* is *ZAT de Bina* and the Light of *Hochma* is found only in *YESHSUT*, the relationship between *Malchut* and ZA works along the same principle, and the Light of *Hochma* is revealed only in *Malchut*. Therefore, only when the Light of *Hochma* fills *Nukva* can it be said that the Light has been revealed, and until that happens, it is considered to be concealed.

WHEN ARE THEY SEEN? WHEN A RAINBOW CAN BE SEEN IN THE WORLD: ZA is called a "rainbow," the world is *Malchut*, and their union is called a "rainbow within a cloud." THE TIME HAS COME TO ERADICATE ALL THE WICKED FROM THE WORLD—as the number of the wicked grows, as more impure forces cling to ZON. The impure forces can influence ZON so greatly that the entire world will be brought to ruin, as has happened in the time of the Flood. If so, there is no salvation for man other than through the revelation of the Upper Light, the Light of *Haya*. That is why *The Zohar* tells us that the world is saved by the flower buds appearing from the earth, meaning that the Light of *Haya* eradicates man's impure forces from the earth (his desires, *Malchut*), and they cannot cling to her and hinder man.

AND HAD THEY NOT APPEARED, THERE WOULD BE NO SALVATION FOR THE WORLD—for initially *Nukva* is built as big as ZA. This is called the "two great celestial bodies," when *Malchut* is on the same degree as ZA, but stands behind him, back to back, unable to receive the Light of *Hochma* in the absence of the Light of *Hassadim*. This is why *Malchut* complains about lacking the Light of *Hassadim* and thus not being able to receive the Light of *Hochma*.

Even though the moon grows as big as the Sun, it cannot shine independently, but only if the Sun (ZA) gives it Light. And since *Malchut* lacks the Light of *Hochma*, such a state is called reversed (*Achor*-back). And a *Zivug* cannot take place in the position of back-to-back (*Achor be Achor*).

However, after *Nukva* is born and grows (receives the properties) from the *Guf* of ZA, as it is written in the Torah (*Beresheet* 2) that Chava (Eve) was born from the body of Adam, she becomes equal to ZA and enters into a *Zivug* face-to-face (*Panim be Panim, PBP*) with him.

Also, *Nukva* still retained the previous Light. Moreover, precisely because she felt the lack of the Light in her initial state, *Malchut* received the Light of *Haya* specifically into her previous sufferings. Similarly, man can feel pleasure only and precisely because of his previous suffering.

Therefore, *The Zohar* tells us that had the flower buds not appeared in *Malchut* during her *Katnut*, when she was standing behind ZA, she would not have been able to receive the Light of *Haya* in her state of *Gadlut*, as she would not have the *Kelim* (desires) to receive this Light. Every new creation is founded on the sensation of darkness, as it is said: the Creator emanates the Light out of Himself, and creates darkness out of nothingness. Man's sensation of darkness signifies his readiness to receive the Light.

**6. Who sustains the world and evokes the revelation of the Patriarchs? It is the voice of the children engaged in the Torah. The world exists thanks to these children. Hence, it is said: "We will make for you pendants of gold" (Shir HaShirim, 1:11). These are the children, youngsters of the world, as it is said: "Make two cherubs of gold" (Shemot, 25:18).**

The Light of *Ruach* is called "the children of the world," and the *Zivug* in this state (*PBA*—face to back) is referred to as THE VOICE OF THE CHILDREN ENGAGED IN THE TORAH. And it is also called "threads of gold" and "two cherubs of gold." Before *Nukva* grew, the impure forces had the power to destroy the world. However, precisely because *Nukva* grows from ZA, the right and left lines merge in her as one, the RAINBOW (right line) shines WITHIN A CLOUD (left line), and the Light of *Haya* can enter *Malchut*. Without this Light, the world can be destroyed as during (in the state of) the Flood.

SO WHO IS IT THAT SUSTAINS THE WORLD: who causes the appearance of the Light of *Haya*? They are precisely the children engaged in the Torah. The "children" designate the Light of the opposite side, the Light of *Ruach*, the sensation of deficiency of the Light of *Haya*, for a "child" alludes to the process of nursing. The children of the house of *Raban* (*Tinokot Shel Beit Raban*)—are the Light of *Haya*, as the word "*Raban*" derives from "*Rav*" (big, *Haya*). They did not transgress, i.e., did not use their *AHP* (egoistic and yet uncorrected desires, for the word "children" designates the small state), their will to receive.

# WHO CREATED THESE

**7. In the beginning, Rabbi Elazar opened, "Raise your eyes and you shall see, WHO HAS CREATED THESE" (*Yeshayahu*, 40:26). Raise your eyes where? To the place on which all eyes depend. Who is He? He is the One who opens eyes, *Malchut de Rosh de Arich Anpin*. And there you shall see that *Atik* is concealed and within it lies the answer to the question: WHO HAS CREATED THESE? WHO? MI, ZAT *de Bina*, the Highest Edge of Heaven, and everything depends on Him. And since the question lies in Him, and He is concealed, He is called MI. For MI is like when the question "Who?" is asked, as there are no questions above Him. The question is found only at the Highest Boundary of Heaven.**

In the beginning, Rabbi Elazar opened, "Raise your eyes on high and look at who has created these." Raise your eyes to what place? To the place, where all eyes depend on Him. And who is He? He is the One who opens eyes. And there you shall know. It is the concealed *Atik*, within which lies the question: who has created these? And who is He? MI = who. He is called by the edge of the Supernal Heaven, where everything belongs to him. Since there lies a question, and He is on a concealed path and does not reveal Himself, He is called *MI*. And because there is no question Above, this edge of Heaven is called *MI*.

In Hebrew, the word *MI* means the question "Who?" as well as the preposition "from." Since Kabbalah tells us about the property of our world's roots, one spiritual object can sometimes reveal an entire range of associations, properties, and categories. In the same way, here the word *MI* is a part of the word *ElokIM*, where the last two letters form the word *MI*. However, at the same time, they carry a variety of additional charges and meanings.

Rabbi Elazar wishes to explain how Heaven and earth were created. Naturally, just like the whole of the Torah, *The Zohar* refers only to spiritual degrees and categories, and does not deal with explanations of the physical

73

origin and development of our world. Moreover, it is impossible to understand the true origin and development of our world without attaining the spiritual world. However, whatever one does attain, he is unable to pass these attainments to others. Hence, even after he attains the full essence of our nature's origin and its actions, he will still be unable to describe it in a form that will be comprehensible to others.

Heaven and earth constitute the seven days of Creation—ZON of the world of *Atzilut*. However, if it is a part of *Atzilut*, then why is it described as *BARAH* (created, from the word *Beria*) and not *ATZIL* (emanated, from the word *Atzilut*)? Yet, precisely herein lies the opportunity to open our eyes to the process of creation.

*Rosh* (head) *de AA* has only *Keter* and *Hochma*. *Malchut* standing below the eyes, below *Sefira Hochma*, is called "the opening of the eyes." After all, only when she opens up does the Light of *Hochma* pass through her from *Rosh de AA* to all the *Partzufim* of the world of *Atzilut*.

It is therefore said that the eyes should be raised up TO THE PLACE ON WHICH ALL EYES DEPEND, for the Light of *Hochma* can fill all the *Partzufim* of the world of *Atzilut* only when *Malchut* opens up in *Rosh de AA*. Hence, the entire secret of the opening lies in *Malchut*. The Light of *Hochma* (the Light of Wisdom) is the Light of the eyes. It comes out of the eyes, and only in this Light can one see.

The word *BARAH* signifies *BAR* (beyond), meaning outside the world of *Atzilut*. This is because *Bina* herself came out of the *Rosh* of AA and stood lower, outside the *Rosh* of AA, giving birth to, that is, precisely *BARAH* (creating) ZON.

In Hebrew, every notion has several possible names that determine the specific action that takes place. Here, the birth of ZON occurred by means of *Bina's* exit and descent from her degree; hence, the birth of ZON is called *BARAH*, from the word *BAR* – outside (of one's degree).

The entire creation consists of only ten *Sefirot*. Yet, since every *Sefira* includes all the others, and since all of them are interconnected, every world, degree, or *Sefira* includes the properties of all the others, and consists of their parts. Therefore, every *Sefira* consists of *Keter*, *Hochma*, *Bina*, ZA, and *Malchut*, each of which in turn consists of five. In all, $5 \times 5 \times 5 = 125$ *Sefirot* or steps of the ladder that separate us (the lowest) from the Creator (the highest).

The property of *Bina* herself is not to receive the Light of *Hochma*. Yet, in order to pass the Light of *Hochma* to ZA and *Malchut*, who desire to receive it for the Creator's sake, since receiving the Light of *Hochma* is the goal of creation, *Bina* allocates within herself a certain part called ZAT *de Bina* or YESHSUT, which receives the Light of *Hochma* from *Partzuf Hochma* and passes it to ZON. The main part, *Bina* herself, is called GAR *de Bina*. The part of *Bina* that receives the Light of *Hochma* is called ZAT *de Bina*.

Therefore, if *Bina* exits the *Rosh* and falls into the *Guf*, as it occurs in the second restriction, this has no effect on *Bina* herself, for she does not suffer from lack of the Light of *Hochma* whatsoever, as though she had never left the *Rosh*. This refers only to the Upper part of *Bina*, GAR *de Bina*, which has no desire for *Hochma*. This part is called AVI, and it spans from the *Peh* (mouth) down to the *Chazeh* (chest) of AA.

However, ZAT *de Bina*, which wants to receive *Hochma* for ZON, just as a mother who wants to receive for her children, feels the exit from the *Rosh* of AA to its *Guf*, for there it cannot receive the Light of *Hochma*, but only the Light of *Ruach-Nefesh*, VAK of the Light. This part of *Bina* is called YESHSUT, and it spans from the *Chazeh* down to *Tabur* of AA.

ZON of the world of *Atzilut*, which receive from YESHSUT, span from *Tabur* to the end of the feet of AA, on the *Parsa*. Thus, there are two *Parsaot* (plural for *Parsa*): one is in the world of *Atzilut*, separating the *Sefirot* of "bestowal" (GE) from the *Sefirot* of "reception" (AHP). This *Parsa* is located at the chest of AA. The second *Parsa* is located between *Atzilut* and BYA. However, we can also say that every *Partzuf* has its own *Parsa*, which separates the desires of bestowal from the desires of reception.

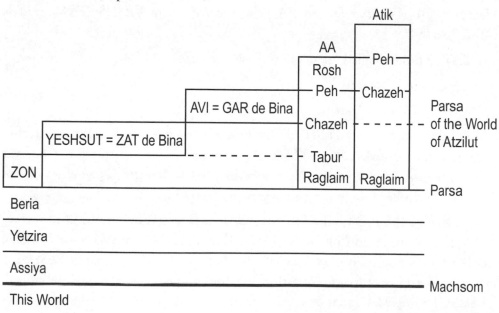

Although GAR *de Bina* are positioned below the *Rosh* of AA, they are considered not to have left it, as they do not feel it, that is, they do not want *Hochma*; they wish only to bestow, and he who wants only to bestow feels perfection wherever he is. All the *Partzufim* and their parts that have nothing to do with reception of *Hochma* (*Keter, Hochma,* and GAR *de Bina*) separate themselves with a *Parsa* from the remaining parts of the world of *Atzilut* that want *Hochma* (ZAT *de Bina* and ZON).

The "existence of the question" that *The Zohar* speaks of signifies the sensation of the lack of Light of *Hochma*, the desire for it. This is felt by ZON, which is why they raise MAN. MAN is a request of the lower one to receive the Light of *Hochma* from the Upper One for the Creator's sake. It is called a "question," for a question is similar to prayer or request. *The Zohar* tells us that the question exists only in YESHSUT, meaning that it receives MAN from below, from ZON.

And before that, it is said of YESHSUT: BARAH (from the word *Beria* = BAR), something that exists outside of its degree. What did it do? BARAH (created) ELEH (AHP, ZON). However, it created them as headless as itself. For the word BARAH (beyond) indicates the lack of a *Rosh* (*Kelim* of the world of *Atzilut*).

ZAT *de Bina* that wait for an "answer to their question," for the Light of *Hochma*, are called MI. It is said BARAH in regards to them because they exited and descended independently from the level of the *Rosh de AA* to below its *Chazeh*. These are ZAT *de Bina*, called YESHSUT or MI, the "Highest Edge of Heaven," for Heaven refers to ZA, who receives from YESHSUT. *Malchut* is called "earth."

ZAT *de Bina* is called "firmament."

ZA is called "Heaven."

*Malchut* is called "earth."

All that exists below YESHSUT (ZON and the worlds of BYA) receives from it. Hence, it is considered that YESHSUT revives the whole of creation: whatever it has, they will receive it, too. However, their MAN determines whether or not YESHSUT will have something to bestow upon them.

THERE LIES NO QUESTION in GAR *de Bina* (AVI). They do not receive MAN for the reception of *Hochma*, and they never feel any lack of *Hochma*, neither for themselves nor so as to give to others. Only ZAT *de Bina* or YESHSUT are created and exist for the question, for the reception of MAN (ZON's plea). YESHSUT raises MAN that is received from ZON to the *Rosh* of AA and receives the Light of *Hochma* from there. *YESHSUT* is called the "Highest Edge of Heaven," for ZA, called "Heaven," receives from it.

**8. But there is another one below, called MA. What is in common between this one and that one? The first one is concealed and is called MI. There exists a question in it for man to inquire and research in order to see and know all the degrees, down to the end of all degrees, which is *Malchut*. That is MA. What does MA mean? MA (what) do you know? What do you see? What do you research? After all, everything is initially concealed.**

Being in a state of *Zivug PBP* with ZA, *Malchut* is also called MA (like ZA) and is considered the lowest edge of Heaven, for she concludes all the degrees and *Atzilut*. ZA, called "Heaven," stands between *Malchut* (lowest edge of Heaven) and *YESHSUT* (Highest Edge of Heaven).

MAN MUST INQUIRE, SEE, RESEARCH—only if one who is below ZON raises MAN (his prayer) to ZON will they raise this MAN higher. For ZON themselves are corrected by the Light of *Hassadim*, and do not want to receive the Light of *Hochma*. And only if a request comes from below, from man, will ZON ascend to *YESHSUT* and ask for the Light of *Hochma*. *YESHSUT* proceeds to raise MAN to AVI, and AVI raise MAN to AA: AVI ascend to the *Rosh* of AA, where there is the Light of *Hochma*, where they make a *Zivug* on this Light.

A *Zivug* of AVI is called "*Aba* and *Ima* looking at each other." To "look" means to receive the Light of *Hochma* (to "hear" means to receive the Light of *Hassadim*). As a result of AVI's ascent to the *Rosh* of AA, *Bina* starts receiving *Hochma* for ZON. All the *Partzufim* of the world of *Atzilut* are corrected by the Light of *Hassadim* in such a way that they do not want to receive the Light of *Hochma* for themselves.

He who is able to raise his request (MAN) to compel ZON to ascend to *YESHSUT*, whereupon *YESHSUT* and AVI will ascend to the *Rosh* of AA together so as to receive the Light for him—such a person is not simply considered a mere "person," but a "righteous"!

The request that one raises to ZON is called one's "soul," for a soul is a vessel, a desire filled with Light. However, the Light inside a vessel is determined by the desire. Hence, the spiritual desire, the intention to act for the Creator's sake is called "a soul." Naturally, if one does not yet have such an intention, he does not have a soul.

The spiritual world is a world of only desires without any corporeal shells. The reader must revise his ideas about the soul, body, connections between worlds, etc., and correct himself continually so as to properly interpret these categories.

So then, man's corrected desires are called "the souls of the righteous." These souls of the righteous ascend to ZON in the form of MAN and compel ZON to ascend to YESHSUT. The presence of ZON creates in YESHSUT a desire to receive the Light of *Hochma*. This compels YESHSUT (ZAT *de Bina*) to ascend to the *Rosh* of AA and there join with GAR *de Bina* (AVI) into one *Partzuf*. And then AVI (AB + SAG = AA + AVI) look at each other, exchange the Light of *Hochma* between them, and pass it down to ZON.

Without a request from below, AVI will be satisfied with the Light of *Hassadim* and will not "look" at one another. Only the request of their children (ZON) compels AVI to face each other (*Panim be Panim*) and make a *Zivug*. In this *Zivug*, *Ima-Bina* receives the Light of *Hochma* for the children, ZON, from *Aba-Hochma*.

However, this occurs BECAUSE MAN INQUIRED—man's question signifies the raising of MAN so as to make AVI look at each other, make a *Zivug* together, and let *Ima* receive *Hochma* from *Aba* for the man that is elevating his soul. The descending Light of *Hochma* is called knowledge or wisdom (*Daat*), for ZON ascend to YESHSUT + AVI, and there stimulate a *Zivug* on the Light of *Hochma*, called "knowledge." Hence, it is written in the Torah: "And Adam came to know his wife."

Thus, to COME TO KNOW means to receive the Light of *Hochma*. ZON that stand in AVI and compel AVI to receive the Light of *Hochma* are called *Daat* (knowledge) or the *Sefira Daat*.

Yet, *Daat* is not an additional *Sefira*. There are only ten *Sefirot*. However, in order to designate the fact that ZON's request for the Light of *Hochma* is inside the ten *Sefirot* of *Partzuf* AVI, we say that AVI have a *Sefira* called *Daat*. In this case, instead of the regular count of *Sefirot*: KHB-HGT-NHYM, we count the *Sefirot*: HBD-HGT-NHYM. The *Sefira Keter* is omitted, and we only mention the *Sefira Daat* after *Hochma-Aba* and *Bina-Ima*. FROM ONE DEGREE TO ANOTHER signifies the passing of the Light of *Hochma* from the *Sefira Daat* of the degree of AVI to the degree of ZA. And TO THE END OF ALL DEGREES—from ZA to *Malchut*, which is called "the end of all degrees."

When the Light is present in *Nukva*, she is called MA, and the Light that she passes to the lower ones is called 100 blessings. There are several states in *Nukva*, *Malchut* of the world of *Atzilut*. We need to know them, for all that we receive, we receive from her alone. In addition to all stages of growth from a point to a full *Partzuf*, a grown *Malchut* has two big states.

*Malchut* attains the first big state when she receives the Light of *Neshama*. This occurs when, due to her MAN, AVI ascend one degree from their permanent place to the *Rosh* of AA. However, although YESHSUT ascends from its permanent place between the chest (*Chazeh*) and the navel (*Tabur*) of AA to where AVI used to be (between the mouth and the chest of AA), it still remains clothed onto the *Guf* of AA, even though it merges into one *Partzuf* with AVI.

And since YESHSUT now clothes the place from the mouth (*Peh*) to the *Chazeh* of AA from the outside, YESHSUT becomes like the *Rosh* of AA, as it merged with AVI in the *Rosh* of AA as one *Partzuf*. Also, YESHSUT ascends from under the *Parsa* of *Atzilut* in the *Chazeh* of AA and stands above it, where the *Rosh* of AA shines.

That is why YESHSUT passes the Light of *Hochma* to ZA, and ZA passes it on to *Malchut*, who fills herself with this Light, called "100 blessings," for, having received this Light, ZON can ascend to the permanent place of YESHSUT between the *Chazeh* and the *Tabur* of AA.

By ascending to this degree, *Malchut* becomes like *Ima*. In the spiritual world, the degree of a spiritual object determines all of its properties. Even in our world, the degree of man's inner development alone determines his properties, thoughts, and desires. And since *Ima* equals 100, *Malchut*, too, is called "100," so as to emphasize the fact that *Malchut* ascended to *Bina* of the world of *Atzilut*.

Now *Malchut* is similar to MI just as YESHSUT was prior to raising MAN and passing the Light. This is because she now clothes the place of the small state of YESHSUT from the *Chazeh* to the *Tabur* of AA, and stands under the *Parsa* of the world of *Atzilut*, below which the Light from the *Rosh de AA* cannot pass.

That is why *Malchut* gained no Light, for the sake of which she had raised MAN. Nevertheless, *Malchut* gains by receiving the properties of *Ima-Bina*, for she ascended to YESHSUT, called *Ima*.

Hence, the Light that *Malchut* received is only considered VAK of the *Gadlut* state, the first state of *Gadlut*. *Malchut* will not be able to receive the GAR of *Gadlut*, the second *Gadlut*, the Light of *Hochma* (*Haya*), as long as she is under the *Parsa* of *Atzilut* in the *Chazeh* of AA. (How *Malchut* receives GAR of the *Gadlut* is explained in items 11 through 15 in the next article).

The Zohar calls *Nukva* that ascended to *YESHSUT* by the word MA (from the word *Me'ah*—100), for by means of this ascent, *Malchut* gained the properties of *Bina*—100 blessings. And she gained the sensation of the question—she feels that it has only *VAK* (a half, a part of the big state). Put differently, she feels the desire for its second half, *GAR*. Nevertheless, she gained a part of the big state, *VAK* of *AVI*.

Thus, *Nukva* became like *YESHSUT* before it raised *MAN*, but gained the properties of *Bina*, 100 blessings. And since this is *VAK* of the Light of the big state, she feels a deficiency (a question), just as *YESHSUT* felt prior to raising *MAN*—at its place, when *YESHSUT* was in the *Katnut* state. When it ascended to *AVI*, *AVI* ascended to *AA*, and *ZON* ascended to the place of *YESHSUT*. *AVI* shine from the *Rosh* of *AA* on the place of *YESHSUT*. *ZON* that stand there now feel the Light that they receive from *AVI*, and realize that this is merely a part of the Light, which generates another question within them.

**9. This is the secret defined by the word MA: WHAT do you testify and WHAT is equal to you? When the Temple was destroyed, a voice came forth and said, "What (MA) shall I indicate to you, and what (MA) shall I equate to you?" (*Eicha*, 2:13). However, here MA means, "What is the covenant, testimony, what (MA) is equal to you?" For every day testifies to you the days of past, as it is said: "This day I call onto Heaven and earth to witness for you" (*Devarim*, 30:19). WHAT is equal to you? It is said: "I adorned you with holy adornments and made you ruler of the world." And it is said: "Is this the city that men called the quintessence of beauty?" (*Eicha*, 2:15). I have called you, "Jerusalem, a city rebuilt by me" (*Tehilim*, 122:3). "What shall I equate to you?" (*Eicha*, 2:13). Just as you sit here, so He sits Above in Supernal Jerusalem. Just as the holy nation does not enter into you, so I swear to you that I will not enter Above until I enter you down below. And this is your consolation—that I will equate you with this degree, with Supernal Jerusalem, which is the Supernal Malchut (Hebrew – Kingdom) that rules over all. But for now you are here, and "Your misery is great, like the sea" (*Eicha*, 2:13). And if you say that there is no existence or salvation for you, then WHO (MI) shall heal you (not Who? with a question mark, but the Upper Force called WHO is what will heal you), that is, that same concealed Upper Degree, which is called MI, Bina that revives all, shall heal and revive you.**

In other words, MA and MI, besides being translated as WHAT and WHO, also designate the names of spiritual objects that perform actions described in *The Zohar*. The destruction of the Temple was the consequence of Israel's transgression of egoistic reception, because they did not want to raise *MAN* for the *Zivug* of *ZON*, and instead wished to receive the Light into the impure forces, their egoistic desires, called "other gods" (*Elokim Acherim*). There is only one Creator.

There is but one property for the Creator, and we know it—the property of bestowal. Drawing closer to this property is defined as working "for the Creator's sake." Any other desire can only mean distancing from this property and from the Creator, for except for this property or its opposite (rather, its absence), nothing else exists in creation. Hence, man's inner movement towards the property of "reception" pushes him away from the Creator, and is therefore called "worshipping other gods." As a result, *ZON* stopped their *Zivug*, the 100 blessings disappeared from *Nukva*, and the Temple was ruined.

The First Temple—*Malchut* ascended to *AVI* and there receives the Light of *Haya*. Its ruin is the fall of *Malchut* to the level of reception of the Light GAR de *Ruach*.

The Second Temple is *Malchut's* ascension to *YESHSUT* and the reception of the Light of *Neshama*. In its ruin, *Malchut* fell to the level of reception of the Light of *Nefesh* in her *Sefira Keter*, while the other nine *Sefirot* fall below the *Parsa*. Such a state is called *Galut*—exile from the spiritual, from the world of *Atzilut*. The single *Sefira Malchut* in the world of *Atzilut* remains as a point below the *Sefira Yesod* of ZA.

ZA is called "six days" and *Malchut* is called *Shabbat* (Saturday). Yet, is *Malchut* really bigger than ZA, as *Shabbat* is bigger (higher) than weekdays? The worlds of *BYA*, including our world, receive the Light, their life-force, from *Malchut*. The "six weekdays" are a state of *ZON* when ZA and *Malchut* are unconnected to one another. *Shabbat* is a state of *ZON* when *Malchut* joins with ZA, a *Zivug* takes place between them, and *Malchut* receives the Light from ZA and passes it on to the whole world.

Since the state of *Malchut* when she passes the Light received from ZA down to the world is important to us, by measuring our states in accordance with what we receive from *Malchut*, we define the extent of maximal reception as *Shabbat*. (Naturally, this has nothing to do with our calendar: weekdays and *Shabbat* are spiritual states that transcend time).

AND A VOICE CAME FORTH AND SAID: "EACH AND EVERY DAY MY COVENANT HAS BEEN IN YOU SINCE THE DAYS OF PAST"— here, *The Zohar* speaks of the Light of *VAK* that *ZON* receive in the state of *Gadlut*, which *Nukva* receives as MA. This Light is called "the past days" (*Yamim*

*Kadmonim*). Therefore, it is written in the Torah (*Devarim*, 4:32): "Ask now of the past days, which were before you, since the day the Creator created man, from one edge of Heaven unto the other, whether there has been any such thing as great as this?..."

The Light of VAK of the *Gadlut* state is called in ZON "the past days," for it is VAK of AVI. YESHSUT is ZAT of AVI. ZAT is an abbreviation of the words *Zayin* (7), and *Tachtonot* (lower, meaning the lower *Sefirot*). ZAT of AVI, meaning the seven *Sefirot* of *Partzuf* AVI, is YESHSUT. These *Zayin* are seven days, the seven primary *Sefirot* of AVI with regard to *Zayin*, the seven days or the seven *Sefirot* of ZON.

Hence, it is written, "MY COVENANT EACH AND EVERY DAY BY HEAVEN AND EARTH" (*Devarim*, 4:26). These words of the Torah speak of the *Zivug* of ZON called "Heaven" (ZA) and "earth" (*Nukva*). "The past days" or "Supernal Days" constitute YESHSUT, and "the low days" or "the present days" are ZON.

In this sentence, the Creator cautions that the *Zivug* of ZON needs to be constantly realized and maintained. Otherwise, the Creator warns that "you will disappear from the earth." And this is the meaning of the Creator's warning about the 100 blessings: they should be guarded and constantly created.

For these 100 blessings that *Nukva* receives from ZA every day in the *Zivug* of MA between them take place during the ascent of ZON to YESHSUT, when ZA becomes like *YeshS* (Israel-Saba) and *Nukva* becomes like T (*Tvunah*). YESHSUT stands for *Israel-Saba* and *Tvunah*. And then, the Light that *Nukva* receives from ZA becomes 100 blessings, like the Light in *Tvunah*.

It is said about it, "the city that united with her," for *Nukva*, called "city," merged with *Tvunah*, and *Nukva* became like *Tvunah*. And *Nukva* receives in *Tvunah* the Light of *Tvunah*, called "holy adornments," and then, like a crown of beauty, she surrounds the earth and receives power over the earth.

However, as a result of Israel's transgressions (the rise of impure desires over the pure ones), the Temple is ruined (the Light disappeared), and Israel is banished from its land (fell to lower degrees). This led to the distancing of *Nukva* (all creatures) from ZA (the Creator), for the lower nine *Sefirot* (desires) of *Nukva* fell to the impure forces (became egoistic). In other words, the nine pure, altruistic desires (forces) lost their screen and became egoistic, and *Nukva* herself turned into a point that stands below the *Sefira Yesod* of ZA.

Hence, it is written: "WHO SHALL REBUILD YOU AND HEAL YOU"— if the sons of Israel return in their aspirations to the Creator (to altruism), called "the return," correct their deeds (desires), and raise their prayers (MAN) for help in their correction to the Creator in ZON, they will once more be able to receive the Upper Light in ZON, *Nukva* will rise again to *YESHSUT*, called *MI*, and will be healed thereby (the Upper Light will enter *Malchut*, the souls, and will impart its properties onto them).

10. **MI—WHO sets the boundary of Heaven Above—YESHSUT. MA—WHAT sets the boundary of Heaven below—ZA and *Malchut*. And this is what Yaakov inherited, as he is ZA that shines from end to end. From one boundary, which is MI, to the other boundary, which is MA. For he, Yaakov, stands in the middle, between YESHSUT and *Malchut*. Hence, it is said, MI BARAH ELEH: MI is YESHSUT, BARAH means created, and ELEH stands for ZA and *Malchut*.**

Actually, it should rather be written, "from the beginning, i.e., from the Height of Heaven down to its end (lowest point) below." Yet it says, "from the boundary of Heaven." MI is YESHSUT that upholds everything with its question, the desire to receive the Light for ZON. MA is *Nukva*. Before *Nukva* raises MAN, she is the very last degree, standing below the *Chazeh* of ZA. Between YESHSUT and *Nukva* stands Yaakov—ZA that clothes AA from *Tabur* to *Malchut* of AA.

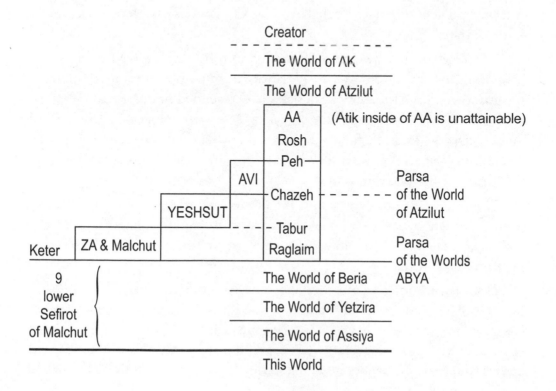

*Arich Anpin* is the central *Partzuf* in the world of *Atzilut*. Since *Atik* is unattainable, everything comes from *AA*, and all the *Partzufim* of the world of *Atzilut* clothe it (receive from it): *Rosh de AA* towers over all, and no one can clothe it, meaning no one can attain its thoughts and reasons for its actions.

The next *Partzuf* is *AVI*. *AVI* clothe (attain) *AA* from *Peh* to *Chazeh*. Below *AVI* stands *Partzuf YESHSUT*, clothing *AA* from *Chazeh* to *Tabur*. *ZA* stands below *YESHSUT* and clothes *AA* from *Tabur* downwards. *Partzuf ZA* is incomplete, as he has only six *Sefirot HBD-HGT* or *VAK*; he is in the *Katnut* state, ending with his *Sefira Tifferet* (his *Chazeh*).

*Nukva* (*Malchut*) stands below *ZA*, or parallel to his last *Sefira Tifferet* (the *Chazeh* of *ZA*). She has only one *Sefira Keter*, whereas her nine other *Sefirot* fell below the *Parsa* to the worlds *BYA*. The entire world of *Atzilut* ends at the *Chazeh* of *ZA*, where the single *Sefira* of *Malchut* stands, who is therefore called a point.

In our world, there is desire and its physical manifestation—action. For example, one wants to receive something, but he does not allow himself to perform the physical act of taking. Meanwhile, his desire to take remains the same. In the spiritual world, there are no bodies, only bare desires. Therefore, the desire itself already constitutes action, like an already completed mental and physical action in our world. Therefore, the desire alone determines man's spiritual state.

Just imagine what it would be like if in our world we judged a person not by his actions, but by his desires! It is terrifying to think how distant we are from spiritual demands. However, our desires are determined by our spiritual degree. And *The Zohar* explains that only by raising *MAN* (the request for correction) can we attract onto us the flow of Upper Light, which will correct and elevate us to a Higher Degree. And we will immediately begin to think and desire whatever that degree will evoke within us.

Therefore, our task is to attain the desire for correction. To this end, we need a "question," perception of our state as intolerable. This is called the realization of evil, i.e., that our egoism is evil, that it brings me harm by severing me from the spiritual.

However, in order for this to happen, we need to come to sense at least a little bit of what the spiritual is and how good it is. Evil can only be realized in contrast with good. Yet, how can we sense the spiritual if we have yet to escape egoism? In what *Kelim* (desires) can we sense this? Even though we lack corrected desires, and therefore cannot sense the spiritual, as a result of studying Kabbalah, one begins to sense the Surrounding Light, which bestows onto him the desire for the spiritual (See "Introduction to the Study of the Ten Sefirot," item 155).

The desire of one who physically exists in our world, but spiritually exists in the worlds of *BYA*—is a desire to enjoy the Light. However, opposite these desires one has an "anti-desire," a screen, which neutralizes his innate will to receive pleasure.

A screen is created (appears, emerges, born) within the *Kli* (desire, man) as a result of man's sensation of the spiritual Light (the Creator). Therefore, all our requests (prayers, *MAN*, "questions") should be about one thing only: for the Creator to grant us the strength necessary to ascend spiritually, to transform our desires or, as Kabbalah defines it, to acquire a screen. It is impossible to annul one's will to receive pleasure. The Creator created it, and it is His only creation. All we can do is acquire a screen (counterbalance) on it, thereby ascending above creation (egoism), and become similar to the Creator! And to the extent of this similarity, to merge with him.

Thus, *Partzuf* Yaakov stands from *MI* (*YESHSUT*) to *MA* (*Malchut*), from end to end. However, what is referred to here is the state of ZON, when they ascend to *YESHSUT* and receive the Light of its degree.

The entire spiritual distance from us to the Creator is divided into 125 invisible degrees, all of them named. These degrees differ from one another only by the magnitude of their screen on man's egoistic desires. Man receives the Light in his corrected, altruistic desires. The volume of the received Light depends on the screen's magnitude (the size of the desire's corrected part).

Every degree is characterized by a particular sensation of the Creator, and this sensation is called Light. Hence, we can designate the spiritual state of the *Kli* (man) in the spiritual world by the name of its degree or the name of the Light it receives, as every degree has its own particular Light. These gradations of the sensation of the Creator are precisely what we call spiritual degrees.

That is why, having ascended to a degree called *YESHSUT*, ZON receive the Light of *YESHSUT*, although *Partzuf YESHSUT* itself ascended, accordingly, to a Higher Degree, and there receives the Light of that degree, called *AVI*. In turn, *AVI* ascend to a degree called *AA*, where they receive the Light of *AA*. We call degrees by the names of the *Partzufim* that abide there in their usual, lowest state. Such a state is called permanent.

Even though by ascending to a Higher Degree, the lower *Partzuf* receives the Light of that degree, which changes its properties, the *Partzuf* remains itself nonetheless, just as a person who acquires new properties remains a person, though now one of another level. Therefore, when it is said, "having ascended to the Upper One, the lower one becomes like him," it implies a change only in the inner properties of man (or *Partzuf*), but not in his identity.

Upon ascending to *YESHSUT*, ZA receives greater Light, for an ascent in the spiritual world signifies an increase in the magnitude of a screen, and, accordingly, reception of greater Light. That is to say, ZA himself grew, but did not turn into *YESHSUT*: previously, at his own place, he had only the Light *Ruach-Nefesh*, but upon ascending and acquiring a screen, he receives the Light of *Neshama* as well.

Therefore, all the places between us and the Creator are established, and the *Partzufim* that are there "stand" on them in their permanent place. However, all the *Partzufim* and the worlds can ascend relative to their permanent, lowest states by one, two, or three degrees. In its lowest state, a *Partzuf* has only *GE* and no *AHP*, and only the Light of *Nefesh-Ruach*.

By receiving the Light of correction from Above, the *Partzuf* can gradually correct its *AHP*: it corrects the *Sefira Bina* and receives the Light of *Neshama*, which designates an ascent of one degree. After that, the *Partzuf* corrects the *Sefira* ZA, and receives the Light of *Haya*, which designates an ascent to another degree, i.e., already two degrees. And after that, it corrects *Sefira Malchut* and receives the Light of *Yechida*, which designates an ascent to yet another degree, a third one.

| | | |
|---|---|---|
| Keter | = Galgalta | ⎫ GE - Katnut (small state) |
| Hochma | = Eynaim | ⎭ |
| — Parsa, Nikvey Eynaim, Masach of Partzuf — | | |
| Bina | = Awzen | (ascent of Bina to GE = ascent by 1 degree) |
| ZA | = Hotem | (ascent of ZA to GE = ascent by 2 degrees) |
| Malchut | = Peh | (ascent of Malchut to GE = ascent by 3 degrees) |

However, the new Light does not enter the just corrected *Kli* (*Sefira*), but comes from Above and enters through the *Sefira Keter*.

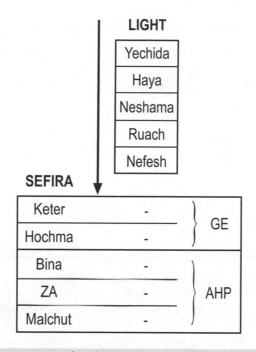

Man's spiritual ascent can be the consequence of two factors:

1. An awakening of a desire from Above, called "special days"—holidays, new moons, Sabbaths. This kind of an ascent is called "an awakening from Above," and leads to the general ascent of all the worlds *ABYA*, and, consequently, of all that inhabits them.

2. Man's efforts in his studies and inner work, his prayer to merit the Creator personally giving him the strength to ascend to a Higher Degree.

Moreover, such an ascent is not limited to only three degrees, but can elevate man along all 125 degrees to the Creator Himself. Ascension to the Highest Degree is precisely the purpose for which man was created. He must accomplish this task while still living in this world. And until he attains this goal, he will have to return to this world again and again.

Although *ZON* are called "the last days," upon ascending and receiving the Light of *YESHSUT*, they receive the name "the days past or first days." In this instance, one boundary of Heaven (*Malchut* or *MA*) ascends and clothes the other boundary of Heaven (*YESHSUT* or *MI*). MA and MI merge in one, and *The Zohar* emphasizes that fact. AND KNOW:

| | | |
|---|---|---|
| MI | – | WHO |
| BARAH | – | CREATED |
| ELEH | – | THIS |

MI is *YESHSUT* that stands in the place of *Bina de AA*, from *Chazeh* to *Tabur de AA*. And although only *Kelim* of *GE* (vessels of bestowal) are present in the world of *Atzilut*, there are *Partzufim* among them that wish only to "bestow": *Atik, AA, AVI*, and those that want to receive for the sake of bestowal, so as to pass the Light on to *YESHSUT* and *ZON*.

**World of Atzilut**

| Atik | These 3 Partzufim form GE of the World of Atzilut |
|------|---------------------------------------------------|
| AA |  |
| AVI |  |

Parsa of the World of Atzilut

| YESHSUT | These 3 Partzufim form AHP of the World of Atzilut |
|---------|----------------------------------------------------|
| ZA |  |
| Malchut |  |

*YESHSUT* and *ZON* want to receive the Light so as to pass it to the souls of the righteous, the people who seek correction. Hence, within the world of *Atzilut* there is a division into two types of *Kelim—GE* and *AHP*. They are separated from each other by the *Parsa* of the world of *Atzilut* that stands in the *Chazeh* of AA.

**World of Atzilut**

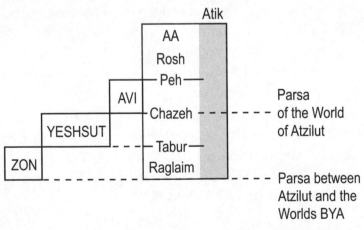

The Light from the *Rosh de AA* does not pass below the *Parsa* of the world of *Atzilut*. Therefore, *YESHSUT* in its permanent state, or *ZON*, when they ascend to *YESHSUT*, cannot receive the Light of *Rosh de AA*. This is why they have the desire to receive the Light of *Hochma*, called "question." The question (desire to receive the Light of *Hochma*) therefore amounts to *MI* (*YESHSUT*, the Light of *YESHSUT*), which is *BARAH* (beyond *ELEH–ZON*), and upon their ascent, *ZON* do not receive the Light of *Hochma*, as they are outside the *Rosh* of *AA*, outside of the Light of *Hochma*, but with a question (a desire for it). This enables them to continue their ascent.

# WHO CREATED THESE (BY ELIYAHU)

11. Rabbi Shimon said: "Elazar, my son, reveal the supernal secret, which the dwellers of this world know nothing about." Rabbi Elazar was silent. Rabbi Shimon wept and paused for a moment, and then said, "Elazar, what is *ELEH?*" If you say that they are like the stars and the signs of the zodiac (destiny), are they not always visible (unlike the changeable signs of destiny)? And in *MA*, that is in *Malchut*, they were created as it is written, "By the word of the Creator were the Heavens made" (*Tehilim*, 33:6), meaning that the Heavens were made by *Malchut*, called the Creator's word. And if *ELEH* speak of the hidden secrets, then there would be no need to write *ELEH*, as the stars and the signs of destinies are visible to all (the word *ELEH* (THIS) tells us that something is clear).

Rabbi Elazar did not reveal the reception of the Light of the first *Gadlut* state (*Ohr Neshama*), and Rabbi Shimon wished to reveal the way to receive the Light of the second *Gadlut* state (*Ohr Haya*). Therefore, he asked Rabbi Elazar to speak and to reveal the way to attain *Ohr Neshama*, which is concealed from people by a supernal secret, for this Light has not yet been revealed in the world, and Rabbi Shimon reveals it here.

The fact is that, although there were righteous who attained the Light of *Haya*, there was no one among them who could explain the path of its attainment in detail, no one who could reveal it to the entire world. This is so because to understand means to attain, to ascend to that degree, which depends only on man's efforts. While there were many people throughout the generations who attained the degree of *ELEH*, revealing it to the world requires an even greater degree, and a special permission by the Creator (See the article *The Conditions for Disclosing the Secrets of the Wisdom of Kabbalah*).

Rabbi Shimon asked him what *ELEH* means, what new things is the Torah telling us with the words, *MI BARAH ELEH* (WHO CREATED THESE), where the word *ELEH* designates *ZON*? After all, if it speaks of the stars and the signs of the zodiac—luck, which signify the Light of *VAK* of the big state, then what is so special about it? After all, *ZON* can receive this Light even on weekdays. There is nothing so extraordinary in this to mention *MI* – WHO CREATED THIS separately.

(One might say that this Light is constant, for only the Light of *VAK* is constantly present in *ZON*, but not *GAR*. And only as a result of *MAN* does *ZON* receive the Light of *VAK* of the big state, the Light of *Neshama*. The answer lies in that this Light can be received at any time, even on weekdays during the morning prayer. However, he still does not understand why these were created in *MA*. After all, Light refers not to *Bina*, but to the *ZON* of the world of *Atzilut*, called *MA*, and exits them, as is written BY THE WORD OF THE CREATOR, where the Creator is *ZA* and His word is *Malchut*.)

**12. However, this secret was revealed on another day, when I was on the seashore. The prophet Eliyahu came to me and said: "Rabbi, do you know the meaning of *MI BARAH ELEH* – WHO HAS CREATED THESE?" I answered: "These are the Heavens and its forces, the works of the Creator, looking at which, people should bless Him, as it is said, 'When I behold Your Heavens, the work of Your hands' (*Tehilim*, 8:4), and 'O LORD! Our Lord! How glorious is Your name throughout all the earth!'" (*Tehilim*, 8:10).**

**13. He replied to me: "Rabbi, the Creator took the concealed and revealed it to the Celestial Council. And here it is: When the most Concealed of all that are Concealed desired to reveal Himself, He first made a single point, which is *Malchut*, and it ascended to His Thought, that is, into *Bina*, meaning that *Malchut* ascended and merged with *Bina*. In her, He shaped all the creatures, and in her confirmed all the laws."**

*Atik* is the first *Partzuf* and the *Rosh* of the world of *Atzilut*. And it is called the most concealed and secret of all the *Partzufim*, and its name—*Atik* (from the word *Ne'etak*—isolated, unattainable) testifies to that fact. No one can attain this *Partzuf* in itself, its properties, but we can attain it the way it appears to us: *Atik* deliberately diminishes and changes itself in such a way that the lower ones could attain the outer form (its properties) in which it appears to them, but not *Atik* itself.

In the words of *The Zohar*, when *Atik* wished to reveal itself to the worlds, although it is a *Partzuf* that acts according to the laws of the first restriction, it "clothed itself in the garments" (an external *Partzuf* that acts according to the laws of the second restriction) with regard to the lower ones so as to enable them to perceive and attain it.

There is an enormous difference between the properties of the sensory organs that perceive sensations of the first and the second restrictions. Just as man in our world is born without sensory organs that can perceive spiritual worlds, which is why he cannot sense them, so is the *Partzuf* that is corrected for the conditions of spiritual work at the level of the second restriction unable to accept (perceive) the Light that descends according to the law of the first restriction. A similar distinction exists between *Partzuf Atik* and the other *Partzufim* of the world of *Atzilut* and the worlds of *BYA*.

To be connected to the lower ones, *Atik* elevated *Malchut de Rosh de AA* within the *Rosh* of the lower-standing *AA* up to the *Sefira Hochma*. As a result, *Sefirot Bina* and *ZON de Rosh de AA* fell from the *Rosh* of *AA* to its *Guf*. After all, *Malchut* ascended from the *Peh* to the *Eynaim* and stood in the *Rosh* at place of *Bina*, whereas *Bina* and *ZON* exited the *Rosh*. The *Guf* (body) begins after *Malchut de Rosh* (after the decision on how to act), wherever it may be.

Here is how one should understand this: the *Sefirot* of the *Rosh* are the thoughts and desires with regards to which the *Partzuf*, man's inner properties (man himself) makes the decisions as to how they can be used in order to advance as much as possible toward the goal of creation. The fact that *Sefirot Bina* and *ZON* exited the *Rosh* of *AA* means that *Partzuf AA* cannot make any decisions with regard to them for lack of a screen on them. This is why they fell into the *Guf*, outside the *Rosh*.

Hence, their remaining role is only to receive the Light from the *Rosh*, just as it is received by all the *Sefirot* of the *Guf*. In other words, they receive the Light that is accepted by the screen of *Sefirot Keter* and *Hochma* that remained in the *Rosh*. Man deliberately restricts the use of his desires, and uses only those desires with which he can work for the Creator's sake.

Therefore, when *Malchut* ascended and stood under the *Sefira Hochma*, *Hochma* became like the male part (bestowing, fulfilling), and *Malchut* became like the female (receiving) part of the *Rosh*. And since *Malchut* took the place of *Bina* (called "thought"), *Malchut* assumed the name "thought," since now it's *Malchut* that makes a *Zivug* and receives *Ohr Hochma*.

A *Partzuf* that receives from *Hochma* is defined as *Bina*, and not *Malchut*. Therefore, although *Malchut* herself is merely a black point (egoistic creature), as a result of her ascent, she becomes *Bina*, i.e., *Malchut* acquires *Bina*'s properties. Hence, *Malchut* is now called *Bina* or "thought."

*The Zohar* calls a "thought" either to *Hochma* or to *Bina*. The difference is that a thought is something that is received from *Hochma*. Hence, *Bina* is called a thought only if she is in the *Rosh* and receives the Light from *Hochma*. In the first restriction, *Bina* always receives from *Hochma*, and is called "thought." However, in the second restriction, *Malchut* ascended above *Bina* and started receiving from *Hochma*. That is why it is *Malchut* that is now called "thought," and not *Bina*.

All the *Partzufim* of the worlds of ABYA are created by this ascent of *Malchut* to *Bina*. Therefore, it is written: IN HER HE SHAPED ALL THE CREATURES, AND IN HER CONFIRMED ALL THE LAWS—*Sefirot Keter* and *Hochma* remained in the *Rosh* of each *Partzuf*, and a *Zivug* was made on these two *Sefirot*. This is why the Light received in *Guf* of the *Partzuf* consists of only two Lights, *Nefesh* and *Ruach*.

Previously, *Malchut* stood in *Peh de Rosh* and the *Rosh* (the part of the *Partzuf* in which it calculated how much Light it can receive for the Creator's sake) ended there. Then, the *Partzuf* would receive that Light from the *Rosh* to the *Guf*, between the *Peh* and the *Tabur*.

But now *Malchut* ascended to *Eynaim de Rosh* and stands under them. This is known as the ascent of *Malchut* to NE (*Nikvey Eynaim* – pupils of the eyes), which are called NE precisely because *Nikvey Eynaim* means *Malchut* of the eyes. Prior to *Malchut*'s ascent to the *Eynaim*, it was as though there were no pupils (NE). It is worth noting that only in *Malchut* (desire) can we feel what surrounds us (the Creator, Light). This is why all of our sensory organs are designed as apertures: *Nekev* (orifice), *Nukva*, *Malchut* in the eyes, *Awznaim* (ears), *Hotem* (nose) and *Peh* (mouth).

Only he who can create desires that work according to the principle of the second restriction through his own strength and effort, and puts *Malchut* after *Keter-Hochma* (thinks in terms of bestowal), can start perceiving through this corrected spiritual sensory organ. Wherever there is a screen, it constitutes that sensory organ with which one can perceive the Upper Light.

Upon her ascent, *Malchut* stood under *Hochma* and made a *Zivug* on her own screen, on *Sefirot Keter-Hochma* (GE). *Sefirot Bina-ZA-Malchut* (AHP) are located below the *Rosh*, in the *Guf* of the *Partzuf*, and passively receive the Light from the *Rosh*. This leads to a division of the ten *Sefirot* of the *Guf*, KHB-ZA-M, in the same way the ten *Sefirot* of the *Rosh* were divided: *Sefirot K-H* of the *Guf* continue receiving from *K-H* of the *Rosh*, and *Sefirot B-ZA-M* of the *Guf*, being unable to receive from the *Rosh*, start receiving from *K-H* of the *Guf*, like the *Sefirot* below the *Tabur* of the *Partzuf*.

As is well-known, every *Partzuf* consists of a *Rosh*, a *Guf*, and extremities. The *Rosh* decides how much Light the *Guf* can receive for the Creator's sake, in accordance with the magnitude of the screen that reflects the Light (pleasure). The decision to accept this Light causes the Light to descend through the screen, from the *Rosh* to the *Guf*, filling it from the *Peh* down to the *Tabur*. Each *Sefira* of the *Rosh* fills its corresponding *Sefira* in the *Guf*.

## Partzuf in the 1st Restriction

| | | |
|---|---|---|
| Keter<br>Hochma<br>Bina<br>ZA<br>Malchut | 5 Parts of the Head<br><br>Mouth | |
| | Keter<br>Hochma<br>Bina<br>ZA<br>Malchut | 5 Parts of the Body<br><br>Tabur |
| | | Keter<br>Hochma<br>Bina<br>ZA<br>Malchut |
| | | 5 Parts of the Extremities<br><br>Feet |

## Partzuf in the 2nd Restriction

| | | |
|---|---|---|
| Keter<br>Hochma | Mouth | 2 Parts of the Head |
| Bina<br>ZA<br>Malchut | Keter<br>Hochma | 2 Parts of the Body<br>Tabur |
| | Bina<br>ZA<br>Malchut | Keter<br>Hochma |
| | | 2 Parts of the Extremities<br>Feet |
| | | Bina<br>ZA<br>Malchut |
| | | Parts outside of Partzuf |

If there are only two *Sefirot K-H* in the *Rosh*, then only the two *Sefirot K-H* remain in the *Guf*. This is because only they can receive from the corresponding *Sefirot* in the *Rosh*. *Sefirot B-ZA-M* of the *Rosh* receive the same Light as *Sefirot K-H* of the *Guf*, which means that they are located under the screen (*Malchut* that ascends and stands under *Hochma de Rosh*). Thus, the *Guf* contains *K-H* that receive, accordingly, the Lights *Ruach-Nefesh*, and *AHP* of the *Rosh* that receive these two Lights of *Ruach-Nefesh*, too.

*B-ZA-M* (*AHP*) of the *Guf* cannot receive the Light from the *Rosh*, as their corresponding *Sefirot B-ZA-M* of the *Rosh* do not participate in a *Zivug*, since they lack the strength of the screen sufficient to reflect the egoistic desires of *AHP de Rosh* so as to receive for the Creator's sake. In other words, since there are no *AHP* in the *Rosh*, there are also no *AHP* in the *Guf*. And since *AHP de Guf* receive no Light from *AHP de Rosh*, they are like the extremities—the end of a *Partzuf*, below its *Tabur*. Hence, at the end of a *Partzuf*, below *Tabur*, there are GE of *Raglaim* (feet) and *AHP de Guf*, which fell there. And *AHP* of *Raglaim* are not parts of a *Partzuf* whatsoever, as they are located at a lower degree.

The Light that cannot be received by the *Partzuf* remains outside, surrounding it, and waits until the *Partzuf* acquires the strength to receive it. It is called "Surrounding Light," and it corresponds to the desires that do not take part in a *Zivug*, those desires that are still uncorrected and lack a screen.

If, previously, before the second restriction, *Malchut* (the last *Sefira* of the *Guf*) was in *Tabur*, now, when only two *Sefirot K-H* remain in the *Guf*, *Malchut de Guf*, too, ascends to *Bina de Guf*, called *Chazeh*. Therefore, when *Malchut* ascends to *Bina de Rosh*, the entire *Partzuf* "diminishes" in size: the *Rosh* reaches only up to the *Eynaim*, the *Guf* only to the *Chazeh*, and the *Raglaim* only to *Tabur*. And that is why this state of the *Partzuf* is called "the state of *Katnut*."

However, if the *Partzuf* receives new strength from Above, acquires a *Masach* (screen), it will be able to resolve to accept the Light for the Creator's sake in its *AHP*, then *AHP de Rosh* will rise again from the *Guf* to the *Rosh*, and complete the *Rosh* to ten *Sefirot*, while the *Sefirot* of *AHP de Guf* will ascend from the *Raglaim* back to their place in order to receive additional Light. And then *Rosh*, *Guf*, and *Raglaim* will all contain ten *Sefirot*. This state of the *Partzuf* is called "the state of *Gadlut*."

In the language of *The Zohar*, the restriction of a *Partzuf*, its transition from the *Gadlut* state to the *Katnut* state is described as a division of each part of the *Partzuf* (*Rosh*, *Guf*, and *Raglaim*) into GE (MI) and AHP (ELEH). All ten *Sefirot* are called by the Creator's name *Elokim*, which consists of the letters *ELEH-IM*, that are further divided into *MI – GE – K-H* and *ELEH – B-ZA-M*. When in *Katnut*, only *Sefirot ELEH* maintain their degree, whereas *Sefirot IM* fall to a lower degree. The word *Elokim* is read from below upwards, the way they are attained by man.

| Partzuf in the Big State | Partzuf in the Small State |
|---|---|

| M - K |
|---|
| I - H |
| E - B |
| L - ZA |
| EH - M |

| M - K | |
|---|---|
| I - H | Parsa |
| E - B | |
| L - ZA | |
| EH - M | |

IN HER HE SHAPED ALL THE CREATURES, AND IN HER CONFIRMED ALL THE LAWS—alludes to the division of each degree into two parts; their new form signifies the division into *ELEH* and *MI*, the separation of the *Kelim* (desires) of "bestowal" and "reception," where, due to the lack of strength to oppose one's nature (egoism), part of the *Sefirot* (desires) remain unused, outside of their degree. Accordingly, their Light remains outside as *Ohr Makif* (Surrounding Light), and waits until the *Partzuf* acquires additional strength to become big and thus receive all the Light.

During the 6,000 years, our entire correction transpires only according to the laws of *Tzimtzum Bet* (second restriction). As soon as the *Partzuf* acquires new strength (*Masach*) to receive the Light selflessly in *Sefirot/Kelim B-ZA-M* (*ELEH*), it will immediately attach them to itself and receive in them the Lights *Neshama-Haya-Yechida*. And it will grow to become a big *Partzuf* consisting of five *Kelim* (ten *Sefirot*) with the five Lights of *NRNHY*.

**14. He confirmed in the sacred and concealed candle (in Malchut that merged with Bina), a concealed image, the Holy of Holies, a secret structure that emerges from the thought, GAR that is called MI, which is the beginning of this structure. It stands and it does not stand; it is great and concealed in the name Elokim (ELEH and IM). It is called MI from the word Elokim, that is, it lacks the letters ELEH of the name Elokim. He desired to be revealed and called by the complete name Elokim, so He clothed Himself in a splendid shining garment, the Light of Hassadim. He created ELEH. The letters ELEH of the name Elokim ascended and combined with the letters MI and formed the complete name Elokim. And until He created ELEH, He did not rise (did not ascend) to the name Elokim. Hence, those who sinned by worshipping the Golden Calf alluded to this secret by saying, "ELEH (this is) your God, Israel!" (Shemot, 32:4).**

"*ELEH* (this is) your God, Israel!"—that is, these egoistic desires (*ELEH*) are your deity, which you must worship until you correct yourself. The use of *ELEH* is the reason for all transgressions and ruin: the breaking of the vessels (*Kelim*), the sin of Adam and the shattering of his soul into 600,000 pieces, worshipping the Golden Calf and the breaking of the Tablets by Moshe, the ruin of the First and Second Temples, and so forth.

As a result of the lower ones raising *MAN*, meaning their request to receive the strength necessary to make a *Zivug* and receive *Ohr Hochma* for the Creator's sake, there descends from Above the Light called *MAD* (*Mayin Dechurin*)—the force that enables the *Kli* to create a *Masach* capable of reflecting Light, thereby resisting its egoistic nature. This force comes in the form of Light, the sensation of the Creator's greatness, and is referred to as the Light of *AB-SAG*, as it descends from the *Partzufim Hochma* (*AB*) and *Bina* (*SAG*) of the world of *AK* (*Adam Kadmon*).

If one ascends from the degree called "our world" to the worlds *BYA*, then wherever he may be in those worlds, his request for spiritual correction will rise through all the worlds and degrees up to *Partzuf SAG*. *SAG* turns to *AB*, receives the Light of *Hochma* from it, and passes it down to all the *Partzufim* along which *MAN* had ascended.

Since the entire world of *AK* exists in the first restriction (*Tzimtzum Aleph*) and above the second restriction (*Tzimtzum Bet*), the Light that comes from it provides the *Kli* that receives this Light with the strength to pass from the small state to the big one. In other words, the Light of *AB-SAG* enables the *Kli* to create a *Masach*, reflect the Light of *Hochma*, and receive it for the Creator's sake. The *Gadlut* state is called "the holy of holies," for being filled with the Light of *GAR* (the holy of holies) is utterly perfect.

The Light of *AB-SAG* first descends to the *Rosh* of *Partzuf AA* and lowers the point (*Malchut*) from the thought (*Bina*) back to its place in the *Peh*, where it was prior to *Tzimtzum Bet*. In consequence, the three *Sefirot B-ZA-M* rejoin the two *Sefirot K-H* and become five *Sefirot* in the *Rosh*, *AHP* (*ELEH*) ascend and join with *GE* (*MI*), and the Creator's name *Elokim* is completed.

However, this does not mean that the *Partzuf* can be filled with the five Lights *NRNHY*; it merely acquires a *Masach*, the strength to receive the Light in all its ten *Sefirot*. Since only *Ohr Hochma* shines in *AA*, this Light cannot fill the elevated *Kelim* of *ELEH*, as they can only receive *Ohr Hochma* if it is clothed by *Ohr Hassadim*. Only the *GAR* of the *Partzuf* (*K-H-B*) can have pure *Ohr Hochma*; the *ZAT* of the *Partzuf* (*Sefirot ZA-M*) can only receive diminished

*Ohr Hochma*—half-mixed with *Ohr Hassadim*. This is called the reception of *Ohr Hochma* in the middle line (consisting of half *Hochma* and half *Hassadim*).

Therefore, says *The Zohar*, THIS STRUCTURE STANDS AND IT DOES NOT STAND—even though all the *Sefirot* are already present in the *Rosh*, they still need to be filled with Light, meaning that *Sefirot ELEH* are not yet revealed in the name *Elokim*. Only the letters *MI* have so far been revealed (filled with the Light).

Hence, first, the *Partzuf* makes a *Zivug* on its *Katnut* state and receives *Ohr Hassadim*. Then, it clothes *Ohr Hochma* into PRECIOUS GARMENT (*Ohr Hassadim*). Only afterwards can the mixed Light of *Hassadim* and *Hochma* fill *Sefirot ZAT* (*ELEH*), and all five *Sefirot* will shine in perfection.

However, before *MI* gives *Ohr Hassadim* to *ELEH* so as to enable *ELEH* to receive *Ohr Hochma* in it, *ELEH* cannot receive *Ohr Hochma*, and only the Light of *MI* shines in the entire name *Elokim*. Further, *The Zohar* tells us that neglect of *Ohr Hassadim* (the intention for the Creator's sake) is precisely what constitutes the entire transgression. And since they transgressed, i.e., neglected *Ohr Hassadim*, that is, since they did not wish to receive with the intention "for the Creator's sake," but desired only *Ohr Hochma*, they caused the separation of *MI* from *ELEH*. Hence, it is written, *ELEH* – THIS (the desires of reception and not *MI*, the desires of bestowal) IS YOUR LORD, ISRAEL—and the Light instantly passed to the impure forces.

The Torah does not tell us about the history of an ancient nation, but about the structure of the spiritual degrees that we must attain. To know the properties of these degrees (whose attainment is designated by the acquisition of their properties), Kabbalah explains to us how they were originally created by a gradual descent (spiritual coarsening) from the Creator Himself.

And in order to give us an opportunity to correct our egoism, the Creator mixed it with altruism at the very creation of the spiritual degrees. This kind of mixing of opposite properties is possible only through an "explosion," since opposite properties cannot be combined otherwise. There were several such mixtures that occurred as a result of explosions (breaking of properties).

One of them is mentioned in the Torah (*Shemot*, 32:4), when, by worshiping the Golden Calf, the sons of Israel (the altruistic desires of "bestowal") suddenly wished to receive the Light for themselves. Consequently, the *Sefirot* (*Kelim*) of GE and AHP mixed together, and the properties (desires) of GE penetrated AHP. Through these altruistic properties that are secretly concealed within a small, egoistic human being, it is possible to awaken him, to evoke in him an aspiration to ascend spiritually and to disregard this world.

Therefore, everything that is written in the Torah should not be perceived by us not as history, but as an instruction manual. All the actions described in the Torah are positive: all the devastations, including the ruin of the First and the Second Temples, wars, adultery and murder. We only need to realize what exactly the Torah is telling us. And one can understand it correctly only if he stops perceiving it as a collection of injunctions referring to the mechanical performance of commandments.

15. Just as **MI** join **ELEH** into one name *Elokim*, when *Hochma* clothes itself in *Hassadim*, so is the name combined by this precious shining garment. The world exists thanks to this secret, as is written, "The world was created by mercy." (*Tehilim*, 89:3). Then Eliyahu flew away, and I did not see him anymore. Yet, it is from him that I discovered that I stood upon the secret and its concealment. Rabbi Elazar approached with the others, and they bowed down before him. They wept and said, "If we have come into this world only to hear this—it is enough for us!"

Rabbi Shimon continues his explanation: There is only one law of reception of *Ohr Hochma*: *Ohr Hochma* can only be received if *Ohr Hassadim* clothes it beforehand. Just as this occurs in *Partzuf Bina*, called "the Upper World," so does it occur in *Partzuf Malchut* (MA, *Nukva* of ZA), called "the lower world." *Malchut* is typically referred to as BON, but when she joins ZA and receives the Light from him, she is called by his name—MA.

The Upper World, *Bina* of the world of *Atzilut*, desires only *Hassadim*, but the lower world, *Malchut* of the world of *Atzilut*, wants *Hochma*. However, Eliyahu the prophet spoke only of the order of Light and the structure of the name *Elokim* in AVI (*Bina de Atzilut*), whereas Rabbi Shimon continues his explanation in the next article and describes the structure and reception of Light in the name *Elokim* in *Malchut de Atzilut* herself.

# THE MOTHER LENDS HER CLOTHES TO HER DAUGHTER

16. Heaven, Earth, and all that inhabit them were created by **MA**, which is *Malchut*, as it is said: "When I behold your Heavens, the work of your hands" (*Tehilim*, 8:4). And before this, it is said, "MA – WHAT (How) majestic Your name is throughout the earth, which You established above the Heavens" (*Tehilim*, 8:2). After all, the Heavens were created by the name (property) **MA** (*Malchut*). It is written "in the Heavens," which refers to *Bina*, called **MI**, the Heavens that are above *ZA*. The explanation for this lies in the name *Elokim*. **MA** (*Malchut*) ascends and enters with her properties into *Bina*, i.e., connects into *Bina*, and receives her properties. *Bina* is called *Elokim*. After He CREATED LIGHT FOR LIGHT, meaning *Ohr* (Light) *Hassadim* (called "precious adornments or garments") so as to clothe *Ohr Hochma*, *Ohr Hassadim* clothes *Ohr Hochma*, which signifies the creation of Light for Light; by the force of the Supernal Name *Elokim* (*Bina*), *Malchut* ascends, and, upon joining *Bina*, receives all of her properties, and includes herself in *Bina*. Therefore, BERESHEET BARAH ELOKIM (In the beginning the Creator created) refers to the Supernal *Elokim*, to *Bina* and not to *Malchut*. For **MA** (*Malchut*) is not created by the name **MI ELEH**.

The lower world (*Malchut*, MA) receives the Light (marked from Above by the name *Elokim*) from *Bina*. This Light brings *Malchut* strength, and the properties suitable for the creation of Heaven, earth, and posterity manifest within her. After all, there cannot be any posterity or birth of new generations without the Light of *Haya*.

And this is what *The Zohar* tells us: so does the lower world (*Malchut*, MA) exist by the name *Elokim*, by the name from the Upper World, which is why there's strength in *Malchut* (*Ohr Hochma*) to create generations. And if *Malchut* has *Ohr Hochma*, then the world can be created by her.

(*Haya* is one type of *Ohr Hochma*. There is one Light that the Creator emanates, or rather, the sensation of the Creator we refer to as Light. This sensation depends on the desires-*Kelim* in which we feel Him. And since there are only two types of desires-*Kelim*, those of "bestowal" and those of "reception," there exist only two types of Light, *Hassadim* and *Hochma*. However, each of them includes several subtypes, and *Ohr Haya* constitutes a particular form of *Ohr Hochma*. This is because *Hochma* is the Light or pleasure that is felt by the will "to receive," whereas *Hassadim* is the pleasure that is felt by the will "to bestow." If only the *Kelim* of bestowal (GE) are present in the *Partzuf*, it is filled with *Ohr Hassadim*; and if it has the strength to receive for the Creator's sake, it is filled with *Ohr Hochma*.) (Do not confuse this with MA, which is used here, where MA = *Malchut* with ZA = MA in *Gematria*).

*The Zohar* explains that the Light descends from the name *Elokim* thanks to the merging of MI and ELEH. ZA is called "Heaven." YESHSUT is above Heaven (ZA). There is no MI in Heaven (ZA), only MA. However, after *Ohr Hassadim* clothes *Ohr Hochma* (the Light ELEH = AHP clothes the Light of MA = GE), all the letters combine and ascend by the name *Elokim* above Heaven = ZA = MA to YESHSUT = *Bina* = MI.

MI (*Bina*) is above the second restriction, above its ban, as her properties are higher, better than those to which the restriction extends: the property of *Bina* is "not to receive anything," which is why the ban of the second restriction—to not receive—simply does not apply to her, for in her essence, she has no desire to receive.

There remains only the ban of *Tzimtzum Aleph*, the restriction imposed on the reception of Light in *Malchut* herself (*Malchut de Malchut*), the central point of all creation, the only creating being. *Malchut* herself is egoistic, but if she has a *Masach* and only receives the Light by means of a *Zivug de Hakaa* (resistance to one's own desire, only for the Creator's sake) on the desires of bestowal, such reception does not occur in *Malchut*, but rather in the first nine *Sefirot*. Hence, *Malchut* can receive the Light in her first nine *Sefirot*.

In other words, if *Malchut* has the will (strength) to receive (enjoy) the Light (pleasure) not for herself, but only because the Creator so desires, then she receives only this amount of Light (pleasure). In order to receive the Light under such a condition, *Malchut* (man's inclination to pleasure and enjoyment) must first reject all incoming pleasure, which *Malchut* perceives to be right there before her. This is referred to as the Light's (the pleasure's) impact against the screen and its reflection off the screen (the reflection of pleasure by force of will so as to not receive, in spite of the natural, primordial desire to receive pleasure).

The reflected pleasure is called *Ohr Hassadim*. Essentially, this is not a Light, but rather *Malchut*'s intention to receive only for the Creator's sake. However, this intention is that necessary and sufficient condition for the subsequent reception of *Ohr Hochma* from the Creator. For after *Malchut* repelled all the Light (expressed her intention to not receive for her own sake), she thereby met the condition of *Tzimtzum Aleph* (first restriction) to only receive the Light of *Hochma* in the intention for the Creator's sake, which is called *Ohr Hozer* (Reflected Light) or *Ohr Hassadim*. And now she can receive *Ohr Hochma*, the pleasure that the Creator wants to bestow upon her.

However, by receiving this Light, *Malchut* is no more a mere recipient-creature. Now, like the Creator, she bestows pleasure upon Him! In this manner, the creature attains the degree of the Creator, becomes equal to Him in properties, for it wants to bestow everything. This is called "being filled with *Ohr Hassadim*." Moreover, *Malchut* receives and enjoys, for if she does not feel pleasure, she will not please the Creator.

Therefore, *Malchut* receives, meaning she is filled with *Ohr Hochma*, full of wisdom and pleasure, from both bestowal and reception for the Creator's sake. And herein lies the perfection of the Creator's Creation: she becomes perfect and similar to the Creator. And this is the perfection of the Creator's works: His creation can ascend to His level independently!

One can imagine one's path from the lows of our world up to the ultimate spiritual peak—the Creator—as a passage through a suite of rooms. In all, between our state and the Creator there are 125 connected, walkthrough rooms. Each room has its own properties, and only those who possess the same properties can be there. If, regardless of reason, man changes his properties, he is automatically moved as though by an invisible current to a room that corresponds to his new properties.

This is how one can move between these rooms: an infinitesimal inner change of properties evokes influence of a spiritual force-field upon man, and he immediately moves to his new place of equilibrium, where his inner properties completely coincide with the external properties of the spiritual field. Hence, there are no guards at the rooms' entrances/exits; as soon as man changes himself so as to match the properties of the next, higher room, he is automatically transferred there by the spiritual current or field.

What properties must one change in order to move from one room to another within this spiritual field? He only needs to alter the type of pleasure to which he aspires. We cannot help receiving pleasure, for such is the entire material of creation, it is all that was created. However, we can change the object of our aspirations, what it is that we wish to enjoy: either coarse reception, reception of mere necessities, or the Creator being pleased with us that we bestow to Him, that we receive because such is His wish.

Our "I," the entity that feels pleasure is present in all of our desires, which change ceaselessly in terms of both magnitude and the desired object. This "I" never disappears. The only thing of which one should rid himself is the sensation that he does something to please this "I." One should aspire to sense the desires of the Creator, how He is pleased with him (just as a mother is pleased with her son's achievements).

After *Malchut* decides to receive only for the Creator's sake, i.e., according to the force of her *Masach* (the force of resistance to her egoistic will to receive pleasure), she receives *Ohr Hochma* only in accordance with the magnitude of the Reflected Light. Or, conversely, one may say that the magnitude of the Reflected Light determines man's willpower and his desire to act for the Creator's sake.

However, the first nine of *Malchut's* ten *Sefirot* are not egoistic, as they are the Creator's properties with which He wishes to correct *Malchut*. Only the last *Sefira* of *Malchut*, *Malchut* herself, the single creation, called *Malchut de Malchut*, is egoistic and remains under the ban of the first restriction: *Ohr Hochma* does not enter where the will to receive pleasure is present. Therefore, the first nine *Sefirot* can receive the Light of *Hochma*.

However, after the second restriction, in order to correct *Malchut* and impart the properties of mercy (*Hassadim*) onto her so she would be able to desire to "bestow," acquire the properties of *Bina*, and convert her initial, primordial egoism into altruism, *Malchut* ascended to *Partzuf Aba*, became *Malchut* in *Partzuf Aba* in *Bina's* place, while *Bina* found herself below *Malchut*. *Bina* herself can receive *Ohr Hochma* without any restrictions, even when below *Malchut*. However, *Bina* adopted the limitations of *Tzimtzum Bet* for the sole purpose of correcting *Malchut*.

Therefore, due to the MAN raised by the lower ones, by man's requests for spiritual correction, the Light AB-SAG descends and lowers *Malchut* from the level of *Bina* back to her own place: *Malchut* descends from *Bina*, and the Light of attainment and wisdom is revealed.

As a result of *Malchut*'s descent, *Bina* purifies herself from all restrictions and limitations and returns to receiving *Ohr Hochma*. And after the *Ohr Hassadim* clothes the *Ohr Hochma*, MI shines in ELEH and the name *Elokim* is revealed, meaning that *Ohr Hochma* shines.

The structure of the name *Elokim* cannot be found in MA, for the lower boundary of Heaven (*Malchut* herself) is limited by *Tzimtzum Aleph*—the ban imposed on the reception of *Ohr Hochma*, and by *Tzimtzum Bet's* 6,000-year long prohibition on the usage of the desires of reception. Hence, *The Zohar* tells us that the name *Elokim* was created with MI, and not with MA, by the property received by *Malchut* upon her ascent to *Bina*.

**17. But as the letters ELEH descend from Above, from Bina down to Malchut, for the mother temporarily lends her clothes to her daughter and adorns her with her own adornments, the name Elokim descends from Bina (mother) to Malchut (daughter). When does she adorn her with her own adornments? When she sees the male essence before her. It is then written of her, "Three times in the year shall all your males appear before the Lord Creator" (Shemot, 34:23). For Malchut is then called by the male name "Master." As it is written: "Behold the Ark of the Union, the Master of all the earth" (Yehoshua, 3:11). The Torah is the Union and the Ark is Malchut, called by the male name "Master." For she received the Kelim (properties, desires) called "clothes," and the Light called "adornments" from her mother, Bina. The letter Hey (A from MA) then leaves MA (Mem + Hey) and the letter Yod (I) enters in its stead, and just like Bina, Malchut assumes the name MI. And then she adorns herself with male clothes, with the clothes of Bina, to accept all the husbands of Israel.**

As it is written (item 13), *Tzimtzum Bet* is in force from the *Rosh* of AA downwards, for *Malchut* of AA ascended to *Bina* and created all the lower *Partzufim* of the world of *Atzilut* in the property of *Tzimtzum Bet*. Thus, each *Partzuf* of AA, AVI and ZON has only two *Sefirot K-H*, and three *Sefirot B-ZA-M* separated themselves (their properties) from that degree, and moved to a lower one (their properties became equal to it). This is how B-ZA-M (AHP of *Partzuf* AA) fell to *Sefirot K-H* (GE) of *Partzuf* AVI, B-ZA-M (AHP of *Partzuf* AVI) fell to *Sefirot K-H* (GE) of *Partzuf* ZON, and B-ZA-M (AHP of *Partzuf* ZON) fell below *Parsa* to the worlds of BYA.

*Sefirot K-H* (GE) that remained in their degree in their *Partzuf* are called MI, and *Sefirot B-ZA-M* that separated (in their properties) and descended (by equivalence in properties) to a lower *Partzuf* are called ELEH.

THE CREATOR

THE WORLD OF ATZILUT

| | | | | | |
|---|---|---|---|---|---|
| K | | | | | AA (the 1st Restriction is in force above AA) |
| H | | | | | |
| B | | | | | |
| ZA | K | | | | AHP of AA fell to GE of AVI |
| M | H | | | | |
| | B | | | | |
| | ZA | K | | | AHP of AVI fell to GE of ZON |
| | M | H | | | |
| | | B | | | |
| | | ZA | K | | AHP of ZON fell to GE of BYA |
| | | M | H | | |
| | | | B | | |
| | | | ZA | | AHP of BYA fell to the point of our world - in the sensation |
| | | | M | | of a person who has attained the level of "our world" |

BUT AS THE LETTERS *ELEH* DESCEND FROM ABOVE—when *Malchut* is expelled from *Bina*, the letters *ELEH* get detached from *AVI* and fall to *ZON* (a lower degree), and clothe themselves in *ZON*: *ELEH* of *Aba* (*YESHS* – *Israel Saba*) clothe *ZA*, and *ELEH* of *Ima* (*Tvuna*) clothe *Malchut*. *Bina* of the world of *Atzilut* is a complex *Partzuf*: her *GE* constitute *AVI* (two *Partzufim*), and her *AHP* have the name of a separate *Partzuf YESHSUT*, for they fulfill separate functions with regard to *ZON*: *Bina*: *GE* = *MI* = *GE* of *Aba* + *MI* = *GE* of *Ima*. *ELEH* = *AHP* of *Aba* = *YESHS* (*Israel Saba*) + *T* (*Tvuna*) = *ELEH* = *AHP* of *Ima*.

When *Ohr Haya* descends from Above (as a result of which *Malchut* descends from *Bina's* level back to her own place), three *Sefirot B-ZA-M* thereby return to their degree, and correspondingly, *Sefirot KHB* (called the "holy of holies") enter the now complete *Partzuf* consisting of five *Sefirot*. (Here, the Light is called by the name of the *Sefirot* it fills.) Previously, there was only *Ohr Ruach-Nefesh* in *K-H*, and now *Ohr Neshama-Haya-Yechida* was added to *KHB*, while *Ruach-Nefesh* descended to *ZA-M*.

However, when *AHP* of *Rosh de AA* (*B-ZA-M* of *Rosh de AA*) that fell to its *Guf* ascend (return from *Guf* to *Rosh de AA*), the *Kelim* of *GE de AVI* ascend along with them to *Rosh de AA*. (These are the *Kelim* of *GE de AVI* that were clothed in *AHP de AA* in their small state, when *AHP de AA* had fallen to *GE de AVI*.) Once there, the *Kelim* of *GE de AVI* receive the Light called "holy of holies" that shines in *Rosh de AA*.

The reason for this is that when the Upper One descends to the lower one, it becomes like the lower one. And when the lower one ascends to the Upper One it becomes like the Upper One. This is because no space or motion exist in the spiritual, and only a change of properties instantly and automatically moves a *Partzuf* or its part in spiritual space, closer (higher) to the Creator or farther away (lower) from Him. Therefore, spiritual ascent itself implies a change of properties of the lower one to those of the Upper One, and a descent of the Upper One signifies that its properties became equal to the properties of the degree to which it descended.

Hence, in *Katnut*, when *Sefirot B-ZA-M = AHP de Rosh* of *Partzuf AA* separate from its head and fall (move according to their now inferior properties) to its *Guf*, from *Peh* to *Chazeh*, where *Partzuf AVI* clothes *Partzuf AA*, they (*B-ZA-M = ZON = AHP de Rosh* of *AA*) become like *AVI* in their properties, without *Ohr Hochma*, and only with the Light of *Bina, Hassadim*.

That is why, in *Gadlut*, when *B-ZA-M = AHP de AA* return to the *Rosh* (the degree that is higher than *Guf*), they take with them *GE* of *AVI*, as they all became one degree while in *Katnut*. Therefore, in *Gadlut*, *GE* of *AVI* ascend from *AHP de Rosh* of *AA* to *Rosh de AA* and become equal to it (in their properties), where they receive the Light called "holy of holies" that shines in *Rosh de AA*.

*ZON* ascend to *AVI* in the same way: after *AVI* receive the Light in *Rosh de AA*, they acquire strength (screen), and lower *Malchut* from *Bina* back to her place in *Malchut*, thereby enabling their *Sefirot B-ZA-M = AHP* to return to their degree, *AVI*, as in *AA*. However, when the *Kelim-Sefirot B-ZA-M – AHP de Bina* that were inside *K-H = GE de ZON* ascend to *AVI*, they also take with them *Sefirot* of *ZON*, which they've clothed—*K-H = GE de ZON*. Thus, *K-H = GE de ZON* ascend to *AVI* and there receive the Light called "holy of holies," the Light of *Haya*.

Therefore, it is written that *Ima*-MOTHER DESCENDS TO HER DAUGHTER TO DRESS AND ADORN HER: the letters *ELEH* or *Ima* (*Bina*) in her small state descend to *Malchut*. This means that THE MOTHER DESCENDS TO HER DAUGHTER, for the three *Sefirot* of *Ima* assumed the property of *Malchut*, thereby separating from *Bina* and becoming a part of *Malchut*. This is akin to *Bina* giving part of her *Kelim* to *Malchut*. Yet, this gift is temporary, as though *Bina* LENDS, GIVES (these *Kelim*) FOR TEMPORARY USE, and thus, *Malchut* uses them temporarily.

And then, *Ima-Bina* (mother) ADORNS HER DAUGHTER WITH HER ADORNMENTS. This is so because in *Gadlut*, when the three *Sefirot ELEH* return to *Bina*, *Malchut* ascends to the degree of *Bina* together with them, and there receives the Light of "holy of holies." And since an ascent to *Bina* implies becoming like *Bina* (in properties), she now has the right to receive the same Light as *Bina*.

It turns out that, as a result of the mother lowering her *Kelim* (properties) ELEH to her daughter by intentionally assuming the properties (desires) of *Malchut* instead of her own properties (desires), thereby entering the small state and willingly diminishing herself, upon receiving the properties of *Malchut* instead of properties of *Bina*, mother *Bina* adorned her daughter *Malchut* with her adornments, meaning the Light that subsequently comes in the state of *Gadlut*: the Light of *Bina* entered *Malchut*. This is described as "*Malchut* received her adornments."

There are two kinds of adornments that the daughter *Malchut* receives from her mother *Bina*: the first is *Ohr Hochma* (*Ohr Haya*, the Light of GAR), the Light of perfection, for it imparts the property of perfection to the *Kli* that it is filling, the Light that *Malchut* receives from *Ima* (Supernal Mother), who stands between *Peh* and *Chazeh* of *Partzuf AA*, above its *Parsa*. The second adornment is *Ohr Neshama*, which still designates imperfection, as it is received from the lower mother, *Partzuf* of *Tvuna* that stands between *Chazeh* and *Tabur de AA*, below its *Parsa*.

Naturally, to receive either Light, *Malchut* must ascend to the corresponding degree. In other words, she must change her properties so as to be able to receive, to merit that Light.

When *Malchut* ascends to *Tvuna* and receives her adornments from *Tvuna*, these adornments are still imperfect, for *Malchut* remains with a "question" (without the Light of *Hochma*), as *Tvuna* was before the raising of MAN. This means that to attain perfection, *Malchut* still needs to receive MAN from the lower ones, called the "husbands of Israel." In this state, the lower ones, called the righteous or "the husbands of Israel," receive the Light from ZA, which ascended to YESHS = *Israel-Saba*.

However, when *Malchut* ascends another degree, to the place of the Supernal Mother, *Bina*, above *Chazeh de AA*, and there receives her adornments from *Ima* and not from *Tvuna*, then these adornments are perfect, for they contain *Ohr Haya*; there is no more "question" in her, as she is considered a male, bestowing *Kli*, and the husbands of Israel receive from her.

And all the husbands of Israel appear before her and receive the Light from her. And *Malchut* is CALLED MASTER (Hebrew – *Adon*). The regular *Malchut* is called by the Creator's female name *Adonay* (mistress) or *ADNI*, whereas in this state she is called by the male name *Adon* (master).

And this is because *Malchut* no longer has a question, for *MAN* is no longer raised within her, as she has reached perfection (Light of *Haya*) and is therefore called "husband" or master (*Adon*). Hence, the prophet said: BEHOLD THE ARK OF THE COVENANT, THE MASTER (*Adon*) OF ALL THE EARTH (*Yehoshua*, 3:11). *Malchut* is called the "Ark," for ZA, who bestows upon her, is called the "Covenant." *The Zohar* calls *Malchut* the "Master of all the earth" or "husband."

As a result of the letter *Hey* in the word *MA* (*Mem-Hey*), signifying the female essence, leaving *Malchut*, for the letter *Hey* signifies the presence of a question in *Malchut*, i.e., the absence of *Ohr Hochma*, whereas *Ohr Hochma* brings absolute knowledge, all questions disappear, and with them the letter *Hey*. The letter *Yod* ascends to the place of *Hey*, and *Malchut* assumes the name *MI* as *Ima*, which signifies *Malchut*'s reception of the name *Elokim*, as the name *Ima*.

**18. Israel receives the last letters (ELEH) from Above, from Bina down to that place, i.e., to Malchut, who is now called MI, just like the name Bina. I pronounce the letters ELEH and my whole soul weeps so as to receive these letters ELEH from Bina into the house of Elokim, which is Malchut. So that Malchut would be called Elokim, just as Bina is called Elokim. How can I receive them? "With joyous songs of praise sung in the voice of the Torah, and festive throngs" (Tehilim, 42:4). Rabbi Elazar said, "My silence has erected the Temple Above, which is Bina, and the Temple below, which is Malchut. Of course, as people say, 'A word is worth a gold coin (Hebrew – Sela), but silence is worth two.' So the words 'a word is worth a gold coin' mean that I spoke and came to regret it. Silence, my silence, is worth twice as much, for the two worlds, Bina and Malchut, were created by this silence. For had I not kept silent (see item 11), I would not have attained the unity of both worlds."**

After *Hey* has left MA and *Yod* ascended in her place, thereby forming MI, Israel elevates the LAST LETTERS *ELEH* to *Malchut* by raising MAN. As we've already explained, in *Katnut*, *ELEH* of the Upper One fell to GE of the lower one. Hence, they refer to the lower one in *Gadlut* as well. For when B-ZA-M = *ELEH* of the Upper One return to its *Rosh*, they thereby elevate GE of the lower one, too. The lower one thus acquires the *ELEH* of the Upper One and the Light with which they filled themselves in their present *Gadlut*.

To equalize with the lower one and enter the state of *Katnut*, the Upper One deliberately makes *Tzimtzum Bet* on its *AHP*. And upon connecting to the lower one, the Upper One returns to the state of *Gadlut*, and passes the Light to that part of the lower one which they've both occupied in the state of *Katnut*.

This scenario is similar to one when a good, strong person joins a company of wicked men, and connects with them by pretending to be like them. And when such contact is established between them, he begins to correct them, little by little, precisely through this connection that has formed between them beforehand.

Each *Partzuf* in the small state is divided into two parts: GE and AHP. However, since there is a "column" of *Partzufim* between our world and the Creator, there is a connection between them via the common parts of the upper and the lower ones. Precisely because there is a part of an Upper One in each lower one, the lower one can receive strength from Above, through this common property, and ascend independently up to the Creator Himself.

Each Upper One that falls to the lower one completes its *Kelim* to ten *Sefirot*: AHP fall to GE of the lower one, and together they make up ten *Sefirot*, since they stand at the same level. In turn, AHP of the lower one falls into GE of the next lower one, and so on.

Afterwards, in *Gadlut*, when GE of the Upper One receive the strength to attach their AHP to themselves and elevate them, GE of the lower one ascend together with AHP, as they were joined below. Therefore, upon ascending, GE of the lower one continue to be joined with AHP of the Upper One, and together they form a *Partzuf* of ten *Sefirot*.

I PRONOUNCE THE LETTERS *ELEH*: Israel (one who wishes to receive the properties of the Creator) raises MAN (prayer for it) to receive in *Malchut* the Light of *Gadlut* (for self-correction) with the help of the letters *ELEH*, *Ima-Bina*. This is achieved by praying near the Gates of Tears, after which no one ever returns empty-handed, that is, after raising MAN, *ELEH* descend from AVI to *Malchut*, the house of *Elokim*. This is because after receiving *ELEH*, *Malchut* herself receives the name *Elokim*, just like *Ima*.

A WORD IS WORTH A GOLD COIN, BUT SILENCE IS WORTH TWO: the words (spiritual action) of Rabbi Elazar (the spiritual *Partzuf* of that name) elevated *Malchut* to *Tvuna*, below *Chazeh de AA*, where there is still no Light of *Hochma*, which designates the presence of a question in *Malchut*, a request for *Ohr Hochma*. And this is called "gold" (Hebrew – *Sela*, a gold coin), for that is the name of *Malchut*.

However, Rabbi Elazar's silence enabled Rabbi Shimon to reveal *Ohr Haya* by raising *Malchut* to the Supernal Mother, whereupon both worlds were simultaneously created, for the lower world, *Malchut*, was created together with the Upper World, *Bina*, of which *The Zohar* speaks: SILENCE IS WORTH TWICE (two worlds) AS MUCH.

**19. Rabbi Shimon said, "From here on the perfection of the written is said to bring forth their host by number." For these are two degrees, and each must be recorded, that is, noted: one is called MA and the other MI. MI is the Upper One, and MA is the lower one. The Upper Degree registers, speaks, and brings forth their hosts by number, where the letter *Hey* alludes to the one that is known and unequaled, namely MI. This is similar to the phrase, "*HaMotzi Lechem*"—He who brings forth bread from the earth (an appeal to the Creator), where the letter *Hey* refers to the knowledge of the known, lower degree, namely MA. And together they are one degree, *Malchut*. However, the Upper One is MI *de Malchut* and the lower one is MA *de Malchut*, the one that brings forth their host by number, for the number 600,000 refers to the number of stars that stand together, and they bring forth innumerable hosts.**

*The Zohar* alludes to the words of the prophet (*Yeshayahu*, 40:26): "Raise your eyes to the height of Heavens and see: WHO HAS CREATED THESE (them) – MI BARAH ELEH? He that brings out their host by number, He calls them all by name; no one shall be hidden from the greatness of His might and the force of His power."

The word "recording" means "marked by the letter *Hey*," for two degrees must be recorded in *Malchut*: MI and MA. With the help of the Light that is received at the time of ascent above *Chazeh de AA* to the Upper World, *Malchut* becomes like the upper world and assumes the name MI, for the letter *Hey* exits MA (*Mem-Hey*), and the letter *Yod* ascends to its place. Thus, *Malchut* is called MI, like the Upper World, and is adorned with the male property.

Nevertheless, MA, the previous degree of *Malchut*, does not disappear. The reason for this is that the degree of *MI* is essential in order to pass the Light, the perfection of the "holy of holies" to the generations, the posterity of *Malchut*, NRN of the righteous, the lower ones. However, the birth and procreation of these generations (sons) depend on the name MA. Hence, if either (MA or MI) is missing in *Malchut*, she will not be able to beget future generations, to create new souls (lower *Partzufim* filled with Light).

Therefore, *Malchut* BRINGS OUT THEIR HOST BY NUMBER—this is the degree of *MI*, which *Malchut* inherits from the Supernal Mother, for the letter *Hey* before the words "brings out" (*Motzi* = *HaMotzi*) alludes to the fact that *Malchut* contains the perfect Light, called "adornments," which she receives from *AVI*. This is the maximal Light that may fill *Malchut* during the 6,000 years.

The same letter, *Hey*, designates the presence of the Light of *YESHSUT*, the degree of *MA* within *Malchut*. For this degree must also be recorded, be present in *Malchut*. And these two degrees, *MI* and *MA*, are present in *Malchut*: *MI* above and *MA* below.

*The Zohar* calls *Malchut* the "world being revealed." That is to say, whatever *Malchut* reveals, the lower ones receive. Those individual attainments, individual sensations of the Light that descend from *Malchut* are what they call "their world." Similarly, whatever we feel in our sensory organs is what we call "our world." But this is nothing more than what we receive from *Malchut* of the lowest degree in the world of *Assiya*, *Malchut* of the previous degree.

However, we should know that the actual notion of "our world" indicates the true attainment of the degree called "our world," i.e., man's sensation of his ultimate disconnection from the Creator, total helplessness, and the realization of his absolute egoism. One can attain this sensation only if the spiritual Light shines on him from Above, in contrast to which he will see his true spiritual state. However, in order to reach such a state, one must make great efforts in the study of Kabbalah so as to draw upon himself the influence of the Surrounding Light ("Introduction to The Study of Ten Sefirot," item 155).

However, when man attains this state, he immediately raises such a request to the Creator that his *MAN* is not left unanswered, and he receives the strength to transcend "our world" and ascend with his properties to a Higher Degree— *Malchut* of the world of *Assiya*. And then it is she that becomes his world.

Here we are speaking about very high degrees. The *Malchut* that is being revealed is *Malchut* of the world of *Atzilut*, *Nukva de ZA*. And the fact that *The Zohar* calls her "Supernal" indicates the state of *Malchut* when she attains the degree of *MI* during her ascent and clothing the Upper World, the Supernal Mother. Therefore, *Malchut* herself is then called "Supernal," and the degree of *MA* is, accordingly, called "lower."

KNOWS ALL THE HOSTS BY NUMBER: number designates perfection. Light without a number indicates that the Light is imperfect, whereas the Light with a number is perfect. The action of *ZA* with regard to passing the Light from *Bina* to *Malchut* is described in the phrase: THE HEAVENS TELL OF THE CREATOR'S GREATNESS. THE HEAVENS (ZA) TELL (Hebrew—*Mesaper*, from the word *Mispar*—number, the Light's perfection). ZA passes this Light from *AVI* to *Malchut*, called THE CREATOR'S GREATNESS.

This Light is called 600,000, for the degree of *Malchut* designates units, the degree of *ZA*—tens, the degree of *YESHSUT*—hundreds, the degree of *AVI*—thousands, the degree of *AA*—tens of thousands.

There are two parts in *AVI*: their own part, where they are regarded as thousands, and the part from *Ohr Hochma* that is received from *Rosh de AA*, where they are regarded as *AA*, that is, tens of thousands. However, they cannot be considered a complete degree of *AA*, but only as its *VAK*, for they clothe *AA* from the *Peh* down to the *Chazeh*. And since *VAK* = *Vav Ketzavot* = 6 *Sefirot* x 10 = 60, the degree of *VAK de AA* equals 60 x 10,000 = 600,000.

Therefore, when *Malchut* ascends to *AVI*, she receives a complete, perfect number—600,000, where 60 signifies that it is merely *VAK*, for *Malchut* has not yet reached *Rosh de AA* and that she still lacks this degree. And the degree of 10,000 refers to *AA*, the part that clothes in *AVI*, for *AVI* are *VAK de AA*. Therefore, *Malchut* contains the number 600,000.

Thus, two degrees are recorded in *Malchut*:

- MI, the degree of *AVI* that clothes in *Malchut*, through which *Malchut* receives the degree of the Upper World and is called accordingly, while the Light in it is called 600,000.

- MA, the degree of *YESHSUT* that clothes in *Malchut*, through which *Malchut* has a question, the sensation of lack of *Ohr Hochma*, and the request for its reception. *Malchut* is therefore called the "lower world."

These two degrees create one *Partzuf* within *Malchut*: her part that is above the *Chazeh* is clothed in *AVI*, and her part that is below the *Chazeh* is clothed in *YESHSUT*. Therefore, in the generations, in *Malchut*'s descendants, each *Partzuf* consists of two parts (degrees): from the Upper Part (MI) there is a Light of 600,000, and from the lower part (lower world, MA), there is an absence of number (perfection) in each descendant.

The phrase, THEY BRING FORTH INNUMERABLE HOSTS is not interpreted as infinitely big. Rather, "Innumerable" indicates the imperfection of the Light that is received in the lower part, as it comes from *YESHSUT*, the degree that is without a number.

*Malchut*'s descendants are therefore defined as imperfect, as these two degrees exist in her as one, and are connected as one. Hence, there are two degrees in *Malchut*'s descendants: the Upper One—600,000, and the lower one—without a number. However, the lower one is defined as supplement to perfection and is not considered a flaw.

The reason for this is that the blessing of the seed, propagation depends only on the lower world, MA, without a number, as it is said in the Torah that Avraham complained that he is childless (*Beresheet*, 15:5), and the answer was: "Look now toward Heaven, and count the stars. Will you be able to count them? So shall be your descendants." From this we see that the blessing of the seed comes from the lack of a number, i.e., the name MA.

Hence, after all the perfection that *Malchut* attains from the Light of AVI (MI), *Malchut* has an additional blessing from MA, which is called the "lack of a number," and both these degrees are included in her descendants—the souls and generations.

**20. All of these 600,000 and all their innumerable hosts, He calls the names. What does this mean: "calls the names?" If you say that He calls them by their names, it is not so, for then it would have said, "calls by name." However, when this degree does not ascend in the name *Elokim*, but is called MI, it does not beget and does not reveal those that are concealed within it. And although they were all concealed within it, meaning that even though the letters ELEH have already ascended, the "precious garment" of *Ohr Hassadim* is still concealed. And while it is concealed, it is not called by the name *Elokim*. For He created the letters ELEH and they ascended in His Name—clothed themselves in "precious garments" of *Ohr Hassadim*, as a result of which ELEH combine with MI, and are called *Elo-im*. Then, by the power of this name, He brought them forth in perfection, defined as CALLS THEIR NAMES, which means that He called by name and brought forth every type and species to exist in perfection. Hence, it is said: HE BROUGHT FORTH THEIR HOST BY NUMBER—called them all by name, that is, by the name *Elokim*.**

It was already mentioned that the perfection of the Light, which is the Creator's name *Elo-im*, descends to the souls, generations, descendants, two degrees joined in one. This degree includes 600,000 from the Upper Degree, and innumerable hosts from the lower, and the Creator's name descends on both of them.

The blessing of the seed depends entirely on MA, for it is determined by *Ohr Hochma*, as this Light designates perfection. Whereas the Light without a number, *Ohr Hassadim*, comes precisely from the name MA. As is already known, *Ohr Hochma* is accepted only when clothed in *Ohr Hassadim*. Until such clothing occurs, even though ELEH ascend to MI, the name *Elokim* (ELO-IM = ELEH + IM) does not act.

Hence, it is written that *MI DOES NOT BEGET (ANY OFFSPRING)*, even though the point of *Malchut* left the thought (*Bina*) and descended back to her place, and all ten *Sefirot* and the Light returned to the *Partzuf*, THE NAME *ELEH* IS still CONCEALED, for she still cannot receive *Hochma* in the absence of *Hassadim*.

However, BECAUSE HE CREATED *ELEH*, meaning that after He added a *Zivug* to the screen of MA (lower world, *Malchut*), there appeared *Ohr Hassadim*, called WITHOUT A NUMBER. And *ELEH* were filled with *Ohr Hassadim*, which means *BARAH* = CREATED *ELEH*, as clothing in *Ohr Hassadim* is called *BARAH* (creation). Only after this are they called *ELOKIM*, for only after the reception of *Ohr Hassadim* can they receive *Ohr Hochma*, called "the Light of a number," the Light of 600,000, as a result of which, the letters combine and form the complete name *Elokim*.

The same perfection (clothing of *Hochma* in *Hassadim*) also extends to the souls and descendants that emerge from the name *Elokim*. AND HE IS CALLED BY THIS NAME: all that emerges is called by this name, with these properties He creates all descendants—*Partzufim* from His *Zivug* on *Ohr Hochma*. THE NAME 600,000 is *Hochma*, TOGETHER WITH *HASSADIM*, so that they will have the perfection of the name, so that Light will clothe Light, as they are clothed in the NAME. It is therefore written: SEE, I CALL THEM BY NAME, for "to call" means to revive and bring to perfection.

**21. He asks, "What is the meaning of 'by the greatness of His might and wealth?'" This is the head of the degree, where all desires ascend and remain concealed. The strong one that ascended in the name *Elokim*, as it is said, "This is the secret of the Upper World, called MI." No man is missing from the 600,000 that He created by the power of this name. And because no one is missing from these 600,000, it follows that wherever the sons of Israel perished and were punished for their transgressions, we subsequently find that not one from the 600,000 had disappeared, so that everything would remain the same Above and below. And just as no one had disappeared from the 600,000 Above, no one has disappeared from this number below.**

FROM THE GREATNESS OF HIS MIGHT AND WEALTH signifies *Keter de AVI*, called the HEAD OF DEGREES. This is *Bina* of AA, which became *Keter de Partzuf AVI*, WHERE ALL DESIRES ASCEND (MAN of the lower ones), and receive all the degrees from there. This degree is filled with *Ohr Hassadim*, and exists in perfection even in the absence of *Ohr Hochma*, as its Light of *Hassadim* comes from GAR de BINA of AA. In other words, it has such a powerful Light of *Hassadim* that although this degree emerged from *Rosh de AA*, it is not regarded as having left it, for it feels no need for *Ohr Hochma*. This degree, *Keter* of *AVI*, is the *Rosh* of all the degrees in the world of *Atzilut*, from where *AVI*, *YESHSUT* and *ZON* receive the Light.

THE STRONG ONE IS THE SECRET OF THE UPPER WORLD, the property of *MI* that is present in *Malchut*, from where the number 600,000 descends, for she clothes the Upper World, *AVI*. Therefore, it is written that NO ONE DISAPPEARS FROM THOSE 600,000 because there *Malchut* receives *Ohr Hochma*, called "600,000." Hence, it is said that AS NO ONE DISAPPEARED ABOVE, SO IT IS BELOW, for *Malchut* clothes *AVI*, described in the phrase: THE MOTHER ADORNS HER DAUGHTER WITH HER OWN ADORNMENTS, by which *Malchut* becomes completely similar to *AVI*. And just as the Light of *AVI* is perfect (which is why it is called "600,000" and NO ONE HAS DISAPPEARED, i.e., no lack of *Ohr Hochma* is felt), *Malchut* is perfect in this number, which means NO ONE HAS DISAPPEARED below.

# THE LETTERS OF RABBI HAMNUNA-SABA

**22. Rabbi Hamnuna-Saba said: "In the first four words of the Torah, IN THE BEGINNING THE CREATOR CREATED *Et* – *Beresheet Barah Elokim Et*, the first two words begin with the letter *Bet*, and the following two begin with *Aleph*" (The letter *Aleph* is pronounced both as "A" and "E"). It is said that when the Creator thought to create the world, all of the letters were still concealed, and even 2,000 years before the creation of the world, the Creator gazed into the letters and played with them.**

In the language of Kabbalah, the same sentence appears in the following way: when the Creator (*Bina*) decided to create the world (ZON of the world of *Atzilut*), the *Kelim* of ZON (*Zeir Anpin* and *Nukva*) were still in *Bina*. *Hochma* and *Bina* (*Aba ve Ima* – AVI) are called 2,000 years. Before the creation of the world (the birth of ZON), all the letters (the *Kelim* of ZON) existed in AVI in the form of MAN, and MAN always stimulates a desire in the Upper One to attend to it.

With regard to the lower *Partzuf*, the Upper One is called the Creator, for it truly begets it, and whatever the lower one receives, comes directly from its Upper One. Moreover, one may say that this is all that the Upper One desires, its entire existence is meant exclusively for the lower one. Therefore, the Upper One always waits for the lower one's genuine request for the desire to ascend spiritually, which is called MAN. Provided this desire is sincere, the Upper One immediately responds and passes the powerful Light of correction to the lower one.

Since the lower one is ZON of the world of *Atzilut*, and all that is below this *Partzuf* (all the worlds of ABYA and our world) is considered a part of it, AVI of the world of *Atzilut* constitute the Upper *Partzuf*. The desires and properties of ZON are called "letters," and here *The Zohar* explains the properties that ZON (the spiritual worlds and our world, we ourselves) were

117

created with, which properties are desirable, which require correction, and how this correction is achieved.

Since the properties of the future Creature are determined by the Creator's purpose in creating it, it is said that even before the creation of the world, the Creator played with the letters. The word "played" suggests that the Creator's interaction with the Creature is like His game with the leviathan (the legendary sea monster), with the property that is opposite from Him. At the end of correction all the letters unite and combine into the one name of the Creator.

The order of the Hebrew alphabet indicates the descent of the Direct Light from Above, the Inner Light that fills the *Partzuf*. The reverse order of the letters from the end of the alphabet alludes to the ascent of the Reflected Light. The direct order of the alphabet refers to mercy, whereas the reverse order—to the strict law and restrictions on using egoistic desires.

When Adam sinned, the letters detached themselves from him, and only the letters *Shin* and *Tav* (the *Kelim* for the Light of VAK of *Nefesh*) remained in him. The *Kelim* for the Light of *Neshama* are represented by the letters from *Aleph* to *Yod*; the letters from *Yod* to *Kuf* are the *Kelim* for the Light of *Ruach*, and the letters *Kuf* and *Reish*—the *Kelim* for GAR of *Nefesh*—disappeared from him.

This is why Adam gave his son, born after his sin, the name *SHeT* (Seth): *Shin-Tav*, according to the two last letters of the alphabet—the *Kelim* that remained in him. The *Kli Shin-Tav* are only fit for the Reflected Light from below upwards, but not for the reception of the Upper Light from Above downwards. However, after it receives *Yesod* of *Zeir Anpin* (the letter *Yod*), *Shin-Tav* turns into a combination *Shin-Yod-Tav*. And if the Creator creates the world by the letter *Bet*, it then enters between *Shin* and *Tav* and forms the word *Shabbat* (Sh-B-T), the state of spiritual perfection, the goal of creation. For this reason, the first word in the Torah—*Beresheet* consists of: *Bara* (created) Sh(in)-Y(od)-T(av).

**23. When the Creator thought to create the world, all the letters of the alphabet came to Him in reverse order from last (Tav) to first (Aleph). The letter Tav entered first and said, "Master of the world! It is good, and also seemly of You, to create the world with me, with my properties. For I am the seal on Your ring, called EmeT (truth), that ends with the letter Tav. And that is why You are called truth, and why it would befit the King to begin the universe with the letter Tav, and to create the world by her, by her properties."**

The Creator answered: "You are beautiful and sincere, but do not merit the world that I conceived to be created by your properties, since you are destined to be marked on the foreheads of the truly faithful who fulfill all of Torah from *Aleph* to *Tav* (from the first letter to the last), and perished because of you" (Talmud Bavli, *Shabbat*, 55)

What does a particular name of the Creator mean? The name of the spiritual object indicates the way one can receive the Light that fills it, the way one can attain its spiritual degree. Generally speaking, the twenty-two letters are the ten *Sefirot-Kelim* in the *Ibur* (embryonic phase) of the future *Partzuf* in the *Sefira Yesod*, for that is where the screen of the embryo of the new *Partzuf* is located. That is why *Yesod* is called a "number," as it measures the size of a new *Partzuf*.

Bearing in mind that each name determines specific spiritual properties and states of an object, one can understand what is meant by a change of name, place, or action.

*HaVaYaH* is the basis of all the letters, but the filling of each letter clarifies the letter itself. The filling of a letter is heard as the letter is pronounced. As we read the letter *Yod* in the word *HaVaYaH* (*Yod-Hey-Vav-Hey*), we actually pronounce three sounds (y-o-d); although we write only one letter, the sounds "o-*Vav*" and "d-*Dalet*" are heard together with the sound "y." When we say "*Hey*," the sound "ey"—*Yod* or "ey"—follows the sound "h." Therein lies the clarification of the name *HaVaYaH* in the process of its emergence.

The Creator's form-properties are revealed in His deeds; hence, the three lines in *Bina* (the Creator) are imprinted and act in His created beings (the lower worlds) as a seal and its imprint. Therefore, the name *MB* exists in *Bina*, as well as in *ZA* and *Malchut*. However, in *ZA*, this name is divided into the ten sayings and thirty-two forces of creation of *Elokim*, which create *Malchut*, the creature.

*Bina* is designated by the letter *Mem*, *Malchut*—by *Bet*; the name *MB* designates the creation of *Malchut* by *Bina*. The letter *Aleph* designates *ZA*, which passes all the twenty-two letters (from *Aleph* to *Tav*) to *Malchut* (*Bet*). This is why *Malchut* is called *ET* (*Aleph* pronounced as 'E'-*Tav*).

*Malchut* is the central part of creation and its purpose. She is the only creation and includes all the worlds with all that inhabits them, us included. Depending on its states, parts of *Malchut* or *Malchut* herself (which is one and the same) have different properties designated by the different letter combinations. For this reason, *Malchut*'s parts receive various "codes" (combinations) of letters (properties) or names.

All the words in the world originate here, in *Malchut*. There is not a single property in the world that is not included in *Malchut*. Each property of *Malchut*, each of the creatures (for all creatures are her parts) is designated by the property that distinguishes it from the others, by the unique set of letters-properties that forms its name.

*Malchut* is called *Shechina* (Divinity), as she is filled with the Light, *Shochen* (Dweller—the Creator). The Creator is called *Shochen* when *Malchut* feels Him as such, within her. If man, being part of *Malchut*, purifies himself of egoism, either partially or completely, and thus fills his corrected desires with the Light (the Creator), he becomes part of the *Shechina*.

*Malchut* consists of four parts that are named by their properties (also called faces): face of a lion, face of an ox, face of an eagle, and face of a man. Alternately, *Malchut* is likened to a spiritual kernel, surrounded by four shells, which correspond to the four *Klipot* (impure forces): *Ruach Se'ara* (Stormy Wind), *Anan Gadol* (Great Cloud), *Esh Mitlakachat* (Blazing Flame), and *Noga* (Radiance).

Kabbalah can describe spiritual actions either as names of *Sefirot* and *Partzufim* or as names of *HaVaYaH*, *EKYEH*, and so forth, with their fillings and *Gematriot* (plural for *Gematria*—the numeric value). Although the most frequently used language is that of *Sefirot* and *Partzufim*, sometimes the language of *HaVaYaH* with its fillings can also be applied, even in parallel or simultaneously with the former.

Most Kabbalistic terms are composite: *Maatzil* (the Creator) comes from the word *Tzel* (shadow), as the Creature emerges from the Creator's concealment, from His restrictions. Another name for the Creator is *Boreh* (combination of *Bo*—come and *Re'eh*—see).

A name denotes attainment. Upon attaining an object, man gives it a name. Similarly, man gives a name to the Creator according to the property that he attains, depending on how he feels the Creator. There are several kinds of names to the Creator, based on His properties. For example, the Creator's name EMET—"Truth" is based on the sensations of His Light within the *Partzuf*.

Below are the names of the Creator with the corresponding names of the *Sefirot*:

- **Keter:** *Aleph-Hey-Yod-Hey* (EKYEH)
- **Hochma:** *Yod-Hey* (YA)
- **Bina:** *HaVaYaH* with the punctuation *Segol-Holam-Hirik*, as *Elokim*: Yod (Yod-Vav-Dalet) - Hey (Hey-Yod) - Vav (Vav-Aleph-Vav) - Hey (Hey-Yod).
- **Hesed:** *Aleph-Lamed* = EL (pronounced *KEL*)
- **Gevura:** *Aleph-Lamed-Hey-Yod-Mem* (ELOKIM)

- **Tifferet:** Yod-Hey-Vav-Hey (HaVaYaH without punctuation)
- **Netzah:** HaVaYaH TZEVAOT
- **Hod:** ELOKIM TZEVAOT
- **Yesod:** Shin-Dalet-Yod = SHADDAY
- **Malchut:** ADONAY (pronounced ADNI)

Merging the two worlds, the Upper and the lower, is designated by the words HaVaYaH-ADNI, implying the ascent of Malchut-ADNI to the level of Bina-HaVaYaH with the punctuation of Elokim.

The name ZA of HaVaYaH comes from the right line (Hesed), and the name ADNI, from the left line (Gevura). Joining of these two lines forms the middle line, where the Light of Hochma shines on account of the presence of the Light of Hassadim from the right line. Such state is designated by a combination of the two names HaVaYaH-ADNI:

YOD-Aleph-HEY-Dalet-VAV-Nun-HEY-Yod. The union (Zivug) of ZA and his Nukva is designated by mixing the two names.

HaVaYaH-ADNI: Yod-Aleph-Hey-Dalet-Vav-Nun-Hey-Yod. The opening Yod indicates the Light of Hochma in ZA, the Yod at the end refers to the passing of this Light to Nukva.

As a result of the second restriction, Malchut ascended to Bina, and governs Bina and ZA with her desire. Since it is impossible to receive the Light of Hochma in the three Sefirot—Bina, ZA, and Malchut, which are governed by Malchut's egoistic desire, the Light of Hochma is absent in the Partzuf, and only the Light of Hassadim is present.

This is designated in the following way: the letter Yod enters the word Light (Ohr contains the letters Aleph-Vav-Reish, signifying the Light of Hochma), and forms the word Avir (air, containing the letters Aleph-Vav-Yod-Reish), signifying the Light of Hassadim. If the Partzuf returns to the Gadlut state, the letter Yod exits it, and it is refilled with the Light of Hochma. Consequently, Avir (air) becomes Ohr (Light).

Unfilled HaVaYaH designates Partzuf Keter. HaVaYaH with the filling of AB (72) designates Partzuf Hochma (AA). HaVaYaH with the filling of SAG (63) designates Partzuf Bina (AVI). Together, these three HaVaYaH form MB (42) letters—the sacred name of the Light that corrects the souls by its influence on the Kli, the screen.

All that was created is the desire to receive pleasure, which we call "creature." Only this desire was created, and nothing else. All the worlds and all that inhabits them, our world with everything within it, are but degrees of the desire to receive pleasure. The intensity of the desire determines its place in the spiritual realm, where all creation and our world—as its lowest point—are located. Man's actual location (the world, his spiritual degree) determines the particular kind of pleasure he desires, how he chooses to enjoy.

In order for the creature to emerge from the Creator, the Light emanating from Him must descend through four stages, whereas the fifth stage already perceives itself as a separate and independent (from the Creator) desire to enjoy precisely the Light emanating from the Creator.

Upon emerging from the Creator—a result of a sequential emanation of His Light—the desire to receive pleasure (Kli-vessel) also consists of five parts designated by the letters: the tip of the Yod, Yod, Hey, Vav, Hey. These five parts (four letters) are called the Creator's name HaVaYaH, because the Kli gives the Creator a name according to its sensation of Him, according to its sensation of the Light that fills it. The Light that fills the Kli is called "filling."

The Kli created by the Creator is divided into five parts, called "worlds." Each world is in turn divided into five more parts, called Partzufim (faces). Then, each Partzuf (singular for Partzufim) consists of five parts called Sefirot. In all, there are 5 x 5 x 5 = 125 spiritual objects or degrees from the lowest degree to the Creator Himself.

Each Partzuf consists of five parts (Sefirot), designated by a dot and four letters: Keter-dot + Hochma-Yod + Bina-Hey + ZA-Vav + Malchut-Hey = HaVaYaH. The difference between each of the 125 Partzufim lies in the type of Light that fills them, whereas the core of the Kli, the letters HaVaYaH, remain the same. A desire cannot appear unless the Creator's Light had previously passed through the five stages; only the fifth stage is considered a birth of a new creation (desire).

The whole universe (all the worlds) is nothing but the ten Sefirot or the Creator's name HaVaYaH.

| SEFIRA | LETTER | PARTZUF | WORLD | LIGHT |
|--------|--------|---------|-------|-------|
| Keter | A dot, the tip of the letter Yod | Galgalta | AK | Yechida |
| Hochma | Yod | AB | Atzilut | Haya |
| Bina | Hey | SAG | Beria | Neshama |
| ZA | Vav | MA | Yetzira | Ruach |
| Malchut | Hey | BON | Assiya | Nefesh |

A filling of *HaVaYaH* with Light is referred to as its revelation. Thus, the letters emerge from the state of concealment when they are not filled. In all there are five *Partzufim*: *Keter* (*Galgalta*), AB, SAG, MA and BON. The first—*Partzuf Keter*—is the main one and the source of all the rest. Its ten *Sefirot* is plain (inner) *HaVaYaH*, for each of the four letters of its *HaVaYaH* comes outside, revealing a new *Partzuf* that clothes it.

So then, out of *Partzuf Keter-Galgalta*, from the letter *Yod* comes *Partzuf Hochma* (AB), from the letter *Hey*—*Partzuf Bina* (SAG), from the letter *Vav*—*Partzuf ZA* (MA), and from the letter *Hey*—*Partzuf Malchut* (BON). Thus *Partzuf Keter* is designated by plain *HaVaYaH*, and the *Partzufim* that clothe it are designated by filled *HaVaYaH*. The recording of *HaVaYaH* with the Light that fills it is called *Miluy* (filling). For the purposes of brevity when naming a *Partzuf*, the notion of *Gematria* was introduced. *Gematria* is the numerical value of the Light that fills the *Partzuf*.

Wisdom (*Hochma*) is called calculation (*Heshbon*), *Gematria*. A calculation is made only in a place where Light is received: (i) a preliminary calculation is made as to how much Light the *Partzuf* can receive for the Creator's sake; (ii) the Light is received in accordance with the calculation; (iii) calculation of the received amount, called *Miluy*, *Gematria*.

*Malchut* cannot receive the Light of *Hochma* without the Light of *Hassadim*, and in that event, *Hochma* cannot shine in her. Then *Malchut* ascends to *Bina* and becomes like an embryo inside of her, by which she receives the right line—*Hassadim*. Upon joining the past and the present states, *Malchut* receives *Hochma* into *Hassadim*, and the Light of *Hochma* shines in her. All these actions of *Malchut* are accompanied by calculations, called *Gematriot*.

The *Gematria* (numerical value) of the *Partzuf* unfilled with the Light, the *Gematria* of the empty *HaVaYaH* is as follows:

*HaVaYaH* = *Yod* + *Hey* + *Vav* + *Hey* = 10 + 5 + 6 + 5 = 26. The *Gematria* of a filled *HaVaYaH* is formed by filling each letter; In Hebrew, each letter has a full name: A-*Aleph*, B-*Bet*, etc.. Hence, there are four kinds of fillings in *HaVaYaH*: 1) AB, 2) SAG, 3) MA and 4) BON.

1) *HaVaYaH* with the filling of AB:
*Yod*: *Yod* + *Vav* + *Dalet* = 10 + 6 + 4 = 20
*Hey*: *Hey* + *Yod* = 5 + 10 = 15
*Vav*: *Vav* + *Yod* + *Vav* = 6 + 10 + 6 = 22
*Hey*: *Hey* + *Yod* = 5 + 10 = 15

In all: 20 + 15 + 22 + 15 = 72 = AB, where "A" designates the letter *Ayin* = 70, and not *Aleph* = 1. *HaVaYaH* filled with this Light is called *Partzuf AB* (*Partzuf Hochma*), for the letter *Yod* with its filling signifies the Light of Wisdom, *Ohr Hochma*. Such a filling is called "*HaVaYaH* with the filling of *Yod*."

2) *HaVaYaH* with the filling of SAG: the *Partzuf* that is filled with Light of Mercy, *Ohr Hassadim*, is called SAG, for its *Gematria* is this:

SAG = *Samech* (60) + *Gimel* (3) = 63:

*Yod*: *Yod* + *Vav* + *Dalet* = 10 + 6 + 4 = 20

*Hey*: *Hey* + *Yod* = 5 + 10 = 15

*Vav*: *Vav* + *Aleph* + *Vav* = 6 + 1 + 6 = 13

*Hey*: *Hey* + *Yod* = 5 + 10 = 15

In all: 20 + 15 + 13 + 15 = 63 = *Samech* + *Gimel* = SAG

If the *Kelim* and their filling originate from the first restriction, the letter *Yod* is present in the filling of *HaVaYaH*. And if the *Kelim* are filled with the Light of the second restriction, it is the letter *Aleph*, present in the filling of *HaVaYaH*. The difference between the *Gematriot* of AB and SAG lies in the filling of the letter *Vav*: *Gematria* of *Vav* in *Partzuf AB* is twenty-two (from the filling of *Ohr Hochma*), whereas *Gematria* of *Vav* in *Partzuf SAG* is thirteen (from the filling of *Ohr Hassadim*). From the aforesaid, it is clear that *Partzuf AB* originates from the first restriction, whereas the letter *Vav* (ZA) in *Partzuf SAG* originates from the second restriction.

3) *HaVaYaH* with the filling of MA:

*Yod*: *Yod* + *Vav* + *Dalet* = 20

*Hey*: *Hey* + *Aleph* = 6

*Vav*: *Vav* + *Aleph* + *Vav* = 13

*Hey*: *Hey* + *Aleph* = 6

Such a filling of *HaVaYaH* is called 20 + 6 + 13 + 6 = 45 = *Mem* (40) + *Hey* (5) = MA (the letter *Hey* is pronounced as "ah").

4) *HaVaYaH* with the filling of BON:

*Yod*: *Yod* + *Vav* + *Dalet* = 20

*Hey*: *Hey* + *Hey* = 10

*Vav*: *Vav* + *Vav* = 12

*Hey*: *Hey* + *Hey* = 10

Such a filling of *HaVaYaH* is called 20 + 10 + 12 + 10 = 52 = *Nun* (50) + *Bet* (2), pronounced as BON for easier articulation. This is the *Gematria* of

*Partzuf Malchut*, and it is equivalent to twice the value of the unfilled *HaVaYaH*: *HaVaYaH* = 26, and 26 x 2 = 52 = MA.

*Partzuf Malchut* cannot receive the Creator's Light due to the absence of a screen. Instead, it can only passively receive what *Partzuf ZA* gives it. Hence, the twofold twenty-six indicates that whatever *Malchut* has comes to her from ZA.

From the four kinds of *HaVaYaH*, it becomes clear that the root of creation is neither *Partzuf Hochma* nor *Bina*, but only ZA, as it is the first *Partzuf* built on the second restriction.

The primary ten *Sefirot* are located in *Partzuf Keter*, whereas *Partzufim AB*, SAG, MA, and BON are merely branches stemming from the first *Partzuf*. However, when the Light spreads within the *Partzuf*, it contains five inner Lights NRNHY and five outer Lights. The five outer Lights of *Bina* come out of the right ear, and the five inner Lights of *Bina* come out of the left. The five outer Lights of ZA come out of the right nostril, and the five inner Lights of ZA come out of the left.

Since the two *Malchuyot* (plural for *Malchut*) are remote from one another, as a branch in our world, man's ear holes are also separated and distanced. The two nostrils are separated by a smaller distance, whereas the five inner and outer Lights of the common Light of the *Peh* (mouth) come out of the same opening. Thus, as they exit the mouth, they collide and interweave, and as a result of their collisions, letters (*Kelim*) are born.

Since twenty-two letters originate from *Bina-SAG* = Samech + Gimel = 60 + 3 = 63, the opening through which they come out is called 63 + 22 = 85 = Peh + Hey = PeH (mouth). The letters come out of the *Peh* of ZA, for *Yesod* of *Ima* is located there.

We received our entire Torah, all of the knowledge about the spiritual worlds, from our Great Patriarchs, who ascended spiritually above our world, sensed the Upper Worlds, and described them to us. This is how we received the whole Torah—both the written and the oral parts.

We cannot imagine the spiritual world because our sensory organs cannot detect it. Thus, to describe the objects and concepts still unattainable by us, Kabbalists use several techniques, languages. The whole Torah speaks only of the creation, governing, and correction of the world; never about history, geography, or anything else. As it is said in the Torah itself, the Torah is the sacred names, that is, manifestations of the Creator, the degrees and methods of His attainment.

Kabbalists, those who ascend to the spiritual world and thus establish direct contact with the Creator, convey this information to us using four languages:

1. The language of the *TaNaKh* (Torah—Pentateuch, **N**evi'im—Prophets, **K**etuvim—Writings/Hagiographa). This is the language of the written Torah.
2. The language of laws.
3. The language of legends.
4. The language of *Sefirot* and *Partzufim*—the language of Kabbalah.

All the languages speak about the same thing—the attainment of the Creator by us, those living in this world. For this is the sole purpose of our creation, and according to the Creator's design, we must devote all of our physical, mental, and spiritual abilities only to it. And if we were to aspire only to this, we would naturally use our language only for this purpose. After all, everything that is given to us is only for the fulfillment of this exclusive goal—the attainment of the sensation of the Creator, while still in this life.

And this is why the first language mastered by humankind was Hebrew. However, as they distanced from fulfilling their mission, humankind conceived other languages. All the other languages in the world have their inner meaning, too, but since their alphabets were not revealed to us by Kabbalists, we study the spiritual forces depicted in the Hebrew alphabet, the source of all the others.

Every *Partzuf* is divided into two parts: right and left. The right part consists of *Ramach* = *Reish* – *Mem* – *Chet* = 248 parts (organs) filled with the Light of *Hassadim*; and the left part consists of *Shasah* = *Shin* – *Samech* – *Hey* = 365 parts (tendons) filled with the Light of *Hochma*. ZA is called a "voice"; he is generally the Light of *Hassadim*. But when he joins with *Malchut*, called "speech," *Malchut* receives the Light of *Hassadim* with *Hochma* from ZA, and thus "speech" is formed.

The seven primary *Sefirot* of ZA are called "Seven Heavens." The seventy names of ZA originate from the 70 (7 x 10) *Sefirot* of ZA. ZA himself is called "Heaven" and *Malchut* is called "earth." The *Sefirot* of ZA are also called *Ruach*, owing to the Light of *Ruach* within them, which ascends to *Bina* (ears) and transforms into sound: *Hochma* in the left ear and *Hassadim* in the right.

There is a difference between language and alphabet, as in our world there are people who can speak, but cannot read or write. The most ancient spoken language is that of the *TaNaKh*, which dates back to Adam. The language of laws originated from it, followed by the language of legends. All of these languages combined and each of them in particular are used in our holy scriptures.

The language of Kabbalah was the last to develop. It is the most difficult language, since proper understanding of it requires sensing the spiritual categories that this language narrates. Kabbalah is also the most precise language of all. It is the only language that can accurately render all the spiritual information.

However, only through direct study with a Kabbalist-teacher can a student learn it and grasp its information. And since for many generations there were only a few Kabbalists, unconnected with one another, the language of Kabbalah was the last to evolve. Even today it can only be "learned" directly from a Kabbalist-teacher.

Initially, Kabbalists enciphered their knowledge of the spiritual world as letters, whose outlines reflected the interrelationships of spiritual forces. In other words, each spiritual degree is characterized by a unique interrelationship of spiritual forces. By assigning each spiritual property with a particular symbol, one can depict the interrelationship, as well as the general product of the union of spiritual forces of each degree, i.e., its essence.

Thus, Kabbalists created the twenty-two letters of the Hebrew alphabet. *The Zohar* pays much attention to analyzing the connection between the letters, which helps a student to synthesize his knowledge and find new ways of discovering spiritual forces and their actions within.

As our forefather Avraham writes in his *Book of Creation* (*Sefer Yetzira*), letters represent the stones from which the building-word is constructed. As our sages tell us, the world was created with the letters of the "sacred language," each letter representing a certain holy, spiritual, altruistic force of creation.

The properties of this force are reflected in the letter's outline, its importance with regard to other letters, its potential combinations with the others, its potential punctuation marks, its crowns and notations, its numerical value (*Gematria*) and variations.

However, this only concerns separate letters and their combinations. There are also certain rules that enable us to determine the properties of spiritual forces not from letters, but from whole words. Moreover, quite often we can replace letters or even parts of a word with similar ones.

The language itself, the roots of its words, indicate the properties of the spiritual object they describe. For example, Adam originated from *Adama*—earth, which emphasizes his insignificance, and from the word *Adameh*—similar (to the Upper One), which emphasizes his eminence. The name Yaakov comes from the word *Ekev*—to get around (*Esau*). There are many such examples in the Torah, for everything is named after its root, as after the patronymic name of one's father.

Once we have established that certain combinations of letters (*Kelim*, language of letters) can be used instead of the language of *Sefirot* and *Partzufim* when describing spiritual actions, the entire description of the spiritual worlds amounts to portraying objects and actions in the form of letters and their combinations. This is how the whole of the Torah is written, in words. Thus,

a) The shape of each letter and the elements of its structure indicate all the properties and the general state of a spiritual object, *Sefira*, or *Partzuf*, which this particular letter depicts;

b) The order of letters in a word indicates the connection between spiritual objects, *Sefirot*, and their shared properties and actions. Attainment of a word's spiritual meaning signifies an ascent to the spiritual level of the object. When that happens, he who attains it becomes this very word, assumes its name. Man's name keeps changing as he ascends the spiritual degrees; it is determined by the degree he is on, as he assumes the name of that degree. It is therefore said that everyone can become like Moshe, i.e., attain the degree called "Moshe";

c) The word itself in its "corporeal" reading, its "corporeal" meaning indicates the spiritual root and its branch—consequence in our world;

d) A combination of words indicates an entire spiritual process, which, as a rule, has a corresponding action (commandment) in our world.

Names change depending on the aspect that requires clarification:

a) By elements of *Sefirot*:

| | | |
|---|---|---|
| Keter | - | has none |
| Hochma | - | fire |
| Bina | - | water |
| ZA | - | air |
| Malchut | - | earth |

b) By colors:

| | | |
|---|---|---|
| Keter | - | has none |
| Hochma | - | white – the basis of all colors |
| Bina | - | red – most prominent |
| ZA | - | green – most perfect |
| Malchut | - | black – cannot be changed by any other color |

Colors are present only in the *Guf* (body) of the *Partzuf*, but never in the *Rosh* (head). These colors are projected onto *Malchut* from Above, and she passes them on to all the lower ones.

c) By lines:

| | | |
|---|---|---|
| Hesed - right | | - white |
| Gevura - left | | - red |
| Tifferet - central, includes all the colors | - green |

Quite often, colors and elements are used instead of the names of *Sefirot* and their properties: fire, water, air, earth (*The Zohar, Vayera*, item 32). *Malchut* is called "earth," but *Malchut* that ascends with her properties to *Bina* is called "earth of the Temple." In the Temple, the four sides of the world—*Hochma, Bina, Tifferet* and *Malchut* join the four elements of the world—fire, water, air and earth. Out of the two points of *Bina* and *Malchut*, which are joined together, the Creator made one *Partzuf* —Adam.

The four foundations of the world, or the four sides of the world:

| Fire | North | *Shuruk* | Left Line | *Gevura* |
|---|---|---|---|---|
| Air | East | *Hirik* | Middle Line | *Tifferet* |
| Water | South | *Holam* | Right Line | *Hesed* |
| Earth | West | – | – | *Malchut* – receives from all |

**Four fundamental metals** are created as a result of a *Zivug* of the four foundations with *Malchut*: gold, silver, copper and iron. All of these names, as well as many others, are used in the Torah instead of the names of the ten *Sefirot*. Therefore, although the languages of the Torah, legends, the Talmud, and the Scriptures are extraordinarily vivid, only the concise language of Kabbalah provides an accurate description of the spiritual worlds.

The four kinds of symbols used with letters:

**Taamim**—tone modulations used in pronouncing letters—signify the Direct Light, which spreads from Above downwards in the body of the *Partzuf*.

**Nekudot**—letter punctuation marks—signify the Light during its gradual exit from the body of the *Partzuf* from below upwards.

**Tagin**—crowns above the letters—represent *Reshimot* (reminiscences/records) of the previously present Light (*Taamim*). *Tagin* originate from GAR *de Bina*.

**Otiot**—letters—represent *Reshimot* of the Light's exit from the body of the *Partzuf* (*Nekudot*). Letters originate from *Zat de Bina*.

The ten *Sefirot* are divided into three primary parts—*Taamim*, *Nekudot*, and *Otiot*:

| | | |
|---|---|---|
| Taamim | - | Keter |
| Nekudot | - | Hochma |
| Otiot | - | ZAT de Bina and ZON |

According to the Light in them, *Sefirot* are divided into:

| | | |
|---|---|---|
| Taamim | - | Hochma |
| Nekudot | - | Bina |
| Otiot | - | ZON |

The letters were created in the following order: the letter *Aleph*, which was initially on the right side, begot the letter *Shin*, which emerged from it and moved to the left side. The letter *Shin* consists of three sides: the left, the middle, and the right. The letter *Vav* is thereby formed by three letters, and upon joining with *Aleph*, it formed the word **Aleph-Shin** = *ESH* (fire) in the left side.

Out of the interaction of the right and the left sides these two letters came forth in contradiction between them, as the right line includes water, while the left line includes fire. Their collisions begot the letters *Reish*, *Vav*, and *Chet*, which formed the word *Ruach* (wind). This wind entered between the two sides (fire and water) and joined them together, thereby establishing the order of the first letters and their perfection.

At first, *The Zohar* offers a general description of the three lines in ZA, designated by the three names of the Creator: *El*, *Elokim* and *Elokeinu*, and then proceeds to clarify the descent of the degrees of filling ZA and *Malchut* with the Light of *Hochma* in the form of letter combinations, in the order of the degrees' descent from Above downwards. *Mayim* - water, *Esh* - fire, *Ruach* - wind constitute the three lines in ZA from *AVI*. This is why the first letters in ZA come from *AVI*.

Then the following combinations emerged: *Aleph* revealed *Mem* from its right side, so *Mem* stands to the left line of *Aleph*. *Mem* revealed *Shin* as the middle line, as *Mem* initially consists of the left line, for it exists in the form of a concealed letter *Mem* in the word *Elokim*, which pertains to the left line, and so forth. This is how all the letters of the Hebrew alphabet were born.

# THE LETTERS
# OF THE HEBREW ALPHABET

| LETTERS | NAME | PRONUNCIATION | GEMATRIA |
|---------|------|---------------|----------|
| א | *Aleph* | [a], [e] | 1 |
| ב | *Bet* | b, v | 2 |
| ג | *Gimel* | g | 3 |
| ד | *Dalet* | d | 4 |
| ה | *Hey* | [a], [e] | 5 |
| ו | *Vav* | v, [u], [o] | 6 |
| ז | *Zayin* | z | 7 |
| ח | *Chet* | h | 8 |
| ט | *Tet* | t | 9 |
| י | *Yod* | y, i | 10 |
| כ (ך) | *Chaf* | h, k | 20 |
| ל | *Lamed* | l | 30 |
| מ (ם) | *Mem* | m | 40 |
| נ (ן) | *Nun* | n | 50 |
| ס | *Samech* | s | 60 |
| ע | *Ayin* | [a], [e] | 70 |
| פ (ף) | *Peh* | p, ph | 80 |
| צ (ץ) | *Tzadik* | tz | 90 |
| ק | *Kuf* | k | 100 |
| ר | *Reish* | r | 200 |
| ש | *Shin* | sh, s | 300 |
| ת | *Tav* | t | 400 |

The letters *Aleph* and *Ayin* do not have any particular sound, and only the accompanying punctuation mark determines their pronunciation.

The letters *Bet, Chaf* and *Peh* with a dot inside them are pronounced as "b," "k," and "p." The absence of a dot changes their pronunciation to "v," "ch" and "f."

The letter *Hey* is not pronounced, but rather aspirated.

The shapes of the letters *Mem, Nun, Tzadik, Peh, Chaf* (pronounced MANTZEPACH) change when placed at the end of a word, as seen in the table of letters.

The shape, external form of letters: the protruding element of a letter indicates that the Light in this part of the letter is greater than in the other. The filling (*Miluy*) indicates the height of the degree. A punctuation mark (*Nikud*) indicates the origin of each part of the *Partzuf*: whether it came from the Upper *Partzuf* (and constitutes its part in the present one), from the lower *Partzuf*, or from itself.

The *Kelim-Sefirot* themselves are called "letters," and their punctuation marks (*Nekudot*) indicate the Light that enters and exits them. The Light of *Bina*, *ZA*, and *Malchut* can enter the *Kelim*, but the Light of *Keter* or *Hochma* cannot. A dot above a letter (*Holam*) signifies the Lights *Keter* and *Hochma*, which never clothe the *Kli*, hence the location of the dot above the letter.

Two horizontally positioned dots (*Tzere*) allude to *Sefirot Hochma* and *Bina*, that *Bina* does not receive the Light of *Hochma*, and contains only the Light of *Hassadim*, the Light of Mercy (*AVI* back-to-back). *Bina* herself is also called *Tzere*, for *ZA* receives everything from her. If there is a third dot (*Segol*) between these two dots, it means that *ZA* raised his request for the Light of *Hochma* to *AVI*. Such a request of *ZA* in *AVI* is called *Daat*. *Daat* receives the Light of *Hochma* in order to pass it on to *ZA*. The punctuation mark *Kamatz* (a "T" shaped mark under the letter) indicates that *ZA* collects (*Mekabetz*) the Light of *Hochma*.

A dot indicates *Malchut* with a reflecting screen, but not a receiving one. Such a form testifies to the absence of Light in the *Kli*; it is merely a black dot, as the law of restriction rules over it.

The *Sefira Hod* is an inclusion of *Malchut's* properties into *ZA*, out of which *ZA* makes a whole *Partzuf Malchut*. The letter *Hey* in the word *Hod* signifies *Keter* in *Malchut*, and the nine lower *Sefirot* of *Malchut* are located among the impure forces that cling to them. This is designated by an elongated leg of the letter *Kuf* (dipping below the line), which indicates that the impure forces receive their strength from the spiritually pure forces through this element, the *Kuf*.

The white background is a plain, indistinguishable and thereby imperceptible Light (by us). Whatever we can distinguish may only be expressed by restricting the diffusion of this white color. The forms and degrees of its restriction are called letters. That is why we see black outlines on white background, and attain only the black restrictions.

We can describe the diffusion of Light in the worlds using attraction and restriction of the Light. And these two forces must act simultaneously. Similarly, when we perceive something in our sensory organs, we only sense it by way of restriction, as the object's surface or a light wave collides with our sensory organ, which restricts its expansion, and can thereby perceive it.

The spiritual roots of the forms are as follows: A circumference originates from the first restriction of the Light in the world of *Ein Sof* (Infinity), the first restriction on the diffusion of Light. Since this restriction was equal and uniform, it assumed the form of a circumference.

A vertical line, length without width, signifies that the notion is unattainable by us, and is therefore called a "thin line" of the diffusion of the Light of *Hochma*. The Light of *Hochma* can only be received with the help of the screen in *Malchut*, which creates Reflected Light that clothes the Light of *Hochma*. Therefore, the Upper Light that comes to the *Kli* is called a line.

A horizontal line, width without height: when a vertical line—the diffusion of the Light of *Hochma* from Above downwards—collides with the screen, their collision (of desires) compels the vertical line to shift into the horizontal line (to the right), resulting in a shape of the English letter L. Its width is determined by the force of the Reflected Light that ascends from the screen from below upwards.

A rectangle is formed by the interlacing of the descending Light of *Hochma* and the Reflected Light: five vertical descending lines—five *Sefirot* of the Light of *Hochma* and five horizontal lines from right to left—five *Sefirot* of the Light of *Hassadim*. The size of the rectangle's side is called *Amah*, consisting of five parts—*Tefachim* (plural for *Tefach*). (Both *Amah* and *Tefach* are distance measuring units.) This is why we describe the *Kli* as a rectangle.

The two kinds of diffusion of Light, the Light of *Hochma* and the Reflected Light, are called the right and the left cheeks, respectively, which turn into the upper and the lower lips. Since, after the first restriction, the Light may not be received in *Malchut*, the Reflected Light is only received in four parts of the *Kli*, not in five. This is why there are 4 x 4 = 16 teeth on the lower jaw and 16 teeth on the upper jaw (The Reflected Light stems from resistance, from "chewing" the Light before receiving it inside).

In the second restriction, a Triangle is formed, as *Malchut* ascends to *Bina* and forms a slanted line. Thus the combination of the Direct Light with the Reflected Light and restrictions beget various spiritual forms.

The Light of *Hassadim* is defined as "protruding," for a protrusion beyond the limits of a spiritual body means that:

1) The Light is so great that it comes out by elevating, protruding the limits;

2) It originates from the middle line, *Tifferet*.

A cavity in the body occurs due to the following reasons:

1) The Light is insufficient; the Light cannot shine there;

2) The Light of *Hochma* is present, but the lack of *Hassadim* prevents it from shining.

## PUNCTUATION MARKS IN THE HEBREW ALPHABET (NEKUDOT)

| Sefira | Punctuation Mark | | Pronunciation |
|--------|------------------|---|---------------|
| Keter | Kamatz | ⊡ | a |
| Hochma | Patach | ⊡ | a |
| Bina | Segol | ⊡ | e |
| Hesed | Tzere | ⊡ | e |
| Gevura | Shva | ⊡ | - |
| Tifferet | Holam | ⊡ | o |
| Netzah | Hirik | ⊡ | i |
| Hod | Kubutz | ⊡ | u |
| Yesod | Shuruk | ·⊡ | u |
| Malchut | No Mark | ⊡ | - |

*Nekudot* are defined by three lines:

### IN THE ROSH (HEAD)

| | | | |
|--------|---|----------|---|
| Kamatz | - | Keter | - right line |
| Patach | - | Hochma | - left line |
| Tzere | - | Bina | - middle line |
| Holam | - | Tifferet | - middle line |

### IN THE GUF (BODY)

Segol   - Hesed   - right line
Shva   - Gevura   - left line
Shuruk   - Tifferet   - middle line

### IN THE EXTREMITIES

Hirik   - Netzah   - right line
Kubutz  - Hod   - left line
   - Malchut  - middle line (has no designation)

The levels of *Nekudot*:

Above the letters  - Light of Neshama
In the letters    - Light of Ruach
Under the letters  - Light of Nefesh

*Zivug de Nekudot* is the *Zivug* between *Hochma de Aba* and *Hochma de Ima*.

*Zivug de Otiot* is the *Zivug* between *Bina de Aba* and *Bina de Ima*.

The letters combined together designate Reflected Light during the screen's ascent from *Tabur* to *Peh*. They are combined, for they all ascend to their root, which unites everything, whereas the use of the will to receive, even for the Creator's sake, causes separation.

A state of separated letters occurs when the Light enters the *Kli* (vessel, the letters of *HaVaYaH*); the four letters thereby separate, since the Light makes a distinction between the *Sefirot*: depending on their different properties, it clothes in them in different ways.

*HaVaYaH* with filling *Aleph* comes on a screen with *Aviut Aleph* (thickness one), *HaVaYaH* with filling *Hey* comes on a screen with *Aviut Bet* (thickness two). A plain name refers to *Aviut Shoresh* (zero thickness) with the Light of *Nefesh*. Plain letters refer to a *Partzuf* with a screen of *Aviut Aleph*.

The truly faithful, who believe in the three fundamentals: the Creator, His Providence and the Torah, need the two lines to be in constant balance for their spiritual advancement. The left line is wisdom, the Light of *Hochma* that enters the desire to receive, which pertains to the left side, and the right line is faith, the Light of *Hassadim* (mercy), the altruistic desire to bestow.

Existing in knowledge only means that man is under the rule of the impure forces (*Klipa*) of the left side, which renders him totally unable to feel the spiritual, leaving him in spiritual darkness. Alternately, existing only in faith means that man is under the rule of the impure forces (*Klipa*) of the right side that convinces him that he has achieved perfection, that there is nothing else to work on, nothing to correct within him. This, too, denies him the opportunity to advance.

*The Zohar* continues: And the Creator answered further (the letter *Tav*): "The word *MaveT* (death) ends with you. And since these are your properties, you are not suitable for Me to create the world with you." Immediately following, the letter *Tav* departed from Him.

The moment the Creator set about creating the world-ZON by selecting their properties, all twenty-two letters of ZON appeared before Him, starting from the last—*Tav*, and ending with the first, *Aleph*—the head of all letters. The reason for the letters coming in reverse order is that they constitute the MAN of ZON, the *Kelim* of ZON, which emerge from below upwards. The usual alphabetical order corresponds to the Light (MAD), which descends from Above downwards. But the order of MAN is opposite to that of MAD, for it ascends from below upwards.

Letters are none other than desires, properties, and thoughts that, in man's opinion, are suitable for the attainment of the spiritual, the Creator, of His Providence. Man skips from one thought to another: one moment he thinks that it is possible to attain the Upper Worlds with one property, next he believes he can enter the spiritual realms by mastering another property, then he begins to stubbornly observe all the commandments and pray zealously, or disregards all the actions and plunges into contemplation and reading. Sometimes he craves only knowledge, and sometimes only faith, right down to fanaticism.

Just as there are two extremes in our world—knowledge and faith, in the spiritual world, as man now consciously ascends the spiritual ladder to the Creator, there is spiritual work in the attainment of knowledge and faith. Hence, Rabbi Yehuda Ashlag's commentary on *The Zohar* is entitled *The Sulam* (The Ladder).

Each of the twenty-two Hebrew letters represents a certain property. At times it seems that the property of the letter *Tav* is suitable for the attainment of the spiritual; at times he believes that some other letter is more appropriate. This occurs because in the process of his spiritual ascent, man begins to increasingly understand the true Goal of creation and the Creator, which is exactly what is demanded of him.

Thus, he continues to sort through it all, until his search yields the truth: only with the help of the letter *Bet*, which stands at the beginning of the word *Berachah* (blessing)—contact with the Creator,—only with the help of this force can one achieve the goal.

Therefore, *The Zohar* tells us how the letters—properties, forces, and desires—come to the Creator. By offering up his prayer (MAN), man asks for some property that seems like a real goal to him. And each letter tries to prove that it is best suited for the attainment of the sensation of the Creator and merging with Him. But the Creator shows that the best and the only letter is *Bet*, as only it can help man to establish contact with Him. This is why the Torah begins with this letter.

The description of the spiritual forces designated by each letter is incredibly deep, and in order to attain full clarity we need to bridge several other preliminary explanations: the creation of the world includes its existence and process of perfection so that the world could attain the goal for which it was created.

The Creator created the world consisting of two contrasting forces; against each pure, altruistic force, He created an impure, egoistic one, which is its equal and opposite. Just as there are four pure worlds *ABYA*, the Creator created opposite them four impure worlds *ABYA*.

Therefore, in our world—the last degree of the world of *Assiya*—a spiritually evolved person that senses the Creator and has entered with his properties into the spiritually pure world, looks no different from an egoistic and spiritually undeveloped person, who has not attained the spiritual realm. This means that one who does not perceive the spiritual is totally unable to differentiate between spiritual purity and impurity.

We see that in our world one cannot advance with the help of the pure forces. On the contrary, it is his egoistic aspirations that provide man with the strength to conquer everything in the world. How often do we see fervent fanatics immersed in their impure desires to capture for themselves both this world and the next, whereas one that aspires to the Creator has no strength for even a slightest spiritual movement! In our world there is no proof or confirmation that man advances on the right path. And under no circumstances should one draw conclusions based on one's life experience or "common sense."

So how can a person in this world exist and advance towards the Goal of creation if he is unable to tell good from bad, pure from impure? There is one sign by which one can distinguish purity from impurity: impure forces bear no spiritual fruit. Thus, those that advance through the impure worlds *ABYA* do not attain anything spiritual, whereas those who are connected to the pure forces reap spiritual fruit on their path.

As it is explained in the "Introduction to The Study of Ten Sefirot" (items 19-23), if man advances along the right path, he attains the secrets of the Torah in three to five years. The Creator helps those who wish to acquire altruistic desires over and above their own requests, and thus one attains the desired goal. From below, man aspires to the Creator with his small desire (*MAN*), and from Above, the Creator pours onto him tremendous spiritual desires and strength (*MAD*).

This is the only opportunity to check whether or not the path that one is on is correct, whether it leads to altruism or to even bigger egoism. By no means can one consider his well-being, soaring elation, his happiness and success in life as proofs of correct advancement. It is precisely in those states of feeling perfection, well-being, and contentment that he must ask himself: "Have I attained the secrets of the Torah?" And until he has attained them, his "perfection" is impure.

Man should always strive for the middle line—a balance of faith and knowledge—in the following three notions: the Creator, His Providence, and the Torah. And under no circumstances should he advance by either faith or knowledge alone. If he only wants to attain the Creator, His Providence or the Torah, he enters spiritual darkness, for it is impossible to receive the Light of Wisdom (*Ohr Hochma*) without the Light of Mercy (*Ohr Hassadim*).

Such a state is referred to as the left impure force, "*Klipat Esau.*" And if man strives to advance through faith alone, he enters the impure force of the right side, "*Klipat Yishmael,*" which tells him he is in a state of perfection. In this case, he sees no point in his work and is thus unable to continue to advance.

In other words, even if one is full of joy, which is exactly what the Torah urges him to feel (to perceive the Creator's Providence with joy, for joy signifies justification of creation, understanding that His Providence is always just and kind), unless he has attained the secrets of the Torah, his path is considered erroneous, as he lacks the intention "for the Creator's sake," which reveals the secrets of the Torah.

This article explains the particular properties of the Hebrew letters—how all the letters come before the Creator, each asking Him to create the world with its property. Each of the twenty-two letters represents a spiritual degree in the worlds *ABYA*, and each believes that its pure spiritual properties are most suitable for the task, that by attaining its degree and acquiring its properties, the inhabitants of the world will be able to elevate the pure forces over the impure ones, so much so that they will reach the end of correction, the Goal of creation.

However, the Creator answers each letter that against it are the corresponding impure forces, and therefore man will be unable to properly separate the pure forces from the impure ones, and afterwards, utilize the pure forces to achieve the goal. This occurrence repeats itself until the appearance of the letter *Bet*, which represents the degree called "the Creator's blessing," against which there are no impure forces of any kind.

And the Creator consented to create the world with the letter *Bet*, with its property; for it has no impure counterpart, only *Bet* presents an opportunity to carry out an analysis between good and evil, to determine when man works for himself and when he works for the Creator's sake. Therefore, only by its force, by its property can the world exist: so as to extract from the "mixture" of one's desires only what's pure, and elevate them above the impure, down to complete eradication of the latter, and the consequent attainment of complete correction of one's nature.

As it follows from *The Zohar*, only the Creator's help, called "a blessing," is the force of man's salvation, the only thing capable of freeing him from the rule of the impure forces. And this force, called "blessing," descends only upon those that advance along the right path.

The right path is a combination of three conditions: (i) one's efforts in studying (only!) genuine Kabbalistic sources; (ii) contact with a true Kabbalist, whom he accepts as his teacher; and (iii) contact with like-minded people, who seek spiritual elevation. A more detailed explanation will be provided to serious students only.

All twenty-two letters are divided into three degrees: *Bina, Zeir Anpin* (ZA), and *Malchut*, since there are no *Kelim* (letters) above *Bina*. Twenty-two letters in *Bina* are called "big," twenty-two letters in ZA are called "medium," and twenty-two letters in *Malchut* are called "small."

Each of the three *Sefirot* of *Bina*, ZA, and *Malchut* are further divided into three degrees: The twenty-two letters of *Bina* contain their own *Bina*, ZA, and *Malchut*. Likewise, ZA has his own ten *Sefirot*, in which his *Bina*, ZA, and *Malchut* also contain twenty-two letters. The same applies to *Malchut*.

The twenty-two letters of each degree are divided into three types. The letters from *Aleph* to *Tet* (1–9) are considered units; these are the nine *Sefirot* of *Bina*. The letters from *Yod* to *Tzadik* (10–90) are considered tens; these are the nine *Sefirot* of ZA. And finally, the four letters *Kuf, Reish, Shin* and *Tav* (100–400) are considered hundreds; and these are the four *Sefirot* of *Malchut*, since *Malchut* is located below and downwards of *Chazeh de* ZA, which corresponds in height to the four *Sefirot* of ZA.

*Bina*, units, big letters, nine letters: *Aleph, Bet, Gimel, Dalet, Hey, Vav, Zayin, Chet, Tet*.

ZA, tens, medium letters, nine letters: *Yod, Chaf, Lamed, Mem, Nun, Samech, Ayin, Peh, Tzadik.*

*Malchut,* hundreds, small letters, four letters: *Kuf, Reish, Shin, Tav.*

However, it is known that units are in *Malchut,* tens are in ZA, and hundreds are in *Bina,* which contradicts the aforesaid that units are in *Bina,* tens are in ZA, and hundreds are in *Malchut.* Such inverse dependence is caused by the inverse relationship between the Lights and the *Kelim:* the lowest Light enters the Highest *Kelim.* The Upper *Kelim* are the first to emerge, from *Keter* down to *Malchut* (*Keter, Hochma, Bina,* ZA, and *Malchut*), whereas the first to enter them is the smallest Light, *Nefesh,* followed by *Ruach, Neshama, Haya* and *Yechida.*

Therefore, if there are only units in the *Kelim,* from *Aleph* to *Tet,* then only the Light of *Nefesh* is present. And if tens are added to the *Kelim,* the Light of *Ruach* appears, and if hundreds are added to the *Kelim,* the Light of *Neshama* fills them.

This is why hundreds are defined as *Bina,* tens as ZA, and units as *Malchut.* However, with regard to the *Kelim,* the order is inversed: units are in *Bina,* tens are in ZA, and hundreds are in *Malchut.*

| Bina: | Light (100) | - Kelim (1) |
|---|---|---|
| ZA: | Light (10) | - Kelim (10) |
| Malchut: | Light (1) | - Kelim (100) |

The letters descend from *Bina* to ZA and from there to *Malchut.* When they descend from *Bina* to ZA, they descend as three lines: 22/3 = 7 letters in each, with the remaining letter being added to the middle line. These twenty-two letters descend in three lines to *Malchut,* which consists of five final letters MANTZEPACH, thereby bringing the total number in *Malchut* to 22 + 5 = 27 letters.

The middle line is called "Heaven," "firmament." Therefore, when *The Zohar* speaks of letters in the firmament, it means that the two middle lines, 7 + 7 = 14 = *Yod* + *Dalet* = *Yad* (hand) writes all the twenty-two letters in the firmament (ZA) through the middle line. That is how one should interpret the words of the Torah regarding the letters that appear in the sky or having seen the hand that writes the letters in the sky.

The twenty-two letters of the Torah are the *Kelim* to be filled by the Light of NRN. Units—from *Aleph* to *Yod*—are the *Kli* intended for the Light of *Bina* (*Neshama*). Tens—from *Yod* to *Kuf*—are the *Kli* meant for the Light of ZA (*Ruach*). Hundreds—from *Kuf* to *Tav*—are the *Kli* for the Light of *Malchut* (*Nefesh*).

Letters are the *Kelim*, into which the Light clothes; in all, there are twenty-two special properties, and thus twenty-two symbols of their description, called letters. Just as the combinations of the twenty-two letters suffice for the description of all existing knowledge, the various couplings, unions (*Zivugim of Sefirot*) of the twenty-two *Kelim*, properties, desires of the *Partzuf* are sufficient for receiving and bestowing Light, fulfilling all spiritual actions and bringing all the letters (man's desires) to correction.

Letters represent the various correlations of ZON:

a) ZA, consisting of six parts of his extremities, husband to *Malchut*, designated by the letter *Vav*, *Sefira Yesod*—level of an embryo;

b) ZA designated by the letter *Vav*, *Sefira Tifferet*, consisting of six parts of his hands—level of nursing;

c) ZA that stands between *AVI*, while *Nukva* must ascend to him, thereby reaching the level of reception of *Ohr Hochma*.

d) ZA, the letter *Vav*, above him are ten *Sefirot Keter-Hochma*, below him are ten *Sefirot Bina-Tifferet-Malchut*—and together they make up the letter *Aleph*. And the final corrected state will come when *Malchut* ascends to *Keter* of ZA (the Upper *Yod* in the letter *Aleph*) at the end of correction. When *Malchut* ascends above *Parsa* (*Vav*), she receives the Light herself, whereas when she descends below *Vav*, she receives from ZA. As *Malchut* ascends, she forms *Taamim* (tone marks), when she descends, she is called *Nekuda* (point), and when she merges with ZA, she is referred to as a point inside *Vav* (*Shuruk*).

The order of **ATBaSH**: There is a special combination of letters, e.g. the first with the last ('A' through 'T'), the second with the second last ('B' through 'Sh'), etc., which designate the conditions for diffusion of the Upper Light from Above downwards.

**MANTZEPACH**: All the worlds and *Partzufim* were created with the twenty-two letters of *Malchut*. The screen is located in the head of the *Partzuf*, preventing the Light from entering. It repels the Light, calculates how much it can receive for the Creator's sake, and only then accepts it.

Each of the five levels of the will to receive that exist in *Malchut*, in the *Guf* of the *Partzuf*, has a corresponding restriction in the screen, located in the *Peh*, to prevent the Light from entering the body. Therefore, the screen in the *Peh* consists of five parts, forces.

These five restrictive forces of the screen, five exertions of the screen are designated by the five final letters of the alphabet: Mem-Nun-Tzadik-Peh-Chaf (abbreviated as MANTZEPACH). They are called "final letters" because they are written only at the end of words. These forces determine the reception of Light in the body of the Partzuf, and therefore beget the other twenty-two letters (Kelim, corrected desires, which receive the Light). Although the five letters MANTZEPACH are only found at the end of words, in oral speech they represent the five groups of pronunciation of the twenty-two letters. And the letters MANTZEPACH stand at the head of each group.

Out of the five letters MANTZEPACH originate five groups of sounds:

1. Peh–Keter: a group of four sounds-letters emerges from the throat; they are called AChHA—Aleph-Chet-Hey-Ayin. Aleph is the Light of Partzuf Keter of Atzilut, concealed from the lower ones and called Atik. Chet is the Light of Partzuf Hochma of the world of Atzilut, called Arich Anpin and also concealed from the lower ones. Hey is the Light of Partzuf Bina of the world of Atzilut, called Ima (mother), who receives the Light of Hochma from Aba (father) in order to pass it on to her children (ZON). Ayin is the Light of Zeir Anpin's face. Since the Light of ZA that enters Malchut is called "the Torah," it is said that the Torah has Ayin (70) faces, that the Creator (ZA) has Ayin (70) names. After all, with regard to Malchut, ZA is the Creator. Therefore, seventy souls descended to Egypt, and so forth.

2. Chaf–Hochma: a group of four sounds-letters emerges from the palate; they are called GIChiK—Gimel-Yod-Chaf-Kuf. The letters AChHA transfer the Light to the letters GIChiK: Aleph passes the Light to Gimel, which carries reward (Gemul—Gimel) for the righteous. Chet passes the Light of Hochma to Yod, but this Light is concealed. Hey illuminates Chaf with the Light of Bina, which carries joy. Ayin illuminates Kuf. Just as Ayin = 70, as it consists of seven Sefirot, Hesed-Gevura-Tifferet-Netzah-Hod-Yesod-Malchut, each containing ten Sefirot of its own, Kuf = 100, as it consists of ten Sefirot from Keter to Malchut, each consisting of its own ten. Hence, the palate fully complements the throat.

3. Nun–Bina: a group of four sounds-letters emerges from the tongue, called DaTLaT—Dalet-Tet-Lamed-Nun-Tav.

4. Mem–ZA: a group of four sounds-letters emerges from the lips, called BOMoCH—Bet-Vav-Mem-Chaf.

5. Tzadik–Malchut: a group of four sounds-letters emerges from the teeth, called ZaSSHRaTZ – Zayin-Samech-Shin-Reish-Tzadik.

Voice and speech: Voice is formed in ZA, speech—in Malchut. If he who is righteous, and who exists in the worlds BYA, raises his prayers (MAN) to

*Malchut* of the world of *Atzilut*, he causes ZON to ascend to *AVI*, and unites them in a constant *Zivug* so as to assure the Light's descent to the lower ones. ZON receives the Light from *AVI*; this Light is called "voice" and "speech," and this is the power of the righteous—to create the pure and destroy the impure with their voice.

Man's speech is conceived in the lungs: as the air exits the lungs and reaches the mouth, it turns to voice, and as it leaves the mouth, it becomes speech. Two lips accept the voice from the two parts of the lungs (the left and the right) and turn it into speech. Each lung consists of five parts so as to pass to the five parts in the mouth: to the guttural letters AChHA, the labial letters BOMoCH, the palatal letters GIChiK, the lingual letters DaTLaT and the dental letters ZaSSHRaTZ.

The seven primary *Sefirot* of ZA are called "Seven Heavens." The seventy names of ZA originate from the seventy (7 x 10) *Sefirot* of ZA. ZA himself is called "Heaven," and *Malchut* is called "earth." The *Sefirot* of ZA are also known as *Ruach* (because of the Light of *Ruach* in them), which ascends to *Bina* (ears), where it turns to sound, with *Hochma* in the left ear and *Hassadim* in the right.

## THE LETTER TAV

Each of the twenty-two letters corresponds to a particular spiritual degree, on which it acts. The letter itself is that spiritual degree. Hence, the letter *Tav* claims that its properties are the most suitable for the creation of the world, that its properties can bring the world to correction and to the goal of creation, for it defines the property of "truth," the Creator's seal.

The impure forces exist solely on account of the miniature Light received from the pure forces; this Light is called *Ner Dakik* (tiny candle). Without this Light, the impure forces would neither be able to exist nor to function—tempting man with the pleasures they received from the tiny spark of Light that fell from the pure *Sefirot*. Therefore, the last, lowest pure degree lets a little bit of the Upper Light down to the impure forces.

Without the support of the pure forces, the impure forces would instantly disappear. A question arises: who needs them to exist and what for? Obviously, the impure forces were created on a par with pure ones by the Creator Himself, for there is no other power in the entire universe besides Him.

It was necessary to create impure forces in order to concentrate them in the enormous desires to receive pleasure, in immense egoism. The system of the impure worlds of *ABYA* serves as a kind of storehouse of desires to receive pleasure, from which, to the extent of his correction, man can take more and more new desires so as to correct them. Thus, by attaching uncorrected impure forces to himself and correcting them, man can gradually ascend higher and higher, up to the level of the Creator. For this purpose the Creator created impure forces and sustains them through the system of pure ones.

The impure system of the worlds ABYA exists on the same level, parallel to the pure one. Our world is located under these two spiritual systems. Our world is also called egoistic and impure, but its forces and desires are so insignificant that they are located below the worlds of the impure *ABYA*.

When, with the help of Kabbalah, one surmounts the level of our world's egoism, he enters the pure world of *Assiya*. And immediately after, the impure world of *Assiya* begins to influence him, tempting him with its false pleasures. By overcoming the temptations of the impure world of *Assiya*, one ascends spiritually. But until one surmounts the impure desires of his body, of our world, he will not begin to sense, or enter the spiritual worlds, for he would not be able to withstand the impure forces that act there.

Unlike the forces that act in the spiritual world, man in our world is only influenced by the small egoistic force called his "body," his ego. Man can struggle with this force, either winning or losing his battles. But even if he is defeated, man retains that tiny spark of Light (*Ner Dakik*), which sustains his existence.

Rabbi Yehuda Ashlag gives the following example: man's work in this world resembles writing on a school blackboard, where any mistake may be wiped off without harming the writer, where he can make corrections and write anew, until he learns to write correctly. Only when he learns to write correctly is he allowed to enter the spiritual realm.

Therefore, our world is the most insignificant of all. Everyone must begin here, and everyone is bound to return here, and be born again and again until he crosses the boundary between our world and the spiritual one. (There are many additional conditions required for the soul to not descend to this world anymore, and those who will merit, will understand).

Hence, the vertical line, the leg of the letter *Kuf*, descends below the writing line, which signifies the Light descending through this letter down to the impure forces. And no other letter descends below the writing line, like the *Kuf* does.

For the impure forces to exist (any creature, whether pure or impure, can only exist by receiving Light), the last, lowest degree of pure forces descends into the impure forces and gives them the Light necessary for their existence and realization of their role: to entice man with their pleasures and convince him to act according to the law of the impure forces.

At first, the left leg of the letter *Tav* also descended below the writing line. But the Creator saw that the impure forces would then be too closely connected to pure ones, so He severed this connection and returned the left leg of the letter *Tav* back to the writing line, to the level of the pure forces.

As a result of this shortening, the left leg of the *Tav* doubled in thickness, as it folded in two, and no Light passes to the impure forces anymore. On the contrary, it even becomes the Creator's seal by holding the impure forces at bay and preventing them from stealing the Upper Light, for as soon as any impure forces touch it, they instantly die.

And all the life-force necessary for the sustenance of the impure forces is passed by the Creator through the letter *Kuf*, because, being the first letter of *Malchut*, it is remote from them; thus, there is no fear or risk that its connection to the impure forces would become too strong.

*Malchut* consists of only four letters from Above downwards: *Kuf*, *Reish*, *Shin*, and *Tav*. *Kuf* is the first, *Tav* is the last, and below it are the impure forces. Therefore, if they receive the Light they need according to the thought of creation from *Kuf*, the furthest letter from them, the impure forces have no way of "stealing" more Light than *Malchut*, who consists of four letters, is obliged to give them.

This is why this letter is called *Kuf*, to show that it gives strength to the impure system of ABYA—a fake (nonexistent) man, just as a monkey (*Kof* in Hebrew) resembles a human being.

And it misleads people by pretending to be the truth and claiming that its path leads to the attainment of spirituality, the Creator, *Lishma*, the sensation of the Creator. However, the pure forces maintain that only with the help of the Torah can man attain adequate correction of his properties so as to merge them with the Creator.

And this is what the letter *Tav* claimed: because it is the Creator's seal of truth, it stands at the end of the pure system and does not allow the impure forces to cling to pure ones, and pose as if they are pure. This is why its properties are worthy of becoming the basis for the creation of the world—so that via the analysis of good and evil, purity and impurity, inhabitants of this world may be sure that by acquiring its properties they will achieve the goal of their creation.

The four letters *Kuf-Reish-Shin-Tav* make up the four *Sefirot* of *Malchut* of the world of *Atzilut*: *Keter-Hochma-Bina-Tifferet*, where *Tifferet* consists of six *Sefirot*—*Hesed-Gevura-Tifferet-Netzah-Hod-Yesod*. But when the letter *Kuf* is by itself, without *Reish-Shin-Tav*, the Torah, which spreads to the worlds BYA, also shines upon the impure forces, and the angel of death receives the strength to destroy all that lives. This state is designated by the letter *Kuf*. But when *Malchut* is corrected, she is designated by the letter *Hey*, whose difference from *Kuf* lies in the long leg of the *Kuf* (*Malchut de Malchut*).

This long left leg, which turns the *Hey* into *Kuf*, indicates that the Light descends from the pure forces (*Partzufim*) to the impure worlds of BYA, the impure forces referred to as death. And when *Malchut* joins with *Bina* and receives the strength from *Bina* to ascend and receive the Light, the other letters join *Malchut*, and she draws the Light of life from *Bina*.

In this state, the left leg of the *Kuf* is reduced in half, turning the *Kuf* into *Tav*, whose left leg is twice as thick, due to its shortening. The part of *Malchut* that passed Light to the impure forces now ascended out of them, hence there are two kinds of *Malchut*: *Miftacha* (key)—the part that joined with *Bina*, and *Man'ula* (lock)—the part that ascended out of the impure forces.

These two parts of *Malchut* manifest in different ways: *Miftacha*—openly and *Man'ula*—secretly. Two paths of bringing man to correction emerge from them: the good path of the Torah and the path of suffering.

However, after *Malchut* corrects her properties and joins with *Bina*, she no longer parts from *Bina*, but, upon receiving Light from her, *Malchut* pours it onto the worlds, and the impure forces lose their strength to sow death and rule over the world. And if a case arises where a sinner must be punished, the impure forces must first receive permission to punish him, for without permission they may not reveal the *Man'ula*.

Thus, after *Malchut* joins with *Bina*, thereby correcting her properties, the impure forces are no longer free to rule the world, unless they are permitted. The reason for this is the letter *Tet*, the last letter of *Bina*, which sends the Light of life to all with the help of the *Miftacha*. After *Malchut* joins with *Bina*, she becomes a *Miftacha*, and does not let go of this connection. Respectively, the impure forces, the leg of the letter *Kuf*, can no longer sow death.

Three places emerge from this: (i) where only the properties of the letter *Tet* rule by shining with the Light of life of this world; (ii) the entire world after *Malchut* joins with *Bina*, defined as *Miftacha*, when the letter *Tet* shines upon all, but permits the punishment of sinners according to the rule: "You advance towards the goal either by the path of the Torah or by the path of suffering"; (iii) hell, the place of eternal punishment by the letter *Kuf*, in contrast with the first place, ruled by the letter *Tet*, where life is eternally prosperous.

All the letters with all their secret properties, described by those who understand them, are located in the Temple. All the Upper and lower worlds are created and function in the framework of their laws-properties, and the Supernal Name, the Creator's name *HaVaYaH* rules over all.

The *Mishkan* (tabernacle) in the Temple was also designed with the help of letters, for its builder, Betzalel, knew how to join the letters that made Heaven and earth. And since he was unique in possessing this wisdom, he was entrusted with the building of the sanctuary.

As the Creator chose Betzalel Above, so He wished him to be chosen below, as He said to Moshe Above: "Choose Betzalel." So Moshe said to his people below: "The Creator has chosen Betzalel." For such was Betzalel's name-property (*Be Tzel El*)—"In the Creator's shadow."

The Creator is called ZA or the *Sefira Tifferet* in *Partzuf* ZA, which shines upon the *Sefira Yesod*, called *Tzadik* (righteous one). Betzalel is called *Yesod*, which receives the Light of *VAK*—an incomplete Light—from *Tifferet*, which is hence called "sitting in the shadow," and, in turn, shining into *Malchut*. Thus, like *Tifferet*, the *Sefira Yesod* that passes this Light also consists of six *Sefirot*: *Hesed-Gevura-Tifferet-Netzah-Hod-Yesod*.

The name of the letter *Tav*, "truth," indicates that in order to reach its level, its degree, one must attain the property of truth. Therefore, the letter *Tav* claimed that with its properties man can fully analyze good and evil, renounce his impure desires as false, and to the degree that he renounces them, draw closer to the pure desires (forces), and thereby be certain that he will reach the goal of creation—correction of all his desires (*Gmar Tikkun*, end of correction).

This corresponds to the saying: "The Creator is close only to those who truly ask Him for help." For only with His help can one achieve correction and spiritual elevation. However, this help only comes to those who genuinely, "truly" demand it. As soon as man is able to cry out wholeheartedly for the Creator's help, he instantly receives it. And if he does not receive an answer from the Creator—it is a sign that his request is not yet complete, that he did not yet fully realize his egoistic nature and properties as worthless, has not yet fully felt his helplessness and inability to exit and correct his properties by himself. This is why letter *Tav* was certain that once man acquires its property of truth, he will be able to reach the goal.

But the Creator answered her that it is not worthy of becoming the basis of creation, for the forces of judgment that would arise from it would be so strong that even the complete righteous, who fulfilled the entire Torah from *Aleph* to *Tav* (A to Z) and reached the property of truth, will nevertheless be punished by it, for they have not destroyed all the sinners, as it is written in the Talmud (*Shabbat*, 55).

Furthermore, the Creator declines its request, for it is also the seal of death, as its power brought death to this world. For man is bound to die, as the serpent forged its seal and deceived Adam in his understanding of the Tree of Knowledge. This is why the world cannot exist with its properties.

## THE LETTER *SHIN*

**24. The letter *Shin* appeared before the Creator and said: "Maker of the world, it befits the world to be created with me, for Your own name *Shadday* begins with me." The Creator replied: "You are fine, handsome, and truthful, but since the letters (properties) of the word *Sheker* (falsehood) took you to be with them, I cannot create the world with your properties, for *SheKeR* (falsehood) exists only because the letters *Kuf* and *Reish* took you."**

*Malchut* consists of ten *Sefirot* and has two endings:

1) If she has only her own properties, she contains all ten *Sefirot*, from *Keter de Malchut* to *Malchut de Malchut*. In this case she firmly restricts the diffusion of Light and is designated by the letter *Tav*;

2) If *Ima-Bina* of the world of *Atzilut* fills *Malchut* with her Light, *Partzuf Malchut* ends not in the *Sefira Malchut*, but in the *Sefira Yesod*, and is designated by the letter *Shin*.

The three tips of the letter *Shin* are called its crown and signify the Light of *Bina*, *Ohr Hassadim* (the Light of Mercy), which descends from *Partzuf Ima-Bina* into *Partzuf Malchut*. This Light of *Bina*, *Ohr Hassadim* (the Light of Mercy), creates new altruistic properties in *Malchut*, altruistic intentions to receive the Light for the Creator's sake, after which *Partzuf Malchut* can receive the *Ohr Hochma* (Light of Wisdom) from ZA (Talmud, *Sanhedrin*, 22). When bonded so, ZA and *Malchut* are called "husband and wife," and the Light that *Malchut* receives from ZA is called "100 blessings."

This new ending of *Partzuf Malchut* in the *Sefira Yesod* instead of in the *Sefira Malchut* is therefore called *Yesod de Nukva* or "the central point of existence," for all that exists in the world originates from it and exists thanks to it. *Partzuf Malchut* is the sum of all the creatures, and we are all its parts. All the worlds and all that inhabit them constitute various parts of *Partzuf Malchut* of the world of *Atzilut*.

Each Upper *Partzuf* is considered the Creator of its adjacent lower *Partzuf*, for the latter originates (born) from it. Therefore, in relation to all the creatures, *Zeir Anpin* of the world of *Atzilut* is considered and called "the Creator," our Creator.

And, like the *Tav*, the letter *Shin* is called "truth" and "the Creator's seal," for a seal signifies the end of a spiritual object—*Partzuf*, like a seal fixed at the end of a letter, written in the name of the Creator. The Creator's seal is similar to Himself; this is why the seal is called the mark of truth, for only the presence of a seal gives a letter the force of truth, and confirms the truthfulness of its content.

However, the significance of the letter *Shin* is greater than that of the letter *Tav*, for *Shin* is the first letter of the word *Shadday*, one of the Creator's names-properties, designating His power, by which He said "*Dai*" (enough) to creation—stop and do not descend further (Talmud, *Hagigah*, 12)—do not descend below the letter *Shin*.

This reveals that the world and its inhabitants can only exist with the help of the letter *Shin*, thanks to its property that restricts the diffusion of Light. The Creator said: "Stop, Creature, at the letter *Shin*, and do not spread to the letter *Tav*," for if the Light had spread to *Tav*, the impure forces would have received such great strength that man would have no hope of escaping them and reaching altruistic properties. This is why the ending point of *Shin* is called "the central point of existence."

Therefore, after the letter *Shin* saw the Creator refuse the letter *Tav*, precisely because ending the diffusion of Light with *Tav* creates conditions for correction of the world that are too difficult for man to meet, the letter *Shin* claimed that its property of *Shadday* is suitable for the creation of the world, and was certain that the Creator would choose it—its properties—as the basis of creation, for it possesses all the advantages that *Tav* lacked, which was the reason for the Creator's refusal.

And it has *Tav's* advantage, as well: it is the Creator's seal—truth. Moreover, it has an additional advantage: it is called by the name *Shadday*, the new ending of *Malchut* for the inhabitants of the world, instead of the ending by the property of the letter *Tav*. Based on all that, the letter *Shin* found the strength and courage to appear before the Creator with the proposition to create the world with it.

But the Creator answered that precisely because of *Shin*'s additional advantages compared to those of the letter *Tav*, the impure forces opposite it are strengthened. For opposite each letter (spiritually pure forces or properties) there is an opposing impure force (egoistic desire), as it is written: "The Creator had made one opposite the other" (*Kohelet*, 7:14).

The strengthening of the impure forces from the properties of the letter *Shin* occurred as a result of her properties joining the impure properties of falsehood, forging spiritual purity of the letters *Kuf* and *Reish*: falsehood would be unable to exist in the world, for it would be recognized at once, had the letters *Kuf* and *Reish* not put *Shin* at the head of the word *SheKeR* (falsehood). And when truth stands at the head of the word that designates the property of falsehood, man naturally tends to err.

There are two sources of impure forces: the first is a small luminescence (*Ner Dakik*), which the pure force itself (the Creator) sends to the impure forces (desires) so as to sustain them. This is done so they would not disappear until there is a need to "punish" the sinners with them. However, these are small forces—their height is not great, for they receive only a small luminescence, sufficient to sustain their life.

This small luminescence descends into the impure forces from the letter *Kuf*, which results in these impure forces becoming similar to man in the worlds *BYA*, as a monkey in comparison to a human being, as it is said: "The Creator had made one opposite the other" (*Kohelet*, 7:14).

The second source of impure forces arises from the lower ones' spiritual fall: as a result of people's evil, egoistic actions, the Light passes from the system of the pure forces into the impure. And the first transgression is Adam's sin, by which the system of the impure forces assumed an identical formation to that of the pure system, stationing itself opposite, parallel to it. As a result, the impure worlds *ABYA* emerged opposite the pure ones.

The second source of impure forces is the letter *Reish*, which indicates that the impure forces rise and attach themselves to the pure forces, right up to the level of *Bina* of *Malchut*, designated by the letter *Dalet*.

As was previously stated, the twenty-two letters of *Partzuf Malchut* of the world of *Atzilut* are divided in three groups of letters: units in *Bina*, tens in *ZA*, and hundreds in *Malchut*.

| PARTZUF | SEFIROT | LETTERS |
|---------|---------|---------|
| BINA (IMA) | Bina<br>ZA<br>Malchut | Aleph-Tet<br>Yod-Tzadik<br>Kuf-Tav |
| ZA | Bina<br>ZA<br>Malchut | Aleph-Tet<br>Yod-Tzadik<br>Kuf-Tav |
| MALCHUT | Bina<br>ZA<br>Malchut | Aleph-Tet<br>Yod-Tzadik<br>Kuf-Tav |

The letters *Aleph-Bet-Gimel* correspond to *Sefirot Keter-Hochma-Bina*, called "the head" of a spiritual object (*Partzuf*). The letters from *Dalet* to *Tet* refer to the body of the *Partzuf*.

| | | |
|---|---|---|
| Aleph - Keter<br>Bet - Hochma<br>Gimel - Bina | **HEAD** | |
| Dalet - Hesed<br>Hey - Gevura<br>Vav - Tifferet<br>Zayin - Netzah<br>Chet - Hod<br>Tet - Yesod | **BODY** | |

The body only receives what descends to it from the head. Therefore, *Dalet*, the first letter of the body, through which the body receives Light from the head, is called *Dalah ve Aniyah* (poor and destitute). *Dalet* only receives what *Gimel* gives it. Since *Gimel* contains the Light of *Hassadim*, that is, what descends into *Dalet*.

And this is why the letter *Gimel* is called *Gomel Hassadim* (merciful One) (Talmud, *Shabbat*, 104), according to its action with regard to *Dalet*, which would otherwise be completely without Light. The protruding sharp angle on the right side of *Dalet* is the sign of *Dalet's* abundance of *Ohr Hassadim*.

However, opposite the pure (altruistic) *Malchut*, stands the impure *Malchut*, who is pride and does not wish to receive the Light from *Gimel* and rely on it. Instead, she rises up in the desire to be the head, and in so creates the sharp angle of the *Dalet*. That indicates that the presence of *Ohr Hassadim* disappears, transforming it into the letter *Reish*, which is written as it is pronounced—with two letters: *Reish* and *Shin*.

The true merging of the pure ZA and *Malchut* is called *ECHaD* (one), consists of the letters *Aleph*, *Chet* and *Dalet*, for the letters from *Aleph* to *Chet* are the nine *Sefirot* of ZA. He passes the Light from *Gimel* of *Bina* to *Gimel* of *Malchut*, resulting in *Malchut* being filled with the Light of *Hassadim*, thereby becoming *Dalet* with a protruding right angle. As a result of this, ZA and *Malchut* become one.

When the lower ones (people) sin in their actions (intentions), they give the impure *Malchut* the strength to cling to the pure one—*Dalet*, to erase the sharp angle of the Light of *Hassadim* and turn it into the letter *Reish*. Thus, the word *Echad* (one) becomes *Acher* (other, alien, foreign): *Aleph-Chet-Dalet* of the word *Echad* are transformed into *Aleph-Chet-Reish* of the word *Acher*, for instead of the connection with the Creator emerges a connection with other, impure forces, called "*Elokim Acherim*" (other gods), which cling to ZA and *Malchut* of the pure world of *Atzilut*.

This leads to the letters *Kuf* and *Reish* distorting the Creator's seal (*Shin*), the letter of truth. As a result, *Yesod* of *Malchut*, which receives from *Yesod de* ZA, becomes linked to the impure source instead of the pure, for a new *Yesod* of the impure *Malchut* was formed with the help of the letter *Shin*.

From here the impure forces develop up to ten *Sefirot* with a head and a body, whereas *Shin* becomes the source of all that desolates, for destruction of purity begets impurity. And from this emerged the system of the impure worlds ABYA of the impure man.

Thus, we have learned how the letters *Kuf* and *Reish* became the two sources of emergence and development of impure forces. And since the impure forces pose as pure, they are called false, counterfeit letters whose purpose is to annihilate the system of the pure forces and their unity with the Creator, so as to forge themselves out of the devastation of the pure forces.

The birth of the impure forces from the destruction of the pure ones is possible on account of the letter *Shin*, *Yesod* of *Malchut*, joining with the impure forces as a result of the forging of the letter *Reish* out of *Dalet*. Thereby,

*Echad* turns into *Acher*, and the system of the impure forces (*Elokim Acherim*, other gods) is created.

And had the letters *Kuf* and *Reish* not captured the letter *Shin*, such an enormous system of impure forces, so capable of lying and falsifying everything in the eyes of man, would not have come into being.

Therefore, the Creator answered the letter *Shin*: "Though you are good, you will stand at the head of the word *Sheker* (falsehood) together with the letters *Kuf* and *Reish*. Indeed, upon capturing you, with your power they will be able to create an entire system of impure forces of falsehood and forgery. Hence, I cannot create the world with your properties, for since there is an impure system opposite from you, it is impossible to achieve the goal of creation with you."

## THE LETTERS *KUF* AND *REISH*

**25. From the aforesaid, it follows that whoever wishes to tell a lie will succeed if he first tells the truth as a base on which the lie will then grow and start to act. And this is because the letter *Shin* is a letter of truth, in which the Patriarchs had been united, for the three lines in the writing of the letter *Shin* (ש) signify the three Patriarchs, who designate the *Sefirot*-properties *Hesed-Gevura-Tifferet*.**

The letters *Kuf* and *Reish* indicate the evil side, as they form the impure side, called *KaR* (cold), which lacks warmth and life, for it draws its sustenance from *Malchut* when she turns from living water into ice. However, to create an opportunity to exist, these letters attach the *Shin* to themselves, thus creating the combination *KeSHeR* (tie, knot), which embodies strength and survival.

For the Light of *Hesed-Gevura-Tifferet* of *Bina*, which she receives from *Yesod de ZA*, creates a new ending in *Malchut*, a new *Kli*-desire to receive the Light called "100 blessings" from ZA. And since *Hesed-Gevura-Tifferet* are called the Patriarchs, and the Light that passes to *Malchut* descends from them, the letter *Shin* that designates them is called "truth."

By eliminating the sharp angle of the letter *Dalet*, the impure forces turn it into the letter *Reish*. By this, they convert the word *ECHaD* into *ACHeR*, thereby stealing *Yesod* of the pure *Malchut*, designated by *Shin*. Also, with the letter *Shin* they build the *Yesod* of the impure *Malchut*, which leads to a very strong clinging of impure forces to pure ones. This clinging is called *KeSHeR*, the reciprocal tie joining pure and impure forces, a knot that is not easily severed.

From the aforesaid, we see that the reason for the letters wishing for the world to be created with them is that each of them believes that only its properties can correct the world. The letter *Shin* thinks that the Light of *Hassadim* will bring the souls to the goal of creation. However, the letters *Kuf* and *Reish*—*KaR* (cold)—do not desire this Light, for receiving the Light of Mercy for the sake of bestowal is pure, but receiving it for the sake of pleasure is impure.

## THE LETTER *TZADIK*

26. Subsequently, the letter *Tzadik* appeared before the Creator and said: "Master of the world, You should create the world with me, for *Tzadikim* (the righteous) are marked by me. You, who is called a *Tzadik* (righteous one), are also recorded within me, for You are righteous and You love righteousness. Therefore, my properties are suitable to create the world by."

The Creator answered: "*Tzadik*, you are truly righteous, but you must remain concealed and not be revealed to the extent required were the world to be created by you, so as to not give the world an excuse." The concealment of the letter *Tzadik* is necessary, for first came the letter *Nun*, which was then joined by the letter *Yod* from the Creator's Holy Name *Yod-Hey-Vav-Hey* (*HaVaYaH*), who stood above it as a mark of the bond between the Creator and His creations, mounted the letter *Nun* and joined it on its right hand side, thereby creating the letter *Tzadik*.

The reason for the necessity of concealing the letter *Tzadik*, which makes it unsuitable for the creation of the world with it, is that when the Creator created Adam, i.e., ZA, He created him as two *Partzufim*-objects—male and female, connected to each other back to back. This is why the letter *Yod* stands with its back to the back of the letter *Nun*, both facing opposite directions, just as the letter *Tzadik* is depicted: the face of *Yod* turned upwards, while the face of *Nun* is turned downwards.

And the Creator also said to *Tzadik*: "In the future I will revoke the relationship of back-to back, and will join them face-to-face. In another place shall you so rise as such, but not at the beginning of creation. For in the beginning of creation, you must be connected back-to-back by the letters *Nun* and *Yod*, for this form indicates that the Light in you is concealed. Therefore, the world cannot be created with you." The letter *Tzadik* then left.

*Tzadik* came to suggest that the world should be created with its properties, for when it saw that the *Tav's* request was turned down by the Creator due to its heavy laws, and the letter *Shin*—due to the impure forces clinging to it—it thought that its properties could be suitable for the creation of the world. After all, it, too, contains the Creator's seal, and no impure forces cling to it.

That is why *Tzadik* said to the Creator that the righteous are sealed by its name as a mark of their union with Him, by circumcision and turning up of the place of contact (*Zivug*) with the Creator, which, thanks to these corrections, repels all the impure forces.

The Creator, called *Bina*, is also marked by *Tzadik*, for He is righteous like ZA, since the Upper Part of *Bina* of the world of *Atzilut* (*Aba ve Ima*—AVI) corresponds to the male and female parts, like ZA and *Malchut*. And AVI are forever joined so as to send down the Light of Mercy and thus sustain the existence of all that are below them. This is why *Tzadik* thought itself suitable for creating the world, for the world lives by the Light of Mercy, and can reach the goal with its help.

The letter *Tzadik* is called the *Sefira Yesod* of ZA. When *Yesod* joins with *Malchut*, it is defined as *Tzadik* (righteous), for the nine *Sefirot* of ZA are from *Yod* to *Tzadik*, and *Kuf* is the beginning of *Malchut*, which consists of four *Sefirot*—*Kuf*, *Reish*, *Shin*, and *Tav*.

When *Malchut* is joined with *Yesod* of ZA, *Kuf* is joined with *Tzadik*, and *Yesod* is called *Tzadik* (righteous). And to this the Creator replied to *Tzadik* that it is *Tzadik* in *Yesod* of ZA: "And you are *Tzadik* in Me, for AVI are forever joined so as to pour down the Light of Mercy and sustain the existence of the lower ones. And you are righteous, for *Malchut* is also connected to you, just as in the alphabet, *Kuf* follows *Tzadik*. Yet, in spite of all that, you do not merit for your properties to become the basis of the world."

*Yesod* of ZA includes in itself *Malchut* in the form of the letter *Kuf* in the word *TzadiK*. And when *Malchut* is included in *Yesod* as *Tzadik*, it is designated by the letter *Nun*, for *Nun* is *Gevura* of ZA (*Yod-Keter*, *Chaf-Hochma*, *Lamed-Bina*, *Mem-Hesed*, *Nun-Gevura*).

When ZA grows and becomes big, his *Sefirot Hesed-Gevura-Tifferet* become *Sefirot Hochma-Bina-Daat*. Thus, *Gevura* becomes *Bina*. And when ZA becomes small once again, *Bina*, too, returns to being *Gevura* (*Nun*). This fall is designated by *Nun*'s head looking down.

The letter *Tzadik* consists of the letters *Nun* and *Yod* connected back-to-back. The letter *Nun* designates *Malchut* with the properties of the *Sefira Yesod* included in her; *Yod* designates the actual *Yesod* of ZA. Their connection—back-to-back, facing out in opposite directions—indicates that impure forces cling to their backs.

They conceal their backs from strangers since there is a flaw in their backs—the desire to receive the Light of Wisdom (*Ohr Hochma*). This flaw must be concealed so as to prevent the impure forces from clinging to their backs. Therefore, the letter *Tzadik* is unsuitable for the world to be created by its properties. Its very shape reveals an opportunity for the impure forces to cling to it; this is why Adam (created out of ZA and *Malchut* when they are joined as *Tzadik*) is also created consisting of two halves, male and female, joined at their backs.

And if the letter *Tzadik* were to argue that in the big state, in the presence of *Ohr Hochma*, ZA and *Malchut* unite face-to-face, it would be told that such connection is impossible at their place, but only during their ascent to AVI. For if such a connection were possible in their own place, the impure forces would immediately cling to them. For this reason, the letter *Tzadik* is unworthy of becoming the basis of the universe.

## THE LETTER *PEH*

**27. The letter *Peh* entered and said: "Master of the world, it would be good to create the world with me, for the future liberation of the world is inscribed in me, as the word *Pedut* (liberation, redemption) begins with me. That is, liberation is deliverance from all suffering. And it is therefore fitting to create the world with me."**

**The Creator answered her: "Though you are fine, the word *Peshah* (transgression) begins with you and is secretly denoted by you, like a serpent that strikes and hides its head in its body. So a sinner bows his head, hiding from others' eyes, but stretches out his hands to sin. So is the shape of the letter *Peh*, whose head is hidden inside it." And the Creator also said to the letter *Ayin* that it would be unfitting to create the world with its properties, for within it is the property of *Avon* (crime, sin). And though *Ayin* tried to object, saying that its properties are contained in the word *Anavah* (humility), the Creator refused it nonetheless.**

*Pedut* (Liberation) begins with the letter *Peh*, meaning that the property of *Peh* is contained in future liberation. This is why the letter *Peh* claims that it is worthy of being the basis of the world. Indeed, both *Galut* (exile) and *Ge'ula* (redemption) depend on *Malchut*: when *Malchut* has no inner Light of *Hochma*, the people of Israel are exiled from the land of Israel. For in our world, the land of Israel corresponds to *Malchut* of the world of *Atzilut*, the spiritual land of Israel.

Just as in the spiritual world, ZA (Israel) distances from *Malchut* (the land of Israel), the people of Israel separate and leave their land in our world. And when the children of Israel correct their actions, they cause ZA (Israel) to fill his *Malchut* (the land of Israel) with Light, build her with his Light and unite with her face-to-face. As a result, the children of Israel of our world merit redemption and return to their land.

The Light from ZA, which builds and fills *Malchut*, descends from *Sefirot Netzah* and *Hod* in ZA. *Hochma* of *Malchut* clothes in *Netzah* and *Bina* of *Malchut* clothes in *Hod*. The letters *Ayin* and *Peh* are *Netzah* and *Hod* in ZA. This is why *Peh*, the *Sefira Hod* in ZA, claimed that it was suitable to be the basis of the world, for the Light of *Hochma* that brings redemption to the entire world stems from *Peh* to *Malchut*. Thus, if the world achieved its property, it would undoubtedly reach the end of correction—complete redemption.

The letter *Peh* thought that it was more suitable to become the basis of the world than *Ayin* because although *Ohr Hochma* enters *Netzah-Ayin* and *Hod-Peh*, and is mainly present in *Netzah-Ayin*, redemption depends on *Hod-Peh*, nonetheless. That is because initially, *Bina* liberates *Malchut* from her restrictions and thereby redeems her.

By receiving from *Bina* her properties of mercy, *Malchut* merits redemption. This is fulfilled in the following way: *Bina* transcends her own properties and joins with *Malchut*, as a result of which, upon receiving the Light of *Hassadim*, *Malchut* can now receive the Light of *Hochma*. The restrictions imposed on the reception of Light mostly affect the left side, i.e., *Hod-Peh* in ZA. And that is why the letter *Peh* thought that since the Light of *Bina* enters it, and not *Netzah-Ayin*, it is better suited to become the basis of the world.

However, all the individual corrections made during the 6,000 years of the world's existence until the end of correction are considered incomplete, for the Upper Light, which allows for the discovery and analysis of all the impure forces within oneself, is not present in its entirety. Therefore, the Light may not be received in the worlds of BYA, below *Parsa*, below the boundary that separates the world of *Atzilut* from the worlds of BYA.

*Parsa* is *Malchut* that ascended to *Bina* in order to restrict the diffusion and reception of Light into those parts of her that are located below *Bina*. And as a consequence of Adam's attempt to nevertheless receive the Light under the *Parsa*, impurity slipped into *Malchut*, of which it is said that the serpent appeared before Chava (Eve) and brought impurity upon her (Talmud, *Shabbat*, 146). This impurity will only be corrected at the end of correction.

The thing is that the absence of the Upper Light in the force capable of discerning good from evil in all of *Malchut's* thickness gives rise to a flaw called "tears"—two tears that fall into a vast sea from the two eyes of *Hochma* and *Bina* that are concealed from all.

The two eyes are *Hochma* and *Bina*, and the tears signify the flaw in them from the presence of the impure force that appeared in them as a result of Adam's sin. This led to the ruin of the two Temples. These tears in *Malchut's* eyes will only dry at the end of correction, when death disappears from the world and all the Light shines in *Hochma* and *Bina* (item 56).

So the letter *Peh* was told that although it brings the world *Pedut* (redemption) with its Light, and although all redemptions pass only through it, this Light is incomplete. All the individual corrections are imperfect, for they come and go, just as the two Temples.

For the properties of *Peshah* (transgression) and *Pedut* (redemption) in the letter *Peh* are not sufficiently perfect and complete so as to withstand the sin of Adam, for in the absence of the full Light of *Hochma*, there is clinging of impure forces. Hence, the letter *Peh* is unworthy of being the basis of the world.

And since the property of *Peshah* (transgression) is concealed, the force of the serpent is present therein, deceiving people and leading them to their death. And it is impossible to kill it, just as a snake bites and immediately hides its head in itself (similar to the head of the letter *Peh*), which makes it impossible to kill it, for one may only kill the serpent within oneself by striking the "head." This is why the letter *Peh* is unsuitable for the creation of the world.

## THE LETTER AYIN

*Bina* of the world of *Atzilut* is called *Ima Ilaa* (Supernal Mother) and also *Anavah* (modesty, humility). (Here, the capital "A" designates the letter *Ayin*, not to be confused with *Aleph*). The *Sefira Netzah* of *Zeir Anpin* (designated by the letter *Ayin*) clothes into *Malchut* with all of its Light, and ascends to *Bina*, who adorns her with her own adornments: *Bina* clothes into *Netzah* of ZA. But since the letter *Peh*, signifying *Peshah* (transgression) is concealed in *Netzah*, the Creator refused to create the world with its properties, as it is written in item 27.

Two words render the meaning of the word "transgression" in Hebrew: *Peshah* and *Avon*. However, "transgression" is mainly concentrated in the letter *Peh*, for *Malchut* of ZA connects into the *Sefira Hod* of ZA.

As a result of Adam's sin, *Klipot* (shells, impure forces) cling to *Malchut* of ZA. But *Netzah* of ZA is a property of ZA himself, and impure forces cannot cling to it. Yet, as it is written in the Talmud (*Baba Kama*), even *Netzah* is subject to *Klipot* clinging to it.

This flaw—the ability of the impure forces to cling to *Netzah* of ZA—is called "transgression." However, the word *Avon* (not *Peshah*) indicates that *Netzah* is pure and direct, and that the transgression is caused by its connection with the *Sefira Hod*.

The reason the Creator turns to the letters *Peh* and *Ayin* at the same time is that *Netzah* and *Hod* are like two body parts—two legs. This is why they both appeared before Him with their requests. However, *The Zohar* clarifies each of them (their properties) one at a time.

## THE LETTER *SAMECH*

**28. The letter *Samech* appeared before the Creator and said: "Creator of the world, it would be good to create the world with my properties, for within me is *Smicha* (support) for the fallen, as it is written: 'The Creator supports (*Somech*) all who fall.'" The Creator replied: "That is why you are needed in your place; do not move from it. If you move from your place, contained in the word *Somech*, those who fall will lose your support, for they rely on you (your properties)." Having heard this, the letter *Samech* departed.**

The letter *Samech* stands for *Sefira Tifferet* in ZA, i.e., *Bina* in the body of ZA. Since *Sefirot Keter-Hochma-Bina* (KHB) were transformed into *Hesed-Gevura-Tifferet* (HGT) in ZA, they were emptied of the Light of *Hochma*, and were left with only the Light of *Hassadim*, thus changing their name from KHB to HGT.

As we know, *Bina* consists of two parts: the Upper Part, called GAR: *Gimel* (three) *Rishonot* (first ones)—the first three *Sefirot KHB*, and the lower part, called ZAT: *Zayin* (seven) *Tachtonot* (lower ones)—the seven lower *Sefirot* from *Hesed* to *Malchut*. The Upper Part of *Bina* is called *Aba ve Ima* (AVI). Being filled with the Light of Mercy, *Aba ve Ima* exist in a state of perfection—without any desire to receive, but only to bestow.

AVI are designated by *Samech* (numerical value – 60), for they include the first three *Sefirot KHB* and three *Sefirot* of ZA, which, in view of the absence of *Ohr Hochma* in ZA, are not called KHB, but rather HGT. Therefore AVI consist of six *Sefirot*, each consisting of ten, totaling 60 = *Samech*.

ZAT of *Bina* receive the Light from Above and pass it on to ZA. This part of *Bina* has the property of ZA, rather than of *Bina*, as it needs to receive exactly what ZA needs, and then pass it to him. Since, unlike *Bina*, who does not wish to receive anything, ZAT of *Bina* need to receive *Ohr Hochma* for ZA, they feels a lack for it, and thus separate from *Bina* and an independently existing object-*Partzuf* forms out of her lower part.

This *Partzuf* is called YESHSUT, and it is designated by the letter *Mem* (numerical value – 40), for it consists of four *Sefirot—Tifferet-Netzah-Hod-Yesod* of *Partzuf* AVI. Owing to its shape (properties), the block-letter *Mem* is called *Mem Stumah* (closed).

However, this separation of AVI into two parts occurs only when they have no Light of *Hochma*, but only the Light of *Hassadim*. Consequently, the Upper Part of *Bina* remains in its perfection, whereas the lower part feels a flaw in its state by not receiving *Ohr Hochma*. And since spiritual objects are separated by the differences in their properties, the sensation of imperfection separates the lower part of *Bina* from the Upper.

However, if those below improve their "intentions" (called "actions" in the spiritual), and ask ZA for help in correcting their actions, overcoming the egoism of impure desires, and acquiring spiritually pure, altruistic desires, ZA then turns to the superior YESHSUT, which turns to AVI. AVI then send their request even higher, receive the Light of *Hochma* and pass it to YESHSUT.

Finally, YESHSUT and AVI unite into one *Partzuf*, for having received *Ohr Hochma*, YESHSUT becomes as perfect as AVI are perfect being filled with *Ohr Hassadim*. YESHSUT passes the Light of *Hochma* down to ZA, who then passes it to *Malchut*. The Light that *Malchut* receives from ZA is referred to as 100 blessings, for *Samech* = 60 joins with *Mem* = 40.

However, when man sins in his intentions (desires, actions), he does not turn to *Malchut* with a request for help, causing the Light of *Hochma* to disappear from ZA, and ZA returns from *Gadlut* (big state) back to *Katnut* (small state). (When ZA contains the Light of *Hochma*, he is called "big"; and when he is filled with only the Light of *Hassadim*, he is called "small"). And the united *Partzuf Bina* is once more divided into AVI and YESHSUT.

In this small state (*Katnut*), ZA and *Malchut* are in danger of impure forces (*Klipot*) clinging to them. To make certain this does not happen, for then they may fall from the world of *Atzilut* below the *Parsa* into the worlds BYA, AVI send them the property of *Samech* (the Light of Mercy). And although it is only the Light of *Hassadim* without the Light of Wisdom (Light of *Hochma*), it provides ZA and *Malchut* with the sensation of perfection in acts of bestowal, and thus impure forces can no longer cling to them, for the sole intention of the impure forces is to receive the Light of Wisdom from a pure *Partzuf*.

And this is why the Light that fills ZA in *Katnut* is called *Samech*, which testifies to its action: *Samech* "supports" ZA and *Malchut* so that they wouldn't fall from the world of *Atzilut* below the *Parsa*.

That is why the letter *Samech* thought that if the world were created with its properties, it would be able to reach the goal of creation and merge with the Creator. Its Light could shine in ZA and *Malchut* even in their small state, and the *Klipa* (impure force) would not attempt to snatch the Light from them. On the contrary, the impure, egoistic forces would flee from its Light. *Samech* believed that if the world were to be created with its properties, it would be able to protect all creatures, even when their actions were corrupted, for even in such a state, the impure force would not be able to harm them.

But the Creator said to *Samech* that precisely because its role is to support those who fall and to protect the lower ones in times of their spiritual descent, it must stay in its place and not move from it. For if the world were created by it, its power would always prevail over all, ridding ZA and *Malchut* of the chance to grow out of their small state.

And if ZA and *Malchut* don't stimulate the lower ones (people) to raise MAN—request for help in achieving *Gadlut*, the Upper Light will not be able to descend to bring the creatures to the end of correction and redemption. Therefore, the letter *Samech* must support the lower ones until they merit more. But when they do merit, they will be able to receive the great Light called "100 blessings" into their entire *Partzuf*. So the Creator refused to create the world with the letter *Samech*.

"Because the lower ones need *Samech* only in their *Katnut*, in the absence of the Light of Wisdom (*Ohr Hochma*), ZON need you and you can help them. However, they need you only in their *Katnut*. But you do not help to bring them to perfection, and so you cannot be the basis of the world."

## THE LETTER NUN

**29. The letter Nun entered and said to the Creator: "It would be good for You to create the world with me, for Norah Tehilot (great praises) is written with me, as well as 'Praising of the righteous.'"**

The Creator replied: "Return to your place, for you are the reason that the letter *Samech* returned to its place. And rely on it for support. For the letter *Nun* exists in the word *Nefilah* (fall), which must be corrected by the letter *Samech*. This is the reason why it needed to return to its place—so as to strengthen the lower ones." The letter *Nun* left Him at once.

When *Nun* saw that the Creator sent the letter *Samech* away (as its properties are only used in the state of *Katnut*, that is, only to support those who had fallen from the *Gadlut*), it thought that it was worthy of being the basis of the world. This is because not only does *Nun* have all the advantages of *Samech*, but it can also use *Ohr Hochma*, the Light of *Gadlut*. Thus, the reason for the Creator's refusal to *Samech* does not apply to *Nun*.

The *Sefira Gevura* in ZA is called *Nun*, for it is entirely mitigated by *Bina's* property of mercy, called *Nun* = 50 gates of *Bina*. It is this property of *Gevura* that gives ZA the name *Norah Tehilot* (great praises). *Ima-Bina* is called *Tehilah* (praise), and since *Gevura* descends from *Bina*, it is referred to as *Norah Tehilot*, while *Nun* is used in the *Sefira Yesod*, in the *Gadlut* of ZA during his *Zivug* with *Nukva*. Like *Ima*, this is whence *Nukva* receives the name *Tehilah*, while ZA becomes one in both *Tehilot—Ima* and *Nukva*.

Therefore, the letter *Nun* said that, being in *Gevura*, the left line of ZA, it attracts the Light of Mercy emanated by *Samech* (*Bina*, *Ima*), which is also called the "Upper *Tehilah*," as a result of which ZA acquires its properties and the name *Norah Tehilot* to match them. This is why *Nun* has all the properties of *Samech*: the Light of Mercy that bestows perfection and repels the impure forces-desires.

The letter *Nun* added: "However, I have an additional advantage in that I am used during the big state of ZA in his *Yesod*, in the letter *Tzadik*, of which I am the left element." This *Nun* in the letter *Tzadik* is that same *Nun* that is defined as *Norah Tehilot* (praises of the righteous), for even when ZA achieves *Gadlut* during the ascent of ZON to *AVI*, *Nun* also acts in *Yesod* of ZA, connecting *Nukva* back-to-back with ZA, so that ZA receives the Light of Mercy from *AVI* (*Samech*).

And so *Nun* is called "praises of the righteous," for *Yod* (righteous one, the basis of the world) mounts it. *Nun* is called "great praises," for it attracts the Light of Wisdom to *Malchut* in the state of *Gadlut*.

Therefore, we find that *Malchut* receives all her beauty from *Nun*, which is located in *Yesod* of ZA. This is why the letter *Nun* claimed that it merits for the world to be created with its properties, for its luminescence adds to the Light of Wisdom that unites and revives ZON, and does not merely support them, like the letter *Samech*.

So the Creator answered it: "You are wrong in thinking that you merit leading the world to complete correction by your properties, without the clinging of impure forces, for even your properties need to be supported by the letter *Samech*. Indeed, this is precisely why you are connected back-to-back with the letter *Yod*, and the Light of *Samech* guards you against the clinging of the impure forces onto you. And that is why your properties, which rely upon the strength of *Samech*, are merely ones of support. Hence, you are unworthy of becoming the basis of the world."

## THE LETTERS *MEM* AND *LAMED*

**30. The letter *Mem* entered and said: "Master of the world, it would be good for You to create the world by me, for *Melech* (King) is called by me." The Creator replied: "That is so, but I shall not create the world by you, for the world needs a King. Return to your place. Also, I shall not create the world with the letters *Lamed* and *Chaf* that form the word *MeLeCH* (King), as the world cannot exist without a King."**

The letter *Mem* is the *Sefira Hesed* in ZA, which receives the Light from its corresponding *Sefira Hesed* in *Bina*. When, in addition to the Light of Mercy in his small state, ZA receives the Light of Wisdom and becomes big, his *Sefirot HGT* turn into *Sefirot Hochma-Bina-Daat* (*HBD*). In other words, *Hesed* in ZA ascends and becomes *Hochma*, thereby revealing a new Light, the Light of *Hochma*, the Light of the Creator's face.

This is why the letter *Mem* claimed that it was suitable for the world to be created by it, for it reveals the Creator's Light to the world, thereby eliminating any risk of impure forces clinging to it, and so the world is guaranteed complete correction.

But the Creator answered that it is forbidden to reveal this Light to the world, for the world needs for this great Light to first clothe itself in the three letters of the word *MeLeCH*. In other words, the great Light may be revealed in the world only if *Mem* joins with the letters *Lamed* and *Chaf*. So the Creator said, "Go and join with them."

*Mem* in the word *Melech* is *Hesed*. *Lamed* is *Bina*, which passes the Light to ZA. The letter *Chaf* is *Malchut*, *Nukva* of ZA, for there cannot be a *Melech* (King) without *Malchut* (Kingdom). Also, all of the Light becomes revealed only thanks to *Malchut*.

In this case, *Malchut* shines from ZA in three places:

1) *Malchut* becomes a *Kisseh* (throne) for a *King* (ZA). A *Kisseh* derives from *Kissui* (cover, concealment), so it is designated by the bent letter *Chaf*.

2) *Malchut* clothes ZA. Because the great Light is revealed only to Israel, *Malchut* clothes ZA, and when her kingdom is revealed, ZA frees himself from her garment and throws it over all the nations of the world, idolaters, and the Light of his face pours upon Israel. And all the righteous then point their finger at the Creator and say: "This is the Creator, to whom I aspired!" This diffusion of Light is designated by the letter *Chaf*.

3) *Malchut* becomes a crown on the head of ZA. And this is the property of the letter *Chaf*, of *Keter* (crown of ZA).

## THE LETTER CHAF

**31. At this time the letter Chaf descended from the Kisseh – the Creator's throne, and stood before the Creator. It trembled and said to Him: "Creator of the world, with my properties I merit to become the basis of the world, for I am Kavod – Your Glory." When the letter Chaf descended from the Creator's throne, all the worlds trembled, and the throne itself, verging on collapse. The Creator then answered: "Chaf, what are you doing here? I will not create the world by you. Return to your place, for you exist in the word Kelayah (destruction) and in the word Kalah (bride)."**

The Creator's throne is the world of *Beria*. The appearance of the letter *Mem* before the Creator led to the letter *Chaf* falling from His throne. As a result, *Hochma* and *Bina* of the world of *Beria* trembled, as well as all the lower worlds with all their inhabitants.

All the arguments that the letters raised in their wish for the world to be created with each of them is like raising MAN—a request for precise measure of help from Above in the form of Upper Light (called MAD), corresponding to that particular letter.

If so, ZON will rule the world, and this ruling is effected by the very Light descending from ZON in the exact quantity of MAD that each letter evoked and caused, for the MAD precisely corresponds to the MAN in both quantity and quality, whereas MAN is the actual property of the letter. Hence, each letter argues that it can draw the kind of Light from Above that will surely bring all creatures to the goal.

Similarly, the Creator's answers to each of the twenty-two letters of ZON *de Atzilut* constitute the descending MAD (the Upper Light, strength, help) that precisely corresponds to the MAN raised by that particular letter. And when the

Upper Light that descends from a particular letter begins to rule the world, this signifies the Creator's reply to that letter. Since the impure forces cling to one of the letter's properties, as the Creator created two precisely balanced, opposing systems of pure and impure forces, this reveals the letter's inability to rule the world. And thus, the Creator dismissed each letter's individual claim to build the world by its property in order to bring it to the goal of creation.

Herein lies the Creator's "game" with each of the twenty-two letters, giving each the opportunity to reveal its properties, power and forces, until it becomes clear from their aspirations and analysis, which of them truly merits the world being governed by it.

From this we see that when the letter *Mem* began to reveal its great Light in the world, in doing so, it caused the fall of the *Kisse* (throne). This is so because the *Kisse* has two properties: (i) it covers and conceals the Creator, where the word *Kisse* derives from the word *Kissui*; (ii) it reveals the Creator's greatness in the worlds with the help of the three letters *MeLeCH*. Then, *Malchut* that became a *Kissui*, the Creator's cover, ascends and turns to *Chaf*—the Creator's own garments—thus revealing the King (Creator), and it becomes a crown on His head.

But as soon as the letter *Mem*, which was not clothed in *Chaf*, began to reveal the Light of the Creator's face, the letter *Chaf* fell from the *Kisse* (the throne of His Glory), stopped concealing Him, and stated that from now on only the Creator's revealed glory would rule over it, without any kind of concealment, as desired by *Mem*.

Owing to *Chaf*'s fall from the throne, two hundred thousand worlds that originate from *Hochma* and *Bina* of the world of *Beria*, as well as the worlds below them, shook and trembled on the verge of collapse. For the entire connection between the lower degree or *Partzuf* and the one above it lies in the fact that *Malchut* of the Upper Degree becomes *Keter* of the lower. And the property of the letter *Chaf* consists in clothing *Malchut* of an Upper spiritual object in *Keter* of a lower one.

There are three distinctive features to the throne: (i) six steps leading to the throne, six *Sefirot*—*Hesed-Gevura-Tifferet-Netzah-Hod-Yesod* of the lower one; (ii) four legs of the throne, the Light in *Sefirot Keter-Hochma-Bina-Daat* of the lower one; (iii) *Malchut* of the Upper One that descends to the lower one, clothes into it, and all the Light from the Upper One is passed through her to the lower one.

Thus, when *Chaf* fell from the throne of the Creator's glory, the connection between the world of *Atzilut* and the throne (world of *Beria*) was severed. This is so because *Chaf* (*Malchut* of the world of *Atzilut*) that clothes in *Sefirot Keter-Hochma-Bina-Daat* of the world of *Beria* pours all the Light onto the world of

*Beria*, called the throne of His glory. But when *Chaf* fell from the throne, the connection between the world of *Atzilut* and the world of *Beria* was severed, *Chaf* trembled, for it lost the power to bestow upon the world of *Beria*, and two hundred thousand worlds (*Hochma* and *Bina* out of *Sefirot Keter-Hochma-Bina-Daat* of the world of *Beria*) trembled in fear of collapsing, for they lost all of their life-force, which they receive from the world of *Atzilut*.

Similarly, in the world of *Atzilut*, *Bina* of the world of *Atzilut*, the Creator, is connected with ZON. This is because *Partzuf Bina* of the world of *Atzilut* consists of ten *Sefirot*, and her last *Sefira*, *Malchut*, clothes in ZA of the world of *Atzilut* with the property of the letter *Chaf*. *Malchut* of the *Sefira Bina*, which clothes in ZA, is the letter *Chaf*. And this letter *Chaf* is the Creator's throne in ZA. For the Creator is *Bina*, *Sefira* above ZA. And ZA becomes a throne for *Bina*. And during the fall, the connection between *Bina* and ZA is severed, since *Chaf* is *Malchut* of *Bina*; it clothes into ZA and passes all the Light to him.

And it therefore trembled (lost its ability to bestow upon ZA), and so did two hundred thousand worlds, which are the Light for ZA, called *Hochma* and *Bina* or *KHBD*—the four legs of the throne—for all the Light departed from them. And the worlds trembled in fear of collapsing, that is, *Sefirot Hesed-Gevura-Tifferet-Netzah-Hod-Yesod* in ZA that include all the worlds below them, for all the Light of *Bina* departed thence.

The Creator told the letter *Chaf* that because it fell from the throne of His glory, the first three *Sefirot* of ZA trembled, and all the other worlds are on the verge of total collapse and destruction without any hope of restoration; hence, *Chaf* must return to its place in the throne of glory.

*Chaf's* return to its place in the Creator's throne takes place just as He refuses to create the world with the letter *Mem*, for the world needs a King. That is, the trembling of the letter *Chaf* as it fell from the Creator's throne, which in turn, made the worlds tremble in fear of possible collapse, and the Creator's answer to the letter *Mem* transpire simultaneously.

## THE LETTER YOD

**32. The letter Yod entered and said: "Maker of the world! It would be good to create the world by me, for Your Holy name begins with me." The Creator replied: "It is sufficient that you are inscribed in My Name, in Me, and all of your aspirations are to Me, and you should not be uprooted from it all."**

Since *Yod* is the first letter of the Creator's name *HaVaYaH* (*Yod-Hey-Vav-Hey*), the beginning of the Creator's revelation to creatures, the first degree of the Upper Light, the letter *Yod* argued for the world to be created with its properties, for the world would then be absolutely guaranteed complete correction. However, the Creator objects to it. As was already stated, the letters' questions and the Creator's answers signify the Creator playing with each letter, where the letters' questions are their *MAN*, and the Creator's answers are *MAD* in the form of the Upper Light.

So, by telling *Yod*, "It is sufficient," the Creator thus explained the creation of restriction—that the Light is only allowed to descend to its level, but no further. And this restriction is fixed in the Creator's name *Shadday* (*Shin-Dalet-Yod*). After *Yod* began to spread with the great Light, the Creator stopped it, forbidding it to spread to the letter *Tav*, but only to *Shin* (as was said above, in item 25). He said to it: "Enough, and do not spread further. Otherwise you will not be able to remain forever in My Name *HaVaYaH*."

As the sages said: "My Name is not pronounced as it is written. For it is written *HaVaYaH*, but pronounced *Adonay*" (Talmud, *Pesahim*, 50). Indeed, the name *HaVaYaH* is not subject to change, as it is written: "For I, the Lord (*HaVaYaH*), do not change" (*Malachi*, 3:6). For corruption and its correction emerge in the days of the world's existence, meaning that constant changes are coming. Therefore, until the end of correction, the Creator is called *Adonay*, for this name is subject to change, and not *HaVaYaH*, which can never be altered.

Yet, in the future, after the end of correction, *HaVaYaH* will be pronounced as it is written. Therefore, the Creator said, "If I see some fault or evil in you, by this you will be removed from My Name, for My Name, *HaVaYaH*, may not contain anything flawed or corrected—neither corruption nor correction. And this is why the world cannot be created by your properties." There are three degrees in the letter *Yod* of the name *HaVaYaH*: in the *Sefira Hochma* of ZA, in *Hochma* of AVI, and in *Hochma* of *Arich Anpin*, called "concealed wisdom."

*HaVaYaH* begins with a dot, which then turns into *Yod*. Subsequently, *Yod* (*Ohr Hochma*) spreads to the sides and downward and turns into the letter *Dalet*, which consists of a horizontal roof-like line that indicates the property of *Bina-Ima* (mercy, *Hassadim*, width). When *Ohr Hassadim* stops spreading in width, *Ohr Hochma* begins to spread downward in the form of a vertical line. This is the leg of the letter *Dalet*, the property of *Hochma-Aba*.

The common property of AVI is designated by the letter *Dalet*. AVI beget ZA, designated by the letter *Vav* inside the *Dalet*, and eventually forms the shape of the letter *Hey*. Thus, the request of *ZA* (*Vav*) to receive from *AVI* compels them to unite their properties of *Hochma* (vertical line) and *Hassadim* (horizontal line), with the help of the letter *Yod*. Consequently, *AVI* receive the Light from *Yod* and pass it on to *ZA*.

The screen with the desires of *Malchut* is called "a point," since the collision between the screen and the coming Light yields Reflected Light. And since the received Light always consists of ten Lights, the screen is called "ten points."

*Yod* designates the spreading of *Nekudot* inside *Partzuf Keter*, from the Light of *Hochma* downwards, while *Vav* signifies the spreading of *Nekudot* inside *Partzuf Hochma*. However, there is no sign in *HaVaYaH* that indicates the diffusion of Light in *Keter*.

Entrance or exit of the letter *Yod* in a word signifies either presence or absence of the Light of *Hochma*. There are four kinds of correction:

1. The First *Ibur*—conception of the small state of ZON. This is an absolutely passive spiritual state, where the letter *Yod* enters the word *Ohr* (Light) and transforms it into *Avir* (air), becoming the VAK of the *Partzuf*.

2. The letter *Yod* exits the word *Avir*, which converts it back to *Ohr*: the Light of *Hochma* enters VAK of *Partzuf*;

3. The Second *Ibur*—conception of the *Gadlut* state of ZON: AHP of *Bina* ascend from ZON to *Bina*, and GE de ZON ascend with them, for they were together in the *Katnut* state, defined as conception of GE de ZON;

4. The diffusion of the Light of *Hochma*.

## THE LETTER *TET*

33. The letter *Tet* entered and said: "Maker of the world, it would be good to create the world with me, for it is by me that You are called *Tov* (Good)." The Creator replied: "I will not create the world by you, for your goodness is concealed within you and is invisible. Therefore, it cannot take any part in the world that I wish to create, and will only be revealed in the world to come. And since your goodness is concealed within you, the gates of the palace will sink into the ground, for the letter *Chet* is opposite from you, and when you join together, the word *CHeT* (sin) will be formed. This is why these two letters are not recorded in the names of the holy tribes." The letter *Chet* immediately moved aside.

The letter *Tet*, whose numeric value of nine, is the inner property of the *Sefira Yesod* in ZA, while the outer property of *Yesod* in ZA is the letter *Tzadik*, whose numeric value of ninety, and it joins with *Nukva de* ZA, forming the notion of *Tzadik* (righteous one). Besides being the inner property of *Yesod* in ZA, *Tet* is also the ninth letter among the letters of *Bina* in ZA.

Also, *Tet* is called *Tov* (good). And since *Tov* is called *Tzadik*, for it is the inner Light of *Yesod*, called *Tzadik*, to whom no impure forces could cling, *Tet* calls on the above to justify its claim to become the basis of the world.

In the Talmud (*Hagiga*, 12), the sages wrote: "In the Light by which the Creator created the world, Adam saw from one end of the world to the other. But the Creator saw that the deeds of the generations of the Flood and the builders of the Tower of Babel are detrimental, and concealed that Light for the righteous in the future." Because the Creator saw that their actions will bring the threat of the clinging of the impure forces, He concealed this Light, Thus, the Light descended secretly from the Supernal Righteous (AVI) to the righteous one (*Yesod* in ZA), the letter *Tet*.

And so the Creator told *Tet* that because He must conceal it from the sinners and only the righteous will be worthy of it in the world to come, it cannot partake in the creation and correction of the world, for the world is ZON, and the letter *Tet* is constantly in danger of being clung to by impure forces.

And since this Light shines only secretly inside *Yesod* of ZA, and not openly, *Nukva* will not be able to receive this Light directly, but only through its concealment in her. Therefore, the gates of *Nukva* sink into her *Sefira Yesod*, which safeguards them against the clinging of the impure forces, and they are confident that the impure forces will not be able to rule over her gates. For even at the time of the ruin of the Temple, the impure forces could not rule over the gates of the Temple, and sank into the ground, that is, the ground consumed them. "But because you are in need of such protection, I cannot create the world with you," the Creator answered *Tet*.

There are two pipes (channels) in *Yesod de* ZA in the world of *Atzilut*: the right one serves for the birth of the souls, and the left one for throwing away waste to the impure forces. The letter *Chet* is *Hod*, whose property is *Malchut* in ZA, the left pipe in *Yesod* of ZA, for the properties of the letter *Chet* are the properties of *Kuf* included in *Yesod*, whereas *Kuf* emanates *Ner Dakik* (tiny Light) to the impure forces, from which they receive the strength to be similar to an image of a pure man, as a monkey compared to a man, for the Creator created purity parallel to impurity.

These two pipes are located very close to each other, separated only by a thin partition, called "a garlic husk." Consequently, the left pipe has the strength to rule over the right one, thereby forming *CHeT* (numerical value 8 + 9 = 17).

The numerical value of *CHeT* (17) equals that of the word *TOV* (9 + 6 + 2 = 17), which means that the impure force opposes the pure one. And if the right pipe (the letter *Tet*) prevails, the word *CHeT* (sin) will turn into *TOV* (good, goodness).

Since the left pipe (*CHeT*) has the strength to rule over the right one (*Tet*), the impure forces can suck the Upper Light for themselves. This would give power to the sinners of the world. This is why neither *Chet* nor *Tet* are present in the names of the twelve tribes of Israel, to show that they (the tribes) are above the letter *Chet*, the root of all the opposing impure forces.

When all the letters merited receiving a blessing through the letter *Bet*, they lined up in their alphabetical order, in which the letters *Tet* and *Reish* joined. The letter *Tet* ascended, but did not take its place until the Creator asked her: "*Tet*, why did you ascend, but do not take your place?" It replied: "You created me to begin the words *Tov* (goodness) and Torah, as it is written: 'And the Creator saw that the Light was good.' How then can I join and stand beside the letter *Reish*, when it begins the word *Rah* (evil)?"

The Creator answered: "Return to your place, for it is precisely you that needs the letter *Reish*. For man, whom I intend to create, combines all those properties—you as the right property, and *Reish* as the left." After that, both *Tet* and *Reish* returned to their places.

Three lines emerge in ZA of the world of *Atzilut*. However, they emerge from their source, *Bina*. (As a result of the second restriction, *Malchut* ascends to *Bina*, which leads to *Sefirot Bina-ZA-Malchut* falling into a lower *Partzuf*, into ZA.) *Bina* is called *Eloh-im* (*Aleph-Lamed-Hey-Yod-Mem*), and as a result of second restriction, her part *Aleph-Lamed-Hey* (the *ELEH* of the word *Eloh-im*, AHP) fell into a lower *Partzuf*, to ZA. Only the letters *Yod-Mem* (the *IM* of *Eloh-im*) remained in *Bina*. This means that only half, (VAK, GE) remained in her from the previous level of GAR. Whatever is left is designated by a sign called *Holam—Vav* with a dot above it, as this is the right line, *Ohr Hassadim*.

Then, in the big state, the letters *Aleph-Lamed-Hey* (ELEH) returned to *Bina* and joined with *Yod-Mem* (IM). Subsequently, the level of GAR returned, yet the Light of *Hochma* in *Bina* was incomplete, for the Light of *Hassadim* disappeared and the Light of *Hochma* cannot shine without the Light of *Hassadim*. The returned letters A-L-H are *Shuruk–Vav* with a dot inside it, because, due to the restrictions in it, it constitutes the left line.

These restrictions are effective until ZON, upon ascending to *Bina*, begin to receive the Light, and the middle line emerges and reduces GAR of *Hochma* in the left line. As a result, the right line joins with the left: *Ohr Hochma* shines in the *Ohr Hassadim*. This middle line is called *Hirik–Vav* with a dot under it, or the screen of *Hirik*, for the Light enters the *Partzuf* because of it.

And since *Bina* regained GAR with ZA's help, ZA, now that he had acquired the three lines, begins to receive this Light from *Bina*, too. *Yod-Mem* (IM), *Tet* and *Holam* constitute the right line, *Aleph-Lamed-Hey* (ELEH), *Reish* and *Shuruk* constitute the left.

Now let us translate this into the language of *Sefirot*. When *Bina* returned once more to the state of *Gadlut*, ELEH returned to IM, the left line merged with the right, and this drove *Tet* (right line, *Hassadim*) away from *Reish* (left line). This is because being opposite to each other, they cannot stand side by side until the Creator (ZA, middle line) reduces the GAR of both the left and right lines by the force of His screen, which is expressed by the words: "And the Creator commanded it to return to its place."

GAR *de Hochma* is called *Man'ula*—the lock that prevents the Light from entering a *Partzuf*, and its diminution is called *Miftacha*—the key that opens a passage for the Light, VAK of *Hochma*, to spread in the left line into a *Partzuf*. Then, *Tet*, the right line, receives *Ohr Hochma* from the left, joins with *Reish*, receiving from it the Light of *Hochma*. Otherwise it would have remained in VAK. Adam, too, is created from the union of these two lines.

But why was the letter *Tet* reluctant to join with the letter *Reish*, and had to be forced to do so by the Creator? In the spiritual world, a root rules over all its branches, and the branches submit to its rule. Therefore, *Tet* did not wish to join with *Reish*, as it was then bound to become a branch and submit to its root, *Reish*.

However, the Creator wanted *Tet* to receive the Light of *Hochma* from *Reish* so that this union would enable man to receive the Light of GAR. Thus, when ELEH return to *Bina*, He made it so *Bina*'s restrictions would be weakened so as to allow the *Reish* to join with the *Tet* and receive the Light of *Hassadim* from it. It follows that *Tet* becomes the root with regard to *Reish*, for without its *Hassadim*, *Reish* would be unable to shine, due to the restrictions placed on its Light.

# THE LETTER ZAYIN

**34.** The letter *Zayin* entered and said: "Maker of the world, it would be good to create the world by me, as *Shabbat* is preserved with me, for it is written: 'Remember (*Zachor*) the day of *Shabbat*, so as to keep it.'" The Creator replied: "I will not create the world by you, for within you is a force of war, as sabers and swords, called *Klei Zayin* (weaponry), are made by you. And you are like the letter *Nun*, with which the world was not created, for within it is *Nefilah* (fall)" (item 29). Having heard that, the letter *Zayin* left Him.

The letter *Zayin* is depicted as a combination of *Vav* and *Yod*, as a head over it, which signifies the big state and the great Light in *Malchut*, ZA's wife, for *Malchut* includes herself into her husband, ZA (designated by *Vav*), and becomes a crown (*Yod*) on his head. Together, these two letters, *Vav* with *Yod* standing above it, form the letter *Zayin*.

Therefore, it is written: "Remember the day of *Shabbat*, so as to keep it holy." As a result of *Shabbat*'s elevation, that is, *Nukva's* ascent to the head of ZA, when she becomes his crown, she includes herself in the word *Zachor* (remember) and receives the name *Nukva Kedoshah* (holy *Nukva*). This is why the letter *Zayin* claimed that since this Light is so great and holy that it brings absolute rest on this day, for purity is completely separated from impurity in this state called *Shabbat*, it is worthy of becoming the basis for the creation of the world.

*Zayin* is the *Sefira Netzah* in ZA. When *Nukva* is included in *Netzah* and merges with its properties, she gains the strength to ascend along with ZA to AVI. There she becomes a crown on his head, by which he is adorned, which signifies the day of *Shabbat*. However, since this correction occurs solely as a result of her inclusion in the male essence and their ascent to AVI, and not in her regular place, where she normally abides with ZA, *Nukva* cannot be corrected completely during the 6,000 years.

The reason for this is that when *Nukva* returns to her place on weekdays, her connection with the letter *Zayin* is defined as a *Kli Zayin* (weapon), and all the wars with the impure forces emerge from her, like the weekdays that prepare *Shabbat*.

For every man must defeat the impure force within him on the weekdays, and thus merit the King's daughter—*Shabbat*. However, during the 6,000 years, the Light of *Shabbat* is insufficient for the neutralization of the impure forces, for weekdays return and surround the *Shabbat*. This continues until the end of correction, when there will be only *Shabbat* as the day of absolute perfection for all eternity.

This is also why the Creator replied to *Zayin*: "I will not create the world with you, for when you are in your place, your Light is not yet perfect. Only after you defeat the impure forces in war will man be able to attain you." And the shape of the letter *Vav* (ZA) resembles a spear, ready to strike and pierce through the impure forces. For *Gevurot* (courage) signifies the left line of *Bina's* male part (*Nun*).

## THE LETTERS *VAV* AND *HEY*

**35. The letter *Vav* entered and said: "It would be good to create the world with me, for I am a letter from Your Name *HaVaYaH* (*Yod-Hey-Vav-Hey*)." The Creator replied: "*Vav*, both you and the letter *Hey* should just be glad to be contained within My Name. This is why I will not create the world with your properties."**

Although the letter *Yod* expressed a similar request, *Vav* thought that *Yod* had been turned down because of its excessive size (spiritual force). This is why *Vav* claimed that it would be good to create the world with its properties, i.e., according to the letters *Vav-Hey* in the name *HaVaYaH*, with the Light of the Supernal *Bina* (*Ima*) of the world of *Atzilut*.

The Creator responded with the same answer he had given to the letter *Yod*—that He restricted it by saying to *DaY* (*Dalet-Yod*): "Stop at the letter *Shin* and spread no more, so that the impure forces would not cling to you." Hence, the letters *Vav* and *Hey* are not suitable for the world to be created with their properties, for even they need protection against the impure forces.

*Sefira Tifferet* is designated by the big letter *Vav* (*Vav* with a head), for it has all six (*Vav*) *Sefirot*: *Hesed-Gevura-Tifferet-Netzah-Hod-Yesod*. *Yesod* is the *Sefira* that is responsible for passing the Light from ZA to *Malchut*. This is why it has the same Light as in *Malchut*—NHY without HGT, and this is also why *Yesod* is called the small *Vav* (*Vav* without a head).

## THE LETTERS *DALET* AND *GIMEL*

**36. The letters *Dalet* and *Gimel* appeared before the Creator. However, the Creator told them right away: "It is enough that you are both together, so that as long as the poor exist on earth, there is someone to treat them with mercy (*LiGmol Hesed*)." The letter *Dalet* derives from *Dalut* (poverty), while *Gimel* renders mercy to it (*Gomelet Hassadim*). "Therefore, you cannot part, and it is enough for you to aid one another in this way."**

It was already stated (item 24) that although *Dalet* receives the Light from *Gimel* and its sharp right angle protrudes from the Light of *Hassadim*, the impure forces are nonetheless strong enough to cling to it, separate it and make the sharp angle smooth, thus transforming it into the letter *Reish*.

This is why the letter *Dalet* requires special protection so as not to be corrupted and to be able to continue being fulfilled by *Gimel* so as to keep the needy ones (*Dalut*) in the world from disappearing. Thus, it is sufficient for these two forces to sustain and complement one another, to fulfill one another in reciprocal union so as to prevent the impure forces from ruling. And this role is enough from them. This is why the Creator did not want to create the world with them.

# THE LETTER *BET*

**37. The letter *Bet* entered and said to the Creator: "Maker of the world, it would be good to create the world by me, as by me You are blessed Above and below. For *Bet* is *Berachah* (blessing)." The Creator replied to *Bet*: "Of course, I will create the world by you, and you shall be the basis of the world!"**

The letter *Bet* is the property of *Hochma* (wisdom), or rather *Hesed* in *Hochma*, a point in a palace, for *Ohr Hassadim* is a palace for *Ohr Hochma* and is called *Berachah* (blessing). Passing through all of the worlds from the Creator down to the lowest degree of the lowest world, this Light does not diminish in any way.

Rather, just as this Light is at the Highest Degree that receives it from the World of Infinity, it is just as great, magnificent, and mighty in the world of *Atzilut*, and likewise all the way down to the world of *Assiya*. And it does not get coarser or weaker as it passes through all the screens from Above downwards.

That is why the letter *Bet* vied for the world to be created with its properties, as the Light of blessing is the same both Above and below; no screen can weaken it and no coarse desires can harm it.

This is also why the property of mercy (*Hassadim*) is most suitable for the creation of the world, for no impure forces can cling to it. This is because the impure forces can only cling to a place where there is a deficiency. And since there is no deficiency of any kind in the property of mercy, there can never be any contact between *Bet* and the impure forces.

The Creator agreed with *Bet* that its property is perfect and suitable for the creation of the universe by Him. As it is said: "*Olam* (world) *Hesed* (mercy)

*YiBaneh* (will be built)," where *YiBaneh* means *Boneh* (building) and *HaVana* (understanding). (In Hebrew, the letters *Vav* and *Bet* are denoted by the letter *Bet*). This is because the Creator determined that this property is entirely sufficient for precisely evaluating and separating pure from impure.

And if man seeks an idol in the Creator's stead, a *Berachah* (blessing) does not descend upon him, for blessing stems from the Creator alone. Thus, it is possible to determine who is righteous and who is a sinner, who works for the Creator's sake and who works for himself, for the world is built by mercy.

Yet, the Creator did not order the Light of Mercy to rule the world. He merely intended it for a good beginning, sufficient to bring the world to perfection. This is because the Light of *Hassadim* is incomplete (*VAK*, and not *GAR*), insufficient for begetting new souls, for their union and multiplication, as no *Partzuf* (spiritual object) can beget until it attains the full Light of *Hochma*, termed *GAR* or head. Until then, the *Partzuf* remains in a state of imperfection.

Our normal (the lowest possible) state is determined by the property of the letter *Bet*. Hence, the Creator laid it as the basis for the creation of the world. In other words, the basis of a state is a state of a pure *Partzuf* (object), when nothing at all can diminish or impede it.

In such a state, an addition of *Ohr Hochma* to *Ohr Hassadim*, necessary for the birth of a new *Partzuf* is no longer considered basic and essential. Rather, it is defined as an addition, i.e., it depends solely on the good deeds of the lower ones. And the fundamental Light, *VAK*, will never be lacking.

## THE LETTER *ALEPH*

**38. The letter *Aleph* stood outside and did not enter to appear before the Creator. The Creator said to it: "Why do you not come to me like all the other letters?" *Aleph* replied: "Because I saw all the letters leaving your presence without the desired answer. And besides, I saw You presenting the letter *Bet* with this great gift. And, indeed, the King of the universe cannot take back his gift and give it to another!" The Creator replied: "Although I will create the world by the letter *Bet*, it is you who will stand at the head of all the letters, and there shall be no unity in Me, but through you alone; all accounts and deeds of this world shall always begin with you, and all of unity shall be in you alone."**

As we already know, all the letters' questions are *Aliyat MAN*—their individual requests, prayers, desires to ascend to the Creator. And the Creator's answers to them are called *Yeridat MAD*—the descent of the Light from Above, giving strength and abundance according to the letters' requests. The great perfection in the letter *Aleph* stems not from the lower ones' request for spiritual ascent and correction, but from a force (Light) descending from Above and elevating those that dwell below.

This is why from the beginning of correction to its end, *Aleph* (unlike the other letters, whose properties fuel the process of correction during the 6,000 years) is never stimulated to raise its request to the Creator. And only if the Light that bestows strength for spiritual ascent descends from Above and begins to shine upon *Aleph* will it be stimulated. However, this will only take place at the end of correction.

*Aleph* did not raise its plea (MAN) to the Creator, for it saw that all the other letters asked, but to no avail, for there was an opposite property in the system of the impure forces against each of their properties. Therefore, *Aleph* decided that it was no better than the rest, that there is a corresponding impure force against it as well.

Furthermore, it raised no requests (MAN) to the Creator because it saw that the Creator decided to create the world with the letter *Bet*, mercy. And since it had no doubt that His decision was irrevocable, it decided not to ask Him.

Although it is true that the world was already created with the property of *Bet*, and that the Creator will not turn His gift over to another letter, the *Partzuf* that was created by the property of *Bet* is incomplete, small, *VAK* without a head. And since a *Partzuf* needs a head in order to reach the state of *Gadlut*, which is possible only when the *Partzuf* is filled not only with the Light of Mercy (*Hassadim*), but also with the Light of Wisdom (*Hochma*), more letters are necessary for the connection, conception and birth of a new *Partzuf*, a new state.

A state of *Gadlut* can only be achieved with the help of the property of the letter *Aleph*. Only *Aleph* can bring a *Partzuf* to *Gadlut*, to supplement its body, *VAK*, with a head, *GAR*, *Mochin*—the Light of *Hochma*. The letter *Aleph* brings the union between *ZA* and *Malchut* in a face-to-face position, whereas previously, in *Katnut*, while being filled with only the Light of Mercy, *ZA* and *Malchut* were connected back-to-back. This is why *Aleph* creates a head for all the letters, and hence stands at the head of the alphabet.

The Creator said: "That is why My Unity in the world is expressed only through the property of the letter *Aleph*. Furthermore, all rewards and punishments, distancing and drawing nearer, as well as the aspiration for spiritual correction (*Teshuvah*), all of which lead to the achievement of the end of correction, will only happen by the property of the *Aleph*. I have made *Bet* the basis of the *Partzuf* so that it would be in no way dependent on the deeds of the lower ones. Thus, even if they begin to sin, those above will remain unaffected."

He continued: "But the Light in you, *Aleph*, is directly related to the actions of the lower ones. So if they sin, the Light of Wisdom (the Light of GAR in you) will immediately disappear. But if they correct their actions (*Teshuvah*), the Light of *Hochma* will return. And My unity with all the creatures at the end of correction will only be realized through the letter *Aleph*."

Letters are *Kelim* (plural for *Kli*—vessel), desires. And this refers to both the individual letters of the alphabet and those that form words. In the names of spiritual objects, letters signify the force of their desire, which the Light can fill. Letters of a simple name, without filling, designate its basis without Light—*Kli* of *Aviut* zero with the Light of *Nefesh*. Letters of a fulfilled name designate the magnitude of desires that are filled by Light.

There are two sources of letters: *Yod* and *Aleph*. *Yod* is a genuine source, for when we write something, we begin with a dot (*Yod*), and then, as we proceed from the dot in one of the four directions, we get a line. Letters are *Kelim*, desires, in which the Light (pleasure) is received.

A desire for something specific may only emerge if: (i) the initial, still unconscious desire is filled with delight, and (ii) the delight exits the desire. It is the memories (*Reshimot*) of past pleasures that lead to the emergence of a true desire to receive it, to feel it once more. And this is the very desire that is called *Kli*.

A filled *Kli* cannot be called a desire, for it is satisfied. Therefore, expulsion of the Light and sensation of spiritual descent constitute the period of the creation of new *Kelim* for future receptions of Light, for new attainments. Because the first restriction is the reason for the disappearance of Light from all the vessels, its black dot, *Yod*, is the basis of all the letters-*Kelim*.

However, the second restriction is the only true root of all the worlds, because the first restriction was only made on a point, (Phase Four, *Malchut*, the fourth letter *Hey* in the Creator's name *HaVaYaH*). The second restriction, however, was made on *Bina*, in whom the two points, *Bina* and *Malchut*, were joined. The union of the two points forms a line, either vertical or horizontal. If it is a horizontal line, it is called "firmament" or *Parsa*.

The sum of consequences of both the first and second restrictions forms a slanted line (\); GE (*Keter-Hochma*) is depicted to its right, and AHP (*Bina-ZA-Malchut*) to its left. *Keter-Hochma* remain on their previous level and are designated by the letter *Yod*, the first root of the world, whereas, a result of the second restriction, designated by a slanted line (\), *Bina-ZA-Malchut* fell to a lower level. And since the letter *Yod* is the first, though a very remote root of the worlds, and all the worlds were created afterwards and in accordance with the law of the second restriction, the letter *Aleph* stands at the head of the alphabet.

The kind of Light that fills the spiritual *Kli* or *Partzuf* can also be seen from its designation: if it is filled with the Light of Wisdom (*Ohr Hochma*), the filling is designated by the letter *Yod*; and if it is filled with the Light of Mercy (*Ohr Hassadim*), it is the letter *Aleph*.

**39. The Creator made the Upper letters, which refer to the *Sefira Bina*, large, and the lower letters that refer to *Malchut*—small. Therefore it is said: "*Beresheet Barah*" (in the beginning He created)—two words that begin with *Bet*, and then *Elokim Et* (the Creator Himself)—two words that begin with *Aleph*. The first set of *Aleph* and *Bet* are letters of *Bina*, and the second set of *Aleph* and *Bet* are letters of *Malchut*. And they should mutually affect one another with their properties.**

When the Upper One wishes to give Light to the lower one, it should clothe in the lower one, signified by the first two letters *Bet* and the two letters *Aleph* in the first four words of the Torah. For the first, Upper *Bet* is *Bina*, the second, lower *Bet* is ZA, and the first *Bet* clothes into the second one.

Similarly, the first *Aleph* refers to *Bina* and clothes into the second *Aleph* in ZA so as to fill it with Light. Therefore, the two letters *Bet* are like one letter *Bet* and the two letters *Aleph* are like one letter *Aleph*, since the lower letter merely constitutes the influence of the Upper One, which tells us that the Upper *Partzuf* fills the lower one.

The world cannot be created with *Aleph*, for the word *Arur* (cursed) begins with it, and had the world been created with *Aleph*, the impure forces, called "cursed," would have received great power from the pure forces, called *Baruch* (blessed). This is why the world (*Nukva* of ZA) is created with the letter *Bet*. Likewise, Adam in *Nukva* of ZA is also created by the power of *Bet*. Thus, *Malchut* of the world of *Atzilut* constitutes the root of all creation, all the worlds, and all that inhabit them.

# SUPERNAL WISDOM

**40. Rabbi Yudai asked, "What does the word BERESHEET mean?" It is the wisdom, upon which the world, ZA, is established to enter the concealed supernal secrets, namely the Light of Bina. Here are the six Supernal and great properties, VAK de Bina, from which everything emerges. The six river mouths, VAK de ZA, that flow into the Great Sea (Malchut) were formed from them. The word BERESHEET consists of the words BARAH (created) and SHEET (Aramaic: six), meaning that six properties were created. Who created them? He who is unmentioned, concealed, and unknown: Arich Anpin.**

There are two types of *Ohr Hochma* (Light of Wisdom) in the world of *Atzilut*:

1. The original Light, *Ohr Hochma* of AA, called "the concealed *Ohr Hochma*." This Light of *Hochma* is present only in *Partzuf* AA and does not spread to the lower *Partzufim*.

2. *Ohr Hochma* that descends via thirty-two paths from *Bina*, who ascended to *Rosh de AA* to receive *Ohr Hochma* and pass it to ZA. Hence, the word *Beresheet* means *Be-Resheet*, with-*Hochma*. However, this is not the true *Ohr Hochma* that is concealed in AA, but rather the Light that descends via thirty-two paths from *Bina* to ZA and sustains ZON.

It is written that the world is established on the "concealed supernal secrets," for when ZON (called "world") receive the Light of *Hochma* of thirty-two paths, they ascend to *AVI*, the concealed supernal secrets. Hence, it is said that ZON enter the concealed supernal secrets and attain the degree of *AVI*, as the lower one that ascends to the Upper One becomes equal to it in its properties.

The word *BERESHEET*, besides being divided into *BE-RESHEET*, is also divided into *BARAH-SHEET* (in Hebrew, both words are spelled the same), which translates as CREATED SIX—created six *Sefirot* (properties), called *VAK* (abbreviation of the words *Vav Ketzavot*, six extremities/properties of ZA, from which all creatures emerge).

The *Sefira Bina* fulfills the function of the *Sefira Hochma*, the source of *Ohr Hochma* for ZON. Because *Malchut* ascended to *Bina*, and *Bina* departed from *Rosh de AA* and became like its *Guf* (body), she cannot receive the *Ohr Hochma* of AA.

But then, thanks to the MAN raised by the lower ones, human beings who are spiritually present in the worlds of BYA, *Bina* returns to *Rosh de AA*, receives *Ohr Hochma* from AA, passes it to ZON, and ZON pass it to all the worlds. It follows that all the worlds emerged from these six properties (extremities), into which *Bina* was divided.

It is therefore written that all six riverheads originate from *Bina*, and descend into the Great Sea. *Bina's* division into six properties, VAK, when she exits *Rosh de AA*, is called "six sources," for this is only a source of Light for ZA. But then, when *Bina* returns to *Rosh de AA*, they become *Ohr Hochma*, called the rivers that descend to *Partzuf* ZA.

And they are called "six rivers," as it is written: "He will drink off the brook in the way; therefore, will he lift up the head" (*Tehilim*, 110:7). Afterwards, ZA passes this Light into the Great Sea, to his *Nukva*. The rivers and brooks signify the Light of ZA. VAK *de Bina* is considered the sources of the Light of Wisdom, *Hochma*, for it emerged from *Bina* in the form of VAK with the sole purpose of creating a source of Light for ZON. And had *Bina* not emerged, ZON would have had no chance of receiving the Light.

The word *Beresheet* has several meanings: *Bere* = *Barah*—created six properties without *Ohr Hochma*, as the word *Barah* signifies concealment. Hence, the word *Beresheet* has two meanings:

1. *Hochma*, as the word *Resheet* means *Hochma*.

2. *Barah Sheet*, which shows how the *Sefira Hochma* was divided into six parts without a *Rosh*, without *Ohr Hochma*. These six parts are the source of Light for ZON (called the "world"), and these six parts of ZA together with *Malchut* are called the "seven days of creation."

However, since the word *Barah* is inside the word *Beresheet*, this means that it was created by "Him who is concealed and unknown," i.e., the concealed *Hochma* of *Arich Anpin*, for it expelled *Bina* from its *Rosh* and turned her into VAK. In other words, it created the six parts described in *Beresheet*.

*Beresheet* designates *Hochma*. The Light cannot descend to ZA until *Ima-Bina* comes outside, for because of *Tzimtzum Bet*, ZAT *de Bina* fell to ZON. Hence, when *Bina* is in *Gadlut*, ZA receives *Ohr Hochma* in his *Kelim*, the desires of *Bina*. The word *Barah* in *Beresheet* = *Barah Sheet* also means *Bar* (Hebrew, to exit, to transcend).

# THE LOCK AND THE KEY

**41. Rabbi Chiya and Rabbi Yosi were walking along a road. As they reached a field, Rabbi Chiya said to Rabbi Yosi, "The words BARAH SHEET (created six) certainly allude to BERESHEET, for the six Supernal Days, VAK de Bina, shine on the Torah (ZA), while the others, GAR de Bina, are concealed."**

ZA of the world of *Atzilut* is called the Torah. The six Supernal Days are *VAK de Bina* that are above *ZA*. Hence, the first word of the Torah, *BERESHEET* = *BARAH* (created) and *SHEET* (six) indicates that the *Sefira Bina* turns to the *Sefira Hochma* in order to receive *Ohr Hochma* and pass it to *ZA*. Since *ZA* is unable to receive all the *Ohr Hochma* (*GAR de Hochma*, the Light of the ten *Sefirot*) from *Bina*, but only *VAK de Hochma* (Light of six *Sefirot*), this is stressed in the word *BARAH SHEET*—CREATED SIX. This means that *ZA* receives from *Bina* the Light of only six *Sefirot*, *HGT NHY* or *VAK de Hochma*, whereas *GAR de Hochma*, the Light of *Sefirot KHB*, is concealed from him.

The reason for this is that although *Partzuf Atik* belongs to *Tzimtzum Aleph* (the first restriction), it is obliged to shine down on all the other *Partzufim* of the world of *Atzilut*, and on all the worlds *BYA* with the Light of *Tzimtzum Bet*. Therefore, with regards to the lower *Partzufim*, it appears as a *Partzuf* that belongs to *Tzimtzum Bet*.

In other words, it deliberately imposed on itself an outward (with regards to others) restriction of its Light, to enable the lower *Partzufim* to receive from it. Hence, it elevated *Malchut* from the *Peh* to the *Eynaim* and made a *Zivug* on the screen that stands in *Nikvey Eynaim*, thus begetting *Partzuf AA*.

This is why *AA* is a *Partzuf* with properties of the second restriction, and acts as *Keter* of the entire world of *Atzilut* instead of *Atik*. This was designed so by *Partzuf Atik* itself, which split into two parts: *GE* remained in *Atik*, and *AHP* became part of the second *Partzuf*, *AA*. And since *Malchut* ascended to *NE*

(*Nikvey Eynaim*), *Partzuf* AA remained without *Malchut*, the *Sefira Ateret Yesod* was used in its stead, and *Malchut* became concealed in the NE of *Partzuf Atik*. Also, GE *de Atik* became concealed from the lower *Partzufim*, *Malchut* stood in NE of *Rosh de Atik*, AHP *de Atik* became GE *de AA*, and *Ateret Yesod* became *Malchut de AA*.

All the subsequent *Partzufim* of the world of *Atzilut* emerged similar to these *Partzufim*. Thus, they all split into two parts, GE and AHP: *Partzuf Bina* was split into two *Partzufim*: GE *de Bina* formed *Partzuf* AVI and AHP *de Bina* formed *Partzuf* YESHSUT. *Malchut* ascended and remained in AVI, while *Partzuf* YESHSUT remained without *Malchut*.

The same applies to ZON: GE formed the big ZON and AHP formed the small ZON. *Malchut* remained in NE of the big ZON, while the small ZON have only nine *Sefirot* without *Malchut*, which is replaced in them by *Ateret Yesod*, as in *Partzuf Atik*. Therefore, just as *Keter* (*Atik*) split into two parts: GAR = *Atik* and ZAT = AA, so was *Bina* divided into GAR = AVI and ZAT = YESHSUT, and ZON into GAR = the big ZON and ZAT = the small ZON: *Malchut* remained in GAR and *Ateret Yesod* replaced it in ZAT.

As a result, the Upper Part of each degree remains concealed, just like *Partzuf Atik*, for *Malchut* does not descend from the place where she had ascended (NE) to her previous place in the *Peh*. And although in *Gadlut*, AHP return to their place or ascend to their own GE (which is one and the same), GE do not become filled with *Ohr Hochma* (the Light of GAR) as a result, since *Malchut* remains concealed in GE. Moreover, *Malchut* exists under the ban of *Tzimtzum Aleph* on the reception of *Ohr Hochma*. Hence, GE remain with *Ohr Hassadim*.

Only the lower part of each degree is filled with the Light of GAR (*Hochma*) in *Gadlut*: there was *Avir* (air) = *Aleph-Vav-Yod-Reish*, then the letter *Yod* departed from this word, and only the letters *Aleph-Vav-Reish* remained to form the word *Ohr* (Light)—*Ohr Hochma* or GAR.

It follows that all *Partzufim* of the world of *Atzilut* have GE, GAR of *Kelim*, *Sefirot* KHB HGT with *Ohr Hassadim*, the Light of VAK, whereas AHP, *Sefirot* NHY, *Vak de Kelim* in the *Gadlut* of the *Partzuf* are filled with *Ohr Hochma*, the Light of GAR. GE (GAR *de Kelim*) are filled with the Light of VAK (*Ohr Hassadim*), and AHP (VAK *de Kelim*) are filled with the Light of GAR (*Ohr Hochma*). It is therefore said that there's no greater Light for ZA in the world of *Atzilut* than the Light of VAK = six days, while GAR are concealed even in the *Partzufim* above ZA.

**42. However, it is said in the secrets of creation of BERESHEET that He who is Holy and Concealed established the laws in *Bina*, in the secret and concealed, meaning *Malchut* of *Partzuf Atik*, which is a *Partzuf* with *Malchut* of *Tzimtzum Aleph*, who ascended to *Bina* and removed *AHP de AA* below its *Rosh*. And the same law that He established in *Bina* He established and concealed within, and everything is locked under one key. And He hid this key in a hall. And although everything is hidden in that hall, the most important thing is in that key, for it locks and unlocks everything.**

HE WHO IS HOLY AND CONCEALED is *AA*, for its *Hochma* is concealed. THE LAWS ARE ESTABLISHED IN IT, meaning in *Malchut de Atik*. The deficiency of the *Kelim de AHP* is confirmed. *Malchut* of *Tzimtzum Aleph*, called "the central point of all creation," is also the sole creation on which *Tzimtzum Aleph* was imposed. Contrary to her, if the screen stands not in *Malchut*, but in *Yesod* or, more precisely, in *Ateret Yesod*, the place of the covenant (circumcision), the place of the *Zivug* that was permitted after *Tzimtzum Bet*, this screen allows for the reception of Light. Hence, it is called the "point of population," and not the "central point."

- *Keter*
- *Hochma*
- *Bina*
- *ZA Yesod*
- *ZA*–*Malchut* that received *ZA's* properties to "bestow," the populated place
- *Malchut*—no *Zivug* can be made; the deserted place

The thing is that there is no *GAR* in *AA*, for the Supernal *Malchut* of *Atik*, within *AA*, is already corrected to the point of being in *NE* of her own *Partzuf*. In *Gadlut*, the screen descends from *NE* to *Peh*, which makes *AHP* return to their place, and a *Zivug* transpires on all ten *Sefirot*, which receive the *GAR* of the Light, *Ohr Hochma*.

Therefore, the screen in *NE* is called a "lock," for it blocks the entry of *GAR* of the Light into the *Partzuf*. The *GAR* of the Light are called *Ohr Hochma*. Yet, by descending from *NE* to *Peh*, the screen lets the Light into the *Partzuf*, and is therefore called *Nikvey Eynaim* (pupils of the eyes).

Although *Atik* itself is in *NE* together with *Malchut*, it affects *AA*, and not *Atik* itself, as *AA* was created by the screen, located not in *Malchut*, but in *Ateret Yesod* (or simply in *Yesod*), and there is no *Malchut* in it. This is why it is not

*Malchut* that rules in *NE de AA*, but *Ateret Yesod*. And this is why, unlike the Light of *Atik*, its Light can be attained, for *Malchut* in *Atik* is the central point, which does not make a *Zivug* on *Ohr Hochma*. Although with regards to *Atik*, *AA* is *AHP* of *Atik*, *AA* itself has its own GE and *AHP*.

Subsequently, *AA* created *AVI* and confirmed the absence of *Ohr Hochma* in them, due to the absence of *AHP de Kelim*. These *AHP* are the HALL in which the entire Light of *Hochma* is concealed (GAR *de Neshama*, GAR *de Haya*, and GAR *de Yechida*). This KEY IS KEPT HIDDEN IN A HALL: *Bina* is a hall for *Ohr Hochma*. *Malchut* ascends to GAR *de Bina* (*AVI*) and rules there, but the absence of *Ohr Hochma* is not felt there, for the properties of *AVI* want only *Ohr Hassadim*; this is what is important to them, as it completely substitutes the *Ohr Hochma*. And *VAK de Bina* is ruled by the key, *Ateret Yesod*.

IN THAT KEY, FOR IT LOCKS AND UNLOCKS EVERYTHING—concealments and revelations are made by *Malchut* that stands in *NE*: when *Malchut* ascends to *NE* she conceals *Ohr Hochma*, since in such a case, the *Partzuf* remains without its *Kelim* of *AHP*—it cannot use its desires to "receive" for the Creator's sake. Consequently, it contains no *Ohr Hochma*, for *Ohr Hochma* can only be received in *Kelim de AHP*.

And when a *Partzuf* receives strength from Above to resist the egoistic desires of reception of its *Kelim de AHP*, and can receive for the Creator's sake, this means that it has acquired a screen against its desires, and can also work with them for the Creator. It then brings its *Malchut* back from the *NE* to the *Peh*. Put differently, it elevates its *Kelim* (desires of *AHP*) to the *Rosh* and begins to calculate how much Light it can receive within them for the Creator's sake. However, the received pleasure must not be too great, or it will make the *Partzuf* enjoy it egoistically. Afterwards, the *Partzuf* receives *Ohr Hochma* in its *Guf*.

Thus, only *Malchut* that stands in *NE* allows or forbids the Light from entering the *Partzuf*. And since she must let the Light into the *Partzuf* in ZAT (where the rule belongs not to *Malchut* that ascended to *NE*, but to *Ateret Yesod*, called "key"), whereas the GAR of each *Partzuf* remain with *Ohr Hassadim* (they desire only the Light of *Hassadim*), letting the Light in or preventing it from entering the *Partzuf* depends only on the key, and not on *Malchut* herself.

**43. That hall conceals tremendous treasures piled one upon the other. And there are fifty tightly closed gates in that hall, which are meant to block access to the Light. They were divided into four sides and became forty-nine gates, for one gate has no side, and it is unknown whether it exists above or below. Hence, it remained closed.**

There are many types of GAR: GAR of *Ohr Neshama*, *Haya*, or *Yechida*. Each of them contains countless individual degrees and details. Hence, it is written, ONE UPON THE OTHER. Yet, as long as *Malchut* stands in *NE*, all these degrees of Light remain concealed and unknown.

A gate signifies a vessel—a desire to receive the Light. In the spiritual world, there are no bodies, only desires. The desire itself is called "a body." If there is no desire, there is no body, as there is no vessel to receive the Light (pleasure). The bigger the desire, the "bigger" the body. However, all the bodies are similar in structure; just as a human body in our world consists of 613 parts, the spiritual body consists of 613 spiritual parts (desires).

If one is able to use one of the desires of his spiritual body for the Creator's sake, such action is referred to as a *Mitzva* (commandment, good deed). The received Light is called "Torah."

A spiritual *Partzuf* has a *Rosh* (head), the place where decisions are made. It contains only those desires that are known to be fit with a screen (resistance to the desires) to use them spiritually, altruistically, and to "reverse" them from "for one's own sake" to "for the sake of the Creator." If one has fulfilled all 613 commandments of the Torah and the seven *Mitzvot* (plural for *Mitzva*) of the nations of the world (620 *Mitzvot* in all), he thereby ascends 620 degrees and completely merges with the Creator.

To observe all the commandments means to completely fill one's spiritual *Partzuf* with the Light of the Torah by fulfilling observant commandments (*Mitzvot Aseh*—positive *Mitzvot*) and prohibitory commandments (*Mitzvot Lo Taaseh*—negative *Mitzvot*). The fulfillment of the later lies in the unwillingness to receive the pleasure that is found within them.

There are two types of desires or gates: when they are closed and receive nothing, and when they open and receive the Upper Light. When they are all closed, there are fifty of them. However, only forty-nine of the fifty can be opened. There are ten *Sefirot KHB HGT NHYM* or five *Sefirot KHB ZA-M* (as *ZA* consists of six *Sefirot HGT NHY*). However, *Malchut* also consists of these six, and hence includes all ten *Sefirot*. And since each of the five *Sefirot* consists of ten, in all they make up fifty.

However, since a *Zivug* is made not on *Malchut*, but on *Ateret Yesod*, *Malchut de Malchut* itself does not receive the Light. Instead, Light is received by the four *Sefirot KHB ZA* that precede *Malchut*. Each of them consists of ten, hence 4 x 10 = 40 plus nine *Sefirot* from *Keter* to *Yesod* in *Malchut* herself yields 40 + 9 = 49.

Only one *Sefira* (*Malchut de Malchut*) out of the fifty does not receive the Light. This is because until all the *Kelim* (desires) have been completely corrected, the Light cannot enter it, as it is known in advance that *Malchut de Malchut* has no strength to oppose such a powerful egoistic desire to receive pleasure.

Instead of being in *Malchut de Malchut*, the screen stands in *Yesod de Malchut*, and this place is called *Brith* (Covenant), the place where the *Mitzva* of circumcision must be kept, so as to make a *Zivug* not on *Malchut* herself (on the first restriction), but on *Yesod*, or rather, *Ateret Yesod* (on the second restriction). *Malchut de Malchut* itself is called "*Shaar Nun*" (the 50th gate). This refers to *Malchut* of each *Partzuf* in the worlds *ABYA*.

And although *Malchut* of *Partzuf AVI* descends from *NE de AVI* to her place in *Peh*, while *AHP* and *YESHSUT* that clothe them ascend to the degree of *AVI*, and *AVI* merges with *YESHSUT* into one *Partzuf*, as a result of which, *Ohr Hochma* descends to them from *AA*, *AVI* are unwilling and therefore do not receive anything from *Ohr Hochma*, and remain only with *Ohr Hassadim*, as though *Malchut* had never even descended from *Eynaim* to *Peh*.

Therefore, it is impossible to tell by the Light of *AVI* whether *Malchut* is located at the *NE* or at the *Peh*. On the contrary, by looking at *AVI*, it always seems to us that *Malchut* stands at *NE*. Only by the state of *YESHSUT* can we determine *Malchut's* location, for when she ascends to *AVI* in *Gadlut* (big state), *YESHSUT* receive *Ohr Hochma*.

Although *Malchut* herself can receive *Ohr Hochma* in *AVI*, since *AVI* receive no *Ohr Hochma* whatsoever, they do not utilize their own *Malchut*. Since *YESHSUT* already has *Ateret Yesod* instead of *Malchut*, it receives the Light or "opens up," whereas *AVI* remain closed.

However, the absence of the 50th gate, the *Zivug* on *Malchut* herself in *YESHSUT*, causes the absence of the corresponding Light of *Hochma* in all the *Partzufim*. It is written about it: "fifty gates of *Bina*, and all are given to Moshe, except for one, the last secret of the absence of the Upper Light." For this Upper Light can be received only within the *Kelim* (desires) of *Malchut* herself, of primordial egoism, which will occur at the end of all the corrections, at the completion of the 6,000 years.

**44. Those gates have one lock with a narrow space inside for inserting the key. It is unmarked, and recognized only by the impress of the key, which is unknown in that narrow space, but only in the key itself. And it is written of this secret: *BERESHEET BARAH ELOKIM* (IN THE BEGINNING THE CREATOR CREATED). "In the beginning" is the key, and all is concealed**

within it, as it unlocks and locks. And six gates are contained in this key, which locks and unlocks. When it locks those gates, encloses them within itself, it is written IN THE BEGINNING (*BERESHEET*): a revealed word, though it is usually concealed. *BARAH* (CREATED) is a concealed word everywhere, implying that the key unlocks it and locks it up.

*Malchut* that stands in *NE* is called a "lock," for she prevents *Ohr Hochma* from entering the *Partzuf*. The entire *Partzuf* ends in *Hochma* (the Light can only be in *K-H*). Hence, it is merely *Nefesh-Ruach*. After all, in the absence of *Kelim-Sefirot B-ZA-M*, the Lights *Neshama-Haya-Yechida* are absent. *Yesod de Malchut* is the 49th gate, the maximum that can be before the end of correction, for *Malchut de Malchut* itself is the 50th gate.

If the key (*Ateret Yesod* of the Light) enters *Yesod de Malchut* (the 49th gate), then this Light lowers *Malchut* to her place, from *NE* to *Peh*. This Light opens the *Partzuf* and *Ohr Hochma* fills it. This is why *Ateret Yesod* is called a "key."

However, there is a special *Reshimo* that allows one to not use *Malchut de Malchut* as a place of *Zivug* before the final correction of all the others (except for *Malchut de Malchut*, *Kelim*-desires). This *Reshimo* is in *AVI*: since they never receive *Ohr Hochma* (they do not use this key), their real *AHP* do not ascend. Nevertheless, even their false *AHP* is sufficient to let *YESHSUT* receive *Ohr Hochma* and realize that knowledge signifies the presence of *Ohr Hochma*.

If the Light that corresponds to *Ateret Yesod* enters the corresponding *Sefira* in *Malchut* (in *Yesod de Malchut*, the 49th *Sefira*), then *Malchut* (the 50th gate) does not forbid this Light to fill the *Partzuf*, does not "lock up" the *Partzuf*, as she contains the *Reshimo* of prohibition only on that which enters *Malchut* herself. The reason for it is that the *Reshimo* (the key's memory) rules in *ZAT de Bina*, that is, in *YESHSUT*. Hence, this Light is called a "key."

And the word *BERESHEET*–IN THE BEGINNING–includes in itself only the key (*Ateret Yesod*, the 49th *Sefira*), excluding *Malchut de Malchut*, the 50th gate. However, none of the *Sefirot KHB* of all the *Partzufim* of the world of *Atzilut* receive *Ohr Hochma*; *Ohr Hassadim* shines within them instead.

Therefore, the words IN THE BEGINNING CREATED (*BERESHEET BARAH*) mean CONCEALED HOCHMA, for the word *BARAH* (created) is derived from the notion of *BAR* (beyond), which signifies moving *Malchut de Malchut* beyond the reception of *Ohr Hochma*; hence, this part of the *Kelim* was locked up by the absence of Light.

# Avraham

45. Rabbi Yosi said, "I heard from the great source of Light, i.e., from Rabbi Shimon Bar-Yochai, that BARAH is a concealed word, the key to which locked it up and did not unlock it. And since the key locked up the word BARAH, there was no world and no possibility of its existence, and nothingness enveloped all. And when nothingness rules, there is no world, nor its existence."

46. So when did this key unlock those gates, and everything became ready for the existence and evolution of the generations? When Avraham appeared, as he is the property of *Hesed* (mercy), of which it is written, "These are the generations of Heaven and earth *Be-Hibar'am* (with which He built)." However, one should pronounce the word not as *Be-Hibar'am*, but as *Be-Avraham* (in Hebrew, these two words consist of the same letters, but in a slightly different order). Then, all that was concealed in the word BARAH was revealed as letters, meaning that the *Kelim* opened up to listen. And there appears the Pillar of Procreation, the sacred *Yesod*, upon which the world's existence is based, for the word BARAH consists of the same letters as the word AVAR (passed).

He asks: "When it is revealed, can one act and produce generations?" This question includes three questions:

1. When will it be revealed? When *Malchut* descends from the *Eynaim* (where she ascended as a result of *Tzimtzum Bet*) to her previous place in the *Peh*, which leads to the revelation of the forty-nine gates of *Hochma*;

2. When can it be used? When *Ohr Hochma* clothes in *Ohr Hassadim*, as a result of which *AHP* can receive *Ohr Hochma*, for unless it is clothed in *Ohr Hassadim*, *MI* = *GE* cannot shine within *ELEH* = *AHP*, as the Light is not yet suitable for reception and use by the lower ones;

3. What does it mean to produce, multiply generations? Generations are the souls that exist in the worlds *BYA*, begotten by *ZA de Atzilut*. After *ZA* receives the Lights of *Hochma* and *Hassadim* (the Light of perfection), this Light enables him to make a *Zivug* with *Nukva* and beget the souls of the righteous.

**WORLD OF AK**

**WORLD OF ATZILUT**: AA of the world of Atzilut

AVI of the world of Atzilut

ZON of the world of Atzilut produce and feed the souls of the righteous

—— Parsa – – – – – – – – – – – – – – – – – – – – – – – – –

**WORLD OF BERIA**

**WORLD OF YETZIRA**     the souls of the righteous in the worlds BYA

**WORLD OR ASSIYA**

—— Machsom, the transition from egoism to altruism – – – – – – – – –

**OUR EGOISTIC WORLD**

Avraham is the property of the *Sefira Hesed* in *Partzuf ZA* during its *Gadlut* (big state), when *Hesed* ascends and becomes *Hochma*: *Sefirot HGT* become *HBD*:

**PARTZUF ZA**

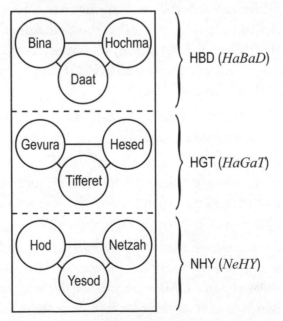

Before Avraham appeared, everything was concealed in the word *BARAH* and nothingness ruled over the world—there was neither *Ohr Hochma* nor *Ohr Hassadim* in ZON. However, when Avraham (the Light of *Hesed* that descends to ZA) appeared, the gates were opened for *Ohr Hochma*, for *Malchut* descended from *Eynaim* to *Peh*, and YESHSUT merged with AVI into one degree, which led to the descent of *Ohr Hochma* to YESHSUT, for *Ohr Hassadim* of Avraham's properties was already present in ZA.

*Ohr Hochma* then clothed in *Ohr Hassadim*, MI (GE) joined ELEH (AHP), the Creator's name ELO-IM was completed, and *Hochma* filled ZA. Then *Malchut* descended from *Eynaim* to *Peh* in ZA, and ZA received new AHP from *Bina*, thereby entering *Gadlut* and passing the Light through his *Yesod* into *Malchut*, called the "lower world." As a result, *Malchut* begets the souls of the righteous.

**47. When Yesod of ZA joins the word BARAH (Malchut), there occurs a concealed and supernal division of the Creator's name and greatness, called MI, and ELEH comes into being. Also, the sacred name MA comes from BARAH. The sacred concealed ELEH exists just like Yesod. Yet, when Yesod attains its complete state, the Partzuf attains its complete state, the letter Hey corresponds to Yesod and the letter Yod—to ELEH.**

Here, *The Zohar* clarifies which Light is present in ZA, depending on his states. In the *Sefira Yesod* of *Partzuf* ZA there is an end, meaning a place of contact with *Malchut*, the place of the covenant between the Creator (ZA) and the *Shechina* (the souls of the righteous), also called "Israel" or *Malchut*. This place of contact is called *Ateret Yesod* (encirclement of *Yesod*) or *Keter de* ZA (the crown of ZA).

The word *BARAH* signifies *Katnut* (small state), which comes as a result of *Malchut's* ascent to NE. AVI never abandon the properties of GAR *de Bina* (properties of mercy); they do not desire to receive. Having ascended and standing in them, *Malchut* is called *Man'ula* (lock), which prevents the Light from spreading below her. *Ateret Yesod de* ZA is called *Miftacha* (key), for it is through its property that the Light can be received in the *Partzufim* located below AVI.

This is possible on condition that ELEH = AHP ascend to MI = GE. *Ohr Hochma* can be received in the *Kelim* ELEH that wish to receive it, but only upon their ascension above *Parsa*. However, until the properties of *Malchut* acquire the property of *Bina*, until they are "softened" by this property, there is no way to receive the Light, and *Malchut* is called "the 50th gate."

Hence, we see that the words MI BARAH ELEH signify not the question, "Who created these?" but the action: MI = GE BARAH (created) ELEH = AHP by the descent of *Malchut* from *NE* back to *Peh*. As a result, *ELEH* = *AHP* ascended to the *Rosh* and there received the Light of *GAR* (*Hochma*).

Upon descending to *Peh*, *Malchut* is called MA, as that is the name of the lower world. Her screen in the *Peh* makes a *Zivug*, onto which descends *Ohr Hassadim*, called "Light of blessing," for it abolishes the prohibition and the lock imposed on the diffusion of Light.

**48. When the letters Hey and Yod wished to complement one another, the letter Mem emerged from them, and the word ELO-HIM = ELE + Hey + Yod + Mem was formed by the union of both sides. The word AVAR + Hey + Mem = Avraham originated from ELEH. However, one might say that the Creator took the words ELEH and MI, joined them and formed the word ELOKIM, whereas the words MA and AVAR formed the word Avraham, where the word MI designates the fifty gates of Bina, and the word MA refers to the numerical value of the holy name, for HaVaYaH with the filling of the letter Aleph forms the Gematria of MA—45.**

Both this world and the world to come exist in these two letters, *Yod* and *Hey*. This world is in *Yod*, and the world to come is in *Hey*. Hence, the world to come was created with *MI*, and this world with *MA*.

It is therefore written: "These are the created (*Be-Hibar'am*) generations of Heaven and earth," where the letters *Be-Hibar'am* make up the word "Avraham," for there was no perfection until the letters formed this word. Therefore, the Creator's name *HaVaYaH* is first mentioned in the Torah only after the name Avraham.

*Ohr Hassadim* in MA and *Ohr Hochma* in *ELEH* wished to complement one another and be complemented within one another. As a result, *Ohr Hochma* clothed in *Ohr Hassadim*, and *Malchut* receives from both *Hassadim* and *Hochma*. In so doing, MA and MI join and create MM, i.e., *Malchut* that receives *Ohr Hochma* clothed in *Ohr Hassadim* from Above.

# The Vision of Rabbi Chiya

**49.** Rabbi Chiya prostrated himself on the ground and kissed it. He wept and said: "Dust, how hard and heartless you are, how many you have consumed, all the pillars of Light and all the great souls were consumed by you. And the greatest of all, Rabbi Shimon, the Light of the entire world, of all the worlds, who illuminates and governs over the descending Light, upon which our world exists, is also consumed by you, and yet you govern the world?" But then he collected himself at once and said: "Do not be proud, dust, for the pillars of the world will not be betrayed to you, and Rabbi Shimon will not be consumed by you!"

*Malchut* is the sole creation. And this sole creation is nothing but a desire to receive pleasure. It was made this way, and its essence cannot be changed. Yet, what can be changed is the intention—for which or whose sake to receive the pleasure.

As a result of *Malchut's* union with *Bina* with an altruistic will to bestow delight, give pleasure, *Malchut* acquires *Bina's* desire in addition to her own. That is, an additional desire appears in *Malchut*—to bestow, opposite to her nature.

Only this desire of *Bina* in *Malchut* can result in a *Zivug* and reception of Light. When *Malchut* receives all the desires that she possibly can from *Bina*, and fills them with Light, only her own initial egoistic property will remain uncorrected, but even that will be corrected from Above by the Creator Himself. The order of correction and reception of Light in *Bina's* properties inside of *Malchut* is referred to as the reception on the *Zivug* of *Yesod*, and it takes place sequentially along 6,000 degrees, called "6,000 years."

*Malchut de Malchut* of the world of *Atzilut* cannot receive any Light during the 6,000 years until all of its parts are completely corrected. All the *Zivugim* (plural for *Zivug*) throughout the 6,000 years are made not on *Malchut* herself, but on the properties she received from *Bina*. The place of such a *Zivug* is called *Yesod de Malchut* or *Ateret Yesod.* Whereas *Malchut* herself (egoistic desires) remains closed to the Light, and is therefore called the "closed gates."

The reception of Light during the 6,000 years, correction of the *Partzufim,* and the gradual filling of *Malchut* with the Light, takes place with the help of *Bina's* desires in *Malchut,* which are called *Miftacha* (*Yesod de Malchut*), for the impure (egoistic) force has no power over this part of *Malchut.*

*Yesod de Malchut* means that *Malchut* only acts with the properties she received from a Higher *Sefira*–*Yesod,* which is free from the influence of the impure forces (*Klipot*). All the properties, except for those of *Malchut,* are altruistic, since they originate from *Bina.* However, since we wish to emphasize that a *Zivug* is made on an altruistic desire, above the egoistic desire of *Malchut,* we usually say *Yesod* instead of *Bina.* And since *Yesod* is the *Sefira* immediately above *Malchut,* we say that a *Zivug* is made not on the egoistic desires of *Malchut,* but on *Yesod.* And since, upon acquiring the properties of *Yesod,* *Malchut* can receive the Light, such reception of Light on *Yesod de Malchut* is called "*Miftacha*" (from the word *Mafte'ach,* key)–the key that opens the way for the Upper Light.

However, since *Malchut* herself, that is, *Malchut de Malchut* ("closed gates") remains inaccessible to the Light for 6,000 years, Rabbi Chiya (a particular spiritual degree) could not understand how Rabbi Shimon (the spiritual *Partzuf* called Rabbi Shimon) could achieve such complete perfection. Indeed, Rabbi Shimon is a *Partzuf* of such spiritual height that it receives the Light of *Yechida.* And it is impossible to receive this Light without utilizing a *Zivug* on *Malchut de Malchut* itself.

And yet, this part of *Malchut* remains uncorrected until the completion of the 6,000 years (the end of correction), and thus cannot be used. By defying these desires, it is as though one has already partially corrected it. And all the prohibitory commandments refer to *Malchut de Malchut*; hence, the ban imposed on its use is called "a restriction."

Yet, if it is impossible to fill the "stony heart" (*Lev HaEven*), i.e., *Malchut de Malchut* (the root of egoism, the basis of creation), with Light, how can even a single soul achieve complete correction? After all, complete correction implies the reception of Light in the entire *Malchut.* Each soul, each part of *Malchut* that man is destined to correct contains a part of all the other parts of *Malchut,* including a part of *Malchut de Malchut,* which he may not work with until the end of correction.

On the other hand, Rabbi Chiya sees Rabbi Shimon in a state of complete correction. So how could the latter have attained such state? This contradiction roused Rabbi Chiya so greatly that he prostrated himself on the ground and cried out.

It is impossible to constantly "translate" the words of the Torah or *The Zohar* into a language we can understand, that "ground" signifies egoism and "dust" refers to the impure forces, that "crying out" implies raising MAN, and so forth. All the words and definitions in the text of *The Zohar* should be perceived sensuously rather than literally, as physical actions of our world. In other words, whatever *The Zohar* speaks of is related only to inner, spiritual sensations and experiences of one who perceives the spiritual realm.

All the worlds constitute the "environment," the spiritual sphere, within which the Creator made His only creation—man (Adam). Everything else was created only in order to help man to achieve his spiritual mission of becoming like his Creator.

Just as in our world, the world itself and all its inhabitants, except man, are robots operated by their animal nature, rather than creatures with free will, in the spiritual worlds, all the spiritual beings, except for the soul, are operated by their spiritual nature. Upon being born in our world, man, too, is an animal without freedom to act against his egoistic desire to receive pleasure. He usually stays that way throughout his existence on earth, being not at all different from the still, vegetative, and animate levels of nature, automatically following orders of his inner master, egoism.

Only with the help of Kabbalah can one gradually receive Upper, spiritual strength, and consequently acquire freedom of choice, that is, liberate himself from the influence of the impure, egoistic forces, and become free in his desires, like the Creator. However, such an opportunity is only given to one who can control his automatically-driven, egoistic nature: according to the strength of his screen, man ascends (moves inwardly, in his sensations) from this world to the spiritual.

After creating the spiritual worlds as a home for his future creation, the Creator created the creature (soul, Adam). The soul constitutes the desire to delight in the sensation of the Creator, of His Light. The sensation of the Creator is called "Light." There is nothing else in the entire universe besides the Light and the soul!

Although the soul itself is *Malchut de Malchut* (the only egoistic creation), the Creator imparted onto it the property of altruism, having created it mixed with the *Kelim* (desires) of *Bina*, thereby demonstrating how wonderful it would be to be like Him.

While performing altruistic actions, the soul (Adam) decided to use its natural egoism, *Malchut de Malchut* itself, to receive the Creator's Light with altruistic intentions. Yet, when it began to let the tremendous Light of *Yechida* into *Malchut de Malchut*, it could not resist and wished to enjoy it egoistically. This change in the soul's desires is referred to as its fall.

As a result of the fall, Adam's soul split into myriad parts (600,000), all of which fell into captivity of impure, egoistic forces (acquired egoistic desires). After the fall, Adam corrected some of the souls (obtained an anti-egoistic screen), but only partially. And then, of the total number of souls, some were selected for correction, lowered into this world, and clothed into bodies, generation after generation.

The descent (distancing from the Creator) into our world (egoistic sensations of only one's own desires) occurs as a result of attaching an additional "makeweight" of egoism to the soul. In the spiritual world, movement (farther from the Creator or closer to Him) and distance (from Him) are determined by the correlation of egoistic and altruistic desires within the soul.

The purpose behind the souls' descent to our world is to transform one's egoistic desires with the help of Kabbalah, and to return to the Creator with one's intentions, by performing altruistic actions. The souls' descent continues until each of them and all of them together achieve complete correction.

And the most exalted souls that refer to the degrees of *Yechida* and GAR of *Haya* depend on the correction of *Malchut* herself in *Malchut* of the world of *Atzilut* ("closed gates"). These will only be corrected at the completion of the 6,000 years, after the correction of all the rest. This is due to the inverse relationship between the souls and the Light that fills them: the more egoistic the soul is, and the lower it is located, the greater the Light that enters the general *Partzuf* (the common soul) at the time of its correction.

| THE LIGHT OF SOULS | Yechida | Haya | Neshama | Ruach | Nefesh |
|---|---|---|---|---|---|
| MALCHUT (types of souls) | Keter | Hochma | Bina | ZA | Malchut |

This is why these exalted souls are consumed by dust (impure force), i.e., the impure force rules over them with its enormous and insolent power, for it is certain that no one and nothing can save these souls from captivity.

This is why Rabbi Chiya wept: "Dust, how cruel you are!" That the most exalted souls are "consumed by you without any hope of escaping you!" In other words, the actual root of creation, the primordial egoism cannot be corrected.

It turns out that as a result of the exalted souls' captivity by the rule of the impure forces, all the righteous that bring Light to the entire world cannot achieve perfection themselves. Since all the souls are interconnected, not a single individual soul can arrive at the end of correction until all the souls are corrected. This is why they are susceptible to the ruthless rule of the dust.

At first, Rabbi Chiya wanted to say that Rabbi Shimon himself was also consumed by dust, i.e., did not achieve complete correction. He had heard that Rabbi Yosi also reasons that the closed gates are closed for all. Yet, after some contemplation, he inquired: "If Rabbi Shimon revives all the worlds and governs them, how can it possibly be that he has not reached perfection?"

Therefore, he concludes that Rabbi Shimon was not consumed by the dust, that he did achieve complete correction and is probably in a state of absolute perfection. The thing that Rabbi Chiya could not understand, however, is how any individual soul could achieve the end of correction prior to (without) the complete correction of all the others. This, Rabbi Chiya could not explain to himself.

**50. Rabbi Chiya stood up and started to walk and weep. Rabbi Yosi joined him. He fasted for forty days so that he might see Rabbi Shimon. He was told he still was not worthy of seeing him. He wept and fasted for another forty days. He was then shown a vision: Rabbi Shimon and his son Rabbi Elazar were discussing him, Rabbi Chiya, the words he said to Rabbi Yosi, and thousands are listening in on their discussion.**

Although the fasting that *The Zohar* speaks of is a spiritual act, in our world such a description is a good example of how strong a desire should be in order to be answered from Above. Other spiritual actions include weeping, tears—the small state (*Katnut*) of a spiritual *Partzuf*, in this case referred to as "Rabbi Chiya." Naturally, Rabbi Shimon and all the other characters of *The Zohar* are spiritual *Partzufim*, rather than people of our world.

Truth be told, the spiritual level of a person known by a certain name in our world may coincide with his spiritual root described in the Torah. However, elucidation of this matter exceeds the scope of this particular article. It is nonetheless essential to note that Pharaoh in the corporeal Egypt, naturally, was not a spiritual Pharaoh, the way he is described in *The Zohar* (the *Partzuf* that includes all of *Malchut*), and Laban, portrayed in the Torah as a villain, is in fact the Supernal Spiritual Light of *Partzuf AB*, the Supernal Light of *Hochma*. This will be explained later on.

The strong desire to attain the degree of Rabbi Shimon allowed Rabbi Chiya to see him, for he was certain that Rabbi Shimon had not been consumed by the dust. He came to this conclusion precisely because of his conversation with Rabbi Yosi, and hence passionately desired to see Rabbi Shimon.

**51. In that same vision, Rabbi Chiya saw several great celestial wings: how Rabbi Shimon and his son Rabbi Elazar mounted them and soared to the Assembly of Heaven, while the wings waited for them. Afterwards, they both returned to their place and shone brighter than ever before, brighter than the light of the sun.**

The Heavenly Assembly refers to the Assembly of the angel Matatron. However, his full name is not pronounced, and the name Matat is used instead, for pronouncing a name is equivalent to an action, which is not always desirable. The term Supernal Assembly refers to the Assembly of the Creator Himself, while the Heavenly Assembly refers to the Assembly of Matat.

The wings that were waiting for Rabbi Shimon and his son Elazar are angels (spiritual forces, similar to robots or draft animals in our world), whose task is to help the souls to ascend from one spiritual degree to another. And just as these wings must assist the souls in their ascent, they must assist them to descend to their places. Therefore, it is said that the wings were waiting for Rabbi Shimon and his son Rabbi Elazar to bring them back down.

And when Rabbi Chiya saw them returning from the Heavenly Assembly back to their place (to Rabbi Shimon's Assembly), he noticed a new light on their faces, and radiance surrounded them that was brighter than the sun.

**52. Rabbi Shimon opened and said: "Let Rabbi Chiya enter and see how much the Creator renews the faces of the righteous in the world to come. Happy is he who comes here without shame. Happy is he who stands in the other world as a rigid pillar opposite all." And Rabbi Chiya saw himself entering, and Rabbi Elazar and all the other pillars of the world that were there stood up before Rabbi Chiya. And he, Rabbi Chiya, was ashamed; he entered, bending, and sat at the feet of Rabbi Shimon.**

Rabbi Shimon opened (opened the way for the Light) and said: "Happy is he who enters without shame." And all that were present there felt no shame. Only Rabbi Chiya was ashamed. This is because they had the strength to withstand the power of the dust, and Rabbi Chiya did not. They were all perfect, whereas Rabbi Chiya had a flaw—the desire to attain. And this is what he was ashamed of.

**53. A voice sounded: "Lower your eyes, do not raise your head, and do not look." He lowered his eyes and saw Light that shone from afar. The voice returned and said: "The Supernal Ones, concealed and enclosed, who have eyes that watch over the entire world, look and see: the lower ones are sleeping, and the Light of their eyes is concealed in their pupils. Wake them!"**

After he followed the instruction to lower his eyes and not raise his head (not use his desire to receive Light, but only desires to bestow), he merited hearing

(Light of *Hassadim*) the appeal, with the help of which he attained everything he wished. The voice divides all souls into two groups: the first is a group of Supernal Holy Ones that are concealed, who merited their eyes to be opened to behold the entire world, and the second group of souls have the Light of their eyes concealed in their eye-sockets, which is what blinded them. This is why the voice called upon the souls of the first group to behold, i.e., to use the reception of the Upper Light, to draw the Upper Light together with the second group.

**54. Who among you turns darkness into Light and savors bitter as sweet even before he came here, that is, while still living in the other world? Who among you hopes and waits each day for the Light that shines when the Lord distances, when His greatness grows and He is called the King of all kings of the world? For he who does not wait for this each day while living in this world, has no place in the other world either.**

The Creator's goal is for man to fully attain Him while still living in this world, to feel Him as he did prior to descending into this world, prior to incarnating in a physical body. From this the division of people of our world into two groups is clearly evident, and the voice appeals to them.

The voice emphasizes to each group their main advantage. To the souls of the first group, it says that they turned darkness into Light. These are the souls of the world of *Atzilut*, for the Creator created two opposite systems in the worlds BYA: the system of darkness and bitterness opposite the system of Light and sweetness. Therefore, in the Torah of the worlds BYA there is a division into suitable and unsuitable, pure and impure, permitted and forbidden, holy and unholy, whereas the Torah of the world of *Atzilut*, which consists wholly of the Creator's names, contains nothing impure whatsoever.

And the sinner Laban is regarded as a holy name in the world of *Atzilut*, as well as the Pharaoh. And all the names that represent impure forces in the worlds BYA become corrected in the world of *Atzilut*, exalted and pure spiritual objects and forces with corresponding holy names. Therefore, the souls that have attained the Light of the world of *Atzilut* transform all darkness into Light and all bitterness into sweetness. In other words, the whole difference between the holy, pure, and good, and their opposites lies in the correction of the desire and in acquiring an anti-egoistic screen over the will to receive.

And to the second group the voice said that they're waiting for the Creator's help, and He will rise (*Shechina*, His manifestation to the lower ones) from the dust (in their sensations). But those who do not wait for Him, being preoccupied with other aspirations, will not rise from the dust, and the sensation of the Creator will remain concealed from them.

**55. In his vision, Rabbi Chiya saw many of his friends gathering around the standing pillars. And he saw them being elevated to the Heavenly Assembly, some are elevated, while others are lowered. And above them all, he saw Matat, the owner of wings, approaching.**

As the voice was calling, Rabbi Chiya saw several souls of the righteous, belonging to the two groups, standing around the two pillars that were already present in Rabbi Shimon's assembly, and whom he had already seen ascending to the Heavenly Assembly. Some were ascending, and some were descending; moreover, this motion ensued in mutually opposite directions.

This way the two groups help one another according to the calling voice, which instructs the first group to descend and the second to ascend. Rabbi Chiya saw also that due to the excitement of all these souls over their aspirations, i.e., the power of the two groups, Matat descended from the Heavenly Assembly to the assembly of Rabbi Shimon and swore an oath.

**56. The angel Matat swore that he heard from behind the curtain how each day the Creator remembers and grieves over _Malchut_, cast into the dust. And when He remembers her, He strikes 390 firmaments, and they all tremble with terrible fear before Him. And the Creator sheds tears for the _Shechina_ (Divinity), _Malchut_ that has fallen to the dust. And those tears simmer like fire, and fall into the Great Sea. And by the power of these tears, the Ruler of the Sea, called Rachav, is revived, blesses the Creator's holy name, and vows to swallow up everything, from the first days of creation, and to absorb all within himself, when all the nations gather against the holy nation, and the waters will dry, and Israel will walk through dry land.**

This vow signifies that the Creator never forgets, but remembers each day that the _Shechina_ lies in the dust. However, this does not refer to the entire Holy _Shechina_: this, the Creator need not vow, for it is revealed and seen by all who dwell in the Upper Worlds that everything He does is for the _Shechina_ (_Malchut_) alone.

But this refers only to _Malchut de Malchut_. She is the one Rabbi Chiya thinks about being held captive by the impure forces, completely abandoned. Hence, he wept: "Oh dust that consumes all!" And here, the angel Matat, who has come to the Assembly of Rabbi Shimon, revealed to Rabbi Chiya a great secret—that the Creator's rule is absolute, and He remembers _Malchut de Malchut_ each day.

A _Zivug_ (union of the _Masach_-screen and the Light-pleasure) is defined as a stroke of Light onto the screen, a result of the desire to enter and cross the screen's barrier, while the screen restricts and repels it. This act of repelling is called the Returning (reversed) Light, as it rises from the screen from below upwards and clothes the coming Light.

This may be compared to the example of the host (Creator) offering delicious food (Light) to his guest (Kli), who wishes to enjoy the delicacies. However, as a result of the shame from being the receiver, the guest refuses to receive, and the screen repels the food (Light). It is as though the guest (Kli) says to the host (Creator) that he refuses to receive the pleasure (Light) for himself, for his own enjoyment. This repelling of the food (Light) forms the Reflected Light, for it stems not just from not wanting to feel shame, as it is in our world, but from the spiritual Kli's desire to be like the Creator.

The Reflected Light is that altruistic intention, desire. This is also the spiritual Kli, and only within it can the Light be received; only in this intention can one feel the Creator.

After the Kli was able to repel all the pleasure coming to it, and demonstrated that it could meet the condition of the first restriction (to refrain from egoistic reception), it began to calculate how much Light it could receive for the Creator's sake. The Kli receives only the amount of pleasure that it is certain it can receive for the Creator's sake.

The delight that was received inside the Kli is referred to as the Inner Light. The amount of Light received inside the vessel determines the degree of similarity to the Creator; the Kli acts like the Creator: just as He desires to bestow pleasure upon the Kli, so the Kli wishes to bestow upon Him, to the extent of the Inner Light received. Therefore, the size of the Kli, (from Peh to Tabur, where it receives the Light) determines the degree of merging with the Creator. In this place, the Kli is merged with Him in properties and intentions.

If the Kli's powers of resistance are not sufficient to receive for the Creator's sake, and it can only refrain from reception, the Kli is considered to be in the "small" state, Katnut. The Kli that was created by the Creator is the strongest. However, afterwards, as it begins to descend, its screen gradually weakens until the Kli can no longer receive for the Creator's sake. It is left with just enough strength to not receive for itself. This is why from this state onward there is a ban on reception of Light into the Kli's desires "to receive." The Kli may only use its GE, but not its AHP. And the boundary beyond which the Light cannot spread is called Parsa, the firmament. This barrier is built from Above; thus, even if the Kli suddenly wishes to receive the Light for itself, it will not be able to do so.

The screen divides the firmament and consists of four parts: Hochma, Bina, Tifferet, and Malchut (HBTM), the four letters of HaVaYaH. Because Malchut joined with Bina and thereby corrected her egoistic properties into altruistic ones, the screen is located not in Malchut, but in Bina. Bina is counted as hundreds; therefore, the four parts HBTM equal 400. However, there is no Zivug (reception of Light) on *Malchut de Malchut* itself (after all, it is called the "closed gates"). This means that *Malchut* contains ninety *Sefirot*, and not 100: 9 *Sefirot*, each consisting of ten.

Therefore, the screen that is called "the firmament" and that makes a *Zivug* with the Upper Light by reflecting it consists of 390 parts, for the part of *Malchut de Malchut* is lacking. The firmament is therefore said to consist of 390 firmaments, and on it a daily *Zivug* with the *Shechina* is made, whereas a *Zivug* on the dust, which signifies the ten parts of *Malchut de Malchut*, is forbidden. The impact between the screen and the incoming Light resembles shuddering from fear to receive the Light inside of oneself, beyond the limits of one's restrictions.

There are five *Sefirot* in the *Rosh* (head) of a *Partzuf*:

| | | |
|---|---|---|
| Keter | - Galgalta (or Metzach) | - forehead |
| Hochma | - Eynaim | - eyes |
| Bina | - Awznayim | - ears |
| ZA | - Hotem | - nose |
| Malchut | - Peh | - mouth |

Just as the secretion from one's physiological eyes is called tears, the secretion of the Light of *Hochma* from the part of the spiritual *Kli* called "eyes" is referred to as "tears." Tears constitute the part of the Light that is rejected by the *Partzuf* due to the absence of a screen on *Malchut de Malchut*. All the Light that comes to a *Partzuf* wishes to enter and fill it with its pleasure, even the part of the *Partzuf* that has no screen to receive with altruistic intentions. Therefore, the screen immediately repels this portion of the Light.

But between the strike of the Light from Above and the resistance of the screen from below, tiny drops of Light seep through the screen, which, due to its hurry, is unable to repel them. These drops have nothing to do with the level of *Hochma* of the *Partzuf*, as they lack the clothing of the Reflected Light. They exit the *Partzuf Hochma* and receive the name "tears." But it is nonetheless Light!

This is similar to a state where we are filled with tears of compassion for another person. Indeed, all that exists in our world exists because it derives from its spiritual prototype, and all that transpires in this world, transpires only because it stems from its Upper, spiritual root.

After all, the fact that the Upper Light strikes the screen, trying to break through its restriction, stems from its origin in the Highest Place, the Creator Himself, and is unrelated to the creature's desire to receive this Light within the bounds of its altruistic capabilities. The Light stems from the world of Infinity, from the Creator Himself, long before the *Kli* appeared and wished to restrict itself.

The Upper Light wishes to fill the desire to enjoy that it created, as it is said, "the Creator wishes to dwell in His creatures below." The Light and the Creator are one and the same; after all, man defines the sensation of the Creator as spiritual Light. And this Upper Light strives to force its way through the screen and enter man's desires, but the screen hurls it back. Thus, this repelled Upper Light becomes Reflected Light, which designates man's altruistic intentions to bestow delight upon the Creator.

As a result of the collision with the screen, portions of the Light fall outside, for these tears originate from the Creator's love and compassion for His creation. In our world, this spiritual action results in an emission of tears in an individual overwhelmed with suffering and love. However, spiritual tears do not disappear.

This is described in *Song of Songs* (8:6): "For love is as strong as death, jealousy is as cruel as hell; the flashes thereof are flashes of fire, the very flame of the Lord!" This is because these tears stem from the Upper One's love and compassion for the lower one. And just as flaming tears shed by someone in our world burn, so do the boiling and burning Upper tears burn like fire, like the very flame of the Lord!

Being related to the property of *Hochma*, *Malchut* is called "sea." It is therefore said that the tears (Light of *Hochma* without first being clothed in Light of *Hassadim*) fall into the sea, *Malchut*. And it is written that the many sea waters will not extinguish the Creator's love for His creatures, expressed in these tears.

It was said during the creation of the world: "Let the waters be gathered together unto one place" (*Beresheet*, 1:9). But the angel that governed the sea did not wish to swallow these waters, and was hence killed (was emptied of Light). Now, as the tears fall, he is revived.

The reason for this is that during the creation of the world, *Malchut de Malchut* itself had not undergone any kind of correction, as the Creator created the worlds ABYA in a special correction, called MAN *de Bina* or *Ateret Yesod*, and not MAN *de Malchut* or *Malchut de Malchut*. In other words, correction is possible only if man corrects not *Malchut de Malchut* itself (his essence), but, while completely refraining from its use (use of egoism), he acquires higher, altruistic desires from *Bina* and receives the Creator's Light in them (in *Sefirot KHB-ZA de Malchut*, in 390 *Sefirot*).

These higher, altruistic desires are referred to as desires of *Bina* or as MAN *de Bina*, and the reception of Light in them (*Zivug*) is made not on egoism (*Malchut* herself), but on the will to bestow, called *Ateret Yesod*. This *Zivug* is therefore sufficient to fill only the first nine *Sefirot* in *Malchut*, but does not fill *Malchut* herself.

Prophet Yeshayahu (Isaiah) writes in this regard: "Who are you with, partners? I started the worlds, and you are to complete them!" The correction of *Malchut de Malchut* is incumbent solely upon the creatures. Hence, when the sea ruler was told: "Let the waters be gathered together unto one place," he objected and did not wish to swallow up the created waters, for due to the uncorrected state of *Malchut de Malchut*, the impure forces prevailed and ruled over him. And that is why he was killed.

However, these tears correct *Malchut de Malchut*, and thus revive the sea ruler so that he would rise from the dead, sanctify the name of the Lord, fulfill the Creator's will, and swallow up the primeval waters. For then, all the impure forces, all the evil in the world will disappear and all (desires) will gather in one place (property), whose name is *Atzilut*. This is because the world of *Atzilut* will spread from the end of the world of AK down to our world, and there will come the end of correction, for the worlds of BYA will return in their properties to the world of *Atzilut*.

In the future, at the end of correction, after the correction of the first nine *Sefirot* of *Malchut*, when only *Malchut de Malchut*, the last, tenth *Sefira*, remains to be corrected, when all the nations of the world (*Malchut de Malchut*) unite to destroy Israel (the first nine *Sefirot* of *Malchut*, the desire to correct all the ten *Sefirot* of *Malchut*), the act of the sea ruler will be revealed in that he will swallow up all the primeval, evil waters, and the waters (severe restrictions) will dry up, and the sons of Israel (those who aspire for the Creator) will walk through dry land.

The prophet Micha (Micah) says of this: "As we fled the land of Egypt, we saw wonders." However, this was only the beginning, for it was only in the End Sea (the Red Sea; the Hebrew name signifies the end of *Malchut*, or *Malchut de Malchut*), and only for a limited time. But, at the end of correction, death will disappear forever.

This is how Matat explained his oath: the Creator never forgets *Malchut*, which is cast in the dust. For even though a daily *Zivug* with the *Shechina* is made on only 390 firmaments, on the nine *Sefirot* of *Malchut* and not on *Malchut de Malchut* itself, which remains lying in the dust, and, as it seems to us, completely forgotten by the Creator, nothing could be further from the truth. In truth, He corrects it with each *Zivug*, because with each *Zivug*, as a result of the 390 firmaments being struck, the tears fall outside. And these tears are not lost, but fall into the Great Sea (*Malchut de Malchut*), which receives from them slow, yet gradual corrections, even if it is the Light of *Hochma* without the clothing of the Light of *Hassadim*. As it becomes more and more corrected, the sea ruler is revived until the tears accumulate to the necessary amount for the correction of the entire *Malchut*, so that all of her intentions would be for the Creator's sake.

This will occur when all the nations of the world unite to attack Israel. Then, the sea ruler will rise back to life and swallow up all the primeval waters, for *Malchut de Malchut* will receive the lacking correction, for each day the Creator cares for her until she, His only creation, reaches her final correction.

And here Rabbi Chiya's delusion was revealed to him: he understood that nothing disappears in the dust, but, on the contrary, each day *Malchut* undergoes corrections, just as Matat swore.

**57. Through all this, he heard a voice: "Clear this place, clear this place! The Mashiach (Messiah), the King-Redeemer is coming to the assembly of Rabbi Shimon," for all the righteous gathered there are the heads of groups and assemblies, whereas all of the assembly members ascend from this assembly to the Assembly of Heaven. And the Mashiach visits all these assemblies and seals the Torah that stems from the mouths of the righteous. And at that moment, the Mashiach comes to the assembly of Rabbi Shimon, surrounded by the heads of all the Supernal assemblies.**

As a result of the great revelation—the end of correction—concealed in the oath of Matat, all of the righteous present at Rabbi Shimon's Assembly were elevated, especially the two groups of the righteous that caused Matat to appear and take his oath. As a result, all of them attained Upper Degrees and reached the levels of "heads of assemblies," for each assembly has members and a head, and the difference between them is similar to the difference between *VAK*, *GE* of the degree or *Partzuf*, from *GAR*, the complete *Partzuf*.

Hence, it is written that the place should be cleared for the *Mashiach*. After all, when Matat revealed the secret of the end (of correction), and specifically how creation will be delivered from egoism, a voice appeared and commanded to prepare a place for the *Mashiach*, the King-Redeemer, for the end of correction is connected to the King-*Mashiach*.

However, only the righteous of Rabbi Shimon's assembly, who are above all the heads of assemblies, merit his coming, for only those who are on the same spiritual level as the King-*Mashiach* (all those who have already corrected all of their other properties—the first nine *Sefirot* in their part of desires-*Malchut*—all of the properties except for the original egoism, *Malchut de Malchut*) can merit the revelation of his face.

The level of the *Mashiach* is the Light of *Yechida*. And if all the members had not reached the level of the heads of the assemblies, the *GAR* of the degrees, i.e., corrected all that they could, they would not have merited the revelation of the *Mashiach's* face. But the heads of the Assemblies are not *GAR* of the low degrees. Rather, they represent a level so high that all the members have merited reaching the Heavenly Assembly of Matat.

And now all the members merited becoming the heads of the Assemblies, wherefrom they merited an ascent to the Heavenly Assembly. Moreover, thanks to their corrections, they merited the *Mashiach* himself coming to all these assemblies to be adorned with their deeds in the Torah. And now all the members have merited reaching the level of the assemblies' heads. This is why the *Mashiach* is adorned with the Torah of the assemblies' heads. Thus, thanks to them, the *Mashiach* himself ascends to a Higher Degree.

**58. At that time, all the members stood up. Rabbi Shimon stood up, too, and his Light rose to the firmament. The *Mashiach* said unto him: "Happy are you, Rabbi, for your Torah has risen in 370 beams of Light, and each beam divides into 613 beams (properties) that ascend and bathe in the rivers of the holy *Apharsemon* (persimmon). And the Creator confirms and signs the Torah of your assembly, of the assembly of Chizkiyah (Hezekiah), the King of Judah, and the assembly of Achiyah ha Shiloni (Ahijah the Shilonite)."**

When the *Mashiach* revealed himself to them and came to Rabbi Shimon's Assembly, all the members stood up (ascended from the level of *VAK* to *GAR*), and Rabbi Shimon stood on the same degree as the *Mashiach*. And the Light rose to the height of the firmament. This indicates that Rabbi Shimon has attained the Light of the ten firmaments, the previously missing tenth firmament on account of the closed gates of *Malchut de Malchut*, and has attained the Light of *Yechida*, which he now was able to receive, as he could make a *Zivug* on *Malchut de Malchut*. And the Light of *Yechida* that shines from this *Zivug* is called *Mashiach*. The "sitting" level is 390, or *VAK*; the "standing" level is 400, or *GAR*.

The *Mashiach* said to Rabbi Shimon that his Torah gave rise to the Light of *Yechida* in *Partzuf Atik*, because:

Units (0 – 9) are in *Malchut*;
Tens (10 – 90) are in *ZA*;
Hundreds (100 – 900) are in *Ima*;
Thousands (1,000 – 9,000) are in *Aba*;

Tens of thousands (10,000 – 90,000) are in *Arich Anpin*;
And hundreds of thousands (100,000 – 900,000) are in *Atik*.

Since each *Sefira* of *Atik* equals 100,000, the four *Sefirot* of *HaVaYaH* (*HBTM* of *Atik*) total 400,000.

However, in this case, he should have said that the Torah performed the deed in 400,000; yet, he said that the Light emanated by *Ima* is not used on 400, but only on 370, for although the Torah had reached the zenith of the firmament, it still could not reach GAR of the last, Supernal Hundred. Hence, there are only 370, while the Upper Thirty are absent in *Ima*.

The same applies with regard to thousands—the Light of *Aba* does not use GAR of each thousand, but only VAK, i.e., 600 instead of 1,000. Instead of the GAR of each thousand, it uses thirteen (*Hochma* of the "thirty-two *Netivot* (paths of) *Hochma*"). The number thirteen signifies *Hochma* of the "thirty-two *Netivot Hochma*," the weak Light of *Hochma*, called the holy *Apharsemon*.

It is therefore said that the Torah attained 370 Lights, and each of them divides into 613 beams; thus, in the 400 of *Ima*, thirty of the Upper Light of *Hochma* are absent, which leaves it with only 370. And each thousand lacks the Upper 400 (GAR *of Hochma*). Instead of using the thirteen paths of the holy *Apharsemon*, each thousand contains no more than 613, for all the supernal secrets are concealed in Rabbi Shimon's assembly. And the Creator Himself sealed them, for He ascends and becomes adorned with the achievements of all the righteous in the Torah.

We know from the Talmud (*Sanhedrin*, 99:1) that everything the prophets ever said refers only to the days of the *Mashiach*'s coming, but in the future (*Yeshayahu*, 64), everyone will behold the Creator themselves. For all the degrees and levels that refer to the days of the *Mashiach* will then be corrected, and all the secrets of the Torah will be revealed, everyone will attain complete revelation of the Light, of the Creator, as it is said, everyone will see with their own eyes (sight implies GAR *de Hochma*).

From the aforesaid, it becomes clear that there exists an opportunity to correct one's individual *Malchut de Malchut* even before all the souls achieve it in the future. In such a case, man reaches his *individual* level of attainment of 400, although his *general* level cannot be higher than 370, as in the case of everybody else. This is the degree that Rabbi Shimon, Rabbi Chizkiyah, and Achiyah ha Shiloni had reached.

**59. The *Mashiach* said: "I have come here not to confirm the Torah of your assembly, but only because the 'owner of wings' is on his way here. For I know that he shall not enter any other assembly, but only yours." Meanwhile, Rabbi**

Shimon told him of the oath taken by the "owner of wings." Right then the *Mashiach* trembled in awe and raised his voice, and the Heavens shook, and the Great Sea boiled, and the Leviathan stirred, and the entire world threatened to overturn.

At that moment, he saw Rabbi Chiya in Rabbi Shimon's adornments. He asked, "Who gave man in this world the adornments, garment of the other world?" (garment of the other world onto the body of this world). Rabbi Shimon answered, "This is Rabbi Chiya, the cresset of the Torah!" He said to him, "Gather him and his sons (those who have left this world), and they shall join your Assembly." Rabbi Shimon said, "Time was granted to him, he was granted time" (Rabbi Chiya's time has not yet come).

The *Mashiach* said to Rabbi Shimon that he came not for the sake of the Torah, but because the "owner of wings" has come to the assembly, wishing to know what Matat had said. For Matat had revealed that the end of correction would be preceded by terrible suffering for Israel—the Heavens and the Great Sea would tremble, and the world would be on the verge of collapse, as predicted in the Talmud (*Sanhedrin*, 97): "All is broken." Hence, he raised his voice, wishing to mitigate all this upheaval.

The *Mashiach* was surprised to see Rabbi Chiya's garment (that Rabbi Chiya exists in a physical body of our world, in the property of this world), for if he had merited the appearance of Matat and his oath, he had attained the degree of complete correction of all his evil. And since he merited seeing the *Mashiach's* face, to receive the Light of *Yechida*, he had obviously completed his work in this world, and there is nothing left for him to do here. Hence, he should leave it and enter Rabbi Shimon's assembly in the Garden of Eden.

But Rabbi Shimon persuaded Rabbi Chiya that he needs to continue performing new, additional corrections in this world. And both the *Mashiach* and Rabbi Shimon explained to Rabbi Chiya what else specifically he still needed to do in this world.

**60. Rabbi Chiya trembled in awe when the *Mashiach* left, and his eyes fulfilled with tears. For the *Mashiach* left Rabbi Shimon's Assembly weeping from the great desire for the final correction and redemption. And Rabbi Chiya was also anguished from the fervent desire to reach the end of correction. Rabbi Chiya cried and said: "Happy is the lot of the righteous in the other world, and happy is the lot of Rabbi Shimon bar Yochai, who has merited all of this."**

# WHO IS YOUR PARTNER?

**61. Beresheet:** Rabbi Shimon opened: "Put my words in your mouth. How much effort should man exert in the Torah day and night, for the Creator is attentive to those who study it. And with every word that man attains by his efforts in the Torah, he builds a firmament."

The Creator gave the righteous the power of His speech. And just as the Creator creates the creature by the power of His word, so the righteous create new Heavens by its power. This is why Rabbi Shimon opened his speech by explaining the words, "In the beginning, the Creator created Heaven and earth," as the word *Barah* (created) also means "closing" and "limiting." And we must understand why the Creator had created it in such a closed form. He answers, "To put the correction of Heaven and earth in the words of the righteous, to make them His partners—participants in the creation of Heaven and earth."

There are two kinds of renewal of Heaven and earth that the Creator enclosed in the mouths of the righteous:

1. The correction of Adam's sin, the correction of the past. Even before the creation of Adam, the Creator had made a secret correction of Heaven and earth, as it is described in the beginning of the Torah, in the chapter *Beresheet*: *ZON de Atzilut* ascended to *AVI* and to *AA*, while Adam ascended to *ZON* and *YESHSUT*. As a result, Adam received the Light of *NRN de Atzilut*, for he clothed *YESHSUT* and *ZON de Atzilut*, i.e., ascended to their level.

Adam is located within the worlds *BYA* and he ascends together with these worlds. All the worlds can ascend above their permanent state or descend to their places with Adam inside of them. Adam's spiritual level and the Light that he receives are determined by his location (see page 212).

| DURING ASCENT | PERMANENT STATE |
|---|---|
|  | Atik |
| AVI | AA |
| ZON | AVI |
| Adam - Beria | YESHSUT + ZON |

—————— Parsa of the world of Atzilut ——————

| DURING ASCENT | PERMANENT STATE |
|---|---|
| Adam - Yetzira | Beria |
| Adam - Assiya | Yetzira |
|  | Assiya |

In other sources, such as the Talmud (*Bava Batra*, 58:2), this is described as Adam's ascent to the level of the sun (ZA *de Atzilut*). This Light is called "*Zihara Ilaa*" (*Zihara* is the Aramaic word for *Zohar* in Hebrew or "radiant Light" in English).

As a result of his sin, Adam fell spiritually to the level of our corporeal world (Talmud, *Hagigah*, 12:1). And instead of NRN *de Atzilut* that he used to receive before his fall, he now receives the Light from the worlds BYA that are below *Parsa*. And as a result of Adam's sin, Heaven (ZA) and earth (*Malchut*) of the world of *Atzilut* descended to the level of VAK *de ZA* and the point of *Malchut* respectively, as they descended below *Tabur de Partzuf AA*.

And the righteous that live in this world, but already exist spiritually in the spiritual worlds of BYA, are entrusted with the task of correcting all that transpired through Adam's fault, and to return, to renew the Heavens and the earth (ZON *de Atzilut*) and elevate them to AVI and AA—ZA to AA and *Malchut* to AVI, as it was before the sin. And as a result of their work, the righteous will receive the Light of the world of *Atzilut* that the corrected Adam is entitled to, for they (their souls, spiritual *Kelim* or inner spiritual *Partzuf*) are his parts.

2. However, even before the sin, Adam was not in the perfect state for which the Creator had created him. Hence, after the righteous correct the consequences of Adam's sin and attain NRN *de Atzilut*, which existed in Adam before the sin, new work awaits them—to receive new Upper Light that has yet to descend. In other words, if the first goal is to correct the sin, the second is to attain even more. It is called to "create new Heaven and earth," new properties of ZON, in which new, Higher Light can be received.

This new level or degree that has never been present in any *Kli* is described as "neither hath an eye seen the Creator beside thee," and the degrees which the righteous attach to the worlds are called "new Heaven" and "new earth," for they are truly new and have never before existed in reality.

And this Heaven and earth, which the righteous correct to the level that preceded Adam's sin, during the creation (*Beresheet*), are not called new, as they've already existed and the Creator Himself corrected them even before Adam's sin. Hence, they are called renewed, and the righteous who correct them are not called the Creator's partners.

"Encloses in their mouths" implies reception of such Upper Light that was neither received by Adam nor emanated from the Creator. And now, by the actions of the righteous, which are called partners, participants and co-creators, it comes out and shines in creation. Thus we see that all the righteous are divided into two groups: those who correct Adam's sin and those who create new degrees of attainment. The latter are called the Creator's partners.

ZA is called voice and *Malchut* is called speech. When a righteous person studies the Torah and thereby raises MAN (by the voice and speech of his Torah) from his soul to ZON, his voice ascends to ZA and his speech ascends to *Malchut*. The voice of the Torah that ascends with MAN to ZA is called the Creator (*Kadosh Baruch Hu*).

Also, each renewed word in the Torah builds a new firmament. A word means speech, and any speech that renews the Torah by those who study it ascends in the form of MAN to *Malchut*, who is called "word and speech." This creates a new firmament in the form of a screen, on which a *Zivug* between the Creator and the *Shechina* is made. This is what the righteous, who study the Torah, attain by raising MAN!

However, renewal in the words of the Torah does not imply anything new in the voice of the Torah. For *Malchut* has to recreate herself for each new *Zivug*, for after each *Zivug*, *Malchut* returns to the state of virginity thanks to the MAN raised by the righteous, who constantly renew her properties, her *Yesod*—the *Kli* for the reception of Light from ZA. Hence, it is written that the Torah is renewed by each word, for a word (*Malchut*) is renewed by the speech of the righteous in the Torah, as, after each *Zivug*, the previous *Kli* disappears and a new one appears.

**62. We have learned that just as the Torah is renewed by one's mouth, that renewal ascends and appears before the Creator. And the Creator accepts this wisdom, kisses it, and adorns it with seventy adornments. And the renewed wisdom itself ascends and settles on the head of the righteous that revive the**

worlds, and then flies, soaring through 70,000 worlds, until it ascends to *Atik*, the *Sefira Keter*. And all that exists in *Atik* is concealed, Supernal wisdom.

When a person raises MAN from his Torah, this word, which is *Nukva de ZA*, ascends and connects to the Creator in a *Zivug* with Him. The Creator takes this word, kisses, and adorns it, and these are the two types of *Zivugim* (plural for *Zivug*) in ZON:

1. *Zivug de Neshikin* (kisses);

2. *Zivug de Yesodot* (bases/foundations).

Each *Zivug* consists of two *Zivugim*, for a *Zivug* on *Ohr Hochma* must clothe itself into the *Partzuf* (garment) of *Ohr Hassadim*. Therefore, a preliminary *Zivug* must be made on *Ohr Hassadim*, whose role is to become a garment for *Ohr Hochma*. This is why each *Zivug* consists of two *Zivugim*:

1. *Zivug* on the degree of *Hochma*, called *Zivug de Neshikin*, because it stands at the *Peh de Rosh* of the *Partzuf*, at the level of *Rosh* and GAR.

2. *Zivug* on the degree of *Hassadim*, called *Zivug de Yesodot*, because it takes place at the level of the bodies of the *Partzufim*.

Therefore, it is said that the Creator took *Nukva* in this word and kissed her, i.e., made a *Zivug de Neshikin* at the level of GAR, and then adorned her, i.e., made a *Zivug de Yesodot* at the level of *Hassadim*. As a result, *Ohr Hochma* clothed in *Ohr Hassadim*, and *Nukva* received the complete Light.

IN SEVENTY ADORNMENTS: the complete Light of *Nukva* is called "seventy adornments," because *Malchut* is the seventh day, and when she receives from ZA, her *Sefirot* become tens, just as the *Sefirot* of ZA; this turns *Malchut* into $7 \times 10 = 70$. *Mochin* (wisdom), *Ohr Hochma* is called *Atara* (adornment or crown). Hence, what she receives is called "seventy adornments." After *Malchut* receives the Light of *Hassadim*, with the help of the MAN of the righteous, she becomes fit to receive the Upper Light of *Hochma*, the seventy adornments.

As was said above, there are two kinds of renewal of Heaven and earth (ZON):

1. When everything returns to the state preceding Adam's sin. In that instance, *Malchut* is called the "word of the Torah" (VAK), where the Torah is ZA.

2. When Heaven and earth are created with a new Light, which even Adam did not attain prior to his sin. And this attainable word is called GAR.

It is written (Talmud, *Berachot*, 7:1) that the righteous sit with adornments on their heads, for *Malchut* ascended to adorn the head of the righteous (ZA) in his *Yesod*, called *Chai Olamim* (reviver of worlds), or, rather, in his *Ateret Yesod*–the place of circumcision. And this transpires thanks to the MAN raised by the righteous that have already attained the Upper Light of Adam's *Zihara Ilaa*, just as Rabbi Shimon and his friends have already attained it.

*Ohr Hochma* is called *Ohr Haya*. Since ZA desires only *Hassadim*, he can receive *Ohr Haya* only with the help of his *Nukva*, *Malchut*. It turns out that ZA lives, i.e., receives *Ohr Haya*, only if he is in a *Zivug* with *Nukva*, called *Olam* (world). That is how the name *Chai Olamim* (reviver of worlds) originated.

Also, *Nukva*, the adornment on his head, becomes important (*Keter* – crown) because ZA receives this Light only thanks to his *Malchut*. Although *Malchut* was born from ZA, since it is *Malchut* and no other that evokes, makes reception of the Light of Life possible, ZA calls her his mother. Indeed, ZA receives *Ohr Haya* (the Light of Life) from her.

Therefore, it is written that *Malchut* flies and soars in 70,000 worlds, and after her *Zivug* with ZA on his *Atara* (adornment on his head), she ascends even higher, to AA, where the seven *Sefirot* of *Malchut*, called 70,000 worlds, become corrected, as one *Sefira* of ZA equals 10,000. After that, *Malchut* ascends higher still–to *Atik*. And all of these ascents of ZON to *Atik* transpire thanks to the efforts made by the righteous that raise MAN: a *Zivug* on *Atara* elevates ZON to AVI, from which they ascend to AA (70,000 worlds), and from there to *Atik*, the highest possible point of ascent.

It is therefore written that all the words of *Atik's* Supernal wisdom are locked, since *Malchut* receives the Upper Light upon ascending to *Atik*, and each degree that she receives from *Atik* is called "concealed," "Supernal wisdom," i.e., GAR *de Hochma*. This is because words of wisdom signify the degree of *Hochma*, and the words "concealed," "secret," and "Supernal" refer to GAR. Also, they are revealed only to those who attain the level of *Atik*, but not below, as *Tzimtzum Bet* (the second restriction) already exists in AA.

**63. And when this hidden wisdom, which is renewed here in this world, ascends, she joins Atik, ascends and descends, enters 18 worlds, where no eye has seen the Creator besides you. They emerge from there and appear before Atik, complete and perfect. Meanwhile, Atik tests her and finds her most desirable above all else. He then takes her and adorns her with 370,000 adornments. And she, the renewed Torah, ascends and descends, and is transformed into a firmament.**

During the ascent of *Malchut* to *Atik*, she joins the *Zivug* that transpires there, and creates *Ohr Hozer* (Reflected Light) by accepting *Ohr Yashar* (Direct

Light) at the level of *Atik's* properties. The ascent of *Malchut* means that *Malchut* elevates *Ohr Hozer* from herself upwards. *Malchut's* descent means that she sends *Ohr Yashar* from Above downwards. And then *Malchut* receives the hidden, secret, and Supernal wisdom. The word "joins" signifies her contact with the *Ohr Hozer* and the *Ohr Yashar* within *Atik* itself.

This *Zivug* is made in *Atik* on its *Yesod*, but not on *Malchut*, since *Malchut de Atik* is concealed until the end of correction. Like *Yesod de ZA* during its ascent to *AVI*, this *Yesod* is called *Chai Olamim*. The difference between them is that *Yesod de Atik* is called "No one else but you can see the Creator," for a *Zivug* on *Yesod* elevates *Ohr Hozer* and clothes *Ohr Yashar* with it. This screen is defined in *AVI*, below *Atik*, as wings that block the Upper Light. This shows that the screen possesses a force of restriction, law, judgment. This is why *Ohr Hozer* is also called "the Light of Restriction." Thus, *Ohr Hozer* exists in *AVI*.

Conversely, the screen in *Yesod de Atik*, of which it is said that there "the Creator no longer hides from you" (*Yeshayahu*, 30:20), while it does raise *Ohr Hozer*, it does not conceal the Creator thereby, does not have the properties of wings. This is the reason why it is called *Chai Olamim* (reviver of worlds).

Nevertheless, it remains concealed until man attains that level himself, as is written: "Only your eyes shall see the Creator." There are no wings or anything else there that conceal Him from outsiders' eyes, for no restrictions are imposed and everything is revealed. And neither are there any restrictions in *Ohr Hozer*, but only mercy and benevolence, as in *Ohr Yashar*.

The name *Chai Olamim* implies that a *Zivug* is made not on ten *Sefirot* of *Ohr Yashar* from Above downwards and ten *Sefirot* of *Ohr Hozer* from below upwards, and not on the whole of the twenty *Sefirot*, i.e., not on *Malchut* herself, but on *Yesod de Malchut*. In this instance, there are nine *Sefirot* of *Ohr Yashar* and nine *Sefirot* of *Ohr Hozer*, as *Yesod* is the ninth *Sefira*: $9 + 9 = 18 = 10 + 8 = Yod + Chet$, which is pronounced in reverse order as *Chet-Yod* (*Chai*), for this is the Reflected Light. The word "life" (*Chaim*) is derived from the word "alive" (*Chai*), for he who is able to make a *Zivug* on *Yesod* receives the Upper Light of life, *Ohr Hochma*.

Tremendous Upper Light manifests in *Atik* as a result of this *Zivug*. This is because all the worlds and all that inhabit them join *Nukva*, and together they attain true perfection, the level for which they were initially conceived and created by the Creator.

Hence, it is said that word flies in the firmament, which signifies the creation of *Ohr Hozer* from below upwards, which leads to *Ohr Yashar* descending from the Creator, from Above downwards. And the clothing of *Ohr Hozer* on *Ohr Yashar* creates a firmament, because the screen that appears in *Malchut* for the creation of *Ohr Hozer* comes as a result of the good deeds of the righteous, their MAN (requests for spiritual ascent) aimed at pleasing the Creator. So then, after this screen makes a *Zivug* with the Upper Light, it becomes a firmament, with the help of which, the righteous attain the full height of the degree on which they have now made a *Zivug*.

This occurs because when this degree descends to the righteous through the firmament, it clothes in *Ohr Hozer* (garment of this firmament), which, together with the *Ohr Yashar* clothed within it, turn over and they descend below the screen (firmament) and thereby become attainable by the righteous.

Those righteous that have achieved such perfection that they can raise MAN to such exalted *Zivug* have already rid themselves of egoism completely and have no desire to receive anything for themselves. Instead, they raise their MAN (request) with the sole purpose of pleasing the Creator. Therefore, by their corrections (MAN), they correct the screen in *Malchut*, and, by creating *Ohr Hozer* in her, which ascends from the screen of *Malchut* upwards, make her capable of a great *Zivug*. This is because all that ascends is altruism, bestowal, repelling, and rejecting reception for oneself and egoistic pleasure.

Then there is a *Zivug* with the Upper Light, and the Upper Light clothes in the ascending Reflected Light. This descending Upper Light clothes into the Reflected Light and enters into the righteous that have raised MAN. The expression "from below upwards" implies the repelling of Light by a person, and "from Above downwards" designates a person's reception.

And since the Upper Light comes to man through a firmament, it takes the Light reflected from the firmament as its garment, and one receives the Upper Light clothed in Reflected Light. This means that, even after one already receives the spiritual information of the entire degree, he delights in the Upper Light that descends to him only to the extent in which he can please the Creator thereby, i.e., to the extent of his strength, the magnitude of his screen, and the amount of Reflected Light that clothes the Direct Upper Light.

Such reception of the Upper Light (only to the extent of the magnitude of *Ohr Hozer* created by man) is called the reception for the Creator's sake. And wherever one cannot find a way to bestow upon the Creator, he does not receive. Hence, his reception is clothed in bestowal: the Upper Direct Light is clothed in Reflected Light, meaning the lower one receives only the clothed Upper Light from the Upper One, i.e., only through the firmament.

64. And thus, every deed creates firmaments that appear before *Atik,* and he calls them "new Heavens" or, rather, "renewed firmaments," concealed by Supernal wisdom. And all the other parts of the Torah that are not renewed by means of Supernal wisdom appear before the Creator, ascend and become "the lands of life" (*Artzot HaChaim*). They then descend and adorn one land. And it becomes renewed, and a new land comes into being from all that was renewed in the Torah.

The righteous are constantly raising newer and newer MAN, and thus receive newer and newer degrees of attainments from *Atik,* with the help of the firmaments created by the Upper *Zivug.* From these firmaments emerge new Heavens, which are renewed in the degrees of *Atik.* These exalted attainments of the righteous are therefore called the hidden secrets of Supernal wisdom, for they descend clothed in the garments received from the firmaments.

*Malchut* is called "earth" and *Bina* is called "the lands of life" (*Artzot HaChaim*). When *Malchut* attains all the degrees of *Bina,* she acquires the name "the land of life." *Malchut* is also called the "new land," for she exchanges her own properties for those of *Bina.* And everything that was previously *Malchut* now becomes *Bina.*

Therefore, it is written that in the future, *BON* will become *SAG,* and MA will become AB, for Heaven is ZA that now ascended to the degree of *Atik* (AB or *Hochma*). The earth, *Nukva de ZA, Malchut,* became SAG, *Bina.* Hence, the new land and the new Heavens are *Malchut* and ZA that became SAG and AB, *Atik* and AA.

65. It is written, "When the new land and the new Heavens, which I make." It is not written, "I have made," in past tense, but rather "I make," in present tense, for they are constantly made from the renewal and secrets of the Torah. And it is written of this: "And I shall place it in your mouth, and in the shadow of your hands' garments, that I may take the Heavens, and lay the foundations of the land" (*Yeshayahu,* 51:16). It is simply said "Heavens," for it implies the Heavens renewed by the Torah.

Everything that is described in the Torah is written in the present tense, as there is no time in the spiritual; everything is written with regard to the one who attains the Torah at that given moment. This is what *The Zohar* wants to stress here: the matter concerns man's constant work on himself, on his nature. And the righteous that have already attained the Upper Light continue creating newer and newer Heavens and lands, as is written, "The righteous ascend from summit to summit," and this process is infinite.

66. Rabbi Elazar said, "What is the meaning of 'in the shadow of your hands' garments?'". He answered, when the Torah was passed to Moshe, tens of thousands of Supernal angels appeared so as to raise him with the flames of their mouths, but the Creator protected him. So now, when the renewal in the Torah ascends and appears before the Creator, He protects it and shelters the one who performed it, so as to prevent the angels from finding out and envying him, until new Heaven and earth are made out of this renewal in the Torah. Hence, it is said, "To take the Heavens and lay the foundations of the land from the shadow of your hands' garments." It follows that all that is concealed from the eyes achieves a supernal result. This is why it is said, "In the shadow of your hands' garments." Yet, why should it be concealed from the eyes for the sake of a supernal result? Hence, it is immediately said, "So that I may take the Heavens and lay the foundations of the land." As we have learned—so that new Heavens and earth will appear out of this concealment.

The phrase "In the shadow of your hands' garments" alludes to *Ohr Hozer*, the garment that stems from the firmament, clothing and covering of the *Ohr Hochma*. Like a shadow, this garment conceals *Hochma* from outsiders' eyes, so they do not know what is inside. Why are High Degrees concealed from angels? So they would not envy man, for when the angels, which are made of a very light material (without egoism), look at one who is righteous and see his negative properties, they envy him for the High Degree that he has achieved. They then begin slandering that righteous, the properties that they discover in him. This brings harm to the righteous.

Therefore, when a degree clothes into the garment of a firmament (*Ohr Hozer*), this garment measures the degree itself, its magnitude, to prevent man from receiving more than his intention for the Creator's sake allows, i.e., only to the extent of *Ohr Hozer*. Thus, he is protected from the angels' envy and from their ability to harm his spiritual condition, for he becomes equal to them in his properties: his Reflected Light makes him equal.

Like everything else that fills the worlds, *Melachim* (angels) are man's inner properties and forces. In order to avoid harming himself by wishing to attain Higher Degrees before he has acquired *Ohr Hozer*, these degrees must be concealed. However, in addition to *Ohr Hozer*, one should exercise caution against his desire.

This explains the rule: "The eye sees and the heart covets," and man would not be able to protect his intention, to keep it for the Creator's sake alone, and would desire to receive for himself. However, once clothed in the garment of the firmament, he can be certain that he will not receive above his intention to receive for the Creator's sake.

Let us briefly examine how a desire is conceived in man. One looks at something for the first time, not yet knowing what he is going to see. It is as if an object accidentally falls into his field of vision. Naturally, no ban can be imposed on it, as this occurrence is not dependent on man; thus, it is neither rewarded nor punished.

However, when looking at it for the second time—here, man already has freedom of choice. And if the second look is going to result in the desire to receive pleasure, it is forbidden. If man cannot restrain himself, and looks for the second time, his eyes send a signal to his heart, and the heart begins to desire. Thus, man has the power to decide whether or not to allow the desire to be born within him. This is the meaning of the phrase: "The eye sees and the heart covets."

**67. He said to these gates and to the words that were set one upon the other in the renewed Torah: "Who are you with? You are my partners. Just as I make the Heavens and the earth with My words, as it is written, 'By the Creator's word were the Heavens made,' so you create new Heavens and earth by your labor in the Torah."**

The properties of reception are called "gates," because, like open gates, they are always ready to receive. "Words" are the properties of bestowal, of raising MAN to the Creator. The phrase "Set one upon the other" signifies one clothing the other, and so occurs reception for the sake of bestowal.

**68. However, if one were to claim that the renovation of the Torah by one who does not even know what he is saying creates a firmament, then look at one who is not familiar with the secrets of the Torah: since he renews the Torah without having sufficient knowledge, all that he renews ascends, and the reverse side of man (male part of the impure force), and the false tongue (from *Nukva* of the impure force, called *Tehom Raba*—great abyss) comes toward him. This reversed man skips 500 *Parsaot* (measures of distance) to receive this renewal of the Torah, takes it and makes a false firmament out of it, called *Tohu* (abyss).**

As we already know, the righteous raise MAN to please the Creator. This is called the "words of the Torah," for the words are renewed as a result of the Upper *Zivug*, and ZON receive a new Light from this *Zivug*, to the extent that they come to merit the renewal of Heaven and earth by their actions. They thereby become the Creator's partners—fellow workers, for, just like Him, they renew Heaven and earth with their words.

Although one who is not familiar with the secrets of the Torah (the ways of the Creator) so as to know how to protect himself and to not harm the Higher Degrees tells himself that his intention is for the exalted goal, he deludes himself, for he does not know that which his soul surely knows—that his intentions are for himself. Terrible punishment awaits him, for he allows the impure forces to destroy those who labor in the Torah. *The Zohar* explains: if one does not know the exact meanings of the words, i.e., if he raises MAN to the great *Zivug* without a thorough understanding of all the intricate details of the act, the reverse man and the false tongue capture his word.

*Klipot* (one's impure forces) also consist of male and female parts. The male part is called "fruitless return," and the female part is called "falsehood." The male part of the *Klipa* is not as bad as the female part. And when it is by itself, it does not prompt one to lie by the Creator's name; on the contrary, goodness strikes his eye, yet the eye itself is evil. And he who falls into the hands of the male impure force uses the Creator's name in vain, for he detaches himself from the Creator and receives no Light from Him, i.e., he utters words and seemingly acts, but fruitlessly, for these actions are not the screen's interaction with the Light.

Hence, the sages said: "The Creator says of all who is proud: He and I cannot be together" (Talmud, *Suta*, 5:1), for his intentions are to receive everything for himself, for his own benefit, for his pride and vanity, as the sensation of one's "I" is the greatest manifestation of pride. Hence, man falls under the power of the evil eye. Consequently, the MAN that he raises receives no response from Above, and he utters the Creator's name in vain. Therefore, the male part of the impure force is called empty, fruitless, false, vain, unsuccessful, and futile, for the Creator cannot unite with him due to the dissimilarity of their properties.

If, however, one feels not his similarity to the Creator, but rather his oppositeness in properties from Him, and perceives himself as the most evil of all, he can then lower himself before the Creator, suppress all of his properties out of hatred for them, and the Creator Himself will perform the remaining part of his correction. However, one who is proud not only fails to understand the extent of his remoteness from the Creator, he actually believes that he is entitled to receive more than others, and that the Creator owes him something.

*Nukva de Klipa* is called "falsehood." After one falls into the net of the male part of the impure force, the latter makes a *Zivug* with its *Nukva* (impure, bitter, and evil force), which, as a result of its connection to the male part, falsifies the Creator's name, descends and instigates man, and then ascends, complaints against him, and takes his soul. However holy this soul was, *Nukva de Klipa* grabs all of it for itself.

Naturally, this refers to one who works on himself and advances spiritually, for whom working for the Creator's sake is his life's calling. Yet, he may occasionally fail to observe precisely all the restrictions, and thus find himself in such states. An ordinary person, however, who neither works on himself nor studies Kabbalah, is obviously entirely unrelated to either pure or impure spiritual forces.

For example, the male impure force says that one must study the Torah, but then steals the results of his work for itself. As a result, man loses interest in his studies, and must once more consolidate himself in his efforts and advancement. And although he attains the Creator and the revelation of Light to a certain degree, it is nonetheless fruitless, for all of his attainments vanish from him, and he gains nothing from them.

Therefore, the Torah refers to it as the "reverse man," for initially he ate and drank and said "Go," i.e., raise MAN to the Creator and receive the Light for the sake of the exalted goal, but not for yourself. Thus, it pretends that it is not the impure force, but its opposite. However, due to its property called "fruitless return," it then makes a *Zivug* with its *Nukva* (the great abyss), which steals man's soul and destroys him with its falsehood, and man is left without even the slightest part of his soul that is holy and pure!

Hence, it is written that he skips through 500 *Parsaot*: initially, ZON of the impure forces have only VAK in ZA and a point in *Malchut*. Consequently, they can only be equal to ZON *de Atzilut* in their *Katnut* (small state), when they are also VAK and a point, and have neither the power nor the place to connect to *Bina*.

Nevertheless, thanks to the MAN raised by the lower ones, the male impure force is given the opportunity to skip through ZAT *de Bina*, which sustain the pure and holy ZON. ZON contain *Sefirot* HGT NH (*Netzah-Hod*) = 5 x 100 = 500, since a *Sefira* in *Bina* equals 100. And this occurs thanks to the MAN raised by one who is uncertain of his intentions (whether or not he acts for the Creator's sake).

The "reverse man" then makes a *Zivug* with his *Nukva* on this false MAN, and receives the Upper Light for the construction of his *Partzuf*, much like the spiritually pure Heavens that were created on the pure MAN. Also, the new Heavens created on the impure MAN are called "reverse," "empty." And since the impure *Malchut* took part in this, these Heavens are called *Tohu* (abyss/chaos).

**69. And this reverse man then flies across the empty firmament, traversing 6,000 *Parsaot* in one bound. And as soon as this empty firmament stops, an impure woman emerges at once, seizes onto this empty firmament, and partakes in it. She leaves it and slays hundreds of thousands, for as long as she remains in this firmament, she has the authority and power to fly and traverse the whole world in an instant.**

All that stems from the empty firmament stems from the impure force, which is correspondingly opposite the Supernal, holy wisdom of *Ohr Hochma*. The *Sefira Hochma* equals 1,000, and so it is written that it flies across the firmament in 6,000 = six *Sefirot HGT NHY* of *Partzuf Hochma*, each of which equals 1,000.

After the new heavens of the impure male part, called the "empty heavens," were completed, the power of its female half, *Nukva* ("the great abyss"), was revealed. Her force attacked the firmament with falsehood by the Creator's name; she soared through the sky, and the heavens were then called *Tohu*.

Since *Nukva* of the impure forces partakes in this firmament, she becomes stronger and grows even more than the male level of the impure part. This is because the male impure part reaches up to *VAK* of *Hochma*, which equals 6,000 *Parsaot*, whereas *Nukva* grows to the full ten *Sefirot*, i.e., the entire world.

Therefore, she is immensely powerful and can destroy many, for, as Rashi says, "The Creator created one opposite the other." And just as new, Holy Heavens and lands are created thanks to the *MAN* raised by the righteous, new, impure heavens and lands are created through the *MAN* raised by those who do not know exactly how one should work for the Creator.

**70. It is written of it: "Do not facilitate fruitless transgression." Transgression is related to the male part, and is as heavy as wagon shafts. What is this transgression? It is the impure *Nukva*. With reins she draws the male impure part to fruitlessness. And then, as a result, a transgression is committed, as the male part draws itself towards this *Nukva*, who grows strong and flies off to slay people. And many does she slay. And who is it that caused all this? It is those that study the Torah, but do not attain *Ohrah* and *Morah* (Light and bestowal). May the Creator be merciful to them!**

As was already mentioned above, the male impure part is not as evil as the female part. This is so because it makes itself similar to the holy part of the creature; hence, it is called fruitless. However, due to this similarity, it has great power to ensnare man, as, for example, just as the sages do, it encourages people to study the Torah. Yet, its goals are different from that of the Creator; it wants to receive wisdom (*Hochma*), and not to become altruistic.

And after one is caught in its toils, the male impure force makes a *Zivug* with its impure *Nukva*, and, like heavy wagon shafts, they pull man into an abyss so great and dark that he doesn't even realize that he is in darkness. On the contrary, he considers himself wise and righteous. The male part only catches man, binds him, and then brings him to the impure *Nukva* and casts him at her feet. Only then does he falter, falls into the great abyss and perishes.

**71. Rabbi Shimon said to his friends: "I beg of you not to utter any discernments from the Torah, no matter what you may hear from the Great Tree of Truth, so that you would not assist the impure *Nukva* in slaying multitudes of people for naught." They all opened and mouthed: "Save us, O Merciful One! Save us, O Merciful One!"**

Rabbi Shimon said that if you have attained the discernment yourselves, then you are allowed, but if not, you must listen to the Great Tree (the great learned sage, whose wisdom and purity can be trusted) to learn how to work for the Creator.

**72. Come and see, the Creator created the world by the Torah. And He looked into the Torah not once, not twice, not thrice, and not four times. Only after that did He create the world. This should show people how not to err.**

**73. Opposite these four times, the Creator saw, counted, prepared, and investigated what He had created. It is therefore written, "*Beresheet* (In the beginning) *Barah* (created) *Elokim* (the Creator) *Et* (the)"—four words, corresponding to the four above. And then, it is written: "Heaven"—opposite all four words, for the Creator looked into the Torah before He began to manifest His thought into reality.**

The four words signify four time periods or four *Sefirot H-B-ZA-M*. "Saw" designates *Hochma*, "counted"—*Bina*, "prepared"—*ZA*, and "investigated"— *Malchut*. After these four, the Creator created what He created.

We find the same in the Torah: *Beresheet* is *Hochma*, *Barah* is *Bina*, *Elokim* is *ZA*, and *Et* (the) is *Malchut*, which includes everything from *Aleph* to *Tav*—all the letters and all the properties. Hence, she is designated in the Torah by the word *Et* = *Aleph-Tav* (from the first letter of the Hebrew alphabet, *Aleph*, to the last, *Tav*). And after these four, He created the Heavens and the earth, i.e., revealed the next, lower degree, below *Malchut*.

# THE DONKEY DRIVER

**74. Rabbi Elazar, the son of Rabbi Shimon, was on his way to visit his father-in-law, Rabbi Yosi, the son of Lakunya, and Rabbi Aba accompanied him. A man followed behind them, driving their donkeys. Rabbi Aba said, "Let us open the gates of the Torah, as it is time to correct our path."**

In Aramaic, the language in which *The Zohar* was written, "driver" means "one who pricks." This is because the donkey driver's function amounts to forcing the donkeys to move by pricking them with the edge of his stick.

**75. Rabbi Elazar opened and said, "It is written: My Sabbaths you are to observe." Let us see: the Creator created the world in six days. And each day would reveal His deeds, and gave strength to that day. When did He reveal His deeds and give them strength? On the fourth day of creation, for the first three days were concealed completely, and would not be revealed. The fourth day arrived, and He revealed the deeds and forces of all the days.**

The phrase "He gave that day strength" means that He gave everything to the day of *Shabbat*. For the six days are *Sefirot HGT NHY* that reveal on *Shabbat* (*Malchut*) the work and the forces that were carried out during these days.

Yet, if the deeds of all the days are concealed, and only reveal at their end, on *Shabbat*, then why is it written that they are revealed on the fourth day of creation? The thing is that *Malchut* is called both the fourth and the seventh days: she is fourth with regard to the first three *Sefirot HGT*, called the "Patriarchs" (*Hesed* is Avraham, *Gevura* is Yitzchak, and *Tifferet* is Yaakov), and seventh with regard to the six *Sefirot*, after three additional *Sefirot*, called the "Sons": *Netzah* is Moshe, *Hod* is Aaron, and *Yesod* is Yosef.

*Malchut* herself is King David—the day of *Shabbat*. *Malchut* grows and gradually accumulates her corrections in two principal stages, called *Ibur* (conception). The first three days correspond to *Ibur Aleph* (the first conception), and the

223

second three days correspond to *Ibur Bet* (the second conception, *Gadlut*, the reception of *Ohr Hochma*).

In other words, *Malchut* is gradually created from *Sefirot HGT* of ZA in three days, and forms on the fourth day as the *Sefira Netzah de* ZA. Hence, at this stage in her growth, *Malchut* is referred to as fourth from the Patriarchs. And then *Shabbat* comes to our land (*Malchut* is called both land/earth and *Shabbat*). The state that *Malchut* achieves as a result of her growth from *Sefirot NHY* of ZA is called *Shabbat* on earth. And this state she attains as the seventh *Sefira* from all the *Sefirot* of ZA.

The first three days are not revealed in *Malchut*, for as long as a *Partzuf* lacks *Malchut*, it is defined as concealed or secret. The weekdays are defined so. And when *Malchut* completely attains the degree where she stands, she thereby attains herself. This state is defined as *Shabbat*.

However, if *Malchut* receives from the six *Sefirot de* ZA, shouldn't they (the six weekdays) be more important than *Malchut-Shabbat* (inferior *Sefira* with regard to those she receives from)?

The truth is that all the weekdays constitute individual degrees of correction (weekdays' work) that are devoid of *Malchut*. Hence, they are called "weekdays," for a *Partzuf* without *Malchut* is considered a closed degree, unable to receive Light, and is therefore deprived of holiness. After all, in the absence of *Malchut*, there is no GAR of the Light, *Ohr Hochma*. And only when *Malchut* is revealed in the *Partzuf* (signifying the arrival of *Shabbat*) is the holiness of the ENTIRE degree revealed; ENTIRE, because all six days receive what they have earned, and the Light shines in all the weekdays thanks to them alone.

When the first three days of creation HGT emerged before the emergence of *Malchut*, these three *Sefirot* were devoid of Light, i.e., they were concealed. And when *Malchut* appeared, the fourth day arrived, and the importance and holiness of all four days manifested, for *Malchut* complements the entire degree, and the perfection of creation becomes revealed thanks to her. In the language of Kabbalah, this is described in the following way: all six days of creation are *Ohr Hochma*, and *Shabbat* is *Ohr Hassadim*. *Ohr Hochma* is present on weekdays, but cannot shine for lack of *Ohr Hassadim*, and when *Ohr Hassadim* arrives on *Shabbat*, all the *Ohr Hochma* shines thanks to this *Ohr Hassadim* of *Shabbat*.

**76. There is fire, water and air—HGT—the three first days of creation. Although they are the initial Supernal foundations of all that will follow, their actions are not revealed until the earth, meaning Malchut, reveals them. Only then does the work of each of the Supernal foundations reveal itself. Hence, the power of the first three days is revealed only on the fourth.**

77. However, the third day may be better described as one that reveals the creation of the first three days, as it is written: LET THE EARTH BRING FORTH GRASS. That is to say, the revelation of the earth's (*Malchut*'s) deeds already took place on the third day. Yet, although it was written on the third day, *Tifferet*, it was actually the fourth day, *Malchut*. *Malchut* joined the third day, for *Tifferet* and *Malchut* are inseparable. And then the fourth day revealed its deeds—to elucidate the work of each and every one of *HGT*, for the fourth day is the "fourth leg" of the Supernal Throne (the *Sefira Bina*), whose four legs are *HGTM* (*Hesed, Gevura, Tifferet,* and *Malchut*).

*Malchut* reveals the holiness and spiritual power of the three days. Therefore, *Malchut* ascended and joined the third day, so as to reveal by the unity of these three days (three lines) their exalted spiritual essence.

It is hence written that the deed is revealed on the fourth day, for *Malchut* alone completes their revelation at the conclusion of the three days. And afterwards, three more days emerge, which are *NHY*. After the revelation of the holiness of the first three days, *HGT*, called the "Patriarchs," which are the foundation of ZA, ZA enters them (his main part is manifested), and the time comes for the Sons (*NHY*, the last three of the six days of creation) to be born.

This is why it is written that ZA is defined as the fourth leg of the throne of *Bina*, and the throne remains imperfect and incomplete until its fourth leg (foundation) manifests. Indeed, ZA is incomplete until *Malchut* manifests within him, i.e., until the fourth day arrives. And only after the emergence of *Malchut* can ZA father the Sons—the three final days of creation.

78. All of the actions of all the *Sefirot*, both on the first three days of creation, *HGT*, and on the last three, *NHY*, are dependent on the day of *Shabbat*, *Malchut*, *GAR* of the entire degree of ZA and its perfection. Hence, it is written, AND THE CREATOR RESTED ON THE SEVENTH DAY, SHABBAT. This refers to the fourth leg of the throne, as the seventh and the fourth days are both *Malchut*. Only the fourth day is *Malchut* that includes the *Sefira Tifferet* of ZA, from his chest upwards. Also, the seventh day is *Malchut* of the entire ZA, and they merge together face to face in a *Zivug*.

Although the first three days, *HGT*, end with the fourth day (the result of their actions), they nonetheless remain not entirely complete; their perfection manifests only on *Shabbat*, together with the last three days, *NHY*.

It is therefore written that *Shabbat* is the fourth leg of the throne, even though it is the seventh day, for, although it emerges after the Sons, it also completes the deeds of the Patriarchs, as the first three days did not complete their corrections on the fourth day, and a seventh day, *Shabbat*, is needed to complete them.

The reason for this is that on the fourth day, *Malchut* is in the state of *Katnut*, called the small phase of the Moon. As a result, the Moon (*Malchut*) returns to the state called *Shabbat*, when all the Light of all the days of creation manifest and shine within her. This is why the Light of the first three days of creation becomes revealed only on *Shabbat*.

**79. Yet, if *Shabbat* is *Malchut*, then why does the Torah say, "My Sabbaths you are to observe," implying two? It is written of the two parts of *Shabbat*: the night (*Malchut*) and the day (ZA) that shines in *Malchut*. Thus, there is no division between them, for they merge face to face in a *Zivug*, and are therefore called two Sabbaths.**

He asks: two *Malchuyot* (plural for *Malchut*) of the fourth and the seventh days are completely separate, as is written, "You shall keep my Sabbaths," implying two? Yet, when we clarify that the fourth day manifests in perfection only on the seventh day, it becomes clear that there is only one *Shabbat*. But what is meant here is ZA and *Malchut* that shine in the holiness of *Shabbat*, for this day is the male, bestowing part (*Zachar*) that manifests in the female part (*Malchut* or *Nukva*). Hence, they are called Sabbaths (plural). However, by merging in perfection, they become a single whole. As a result, ZA also assumes the name of *Shabbat*.

**80. Following behind them with the donkeys, the donkey driver asked: "Why is it said, 'You shall fear sanctity?'" They replied: "This refers to the sanctity of *Shabbat*." The donkey driver asked: "What is the sanctity of *Shabbat*?" They replied: "It is the sanctity that descends from Above, from AVI." He said to them, "If that is so, then *Shabbatot* (plural for *Shabbat*) are without sanctity, for sanctity descends on it from Above, from AVI." Rabbi Aba answered him: "It is indeed so." And it is said: "And call *Shabbat* a delight, a holy day dedicated to the Creator." *Shabbat* and a holy day are mentioned separately. The donkey driver asked: "If that is so, then what does a holy day mean to the Creator?" He replied: "That is when sanctity descends from Above, from ZA, and fills *Shabbat*, *Malchut*." The donkey driver objected, "But if sanctity descends from Above, then *Shabbat* itself is not a holy day. And yet, it is written, 'You shall sanctify *Shabbat*,' meaning *Shabbat* itself." Rabbi Elazar said to Rabbi Aba, "Leave this man alone, for there is much wisdom in him, of which we do not know." So he said to the donkey driver, "Speak, and we shall listen."**

The donkey driver's question is this: if *Shabbat* is ZA, then why is it described as holy? After all, sanctity is the property of *AVI*, and only *AVI* are called holy.

Hence, he objected that *Shabbat* should be separated from sanctity. *Shabbat* (ZA) is not holiness in itself, but because it receives holiness from Above, from *AVI*. That, which ZA receives from *AVI* is what is called the Creator's holiness.

**81. The donkey driver opened and said, "It is written: *Shabbatot*, i.e., there are usually two. And this alludes to the border of *Shabbat*, which is 2,000 *Amah* (cubits) in each direction from the city. This is why the word *Et* was added before the word *Shabbatot*, which designates the plural form—both the Upper *Shabbat* and the lower *Shabbat* joining into one."**

Although it is said: "Man shall not leave his place on the seventh day" (*Shemot*, 16), i.e., the singular form is used, in many places in the Torah, the word *Et* is used; for example, in the sentence: "**Et** 2,000 *Amah* in each direction from its place." The word *Et*, consisting of the first and the last letters of the alphabet, *Aleph* and *Tav*, designates *Malchut* entering into union with ZA, which signifies the state of *Shabbat*; hence, the Light of *AVI* becomes revealed and shines (as a supplementary luminescence) upon ZON. This is because *AVI* are called "two thousand," and so the word *Et* is present here to designate a supplement of Light to *Shabbat*.

There exist a *Shabbat* Above and a *Shabbat* below: the Upper *Shabbat* is *Partzuf Tvuna*, and the lower part of *Partzuf Bina*, whereas the lower *Shabbat* is *Partzuf Malchut*, *Nukva de ZA* of the world of *Atzilut*. In the world of *Atzilut*, *Partzuf Bina* is divided into two *Partzufim*: the Upper Part of *Bina* is called *Partzuf AVI* and the lower part of *Bina* (the part where she receives the Light from the Upper Part so as to pass it to ZA) is called *Partzuf YESHSUT* (*Israel Saba ve Tvuna*) or simply *Tvuna*. The relationship between *Bina-AVI* and *Tvuna* is similar to that of ZA and *Malchut*. *Bina* is called the "Upper World" and *Malchut* is called the "lower world." On *Shabbat*, ZON ascend to *Bina*, ZA to *AVI*, and *Malchut* to *Tvuna*.

On *Shabbat*, *Malchut* merges with *Tvuna*. However, this does not mean that no difference is left between them, for *Malchut* receives the Light from *Tvuna* only because she ascends to *Tvuna*'s level. Yet, at her place on the last, lowest degree of the world of *Atzilut*, *Malchut* is unable to receive the Light from *Tvuna*. And to the extent that *Malchut* cannot yet receive the Light from *Tvuna* in her regular state, she is defined as "closed."

Also, *Tvuna* suffers from *Malchut* being closed because while in her place, *Malchut* cannot receive the Light from *Tvuna*, for the revelation of *Tvuna* is possible only through *Malchut*. On *Shabbat*, *Tvuna* and *Ima* join to form one *Partzuf*, which is not closed. Yet, since its Light shines only when *Malchut* ascends to it, *Tvuna* feels the closed state of *Malchut*, and suffers, too.

82. One *Shabbat* was left, unmentioned Above, and felt ashamed. She said to Him, "The Creator of the universe, from the day I was created, I am called *Shabbat*, but there is no day without night." The Creator replied to her: "My daughter, you are *Shabbat*, and I have given you this name. But now I am surrounding and adorning you with the most exalted adornment." He then raised His voice and proclaimed, "Those who sanctify shall fear. And this is the night of *Shabbat* that radiates fear." But who is she? It is the merging together of I (*Malchut*, the nights of *Shabbat*) with the Creator Himself (*ZA*) into a single whole. And I've heard from my father that the word *Et* refers to the boundaries-borders of *Shabbat*. *Shabbatot* (two Sabbaths) denote a circle and a square within, which total two. According to them, there are two sanctities we should mention during the *Shabbat* blessing: *Vayechulu* consists of thirty-five words, and *Kiddush*, too, consists of thirty-five words. Collectively, they make up to the seventy names of *ZA*, with which *ZA* (the Creator), and *Malchut* (the Assembly of Israel) adorn themselves.

83. Since the circle and square are *Shabbatot*, they are both included in the instruction, "My *Shabbatot* you are to observe." However, the Upper *Shabbat* is not included in the instruction "Observe," but rather in "Remember." For the Supernal King, *Bina* is as perfect as memory. This is why *Bina* is called "King," whose perfection lies in peace and in memory. Hence, there is no contradiction Above.

*Malchut de Malchut* is called the central point of creation, and receives no Light even on *Shabbat*, as, being a *Man'ula* (lock), she is closed to the Light. And the entire Light enters her only in the form of *Miftacha* (key), into *Yesod de Malchut*, in *Malchut* that joins *Bina* with her properties, while *Malchut* herself is therefore referred to as "locked."

This central point of creation is the only thing that the Creator created, and is comprised of all the creatures, including human souls. And she argues with the Creator that in the beginning of creation, in the world of *AK*, the entire Light was revealed and shone upon the creatures thanks to her, for there was no other *Malchut* in the world of *AK*, except for the central point. And only due to *Tzimtzum Bet* (second restriction), now in the world of *Atzilut*, was she restricted and closed to the reception of Light.

And this is a great and wonderful secret, for, as *Malchut* objects, even on the first day, it is said: "And there shall be evening, and there shall be morning—one day." (*Beresheet*, 1:6) In other words, unity is revealed in both night and day together. Yet, why is the night of the first *Shabbat* not mentioned in the

Torah, and only the words "on the seventh day" are used? The Creator replied to *Malchut* that a future *Shabbat* is implied—*Shabbat* of the seventh millennium, when the day of *Shabbat* will come and remain forever.

Meanwhile, during the 6,000 years, the Creator elevates *Malchut* to *Bina*, and as a result, she receives Supernal Adornments, greater than the ones she had had in the world of *AK*. For there she acted as the end of all *Sefirot*, but now she has risen to act in the place of *GAR*, in *AVI*, which are called "holy of holies."

If *Malchut* is in *Yesod*, the lack of *Ohr Hochma* is felt. But if *Malchut* ascends to *AVI* (where *Ohr Hassadim* is present, and there is absolutely no need for *Ohr Hochma*), this state is defined as perfect.

*Malchut* is called "fear," for she was restricted to refrain from receiving the Creator's Light within her desire to receive pleasure. Therefore, she does not receive the Light from Above within her desire to receive pleasure. Instead, she receives the Light only in *Ohr Hozer* (Reflected Light), when she refuses to use her egoism.

This occurs in the following way: first, *Ohr Yashar* (Direct Light) comes from the Creator to *Malchut* and wishes to enter her (*Malchut* feels both the delight and her own desire to receive and enjoy it). Secondly, by wishing to be like the Creator, *Malchut* repels the Light (prohibits herself from receiving the delight).

This renunciation of egoistic pleasure is called *Ohr Hozer* (Reflected Light), because *Malchut* repels the Light (pleasure) from her. Thirdly, after *Malchut* has created *Ohr Hozer*, she begins to receive *Ohr Yashar* in it (her new desire to receive only because the Creator wants her to). This reception is possible because *Malchut* has an anti-egoistic force, will power, called a screen.

The spiritual world is a realm of sensations, desires, and forces, not vested in shells-garments, like the corporeal bodies in our world. Similarly, all the characters depicted in Kabbalah do not designate any images; rather, they demonstrate interactions of forces and properties.

Therefore, a circle implies that the Light shines completely unrestrictedly in every place and to the same extent, so there can be no change in its radiance. A square or a rectangle indicates restrictions, which create differences between the sides: right and left, top and bottom. Hence, the head has a round shape with regard to the rectangular shape of the body, for the *Rosh* (head) is free of restrictions, but *VAK* (body) are not.

*Shabbat* is a spiritual state, when ZON ascend to *AVI* and clothe them. As a result, the lower *Shabbat* (ZON) and the Upper *Shabbat* (AVI) merge into one.

The Upper *Shabbat* (AVI) is designated by a circle, and the lower *Shabbat* (ZON) is designated by a square. On *Shabbat*, ZON merge with AVI, depicted as the square's ascent and insertion into the circle.

*Ohr Hochma* is designated by the letter *Ayin*. Since *Ohr Hochma* is revealed only during the ascent of the lower *Shabbat* to the Upper, *Ohr Hochma* is divided into two parts: one half for the Upper *Shabbat*, and one for the lower. Hence, the passage of *Vayechulu* (*Beresheet*, 2:1) consists of thirty-five words that refer to half of the Light of the Upper *Shabbat*, whereas the blessing itself consists of thirty-five words that refer to half of the Light of the lower *Shabbat*. And the common soul, called the "Assembly of Israel" or *Malchut* (*Shabbat*), is adorned with this Light.

Since the circle and the square merge and assume the name *Shabbatot* (two *Shabbats*), the Light of both the circle and the square is defined as protecting— GUARD. And, although the word GUARD alludes to restrictions and borders that one must observe and fear violating, whereas the Upper *Shabbat* (designated by a circle) has no restrictions and borders, due to the joining of the two *Shabbatot* into one, there still appeared restrictions and borders.

The Upper *Shabbat* is called REMEMBER, and not OBSERVE, as it is completely free of restrictions. However, since it merged with the lower *Shabbat*, called OBSERVE, it, too, needs to GUARD, which normally relates to *Malchut* alone. Only due to *Malchut's* ascent to *Bina* did the need to guard, which is present in *Malchut*, arose in *Bina*. But *Bina* herself remains only in the property of REMEMBER, for only egoistic desires to receive pleasure need GUARDING.

The Upper *Shabbat* (*Bina*) is designated by the letters MI = *Mem-Yod*. The lower *Shabbat* (*Malchut*) is designated by the letters MA = *Mem-Hey*, and has the form of a square, which implies a presence of controversy between its properties— the right and the left sides, which give it its square form.

**84. There are two types of peace below: one is Yaakov (*Tifferet*), and the other is Yosef (*Yesod*). Therefore, PEACE is written twice in the greeting: "PEACE, PEACE to the distant one and to the near one." "The distant one" refers to Yaakov, and "the near one" refers to Yosef. Or, as it is written, "From afar I see the Creator," "Came to a stop far in the distance."**

"Below" signifies ZON, containing one of the properties, Yaakov or the *Sefira Tifferet de* ZA. ZON also contain the property called Yosef, or *Yesod*. Both these *Sefirot* indicate the place of a potential *Zivug* between ZA and *Malchut*, for Peace signifies *Zivug*. The Upper *Zivug* (Yaakov) is intended for reception of *Ohr Hochma* from Above, and the lower *Zivug* (Yosef) fills *Malchut* only with *Ohr Hassadim*.

It was already mentioned that it is impossible to receive *Ohr Hochma* without it being clothed in *Ohr Hassadim*. *Ohr Hochma* or the *Zivug* that is made on it is therefore defined as distant, for it must first be clothed in *Ohr Hassadim* before it can receive *Ohr Hochma*. Hence, it is written, "From afar I saw the Creator."

The lower *Zivug* is called "the near one," because the *Partzuf* receives *Ohr Hassadim* without any preliminary actions. Furthermore, with the help of this *Ohr Hassadim*, the *Partzuf* subsequently receives *Ohr Hochma*. This is why the word "peace" is used twice: "Peace, peace to the far and to the near"—a greeting to Yaakov and Yosef, respectively, both of whom take part in the great *Zivug* (the reception of *Ohr Hochma*) in ZA.

These two greetings are defined in ZON as a square, as there is controversy between them, defined as the controversy between the right and the left sides, and they end in the letter *Hey*—*Nukva* or *Malchut*, whereas the Upper *Nukva* (*Bina*) ends with the letter *Yod*, which designates not the female part, but the male. Hence, there is no controversy in her.

Even the notions of "near" and "far" do not exist in *Bina* herself, for she refers to GAR, perfection, and GAR can receive *Ohr Hochma* nearby, meaning they do not need to clothe in *Ohr Hassadim* beforehand, but can receive *Ohr Hochma* without *Ohr Hassadim*. Hence, it is said that the Upper *Malchut* is the King, who has peace. Thus, unlike ZON, two notions of peace are absent in him.

**85. "From afar" is the Supernal Point, standing in His palace, of which it is said, "You are to guard." "You shall fear My sanctity" refers to the point standing in the center, which must be feared more than anything, for its punishment is death, as it is written, "All who transgress in it shall perish." Who are these transgressors? They are those who have entered the space of the circle and the square, and committed a sin. Hence, it is written, "You shall fear!" This point is called "I," and there is a prohibition on its revelation, called *HaVaYaH*. "I" and *HaVaYaH* are a single whole. Rabbi Elazar and Rabbi Aba dismounted from their donkeys and kissed him. They said, "So great is your wisdom, and yet you drive donkeys behind us! Who are you, then?" He replied to them: "Do not ask me who I am, but let us go on and study the Torah. Each of us will speak his wisdom so as to illuminate our path."**

The distant point refers to the point that opens the way to the *Partzuf* for thirty-two streams of *Ohr Hochma*. And this is the letter *Bet* in the first word of the Torah—*Beresheet*, called the "point in the hall," from which *Ohr Hochma* descends to ZON, when ZON ascend to *AVI*. For then, the two *Shabbatot* (the

Upper—AVI and the lower—ZON) merge. It is written about them: "I saw the Creator from afar," for ZON cannot receive *Ohr Hochma* without being clothed in *Ohr Hassadim*.

*Hochma* and *Bina*, called the "point in the hall," are referred to as "distant from ZON," for they need the garment of *Ohr Hassadim* from the lower world, *Nukva*, called MA. *Malchut* of the world of AK is the central point, called the "lock," whereas *Malchut* of the world of *Atzilut* (the point in the hall) is the "key," as the Light from ZAT *de Bina* (YESHSUT) can be received in it.

The circle is called *AVI*, the square—ZON. ZON ascend to *AVI* and thus the square enters the circle. As a result, two properties appear in *Malchut* of *AVI*: the "lock" (*Malchut de Malchut*, the central point or *Malchut de AVI*), and the "key" (the point in the hall, *Yesod de Malchut* or *Malchut de YESHSUT*). *Malchut de AVI* is called space, for she is unattainable, and he who wishes to fill her with Light is punished by death. It is written about it: "You shall fear My sanctity."

The point itself is called "I," and *AVI* is *HaVaYaH* that merges with it. And they are defined as a single whole; hence, the point itself is referred to as *AVI*, meaning that it is characterized as holy, as the property of *AVI*.

As was already mentioned before, *The Zohar* and the entire Torah speak exclusively of spiritual degrees, the structure of spiritual worlds, and the revelation of the Creator's governance to us. There is not a word in the Torah that refers to our world. The whole Torah is, as it is said, "The Creator's sacred names." And those who reduce it from its spiritual heights to the corporeal level with their commentaries cast it down completely.

Rashi says that the Torah only speaks in human tongue, but it tells us of man's spiritual paths toward his Creator. Therefore, when we read that one Rabbi went to visit another, the real meaning is that one spiritual degree, called, for example, Rabbi Elazar, passes to another spiritual degree, called, for example, Rabbi Yosi.

ZA has his own *AVI*, who are called the Upper *AVI*. The wife of ZA (*Nukva* or *Malchut*) contains *AVI*, too, called *YESHSUT*. First, ZA attains the *AVI* of his wife (*YESHSUT* or *Ohr Hassadim*). Then it rises to a Higher Degree and attains the *AVI* themselves—*Ohr Hochma* (also called *Ohr Haya*).

The righteous who ascend the spiritual degrees are the constituents of *Partzuf* ZA. Since the degree of Rabbi Elazar and Rabbi Aba is *Ohr Hassadim* (the Light of *Neshama*), this ascent means it went to (spiritually) see (in *Ohr Hochma*) another spiritual degree.

In the spiritual worlds, the donkey driver constitutes a special spiritual force that helps the souls of the righteous move from one spiritual degree to another. Without this help sent by the Creator from Above, it is impossible to exit your degree and ascend to the next. Hence, the Creator sends a Higher soul from Above to each of the righteous (those who wish to ascend). Each receives his own, according to his degree, properties, and purpose.

And so, at first the righteous fails to recognize this exalted soul; he considers it low, that it leeched onto him on his spiritual path. Such state is called *Ibur*—conception of the righteous' soul. Since the Higher soul has not yet completed its assistance and purpose, it is not yet perceived by the righteous for what it really is.

However, after it completes its task in its entirety, and brings the righteous' soul to the Upper Degree for which it is intended, the righteous then reveals the exalted properties of the soul that helped him. This is referred to as the revelation of the soul to the righteous.

In our case, the soul that was sent to help the souls of Rabbi Elazar and Rabbi Aba was the soul of Rabbi Hamnuna-Saba—a very exalted and perfect soul, the Light of *Yechida*. Yet, initially, it is revealed to the righteous in its smallest scope, called *Ibur*, conception (in sensations). Hence, they perceive it as the level of a spiritual donkey driver—a simple soul.

The Hebrew word for donkey is *Hamor*, which also means matter, *Homer*! Thus, one who can control his donkey, his body, his desires, ascends above matter as a spiritual being. And since he wishes to ascend above matter in his desires, he is considered a righteous. However, here, *The Zohar* speaks of Higher Degrees.

The donkey driver's task is to take the riders, mounted atop of their donkeys, from place to place; yet, he walks in front of his donkeys, thereby leading them through spiritual degrees. Since every word in the Torah has several meanings, due to the multiplicity of the Upper Roots (wherefrom word notions descend), the notion of a "donkey driver" is more precisely referred to as a "donkey guide," and implies properties that are coarse, sinful, and most base.

Therefore, Rabbi Aba said: "Let us open the gates of the Torah, for the time has come for us to correct our path," that is, to open their souls with the help of the secrets of the Torah, so their path would be correct and lead them to the Creator. Rabbi Elazar then began to discuss a passage from the Torah that says, "You shall observe my *Shabbatot*," as he stood at this degree (the Light of *YESHSUT*) in his properties. He therefore concluded that *Shabbat* itself is the property of ZON, which has not yet reached the property of sanctity, but only receives the Light of YESHSUT on Shabbat. It is written about this Light, "You shall fear my sanctity," for when Ohr Hochma passes from YESHSUT to ZA, it evokes fear in them.

And here they receive the donkey driver's help, who reveals to them the secret of Ohr Haya. He explains that the phrase "You shall observe my Shabbatot" signifies the Upper and the lower Shabbatot, which come together, due to the ascent of ZON to AVI. As a result, ZON themselves become holy (the square within the circle) and acquire the properties of Bina: mercy, altruism, Ohr Hassadim. Hence, it is written with regard to them: fear not and observe. For Ohr Haya repels foreign, impure forces and desires, and all restrictions are lifted on Shabbat; hence, there is no fear.

And, according to the donkey driver's explanation, the phrase "You shall fear My sanctity" refers only to the central point that is used in GAR de AVI, in GAR of Ohr Haya, which is unattainable and where fear does exist.

At that, the soul of the donkey driver has fulfilled its role, for it brought them to the attainment of Ohr Haya. Only then did they merit the attainment of the height of the soul that had helped them, since they attained its revelation and were thus able to appreciate it.

This is why Rabbi Elazar and Rabbi Aba dismounted from their donkeys and kissed him, for the attainment of the Upper One is defined as a "kiss." However, this exalted soul has not yet finished aiding them: it must still help them attain Ohr Yechida. Yet, since the attainment of Ohr Haya already provides perfection, they've already attained thereby the degree of the son of Rabbi Hamnuna-Saba.

The level of Rabbi Hamnuna-Saba himself is the degree of attainment of Ohr Yechida. Therefore, by attaining only Ohr Haya, they mistakenly thought that the soul guiding them belongs to the son of Rabbi Hamnuna-Saba. However, after the donkey driver had revealed to them the secret of the attainment of Ohr Yechida, they realized that their companion is none other than Rabbi Hamnuna-Saba himself.

And the reason why they could not recognize him before is that the powers of the helping soul cannot be seen until its role is fulfilled. Hence, they asked him to reveal his name, but he told them not to inquire about his name, for without having completed all the corrections, they do not merit the revelation of the secrets of the Torah. And he must help them in their studies of the Torah, for he still needs to illuminate their path, as they have not yet attained the desired goal.

86. He said to him: "Who appointed you to walk here and be a donkey driver?" He replied: "The letter **Yod** waged war with two letters, **Chaf** and **Samech**, for me to come and join. The letter **Chaf** did not want to leave its place because it has to support those who fall, for without a screen, they cannot survive."

87. The letter **Yod** came to me alone, kissed me and wept with me. It said to me, "My son, what can I do for you? I disappear from many good deeds and from secret, supernal, basic letters. But I shall return to you and will be of help to you. And I shall give you two letters that are more exalted than those that have disappeared—the letters **Yod** and **Shin**. They shall become for you a treasury that is forever full. So, my son, go and drive the donkeys. And that is why I am here in this role."

As we already know, the donkey driver is an auxiliary force given to someone who wishes to ascend to a higher spiritual degree on his path toward the Creator, just as donkeys carry people on their backs, thereby helping them travel from one place to another. As this happens, the righteous one falls from his previous degree and enters the embryonic state of the new degree, just as the soul that came to help him. However, the property of *Ibur*-embryo (*Ibur* is also derived from the word *Haavarah*, crossing) means that all the Light that it had in the previous degree disappears upon the conception (*Ibur*) of a new, Higher Degree.

And that is what they wanted to know of the donkey driver: "How did the Creator bring you here in the state of *Ibur*, in our state of *Ibur*, as a result of which the Light in us has disappeared? Who lowers you from the Higher Degrees?" And that is why the donkey driver replied that the letter *Yod* waged war against the letters *Chaf* and *Samech*, to join with them. The degree of *Hassadim* is called *Samech* (*Ohr Neshama*).

"When the time has come for you to attain *Ohr Haya* (*Yod* from *HaVaYaH*, the degree from which I descended to help you to attain *Ohr Haya*), *Hochma* really wanted to connect *Ohr Neshama* (that was previously in you) to me. And here *Yod* wages war against *Chaf* and *Samech*. *Malchut* of the Upper *Partzuf* clothes in the lower *Partzuf*, designated by the letter *Chaf*. There used to be *Ohr Neshama*, and now there is *Ohr Haya*, whereas *Yod*, which desires *Ohr Neshama* as well, merges with it, and rejects the *Chaf*."

This is so because the connection between the degrees, from the Highest Degree in the world of *Atzilut* to the end of the world of *Assiya*, is realized only by *Malchut* of the Upper One descending to the lower one and clothing in it. *Malchut* of the Upper One herself cannot descend from her degree of *YESHSUT* (the degree of *Neshama*) even for a moment, as the chain connecting the degrees would be instantly broken.

The property of *Samech* is the property of the Light itself, which the soul receives from *Sefirot HBD HGT* of *AVI* (above the *Chazeh*), and which *AVI* pass to *ZON* when the letters are in *Katnut*, and support them (the Hebrew word for support is *Somech*, derived from the letter *Samech*) so that *ZON* will not fall from the world of *Atzilut*.

The letter *Chaf*, *Hassadim*, is unwilling to leave its place and join *Hochma*, as it needs to connect the Upper *Partzuf* to the lower one. Thus, it must always remain in its place, for all the degrees are constant, and only the soul changes while moving from one degree to another within the worlds. This is why the soul is called the "inner part" with regard to the world (the external part)—the soul exists and moves about within the world by changing its properties.

Hence, the Light of the soul did not wish to join the letter *Yod* (degree of *Hochma*, the soul of Rabbi Hamnuna-Saba) as it descended to help Rabbi Elazar and Rabbi Aba. This is because they needed a new Light that would build a new degree within them, the degree of *Ohr Haya*, whereas each new degree is built from scratch, from the state of *Ibur* (conception). As that happens, the entire previous degree with all of its Light disappears. Similarly, in their case, the new degree starts with *Ibur* and reaches the level of *Haya*. This resembles a seed that must first abandon its present form and rot, in order to become a tree afterwards.

It is therefore written that it came to me without the Light of *HBD HGT de AVI*, called *Samech*, the Light of *Hassadim*. *Samech* is the property of mercy, a selfless desire to give, pure spiritual altruism. Hence, it is unwilling to join *Yod*, *Ohr Hochma*. Yet, *Ohr Hochma* cannot enter and fill the *Partzuf* without first being clothed in *Ohr Hassadim*, for this clothing of *Ohr Hochma* in *Ohr Hassadim* means that the *Partzuf* receives *Ohr Hochma* not for itself, but for the Creator's sake. But *Ohr Hassadim*, *Samech*, does not wish to receive anything within itself; it wants nothing to do with *Ohr Hochma*! This is why the letter *Yod* wept, being unable to fill the *Partzuf* with its Light, for *Hassadim* refused to accept *Hochma*.

It is written in this regard: Hence, I must now disappear, and you, the donkey driver, go to the state of *Ibur*, to rebuild the degrees of gradual development of a new *Partzuf*-state with you: *Ibur* (embryo), *Leidah* (birth), *Yenika* (nursing), and *Mochin* (maturity).

And know that such is the order of creating (begetting) each new degree: every time one is to attain a new degree, he must undergo (in his properties) a complete disappearance of the previous degree (level of attainment, Light), and begin anew. He must receive new attainments, from the lowest new degree, *Ohr Nefesh* (*Ibur*), to *Ohr Ruach* (*Yenika*), and so on, as though he had never attained any spiritual level at all.

It is impossible to take with you anything from a previous degree. Hence, one must start anew from the lowest level of *Ibur*, called THE DONKEY DRIVER. *Ohr Haya de AVI* is called YESH (*Yod-Shin*), where *Yod* is *Hochma* and *Shin* is *Bina*. And, of course, they are more important than the *Ohr Neshama* that was in the *Partzuf* before them.

**88. Rabbi Elazar and Rabbi Aba rejoiced, wept, and said, "You sit on the donkey, and we shall drive it." He replied to them, "Have I not told you that it is the command of the King that I act as I do, until the other donkey driver appears" (this hints at the *Mashiach*, who, as it is said, will appear poor and riding a donkey). They said to him, "You have not even told us your name! Where do you dwell?" He told them, "My dwelling place is wonderful and very precious to me. It is a tower that soars in the air, grand and unique. Only two live in this tower: the Creator and I. That is the place, in which I dwell. And I am exiled from there in order to drive the donkeys." Rabbi Elazar and Rabbi Aba looked at him, and his words were unclear to them, for they tasted sweeter than manna and honey. They said to him, "Perhaps you will tell us the name of your father, so that we could kiss the earth at his feet?" He responded, "What for? It is not my habit to boast of the Torah."**

After they have attained the greatness of the donkey driver's degree, they could no longer bear his small state of *Ibur*, which he inhabited for their sake. Hence, they told him that since they have already attained *Ohr Hochma*, he has done enough and can leave the state of *Ibur*. And should a need arise to add anything else to them, they would be able to enter *Ibur* on their own, and he does not need to suffer for their sake.

However, the donkey driver warned them beforehand to not ask him his name, for they still require revelations of secrets of the Torah. Once again, he hinted that it is the degree of *Ohr Yechida* that they lack, which is implied here. This degree signifies the reception of the Light of the King Messiah's face, which he mentioned by hinting at the poor donkey driver, as described by a prophet (*Zachariah*, 9:9). And he is commanded by the Creator to help them attain *Ohr Yechida*.

This is why they asked him about the type of his soul: "For you did not wish to reveal your name, as we have not yet received from you that which we must attain. But if so, at least tell us where you live, what is your degree? At least then we will know what we lack, what else we must receive, attain from you."

He replied that his place is much higher than his present location, for now he himself cannot attain his own individual level. This is a result of the Upper *Partzuf* descending to the place of the lower one and becoming completely identical to it, and while there (in that state), the Upper *Partzuf* can no longer attain its own level. The tower that soars in the air is *Bina, Hassadim*. The *Mashiach*'s tower (the great tower) designates the time (state) of ascent to *GAR de AA*, when *Ohr Hochma* is available.

**89. But the place of my father's dwelling was in the Great Sea. And he was a big fish that continually circled the Great Sea, from one end to the other. And he was mighty and he grew old, until he swallowed up all the other fish in that sea. And then he released them, and they were thriving and filled with all of the very best of the world. And it was in his power to swim across the entire sea in one instant. And He pulled him out and hauled him in with an arrow, like a warrior, and brought him to the place that I told you about, to the tower that soars in the air, but he returned to his place and disappeared in that sea.**

The concealed *Zivug* is called *Shaar HaNun* (the 50th gate). The Great Sea is *Malchut*. All the *Zivugim* from *Partzuf Atik de Atzilut* and below do not include the Great Sea in its entirety, all the *Sefirot* of *Malchut*, but only the first nine *Sefirot* of *Malchut*. Moreover, none of the *Zivugim* include *Malchut de Malchut*.

This *Sefira, Malchut de Malchut*, is the only creation, because all the other *Sefirot* constitute properties of spiritual forces and desires above *Malchut*, existing in and referring to the Creator, the sole purpose of which is the correction of *Malchut de Malchut*. The only *Zivug* on this *Malchut* exists in *Atik*, and it will be revealed to all only at the end of correction.

Rav Hamnuna-Saba emerged from this concealed *Zivug* in *Atik*; hence, the donkey driver calls him "my father." And he says that his father lived in the Great Sea, as this *Zivug* was on the entire *Malchut*, on *Malchut de Malchut*, called the "Great Sea."

Yet, if one were to argue that all *Partzufim* make a *Zivug* on the Light with a screen that stands before *Malchut*, then that *Zivug* was made on the 50th gate, on all the parts of the desire, on the full depth of the Great Sea (*Malchut*), down to the very last of her desires and properties, from *Keter de Malchut* to *Malchut de Malchut*, from end to end of the Great Sea. Nevertheless, this occurs only

In *Partzuf Atik de Atzilut*, but not below it. And this is not the donkey driver himself, but his father.

This occurs because the great *Zivug* absorbs all the other particular *Zivugim* ("swallows all the other fish in the Great Sea") and all the souls in all the worlds, for they are all much weaker than it. Hence, it is as though they do not exist in its greatness and might. And since it includes absolutely everything, they are all called by the name *Nunin*, from the letter *Nun* (50).

This indicates that after all the major corrections that follow this great *Zivug*, all those Lights and souls, absorbed during its *Zivug*, return and are born anew for eternal life, for they are completely filled with Light as a result of the great *Zivug*, when the Light absorbed them completely.

All the *Zivugim* below *Partzuf Atik* stem from unifications of the *Sefirot* with one another. These unifications are defined as interruptions in a *Zivug*, whereas the *Zivug* in *Atik* is direct and without unification. Thus, it is defined as "instant," for it goes on uninterrupted. It is therefore written that "he crosses the entire sea in an instant," without any garments-unifications. And it mounts an attack, for there is great power of reception of *Ohr Hochma* in this *Zivug*; hence, he said: "Begets, like an arrow in the hands of a warrior."

It is written of this *Zivug* in *Partzuf Atik*: "No one else but you saw the Creator." However, no birth is possible without the forces of resistance, since, as is written: "The seed that is not shot like an arrow does not beget." (Talmud, *Hagigah*, 16). Hence, after he had begotten me and hid me in the Great Tower, he returned to his concealed *Zivug*.

**90. Rabbi Elazar contemplated his words and replied: "You are the son of the Holy Source, you are the son of Rabbi Hamnuna-Saba, you are the son of the Source of the Torah, and you drive donkeys behind us!" They wept and kissed him, and continued their journey. Then he said: "If it pleases our master, let him reveal his name to us."**

It is written "looked," because sight signifies *Hochma*, and no other words, such as "said," "heard" (*Bina*) or "thought" could be used in its stead. Since they have not yet attained to the full extent of perfection what the donkey driver had told them, and their attainment reached only as high as *Ohr Haya*, they were delighted with what was begotten by Rabbi Hamnuna-Saba, for Rabbi Hamnuna-Saba is *Ohr Yechida*.

He asked him to reveal his name, that is, to receive his degree, for the attainment of a name denotes the attainment of the spiritual degree. Therefore, the saying, "the entire Torah consists only of the Creator's names," means that the entire Torah constitutes the degrees that one must attain, up to the very highest, called "Love" ("Introduction to The Study of the Ten Sefirot," items 70-71).

Each degree in the attainment of the Upper Worlds has its own name. All the Creator's names: Moshe, Pharaoh, Avraham, the Temple, Sinai—every single word in the Torah—are degrees of perception of the Creator, degrees of attaining Him, for nothing exists besides man and his Creator. Everything else that exists in the world, as it seems to us, are the various degrees of our perception of the Creator Himself. He may appear to us as this world, and He may appear as the world of *Assiya*, as *Yetzira*, *Beria*, *Atzilut*, or He may be revealed completely, without partial concealments of the spiritual world or total concealment of our world. Thus, the word *Olam* (world) is derived from the *Haalamah* (concealment).

**91. He opened and began. It is written, "Benayahu (Benaiah) Ben (the son of) Yehoyada (Jehoiada)." This narrative is beautiful, but it serves to show us the exalted secrets of the Torah. And the name Benayahu Ben-Yehoyada indicates the secret of the Light of Wisdom, *Ohr Hochma*. Ben Ish Chai is the righteous who revives the worlds. *Rav Paalim* means that He is the Master of all that transpires, and that all the forces and Supernal Troops stem from Him. He is called the Creator of Force, the Master of all, and He is in everything.**

It is written in Prophets: "Benayahu, the son of Yehoyada," (*Shmuel* II, 23:20). Here, *The Zohar* reveals to us the exalted secrets of the Torah, for the holy name of Yehoyada consists of two: *Yod-Hey-Vav*, the first three letters of *HaVaYaH*, and *Yeda* (knowledge).

*Keter* of the world of *Atzilut* is called *RADLA* (unattainable head), whereas *Atik* itself surrounds all the other *Partzufim* of the world of *Atzilut*—AA, AVI, and ZON. *Atik* is called *Makif* (surrounding), for the other, lower *Partzufim* cannot attain it or its *Zivug*. Moreover, they cannot attain anything that comes from it. In other words, there is nothing descending *from Atik* to the lower *Partzufim*. Even AA is concealed from them; hence, it is called the "concealed *Hochma*." However, it is not defined as unattainable, like *Atik*, for it contains a *Zivug* on *Ohr Hochma*. Nevertheless, this Light does not descend to the lower ones, but only a small luminescence from it, called *He'arat Hochma*, reaches them.

And all the Light that fills the worlds through the 6,000 years comes from AVI and YESHSUT, who are called *Hochma* of the thirty-two paths or thirty-two forces (*Elokim*) of creation, i.e., thirty-two types of *He'arat Hochma*. This Light of *Hochma* is the result of *Bina's* ascent to AA, where she receives *Ohr Hochma* and shines downward. Therefore, all the Light of *Hochma* that is revealed through the 6,000 years, before the end of correction, is no more than the Light of *Bina*, which received *Ohr Hochma* upon ascending to *AA*.

*AA* is called *Yeda* (knowledge) because it gives *Ohr Hochma* to *Bina*, and knows all the routes of *Ohr Hochma* into *Bina* and through her on to the lower ones. While making a *Zivug*, *AA* itself does not pass its Light downwards, but as *AVI* ascend to *AA*, they receive *Ohr Hochma*, called "thirty-two streams" or "paths of wisdom," which can be attained by the lower ones.

Everything that is written in *The Zohar* refers to all the souls in general. However, there are exceptions that are not normally studied. There exist special, exalted souls that merit becoming a *Kli*, *MAN* for the great *Zivug* of *RADLA* after their exile, and to receive from this *Zivug* in the Upper World the degree of *Yechida*. These are the souls of Benayahu Ben-Yehoyada, Rabbi Hamnuna-Saba and a very few chosen others. These exalted souls reveal themselves to the righteous in this world, and as a result, the righteous merit delighting in *Ohr Yechida*, which shines only in such exalted souls, while still being in this world.

Therefore, the name of Benayahu Ben-Yehoyada indicates that it stems from the inner wisdom, the unattainable Light of *Hochma* of *Atik*. This name also causes the concealment of the Light of *Hochma*, for the name Yehoyada: *Yod-Hey-Vav* + *Yedu* means that only he who attains the first three letters *Yod-Hey-Vav* of the Creator's name *HaVaYaH* shall attain Him, and no other shall.

Therefore, this name remains concealed in its place. At first, the donkey driver explains the quality of this *Zivug* in *Atik*—its height, the power of the Light that emerges onto it in *Rosh de Atik*, which the name of this *Zivug*, "*Ben Ish Chai Rav Paalim ve Mekabtziel*," indicates. And then he explains what is concealed and what descends to the souls.

It was already stated that this *Zivug* takes place at the end of the correction of the entire *Malchut*. Hence, it includes all the individual *Zivugim* and the degrees that emerge on them through the 6,000 years. All the Lights accumulate into one. All the types of *MAN* combine into one and ascend to ask for this *Zivug*, which includes all the suffering and punishments gradually accumulated during the 6,000 years.

Hence, the height and greatness of this *Zivug* and the degree of Light that emerges from it are infinite, and it destroys all the impure forces once and for all. *Yesod de ZA*, from which the Light of this *Zivug* (the combination of all the Lights over the full course of the 6,000 years) is emanated, is called "*Ish Chai Rav Paalim*"—a vivid man of many actions. However, *Malchut*, which contains within her all the MAN, suffering, and work performed during the 6,000 years, is called *Mekabtziel* (gathering one).

The *Zohar* also calls it *Tzadik Chai Olamim*—the righteous, who revives the worlds, for it thereby points to the *Sefira Yesod*, which gives the Light to *Malchut*. The *Sefira Yesod* does not have a place to receive the Light for itself. Hence, it lives (*Chai*) only to pass the Light to *Malchut*. This is why it is called *Tzadik* (the righteous one), who revives the worlds (*Chai Olamim*).

Its other name, *Rav Paalim* (performing many actions) indicates that it includes all the MAD of all the good deeds and all the degrees that were revealed through the 6,000 years. This is because all these degrees are now being revealed all at once in a cumulative, integrated Light, as they leave *Yesod* and enter *Malchut*. And since *Yesod* now gathers all the Light that was emanated during the 6,000 years into one, and passes it to *Malchut*, this action determines its name—*Rav Paalim*.

**92. Rav Paalim is also Mekabtziel—the Exalted Tree, gathering and performing many actions, Supreme Above all. Where did it come from? From which degree did it originate? Once more, the source indicates—from Mekabtziel, for it is an exalted and concealed degree that none has seen. It includes everything, for it gathers all of the Upper Light within it, and everything originates from it.**

*Malchut-Nukva* is also named *Mekabtziel*, for she receives and gathers all the Light from *Yesod* within herself. Hence, *Yesod* is called *Rav Paalim*. The degree that emerges onto this *Zivug* is called the "Supreme and Exalted Tree" that originated from *Yesod* and entered *Malchut*. The *Zohar* goes on to explain that to show us the quality and the origin of this exalted degree, the name *Mekabtziel* (gathering) is used; *Yesod* accumulates the Upper Light and passes it to *Nukva*. And both *Yesod* and *Malchut* are called *Mekabtziel*.

And the degree that emerges onto this *Zivug* of *Yesod* and *Malchut* is called "None but you has seen the Creator." This degree emerges after the complete correction has been achieved, at the moment of attachment of the final correction that completes them all. Therefore, this degree is defined as all-inclusive, for it collects all the Light over the full course of 6,000 years, and thereby manifests at once in its true perfection.

**93. All of the degrees gather in this Supernal, Sacred, and Concealed Hall, where everything is concealed. All of the worlds are inside that hall. All the holy forces are sustained and revived by it, and all are dependant on it.**

*The Zohar* speaks of *Rosh de Atik*, where all the degrees and all the Light of all the worlds are concentrated and concealed. It further explains how this *Zivug* can occur up to the final correction, so it would combine all the degrees emerging one after another during the 6,000 years. And it would emerge instantly during the 6,000 years of the world's existence, when the degrees are in a state of constant ascents and descents, for as soon as a new degree, a new attainment of the Creator, of the Light, is revealed, the present degree disappears. This occurs due to the sin of the lower ones, who cannot retain this degree permanently (world–*Olam*, from the word *Haalamah*–concealment. The complete revelation of the Creator to His Creatures will take place at the end of the 6,000 years; thus, the world-concealment will cease to exist).

So, whenever a degree disappears, it does so only from the sensation of one who attains a new degree. In reality, this degree ascends to *Rosh de Atik* and hides there, so as to, by joining other degrees, be manifested at the end of correction.

In the same way, *Atik* gathers all the degrees revealed in the world during the 6,000 years, and conceals them within itself until the time of the end of correction comes; WHEN IT CORRECTS THE LAST PORTION OF WHAT IT MUST CORRECT, AND THUS CANNOT NO LONGER SIN. AND IT NO LONGER NEEDS TO SIN TO CORRECT THE NEXT PORTION OF EGOISM; HENCE, THIS FINAL DEGREE REMAINS PERMANENTLY AND DOES NOT DISAPPEAR. Then, *Atik* gathers all the degrees, and they all manifest simultaneously.

Everyone has his own *Partzuf Atik*. How can one accelerate his advancement along the degrees of correction in this world and in the spiritual worlds? It is written in the Talmud that an old man bends as he walks, as if he's looking for something that he had lost.

An old man symbolizes someone of wisdom, *Hochma*, for even without having lost anything, he looks beforehand for things he can correct in himself, and thus finds them. Hence, he does not require the previous degree of attainment to disappear from him. And if one does not discover new egoistic properties in need of correction within him, his previous degree disappears and a new one begins. However, this process is considerably slower than when one acts like an old man in search of shortcomings.

Throughout the 6,000 years, *Atik* is defined as unattainable. Therefore, its head is called *RADLA* (an abbreviation for the Aramaic words, *Reisha de Lo Etiada*, the "unattainable head"), whereas the name *Atik* is derived from the word *Ne'etak* (isolated) from the lower ones, for it does not shine upon them.

And, although it accumulates within all the Lights that emerge from it itself and become revealed in the lower worlds, the Light of the end of correction remains concealed nonetheless. It follows that after each degree disappears due to the sins of the lower ones, it ascends to *Rosh de Atik* and conceals itself there.

However, *Guf de Atik*, from its *Peh* downward, is located inside all the other *Partzufim* of the world of *Atzilut*, i.e., it is attainable by them. Thus, by clothing in the *Partzufim* of the world of *Atzilut*, *Atik* shines through them and gives the Light to them and to all the lower worlds of BYA. And any Light that shines on creation during the 6,000 years comes only from *Guf de Atik*, and not from some other spiritual object.

We usually say that whatever is present in the *Rosh* of a *Partzuf* manifests in its *Guf*. This is also true with regard to all the *Partzufim* of the world of AK and all the other *Partzufim* in all the worlds, except in *Partzuf Atik*! This is so because *Atik* remains in *Tzimtzum Aleph* and descends down to our world. However, with regard to other *Partzufim* below it, *Atik* acts as though it is in *Tzimtzum Bet*, making a special *Zivug* on itself and the Light from it descends to the lower worlds.

The Light that comes to revive the worlds is called "sustenance" or *Ohr Hassadim*, and the Light that comes to stimulate the growth of the *Partzufim*, to turn a small *Partzuf* (*Katnut*) into a big one (*Gadlut*) is called *Ohr Hochma*. Both these Lights originate in *Guf de Atik*. *Ohr Hochma*, which makes a *Partzuf* big, is called the Light that elevates the *Partzuf*, for the lying position is called *Ibur* (embryo), the sitting position is called *Katnut* (small), and the standing position—*Gadlut* (big).

**94. He slew two—Ariel and Moav (Moab). Two Holy Temples existed thanks to Atik and received from it: the First Temple and the Second Temple. Since Atik's disappearance, the process that stemmed from Above had ceased. It is as though he struck and destroyed them.**

Only *Malchut de Malchut* must be corrected, and nothing else. All the other properties do not require correction. This *Malchut de Malchut* is *Malchut of Olam Ein Sof* (the World of Infinity), *Behina Dalet*, *Nukva de ZA* or *Partzuf BON*—the Creator's only creation, the will to receive (pleasure) for oneself. It is this desire that caused the breaking of the *Kelim* (vessels)—the sin of Adam.

And all the work of the righteous during the 6,000 years concerns the correction of *Malchut*, so she becomes precisely as she was prior to the breaking of the *Kelim* and the sin of Adam. As a result, the great *Zivug* on *Tzimtzum Aleph* in *Rosh de Atik* will be revealed. The Light of this *Zivug* enables man to sort and separate his impure desires from the pure ones, and thus forever rid himself of the impure egoistic forces. This is exactly what Prophet Yeshayahu writes about: "He will eradicate death forever" (*Yeshayahu*, 25:8).

Since *Malchut*, *Partzuf BON* of the world of *Atzilut*, is completely corrected already and does not require any further corrections, her *Partzuf BON* ascends to the level of *Partzuf SAG* of the world of *AK*. Thus, *Malchut* completely attains the properties of *Bina*.

However, meanwhile, after the great *Zivug* in *Atik*, but before the ascent of *Partzuf BON* to *SAG*, the Light of *Atik* stops shining. As a result, the two Temples were destroyed. The two temples are the two Lights of *Hochma*: the Light of *AVI*, *Ohr Hochma de Haya* that shines in the First Temple, and the Light of *YESHSUT*, *Ohr Neshama* that shines in the Second Temple. And all the Light that Israel received from *Atik* disappears.

However, all these destructions and disappearances of Light are corrections and milestones on the path to deliverance and complete correction. They signify not devastation, but creation of perfection, as they are precisely those final corrections that bring *BON* back to *SAG*.

Since all the roots and sources of what transpires in this world exist in the spiritual realm, and must all manifest once in our world, every spiritual root must "touch" its branch in our world, and it does not matter when this occurs. In the spiritual world, everything unfolds in accordance with a strict cause-and-effect process, whereas in our world those same consequences can manifest at a completely different time.

An example of this is the destruction of the First and the Second Temples. While this event has already transpired in our world, in the spiritual world it occurs only when the last stage of correction is attained. Due to the complexity of time-transcending notions, we will examine this matter in another book. However, one way or another, only our inner spiritual properties can become the Temple in which we will feel the Creator and in which He will forever dwell!

At the end of correction, *Ohr Haya* and *Ohr Neshama* will be called the First and the Second Temples, respectively. Also, until the end of correction, *Ohr Haya*, which is received on the *Zivug* of *Malchut* and included in *Yesod*, is called *Shabbat* (Sabbath), while *Ohr Neshama* is called *Hol* (weekdays). As we can see, there is absolutely no connection between these Lights and the days of the week in our world.

After the destruction of the spiritual Temples (the disappearance of Light), they will be recreated from Above by the screen of *Bina*, called "Heaven." This is because the screen of *Partzuf SAG* is a property of absolute mercy and is completely unrestricted in its actions, desiring only to bestow and refrain from receiving *Ohr Hochma*. Thus, it is beyond the influence of any restrictions and limitations.

As a result of this *Zivug*, the two Temples will be restored forever, and "the Light of the Moon (*Malchut*) shall be as the Light of the Sun (*Bina*)" (*Yeshayahu*, 30:26). The Light of *Bina*, which is now the Light of ZA (called "the sun"), will be seven times more powerful, as *ZAT de Atik*. From there, this Light will descend to *AVI* and create the first seven days of creation, for ZA (the sun) will become like *AB* and contain the Light of *Guf de Atik*. *Malchut* will become like ZA and receive his Light, the Light of the sun.

At the end of correction, a *Zivug* on *Malchut* herself (the primordial, but corrected egoism) will transpire, and all the particular *Zivugim* that were made on all the Lights through the 6,000 years (made not on *Malchut*, but on her inclusion in *Yesod*) will thereby disappear.

The Temple will be restored from Heaven, for *Bina* herself does not wish to receive *Ohr Hochma*. And it will not occur because she cannot, but because she does not want to. This degree is referred to as "in the hands of Heaven." For example, it is written in the blessing on the new moon: "Life, which contains the fear of Heaven, and the fear of sinning." This life is above our reasoning and desires, for it is said that faith must be "above reason"; otherwise, sins will ensue.

Thus, one desires nothing more than to go by faith above his reason and desires, for he is afraid to sin. However, there exists an even Higher Degree: when he no longer fears sinning, as he now has a screen, but still prefers to proceed by faith above reason and desires, for he yearns to be dissolved in the Upper One.

The reason for the Light's disappearance from *Guf de Atik* prior to these corrections is that the two *Malchuyot* (*Bina* and *Malchut*, called SAG and BON) no longer exist. After the great *Zivug* of *Atik*, BON were annulled along with the screen of SAG, as *Guf de Atik* contains the connection between *Bina* and *Malchut*, designed for their interaction during the 6,000 years.

As a result of such interaction between *Bina* and *Malchut*, an opportunity arises to partially, gradually correct *Malchut*. In this mutual *Zivug* with *Malchut*, which is merged with *Bina* (*Bina's* properties), *Atik* first creates AA and then all the other *Partzufim* of the worlds of *Atzilut* and BYA.

And since the screen of *Malchut* (*Masach de BON*) now disappears, the screen of *Bina* (*Masach de SAG*) disappears as well, as they are merged together. In the absence of *Malchut* and the screen, this *Zivug* stops, and all the Light of *Guf de Atik* emanating from this *Zivug* on the mutual screen of *Malchut* and

*Bina* disappears. Therefore, all the Light that descended from its *Guf* (called Temples) disappeared.

In *Rosh de Atik* there is a *Zivug* on *Malchut* of *Tzimtzum Aleph*. Merged with *Bina* and existing for 6,000 years, the screen of *Malchut* disappears. As a result, the Light disappears as well. *Malchut* has yet to ascend to *SAG* to receive her perfection, as there is still no new Light. This complete absence of Light is called "destruction." However, *Malchut* then receives the Light of *AVI*, and the worlds of *BYA* merge with the world of *Atzilut*.

**95. And the Holy Throne (*Malchut*) is overthrown. Hence, the prophet Yechezkel (Ezekiel) wrote, "I am in exile," signifying that the degree called "I," which is *Malchut*, is in exile. Why? "By the river *Kevar*." *Kevar* (already) is the river that had already existed, but has now disappeared. As it is written, "The river is destroyed and dried up." It was "destroyed" in the first Temple and "dried up" in the second. Hence, it is written: "He struck and destroyed both, Ariel and Moav." Moav (or Mi Av) means "from the Heavenly Father." They were all destroyed for Him, and all the Light that shone upon Israel disappeared.**

The word *Kursa*, derived from the word *Kisse* (throne) or *Kissuy* (cover) signifies the combination of the properties of *Malchut* and *Bina*, which leads to the Light descending to *BYA* during the 6,000 years. The Holy Throne is overthrown, because the screen of *Bina* (*Kisse*) has been annulled, as it is said, "I am in exile," where "I" designates *Malchut*.

The entire spiritual complex is structured like a ladder, where *Malchut* of the Upper *Partzuf* becomes (descends to) the *Keter* of the lower one. This is also indicated in the names: *Malchut* is called "I" (*Ani* = Aleph-Nun-Yod) and *Keter* is called "no" (*Ein* = Aleph-Yod-Nun), as it is completely unattainable. Only that which is perceived within *Malchut* can be attained; hence, it is called "I."

Only *Malchut* of the Upper *Partzuf* acts as a link between the *Partzufim*: the Upper One makes a *Zivug* on its *Malchut*, creates *Ohr Hozer*, and receives (clothes) the Upper Light within it, and then *Malchut* of the Upper One descends to the lower *Partzuf* in the form of *Ohr Hozer*. This state of the Upper One clothing in the lower one is called the exile of the Upper One, for the *Zivug* with the Upper Light disappears from it, and the Upper Light disappears from all the *Partzufim*. And the river dries up—the corrected screen is called the "river," for it causes the Upper Light's descent to the lower ones.

However, now that the screen (river) disappears, the descent of the Upper Light disappears as well. The destruction of the river in the First Temple causes the disappearance of *Ohr Haya*; the river in the Second Temple dries up, and *Ohr Neshama* vanishes along with it. The river in the First Temple is destroyed because the *Zivug* in *AVI* is stopped; the Light in *YESHSUT* is exhausted, and the river in the Second Temple dries up.

The source of *Ohr Haya* and *Neshama* is *Aba*, called the "Heavenly Father," for he shines in ZA, called "Heaven," with the Light that elevates ZON to *YESHSUT* (the Second Temple) and to *AVI* (the First Temple). Because the Light stops shining from *Guf de Atik*, all of the Light descending to Israel disappears. This refers not only to the Light of the two Temples, but to all of the Light shining upon Israel, including *Ohr VAK* and the Light in the worlds of *BYA*.

**96. Further, He descended and struck the lion. Initially, when this river rolled its waters down, Israel was in a state of perfection, for they offered up gifts and sacrifices to atone for their sins and to save their souls. Then, the image of a lion would descend from Above, and they would see it on the altar as it trampled the bodies of the sacrifices, devouring them, and all the dogs (all those who slander Israel) would fall to silence.**

The fire that consumes the sacrifices laid on the Temple altar resembled a lion, and towered over the sacrifices, like a lion (Talmud, *Yoma*, 21:2), and that fire burned the sacrifices laid down by the sons of Israel. However, this is a corporeal image that a regular person perceives in our world.

But we shall follow our higher analysis and detach ourselves from this corporeal image; we will explain the action in the spiritual world that this language actually alludes to. All the languages in the Torah, including that which describes a rather corporeal image of sacrifice, speak only of spiritual actions. The most precise language for the description of these actions is the language of Kabbalah. However, this language is clear only to those who have ascended to the spiritual worlds and see both the roots, i.e., the events that transpire in the spiritual worlds, as well as their corporeal consequences.

Before the Light of *Atik* disappeared, when the Upper Light still shone upon Israel, like a river rolling its waters, Israel was in a state of perfection: by means of sacrifice, it raised its *MAN* (request), thus evoking a *Zivug* on its screen, and *MAD* (the Light, abundance) descends on it. As a result of these actions, it grew closer to the Heavenly Father, and all the impure forces distanced from it, for it purified its souls, and purification signifies distancing from the impure forces (desires), the way a soiled garment is cleansed from dirt.

Hence, the Hebrew word for sacrifice is *Korban*, derived from the word *Karov* (near). Thus, sacrifice signifies a person tearing away a part of his inner animal egoism for the sake of drawing closer to the Creator. This is what brings Israel closer to their Heavenly Father.

And since Israel existed in perfection and raised MAN for the Creator's pleasure alone, its MAN would ascend to *Bina*. The Light of *Bina* is called *Ohr Hassadim*, and its form resembles the image of a lion, like the property of bestowal, *Hesed*. This means that the lion-*Bina* receives Israel's good desires and deeds. And it was seen how *Bina* consumes Israel's MAN—*Ohr Hassadim* descends from *Bina* onto this MAN, like a lion trampling his prey (MAN) and devouring it.

A lion devouring its prey is the principal aspect of sacrifice, for it signifies raising MAN to strengthen a screen and create *Ohr Hozer*. And since the magnitude of the received *Ohr Yashar* is determined by the magnitude (height) of *Ohr Hozer*, which creates the screen, it follows that existence and growth of *Ohr Yashar* is dependent on the *Ohr Hozer*. The greater the *Ohr Hozer*, the greater the descending *Ohr Yashar* becomes.

In other words, to the extent that every one of us desires to "bestow," he evokes a corresponding response from Above, from the root of his soul. And just as in our world a living being's life and strength depend on nutrition (it simply dies without it), the Upper Light depends on the Light reflected by the screen. When it stops, the Upper Light disappears from the *Partzuf*, i.e., man stops feeling it.

The Upper Light descends from *Bina* as *Ohr Yashar* (called a "lion"), i.e., in the form of "bestowal," in accordance with *Bina's* nature. And man sees (feels!) how *Ohr Yashar* clothes in *Ohr Hozer*, which ascends from its sacrifice (rejection of egoism), the lion's nourishment.

It devours its prey and thereby grows: the extent of Israel's perfection and their ability to offer sacrifices, to "bestow," determines the magnitude of their MAN and the force with which the *Ohr Yashar* strikes the screen, which reflects the Direct Light (pleasure) from below upwards with all its might. Moreover, it does so in great fear: for what if it fails to reflect the Light and desires to enjoy the Light of this commandment selfishly?

That is precisely where one's work lies. It is called "faith above reason," for it must rise above one's reason (egoism) and intellect. Conversely, those who receive inner confidence that it is enough to advance within one's nature are called "sacred still," a pure inanimate (non-developing) being, as such reason prevents them from spiritual growth.

Therefore, if the height of *Ohr Hozer* is great, it is defined as a lion that tears and devours its prey, as a victor, for it grows and ascends to a higher spiritual level thanks to the efforts of the lower one (man).

The impure force, the selfish will to receive pleasure is called "a dog," as it is written: "The leech has two daughters (who demand): Give-give." (*Mishley*, 30:15). They bark like a dog, and demand (to receive) both this world and the next. And the Higher One ascends, the stronger this impure force, called *Klipa*, becomes. And its strongest part corresponds to *Ohr Yechida*, opposite the lion devouring its prey).

The lion represents mercy and bestowal, unwillingness to receive anything for oneself. As it is written in *The Ethics of the Fathers*, 95: "A *Chassid*, the merciful righteous one, says, 'What's yours is yours, and what's mine is yours,'" so is the impure force (dog) aimed wholly at reception, and has no aspiration to bestow. As it is said in the Talmud (*Bava Batra*, 10:2), "The righteous among the nations of the world: all their mercy is for themselves alone;" hence, they are connected to the impure force of a dog. (Under no circumstances should any of this be interpreted literally, for, as it was repeatedly explained, the whole of the Kabbalah speaks only of man's-prototype. Israel is one's inner aspiration to the Creator, and *Goy* (a gentile) signifies egoism (regardless of and unrelated to one's origin). Relate this to the above-mentioned corporeal and spiritual Temples, where there is no connection between rocks and spiritual objects. It is also unclear to the uninitiated why altruism is the property of a lion, while a dog, a loyal animal, is the root of egoism and impurity).

It is therefore said that when Israel was perfect, it acquired the property of a lion, and all the dogs left it be, for it gave *Malchut* the strength to raise *Ohr Hozer* to great heights (devoured its prey, like a victor), and the impure force, like a dog, was afraid to come near it, and would hide in fear of the lion.

**97. Yet, when sins increased, he descended to the lower degrees and slew the lion. This was because the lion refused to give up its prey as before, and this is as though he killed it. Therefore, he struck the lion and threw it into a pit, to the Evil Side (according to his understanding). The Evil Side saw this and sent a dog to devour the sacrifices from the altar in the lion's stead. What is the name of that lion? And what is the nickname of that dog? Baladan is its name; Baladan is formed by the words Bal-Adam, where the letter Mem is replaced by Nun, for he is not a human being at all, but a dog, and his face is like a muzzle of a dog.**

("He" refers to Benayahu Ben Yehoyada Ben Ish Chai, *Rav Paalim u Mekabtziel*, in whom the degree of *Atik*, all of the Light, shines all at once.) Due to the disappearance of the screens of *Malchut* (BON) and *Bina* (SAG), Israel below could no longer raise MAN (the will to "bestow," the screen, the lion's nourishment). The *Zivug* stopped, and the Upper Light (lion) disappeared in its Root Above.

"Threw it into a pit"—the root of the desire to receive for one's own sake is in the eyes, as Rashi said: "The eye sees, and the heart burns with desire" (The weekly portion *Shlach*). This will to receive for oneself is called an "empty, waterless pit" (*Beresheet*, 37:24). The Upper Light does not fill it. Although it is empty, it is unworthy of being a vessel for the Light, as it is written: "He and I cannot dwell in the same abode" (Talmud, *Suta*, 5).

Thus, the lion was thrown into a pit, for it was struck before the eyes of the impure egoistic force, called an "empty, waterless pit." And these pits now emerge from their hideouts and reveal their power, and in place of a lion appears a barking dog.

ZA-MA = 45 is called Adam = *Aleph* + *Dalet* + *Mem* = 1 + 4 + 40 = 45, when he receives the Light from *Bina*. The property of *Bina* is bestowal. Hence, it is written: "Man is your name" (Talmud, *Yevamot*, 61), referring only to those who attain the property of bestowal, but not to the others, of whom it is said: "Even their mercy is only for their profit" (Talmud, *Bava Batra*, 10:2), and who are therefore called Baladan (Bal-Adan).

**98. On a day of snow, on the day misfortunes descend from the Supernal Court Above, it is written, "Her household shall not fear snow," that is, the Supernal Court, called "snow." For her household is clothed twofold, and can thereby endure a strong fire. So the book says.**

Strictness, judgment (*Din*) or restriction imposed on the use of egoism in the male part is called "snow" that stems from the Supernal Court. These restrictions are very powerful, but are mitigated below the *Chazeh*, where *Malchut* receives them. *Nukva* describes these restrictions in the following way: "Surround me with roses," (*Shir HaShirim*, 2) referring to two fires: the Upper—*Bina*, and the lower, her own—*Malchut*.

After *Malchut* acquires these two fires, she weakens the strictness of the cold snow with her fire. Hence, it is written in *Shir HaShirim* (Song of Songs) that her household shall not fear snow (the Supernal Court), i.e., the restrictions imposed on the male part, for her household is clothed twofold. In other words, on the contrary, the snow helps her withstand the heat of her fire. And only now that the screen and *Zivug* are gone, and the two fires are no more, the restrictions of the snow return.

**99. What is written next? "And he struck an Egyptian." This refers to a secret: every time Israel sinned, the Creator would conceal Himself and restrict them from receiving all the goodness and all the Light that He shone upon them. "He struck an Egyptian." "He" refers to Moshe, the Light that shines upon Israel. For in Egypt he was born, grew up, and attained the Supernal Light.**

The Torah speaks not of man, but of the Light that disappeared and concealed itself. Hence, it is defined as "slain." Gone is the great Light, with which Moshe shone upon Israel. And this Light is called the "Egyptian," for in Egypt Moshe was born, grew up, and attained the great Supernal Light, the Light that delivered Israel from Egypt.

**100. A man of mirror. It is written, mirror and man, as it is written, a Godly man, the husband of that mirror, of the Creator's glory, *Malchut*. For with this degree he merited ruling over the entire land in all of his desire—a feat unmatched by any other.**

The difference between Moshe and the other prophets is that Moshe is the foundation of ZA, as he constructs and passes the Light from ZA to *Malchut*, whereas the other prophets are the foundation of *Malchut*, and receive from her. Hence, it is written of him: "Godly man," the husband of *Malchut*, called the "Creator's greatness." And why is Moshe called the husband of *Malchut*? Because he attained the level of ZA and gives the Light to *Malchut*. Therefore, it is written that his attainments are beyond anyone else's, for the other prophets receive from *Malchut*, and are therefore ruled by her.

He who attains *Malchut* receives from her. The degree called Moshe means that he who attains it gives the Light to *Malchut*, instead of receiving from her. Yet, how can this be? How can one possibly rise above *Malchut* if all our souls originate from her and exist in the worlds of BYA? This indicates the state of ascent above *Malchut*, which is how Moshe ascends to *Bina*.

**101. This is the Creator's staff that was delivered to him, as it is written, "With the Creator's staff in my hand." This is the staff that was created on the evening of the sixth day of the creation, before *Shabbat*. And His Holy Name is contained in it. And with this staff Moshe sinned by striking it twice against the rock. The Creator said to him: "Moshe, it is not for this purpose that I have not given you My staff; thus, it will no longer be in your possession henceforth."**

The words "evening" and "twilight" signify the state of mitigation of *Malchut's* strictness by the properties of *Bina* to an extent that it becomes impossible to distinguish *Malchut* from *Bina*. This is because on *Shabbat*, *Malchut* ascends to AVI and becomes *Bina*. However, on the twilight of *Shabbat*, *Malchut* is not yet *Bina*, but is no longer *Malchut* (everything in the book speaks only of the properties of spiritual objects, for nothing but desires exists in the spiritual worlds. Only in our world are desires clothed in physical bodies).

Hence, it is said that ten things were created in the twilight, when there is no distinction between the thing itself and its origin, *Bina* or *Malchut*, for *Malchut* herself shows no distinction. And such is the property of the staff that was created in the twilight, before the world's first *Shabbat*. Hence, it possesses the holy (special) property of the Creator's name, an allusion to the properties of *Bina*, from which holiness (altruism) descends. And *Malchut* is ready to receive this holiness.

And these two properties of *Bina* and *Malchut* are contained in the Creator's staff, utterly indistinguishable from one another, for they were created in the twilight. Hence, with the help of this staff, i.e., by means of the property of uniting *Malchut* with *Bina*, all the fortunes and wonders, all of the Light can be brought to Israel, for this is the purpose behind the Light's descent from *Bina* to *Malchut*. With the help of this property (the staff), Moshe merited an ascent to *Bina*, up to the degree of "Godly man." Therefore, the staff is called the Creator's staff, according to the name of *Bina*.

*Malchut* is called *Tzur* (rock), and upon ascending to *Bina*, she is called *Sela* (another name for a rock). The inner *Zivug* between ZON (ZA and *Malchut*) in the state of their ascent to *AVI*, when *Nukva* uses *Ima's Kelim*, is called "speech." The outer *Zivug* between ZON, when they are in their own place, is called "*Zivug de Hakaa*" (a *Zivug* by Striking).

It is hence written to Moshe in the weekly Torah portion *Bashalach*: "You shall strike the rock (*Tzur*), and it shall bring forth water" (*Shemot*, 17:6), for a *Zivug de Hakaa* occurs within *Malchut* herself. However, it is written in the weekly portion *Chukat*: "Speak ye unto the rock before all eyes, that it give forth its water" (*Bamidbar*, 20:8), for the "rock" is in *Bina*, and the *Zivug* within her is called "speech."

And herein lies the sin of Moshe: he struck twice: in addition to first striking the *Tzur*, he struck the *Sela*, which lacks the strike, and only has a *Zivug* in the form of speech. Since there is no distinction in the Creator's staff, and it is unclear whether it refers to *Malchut* or to *Bina*, he also applied it to *Sela-Bina*. And the Creator told him that the staff was given to him to use with *Tzur*, but not with *Sela*.

**102. At once He descended to him in strictness and wrenched the staff from the Egyptian's hand, for the moment the staff was taken from him, it was taken for good. And he was killed by it: because of the sin of striking the rock with the staff, he died and did not enter the Holy Land. And that Light was concealed from Israel.**

It was already mentioned in item 94 that as a result of a great *Zivug* in *Atik*, only *BON* were supposed to disappear, but not *SAG*, for *BON* could have immediately risen and forever become like *SAG*. However, as *SAG* and *BON* were merged, *SAG* disappeared together with *BON*.

The Light of Moshe disappeared from Israel for the same reason—because he committed an even greater sin and harmed the union of *BON* and *SAG* by striking the *Sela*. Hence, harsh judgment descended upon him, which refers to the disappearance of the Light of *SAG*. Indeed, *SAG* is no longer connected to *BON* in any way, and the annulment of *BON* has no influence on it.

This is the meaning of what is written in Psalms: "He resembled those who draw axes at a copse of trees, but now all of his adornments are smashed by hatchets and axes" (*Tehilim*, 74:5). Due to *Malchut's* ascent to *Bina*, and her correction there, *Malchut* is like a "copse of trees," for *SAG*, too, is annulled by the merging with *BON*, *Malchut's* ascent, as if struck with "hatchets and axes."

Hence, it is written that the staff was taken from the Egyptian, and will never return to him, for the staff refers to *Malchut*. So the Light disappears for good, because *BON* renews itself afterwards and becomes *SAG* forever. Thus, it is no longer necessary to use the staff for striking.

It is written in this regard that he was slain by the same staff, for had he been careful and used it only once—striking the *Tzur*, but not the *Sela*—*SAG* would not have been annulled together with *BON*, and he would not have died. Instead, he would have immediately risen to *SAG*.

This is why it is written that Moshe shall not enter the Holy Land, Israel, as Israel is *BON* in the state of ascent to *SAG*, and it is called the Holy Land, for the Light of *Bina* (called the Holy Light) shines in it. However, until the end of correction arrives, there are still ascents and descents, which cause destructions (disappearance of the Light) and revelations (shining of the Light). But at the end of correction, *BON* will remain within *SAG* permanently as *Eretz Israel*, and there shall be no more exiles from it.

**103. "The most respected of the thirty" refers to the Upper One that receives from Above and passes downward, one that receives and brings closer. However, he does not go to the first three, but they come to him and give to him wholeheartedly, but he does not come to them.**

*GAR* (*HBD*) are called "thirty," as each of the three *Sefirot HBD* consists of ten, which amounts to thirty. And their Light shines in all of the 6,000 years. The soul of Benayahu appears out of the great *Zivug* of *Atik*, which accumulates all the *Zivugim* during the 6,000 years. Hence, it is called *Rav Paalim* (performing many actions) and *Mekabtziel* (gathering all into one degree-*Partzuf*, called Benayahu Ben Yehoyada).

Therefore, he receives the Light of all of the Supernal Thirty, which descends to his soul. Indeed, he consists of particular *Zivugim* that have transpired through the 6,000 years, which he gathers into one. And, although they give him the best of their properties wholeheartedly, he still cannot draw closer to them and subsequently receive from them. This is because the disappearance of the screen in ZON made the screen in SAG disappear as well. Hence, he cannot come to them, raise MAN, and receive from them further.

**104. Despite not being considered one of them, David heard the meaning that is never detached from the heart, for they can never be separated. David paid attention with all his heart, but he did not pay attention to David. For by the praises, hymns, and mercy that the moon offers the sun, the moon draws the sun closer so as to be with it.**

David is *Malchut*; *Malchut* comes from the word *Melech* (King). Therefore, David is King, for his properties are the properties of *Malchut* (kingdom). And this is the fourth leg (support) of GAR. Hence, it is written that although he cannot be together with the thirty (GAR), he nonetheless clings to these properties, and never detaches himself from them.

This is because *Malchut's* entire perfection is revealed in him, for it stems from the great *Zivug* of *Atik*, which destroys all the impure forces of BON, as it is said: "He destroys evil forever."

Therefore, David resolved to never part with it again, for it is his perfection. However, Benayahu Ben Yehoyada paid no attention to David, as David is the fourth support of GAR. Hence, it is as though he is unable to receive from GAR. And since he cannot receive from David, he pays no attention to him.

With the help of the MAN of *Malchut* (called *Se'ara*—stormy wind), which is raised to ZA (called "Heaven"), as a result of the hymns, praises, and mercy, *Malchut* receives the Light of Benayahu Ben Yehoyada's soul, which is absolute perfection, and merges with it for all eternity.

**105. Rabbi Elazar and Rabbi Aba fell down on their faces before him and could not see him anymore, then rose and went in every direction, but could not see him. They sat and wept, and could not even speak to one another. Then, Rabbi Aba said, "It is true what we have learned, that the Torah accompanies the righteous on all their paths. The righteous of the other world come to**

them to reveal to them the secrets of the Torah. And this must have been
Rabbi Hamnuna-Saba, who came to us from the other world to reveal these
secrets to us. But before we could recognize him, he vanished." They rose and
wanted to lead their donkeys on, but could not. They repeatedly tried to goad
the donkeys, but still they could not move. They grew frightened and left their
donkeys behind. And to this day this place is called "the place of donkeys."

Because they could not bear such a powerful Light, which was revealed to
them upon the disclosure of those secrets, they fell (*Katnut*) and then rose (*Gadlut*),
for it was so unbearable. After they merited receiving from it such a great degree,
this Light disappeared at once and did not reappear, and they could not attain it
anymore. Hence, they wept (a kind of *Katnut*) out of great grief that they had lost
such exalted attainment, and they could not speak (absence of *Kelim*).

The bitterness of their loss made them realize that it was the degree of
Rabbi Hamnuna-Saba himself, and not lower, as they had mistakenly thought
before. The forces that they received from the soul of Rabbi Hamnuna-Saba are
called "donkeys," with which they can raise MAN, the request to attain Higher
Degrees, *Haya* and *Yechida*.

In other words, the soul is a spiritual force of Light; like a pulling force of
a donkey that helps overcome egoistic desires and move from place to place in
the spiritual world, onto a Higher Degree. To raise MAN means to feel what is
lacking and what needs to be attained—this is what man's work is all about.

Such is the work of a righteous soul—it helps man by lifting him up onto
his donkey (egoism) and taking the lead (pulling) in order to illuminate (give
strength) for him the path of the righteous. And now, when its role has been
completed, this soul disappears, although they would have very much liked to
continue ascending and riding its donkeys, i.e., they wished to raise MAN anew
to return and attain once more.

However, they could no longer receive the strength to raise MAN. Thus,
they were struck by fear and left their donkeys in that place, which is hence
called "the place of donkeys," for they could not use them any longer.

**106. Rabbi Elazar opened and said: "Oh, how great is Your goodness, which
You have hidden away for those who fear You! (*Tehilim*, 31:20). How infinite
is the goodness that the Creator shall bestow on humankind in the future,
on those sin-fearing, exalted righteous, who study the Torah as they arrive
at that Upper World."**

The words "great goodness" refer to *Gadlut*, the attainment of the Light of
GAR. For the basis of a *Partzuf* is its VAK—the amount of Light necessary for its

existence, received from the *Zivug* of *AVI*, who make this *Zivug* and emit *Ohr Hassadim*, necessary to sustain the worlds. And all the extra Light, necessary for existence, is called *GAR* or *Ohr Hochma*—the additional, delectable and great Light.

This *Ohr Hochma*, the Light of *GAR*, stems from *Bina*, which is called "the world to come." It is clothed in *Ohr Hassadim* that emerges from a *Zivug* of the *Sefira Yesod* (*Chai Olamim*—life of the worlds), and from there descends to the righteous who fear to sin.

The *Zivug* of *AVI*, when they are at the degree of *Bina*, gives *Ohr Hassadim* to *ZA* for the sustenance of the worlds. However, when *AVI* ascend to *AA* and beget new souls by their *Zivug*, their *Zivug* is inconstant, as it emits *Ohr Hochma*, called "new souls."

**107. The name "great goodness" can be further described as containing all the secrets of the Supernal wisdom, which descend from ZA to *Malchut*. There is a great tree, called ZA or *Rav* (great, strong), and there is a small tree, *Malchut*, which grows from it. And it is elevated to the Highest Firmament.**

In addition to the attainment of the Light of *GAR*, there is also the inner part of the Supernal wisdom with its secrets, which become revealed in the *Zivug* of *Atik* at the completion of the 6,000 years, the end of correction. *MA* designates the lower world, *Malchut*. The great and strong tree is *ZA* in the state of ascent to *Partzuf AB*, as in this state he receives *Ohr Hochma*, and *Hochma* signifies strength (not "reason—strength" but the strength of *Ohr Hochma* lies in the fact that it allows one to go against reason, in defiance of common sense, in faith above reason).

However, when *ZA* is in his place, he is simply called "a tree," for he lacks *Ohr Hochma* and has only *VAK*, *Ohr Hassadim*. *Malchut* is also called a tree and grows together with *ZA*; *ZA* ascends to *Aba*, to the utmost height, to the Supernal Firmament—*Atik*.

**108. The "great goodness" is the Light that was created on the first day of creation and concealed so as to be revealed in the future for the righteous in the other world. Your Deeds are the Supernal Garden of Eden, which the Creator has created by His act.**

The Light that was created on the first day of creation is the Light in which Adam saw from one end of the world to the other. Hence, the word "Light" is used five times in the Torah's description of the first day of creation. This Light is intended for the righteous in the world to come, for it is concealed in *Yesod de Aba* and in *Yesod de Ima*, which are collectively called "righteousness and justice."

(In Hebrew, the words *Tzedek*—justice and *Tzadik*—righteous/just have the same root. This name is given to one who attains the Creator's governance and sees that His governance is just; hence, he justifies all of the Creator's actions, and is thus called righteous. The other meaning of the word 'righteous' refers to man's belief that the Creator is righteous, because in spirituality, one assumes the name of the degree one has attained. If he attains that the Creator is righteous by receiving this knowledge from the degree onto which he ascends, then he is already called by the name of that degree.)

*Ohr Hochma* can be received only in "precious garments," called righteousness and justice, that is, only with these intentions. The above excerpt speaks of an open action, implying unrestricted diffusion of Light, as it will be after the end of all the corrections. In the Torah, such a state is called "the Supernal Garden of Eden."

In the meantime, only the complete and perfect righteous ones, the souls of Benayahu Ben Yehoyada and others that merited reception of Light from the great *Zivug* of *Atik*, gather all the Light of the 6,000 years. These souls' place of rest is referred to as the Garden of Eden.

There exists the lower Garden of Eden of earth, which is VAK, and the Supernal one, GAR. All the souls dwell in the lower Garden of Eden, and only on new moons and Sabbaths do they ascend to the Supernal Garden of Eden, and then return to their place. However, there are individual, special persons (souls), whose place is in the Supernal Garden of Eden. These are the souls of which Rabbi Shimon says: "I saw them ascending, but their numbers were few."

**109. All the righteous stand in the lower Garden of Eden, clothed in precious adornments, similar in quality and form to those which they wore in this world, meaning in the same form as people in this world and according to man's actions in this world. They stand there and fly away through the air, ascend to the Assembly in the Supernal Garden of Eden, fly there and bathe in the dew of the pure river of Apharsemon (persimmon), then come down and fly below in the lower Garden of Eden.**

The main difference between GAR and ZAT with regard to both *Partzufim* and souls is that GAR (*KHB*) do not need the garment of *Hassadim*. They can receive *Ohr Hochma* as it is. However, *Partzufim* of VAK and the souls born from ZON, whose basis is VAK (*Ohr Hochma* clothed in *Ohr Hassadim*), can only receive *Ohr Hochma* when it is clothes in *Ohr Hassadim*.

The *Ruach de Tzadikim* (spirit of the righteous) in the lower Garden of Eden is clothed in *Ohr Hassadim*, just as human souls in this world. And with the help of these precious garments, they can ascend to the Supernal Garden of Eden and there receive *Ohr Hochma*. Afterwards, they return to their place in the lower Garden of Eden, for that is their permanent place.

They ascend by the power of *Ohr Hassadim*, called "air," and fly to the Supernal Garden of Eden to receive *Ohr Hochma*, called the river of *Apharsemon*. However, they cannot stay there, so they immediately descend from the Supernal Garden of Eden to the lower. *The Zohar* compares them to human souls, for both the Upper and the lower human souls need to receive the garment of *Ohr Hassadim* in order to correct themselves and ascend.

**110. And sometimes these righteous appear as people in order to perform miracles, like celestial angels, just as we have seen the luminescence of the Upper Light, but did not merit to see and discover the wisdom's great secrets.**

DID NOT MERIT TO DISCOVER THE WISDOM'S GREAT SECRETS— for the donkey driver had left them and disappeared. There are special souls that abide in the Supernal Garden of Eden. They have risen so high that the souls from the lower Garden of Eden ascend to them only on new moons and Sabbaths, and, being unable to stay there, immediately descend to their permanent place. However, they are nonetheless similar to human souls, which descend from the Supernal Garden of Eden to this world and meet people, just like the angels that seldom descend to this world.

Now they have seen the Light of the Supernal Luminary, the Light of Rabbi Hamnuna-Saba that descended on them from the highest point, the Supernal Garden of Eden, and was revealed before them in this world (while they are still living in this world).

AS PEOPLE refers to the souls that abide in the lower Garden of Eden, which have the form of people, and the Light of the Supernal Garden of Eden influences them. They can receive this Light during their ascent on new moons and Sabbaths, whereupon they merit meeting the souls of the Supernal Garden of Eden, and then descend to their permanent place.

However, one may also say that the words AS PEOPLE refer to the people of our corporeal world, while the souls from the Supernal Garden of Eden sometimes descend to this world and, like exalted angels, appear before the eyes of the righteous.

**111. Rabbi Aba opened and said: "And he who is doomed said to his wife, 'We shall die, for I have seen the Creator.' Even though he was not aware of his actions, as it is written, 'He did not know that it was an angel'; however,**

since it is written, 'Man shall not see Me and live,' we know that he has died. And we have merited this great Light to accompany us, and the world exists because the Creator Himself sent him to us, to reveal the secrets of His Supernal wisdom to us. How joyous is our share!"

When the angel saw him who was doomed, he did not yet have the proper level of attainment; thus, the angel was unwilling to reveal his name. Yet, although he did not know and did not attain him, he still feared the words, "Man shall not see Me and live" (*Shemot*, 33:20).

But we have merited complete attainment, for we came to know his name, Rabbi Hamnuna-Saba. And we live and exist in this world. It is therefore clear that the degree of Rabbi Hamnuna-Saba is called "Show me Your glory" (*Shemot*, 33:18), Moshe's request of the Creator.

But the Creator replied: "You cannot see My face, for man shall not see Me and live." From this we see that they have attained more than Moshe. This state is described by sages as, "There was no prophet more exalted than Moshe, but there was a sage" (*Yalkut Shimoni*, the end). It is also written: "A sage is preferred to a prophet" (Talmud, *Bava Batra*, 12:1). Thus, they have spiritually ascended to merit the appearance of such an exalted soul, while still being in this world.

**112. They walked and came to a mountain. The sun had set. The branches of the tree on that mountain started rattling and singing. As they were still walking, they heard a resounding voice proclaim, "Sons of the Holy Creator, dispersed among the living in this world, illuminated by the sons of the Assembly, gather in your places and rejoice with your Creator in the Torah." They grew frightened and stopped, then sat down.**

"They came to a mountain" refers to the words of King David, who said (*Tehilim*, 24:3): "Who shall ascend the mountain of the Lord, and who shall stand in His holy place?" meaning who is worthy of it? After they climbed the mountain, the sun had set (the Light left the *Partzuf*). But they heard something from the trees, as it is written: "Then shall all the trees of the wood sing for joy" (*Tehilim*, 96:12).

They heard a voice that told them to return to their place, rejoice in the Creator and His Torah, and descend from the mountain. And it calls them by the name of that High Degree, which they've achieved. But it hints that people are not worthy of being at that degree and in this world simultaneously. Yet, although they were frightened, they remained on the mountain, sat down, and did not move. "Grew frightened," "stopped," and "sat down" are the spiritual states of the *Partzuf*.

We see how *The Zohar* explains the path of the righteous, those who cross the *Machsom* (the barrier that separates our world from the spiritual) and start ascending the rungs of the spiritual ladder. This path is diverse, and each book of the Torah describes it in its own way: the language of Kabbalah, legends, judicial laws, historical accounts of the Pentateuch, etc.. *The Zohar* draws a vivid picture for us—like a guidebook for those who will find themselves in the place of these exalted travelers in the spiritual world. Once there, you will see for yourselves what is implied by such notions as "mountain," "tree," and "voice." Then *The Zohar* will become your true guidebook!

It is impossible to provide a more detailed description of the *Partzufim*, i.e., an inner perception of one who ascends spiritually. This is because the reader must first have certain analogous sensations of his own. If one could see only once what the described content (or something similar) really means, one would be able to clearly imagine what it speaks of.

It is the same in our world: even if we have never been to a certain country, we can imagine what others describe to us by analogy with what we already know. But in this case, there is no analogy. One who sees the spiritual world for the first time realizes how wrong all of his previous visualizations have been! Hence, we can say nothing about many of the states described in *The Zohar*.

**113. Meanwhile, a voice called out again, "O, mighty rocks, great hammers of thunder, *Bina* stands upon a pillar, so enter and assemble." At that moment, they heard the mighty voice of thousands of trees, which was saying, "The Creator's voice breaks the cedars." Both Rabbi Elazar and Rabbi Aba fell down on their faces. Great fear fell upon them. They rose hastily and left, not hearing anything else, then came down the mountain and kept on walking.**

It was previously said that they could not load their donkeys, meaning that they were unable to raise MAN, because Rabbi Hamnuna-Saba had already completed his helping mission. This is why they lost the power of their donkeys, and could not continue using them to raise MAN and merit Higher Degrees.

Therefore, Rabbi Elazar said earlier that they did not merit seeing and attaining the secrets of the Supernal wisdom. The fact is that after they attained the level of *Yechida*, i.e., revealed the soul of Benayahu Ben Yehoyada with the help of Rabbi Hamnuna-Saba, the disappearance of the screen (*Masach*) of BON caused the loss of *Masach de SAG*. Hence, they could no longer raise MAN.

The Light stopped descending to them from *Guf de Atik* specifically to give them the opportunity, or rather the strength to recreate *Masach de SAG*.

Consequently, *BON* will become like *SAG*, they will resume raising *MAN*, and will once more be able to ascend from degree to degree.

Hence, as soon as both Rabbi Elazar and Rabbi Aba left their donkeys, they lost strength to raise *MAN* in order to bring *BON* back to the level of *SAG*. However, the voice proclaimed that they are as strong as rock and thunder, for so far they have endured all the trials. And they will gather strength to endure the mighty rocks and to overcome all the obstacles as before, until they obliterate these obstacles, like great hammers of thunder crashing down from Above.

*Bina*, though herself colorless, is called "the source of colors." This is because she is all mercy, whereas all the other properties originate specifically from her by enduring all the trials, like rocks. From all this, *Bina* receives new forms, hence she received the powers of a new screen onto which emerge all the new degrees and *Partzufim*.

Together with the voice that informed them of *Bina's* new powers, they heard another voice, "The Creator's voice breaks the cedars" (*Tehilim*, 29:5), which let them know that all the cedars (obstacles) on their path to higher attainments have been removed. This gave them strength to climb down the mountain and continue their path onto Higher Degrees.

**114. Upon reaching the house of Rabbi Yosi, the son of Rabbi Shimon Ben Yosi Ben Lakunya, they saw Rabbi Shimon Bar-Yochai. They rejoiced. Rabbi Shimon rejoiced, too. He said to them, "You have traveled this path of Heavenly signs and wonders correctly, for as I was sleeping, I saw you and Benayahu Ben Yehoyada, who was sending you two crowns with an old man, so as to adorn you. I am certain that the Creator was on this path too, because I see how your faces have changed." Rabbi Yosi said, "Truly, it is said that a sage is preferred to a prophet." Rabbi Elazar came and put his head on the knees of his father, Rabbi Shimon, and told him of what had happened.**

Here *The Zohar* gives an allegorical explanation of two states: first, they merited attaining the Light of *SAG* (called Rabbi Yosi) once more, and secondly, now *SAG* and *AB* join in a constant *Zivug*. We see this from their meeting with Rabbi Shimon, who signifies *Ohr Hochma*. In other words, they merited their *BON* returning and becoming like *SAG* in its constant and eternal *Zivug* with *AB*.

Benayahu Ben Yehoyada sent them two crowns through Rabbi Hamnuna-Saba: *Ohr Yechida*, called Benayahu Ben Yehoyada himself, and a new Light *AB-SAG*, which they have just attained. This Light also came to them by the powers of Benayahu Ben Yehoyada as a reward for overcoming all the trials, thanks to which they, of all others, merited this degree, which is emanated from the great Light of his soul.

Hence, it follows that he sent them two crowns. However, all these descents on their spiritual path were not failures; rather, the Creator Himself was leading them to that High Degree, which they have now attained. This is why it is written: I AM CERTAIN THAT THE CREATOR WAS ON THIS PATH (with you). However, HOW YOUR FACES HAVE CHANGED, for you have attained something else, described by the phrase, A SAGE IS PREFERRED TO A PROPHET.

**115. Rabbi Shimon was frightened and wept. He said, "I have heard the Creator and I am awed." This verse was spoken by the prophet Havakuk (Habakkuk), when he saw his death and his resurrection by Elisha. Why was he named Havakuk? Because it is written that at around this time there would be a HOVVEK-ET—a son will be embraced. For Havakuk was the son of the Shunamit. And there were two embraces: one from the mother and one from Elisha, as it is written, "He put his mouth to his."**

First, it is unclear how the prophet Elisha could pass a seed in his blessing to the Shunamit, for this seed cannot exist (procreate). Indeed, Elisha was the greatest prophet after Moshe and his soul came from the Supernal Garden of Eden. Hence, his BON (in Hebrew, the words Ben—son and BON are spelled the same way: Bet-Nun) was already absolutely pure and perfect.

Therefore, when he passed his son to her, he tied him to the male side, whereas he tied Havakuk only to the female side. And since the female side, Nukva, is closer to the impure force, it clung itself to him, and he died. Thus, the reason for his death lies in the exalted level of the prophet, for his BON is pure and free from the clinging of impure forces.

Hence, the prophet prayed: "The Creator has hidden it from me and had not told me!" (Melachim II, 4:27). In other words, he had not the slightest clue that he could die by being connected only to BON. That is why it was necessary to return, revive, and attach him to the Upper World, to the resurrection of the dead.

The essence of the embryo is the white (Ohr Hochma) in it, as it is written (Talmud, Nidah, 31:1) that Aba (father) is Hochma, for Hochma is called "white," as it is said, "He made everything with Hochma (wisdom)" (Tehilim, 104). However, there is also a need for clothing in Ohr Hassadim, the intention "for the Creator's sake," as it is impossible to receive Ohr Hochma, the Light of Wisdom, attainment and delight, without the clothing of Ohr Hassadim, without an altruistic intention.

So the mother must provide the red, the screen, which provides *Ohr Hassadim*, required for the clothing of *Ohr Hochma* in it. As a result of the *Ohr Hassadim* embracing (clothing, enveloping) *Ohr Hochma* in itself, an embryo can exist. And here the embryo's entire embrace came only from the mother, the Shunamit, i.e., only from the female side (*BON*).

Hence, when Elisha revived him, he gave him the white (*Hochma*) and the red (*Hassadim*) once more. It follows that it was Elisha himself who embraced him the second time. It is hence said that there were two Havakuks (from the word *Hibuk*—embrace): one from the mother and the other from Elisha.

**116. I have discovered in the book of King Solomon that the name Havakuk consists of seventy-two names. Elisha created it with words. Each word consists of three letters, for the letters of the alphabet that the Father confirmed to him initially flew away when he died. But Elisha embraced him and confirmed in him all these letters in his seventy-two names. In all, there are 216 letters in his seventy-two names, three letters in each.**

The embryo is built of 216 = *RYU* (*Reish* = 200 + *Yod* = 10 + *Vav* = 6) letters, designating *Ohr Hochma*, which descends to *YESHSUT*. This means that the embryo has *RYU* letters, which amounts to the *Gematria* of *RE'IYAH* = *Reish-Aleph-Yod-Hey*, i.e., the Light of vision. *Re'iyah* means vision in Hebrew, and vision is possible only in *Ohr Hochma*, for "seeing" means "attaining," and the Light of the eyes is the Light of *Hochma*.

When a growing *Partzuf* attains *Gadlut*, receives the clothing of *Ohr Hassadim* of the Upper World from *AVI*, and *RYU* clothe in *Ohr Hassadim*, this *Partzuf* is called *AB* (72) names, as each three letters join into one and *RYU* = 216 letters turn into *AB* = seventy-two groups with three letters in each group, or *AB* = seventy-two names.

When *Ohr Hassadim*, the clothing of the *Partzuf*, comes only from the lower world, it is defined as *RYU* = 216 letters. And when it attains *AB*, *Hassadim* of the Upper World, each three letters form a group, and this results in *AB* = seventy-two names, as it is written, HE CONFIRMED IN HIM ALL THESE LETTERS. When Elisha revived Havakuk, the son of the Shunamit, he created the name Havakuk, *AB* = seventy-two letters from *RYU* = 216, for he gave him *Ohr Hassadim* of the Upper World from *AB*.

Because of it, all 216 letters made groups of three and formed three lines from Above downwards: right, left and middle. A cell made of three letters—the right, left, and middle lines, situated horizontally (referring to the same screen and type of *Kli*)—is regarded as one. Therefore, *AB* (seventy-two) letters is used instead of *AB* (seventy-two) names, because each letter is considered to include three, merged into one. When *Ohr Hochma* enters these seventy-two cells, the *Partzuf* is called *AB* and is said to have the complete Light of *Hochma*.

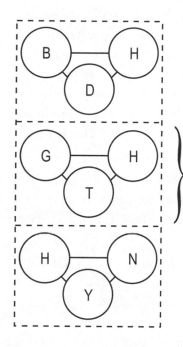 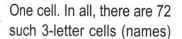

One cell. In all, there are 72 such 3-letter cells (names)

*Ohr Hassadim* is the Light that brings peace in the state of the *Partzuf* at a given moment, for its property is not to wish anything for itself, but to bestow. However, *Ohr Hassadim* received from the lower world is merely comfort "for want of something better," whereas *Ohr Hassadim* received from the Upper World creates such a powerful property of "bestowal" that the *Partzuf* receives *Ohr Hochma*, thereby showing that although it has *Ohr Hochma*, it still prefers *Ohr Hassadim*.

This is similar to a person in our world, who says that he needs nothing. Yet, there is a distinction: does he say this in a state when he has nothing and can have everything he wants, but still wishes to restrict himself to bare essentials and to give away the rest?

Therefore, when the growing *Partzuf* (the son—*BON*) had only *Ohr Hassadim* from the lower world, it could not receive *Ohr Hochma* in it, and was thus called *RYU* letters. But since the impure forces still cling to them and tempt the *Partzuf* to receive *Ohr Hochma* for itself, *Ohr Hochma* cannot be clothed within them.

These *RYU* letters that Havakuk had since the day of his birth FLEW AWAY WHEN HE DIED. Hence, it was essential to give him *RYU* letters and *AB* names once more. And Elisha did just that by HIS SPIRIT, for he was obliged to recreate in him *RYU* letters in order to combine them into *AB* cells with the help of the Upper *Hassadim* (combine everything into three lines), when everything unites into *AB* names.

**117. Elisha confirmed all of these letters in the soul of Havakuk so as to revive him by the letters of the seventy-two names. And he called him Havakuk, for that is his complete name, which describes all of his properties, as it alludes to two Havakuks and to the 216 letters of the Holy Name, as the *Gematria* (numerical value) of the name Havakuk is 216, from which the seventy-two names were formed. By *AB* names he revived him and brought his spirit back, and by *RYU* letters he revived his body and let it live. This is why he is called Havakuk.**

Havakuk = *Chet* + *Bet* + *Kuf* + *Vav* + *Kuf* = 8 + 2 + 100 + 6 + 100 = 216. The word Havakuk indicates two embraces (*Hibukim*, plural for *Hibuk*). Like all Hebrew names, it refers to the property of its bearer. For instance, Yaakov is derived from "*Akev*" ("got around" Esav), and Avraham signifies *Av* —father, *Am*—of the nation).

The first embrace came from *Ima*, but it did not yet allow *Ohr Hochma* into the *Partzuf*, into *RYU* letters, for the impure force clings to the red in *Ima*. But then Elisha embraced him with *Hassadim* of the Upper World that came from *AVI*. This united the letters into groups (names), and *Ohr Hochma* entered and filled these names permanently, since the impure force cannot cling to *Hassadim* of the Upper World.

As in the above example, even if all the *Ohr Hochma* were to be offered, the *Partzuf*, upon receiving protection in the form of a desire for *Hassadim* of the Upper World, receives such great strength (desire) to bestow that it never wants *Hochma*. This is precisely why *Hochma* can fill it for all eternity.

Therefore, the name Havakuk denotes two *Chibukim* (embraces): one from the mother and one from Elisha, thereby imparting him with perfection from all sides: from both the *Ohr Hochma* and the *Ohr Hassadim*. "Embraces" signify *Ohr Hassadim* that stems from *AVI*, and *Ohr Hochma* received within *Ohr Hassadim* is called "the secrets of *RYU*."

It is hence written that HE REVIVED HIS SPIRIT BY *AB* NAMES AND HIS BODY BY *RYU* LETTERS. And he was revived by Elisha's embrace, for *RYU* letters had formed names, that is, the three lines, in which *Ohr Hochma* could be received, thanks to the reception of *Ohr Hassadim* from *AVI* (the Upper World).

The impure forces (man's egoistic desires) cannot attack in this Light. Hence, death (the result of receiving *Ohr Hochma* for oneself) does not exist.

Subsequently, he receives *Ohr Hochma*, which yields the complete correction of his *Guf*.

However, the *Partzuf* (son of the Shunamit) had *RYU* letters from the moment of birth, and they left him when he died. Then why is he called Havakuk (two embraces)? After all, the first embrace of *Ima* (mother) left him the moment of his death, and Elisha revived him from death by embracing him only once. Thus, does he not contain only the embrace of Elisha?

The thing is that Elisha has given him nothing new at the time of resurrection, except for the embrace, the Light from the Supernal *Ima*–SAG, whose Light evokes the resurrection of the dead. And *RYU* letters were simply revived by his lower mother–BON. These are the same *RYU* of BON with which he was born. Otherwise, it would have been an entirely new soul, of which one would not have been able to say that it was dead and then resurrected.

Therefore, now he truly has two embraces, for the first one has now been revived as well, when BON ascended to SAG. And since BON is in the place of SAG, his *Hassadim* are regarded as those of the Supernal Mother. They completely neutralize the impure forces and death, for their properties (desires) are only of bestowal, which the impure force cannot bear. Thus, they can no longer tempt man. This is why he is called Havakuk, after the action of the two embraces.

**118. He said, "I have heard the Creator and I am awed by His Name." I have heard of what I had and have had a taste of the other world at the moment of death, before Elisha resurrected him, and I am awed. He began asking for mercy for his soul. He said, "O, Creator, the deeds that You have performed for me throughout the years were my life." And whoever connects to the past years (the name of the *Sefirot* of *Atik*), connects to life. Throughout the years, bestow life upon the degree that has no life of its own, upon *Malchut de Malchut*.**

His fear comes from the past, previous states, for now he has become perfect on all his sides, and therefore fear has no place. This fear remained from the past, when he left the world. This describes the state between death and resurrection. However, he continues receiving fear from the past state, so it would help him create a screen for raising *MAN*. It is precisely this fear from past times (states) that stimulates him to raise *MAN* (request for mercy).

This is the secret of the future screen, after BON becomes SAG. For then "He will eradicate death forever" (*Yeshayahu*, 25:8), and there will be no force evoking fear of death and suffering or able to cause harm to one's purity and holiness. Hence, there will be no need to shun, no one to beware of or avoid.

So if one has attained such an exalted spiritual state, where could he possibly acquire fear? After all, he will not be able to ascend without it! Only if he takes fear from his past states! For the *Partzuf* retains the memories, records, recollections of past states, even after its ascent to SAG, when BON become like SAG.

If not for the recollections of fear from the past states, the *Partzuf* would not have been able to create a screen in a state when it has nothing left to fear. While explaining this, Rabbi Shimon told them of Havakuk, to teach them how to acquire fear, just as Havakuk did by taking fear from the past.

THE DEEDS THAT YOU HAVE PERFORMED... THROUGHOUT THE YEARS... WERE MY LIFE—because he lived through two periods: the years preceding his death and the years following his resurrection. Between these two periods, there was a state of exiting this world, death (during which he existed in the other world). That is to say, because I remember the time of my death, I thereby connect to life of the Upper World, which Elisha bestowed by resurrecting me.

ZAT *de Atik* is called the "past (sometimes ancient) years," since they receive their Light from *Malchut* of the world of AK, *Malchut* of *Tzimtzum Aleph*. However, ZAT *de Atik* do not shine upon the lower *Partzufim* and worlds with their Light of *Tzimtzum Aleph*. ZAT *de Atik* shine downward during the 6,000 years with diminished Light, restricting it according to the laws of *Tzimtzum Bet*. Only at the end of correction will they begin to pass down all of their Light. It is written in the Torah that the Light that *Atik* had passed during the 6,000 years is designated with the small letter *Hey* in the word Avraham.

However, because Havakuk's death has purified him completely, since at the end of correction he merited merging with the "past years" of *Atik*, he received the required strength in Elisha's embraces and resurrection. It is hence written that after he has purified himself and felt fear at the moment of his death, the power of this fear enabled him to establish contact with ZAT *de Atik* and receive the Light called "eternal life."

For having purified himself through death, BON received complete correction, upon ascending and becoming SAG at the time of death. Subsequently, it reaches the degree of *Malchut de Malchut*, a *Zivug* on which can only be made at the end of correction, and attains this degree, the Light of his life.

119. Rabbi Shimon wept and said: "And I have seen from the Creator what I have heard." He raised his hands above his head, and said: "But you have merited seeing Rabbi Hamnuna-Saba, the Light of the Torah, face to face, while I have not." He fell on his face and saw him who uproots mountains and

lights candles in the Temple of the King (*Mashiach*). He said to him, "Rabbi, in the other world we shall be neighbors with the heads of the assemblies before the Creator." From here on, he called his son Rabbi Elazar and Rabbi Aba by the name Pnei'el (the face of God), as it is written: "For I have seen the Creator face to face."

He praised himself for using the same fear from the past, just like Prophet Havakuk.

All corrections are already ready and waiting in the hall of the King (*Mashiach*), down to the very last detail. They must all be revealed at the end of all corrections, with the appearance of the King. And the souls in that hall are those who merited completion of their individual corrections, for there is an individual correction and a general one.

*Malchut de Malchut* is the only creation, and it is divided into parts called souls. These parts merge with people of our world, and each of them, while existing within man, must attain one's own correction, i.e., gradually replace one's properties (desires) with those of the Creator. This is considered the soul's individual or personal correction. So then, the souls that have attained their individual correction reach and exist in the state called "abiding in the hall of the King-*Mashiach*."

The Light in that hall (the Light of the Torah), also called Hamnuna-Saba, completely liberates man from the impure forces, i.e., purifies him from all his primordial egoistic desires and corrects *Malchut de Malchut*, which "appears to the righteous as a high mountain" (Talmud, *Sota*, 52). This correction is made by creating a new SAG-like screen with the purpose of raising MAN (the request for final correction). MAN is called *Me'orei Esh* (sparkles of fire), as it is written: "Man's soul is the Creator's candle" (*Mishley*, 20:27).

The light of the sun designates the Light's descent, MAD, just as sunlight descends upon us from Above, whereas a fire's flame signifies *Ohr Hozer* that rises from below upwards, like candlelight. *The Zohar* therefore says that these two corrections, aimed at destroying the impure forces and ascending to light the candles in the hall of the King-*Mashiach*, are in the hands of Rabbi Hamnuna-Saba.

And the perfect righteous in need of these two final corrections merit receiving them only through revealing the soul of Rabbi Hamnuna-Saba. And he stated that they (the disciples of Rabbi Elazar and Rabbi Aba) will merit the honor of serving in the hall of the King-*Mashiach* after their death, and will become his neighbors and the heads of the Creator's Assembly.

# THE TWO POINTS

120. Rabbi Chiya began and opened, "The beginning of *Hochma* (wisdom) is fear of the Creator, and those who observe this rule receive all the goodness." He asks, "The beginning of wisdom? One should rather say that the end of wisdom is the fear of the Creator, for fear of the Creator is the property of *Malchut*, which is at the end of *Hochma* (wisdom)." He replies, "Yet, *Malchut* is the beginning of the entrance to the degrees of reception of the Supernal wisdom." Hence, it is written, "Open to me the gates of justice," meaning that the gates of *Malchut*, called "justice," are the Creator's gates. And if man does not enter these gates he shall not reach the Supernal King through any other, for He is concealed and detached, and has erected many gates on the path to Him.

Fear of the Creator is the *Sefira Malchut*. Yet, how can *Malchut* serve as an entrance if she is the last of the ten *Sefirot*? Indeed, she may be called the end of *Hochma* or of a *Partzuf*, but not the beginning. However, this is not an allegorical expression, but the essence itself, for HE IS CONCEALED AND DETACHED and no thought of man can attain Him. Hence, He has put up many gates ON THE PATH TO HIM, and thanks to these gates He grants sufferers the opportunity to draw closer to him, the opportunity for attainment.

This is precisely what the verse, "Open to me the gates of justice," (*Tehilim*, 118) alludes to; these are the very gates that the Creator made, through which people can come to Him. HOWEVER, AT THE END OF ALL THE GATES ERECTED A SPECIAL GATE WITH MANY LOCKS. This gate is *Malchut de Malchut*, the ultimate point of all creation, the ultimate point of all Supernal gates.

And this last gate (from Above downwards) is the first gate to Supernal wisdom (from below upwards), for it is impossible to attain the Supernal *Hochma* (wisdom) without attaining precisely this final gate, as it is the first gate with regard to attainment of the Supernal wisdom. It is therefore written (*Tehilim*, 111:10): "Fear of the Creator is the beginning of wisdom," as fear of the Creator is called the final gate, which stands first on the path to Supernal attainment.

**121. And at the end of all the gates He erected a special gate with several locks, several entrances, and several chambers, one atop of the other. And He said, "Whoever wishes to reach Me, let this be the first gate on his way to Me. Whoever enters through this gate—will enter." Only this is the first gate to the Supernal wisdom, the gate of fear of the Creator, *Malchut*, which is hence called "beginning."**

The locks, entrances, and chambers are three successive processes of attainment, of realizing the spiritual in one's inner sensation. The thought that created the world was the Creator's thought to make a creation (the human soul) in order to fill it with delight. However, it is impossible to feel delight as long as one is removed from the Creator, for He is the only One in existence. And He has created us in such a way that the nearer we come to Him, the greater delight we feel, whereas the farther we are from Him, the more we suffer.

Those of us who live in and perceive only this world can only accept the above words on faith or reject them. However, Kabbalists, who ascend spiritually and draw closer to the Creator, make these assertions and describe their attainments for us. And as to how and when we shall travel the same path to the Creator and attain complete unity with Him, this depends on us alone. However, regardless of whether we want to or not, we will need to travel the entire path from our world to complete unity with the Creator while still existing in this body, during one of our lifetimes in this world. This is the purpose of creation, and until it is fulfilled, man must reincarnate and return to this world, as the sages said: "The Creator wished to dwell in the lower ones."

Our world is built completely opposite from the Creator, as it was created in the property of egoistic will to receive pleasure, and this property is the exact antithesis to the Creator's property (desire) to delight us. Additionally, there is no trace of a will to receive pleasure in the Creator Himself.

It is hence said about a person in our world: "Man is born akin to a wild ass" (*Iyov*, 11:12). Therefore, to those who live in this world, the Creator's governance seems completely opposite to the purpose of creation—to delight the creatures. After all, that is how we perceive His rule over us, and feel the surrounding world in our egoistic sensations.

According to the Creator's plan, one must correct his egoistic desires and make them altruistic, whereupon the Creator fulfills them with supernal, absolute delight (to the extent of their correction). Until one attains this state, he continues to suffer from his desire to enjoy either this world or the spiritual.

These sensations are called "gate locks," for all the numerous contradictions to the oneness of the Creator's actions that we feel in this world separate us from the Creator and prevent us from drawing closer to Him. However, when we exert to observe the Torah and *Mitzvot* with love, with our heart and soul, as devotedly as it was prescribed for us, with the sole intention of pleasing the Creator and without any benefit for ourselves, all of the forces that separate us from Him and every contradiction that we overcome on our path to Him becomes a gate of attainment of His Supernal wisdom, of *Ohr Hochma*. This is because every contradiction reveals its own uniqueness in the attainment of the Creator's governance.

Thus, those very questions and contradictions, which initially seemed to prevent us from accepting the oneness of the Creator's governance, then turn into knowledge, thanks to which we come to understand and attain the oneness of His governance.

And those who merit this transform darkness into Light (within themselves) and bitterness into sweetness. This is how they feel their attainments—in precisely those past sensations of darkness and bitterness. For the forces that repel us from the Creator, that form our minds and are perceived by the body as bitter turn into gates of attainment of Supernal Degrees. This way, darkness becomes Light and bitterness becomes sweetness.

And the more negative the Creator's governance is first perceived, the deeper man eventually comes to realize the perfection of His governance. At last, the entire world ends up on the scale of merit, for every force and insight now serve as SHAAREY TZEDEK (the gates of truth), through which one can enter and receive from the Creator everything that He intended to bestow at the Thought of Creation. Thus, it is written about such contradictions that turn into realization of unity: "These are the gates to the Creator; the righteous shall enter them" (*Tehilim*, 118:20).

Hence, until one merits turning his will "to receive for himself" into the will "to receive for the Creator" with the help of the Torah and *Mitzvot*, all the gates to the Creator have sturdy locks (the sensation of imperfection in the Creator's governance), as they then play their opposite role: to distance and turn one away from the Creator. And they are called locks, for they lock the gates of contact with the Creator and distance us from Him.

However, if we make efforts to overcome them so they stop influencing us and weakening our love for the Creator, we will thus turn these locks into entrances, darkness into Light, and bitterness into sweetness. This is because for every lock we receive a special degree of attainment of the Creator. These degrees become entrances that lead to the degrees of sensation of the Creator Himself. And the degrees themselves turn into halls or chambers of wisdom.

Thus, we see that locks, entrances, and chambers constitute the three types of perception of one material, our will to receive or egoism. Indeed, before we turn the egoistic desire to receive into reception (of pleasure) for the Creator's sake, altruism, this material transforms Light into darkness and sweetness into bitterness, in accordance with our (egoistic) taste. In other words, egoism finds suffering in the same types of influence that bring pleasure to altruism. Therefore, to perceive the Light (delight) that surrounds us, we only need to change our senses. But until we do, this Light will be perceived by us as darkness and suffering.

Initially, whatever examples of the Creator's governance we see, they distance us from Him. This is because we perceive them negatively; at that very moment, our egoism (will to receive pleasure) begets locks. However, once we transform our desires to "reception for the Creator's sake," these locks become entrances, and entrances turn into chambers—vessels of wisdom, *Ohr Hochma*.

As we already know, the end of all the degrees, i.e., the very last degree, below which nothing can possibly exist, is called *Malchut de Malchut*. To attain Supernal wisdom, one must first overcome this last gate, which turns into the first gate to ascend from below upwards, toward the chamber of Supernal wisdom, the *Sefira Hochma*. All gates become entrances and chambers of the Creator's wisdom. This is why it is written, IN THE BEGINNING (the first words in the Torah), for IN THE BEGINNING signifies fear of the Creator, the last gate (*Malchut*), which becomes the first on the path to attainment of the Supernal wisdom.

**122. The letter *Bet* in the word *BERESHEET* (IN THE BEGINNING) indicates that the two are joined together in *Malchut*. Both are points: one is concealed, while the other is revealed. However, since there's no division between them, they are called THE BEGINNING, which signifies only one, rather than two, for he who takes one, takes the other as well, and all is one,**

**for He and His Name are one, as it is written, "And you shall know that this is the Creator's only name."**

The Hebrew letter *Bet* has a numerical value of two, indicating two points. These two points symbolize the correction of the egoistic point of *Malchut*, onto which the point of mercy (*Bina*) imposes a restriction of use. Correction is achieved when *Malchut* (strictness) ascends to *Bina* (mercy), as it is written, "So they both walked" (*Rut*, 1:19), i.e., *Bina* and *Malchut*. Hence, the screen in *Malchut* consists of both points, and they are thereby joined together as one.

It is explained in *Megilat Rut* (*The Book of Ruth*) how *Malchut* (Ruth) merges with *Bina* (Naomi), which then leads to the correction of *Malchut* and the birth of David, the first King (the word King (*Melech*) is derived from *Malchut* (kingdom) of Israel).

HOWEVER, ONE IS CONCEALED, WHILE THE OTHER IS REVEALED, for the judgment in the point of *Malchut* is concealed, whereas only the property of mercy in the point of *Bina* is revealed. Otherwise, the world could not exist, as it is written, "In the beginning, He created the world with the property of judgment, but seeing that it cannot exist, He attached to it the property of mercy" (*Beresheet Raba*, item 1).

Although the restriction is concealed, this does not mean that a *Zivug* is not made on it, since these two points merge into one, and the point of *Malchut* receives a *Zivug* together with the point of *Bina*, though it participates in it secretly. Therefore, it is written, IN THE BEGINNING, for the word "beginning" indicates one point, which includes two that are as one.

Because *Malchut* participates with *Bina* in all the *Zivugim* that are made during the 6,000 years (albeit secretly), she corrects herself to such an extent that at the end of all the corrections, even her property of restriction is corrected, and she acquires the property of *Bina*. It is written of this state that on that day He and His Name will be one.

Since the property of restriction is also concealed within the letter *Bet* of the word *BERESHEET* (in the beginning), this property is called *RESHEET* (first) in *Hochma* (wisdom). However, the correction of this property occurs only at the end of corrections, when the Supernal wisdom is revealed, as the prophet said: "For the earth shall be filled with the knowledge of the Creator" (*Yeshayahu*, 11:9). This is because the last gate will become the first. Hence, it is written, "That they may know that it is Thou alone whose name is the Lord, the Most High over all the earth," (*Tehilim*, 83:19) for the Creator's wisdom will be revealed in our world to all.

**123. Why is *Malchut* called "fear of the Creator?" It is because *Malchut* is the Tree of Good and Evil: If man merits, it is good, but if he does not, it is evil. This is why fear dwells in that place. And this gate leads to all the goodness that exists in the world. ALL THE GOODNESS signifies two gates, two points that are as one. Rabbi Yosi said that ALL THE GOODNESS refers to the Tree of Life, for it is entirely good and completely without evil. And because it is without evil, it is entirely good, without evil.**

It is written of the last gate: THE BEGINNING OF WISDOM IS FEAR OF THE CREATOR. So why is it called "fear of the Creator?" Because this is the secret of the Tree of Knowledge, by which Adam sinned, for the use of that point (egoistic desires) is punishable by death (disappearance of the Light). And great fear is needed to refrain from touching (using) it before all the other desires have been corrected. Nevertheless, at the end of correction, when even this point is completely corrected, death will cease to exist for all eternity. That is why it is called "fear."

The Creator created one creation—the egoistic *Malchut*. The goal of creation is to fill her with the Creator's Light using an altruistic intention. As a result, *Malchut* merges with the Creator and receives limitless delight.

*Malchut*, the only creation, consists of five parts: *KHB ZA-M*. Her parts *KHB ZA*, excluding *Malchut de Malchut*, have altruistic properties, which they received from the Light.

As a result of her decision to refrain from receiving Light into egoistic desires, called *Tzimtzum Aleph* (the first restriction), *Malchut* receives the Light only in her first four desires: *KHB-ZA*. *Malchut de Malchut* remains inaccessible to the Light. So how can she be corrected?

To correct *Malchut de Malchut's* properties (desires), the Creator creates the conditions under which *Bina* and *Malchut* mix, and consequently, *Malchut* acquires the properties of *Bina*.

This process needs to occur more than once, so that all of *Malchut's* parts will be mixed with *Bina*. Every time it takes place in an increasingly deeper layer of *Malchut*, it is called the breaking of holiness, for *Bina* descends and passes her properties to *Malchut*, but she herself breaks during this mixing, as though losing her altruistic properties.

Thus, we can conclude that all the shattering of vessels, the breaking of Adam's soul, the ruin of the First and Second Temples, and other spiritual disasters take place not as punishment, for punishment (as we understand it) does not exist in the spiritual, but only so as to enable the altruistic desires of *Bina* penetrate deeper into the egoistic desires of *Malchut*.

The last point of *Malchut*, the yet uncorrected *Malchut de Malchut*, is that very point the use of which is punishable by death (the Light's disappearance is considered death). It is forbidden to use *Malchut de Malchut* until all the other properties of *Malchut* (KHB-ZA) have been fully corrected. Or rather, if man refrains from using egoism (the point of *Malchut de Malchut*), and uses only his other altruistic desires, he gradually constructs a "non-reception" screen on *Malchut de Malchut*.

Having filled all of his corrected desires with Light, man achieves the end of correction—of what he could correct by himself. As soon as that happens, i.e., as soon as one receives the Light in all of his soul's first nine *Sefirot* (KHB-ZA, excluding *Malchut*), the Light called *Mashiach* descends from Above, which imparts *Malchut de Malchut* with the altruistic property of bestowal, of acting for the Creator's sake. This concludes the entire correction process of man's soul, and he attains complete unity with the Creator. The Creator's goal is for man to attain this state while still living in our world and in his physical body, to combine all the worlds, spiritual and material, within himself.

AND THIS GATE LEADS TO ALL THE GOODNESS, for there is nothing better than the revelation of the Supernal wisdom in the world, included in the Thought of Creation. And since fear of the Creator is the last gate to the Supernal wisdom, it also constitutes the gate to all the goodness.

THESE TWO GATES ARE AS ONE refers to the two points, *Bina* and *Malchut*, which are united in the letter *Bet* of the word *BERESHEET* (IN THE BEGINNING), the first word in the Torah. And the two points are mentioned because they allude to the state following the correction, when these two points are called "the two gates," for both turn out to be good and free from evil, thereby bringing man only perfect goodness.

Nevertheless, until the end of correction, one must strain to separate within him the desires that refer to the point of *Bina* from those that refer to the point of *Malchut*, to reject the desires of *Malchut*, and, in defiance of egoism, use the desires of *Bina*. During man's work on self-correction, called "6,000 years," these two points are referred to as "The Tree of Knowledge of Good and Evil."

RABBI YOSI SAID—Rabbi Yosi does not object to the words of Rabbi Chiya. They are talking about two different states: Rabbi Chiya alludes to a state past the end of correction of *Malchut*, when both points become a gate, and there is no more evil within them. And Rabbi Yosi explains a state in the correction process, when the two points, *Bina* and *Malchut*, exist within us as our Tree of Knowledge of Good and Evil. Hence, he tells us that ALL THE GOODNESS IS (can only be found in) THE TREE OF LIFE.

ZA filled with the Light of *Ima-Bina* is called "The Tree of Life," for he possesses only good properties. And the two points of good and evil, *Bina* and *Malchut*, remain within *Malchut* until the end of correction; hence, *Malchut* is called "The Tree of Knowledge of Good and Evil."

**124. To all those who act, it is the faithful mercy of David that upholds the Torah. Those who keep the Torah seemingly create it themselves. All those who study the Torah—there is no action in them as they study, but those who keep the Torah—in them there is action. And the world exists by this force, eternal are the wisdom and the Torah, and the throne stands just as it should stand.**

It was previously said that fear of the Creator constitutes the last gate, though it is the first gate to the Supernal wisdom. It turns out that ALL THOSE WHO STUDY THE TORAH have already corrected the last gate, and the two points become for them two entrances, all goodness without evil. Hence, it is said that THERE IS NO ACTION IN THEM, i.e., no analysis of good and evil, for they have already corrected everything.

However, those who have not yet reached the end of correction are referred to as those who keep the Torah. There is action in them, for they have not yet corrected good and evil in everyone's Tree of Good and Evil—not everyone has realized in one's inner tree (in all of one's properties) what is good and what is evil with regard to the spiritual truth.

It is therefore said that THOSE WHO KEEP THE TORAH SEEMINGLY CREATE IT THEMSELVES. As a result of man's effort to refrain from their use, all the distracting and impeding forces (thoughts and desires) of the point of *Malchut* become gates, all the locks become entrances, and all the entrances become chambers of wisdom filled with *Ohr Hochma*.

It follows that all the wisdom and the entire Torah become revealed only through the efforts of those who keep the Torah. Hence, they SEEMINGLY CREATE IT THEMSELVES. The forces of good and evil are combined within them, and they become those who keep the Torah, for the Torah is revealed thanks to their inner work of separating and correcting good and evil.

Such people are called "those who act," for they seemingly create the Torah by themselves. After all, without perceiving the Creator (The Torah, Light) as concealed, and then overcoming this concealment, thereby turning it into gates, entrances, and chambers the Torah could never have been revealed.

The perfection of the Creator's actions lies in the fact that by creating man so paltry (with such insignificant egoistic desires, completely opposite to the Creator in his properties, and utterly powerless to change himself), the Creator gave man an opportunity to become like Him (in properties, greatness, and the sensation of creating himself), to create within and by himself all of the worlds and the Torah. By revealing the Light, it is as though man actually creates it.

Thus, since these individuals reveal the Torah, they are regarded as its creators. The word is SEEMINGLY used to indicate that the Torah was created before the creation of our world (Talmud, *Pesachim*, 54:1), and of course, it is the work of the Creator Himself. Yet, without the good deeds of those who keep the Torah, it would not have been revealed to the world. Hence, they are regarded as the makers and creators of the Torah.

The wisdom and the Torah are eternal; that is, they exist even after the end of correction, for fear of the Creator is needed even then. However, once the entire egoism is corrected, there is no place from which to take this fear, for the Tree of Good and Evil becomes only good, and can no longer furnish fear of the Creator.

However, because they received fear in the past, they can continue using it in the present, after the end of correction, when there is nothing left to fear, as there are no restrictions in *Malchut*. And the only reason they can do so is that during the correction they worked on creating within them the sensation of the Creator's absolute rule and the eternity of the Torah. And since this fear is never-ending, the Creator's throne remains forever standing in their attainment.

# THE NIGHT OF THE BRIDE

**125.** Rabbi Shimon was sitting and studying the Torah on the night when the Bride, *Malchut*, unites with her husband, *Zeir Anpin*. And all the friends present in the bridal chamber on that night, the eve of the holiday of *Shavuot* (Pentecost), must stand together with the bridegroom under the *Huppah* (wedding canopy), and be with him this whole night, and rejoice with him in the corrections of the Bride, i.e., study the Torah, then Prophets, then Holy Scriptures, and finally the wisdom, for these corrections are the Bride's adornments. And the Bride receives corrections, adorns herself with them, and rejoices with them all of that night. And on the next day, on the holiday of *Shavuot*, she only comes to the *Huppah* together with them. And her friends, who studied the Torah all night long, are called the sons of the *Huppah*. And as she approaches the *Huppah*, the Creator asks about them, blesses and adorns them with the Bride's adornments. Happy are those who merit this!

All the days of exile are called night, for this is when the Creator's face is concealed from Israel, as the impure forces rule and separate His loyal servants from Him. Yet, this is the time when the bride unites with her husband (in Hebrew, "husband" and "master" are the same word, so one must keep in mind the second meaning of the word as well). The *Huppah* is a wedding canopy, under which the ritual of union between a bride and a bridegroom (their merging in a *Zivug*) takes place.

The union between the bride and her husband (*The Zohar* uses the word "husband" instead of "bridegroom") occurs thanks to the Torah and *Mitzvot* (commandments) of the righteous, referred to as "those who keep the Torah." And all the Supernal Degrees, called "secrets of the Torah," become revealed thanks to them alone, for they are also called MAKERS (as though CREATING the Torah itself), as is described in item 124. Therefore, the time of exile is called the NIGHT WHEN THE BRIDE UNITES WITH HER HUSBAND. AND

ALL THE FRIENDS, THE SONS OF THE BRIDE'S JOY, ARE CALLED THOSE WHO KEEP THE TORAH.

And after THE END OF CORRECTION and complete deliverance, of which the prophet Zachariah writes (14:7): "And there shall be one day, which shall be known to the Creator, neither day nor night, but it shall come to pass come evening time: there shall be light." THE NEXT DAY, THE BRIDE AND HER HUSBAND ENTER THE *HUPPAH*, for *BON* will become like *SAG* and *MA* will be like *AB* (see item 64).

This state is therefore defined as the next day and a new *Huppah*. Whereas at this time (in this state), the righteous are called SONS OF THE *HUPPAH*, in whom there is no action, for then, as it is written: "They shall not do evil upon My holy mountain, for the earth shall be filled with the knowledge of the Creator, as waters cover the sea" (*Yeshayahu*, 11: 9).

And since these righteous elevated *BON* to *SAG* by their actions, i.e., made its properties similar to those of *SAG*, they are considered to have made a new *Huppah*, they are called "sons of the *Huppah*."

The night of *Shavuot* (Pentecost) is when THE BRIDE UNITES WITH HER HUSBAND, for the *Huppah* takes place on the next day, the day of *Shavuot*, the day of the reception of the Torah. On that day, all of creation achieves the state of the end of correction, as it is said: "He will swallow up death forever; and the Creator Himself will wipe away the tears off all faces" (*Yeshayahu*, 25:8).

The Torah describes this state as "engraved upon the scrolls" (*Shemot*, 32:16). In Hebrew, the word "engraved" is *Harut*, but it should be pronounced *Herut* (freedom), freedom from the angel of death. However, the sin of the golden calf followed and the High Degree was lost. Since *Shavuot* is the day when the Torah was received, it is also regarded as the end of correction.

Therefore, all the necessary preparations (the corrections carried out during the concealment period) are completed beforehand, on the night before the holiday of *Shavuot*. This night is hence defined as the night when the bride unites with her husband so as to enter the *Huppah* the following day, on the holiday of *Shavuot*, when all the corrections are completed and liberated from the angel of death, thanks to the actions of the righteous, who erect a new *Huppah*.

All of the bride's friends, those who keep the Torah, also called "sons of the bridal chamber," must be merged with the *Shechina-Malchut* (the bride) all of that night, called "exile." Only then do their acts in the Torah and *Mitzvot* correct and purify the good in her from the taint of evil, so she would emerge with the properties that contain only good, without evil.

Hence, those who keep the Torah should rejoice together with the bride for all the great corrections that they've made in her. Then they joyously continue with their corrections in THE TORAH, then in PROPHETS and finally in the HOLY SCRIPTURES. All the degrees and revelations of the secrets of the Torah, which make up the framework of the *Shechina* herself at the end of her correction, are made exclusively by the righteous, who keep the Torah during the exile.

Therefore, all the degrees that emerge through the righteous at the time (state) of the exile are called the bride's corrections and adornments from the Torah, Prophets and Holy Scriptures, for *Sefirot Hesed, Gevura,* and *Tifferet* constitute the Torah, *Sefirot Netzah, Hod,* and *Yesod* are the Prophets, and *Malchut* is the Holy Scriptures. The Light of *VAK* is called *Midrashim* and the Light of *GAR* is called "the secrets of the Torah." And all these corrections must be made in *Malchut* (the bride) on the night when she completes her corrections (precisely in the darkness of exile from the spiritual does man carry out the work of his inner correction).

It is known that the end of correction does not bring anything new or that was previously unknown. Rather, all the MAN and MAD, along with all degrees and *Zivugim* that have emerged consecutively during the 6,000 years will merge into one degree and become corrected with the help of the Light of *AHP*.

The bride will then enter her *Huppah,* and THE CREATOR WILL ASK ABOUT EVERYONE, about every man who had even once raised MAN for the Supernal, final *Zivug.* For the Creator waits for all the small *Zivugim* to assemble, as though asking about and waiting for each of them. And when they've gathered, a great *Zivug* will unfold, called *RAV PAALIM U MEKABTZIEL* (HE WHO BLESSES AND ADORNS HER). And when all the creatures are blessed and adorned together, correction comes to an end. This is referred to as "the adornment of the bride's crown."

**126. This is why Rabbi Shimon and all of his friends stayed up that night, and each of them renewed the Torah again and again. Rabbi Shimon was joyous, and so were his friends. Rabbi Shimon said to them: "My sons, how blessed is your lot, for it is you who shall accompany the Bride tomorrow to the *Huppah,* for all those who correct Her and rejoice in Her this night shall have their names recorded in the Book of Remembrance. And the Creator shall bless them with seventy blessings and adornments of crowns of the Upper World."**

The Book of Remembrance, mentioned by the prophet (*Malachi*, 3:15): "You will say, 'How futile it is to serve the Creator! When we carried out the Creator's will, and walked heavy-hearted before Him—what is the use of it all? And now we regard the wicked as blessed: they have settled in their wickedness, tried the Creator, and were liberated.' Then those who feared the Creator spoke with each other, and the Creator hearkened and heard, and a Book of Remembrance was recorded before Him for those who fear the Creator and honor His Name. 'They shall become chosen for Me on the day that I shall determine, and I shall spare them, as a man spares his own son, who serves him.'"

But how can we understand that when they spoke ill of the Creator, they referred to fear of the Creator, as the prophet says? Moreover, they were inscribed in the Book of Remembrance as those who "feared the Creator and honored His Name?"

The thing is that at the end of correction, when the great general *Zivug* of *Atik* manifests, great Light will be revealed in all the worlds, and in this Light everyone will return to the Creator in absolute love. The Talmud (*Yoma*, 86:2, "Introduction to the Study of the Ten Sefirot") says: "He who attains the repentance from love shall have his sins turned to merits."

Here, the prophet refers to the sinners claiming the futility of spiritual work: on the great day of the end of correction, when the Light of repentance from love shall shine, all the most malicious and deliberate, worst imaginable sins, will turn to merits, and their words shall be deemed not slight, but fear of the Creator.

Therefore, all the sins, as well as all the good deeds, are recorded before the Creator, for He will need them on that great day of His miracle: all the merits gather and complete the *Kli*, which receives the Light necessary for the final correction. Hence, it is said that the Creator shall record the names of those who fear Him in the Book of Remembrance, for He will need them on that day to complete the common *Partzuf*. This is exactly what the prophet says: those who remain shall be close to the Creator, like sons who served Him.

It is therefore said that everyone and everything will be recorded in the Book of Remembrance, even the sins. However, The Creator will record them as though they are merits, as though they served Him. These are the words of the prophet.

The number seventy signifies the Light of *Hochma*, GAR, adornment, a crown, and the Light of *Hassadim* is called "a blessing," for the world was created with the letter *Bet* (blessing), as it is written: "The world was built by mercy" (*Tehilim*, 89:3), which is *VAK*. But at the end of correction, the Light of *Hassadim* will also be like seventy crowns, like the Light of *Hochma*, for MA and BON will ascend to *AB* and *SAG*. Therefore, *The Zohar* says that the Creator will bless them with seventy blessings and adornments of crowns of the Upper World.

127. Rabbi Shimon opened and said, "The Heavens declare the Creator's greatness. I have already explained this, but when the bride awakens to enter the *Huppah* on the following day, with all the friends who rejoiced with her through that night, she rejoices with them, corrects herself and shines with her adornments."

128. And on the following day, a multitude of masses, hosts, and legions join her. And she, together with all these masses, hosts and legions, awaits all those who corrected her by studying the Torah on that night. This is so because *Zeir Anpin* unites with *Malchut*, and she sees her husband, and it is said: "The Heavens declare the Creator's greatness." "The Heavens" alludes to the Bridegroom (ZA), who enters the *Huppah*. "The Heavens declare," i.e., shine, like the luminescence of a sapphire, upon the entire *Malchut*, from end to end.

The day of the end of correction is called "tomorrow," as it is written in the Talmud: "Do today, and receive the reward tomorrow" (*Eruvin*, 22:1). The masses are the worldly masses who do not serve the Creator, the hosts are those who serve the Creator, and the legions are chariots of warriors in armor—the Supernal groups of angels that accompany the souls, as it is said: "For He bid His angels to guard over you on all your paths" (*Tehilim*, 91:11). Just as the Creator waits for everyone, as was previously stated, so does the *Shechina*.

"Heavens" is the bridegroom entering the *Huppah*—the state of the end of correction, of which it is written: "And the light of the moon (*Malchut*) shall be as the light of the sun (ZA)" (*Yeshayahu*, 30:26). The Creator is called the "Heavens," and at the end of correction He is referred to as the "bridegroom," as it is said: "Just as a bridegroom rejoices over his bride, so shall your Creator rejoice over you." (*Yeshayahu*, 62:5).

Wherever it is said that the Creator descends, it indicates His strictness and judgment, for it speaks of diminishing His greatness in the eyes of the lower ones, as it is said: "His might and greatness are in His place." But at the end of correction, when all sins turn to merits, for it will become clear that all the spiritual descents were nothing other than spiritual ascents, the Creator becomes the "bridegroom" and the *Shechina* becomes his "bride."

The Hebrew word for "bride" is *Kalah*, as in the words *Kalat Moshe* (*Bamidbar*, 7), which describes the completion of the altar. Hence, in the Torah, the word *Kalah* signifies the end of construction. The Hebrew word for "bridegroom" is *Hatan*, and it signifies the descent along spiritual degrees, as it is said in the Talmud: "Descends the steps" (*Yevamot*, 63:1). However, this descent is greater than all the previous ascents, for it takes place on the way towards the bride at the moment of the end of correction.

The *Huppah* represents the total of the Reflected Light received on the MAN raised by the righteous in all the *Zivugim* at all the times during the 6,000 years. This is because now they have all gathered into one great Reflected Light, rising and soaring over the Creator and the *Shechina*, over the bridegroom and his bride, like a *Huppah*—wedding canopy.

In this state, the righteous are called "Sons of the *Huppah*," for each of them has a part in this *Huppah*, to the extent of the MAN they raise to the screen of *Malchut*, which evoked, produced the Reflected Light, corresponding in magnitude to this MAN. At the end of correction, the Creator is called *Hatan* (bridegroom), for He *Nechit Darga*—descends from His degree to his bride, and enters the *Huppah*.

At this time (in this state), the Heavens say—this is a great *Zivug* of the future, as the Talmud says: "The wife speaks to her husband" (*Berachot*, 3:1). The word "speaks" (*Mesaperet*) implies a *Zivug*, and is derived from *Sapir* (sapphire), the name of the *Shechina*, as it is said in the Torah, "...and under His feet—like a pavement of sapphire" (*Shemot*, 24:10).

THE LUMINESCENT SAPPHIRE is the Reflected Light, ascending from below upwards. LUMINESCENT, LIKE LUMINESCENCE—The Reflected Light, LUMINESCENT is equivalent to the Direct Light, LUMINESCENCE. This great *Zivug* gathers all of the Reflected Light from all the *Zivugim* made during the 6,000 years, and the Direct Light will shine in it, as it is said, FROM END TO END.

**129. The Creator's glory = *EL*—is the bride, *Malchut*, called *EL*, as it is written: "*EL* rages each day." She is called *EL* on all the days of the year. And now, on the holiday of *Shavuot*, when she already entered the *Huppah*, she is called GREATNESS and she is called *EL*, greatest of the great, luminescent out of the luminescent, dominion over dominions.**

*El* is the name of great mercy. Yet, here it says: "*El* rages each day," which is contrary to mercy. The Torah says: "And there shall be evening, and there shall be morning, one day." The *Shechina* is a small star, the Moon, which reigns at night. It is called "fear of Heaven," for it is the property of the righteous, who must raise *MAN* through their aspiration to be corrected, thereby evoking the Reflected Light to descend on *Malchut* from Above and correct her.

It is therefore written: "The Creator hath made it so man would fear Him" (*Kohelet*, 3:14). This is so because it is impossible to raise the *MAN* without fear. The absence of fear of the Creator is referred to as *Malchut's* reign at night, in the state of darkness. In the absence of Light, all the restrictions and suffering are revealed, as they are opposite to the property of day, mercy. Thus, fear of the Creator emerges; were it not for this fear, the property of morning and day could not be revealed.

So it is written: "And there shall be evening, and there shall be morning, one day." Night also enters morning, for without a night, there would be no morning, and one cannot do without night. It is hence written that *EL* RAGES EACH DAY. After all, the property of mercy, called *EL*, is revealed only with the help of the night, through the property of RAGE. Hence, this property is also regarded as mercy; and consequently, the *Shechina* is called *EL*.

This is why it is said that the CREATOR'S GREATNESS = *EL*–IS THE BRIDE, MALCHUT, CALLED *EL*, for it is impossible to achieve the state of "day" without the state of "night." So it is in each of the six days of creation, of which it is said: "And there shall be evening, and there shall be morning, one day." We see that the night is included in the name "day." And just as they are all called the six DAYS of creation, the 6,000 years are called "night" in the property of mercy.

And in the great *Zivug* at the end of correction, a day shall come; the light of the moon will become like that of the sun, as the prophet said (*Zachariah*, 14:7): "It shall come to pass, that at evening time there shall be light." This will cause the degrees of *Malchut* to increase twofold, for even during the 6,000 years, the light of the moon was according to the aforesaid, "And there shall be evening, and there shall be morning."

And at the end of correction, when the moon becomes like the sun (ZA), the moon will be twice as great as before, as it will become greatness itself, for its greatness will equal that of ZA, of which *The Zohar* says: THE GREATEST OF THE GREAT, DOMINION OVER DOMINIONS. Although it merged with the light of the morning during the 6,000 years, as it is said, "And there shall be evening, and there shall be morning, one day," now that it is as big as the sun (ZA), it becomes Light, itself, LUMINESCENT OUT OF THE LUMINESCENT. Previously, its Light was solely the result of the inclusion of the properties of Higher *Sefirot* into it.

Also, DOMINION OVER DOMINIONS, for during the 6,000 years, its reign was that of a small star, reigning only at night. Now, however, it also reigns during the day, for it is as big as the sun.

**130. The hour when the Heaven (ZA) enters the *Huppah* and shines upon *Malchut*, all of her friends, who corrected her by studying the Torah, are known by their names, as it is said: "The Heavens declare the work of His hands." "The work of His hands" refers to the members of this covenant, called "the work of His hands." As you say: "Confirm for us the work of our hands," which is the mark of the covenant, imprinted on man's body.**

"Friends" are those who keep the Torah, which includes both good and evil deeds, even those parts of them that are still evil and uncorrected; EACH IS KNOWN BY A NAME (his corrected part), as it is said: THE HEAVENS DECLARE THE WORK OF HIS HANDS. "Heavens" is the Book of Remembrance, which constitutes the Light of the great *Zivug* that leads to repentance (correction) out of love, when sins become merits (Talmud, *Yoma*, 86:2).

And even those who were speaking ill things, it is said about them: "Then they shall impart their fear of the Creator upon one another" (item 126). Therefore, the action defined as "upholding the Torah," which includes both good (for the worthy) and evil (for the unworthy), now becomes completely good and holy. And it turns into THE WORK OF HIS HANDS—the Creator's actions, for THE HEAVENS SPEAK even of the unworthy. It turns out that all the friends have performed only good deeds and carried out holy work, for they would all correct *Malchut*, and ALL ARE KNOWN BY THEIR NAMES.

It is therefore said: CONFIRM FOR US THE WORK OF OUR HANDS (*Tehilim*, 90:17). However, it is unclear whose hands are meant: His or ours? Only one thing is meant here—that the covenant is referred to as "the work of our hands," for its confirmation is *Yesod* (*Yesod* is not only the name of a *Sefira*, it also means "basis," "foundation" in Hebrew), the foundation of the entire construction.

The correction of *Yesod* is *Brit Milah* (circumcision). Hence, it is said that the existence of the covenant is called "the work of our hands," for we separate the *Orlah* (foreskin) from *Yesod* through the work of our hands. But this only concerns the period up to the end of correction. And at the end of correction, THE WORK OF HIS HANDS will be revealed. In other words, the Creator

Himself will detach the *Orlah* from us, and THE HEAVENS DECLARE THE
WORK OF HIS HANDS. But until that state comes, we are entrusted with the
correction of the circumcision. Therefore, we ask: CONFIRM FOR US THE
WORK OF OUR HANDS.

**131. Rabbi Hamnuna-Saba then said as follows: "Do not let your mouth cause
your body to sin," i.e., one must not allow his mouth to get close to evil and be
the cause of sin for the sacred flesh, which bears the mark of the holy covenant
with the Creator. If he does so, he shall be dragged to hell. And the ruler of
hell, called Domeh, stands at the gates of hell with hundreds of thousands of
angels, but he is forbidden to approach those who have kept the holy covenant
in this world.**

There is a warning here: let each man be careful of what he utters, so that
his prayer is pure when he raises MAN with the help of the Torah and *Mitzvot*.
If the impure force clings to his prayer, it will receive his MAN. As a result,
man will develop a grudge against the Creator and foreign thoughts, thereby
causing the *Orlah* to once again cling to the holy covenant. Consequently,
his holy soul will fall into the captivity of the impure forces, and they will
drag it to hell. This is similar to what Rabbi Elazar said about falling into
Lilit's hands (item 68).

THE SACRED FLESH, WHICH BEARS THE MARK OF THE HOLY
COVENANT alludes to the holy soul guarded by the holy covenant, as it is said:
"From my flesh I shall see the Creator," i.e., from my nature, my properties. Yet,
doubts evoke the return of the impure force of the *Orlah*. It touches the holy
covenant, and the Divine soul is instantly driven away. Hence, "The Tree cried
out: Sinner, do not touch me," for this Tree is *Yesod*, *Ateret Yesod* (foreskin—the
very essence of creation, egoism), the Tree of Knowledge of Good and Evil.

DOMEH, THE RULER OF HELL—DOMEH is derived from *Dmamah*—
lifelessness, for he robs man of his soul and leaves him lifeless. This is the angel
that fills man's heart with doubts regarding the Creator's greatness, and creates
within him a sinful desire to perceive His plans as though they were plans of one
born of a woman, i.e., as though they were of this world. And since he likens the
Creator's thoughts in man's perception to those of man, he is named so (*Domeh*
also means likeness, similarity).

At first, man understands that the Creator's thoughts and ways are different
from ours, for the created mind can grasp neither Him nor His thoughts nor
His governance, as our mind is inferior to His. But, through sin, the angel
Domeh plants a silly spirit within man, which forces him to say that the mind

of one born of a woman is similar to the Creator's. This leaves man open to doubts, which DRAG HIM TO HELL.

Therefore, the power of the angel Domeh is in his name, as it is said: "Who is as mighty as You, who is LIKE You, the King that kills and resurrects?" This indicates that the connection with the one who is LIKE him leads to death, whereas in the realization that there is none like Him, man finds life.

However, the doubts and thoughts that man receives from the angel Domeh are countless, as *The Zohar* says, HUNDREDS OF THOUSANDS OF ANGELS ARE WITH HIM, and they are all standing at the gates of hell, through which man is dragged there, though the gates themselves are not yet considered hell.

BUT HE (THE ANGEL) IS FORBIDDEN TO APPROACH THOSE WHO HAVE KEPT THE HOLY COVENANT IN THIS WORLD. And even if one did not fully keep (observe) the covenant, and there is still good and evil in his deeds, he is nonetheless regarded as one who has kept the holy covenant. So, unless one comes to doubt, the angel Domeh is forbidden to drag him to hell.

**132. When this happened to King David, fear enveloped him. Right then, Domeh ascended before the Creator, and said: "Master of the world, it says in the Torah (*Vayikra*, 20:10): 'And the man that commits adultery with another man's wife...' David broke his covenant, is it not so?" The Creator replied to him: "David is righteous, and his holy covenant remains pure, for it is known to Me that Bat Sheva was destined for him since the creation of the world."**

Although David committed no sin, as the Talmud explains (*Shabbat*, 56:1) that he who says that David sinned is wrong, he was enveloped with fear nonetheless, as if he really had sinned, for Domeh cited the Torah in his complaint.

However, Bat Sheva had been destined for David since the creation of the world (Talmud, *Sanhedrin*, 107:1); thus, he did not violate his covenant. Yet, if Bat Sheva had been destined for David, why was she first married to Uriah? After all, a wife is half of her husband's body. And if she is half of David's body, how could Uriah have taken her, if there is nothing in him that corresponds with her?

The fact is that Bat Sheva is David's true *Nukva* (female) from the day of the creation of the world, for David is the male part of *Malchut*, while Bat Sheva is the *Nukva* in *Malchut*. But since, as the world was being created, *Malchut* ascended to *Bina* to receive the property of mercy (bestowal) from her, Bat Sheva, too, required this correction in *GAR*. Without it she could not have given birth to the soul of King Solomon.

And Uriah the Hittite was an exalted soul, the properties of *GAR*, wherefrom the name "Uriah," which consists of Ur = *Ohr* (Light) and i(a)h = i (*Yod*) + h (*Hey*) =

the first two letters of the Creator's Name *HaVaYaH*, is derived. In other words, Uriah signifies "the Creator's Light." And the fact that his name contains only the first two letters *Yod-Hey* = *Hochma-Bina*, and lacks the last two letters *Vav-Hey* = *ZA-Malchut* indicates that his Light is the Light of *GAR*. Therefore, to correct Bat Sheva in the property of mercy, she was joined with Uriah. As a result, she became fit for queenship, and became the Queen of Israel.

**133. Domeh said to Him: "Master of the World, what is revealed to You is concealed from him." The Creator answered: "Whatever David did was done with My permission. For no man goes to war without first giving his wife a *get* (document of divorce)." Domeh then said: "But if this is so, David should have waited three months, which he did not." The Creator replied: "This extension is only necessary to make certain that the woman is not pregnant from her previous husband. But it is known to Me that Uriah never went near her, for My Name is imprinted in him as testimony. Indeed, Uriah is *Ohr-Iah*, the Creator's Light, though it is written *Uriahu* = *Ohr* + *i* + *a* + *hu* (*Yod-Hey-Vav*), without the last *Hey*, *Malchut*, which proves that he did not use *Malchut*."**

The letters *Yod-Hey* in Uriah's name (*Aleph-Reish-Yod-Hey*) indicate that he had never touched Bat Sheva. This is because Uriah refers to *GAR* without *VAK*. And *The Zohar* emphasizes that whenever *VAK* is used, the name *Uriahu* is applied. However, it is written here that Uriah was Bat Sheva's first husband, meaning that he had nothing of *VAK* in him, but only *GAR*—the Light of *Hochma* without the Light of *Hassadim*, for *Vav* signifies *Hassadim*. This is why he could not come near Bath Sheba.

**134. Domeh said to Him: "Master of the World, this is exactly what I have said: if You knew that Uriah had never laid with her, then who revealed it to David? He should have waited three months. And if You will say that David knew that Uriah had never laid with her, why did he send Uriah to his wife, saying: 'Go down to your house, and wash your feet?'"**

Usually the readers of the Torah give this example of "a love triangle" as evidence of King David's less than exalted qualities and of the inconsistency of the Creator's judgment—how He forgave David for "killing" Uriah, and so forth. We must remember that the Torah speaks only of the spiritual worlds and their laws, which have no obvious consequences in our world. There is a cause-and-effect connection: whatever occurs in our world is a result of a Higher cause, but in no way is it vice versa, i.e., whatever is described in the Upper World does not necessarily need to manifest in ours. To consider the Torah a narrative about our world relegates the Torah of the world of *Atzilut*, the Creator's holy names, the Creator's Light, to the lowest level of creation, which is strictly forbidden: "Do not make an idol for yourself."

**135. He replied to him: "Of course, David did not know, but he waited more than three months, as four months had passed." As we have learned, on the 15th day of Nissan, David ordered all the people of Israel to prepare for war, Yoav—on seventh day of Nissan. They conquered the lands of Moav and remained there for four months, until he went to Bat Sheva in the month of Elul. And on Yom Kippur, the Creator forgave him his sin. But there are those who say that David dispatched his orders on the seventh day of Adar, the troops assembled on the 15th day of Iyar, he went to Bat Sheva on the 15th day of Elul, and on Yom Kippur the Creator forgave him and spared him from death at the hands of the angel Domeh.**

Domeh is in charge of adultery. And since David was forgiven on the Day of Atonement, he thereby escaped death at the hands of Domeh. However, death was a consequence of Uriah's death at the hands of Amon's sons, as is recorded in the book of Kings (*Melachim*, 1, 15:5), "For David did that which was right in the eyes of the Lord, and turned not aside from anything that He commanded him all the days of his life, save only in the matter of Uriah the Hittite."

**136. Domeh said: "Master of the World, I have nonetheless one claim against him: why did he open his mouth and say: 'The Lord is righteous, for a mortal does so,' thus condemning himself to death. Hence, I have the power to bring death upon him." The Creator replied to him: "You are not allowed to bring death upon him, for he has repented and confessed: 'I have sinned before the Creator,' even though he did not sin. But he did sin in one matter—the killing of Uriah. I have recorded his punishment, and he had received it." Then Domeh immediately gave up his complaints, and returned, despondent, to his place.**

The last letter *Hey* in the name *HaVaYaH* has two points—restriction (strictness) and mercy. And all the corrections of *Malchut* with the help of the covenant (circumcision) are intended to conceal strictness and reveal mercy. Then, the Creator's name descends into *Malchut*. Even though *Malchut* exists there under the ban of the first restriction (strictness and judgment), and all the impure forces cling onto her, this point is nonetheless concealed, and only *Bina*'s property of mercy is revealed. Thus, the impure forces-desires, which are foreign to holiness and spirituality, are powerless and cannot cling to her.

To violate the covenant means to reveal the strictness and judgment in *Malchut* (the letter *Hey*). As a result, the impure forces immediately cling to her, for this is their property—a part of them. The holy soul, the Creator's name, thereby disappears at once, as it is written (*Iyov*, 4:9): "By the breath of God they perish."

David himself is the part of *Malchut* related to *Malchut's* property of mercy. Hence, he requires special care so as to prevent *Malchut's* property of strictness from being revealed in him. For he who reveals the property of strictness and violates the covenant with the Creator, surrenders himself to the impure forces, which condemn him to death. This is because the property of strictness reveals itself within him before the impure force (the angel Domeh), who wished to cling to David's soul and drag it to hell.

Although he was innocent, David begged the Creator's forgiveness for adultery, and received it. But with regard to David sending Uriah to his death, Domeh had no right to ask the Creator for punishment, as he is only in charge of adultery.

**137. And David said to this: "Were it not for the Creator's help, Domeh had nearly claimed my soul." "Were it not for the Creator's help" means "had the Creator not been my guard and guide against the angel Domeh." "Nearly" means that only the distance as thin as a thread remained for Domeh to drag my soul to hell.**

David is *Malchut*, of whom it is written (*Mishley*, 5:5): "Her feet descend to death," for she is the end, conclusion of holiness (the spiritual). The impure forces originate in *Malchut*, and she sustains them, as it is said (*Tehilim*, 103:19): "His kingdom rules over all."

However, when *Malchut* exists in her corrected property of mercy (item 122), she is defined as consisting of two points: her own point of judgment and the point of mercy that she received from *Bina*. Her point of judgment is concealed, while the point of mercy is revealed. And thanks to this correction, all that the impure forces can get from *Malchut* is a *Ner Dakik* (tiny luminescence), which only sustains their existence, but does not allow for their spreading.

*Ner Dakik*, the source of existence for the impure forces, is also known as *Hoteh Dakik*, a small sin, the root of sins, as it is written (Talmud, *Sukkah*, 52:1): "Initially, the impure force seems as thin as a spider web, but then grows as thick as a shaft." And it is called small (*Dakik*), for judgment and restrictions are concealed within the property (point) of mercy.

However, he who violates the covenant causes the point of judgment in *Malchut* to be revealed. As a result, the impure forces cling to *Malchut* and draw much Light from her, thus receiving the strength to spread and expand. And he who does so is said to be forsaking his own soul, as it is written: "By the breath of God they perish" (*Iyov*, 4:9).

And when he merits returning to the Creator, he returns and corrects *Malchut* with the property of mercy. This is why this process is called *Teshuva* (return), from the word of *Tashuv* (to return) + "A," where "A" (*Hey*) designates the Creator. In other words, it is the return to the property of mercy, whereas the property of judgment goes back to being concealed in the property of mercy, like a small candle, and nothing more.

It is therefore written: WERE IT NOT FOR THE CREATOR'S HELP, referring to His acceptance of my return and repelling the angel Domeh by bringing *Malchut* back to her place (to the property) of mercy, reducing the property of judgment to a mere small candle, a hair's-breadth fire, whose LIGHT SEPARATES ME FROM THE IMPURE FORCE.

This is that minimal Light that must always remain between *Malchut* and the impure force, so as to allow *Malchut* to exist and be sustained by this small Light, called "small sin," so small that DOMEH WOULD NOT DRAG MY SOUL TO HELL FOR IT.

It is precisely the magnitude of this Light that saved me from the hands of Domeh, for had the property of judgment not returned to *Malchut* in the measure of a small sin, I would have fallen into the hands of Domeh.

**138. Therefore, man should be careful not to say what David said, for one cannot say to the angel Domeh that "It was an error" (*Kohelet*, 5:5), as it was with David, when the Creator won the dispute against Domeh. "Why should the Creator be angry over your word" (*Kohelet*, 5:5), i.e., for what you have said. "Destroyed the work of your hands" (*Kohelet*, 5:5) i.e., the sacred flesh, the holy covenant, which you have broken, and are therefore to be dragged to hell by the angel Domeh.**

There are two ways to return to the Creator ("Introduction to the Study of the Ten Sefirot," items 45, 59, 64; Talmud, *Yoma*, 86:2):

1) Repentance out of fear, when intentional sins become unintentional,

2) Repentance out of love, when intentional sins become merits.

Before the end of correction, when the forces of strictness, restriction, and judgment are still needed in the world, as it is written (*Kohelet*, 3:14), "The Creator hath so made it that man should fear Him," *Malchut* must sustain the existence of the impure forces as *Ner Dakik*, so they will not disappear from the world.

Therefore, at such a time (in this state), *Malchut's* corrections are made in two points: mercy and judgment. However, judgment is concealed, while mercy acts openly. This is why the Tree of Knowledge of Good and Evil is feared: if man is worthy—it is good, if not—it is evil (items 120–124).

Therefore, DURING THE 6,000 YEARS, WE RETURN TO THE CREATOR ONLY OUT OF FEAR, which causes our intentional sins to turn into unintentional ones—errors. As a result of our repentance, we bring *Malchut* back to the property of mercy. But strictness and judgment are concealed in her to the extent of a small candle (small sin), since *Malchut* must still remain in the property of fear. Hence, this return is called "the return out of fear."

The small sin that must remain is also called "unintentional sin," an "error," a "mistake," for it is not regarded as a sin in and of itself. Rather, it only leads man to commit an unintentional sin. Man sins intentionally only after having first committed an unintentional sin: he committed something unintentionally, but it turned out that he has sinned.

Thus, this small sin remains in *Malchut*, but although it remains, it is not really considered a sin. Yet, through this concealed judgment and strictness we come to intentional sins. This is why it is said: "Initially, it is as a hair's-breadth," i.e., like a small sin. But then, unless we properly guard our covenant, it "becomes as thick as a shaft," as the property of strictness and judgment becomes revealed in *Malchut*.

It is hence said that Domeh stands at the gates of hell, as the power of a small sin is only an entrance, for it is said that it looks as thin as a spider web. Therefore, our repentance is called "forgiven sins," which turn into unintentional errors, as though they were mistakes. For a small sin remains, which is capable of leading us to intentional sins.

All this refers to the repentance out of fear, whereas the second kind is the repentance out of love, when intentional sins turn to merits (item 126).

Therefore, MAN SHOULD BE CAREFUL NOT TO SAY WHAT DAVID SAID, i.e., not to utter the word that causes the property of judgment in *Malchut* to be revealed (as David had done). FOR ONE CANNOT SAY TO THE ANGEL DOMEH THAT IT WAS AN ERROR, for he is unsure as to whether he can return to the Creator right away, so that his sin would be forgiven and made unintentional, AS IT WAS WITH DAVID, WHEN THE CREATOR WON THE DISPUTE AGAINST DOMEH.

It happened with David because throughout his life all of his actions before the Creator were pure, he had committed no crimes, and the only exception was his act toward Uriah. Hence, the Creator became his defender, and helped him return to Him at once, and his sin was turned into an error, as it is said in *The*

*Zohar* (item 137): WERE IT NOT FOR THE CREATOR'S HELP, DOMEH HAD NEARLY CLAIMED MY SOUL. But other people should fear this angel, for an unintentional sin may lead them to hell at the hands of Domeh.

DESTROYED THE WORK OF YOUR HANDS, THE SACRED FLESH, THE HOLY COVENANT, WHICH YOU HAVE VIOLATED, AND ARE THEREFORE TO BE DRAGGED TO HELL BY THE ANGEL DOMEH. The correction in us called "the holy covenant" is regarded as "the work of our hands," as it is written: "Confirm the work of our hands." The holy soul is called the sacred flesh, as it is said, "Out of my flesh shall I see the Creator" (*Iyov*, 19:26) (item 131). Because of the revelation of the property of strictness and judgment in *Malchut*, the correction of the covenant was corrupted, and Domeh drags the soul to hell.

Therefore, THE HEAVENS DECLARE THE WORK OF HIS HANDS (item 130). In the end of correction, the Heavens will declare the work of His hands, as the reward for all these corrections will be revealed. It will become clear that this was THE WORK OF HIS HANDS, and NOT OURS', and THE HEAVENS DECLARE this. And the great *Zivug* RAV PAALIM U MEKABTZIEL will be made on these actions (corrections) (item 92). DECLARE refers to the Light's descent from Above.

Know that this is the only difference in our world before and after the end of correction. Before the end of correction, *Malchut* is called the Tree of Knowledge of Good and Evil, for *Malchut* is the revelation of the Creator's governance over this world. And until people achieve the state where they can receive His Light (as He conceived and prepared for everyone back at the Thought of Creation), the world will be ruled by good and evil, by reward and punishment.

The reason for this is that our *Kelim de Kabbalah* (vessels of reception) are impure, stained by egoism, which (i) prevents the Creator's Light from filling theses desires, and (ii) separates us from the Creator. And the infinite goodness that He has prepared for us may only be received in altruistic desires, for these delights are not limited by the bounds of creation, like egoistic pleasures, in which fulfillment instantly douses the pleasure.

Hence, it is written: "The Creator hath made everything for His own glory" (*Mishley*, 16:4), i.e., all the deeds in the world were initially created by Him so that we could please Him. Therefore, people in our world are engaged in things that are totally opposite from what they should be doing, according to the purpose of their creation. After all, the Creator clearly states that He created the world for Himself: "I have created it for My glory" (*Yeshayahu*, 43:7).

Yet, we claim the exact opposite—that the whole world was created for us, and we desire to swallow it whole, for our own pleasure, satisfaction, indulgence, and exaltation. So it is no surprise we are unworthy of receiving the Creator's perfect goodness. And thus He rules over us through good and evil, in the form of reward and punishment, for one depends on the other: reward and punishment give rise to good and evil.

Because we use our desires to receive (pleasure), thus becoming opposite from the Creator, we perceive His governance towards us as evil. This stems from the fact that man cannot perceive obvious evil from the Creator, as this would greatly undermine the creatures' perception of the great and perfect Creator, for the Perfect one cannot create evil.

Therefore, to the extent that man feels bad and evil, and denies the Divine Providence, a veil immediately falls over him, and the sensation of the Creator's existence disappears. This is the worst punishment in the world!

Hence, the sensation of good and evil in the Creator's governance gives us a feeling of reward and punishment. This is because he who exerts efforts not to lose faith in the Creator's existence and governance, even if he tastes evil in His governance, is rewarded with finding strength to not lose faith in the governance and good purpose of the Creator's "evil" influence. But if he had not yet merited the opportunity to exert efforts in believing that the Creator pursues a definite purpose by sending him unpleasant sensations, he is punished with remoteness from faith in the Creator and the sensation of His existence.

Therefore, although He has done, is doing, and will do all the deeds in the world, it remains semi-concealed from those who perceive both good and evil. For when they perceive evil, the impure force is allowed to conceal the Creator's governance and faith in Him. Thus, man suffers the worst punishment in the world—the sensation of detachment from the Creator—and becomes filled with doubts and denial of the Creator's existence and governance. And when he returns to the Creator, he receives a corresponding reward, and is able to unite with Him once again.

But through this very governance of reward and punishment, the Creator has prepared for us the opportunity to utilize this governance in order to achieve the end of correction, when all people attain their corrected *Kelim* (desires), and use them to bring pleasure to the Creator, as it is written that He has created everything for Himself! In other words, our bestowal must be absolute.

Then the great *Zivug* of *Atik* will be revealed. In consequence, we will all return to the Creator out of love, all our intentional sins will turn to merits, all evil will be felt as infinite goodness, and His Divine Providence will be revealed in the entire world. Thus, ALL SHALL SEE that only He has done, is doing, and will do all the deeds in the world, and that no one acts besides Him. After the sensation of evil and punishment is turned to one of goodness and reward, and our egoistic desires become altruistic, we are given the opportunity to attain the Maker, for we conform to the work of His hands by blessing and exalting Him above all evil and all punishments we had once suffered.

However, the most important point to stress here is that until the end of correction, all the corrections were considered as THE WORK OF OUR HANDS. This is why we receive rewards or punishments for them. But in the great *Zivug* at the end of correction, it will be revealed that all the corrections and all the punishments are THE WORK OF HIS HANDS.

Thus, it is said, THE HEAVENS DECLARE THE WORK OF HIS HANDS. This is because the great *Zivug* signifies what the Heavens will declare, that all the deeds are the work of His hands, that He has done, is doing, and will do all the deeds in the whole of creation.

**139. Thus, "the Heavens declare the work of His hands." These are the friends who have united in the bride (*Malchut*) by studying the Torah on the night of the holiday of *Shavuot*. They are all participants of the covenant with her, and are called "the work of His hands." And she praises and notes each and every one of them. What is Heaven, firmament? It is the firmament, where the sun, the moon, the stars, and the zodiac are located. This firmament is called the Book of Remembrance, and it declares and records them, so they shall become the sons of His palace, and He will fulfill all their desires.**

*Yesod* of *Zeir Anpin*, onto which a *Zivug* is made for the revelation of all the Supernal Degrees, called the sun, the moon, the stars, and the signs of the zodiac, is referred to as the "firmament." All of the Supernal stars exist on the firmament, called *Yesod* of *Zeir Anpin*. And everything exists thanks to it, for it makes a *Zivug* with *Nukva*, called earth, and shines upon her with all these stars, i.e., gives these stars to her.

It turns out that *Malchut* is smaller than the sun (ZA). But at the end of correction, the light of the moon will be as the light of the sun, and the light of the sun will be seventy times greater than before—*Malchut* will become as big as *Zeir Anpin* during the six days of creation. When will this be? Rabbi Yehuda answers: on the day when death disappears forever, and the Creator and His Name are as one.

The Heaven or the firmament (ZA) is *HaVaYaH*, called "the sun." *Malchut* (*Nukva*) receives from it, and is called "the moon." During the 6,000 years, *Malchut* receives the Light from the six days of creation, but *Zeir Anpin* does not reveal that the Creator and His Name are one. Hence, the moon is smaller than the sun. Its lesser size is a result of *Malchut's* consisting of both good and evil, reward and punishment.

There is a considerable difference between "Him" and "His Name." "His Name" is *Malchut*, where all the *Zivugim*, and all the states of unification and separation are accumulated. But at the end of correction, when death is said to disappear forever, *HaVaYaH* and His Name will be one. The Name (*Malchut*) will be like the Light of *Zeir Anpin*—only goodness without evil, and the private governance will be revealed in her, which means that the light of the moon will become equal to that of the sun.

Therefore at this time (in this state), *Malchut* will be called "the Book of Remembrance," for all human deeds are recorded in her. *Yesod* of *Zeir Anpin* is called "remembrance," for it remembers the deeds of the entire world, studies, and analyzes all the creatures that receive from it.

During the 6,000 years before the end of correction, the Book of Remembrance exists sometimes together and sometimes separately. But at the end of correction, these two degrees will merge into one, and *Malchut* herself will be called "the Book of Remembrance," when ZA and *Malchut* become a single whole, for *Malchut's* Light will equal that of ZA.

Therefore, the firmament is a place where the sun, the moon, the stars, and the signs of the zodiac are located. The firmament is *Yesod* of ZA, which emanates all the Light of the world and sustains all existence. It passes the Light onto *Malchut* when she is smaller than it, and the state, "He and His Name are one" has not yet been achieved. And at the end of correction, it will be exactly like *Malchut*, who is hence called the Book of Remembrance.

Thus, when *Malchut* receives all the properties of *Zeir Anpin* (the firmament, called "Remembrance"), she will become the Book of Remembrance, i.e., she and the firmament will be one.

**140. Day after day brings *Omer*—a sheaf. The holy day out of those days (*Sefirot*) of the King (*Zeir Anpin*) praises the friends, who study the Torah on the night of *Shavuot*. They say to each other, "Day after day shall bring a sheaf," and praise it. And the words "night after night" refer to all the degrees, *Sefirot* of *Malchut*, that reign in the night, praise one another by**

each receiving from a friend, from another *Sefira*. And the state of complete perfection makes them beloved friends.

Having explained that THE HEAVENS DECLARE THE WORK OF HIS HANDS is THE BOOK OF REMEMBRANCE. *The Zohar* continues to clarify the writings in the *Book of Malachi* (3:14-16): "You have said, 'How futile it is to serve the Creator! When we carried out the Creator's will, and walked heavy-hearted before Him—what is the use of it all? And now we regard the wicked as blessed: they have settled in their wickedness, tried the Creator, and were liberated.' Then those who feared the Creator spoke WITH EACH OTHER, and the Creator hearkened and heard, and a BOOK OF REMEMBRANCE was recorded before Him for those who fear the Creator (every day) and honor His (holy) name. 'And they shall become chosen for Me,'—the Lord said,—'on the day that I shall determine, and I shall spare them, as a man spares his son, who serves him,—on the day that I shall work a miracle, on the day of the end of correction.'"

Before the end of correction, before we prepare our desires "to receive" only for the Creator's sake, and not for self-gratification, *Malchut* is called "The Tree of Knowledge of Good and Evil," for *Malchut* governs the world in accordance with man's deeds. Inasmuch as we are not yet ready to receive all the delight that the Creator prepared for us in His Thought of Creation, we have no choice but to submit to *Malchut*'s governance of good and evil.

And this very governance prepares us for the eventual correction of our desires to receive (*Kelim de Kabbalah*) into desires for bestowal (*Kelim de Hashpaa*), thus achieving the goodness and delight that He conceived to bestow upon us.

As was previously stated, the sensation of good and evil creates in us a feeling of reward and punishment. Therefore, when one tries to retain his faith in the Creator while he is feeling evil, but still continues to observe the Torah and *Mitzvot* as he did before, he is rewarded.

And if he cannot overcome this test and is distanced from the Creator, he becomes filled with doubts with regard to the good governance. Alternatively, he stops believing that the Creator governs the world altogether, or feels resentment towards the Creator in response to these unpleasant sensations. The Creator punishes for all thoughts, just as He does for all actions (Talmud, *Kidushim*, 40:1).

It is also said that one's righteousness is of no help to him on the day of his sin. But sometimes man's doubts are so overpowering that he regrets even the good deeds he had previously done, and says (*Malachi*, 3:14): "You have said, 'How futile it is to serve the Creator! When we carried out the Creator's will, and walked heavy-hearted before Him—what is the use of it all?'" He becomes a complete sinner, who regrets his righteous past (complaining that he wasted time and effort instead of enjoying this world like the others!), and his doubts and regrets cause him to lose all of his good deeds, as the Torah warns us: "One's righteousness is of no help to him on the day of his sin."

Yet, even in this state, man can return to the Creator. However, he is said to be beginning on his path anew, as though he is a newborn, for all of his past good deeds are gone.

One should not take the aforesaid literally, even in its spiritual context, for he who works to achieve unconditional altruistic deeds constantly experiences descents and ascents, is filled with doubts, and tries to overcome them. Only one who advances in this manner feels that he is starting his work every time anew, that he understands no more than a newborn baby. Conversely, one who belongs to the masses—who works in his egoistic desires—is constantly filled with self-reverence and thinks that on each new day, he adds to the previous one, and nothing seems to disappear. This makes his spiritual growth impossible.

Only one who truly ascends the spiritual degrees feels like a newborn baby before his Creator at each moment. After all, as he ascends from one degree to the next, the previous state (degree) disappears, and until he attains a Higher Degree, he is in total darkness and feels that he is starting from scratch, rather than supplementing his assets, which is how the spiritually inanimate (*Domem do Kedusha*) fool.

The governance of good and evil causes us to ascend and descend—each in his own way... Each ascent is considered a separate day (sensation of Light). As a result of the great descent that he has just undergone by regretting his past good deeds, man moves into a state of ascent, as one who is born anew.

Therefore, at each ascent, it is as though one starts over on his path to the Creator. Thus, each ascent is regarded as a separate day, for there is a break (night) between these states. And each descent is hence considered a separate night.

This is what *The Zohar* tells us: DAY AFTER DAY SHALL BRING A SHEAF—in each ascent we draw nearer to the Creator's greatest day (the end of correction), HE PRAISED THE FRIENDS AND THEY WOULD SPEAK WITH EACH OTHER. This is because through the great *Zivug* at the end of correction, they will all merit returning to the Creator out of love, for the desire "to receive" will be completely corrected, and they will begin to receive only for the Creator's sake, so as to bestow delight upon Him.

In this great *Zivug* (unity), we will reveal all the supreme goodness and delight of the Thought of Creation. And we will then see with our own eyes that all those punishments we experienced in the states of descent, which made us doubt and regret the efforts exerted in the Torah, all those punishments would correct and purify us. And now, at the end of correction, they are the direct cause for our sensation and reception of the Creator's goodness.

Had it not been for the terrible suffering and punishments, we would not have been able to achieve the state of being filled with perfect delight. Therefore, even these intentional sins turn into merits, as it is said: DAY AFTER DAY SHALL BRING A SHEAF—each ascent in *Malchut*, up to the end of correction, is like a separate day.

This day is revealed by the word, which supports the Torah in all its greatness. What is this word? When they say, "How futile it is to serve the Creator! When we carried out the Creator's will, and walked heavy-hearted before Him—what is the use of it all?"

These words brought punishments that have now become merits, for all the perfection and magnificence of that great day can now be revealed thanks to these very punishments of the past. Thus, those who uttered these words are now regarded as those who fear the Creator and praise His Name. (And these words could only have been spoken by those who made efforts to advance on the Path of Truth, and felt frustrated upon receiving uncorrected egoism of a Higher Degree. In other words, frustration comes only to those who truly work for the Creator's sake.)

Hence, it is said about them: "The Lord said, 'On the day that I shall determine, and I shall spare them, as a man spares his son, who serves him,'" for all the nights—states of descent, suffering and punishments, which sever their connection with the Creator—now become merits and good deeds. And the night turns into day, darkness turns into Light, and there are no divisions between days, and all 6,000 years gather into one great day.

And all the *Zivugim* that were made one after another, revealed the ascents and the separate, consecutive degrees, have now gathered into one degree of one great *Zivug*—Unity, which shines in the world from end to end. Hence, it is written: DAY AFTER DAY SHALL BRING A SHEAF, that is, the intervals between days now become magnificent glory, for they have been turned into merits. Thus, everything becomes the Creator's one glorious day!

And the words "night after night" refer to all the degrees that reign in the night. They praise one another, and each receives everything that man feels as suffering in a state of descent—this is called night. And through such sensations, intervals are formed between the sensations of day.

On the whole, each degree is separated from one another. Night is an aspiration to attain the Creator. And while each night is full of darkness, now all the nights (states of feeling emptiness, hopelessness, heaviness of efforts, the Creator's concealment) gather together and form a unified vessel of reception of Supernal wisdom, which fills the entire earth with Knowledge of the Creator, and the nights shine like days.

For each night receives its own part of Knowledge only by joining with the other nights. Thus, each night is said to help the other nights in the Knowledge. Put differently, man is ready to receive the Knowledge only if he joins with the other nights.

And since night is a feeling of lacking knowledge, attainment, and sensation of the Creator by uniting, they form a perfect vessel of reception of the Knowledge of the Creator. And they praise one another, for each has received his share of the Knowledge of the Creator thanks exclusively to his friend, through uniting with him. Only in unity do they merit reception of the Supernal Knowledge. Hence, it is said that through the perfection achieved by all, the nights became beloved friends.

**141. Does he speak of the others in the world who do not obey the Creator, and whom He does not wish to hear? But they made lines through all the earth, that is, these things make a line out of those that reside Above and out of those that reside below. From the first—firmaments are made, and from the second, from their return—earth. And should you say that they revolve around the earth in one place, it is said that they are also at the end of the world.**

Thus far, we have discussed the most terrible punishments and suffering in the world—being detached from the Creator and losing faith in Him. Moreover, *The Zohar* tells us that all the punishments, all the suffering of hell and of the body, which stem from personal sins and fill this world, also gather and are included into one great *Zivug*, as it is written: "And it shall come to pass, that as the Lord rejoiced over you to do you good, and to multiply you; so the Lord will rejoice over you to cause you to perish, and to destroy you" (*Devarim*, 28:63).

All will gather and become one great Light, and everything will turn to great joy and bliss. It is therefore said that THERE IS NO SHEAF AND NO THINGS IN THE OTHER WORDS OF THE WORLD, which man perceives in this world as suffering. But they will turn to joy and bliss, and thus the holy King, too, shall wish to hear them.

So, all the suffering during the 6,000 years will gather at the end of correction and will become a tremendous delight, as the prophet said: "In those days and in that time, said the Lord, even if the iniquity of Israel shall be sought for, there shall be none" (*Yirmiyahu*, 50:20).

Everything will turn to merits, so much so that they will ask and search "for the past sins that can be included in the *Zivug*, and which can be laughed at, for they were felt as suffering and now they are joy and bliss," but they will not find any. There will be no more suffering in its true form, as it was in the past, although they greatly desire to find it and feel it, for all suffering will have now been turned to great Light.

This Supernal Degree, created by the great *Zivug* out of all the souls and all the deeds, both good and evil, is now defined as a pillar of Light, which shines from one end of the world to the other. And this unity is perfect, as is said by the prophet (*Zachariah*, 14:9): "And the Creator shall be one (for all), and His Name one"—all the senses will grasp the Creator's complete and perfect name, "the Infinitely good."

Precisely because this most Supernal Degree is achieved as a result of bringing together all the suffering and punishments, it fills the entire universe with Light, including earth. However, it should be noted that the suffering of which *The Zohar* speaks is not the suffering of the body's lack of pleasure. It is the suffering caused by the absence of unity with the Creator!

But if suffering is so useful, why is it written, "neither them nor the reward for them?" Suffering is necessary, for it is correction. However, the true suffering, for which man can receive the degree of the end of correction, is caused by temporary distancing from the Torah and *Mitzvot* as a result of feeling the pain of suffering, and this pains the Creator. Thus, the *Shechina* suffers, for when man suffers in his heart, he speaks ill of her, willingly or unwillingly. Although the Torah tells him to be patient, to endure and have faith above reason—selfless faith that all of this is the correction that he must undergo—he debases the *Shechina* by being unwilling to endure them and achieve the end of correction.

Man's soul is also a *Partzuf* consisting of ten *Sefirot*. In its initial, spiritually undeveloped, unborn state, the soul is defined as a point, as a potential future spiritual body. If man works on himself, this point within him gradually acquires a screen, and he makes a *Zivug* on it. He repels all the pleasures for the sake of the Creator's desires, and receives Light in this point. Thus, he "amplifies" it to the size of a *Partzuf* and transforms it into a body, a newborn *Partzuf*.

Afterwards he continues to cultivate his screen, gradually nurturing the small state into the big one, until he receives all of the Light destined for him by the Creator within his spiritual body. This state is called "the end of the personal correction." When all the personal corrections merge into one, the general correction of the entire world (of *Malchut*) will occur. *Malchut* is a *Partzuf* that consists of separate souls; each soul, the *Partzuf* of each soul, is part of *Malchut*, and *Malchut* is a collection, the sum of all the *Partzufim* that are to be made by all the people. To make a *Partzuf* is to acquire a screen and become filled with Light.

THOSE THAT RESIDE ABOVE AND THOSE THAT RESIDE BELOW refers to the order of time in the spiritual, eternal world, which is different from ours. When the Creator wished to create the world, He immediately created everything: all the souls filled with Light in a state of absolute perfection, called "the end of correction," where all the creatures receive the infinite delight that He envisioned.

This ultimate state was born with the Creator's first thought to create the world, and it exists in its final form from the very first moment, for the future, present, and past are merged in the Creator, and the factor of time does not exist in Him.

All human progress is necessary only to enable us to imagine that the following is also possible:

1. Change of time: the stretching of time into infinity, i.e., when time stops and the present merges with the past and the future; when time reverses its course or disappears. Yet, time is the only thing that provides us with a perception of existence. By "switching off" time, we stop perceiving that we exist!

2. Transformation of space: expanding and contracting of space into a point; space taking other forms, other dimensions; infinity and total absence of space altogether.

I've already dealt with these issues in my book, *Kabbalah, Science and the Meaning of Life*, and I would prefer not to digress from the text of *The Zohar*. However, to understand our true state, and not the one we currently perceive, it is essential to remember that notions of time and space do not exist with regard to Creator. In reality, we are completely different and exist in a completely different form and state from what we presently perceive. We feel this way because our sensations are distorted by our egoism, which infuse our senses and possess our bodies, like a cloud.

Therefore, all that is described in the Torah refers strictly to the spiritual realm. This information transcends time, referring at once to our past, present and future, for time exists only with regard to those who are still confined to their egoistic *Kelim* (desires). From this we can understand what is said in the Torah: "The Creator showed Adam each generation and its representatives, and showed it to Moshe as well" (Talmud, *Sanhedrin*, 38:2).

Yet, if the above described unfolded before the creation of these generations, how can the Creator show them to Adam and Moshe? It is possible because all the souls with all their destinies from the moment of their creation to the end of their correction emerged before the Creator in their completeness and reside in the Supernal Garden of Eden. From there they descend and enter the bodies of our world, each at their own "time." And there, "Above," the Creator revealed them to Adam, Moshe, and all the others who were worthy of it. However, this is a difficult notion, and not every mind is ready to grasp it.

Therefore, *The Zohar* says (*Terumah*, 163) that the way the six *Sefirot* of *Zeir Anpin* unite as ONE above *Chazeh de Zeir Anpin*, where they are free from the *Klipot*, *Malchut* unites with *Zeir Anpin* below his *Chazeh*, so that unity exists below, as it does Above. For the Creator (*Zeir Anpin*) is One (male) Above. And *Malchut* becomes One (female), so that One (male) would be with One (female). This is the secret of unity expressed in the words: "He and His Name are one"; "He" (ZA) and "His Name" (*Malchut*) are within one another.

The degree that is born at the end of correction, in the state of "He and His Name are one," already exists Above as the sum of all the 600,000 souls and deeds during the 6,000 degrees (called "years") in the world, which will emerge before the end of correction, but exist in their eternal form Above, where the future is as present.

Therefore, the pillar of Light that will shine upon the world from one end to the other at the end of correction already exists in the Supernal Garden of Eden, which illuminates it with the same brilliance that will be revealed to us in the future. This is because at the end of correction the two degrees will shine as one, and "He and His Name will be one." A pillar (line) of Light will appear, made of those that reside Above (the souls that reside in the Supernal Garden of Eden) and those that reside below (the souls clothed in the bodies of our world). And "One receives One"; these two degrees shine together, and reveal the Creator's unity thereby, as it is said that on that day "He and His Name will be one."

From the aforesaid one can assume that the pillar of Light that shines in the Supernal Garden of Eden descends and shines in the Garden of Eden of our world. But this is not so. Rather, FROM THE FIRST–FIRMAMENTS

ARE MADE, for this degree exits onto a *Zivug* of *Yesod* of *Zeir Anpin*, called "firmament." Therefore, all the *Zivugim* that ascend above the firmament shine upon those that receive them from the firmament and below. The degree above the firmament is referred to as "Heaven," and the degree that receives from the firmament is called "earth."

When the line (pillar) of Light unites the inhabitants of Above and those of below, the distinction between the Supernal Garden of Eden and the inhabitants of this world still remains. This is because the inhabitants of the Supernal Garden of Eden receive from a *Zivug* above the firmament, and what they receive is called "the new Heaven for the inhabitants of Above." And only a small luminescence, called "the new earth," descends below the firmament to the inhabitants of below. This is what *The Zohar* says: "From the first—firmaments are made, and from the second, from their return—earth."

Although in this great *Zivug*, as in all *Zivugim*, all that is decided above the firmament, above the *Zivug*, spreads down to earth, below the line of the *Zivug*, one should not think that this *Zivug* (like all the previous ones) is merely a thin line of Light, called "one," a limited, inner place, as it is written at the beginning of creation: "Let the waters gather together unto one place," i.e., in the inner place of the worlds (and not the outer), a place of Israel.

But the Light of this *Zivug* revolves around the world and fills it whole. This Light reaches even the outer parts of the worlds (the nations of the world), as the prophet writes: "The earth shall be filled with Knowledge of the Creator" (*Yeshayahu*, 11:9).

**142. And since out of them Heavens were created, who resides there? He returned and said, "There is a shelter for the sun in them. This is the holy sun, called *Zeir Anpin*, and it dwells and resides there, and adorns itself with them."**

**143. Since *Zeir Anpin* resides in those firmaments and clothes in them, he emerges like a bridegroom out of his wedding canopy, and rejoices and races along these firmaments, and exits them and enters, and races toward a tower in a different place. He emerges from one end of Heaven, from the Upper World, from the Highest place, from *Bina*. And his season—where is it? It is the opposite place below, i.e., *Malchut*, which is the year's season that forms all the ends and binds everything—from Heaven to this firmament.**

*The Zohar* speaks of the great secret of the sun coming out of its hiding. It is worth noting that Kabbalists often use the word "secret" only to explain and as if reveal the mystery in the passages that follow. The reader should nevertheless understand that there are no secrets in the world. Man attains everything from his degree. Even in our world, in the process of his mental development, man attains new notions on every new degree. And whatever he considered a secret only yesterday now becomes clear and revealed before him.

The same is true with regard to spiritual attainments. Kabbalah is called a secret wisdom, for it is concealed from ordinary people, it is a secret to them. But as soon as one acquires a screen and begins to perceive the spiritual world, he sees the secret becomes a reality. And this process continues until he completely attains the entire universe, all of the Creator's secrets ("Introduction to the Study of the Ten Sefirot," item 148).

The sun emerges from its hiding (sheath—*Nartik*), from under the *Huppah*, and rushes to a tower at a different place—after the great *Zivug* under the *Huppah*. *Zeir Anpin* leaves his hiding and enters *Malchut*, called the tower of *Oz* (strength) of the Creator's Name, for *Malchut* then ascends and unites with ZA, and they become as one.

The end of *Malchut* is called "the year's season." And until the end of correction, the impure forces, called "the end of days," attach themselves to it. Now, after the end of correction, it is still necessary to correct this part of *Malchut*, called "the end of days." To this end, the sun emerges from its hiding, LIKE THE BRIDEGROOM EMERGING FROM UNDER THE *HUPPAH*, and shines, and enters the tower of *Oz* (*Malchut*), races and shines on all the ends of *Malchut* to correct "the year's season" of the lower end of Heaven.

For this last action corrects all the ends of *Malchut* and unites all from the Heavens to the firmament. In other words, *Malchut* receives the Light of THE END OF HEAVENS above the firmament (ZA).

**144. There is nothing hidden on account of the year's season and the phase of the sun that revolves in all directions. And there is no concealment, i.e., not a single Supernal Degree is hidden from him, for all were bound together and everyone appeared before him, and none could be concealed from him. Thanks to him and thanks to them he returned to them, to the friends, in the phase of complete return and correction. All this year and all this time is for the Torah (to study it), as it is written: "The Creator's Torah is perfect."**

After the great *Zivug*, a restriction was imposed on all the Upper Light (item 94). Therefore, a new *Zivug* (TOWER) is necessary, which reveals anew all of the Upper Light that was concealed on account of the disappearance of the degree of BON, before it begins to ascend to SAG. Thus, NOTHING IS

CONCEALED FROM THAT PHASE OF THE SUN THAT REVOLVES IN ALL DIRECTIONS.

Indeed, a *Zivug* between the phase of the sun and the year's season corrects the ends of *Malchut* on all sides, until the correction is completed. Thus, *BON* ascends and becomes like *SAG*, which amounts to the complete correction of *BON*, whereupon THERE IS NO CONCEALMENT, NOT A SINGLE SUPERNAL DEGREE IS CONCEALED FROM HIM, for all the degrees and the Upper Light are once more revealed in their perfection. AND NOTHING CAN BE CONCEALED FROM Him, for all the degrees and Light gradually return to Him, until all become revealed.

It is hence said that the revelation does not occur at once, for while in its phase, the sun travels and shines in sufficient measure for a COMPLETE RETURN, as it is written that He punishes the sinners and cures the righteous, whereupon they all merit the complete revelation of the Star.

**145. The word *HaVaYaH* is written six times, and there are six verses from "the Heavens declare" and until "The Creator's Torah is perfect" (*Tehilim*, 19:2-8). And this is the secret of the word *BERESHEET*, which consists of six letters: THE CREATOR CREATED ET (THE) HEAVENS AND THE EARTH, six words in all. The other sources of the verse from "The Creator's Torah is perfect" and until "they are better than gold" (*Tehilim*, 19:2-8) correspond to the six utterances of the name *HaVaYaH* in them. The sources from "the Heavens declare" through "The Creator's Torah is perfect" are for the six letters in the word *BERESHEET*, whereas the six names are for the six words from "the Creator created" through "the Heavens and the earth."**

It is known that any degree born or revealed in the worlds is first revealed through its letters, which signifies the, as yet, unattainable. Afterwards, it appears in the combination of letters. This degree then becomes attainable, its contents become known, as previously described with the letters *RYU* = 216 and *AB* = 72 (item 116).

The six letters in the word *BERESHEET* contain everything that exists in Heaven and on earth, but in an unattainable form, and are hence designated by these letters alone, without their combinations. Then there are the six words: *Bara Elokim Et Ha-Shamayim Ve-Et Ha-Aretz* (THE CREATOR CREATED THE HEAVENS AND THE EARTH), where everything that the word *BERESHEET* contains (Heaven, earth, and all their inhabitants) is already attained.

The same principle allows us to understand what is included in the six verses from "the Heavens declare" to "The Creator's Torah is perfect." This is just the beginning of the revelation of attaining the end of creation in the form of letters, as with the six letters in the word BERESHEET.

And the complete revelation, the attainment of the end of creation begins with the verse "The Creator's Torah is perfect." This verse contains six names, each of which constitutes unique attainment, thus indicating that only after the completion of this degree do all the letter combinations become revealed and attained in the great Zivug at the end of correction, as it is said, NOTHING IS CONCEALED IN CONSEQUENCE OF HIM.

This is why The Zohar says that THE WORD BERESHEET, WHICH CONSISTS OF six, IS WRITTEN (SPEAKS) ABOUT THIS SECRET. The word BERESHEET contains six letters, where Heaven and earth are concealed, before they become revealed in the six words, THE CREATOR CREATED THE HEAVENS AND THE EARTH.

The same applies to the six verses (Tehilim, 19:2-8): the great Zivug of the end of correction is not yet revealed from THE HEAVENS DECLARE to THE CREATOR'S TORAH IS PERFECT. Only after NOTHING IS CONCEALED IN CONSEQUENCE OF HIM are the six names revealed, which in turn reveal the end of correction in its full perfection.

**146. As they were sitting and talking, Rabbi Elazar, the son of Rabbi Shimon, entered. He said to them: "Certainly, the face of the Shechina has come, hence I called you Pniel (Pnei-face + El-Creator = the Creator's face)" (item 119), for you have seen the Shechina face to face. And now that you have attained Benayahu Ben-Yehoyada, it certainly refers to Atik, the Sefira of Keter, just as everything else that occurred afterwards, as it is written in the Torah: "And he slew the Egyptian." And he who is concealed from all—is Atik.**

It is said in the continuation of "The Donkey Driver," who revealed the soul of Benayahu Ben-Yehoyada to Rabbi Elazar and Rabbi Aba, as a result of which Rabbi Shimon called them Pniel. For the soul of Benayahu Ben-Yehoyada is a spiritual degree destined to be revealed in the future, at the end of correction. This is why they were in a state of concealment of the Upper Light (item 113), as was already mentioned with regard to the Zivug of the sun's phase and the year's season, until they have found Rabbi Shimon Ben Lakunya and others, thus meriting all the Light once again.

Therefore, Rabbi Shimon says to them, YOU HAVE ATTAINED, BENAYAHU BEN-YEHOYADA WAS REVEALED TO YOU. This means that they have already attained the six verses, the essence of THE HEAVENS DECLARE, and exist in the six names. When they have attained the soul of

Benayahu Ben-Yehoyada with the help of the donkey driver, their attainment had not yet been revealed to them, as they still existed in the six verses—the reason for their concealment. But now they have attained and revealed his soul, that it is the great *Zivug* of *Atik*, when everything is revealed to all.

**147. The words, "He slew the Egyptian" are explained in another place, i.e., at a different degree, in a different way. He opened and said, "He slew the Egyptian, a man of good stature, five cubits high." All of this refers to the same secret. This Egyptian is the one who is well-known and is described as "very great in the land of Egypt in the eyes of the Jew," for he is great and honored, as that old man had already explained (item 99).**

The Torah describes the killing of the Egyptian in the book *Shemot* (2:12). As we have already learned from the article about Rabbi Hamnuna-Saba, it is expressed differently at a different degree (in a different language, the language of *Divrey HaYamim*). However, these two verses are the same secret, for it is written in the book *Shmuel* 1 (11:23): "And he slew the Egyptian, a prominent man," while in *Divrey HaYamim* it is written: "And he slew the Egyptian, a man of good stature, five cubits high." Both verses are the same secret, which *The Zohar* continues to clarify.

**148. This case was examined at the Divine Assembly. "A prominent man" and "a man of good stature" are the same, as they constitute *Shabbat* and the bounds of *Shabbat*. As it is written: "You shall measure it from outside the city." It is also written, "You shall not impede limitations in measure." Hence, he was a man of good stature. Precisely such, from one end of the world to the other. Such is he, Adam, the first man. And should you disagree, referring to the written "five cubits," know that these five cubits extend from one end of the world to the other.**

The matter concerns the Divine Assembly, of which Rabbi Shimon said: "I saw those ascending, but how few they were" (Talmud, *Sukkah*, 45:2). There is a lower assembly of the angel Matat. However, the described above takes place in the Supernal Assembly, which will be clarified further.

"A prominent man" is the degree of Moshe, of whom it is written in the Torah: "And there hath not since risen a prophet in Israel such as Moshe" (*Devarim*, 34:10), of whom it is written "My servant Moshe is not so; he is trusted in all My house; with him do I speak mouth to mouth, clearly, and not with riddles" (*Bamidbar*, 12:7-8).

"A prominent man" also constitutes a measure, which extends from one end of the world to the other. Moreover, its form and size correspond to *Shabbat* and the bounds of *Shabbat*, where the bounds of *Shabbat* are the end of its measure. During the 6,000 years, the bounds of *Shabbat* are limited by only 2,000 *Amah* (cubits). However, after the end of correction, the bounds of *Shabbat* will extend from one end of the world to the other, as it is written: "And the Lord shall be King over all the earth" (*Zachariah*, 14:9).

As we already know, the Light can descend and fill the *Partzufim* down to the level of *Parsa* of the world of *Atzilut*. *Shabbat* is a spiritual state when the worlds of *BYA* with all that inhabit them rise above the *Parsa* to the world of *Atzilut*. Above *Parsa* are only pure forces, corrected desires (*Kelim*). Hence, naturally there is no need to separate pure *Kelim* from impure ones and to correct them during *Shabbat*.

However, the Light of *Shabbat* shines not only in the world of *Atzilut*, but beyond its bounds as well. It thus affects the sixteen *Sefirot* from *Parsa* down to *Chazeh* of the world of *Yetzira* so the soul can be in the state of "*Shabbat*" with these desires, too. The language of our world describes this as the permission to transcend the bounds of the city of *Atzilut* (seventy *Amah*) by 2,000 *Amah* down to the *Chazeh* of the world of *Beria*, and then another 2,000 *Amah* from *Chazeh* of the world of *Beria* to *Chazeh* of the world of *Yetzira*. (Seventy *Amah* are regarded as being within the city limits.)

However, after all the *Kelim* (desires) are corrected, there will be no restrictions; the world of *Atzilut* will extend down to our world, and only the state of *Shabbat* will prevail in the entire world—in all desires of all creatures.

It is hence written: A PROMINENT MAN and A MAN OF GOOD STATURE are one and the same, for they constitute *Shabbat* and the bounds of *Shabbat*, as is said: AND YOU SHALL MEASURE FROM OUTSIDE THE CITY, and it is also written: YOU SHALL NOT IMPEDE JUDGMENT IN MEASURE. It follows that an object's measure represents its limit, just as the words A MAN OF GOOD STATURE alludes to the end, the bounds of *Shabbat* after the end of correction, which will extend from one end of the world to the other.

AND HE SHALL BE PRECISELY MAN OF GOOD STATURE indicates that size does not rule over him; rather, he rules over size, and it is he who determines this size according to his own will. SUCH IS HE, ADAM, who, prior to his sin, extended and shone from one end of the world to the other (Talmud, *Hagigah*, 12:1), as the bounds of *Shabbat* after the end of correction.

FIVE CUBITS FROM ONE END OF THE WORLD TO THE OTHER— because the five cubits are the five *Sefirot*: *Keter*, *Hochma*, *Bina*, *ZA*, and *Malchut* that expand and fill everything from one end of the world to the other after the end of correction.

**149. It is, as is written, "like a weaver's beam" (*Shmuel* 1, 17: 7) "as the Divine staff" (*Shemot*, 4:20) that was in his hand, which reveals by the secret name (Light) confirmed in it by the Light of the letter combinations that Betzalel and his disciples engraved, called "weaving," as is written, "He filled them and others, and BOUND them." And that staff—within it shone a secret name, inscribed on all its sides by the Light of the sages, who confirmed the secret name in forty-two properties. And the rest of what is written from here onward is similar to what the old man had already explained. Happy is his lot!**

The secret of the letter combinations in sacred names is called "weaving," like a weaver joins his threads into a fabric, the letters join into combinations of sacred names, which designate man's spiritual level of their attainment. Hence, *The Zohar* says that the Creator's staff in Moshe's hand had engraved the letter combinations of the secret name, which Betzalel and his disciples engraved as they worked on the Tabernacle.

The Creator's staff is therefore called a "weaver's beam." The Hebrew word for "beam" is MANOR (from OHR—Light). This refers to the Light of the letter combinations in the secret name, which Betzalel weaved and engraved, as it is said, "by the Light of the letter combinations that Betzalel engraved."

However, the staff does not shine in all directions until the end of correction, for there is a distinction between the Creator's staff and that of Moshe. It is written of the staff of Moshe: "Put forth your hand and take it by the tail (of a snake), and it shall become a staff in your hand" (*Shemot*, 4:4). This means that it did not shine from all sides.

However, after the end of correction, it will shine in all directions, as it is said: "And the secret name shone from within that staff in all directions by the Light of sages, who confirmed the secret name in forty-two properties." For the secret name that was engraved on the staff shone in all directions, i.e., in the property called "He will eradicate death forever" (*Yeshayahu*, 25:8). It will thus begin to shine evenly in all directions, whereas the Light of the name engraved on the staff is the Light of *Hochma* of the Name MB.

**150. Be seated, dear friends. Be seated and let us renew the correction of the Bride on this night, for whomever joins her on this night shall be guarded Above and below in the coming year. And this year shall pass over him in peace. Such people are described in the verse: "The angel of the Lord stands**

round those that fear Him, and delivers them. O taste and see that the Creator is good" (*Tehilim*, 34:8-9).

As was already stated in item 125, there are two explanations of the aforesaid. The first is that since the day of the giving of the Torah is the Light of the end of correction that abolishes death forever and brings freedom from the angel of death, one should exert to receive this Light on the day of *Shavuot* (Pentecost), as Light is renewed on the holiday and brings deliverance from death.

According to the second explanation, *Malchut* is called a "year," and the renewal of the Light by those who keep the Torah after the end of correction will also bring the complete and final correction of the year (*Malchut*). This is because the renewal of the Light by those who keep the Torah is referred to as the correction of the night of the bride, *Malchut*, called a "year." And this brings us to a corrected year.

# HEAVEN AND EARTH

**151. Rabbi Shimon opened and said, "In the beginning the Creator created the Heavens and the earth." This verse should be examined carefully, for whoever claims that there is another Creator disappears from the world, as it is written, "He who claims that there is another Creator perishes from both the earth and from Heavens, for there is no other Creator, but the Almighty."**

Here *The Zohar* continues to discuss the correction of the bride. It starts with the first sentence of the Torah: IN THE BEGINNING THE CREATOR CREATED, with the root and the source of all the corrections of the bride (*Malchut*) during the 6,000 years.

*Malchut's* entire correction occurs only through her union with *Bina* and the reception of *Bina's* properties. In the verse, IN THE BEGINNING THE CREATOR CREATED, the Creator is called *Elokim*, signifying *Bina*. This means that He created the world by the property of *Bina* for the purpose of correction.

*Elokim* consists of *MI-Bina* and *ELEH-Malchut*. Thanks to the constant union of *MI* and *ELEH*, the world can exist. The Creator is *Bina*, called *Elokim*, and as a result of *Ohr Hochma* clothing in *Ohr Hassadim*, the union of *MI* and *ELEH* provides *ELEH* with the property of *Bina*. It is through this correction that the world is able to exist.

The union of *MI* and *ELEH* does not permit for the existence of other, foreign, egoistic forces within the *Partzuf*. These are the so-called "other gods," who cannot sustain the world, as they separate *MI* from *ELEH* and do not clothe the Light of pleasure (*Hochma*) in the altruistic intention of *Hassadim* (for the Creator's sake), which leads to *Ohr Hochma* departing the *Partzuf*, leaving *ELEH*. Therefore, it is forbidden to believe that man is governed by any other forces besides the Creator, for instead of existence and reception of the Light of Life, such belief brings the world and man only ruin and disappearance of this Light.

**152. With the exception of *ELEH*, everything is written in Aramaic. This is called "translation." He asks: However, should you suggest that it is because the holy angels do not understand the translation, i.e., the Aramaic language, then everything should have been said in Hebrew, so the holy angels would hear and be grateful for it. He replies: This is exactly why it is written in the translation (in Aramaic), as the holy angels neither hear nor understand it, and hence will not envy people, which would be detrimental to the latter. For in this case, even the holy angels are called Creators, and they are included in the group of Creators, but they have not created Heaven and earth.**

Aramaic is referred to as "translation." It is very close to the holy language of Hebrew, but angels neither need nor know it nonetheless. Yet, they know and need all the other languages of the nations of the world. This is so because the translation from the holy language is called its "reverse side," its *VAK* without *GAR*.

In other words, there is an altruistic language, which is hence called "holy," and its reverse, preliminary stage, hence called "translation," is the Aramaic language. No other language in the world but Aramaic can act as translation from the holy language. All the other languages in the nations of the world (egoistic desires) are strictly egoistic and are unrelated to altruism. They are not *AHP* with regard to *GE* (the holy language).

Therefore, the translation is truly close to the holy language. However, there is one distinction here, which renders it unnecessary to angels: the holy language is like the scale pointer that shows the extent of balance between the right and left scales, where the pointer moves between the two scales and delivers its judgment—toward the scale of reward (for merits) or towards the scale of punishment (for sins). It brings everything back to the state of correction, to purity and holiness, and is hence called the holy language ("Introduction to The Study of Ten Sefirot," item 120).

As it is written in item sixteen, Heaven, earth, and all that inhabit them were created by *MA*, i.e., *Malchut*, as it is written, "MA = WHAT = HOW glorious is Your name in all the earth, which You have set above the Heavens!" Indeed, Heaven was created by the name (property) of *MA* (*Malchut*), whereas the Heaven that is mentioned alludes to *Bina*, called *MI*. But all is explained by the name *Elokim*.

The name *Elokim* is revealed in Heaven and earth, which were created by the power of *MA*, by attaching the letters *ELEH* from *Ima-Bina* with the help of *MAN* and good deeds of the lower ones. Therefore, the Light of *GAR*, i.e., *Ohr Hochma*, called *Elokim*, is consistent neither in Heaven (*Bina*) nor on earth (*ZON*).

Typically, only GE are present above the *Parsa*, in ZON of the world of *Atzilut*, whereas their AHP is below the *Parsa*, in the worlds BYA, for ZON themselves are unwilling to receive *Ohr Hochma* unless it is to be passed on to the *Partzufim*—the souls of the righteous—in the worlds of BYA.

When the lower ones, the righteous that exist spiritually in the worlds of BYA, raise MAN from below upwards, from their place in BYA to *Malchut de Atzilut*, MA turns into MI and the letters ELEH join with MI. Together, they create the word *Elokim*, which is the Light of Heaven and earth. However, if the lower ones corrupt their deeds by sinking into egoistic intentions, the Light disappears and leaves *Sefirot K-H* with the Light *Ruach-Nefesh* (called MI or MA), while the letters ELEH fall into the impure forces, for MI is GE and ELEH is AHP.

Therefore, the entire correction depends exclusively on attaching the letters ELEH to MI with the help of MAN. Hence, this correction is called the "holy language," like the scale pointer, which determines the balance between egoistic desires and altruistic intentions, i.e., the reception for the Creator's sake. This is why the scale pointer is set in the middle, and by means of such interaction of the properties of *Malchut* (the will to receive) and *Bina* (the will to bestow), one can achieve the reception of *Ohr Hochma* for the Creator's sake.

The Light is called "holy," as it passes the holy name *Elokim* to ZON, descends from *Bina* to ZON, and transfers the letters ELEH to the pure and holy side, to the scale of merit. This is why the Hebrew word for "scales" is *Mawznaim* (from the word *Awzen*), for the Light in AHP (*Awzen-Hotem-Peh*) is named according to its highest Light, the Light of *Awzen* of the *Sefira Bina* or *Ohr Neshama*.

| Keter | - Galgalta | - Forehead/Skull | - Yechida | } GE |
| Hochma | - Eynaim | - eyes | - Haya | |
| --- | --- | Parsa | --- | --- |
| Bina | - Awzen | - ear | - Neshama | } AHP |
| ZA | - Hotem | - nose | - Ruach | |
| Malchut | - Peh | - mouth | - Nefesh | |

And the language of translation called *Targum* is opposite to the holy language of *Mawznaim* (scales). It is so because when the lower ones do not raise MAN and do not harbor pure intentions, it is defined as an aspiration to use only the desires to receive, designated by the letters ELEH, and which do not aspire to unite with the desire (property) of bestowal (the letters MI-Bina). As a result, *AHP* of *ZON*, called *MA*, descend and Heaven and earth (*ZON*) return to the state of *VAK*.

Such a state is called the language of *Targum*. The *Gematria* of the word *Tardema* (sleep) matches that of the word *Targum*. In Hebrew, the word *Targum* is spelled with the same letters as the words *Tered MA*, which means "descending MA," for through this spiritually impure language, *AHP* = *MA* (designated by the words *Tered MA*) becomes revealed. This leads to the descent from the scale of merit to the scale of punishment. While this is happening, the state of *GE* is called "sleep."

However, all this refers only to *ZON*, to Heaven and earth created in *MA*, the desires of reception. This is because they have emerged as a result of a *Zivug* on *Yesod*, called *MA*. But the holy angels that emerged from the *Zivug de Neshikin* (kissing *Zivug*) of *AVI*, and which have only *MI* but no *MA* (only altruistic desires of bestowal, the property of *IMA-Bina*), permanently exist in the state of *VAK* without *GAR*, that is, without *Ohr Hochma*.

On the other hand, their *VAK* is *Ohr Hassadim* of *MI* = *Ima-Bina*. *Ohr Hassadim* in *Bina* is as important as *GAR*, for it fills desires with just as perfect a sensation as does the *GAR*, to the point that they reject *Ohr Hochma*, just like *Ima*. And there is holiness in them; hence, *GAR* are called holy, as well.

There are two reasons why angels do not respond to the language of *Targum*, which adds *MA* to *ZON* and returns *ZON* to the state of *VAK*:

1. Even when *ZON* are in the state of *GAR* due to the influence of the holy language, angels do not receive *GAR* (*Hochma*) from it, as, just like *Ima*, they want only *Ohr Hassadim*.

2. The addition of the *Achoraim* (*AHP*) does not apply to angels whatsoever; they lack the properties of *MA*. Hence, *The Zohar* says that THE HOLY ANGELS HAVE ABSOLUTELY NO NEED for translation AND DO NOT LISTEN to it. They do not need it because they neither lose anything when it is present nor gain anything when it is absent, as they constitute the property of *VAK* and lack the property of *MA*.

AND THEY SHALL NOT ENVY MAN—this sentence refers primarily to the damnation of other gods, the forces that prevent man from revealing *GAR*, *Ohr Hochma*. As a result, he loses the Light and the letters *ELEH*, for angels do not have the properties of *GAR de Hochma* either, but only *GAR de Hassadim*. Thus, they feel ashamed of their descent to such a low degree, and envy us for considering ourselves significant.

*The Zohar* says that in this case, even the holy angels are called "Creators," but they have not created Heaven and earth and are called "Creators-*Elokim*" (forces) because they come from *Ima-Bina* (called *Elokim*), thus existing in the general *Elokim*. But THEY HAVE NOT CREATED HEAVEN AND EARTH, for they cannot uphold the existence of Heaven and earth in GAR *de Hochma*. However, Heaven and earth (the correction of the world to its ultimate merging with the Creator) cannot exist unless man settles there (man must consist of egoistic and altruistic desires) and sows and reaps (corrects his egoistic desires by uniting with the properties of *Bina*). This existence is possible only in the Light of GAR *de Hochma* (the reception of *Ohr Hochma* for the Creator's sake). Hence, angels do not create Heaven and earth.

**153. He asks: earth is called *Arka*, when it should read, *Ar'a*. He answers: because *Arka* is one of the seven lands below, where the sons of Cain's sons reside. Indeed, after being banished from the face of the earth, they descended there and fathered generations; wisdom became so lost that all understanding was lost, and this is a double land, consisting of darkness and Light.**

Each of the seven *Sefirot* (the six *Sefirot* of ZA and *Malchut*) contain the properties of the other six. Thus, each one of them contains the seven *Sefirot* HGT NHYM. In other words, *Malchut*, too, has seven *Sefirot*, and the lower world contains seven lands, as well, called *Eretz*, *Adama*, *Arka*, *Gia*, *Neshia*, *Tzia* and *Tevel*.

Our land is called *Tevel* and is the highest of the seven lands. *Arka* is the third of the seven lands. The souls of Cain and Abel descend from the word *Elokim*, but due to the impurity that Chava (Eve), Adam's wife, received from the serpent, the soul of Cain emerged first from the letters *ELEH*, followed by the soul of Abel, which emerged from the letters *MI*. These two *Partzufim* were meant to unite and incorporate their properties in one another, which would make the name *Elokim* shine in both of them, as when *MI* is permanently present in *ELEH*. However, the impure force that emerged together with Cain's soul incited him against his brother (*MI* of the word *Elokim*) to the point that he rose against Abel (*MI* in *Elokim*) and slew him. This is because the disappearance of the property of *MI-Bina* from *ELEH* is tantamount to murder.

Without the support of the properties of *MI*, *ELEH* (Cain's own property) fell into the impure forces: from the spiritual level of the holy land to the impure place (of egoistic desires). And he lost his descendants (*Partzufim* filled with Light) because of the rule of the impure forces (the disappearance of the screen).

Thus, the holy language within him was substituted for translation, for he had lost the wisdom (*Ohr Hochma*). After all, the impure forces lack wisdom, as they have only the Light of *HB* without *Daat*.

The slaying of Abel, i.e., the exit of Light from this *Partzuf* (item 152), occurs because *MI* is formed in *ZON* exclusively by the power of *MAN* (raised by the pure thoughts of the righteous in the worlds of *BYA*). Then appear the letters *ELEH*, and the word *Elokim* becomes as complete in *ZON* as it is in *AVI*. *Malchut* ends just like *ZA*, like *Ima*, due to the replacing of the letter *Hey* with *Yod* (item 17).

However, the letter *Hey* does not disappear from *MA* forever. Rather, it simply enters the inner part of *Malchut* and hides there (the will to receive receives its fulfillment from altruistic actions, from *Ohr Hassadim*. Hence, its egoistic aspirations are temporarily unfelt, as they are concealed in *Ohr Hassadim*). Meanwhile, the letter *Yod* is revealed in *MI*.

This is why the Creator's holy name *Elokim* is also found in *ZON*, in Heaven and earth. However, Cain raised *MAN* not in holiness and purity, but wished to use the letters *ELEH*—which relate to him—for his own pleasure. This is described as, AND CAIN ROSE UP AGAINST ABEL, HIS BROTHER, for he put himself above his brother, to rule over *MI* (Abel).

However, *AHP* of *Nukva* (the hitherto concealed letter *Hey* of *MA*) were immediately revealed, and the word *MI* disappeared from *Malchut*. Hence, Abel's soul, which stems from *MI* of *Nukva* (*MI* fill the *Partzuf* with Light and are considered its soul) ascends and disappears as well, as is described by the words, AND SLEW HIM, for the Light's exit from the *Partzuf* is referred to as death.

This is why *The Zohar* describes this process in the following way: The serpent's impure force was within Cain (*Beresheet*, 2:4); hence, he wished to strengthen the letters *ELEH*, annul *MI*, and govern them. That is why he revealed *AHP* of *Nukva* (*MA*) and *MI* disappeared from *Nukva*, whereupon Abel's soul, which descends from *MI*, disappeared as well (AND SLEW HIM).

Thus, Cain himself (*ELEH*) fell under the rule of the impure forces, called *Arka* or *Eretz Nod*, as it is written in the Torah: "And he settled in the land of Nod" (*Beresheet*, 4:16).

*The Zohar* calls it a double land, one that contains both Light and darkness. This is because Light and darkness mix and act (rule) together, as there are two rulers in that land, who divide the power equally between them. One rules over darkness, the other over Light. Hence, in this state one is unable to separate Light from darkness, and only help from Above, the descending Light of reason, enables one to tell between the true Ruler and the lord of darkness.

**154.** And there are two rulers there—one rules over darkness and one over Light, and they become hostile to each other. When Cain descended there, they joined together and became complete. And they all saw that they were Cain's descendants. Therefore, their two heads are like two serpents, except for when the ruler of Light defeats the other, the ruler of darkness. Hence, they enter Light and darkness, and become as one.

We need to review item 14, which expounds on the creation of the holy name *Elokim*. First, the letters *ELEH* ascend and join *MI* to form a simple word, since *Ohr Hassadim* is still insufficient, whereas holiness (*Ohr Hochma*) cannot enter the *Kli* (desire) without being clothed in *Ohr Hassadim*. Hence, it is concealed in the name *Elokim*.

That is why a *Zivug* takes place in *MI*— to receive *Ohr Hassadim*, which clothes *Ohr Hochma*, thereby correcting the name *Elokim*: *MI BARAH ELEH—BARAH* is the source of *Ohr Hassadim*, which clothes *Ohr Hochma*, thus connecting *MI* to *ELEH*, which brings correction to the name *Elokim*. *MI-Bina* consists of *GAR* (*AVI* with the property of pure altruism), who never receive *Ohr Hochma*, and *ZAT* (*YESHSUT*), who do receive *Ohr Hochma*.

Therefore, as the letters *ELEH* begin to ascend to *MI*, they first rise to *ZAT de MI* (*YESHSUT*), who receive *Ohr Hochma*, but are currently concealed in the name *Elokim*. Then transpires the second *Zivug* on *GAR de MI*, *AVI*, altruistic desires, which provide *ELEH* with *Ohr Hassadim*, thus bringing correction to the name *Elokim*.

| | | |
|---|---|---|
| AVI | - GAR de Bina | - Ohr Hassadim |
| YESHSUT | - ZAT de Bina | - Ohr Hochma |
| ZON | | |

Since *ELEH* lacks *Ohr Hassadim*, those deprived from *Ohr Hochma* are called *Partzuf* Cain. Not only did Cain fail to raise *MAN* to receive *MI* with *Hassadim*, he also wished to receive *Ohr Hochma* from *AVI*, thereby destroying the *Partzuf* named Abel, for the egoistic desires of *AHP de Malchut* of *Atzilut* were exposed. The Light disappeared from *Partzuf* Abel, signifying its death, whereas Cain himself fell into the impure forces—*ELEH*.

The place of these impure forces is called *Arka*. Also, two rulers exist there, emerging from the impure *ELEH*: when *AHP de MA* in *Malchut* is concealed, while *AHP de MI* are revealed, they can pass the Light from the perfect, pure, and holy name *Elokim* to the souls. *Ohr Hochma* of *ELEH* (received by

YESHSUT) then clothes in *Hassadim* (received from *AVI*), and the holy name *Elokim* becomes revealed.

However, since the impure forces cling only to the *AHP* of the pure forces (to *MA*), the letters *ELEH* within them exist in two incomplete states: (i) when no *Hassadim* are present at all; (ii) when *Ohr Hochma* in *ELEH* cannot clothe in *Hassadim* due to the lack of *Hassadim de MI*; hence, *ELEH* are kept in darkness.

This is the male part of the impure *ELEH*, as these *Kelim* are intended for *Ohr Hochma*. However, they have no *Hochma* due to the lack of *Hassadim de MI*. Hence, they are kept in darkness, devoid of both *Hochma* and *Hassadim*. Yet, these are great *Kelim*, for if they had been able to receive *Ohr Hassadim*, they would have been able to receive *Ohr Hochma* within it, too.

The female part of the impure *ELEH* stems from *AHP de MA* of the holy *Nukva*, the *Kli* for *Ohr Hassadim*. However, the impure *Nukva* is considerably injured, as she is the basis for everyone's remoteness from the Creator, as she impersonates the holy *Malchut*. Depending on the extent of her corruption, she has a multitude of impure names. Yet, she still retains a tiny Light (*Ner Dakik*), since her *Kelim* stem from *AHP de MA*, the roots of which are *Kelim* of *Ohr Hassadim*.

These male and female parts of the impure *ELEH* are ZA and *Malchut* of the impure forces, the two rulers in *Arka*. The male part rules over darkness and the female part rules over the Light that is there. They complain against each another, since they are opposite. The male part complains because it is the *Kelim* of the letters *ELEH*, which are empty of *Ohr Hochma*; it hates the forces of remoteness from the Creator and forgery, existing within the *Kelim* of the female part of the impure forces, and prefers to remain in its darkness.

*Nukva* of the impure forces, however, who has a small Light of *Hassadim*, does not aspire for *Ohr Hochma*, let alone for the darkness in which her male part abides. Therefore, she complains about the male part and distances from it. As *The Zohar* says, two rulers govern there: one (the male part) over darkness, and the other (the female part) over Light, and they are hostile towards each other, for the male part rules over darkness and the female rules over Light. Hence, they hate, slander, and complain against each other. And since they are thereby distanced from one another, they cannot expand their dominance and are incapable of causing any harm.

However, after Cain had sinned and dropped the pure letters of *ELEH* of his soul into the impure forces of *Arka*, his *ELEH*, which are concealed from *Hassadim*, clothed in the tiny Light present in the impure forces. This revives the small *Kelim de Hochma* in Cain's *ELEH*, for the Light of the impure forces bestows life upon them, just like the pure Light of *Hassadim*.

As a result, the male part of *ELEH* of the impure forces, too, made a *Zivug* with this *Nukva*, who clothed Cain's *ELEH*, since he has these *Kelim*, as well. With the help of this *Zivug*, Cain fathered his descendants, the sparks of *Ohr Hochma* that remain in the letters *ELEH*, which are not mixed with the male impure *Kelim* of *ELEH* that clothed in the Light of *Nukva* of the impure forces.

This is why *The Zohar* says that when Cain descended there, everything merged and became complete, for the sparks of *Ohr Hochma* that remained in Cain's *ELEH* were clothed in the Light of *Nukva* of the impure forces. Consequently, her male impure force wished to enjoy the sparks of *Ohr Hochma* that are in Cain's *ELEH*.

Hence, they made a *Zivug*, i.e., spread and completed one another, and everyone saw that they were the descendants of Cain, that this *Zivug* produced the descendants, the clothing of the sparks of *Ohr Hochma* in Cain's impure *ELEH*. Thus, the sparks of *Ohr Hochma* of Cain's soul were revealed, and everyone saw that they were Cain's descendants, born of a vile *Zivug*.

Therefore, their two heads are like two serpents, for they were born from a union of the male and female parts of the impure *ELEH*, which are initially opposite to one another. Therefore, Cain's descendants have two heads, from the two impure forces. one craves the darkness of the desires to receive *Ohr Hochma*, and the other craves the Light within the impure desires of the impure *Nukva*. And the two serpent heads correspond to the two animals that belong to the system of the pure forces: the bull and the eagle.

However, the two heads exist only when the male part is dominant, when darkness rules. Indeed, by clothing in the Light of *Nukva* in order to enjoy the small sparks of *Ohr Hochma*, the male part also supports (against its will) the dominance of its *Nukva*, for it wants her Light. As a result, their descendants have two heads: the first pulls in one direction and the second in another.

*Nukva* of the impure forces does not need their male part whatsoever, as her male part exists in darkness and cannot give her anything. Therefore, *Nukva* dominates and prevails in her impurity, leaving nothing of the properties of the male part. Consequently, Cain's two-headed descendants become one-headed.

*The Zohar* tells us that the ruler of Light defeats the lord of darkness. When the impure *Nukva*, which has the Light, dominates, she defeats the male impure part, as well as the other male ruler. She defeats the male part, fully subduing it to her rule, and they include themselves in her Light and darkness, and become as one. Consequently, the rule of the male part (darkness) is included under the rule of the female part (Light), and the two heads become one.

**155. For these are the two rulers, called Afrira and Kastimon, who resemble holy angels with six wings. One has the image of a bull, and the other of an eagle. And when they unite, they create an image of man.**

The male impure force is called Kastimon (from the word *Kosti*, devastation), for it is darkness and is unfit for man's life. And the impure *Nukva*, the female part, is called Afrira (from the word *Afar*, dust), and is unfit for sowing. She is called so in order to show that although she contains Light, she is insufficient for sowing the seed and producing harvest to feed human beings.

*The Zohar* also says that she resembles holy angels with six wings, for the six wings of the holy angels correspond to the letter *Vav* in the name *HaVaYaH*. In contrast, there are only four wings in the impure forces, corresponding to the name *ADNI*, indicating the height of the impure forces with regard to the holy angels, opposite them.

The Upper Light is called "wine," bringing joy to the Creator and to human beings. However, wine residue contains *Sigim* or wine yeast. And from this waste emerges the foremost wrecker of the world, for he is still connected to purity (to yeast) and has the image of a man. However, as he descends to bring people harm, he assumes the image of a bull. This is why a bull is the first of the four main types of wrecker.

Hence, *The Zohar* tells us that Kastimon is a wrecker in the image of a bull, thus indicating that it is the basis of all wreckers that are called "the impure bull." It is the *Sigim* of the Supernal *Ohr Hochma* of the holy name *Elokim*, the impure *ELEH* that correspond to the pure *ELEH* of the name *Elokim*. For *Sigim* and yeast stand below it, but since it is still connected to purity, it has the image of man, for *Ohr Hochma* of the name *Elokim* is *Tzelem* (image and likeness) of man, of which it is said: "*Be Tzelem Elokim*—created man in image and likeness."

Yet, when separated from purity (altruism) through deterioration of its desires and, consequently, of its properties, it descends to its place (befitting these properties) in *Arka*, and assumes the image (properties) of a bull. And its *Nukva* assumes (in *Arka*) the form (properties) of an eagle, in congruence with her goal and action of *Linshor* (to fall out)—to bring about the fall of human souls under her power.

Hence, the word *Nesher* (vulture) is derived from the word *Neshira* (fall), just as leaves fall from a tree, for the role of the impure *Nukva* is to seek people out and bring them to a state of night and darkness, to the destruction of the holy covenant, as a result of which people's souls depart from them (item 131).

Therefore, *The Zohar* tells us: "And when they unite, they form the image of man," i.e., if they return and unite with purity, existing as wine yeast, they return and assume once more the image of man, just as before they descended to Arka and became wreckers.

**156. When they are covered with darkness, they turn into a serpent with two heads, and move like a serpent. They soar in the void and bathe in the Great Sea, and when they approach the chains of Aza and Azael, they rile and rouse them and leap into the mountains of darkness, thinking that the Creator wishes to bring justice upon them.**

I suggest that the reader will try to comment on *The Zohar* on his own, without any help, and then compare his thoughts with those stated below. This way, we might understand what Rabbi Yehuda Ashlag has done for us with his commentary. Prior to the appearance of his commentaries on the books of the ARI and *The Zohar*, there was no way for us to understand Kabbalah correctly, and only a handful of people in each generation could climb the spiritual ladder on their own.

Now, however, I assure the reader that simply by constantly reading even my books, which retell the compositions of the great Kabbalists, Rabbi Ashlag and his elder son and my teacher, Rabbi Baruch Ashlag, anyone can attain ascension to the Creator. I think that those who have already read previous books realize that this is truly possible!

As *The Zohar* already mentioned in item 154, when the impure *Nukva* dominates man through her Light, the two heads become as one. However, in the darkness, when the male part, called Kastimon, dominates, they turn into a serpent with two heads, for the male part is unable to annul the power of the female part, as it needs to be clothed in her Light. Hence, the serpent has two heads. And they move like a serpent—aiming to bring harm (the property of the serpent), to tempt Chava to dine on the fruit of the Tree of Knowledge.

By the power of the *Rosh* of the impure *Nukva* they soar in the void, which contains the root of the impure force, called "void" or the greatest fall, as it is written: "They ascended up to Heaven, they descended down to the abyss" (*Tehilim*, 107:26). By the power of the impure male part, they bathe in the Great Sea, in *Ohr Hochma* of the impure forces.

Therefore, *Arka* is called the Land of Nod, as it constantly sways from the rule of the two heads: those that reside there keep alternating between ascending up to the Great Sea and descending down into the void.

The angels Aza and Azael are very exalted angels. Indeed, even after they had fallen from Heaven into our world, into the mountains of darkness, linked by a metal chain, so great was their power that with their help Bil'am (Balaam) attained the degree of prophecy, of which it is written: "Sees the Creator's presence" (*Bamidbar*, 24:4).

This is described as "falls and opens his eyes," for Aza is referred to as "falling" because of his fall from Heaven to earth. And Azael is called "he who opens his eyes" with regard to Aza, at whose face the Creator throws darkness. And with regard to Bil'am's prophetic degree, our sages have said the following: "There has not been a prophet in Israel like Moshe, not in Israel, but there was one among the nations of the world, and his name was Bil'am" (*Bamidbar-Raba*, 14)—so great was his prophetic degree.

And the reason for their downfall from Heaven to earth lies in their complaints against man at the moment of his making. Yet, there were many angels complaining and objecting, so why did the Creator cast down only these two? The answer to this question can be found in items 416-425 of the chapter "*Balak*" in *The Zohar*. Briefly, it says that when the desire to create Adam (or man, since the Hebrew word for man is Adam) appeared in the Creator, He summoned the Supernal angels, seated them before Him, and told them of His desire to create man.

The angels replied: "What is man, that You are mindful of him?" (*Tehilim*, 8:5), meaning what are the properties of this man that You so wish to create? He replied to them: "This man will be similar to Me and his wisdom will surpass yours, for the human soul includes all the angels and Supernal Degrees, just as his body includes all the creatures of this world."

Therefore, at the moment of creation of man's soul, the Creator summoned all the Supernal angels, so they would pass all of their properties and forces to man's soul. It is therefore written: "Let us make man in our image, in our likeness," meaning that man's "image and likeness" includes all of the properties of all the angels.

The words "image and likeness" are written in quotation marks, since the words *Tzelem* and *Demut* (image and likeness) are not mere words that simply describe likeness. Rather, they constitute very meaningful spiritual notions.

But the angels' question should be interpreted as follows: "What kind of a creature is this man and what is his nature? How shall we benefit from passing (including) our properties in him?" The Creator replied to this: "This man will be similar to Me and his wisdom will surpass yours." In other words, the Creator thus promised them that man will embrace all of their qualities (the properties of *Tzelem*), and that he will be wiser than them. However, because of their connection to him, they will also benefit from his great attainments and acquire everything that they presently lack.

This is because the human soul includes all the spiritual degrees and all the utmost properties of all the angels. And just as his body includes all the materials and creatures of our world with all of their properties, so was the Creator's wish that his soul would absorb the whole of creation within it.

It is written in the Torah: "Yaakov and Israel shall be told of the Creator's works (*Bamidbar*, 23:23)." The sages have said that in the future the angels will ask Israel for things that they do not know themselves, for Israel's attainments will be beyond that of the angels. Hence, all the angels took part in the creation of man and integrated all their properties within him.

However, once man was created and sinned, thus becoming guilty before the Creator, the angels Aza and Azael appeared before the Creator with accusations "that man, whom You have created, has sinned before You." For these words, the Creator cast them down from their exulted and holy degree, and thus, they began to deceive human beings.

Of all the angels, only these two, Aza and Azael, came before the Creator to complain about Adam's sins, for only they knew that man shall return to the Creator. However, Aza and Azael also knew that the harm brought to them by man's sin will not be corrected by this return. Moreover, they would prefer man to not return in his desires to the Creator at all. This is why they were the only ones that complained about Adam's sin, because from their perspective, this sin is incorrigible.

The thing is that the breaking of the vessels and Adam's sin constitute the same breaking, disappearance of the screen (anti-egoistic willpower or intention to act for the Creator's sake). The difference is that the breaking of the vessels signifies the breaking of the screen in the *Partzuf* called "world," while Adam's sin is the breaking, disappearance of the screen in the *Partzuf* called "soul." The difference between these two *Partzufim* is that the *Partzuf* called "world" is external with regard to the inner *Partzuf* called "soul." The soul exists within the world and is sustained by it.

The breaking has its causes and consequences. It is necessary for mixing all the properties of *Bina* and *Malchut*, and must transpire both in the spiritual world and within the soul, to impart the properties of *Bina* to *Malchut*, and thus enable her to correct herself.

The breaking of the world of *Nekudim* led to the breaking of the eight *Sefirot Hesed-Gevura*-2/3 of *Tifferet* and 1/3 of *Tifferet-Netzah-Hod-Yesod-Malchut*, four *Sefirot H-B-ZA-M* in each one that in turn consists of ten *Sefirot*, in all: $8 \times 4 \times 10 = 320$ (*SHACH*) parts. As a result of the mixing of all the parts, each part in turn consists of 320 parts. All of these 320 parts, called *Nitzotzin* (sparks), acquired the egoistic will to enjoy by receiving the Creator's Light, which signifies their descent into the impure forces.

In the spiritual realm there are no locations or departments of pure and impure. However, for the purpose of conveying information more vividly, we envision the reception of lower properties as a descent, the reception of more spiritual properties as an ascent, the attainment of equivalence of form as a union, and the emergence of a new property as separation. The appearance of egoistic desires in a spiritual object is considered a descent into the impure forces, although these forces exist within us (and not vice versa), and simply become more apparent. There is nothing surrounding us, for everything is within: all the worlds and desires, both pure and impure.

By studying Kabbalah we attract the emanation of the Light that surrounds our soul (see "Introduction to The Study of Ten Sefirot," item 155), which cultivates within us a desire for correction. Then, as we attain the degrees of the spiritual worlds, we begin to feel the spiritual Light that corresponds to each degree, through which we begin to discern egoistic and altruistic parts in each of our properties.

By comparisons to the Light, we perceive our egoistic parts as evil, and to the extent that we sense it, we distance ourselves from it and refuse to use these desires. Conversely, we perceive our altruistic desires as good for us, but, having no strength to use them, we submit a request, receive the necessary strength, and accept the Light for the Creator's sake, thereby ascending to a higher degree, where this process repeats itself.

The return (*Teshuva*—repentance) means that by raising MAN (request for correction), we elevate some of the 320 corrupt parts from the impure forces, into which they fell, back to the world of *Atzilut*, where they existed prior to Adam's sin. However, we are powerless to sort out and correct, i.e., to elevate the thirty-two parts of *Malchut* herself, which exist in the eight *Sefirot* of this *Partzuf* (world), for their level of corruption is beyond our ability to repair them.

Therefore, out of the 320 (SHACH = *Shin* + *Chet* = 300 + 20) parts, we can, that is, we are entitled to and must sort out and correct only 320 – 32 = 288 parts (RAPACH = 288) by our return to the Creator, i.e., 9 x 32, where nine designates the first nine *Sefirot* in each *Sefira* that we are allowed to correct. Yet, we are unable to correct *Malchut* of each *Sefira*, for this requires a Light of a special power. We will receive this Light from the Creator only after the correction of all the other 288 parts, that is, at the end of correction.

These thirty-two parts of *Malchut*, which are impossible and thus prohibited to correct, are called *Lev HaEven* (*Lamed-Bet Even*—thirty-two stones). As I've repeatedly mentioned, there is no such notion as "prohibition" in Kabbalah; this word is used when it is necessary to point out the futility of trying despite one's weakness and limitation. "Prohibited" means impossible, beyond one's power. Moreover, it is not the Creator's prohibition; rather, as a result of one's personal faith and experience, one should admit that "prohibited" alludes to whatever is still beyond one's power to correct.

Therefore, GAR *de AVI* are concealed, and their Light does not shine. After all, for all of its ten *Sefirot* to shine, a *Zivug* needs to be made on *Malchut* herself, for *Lev HaEven*, the thirty-two uncorrected parts of *Malchut* herself are a supplement to their ten *Sefirot*. And as long as these *Kelim* are missing, a complete *Zivug* is impossible. However, when the complete analysis and correction of the 288 (RAPACH = *Reish* + *Peh* + *Chet* = 200 + 80 + 8 = 288) *Nitzotzin* is completed, *Lev HaEven* will be corrected by itself, and no effort or corrections shall be required on our part.

So the prophet says: "A new heart also shall I give you, and a new spirit shall I put within you; and I shall take away the stony heart out of your flesh, and I shall give you a heart of flesh" (*Yechezkel*, 36:26). Then *AVI* will receive their Light. However, this will occur at the end of correction, and before the end of correction, *AHP* of *AVI* will not be able to receive correction by means of our return, for we will be able to correct all of our egoistic desires, except for our very essence, *Malchut de Malchut*.

These angels—Aza and Azael—are the real *AHP de AVI* that were destroyed during the breaking of the vessels, and were nearly restored before the sin of Adam. However, Adam's sin destroyed them once more, this time until the very end of correction.

Hence, both angels were complaining to the Creator about their Light, which has disappeared because of Adam, for they saw that there was no hope that Adam would correct them through his return to the Creator. Moreover, they saw that by his return, Adam had lowered their degree even more, for now the entire correction and return was limited to only 288 parts, without any participation or even mentioning of the thirty-two forbidden parts, *Lev HaEven*, which refer to the correction of *AVI*, whose Light is the Light of these angels, just as the *Kelim* of the true *AHP de AVI* are their *Kelim*.

Each raising of *MAN* designates cutting off, separation of impurity—*Lev HaEven*—from the food, *RAPACH* = 288 *Nitzotzin*, the parts that can be corrected. It follows that by preventing Aza and Azael from participating in the correction of *Lev HaEven*, we lower them even more. This is why the two angels complained to the Creator and tried to impede Adam from returning. After all, his return lowers them even further, for the thirty-two parts refer to them.

Therefore, when the Creator saw that their complaints threatened to weaken man's strength to return to Him, He told them that Adam's sin did not spoil anything for them. For although there is greatness and holiness in them while they are in Heaven and no impure forces can cling to them, still this perfection is incomplete, as they cannot exist in our world, in a place of impure forces.

The Creator told them: "Hence, you have lost nothing as a result of Adam's sin, for you are no better than him anyway, as your degree is merely the result of the place of your residence." And since the Creator's words constitute His actions, they fell instantly from Heaven to earth (into egoism, of course, not to the physical earth!).

And since they came (spiritually descended) to the corporeal life (as Kabbalah defines it), they began to sort through and analyze the thirty-two parts of complete egoism, called the "daughters of men," of which the Torah says: "And the sons of great (angels) saw the daughters of men (egoistic *Nukva*), that they were fair (they saw in her an opportunity for egoistic reception of pleasure), and they took them as wives (used their egoistic desires), whomsoever they chose (they themselves chose precisely this low state)" (*Beresheet*, 6:2). For they did not want to separate the impurity of the thirty-two egoistic parts and prefer only 288, but took everything they wished, including *Lev HaEven*.

Hence, they also transgressed with *Nukva* Lilit (Lilith) the sinner, and wished to draw the entire world toward sin, to fling it into the last stage of egoism, for they did not wish man to return, as it completely contradicts their root.

What did the Creator do? He put them in iron chains! For the Creator saw that if they had the power to return to Heaven after the sin, all the people would fail in their attempts to aspire to the Creator in their desires, as the dominance of these egoistic angels (forces) in man would be too great. (Rashi—the great eleventh century Kabbalist and Biblical commentator—says that the entire Torah speaks in the words of man. Hence, everything is described in notions of time and sequence of events. Similarly, the Creator seemingly creates and only then sees the results of his work).

Therefore, although their root is quite high, the Creator gave the root of the impure forces His permission to act (here we see that the Creator governs all the forces in creation). This root is called *Barzel* (iron), as it is written: "There was neither hammer nor axe nor any tool of iron heard in the house, while it was in building" (*Melachim*, 1, 6:7), for iron is an impure force.

And since this impure force clang to the two angels and bound them, as if with iron chains, by the desires that it dictates to them, such a state is characterized as being in the mountains of darkness, from which they can no longer ascend until the end of correction.

And when they approach the chain of Aza and Azael, rile and rouse them, it designates the awakening of the fourth part of the will to receive, *Malchut de Malchut*, the greatest desire to receive, called "wrath and rage." And they leap over the mountains of darkness, thinking that the Creator wishes to bring justice upon them, for being bound by iron chains, they could not ascend to their roots and receive *Hochma*.

Therefore, this action is considered leaping, an attempt to ascend, followed by a fall, as a result of which they descend even deeper into the mountains of darkness. And they think that because of their leaps (attempts to receive the Light from their root), the Creator is becoming increasingly stricter with them; thus, they decide to stop leaping.

However, even though they cannot give anything, as their attempts to reach up are mere leaps and falls, it is nonetheless enough for the two rulers to receive *Ohr Hochma* from them, as this gives them the strength to swim in the sea of *Hochma* of the impure force, whereas before they had only the strength to bathe in it.

The reason for this is that there is no action in this exalted impure force, and everything is limited only in thoughts and desires, for such is the essence of the impure forces (desires) that separate us from the Creator—before the level of an action is achieved, purity disappears from it. Therefore, the impure forces will never reach the level of an action.

Hence, the work for the impure forces is called *Avoda Zara* (alien work or idol worshipping), as it is alien to spiritual work "for the Creator's sake," and is performed according to the instruction and desires that the impure forces insert into man's thoughts. In this alien work for an alien master, the Creator punishes even for mere thoughts and desires, as the prophet said: "That the house of Israel may understand in their own heart" (*Yechezkel*, 14:5). And the sages have said that man is accused and punished even for thoughts, desires, and doubts in the alien work that transpires in his heart in exactly the same measure as for a completed action. Hence, the leaps of Aza and Azael are sufficient in their desire to receive *Hochma*, although in reality they received nothing.

**157. And these two Creator-appointed rulers swim in the Great Sea, fly up from there, and at night go to Naamah, the mother of witches, for whom the first people fell (*Beresheet*, 6:1-4). And they wish to approach her, but she leaps 60,000 *Parsa'ot* and assumes several different forms, so that people may be deceived and enticed by her.**

After receiving power from Aza and Azael, they can now make a *Zivug* with Naamah, as the first angels Aza and Azael erred. From that *Zivug* with Aza and Azael, Naamah gave birth to all the spirits and witches of the world. The Torah calls Aza and Azael the "sons of Gods" or the "sons of the great" (*Beresheet*, 6:2).

Yet, how could such exalted angels stoop to such depraved actions with Naamah, and why did she give birth to spirits and witches, and not to people?

The thing is that the Upper World (*AVI*) was created by the letter *Yod*, by the male part, which have nothing of the fourth part of *Malchut*, called *Malchut de Malchut*. However, ZON (the lower world) was created by the letter *Hey*, which includes *Malchut de Malchut*. AVI aspire only to *Ohr Hassadim*, to altruistic actions (bestowal), for *Bina* emerged as such in the four stages of *Malchut's* birth, even before the appearance of the first *Kli* (*Malchut de Malchut*).

Nevertheless, ZON need *Ohr Hochma*, since ZA was created as such in the four stages of *Malchut's* birth. Also, ZA wishes to receive *Ohr Hochma* within *Ohr Hassadim*, which he already has.

The *Zivug* of AVI, called the "Upper World," begets angels who desire *Ohr Hassadim*, just like AVI, from whom they were born. Human souls are born from the *Zivug* of ZON, called the "lower world," and they, like ZON, from whom they were born, desire only *Ohr Hochma*.

The moment the common soul of all the creatures (Adam) was born from ZON *de Atzilut*, ZON existed at the level of the Upper World (*AVI*) and clothed it. Like *AVI*, they, too, ended in the letter *Yod* of the name *HaVaYaH*. And the letter *Hey* of the name *HaVaYaH* was concealed in their posterior side, *Achoraim* or *AHP*.

Hence, Adam's level was quite high because *ZON* was in the Upper World and ended in the letter *Yod*. The level of *ZON* was that of the angels that were born from *AVI*; therewith, *ZON* received *Ohr Hochma* according to their desires, as *ZON* are meant to.

As a result, *ZON* contain the name *Elokim*, Supernal *Hochma*, the perfection of the Upper World. This is because the ban of the first restriction to not receive *Ohr Hochma* does not apply to the letter *Yod*. Cain and Abel were born from this state: Cain was born from *ELEH* and Abel from *MI*. *Malchut* herself (the last letter *Hey* of the name *HaVaYaH*) was concealed in them both, and only the letter *Yod* was revealed; hence, they contained Supernal *Hochma*.

However, on the whole, *Hochma* is received in *Kelim ELEH*, *ZAT de Bina*, by Cain's soul. This property of Cain is concealed in *MI*, as the last *Hey* is concealed inside *Yod*, and Cain wanted to make a *Zivug* with it, to receive *Ohr Hochma* in *Malchut de Malchut*, concealed in Abel's soul.

It is by this that he slew Abel, for after the last *Hey* was revealed, the ban of the first restriction to receive *Ohr Hochma* in it was revealed. Hence, the Creator's name *Elokim* disappeared from them both: *MI*, since it refers to *GAR*, ascended and disappeared (signifying Abel's slaying), and Cain's *ELEH*, since it refers to *ZAT*, fell into the impure forces, called *Arka*.

However, although it fell into the impure forces, sparks of *Ohr Hochma* still remain in these *Kelim* (desires), as it is written that his daughters did not suffer from it greatly, and the sparks of *Bina* still remained in them. From this we can understand that Naamah, one of Cain's daughters, was the most beautiful of all the women in the world, for the sin transpired mainly in Cain's male part, and not in his female part, as is described in the Talmud (*Sanhedrin*, 74:2).

Therefore, after the Creator cast Aza and Azael into this world (created by the letter *Hey*), and they've seen Naamah, a new hitherto non-existent desire appeared within them—the desire to receive *Ohr Hochma*, for in their essence they desire only *Ohr Hassadim*, and only the image of Naamah bore a new desire for *Ohr Hochma* within them.

And since there is no *Hey* (the last *Hey*, on which there is a ban to receive *Ohr Hochma*) in their essence and in that of Naamah (the last revealed one, for it originates from Cain's *ELEH*), they erred in her, thinking that she is able to receive *Ohr Hochma*, and made a *Zivug* with her.

Their error was twofold:

1. Despite the fact that they do not have the last *Hey* from birth, since the place determines, and they exist in this world, the last *Hey* already governs them, and they are forbidden to receive *Ohr Hochma*.

2. They thought that the last *Hey* was absent in Naamah's structure, when in fact, it was concealed. Hence, spirits and witches were born from their *Zivug*.

From this we can understand what is written in the Talmud (*Hagiga*, 16:1), that witches are half-angels half-people, for with regard to their fathers, Aza and Azael, they are angels, whereas with regard to Naamah, they are like people. But she could not give birth to people, for the seed within her came from angels, and not from people.

The reason for the harm that they cause lies in the fact that they were born from depravity, the greatest possible distance from the Creator. Hence, their impurity accompanies them and brings harm wherever it possibly can. Therefore, *The Zohar* says that at night they come to Naamah, the mother of witches, for whom the first people fell (see *Beresheet*, 6:1-4).

Indeed, after they received strength from these angels, who were the first to engage in depravity with Naamah, they could continue to engage in depravity with her. *The Zohar* indicates that this is precisely why they come at night, for the power of *Hochma* of the impure forces rules only in the darkness of night, the time of judgment and restrictions, and also as the consequence of roots, namely Aza and Azael, who reside in the mountains of darkness.

However, after engaging in depravity with them, she leapt 60,000 *Parsa'ot*, i.e., she rose so high that she wanted to annul the *Parsa* below *VAK de AA*, whose each *Sefira* is defined as 10,000; hence, its *VAK* = 6 *Sefirot* equal 60,000.

But as soon as they think to approach her, she leaps 60,000 *Parsa'ot*, but immediately falls back down and is unable to touch them, for there is no action in these upper impure forces, and all transgressions and all errors are only in thoughts and intentions.

Yet, there is still enough power in her to deceive and entice people, even if man does not reach the level of impure actions and is only drawn to her in his thoughts and desires. However, the Creator punishes for such thoughts and desires, as He does for actions, as the prophet warns us: "the house of Israel may understand in their own heart" (*Yechezkel*, 14:5). And the impure force assumes several different shapes, such as depravity with married women, murder and other things laid upon Lilit.

**158. These two rulers soar in the entire world and then return to their places. And they rouse the sons of Cain's sons with a spirit of evil desires to beget children.**

"Soar in the entire world"—they bring harm to man in all of their thoughts, wherever they can, and lure him into the darkness of night. For after man sins, they return to their permanent place in *Arka*, where they rouse the sons of Cain to defile the descendants with impurities.

Moreover, *The Zohar* says that besides pushing the sons of Cain to sin in *Arka*, they also soar in our world (*Tevel*), and compel the sons of this land to sin.

**159. The Heavens that rule there are not like ours, and the land bears neither seed nor fruit by the power of Heaven, as ours does, and the grains grow again only once in several years. Hence, it is written of them that they could not correct *Shemaya* and *Arka*, and perished from the Supernal land, called *Tevel*, where they will not be able to exist, nor rule over it, nor cause human beings to sin because of the night. Hence, they disappeared from *Arka* and from the place of *Shemaya* that were created by the name *ELEH* (as mentioned in item 14).**

Our Heavens receive the Light essential for the birth of subsequent *Partzufim* from ZA, which has *Ohr Hochma*. Hence, our land, which receives in *Malchut de* ZA, receives a grain and a seed.

However, the Heavens in *Arka* do not have the Light to bear fruit and give birth due to the rule of the impure forces that are there. Hence, unlike our land, *Arka* cannot produce; its land has no power to receive and grow a seed, and this property appears in it only once in several years.

Here *The Zohar* speaks of the two rulers: Afriron and Kastimon, who could not correct *Shemaya* and *Arka*, to make them bear fruit. Therefore, these rulers are not allowed to be here and seduce people in our land (*Tevel*), to sin, for when they are here, they bring harm to our land so as to make it like their *Shemaya* and *Arka*.

Therefore, *The Zohar* says that they disappeared from the Supernal land of *Tevel*, from our land, for here they sought to bring harm by the power of the night. They provoke people toward sin by virtue of the night, and it is a curse that hangs over *Arka* because of their rule there.

Our Heavens were created by the name *ELEH*, for our Heavens receive from ZA, which was corrected by *ELEH's* properties, by the words: IN THE

BEGINNING THE CREATOR CREATED, where *MI* is connected to *ELEH*. Hence, our land is corrected by the Supernal holiness and purity. Therefore, these two rulers are not allowed to rule here.

160. Hence, there exists a ***Targum***, a translation (from Hebrew to Aramaic, which **The Zohar** dubs ***Targum***), so the holy angels will not think that it is said about them, so they will not harm us. This is the secret of the word *ELEH*—as we have already stated, it is a holy word that cannot be translated into a ***Targum***.

Everything but the word *ELEH* has been translated into the language of the *Targum*, as it is said in item 149, that *ELEH* disappeared from both *Arka* and *Shemaya*, for the word *ELEH* is untranslatable, as it constitutes the full connection between *ELEH* and *MI*, which causes the descent of *Ohr Hochma*. And should anyone sin and corrupt the letters *ELEH*, as Cain had done, they would fall to the impure forces, so even the holiness of the *Targum* (*VAK* of the pure forces) would depart from them.

# AMONG ALL THE SAGES OF THE NATIONS OF THE WORLD, THERE ARE NONE LIKE YOU

**161.** Rabbi Elazar said, "It is written: 'Who would not fear the King of the nations of the world?' What kind of praise is this?" Rabbi Shimon replied: "Elazar, my son, this has been said in several places. However, one should not understand the verse, 'For among all the sages of the nations of the world, and in all their kingdoms, there are none like You' in its simple, literal interpretation. This is because it naturally gives rise to evil intentions of sinners—those who think that the Creator is not aware of their dark thoughts, doubts and intents. Therefore, their folly must be clarified. A philosopher of one of the nations of the world came to me and said, 'You say that your Creator governs the entire Heavens, and that all the Heavenly hosts are unable to attain Him, nor come to know His dwelling place. However, this does not add to His greatness, as it is written, 'among all the sages of the nations of the world, and in all their kingdoms, there is none like You.' What kind of a comparison is this when He is compared to man, who is nothing?'"

This is similar to what is written about sinners in Psalms (*Tehilim*, 73:11-12): "And they say: 'How does the Creator know? And is there knowledge in Him? Behold the wicked; they are always at peace, rich and powerful.'" This is exactly what the philosopher says. He was one of the greatest sages among the nations of the world, and he came to Rabbi Shimon to dishonor Israel's wisdom and work in absolute faith for the Creator's sake, which ought to be in great wholeness, perfection, purity, and integrity, for no thought can grasp Him.

This sage was a representative of the philosophers who asserted that the main principle in working for the Creator is to attain Him, rather than serve Him in faith, for in their understanding, they attain Him. And now he has come to ridicule Israel's approach.

Hence, he said: "The Creator is above all human wisdom, and thereby He rules, and He bid you to work for Him in faith and purity, and have no doubts in Him, for the human mind cannot grasp Him. After all, even the Heavenly hosts, His legions and angels are unable to attain Him, as it is written of those who say: 'Blessed be the Creator in His place,' for they do not know 'His place.'"

However, the phrase, "as among all the sages of the world, there is none like the Creator" does not imply the Creator's greatness. Indeed, if this prophetic expression is used in order to exalt the God of Israel and show that He is greater than the god attained by the sages of the nations of the world by their human strength and reason, then naturally, this does not add to the glory of the God of Israel, as He is being compared to trifle and transient forces. On the contrary, this statement shows great disdain for your Creator, when you compare Him to the sages of the nations of the world, who are mortal and restricted creatures. Those were the words that the scholarly sage, who represented the wisdom of the nations of the world, uttered before Rabbi Shimon.

Clearly, *The Zohar* is referring to some overseas sage who paid a visit to Rabbi Shimon. Just like all the other names of places and characters mentioned in the Torah, the Talmud, and the Kabbalah, names of places, animals, people, and actions described in *The Zohar* speak only of the spiritual world, the Creator's actions, and how one can achieve the goal of creation. In no way does any of this relate to events in our world!

Therefore, the "sage of the nations of the world" symbolizes man's own egoistic property to research and know everything, instead of having faith above reason, as the Torah demands. This human property, called a "sage of the nations of the world," the egoistic reason, is in a state of constant argument with man's spiritual, altruistic property, called "Israel" or the aspiration to the Creator. Thus, by opposing it, man builds himself and grows.

**162. Furthermore, you claim, as your Torah says, that "There had not risen a prophet since in Israel like Moshe." There are none in Israel, but there is one among the nations of the world! So I claim the same: there is none like You among all the sages of the nations of the world, but among the sages of Israel there is one like You. However, if there is one like Him among the sages of Israel, then He cannot be the Supreme Ruler. Look closely into my words, and you shall see that I am right.**

Here the philosopher (man's egoistic voice) spoke wisely. He understood that should he speak directly, he would hear precise answers to his questions. It is written: "Among all the sages of the nations of the world, there are none like

You," meaning that there is no one that can attain You. For the words, "there are none like You" imply that You have no equals, that it is impossible to attain You, attain Your degree.

However, since the sages of the nations of the world (human reason) take pride in their attainment of the Creator (that they understand His intentions and actions), they consider themselves similar to Him, for attainment means similarity of properties with the attained degree. This is why it is considered a lie, and that there are none like Him, for they do not attain the Creator, but only delude themselves by thinking that they do.

The philosopher (within man) understood that, and hence began (leading man astray from the path of faith, which surpasses and defies reason) with a completely different question: "If it is explicitly said that no one is equal to the Creator among the sages of the other nations, does it not mean that there are those who *can* attain Him among the sages of Israel? Otherwise, why would it be necessary to specify that there are none like Him among the sages of the nations of the world?

"But if this is so, and He is similar to you, then He cannot be the Supreme Ruler! Thus, how can you say that the God of Israel cannot be attained by reason and that He governs all? You speak by means of faith in His greatness, but indeed there are those among your sages who are like Him, i.e., those who attain Him."

**163. Rabbi Shimon said to him, "You object correctly that there are those among the sages of Israel who are similar to the Creator, for who resurrects the dead back to life, if not the Creator Himself? Yet, Eliyahu and Elisha came and resurrected the dead back to life! Who causes rain to fall if not the Creator Himself? Yet, Eliyahu came and abolished rain, and then summoned it through his prayer! Who created the Heavens and the earth, if not the Creator Himself? Yet, Avraham came, and, as it is written, the Heavens and the earth were revived."**

Rabbi Shimon replies that the (inner) sage speaks the truth when he asserts that there are those among the sages of Israel who are similar to the Creator. However, in no way does this revoke the simple faith in the Creator's unattainability by human reason. Of course, He is the master and ruler of the Heavens, and He is so much higher than all of them that even the Supernal angels cannot attain Him and do not know His place.

Yet, the Torah and *Mitzvot* (commandments) were given to us precisely for this purpose—so that by observing the *Mitzvot* (making a *Zivug* between the screen and the Light) and studying the Torah (receiving the Light) for the Creator's sake, we, Israel (those who aspire to the Creator) would completely merge with Him (in our properties), so His Light would permeate us and clothe in us to such an extent that we would merit (begin to desire and receive the power of a screen) carrying out the same actions as the Creator: resurrecting the dead (correcting egoism), summoning rains (*Ohr Hassadim*), and reviving Heaven and earth (filling all the *Partzufim* in all the worlds with the Light of our actions).

In that, we are just like Him, as it is said: "By Your deeds (by experiencing them on myself) I will know You." However, we attain all this only through absolute and devout faith (the property of *Bina*), which leaves within us no desires whatsoever to attain Him with our reason (to verify first and act next), as in the path of sages of the nations of the world (our egoism). Our egoism consists of a *Partzuf* called a "sage of the nations of the world." Its *Rosh* (head) designates knowledge and desire to attain everything, and its *Guf* (body) is the will to receive pleasure for oneself.

The philosopher argues that if Israel can do what the Creator does, then Israel attains Him. This is correct, for if one is able to act like the Creator, then, to the extent of his actions, he attains and perceives Him. After all, it is said: "By Your deeds I will know You." If one acts like the Creator, then he understands the Creator's analogous actions in his own actions, and thus perceives Him. However, one must first advance by faith above reason, and as a result, he attains the Creator's properties, thereby becoming like Him in his actions.

**164. (Rabbi Shimon continues:) "Who governs the sun, if not the Creator? Yet, Yehoshua came and stopped it. The Creator issues His decree, yet Moshe immediately issues a decree of his own, and it is carried out. The Creator wishes to punish, and the righteous of Israel annul His verdict. Moreover, He bid us to closely follow His ways and to be like Him in every way." The philosopher then went and became Israel, and lived in the village of Shachalayim, and they called him Yosi HaKatan (Little Yosi). He studied the Torah a great deal, and was among the sages and the righteous of that village.**

The problem is that if a person does everything only by means of his faith, he denies himself the chance to attain the Creator, for attainment comes through applying reason. However, the moment he begins to apply his reason, he immediately diminishes his faith. So how can one combine faith with reason?

It is true that those who aspire to draw nearer the Creator (those who are called Israel) diminish their simple, devout faith. However, they do this only because He bids them to do so in order to attain His actions, and thus become like Him, as it is said in the Torah: "Follow His way" (*Devarim*, 21). Hence, they observe His commandments. The philosopher was so overwhelmed by this truth that he became "Israel" and started observing the Torah and *Mitzvot*.

He was overwhelmed when he had found that Israel's actions, their attainments of the spiritual worlds, did not diminish their faith above reason, for all of their actions and attainments were based on faith. Israel attains the Creator because He bids them to, not because they desire this with their egoism.

**165. And now the time has come to take a closer look at this verse. It is written that all the nations of the world are nothing before Him. Yet, how does this exalt Him? Hence, it is written: "Who sees the King of the nations of the world?" Yet, is the King of the nations of the world also not the King of Israel? The Creator wishes to elevate Israel in all places; this is why He is called everywhere "the King of Israel." The other nations of the world say that they have another King up in the Heavens, for it seems to them that He governs only them, and not us.**

The nations of the world are certain that their Supernal King is not the King of Israel, that the King who sits in the Heavens and governs them is only their King, and that the King of Israel has no power over them. Thus, it seems to man's egoism that it exists under some other (non-altruistic) system of governance, and not altruism. The egoism fails to realize that the Creator made it exactly the way it is so as to achieve His goal: using egoism, to bring man to altruism, from "for one's own self" to "for the Creator's sake."

**166. It is written: "Who would not fear the King of the nations of the world?" (*Yirmiyahu*, 10:7) That is, their Supernal King is there to threaten and persecute them, and do with them as He pleases. Hence, He should be feared. And all fear Him Above and below. For it is written that among all the sages of the nations of the world (the angels that rule over these nations) and in their Kingdoms (Above) there is none like You. There are four Kingdoms Above that rule over all the nations of the world according to the Creator's will. And there is no one who can do even the smallest action without His personal instruction. The sages of the nations of the world are the forces that rule them from Above, and all the wisdom of the nations of the world comes from these rulers. "In all their Kingdoms" means that the Creator's will rules over them.**

These lines describe how the bride, who is in a state of exile, prepares herself for her future, final correction. The power of the nations of the world (in every one of us) amounts to conquering us (the altruistic desires for the Creator) and placing us under their power (serving only the body). They wish to drive us away from the Creator's rule and let other desires, called "the nations of the world" dominate us. Our egoistic desires, the nations of the world, do so because of their power (tempting us with various pleasures) and wisdom (appealing to our common sense).

Their actions over us (spiritual aspirations) stem from the system of the impure forces and their impure (egoistic) angels (our inner egoistic forces), which give power and reason to the nations of the world. With the help of their wisdom, they (our egoistic desires) lead us (the sons of Israel, those who aspire only to the Creator) to all sorts of doubts and desires to understand the Creator, His ways and thoughts, without any fear or reverence before His greatness and supremacy.

Because of these doubts, we draw far from the Creator and His Supernal Light, which, as a result, passes on to them (our egoistic desires), as it is written, "Tzur (the capital of the impure forces) was built only on the ruins of Jerusalem (the capital of the pure forces)." Thus, they acquire the strength to persecute and humiliate Israel, and force them to submit to their will (suppress the only true path to the spiritual—faith above and in defiance of reason—with their persuasions and proof of their "real" rightfulness). And as it was already explained in the "Introduction to the Book of Zohar" (items 69-71), our inner spiritual enslavement leads to our external, corporeal enslavement, persecution, and humiliation by the nations of the world.

This is the secret of the four Kingdoms that rule over us in our four (spiritual and therefore physical) exiles, which correspond to Sefirot H-B-ZA-M, symbolized by Nebuchadnezzar, as it is written: "Here is that idol, its head made of pure gold, its breast and its arms of silver, its belly and its thighs of brass, its shins of iron, and its feet part iron and part clay" (Daniel, 2:32-33).

When this idol governs us, the nations of the world mock us, claiming that they have a King of their own. However, such was the Creator's plan, as it is said: "The Creator hath so made it, that men should fear Him" (Kohelet, 3:14), for the sensation of the Creator, called Shechina, is also referred to as fear before Him. However, since we do not yet feel the greatness and supremacy of the Creator, we do not merit fearing Him, and live in fear of the King of the nations of the world.

This points to the fact that we have no other way of completely and eternally merging with the Creator other than by means of tremendous fear before His greatness, by assuming His Torah and His desires (Mitzvot) in devout and complete faith, without any doubts in His properties.

Only then will we merge with Him in absolute, eternal union, and the Creator will impart us with all the goodness for which He had created us. He conceived this in the beginning of creation, and it became the purpose behind the whole of creation. This state is considered the complete and final deliverance and correction.

However, before the attainment of such an exalted spiritual state, this is how the prophet describes those who aspire to the Creator: "You have sown much, and brought in little; you eat but you have not enough; you drink but your thirst is not quenched" (*Haggai*, 1:6), for in all of our actions (of those who aspire to the spiritual) the impure force (egoism) constantly takes all the Light for itself. This occurs as a result of our doubts with regard to faith in the Creator, which the impure force itself cultivates within us.

However, the purpose of these punishments is not to cause us grief! Everything happens according to the Creator's plan and serves only to promote us toward correction. Therefore, as long as man can listen only to egoistic arguments, the Creator develops us gradually, using these forces. With their help, we gradually become fit to feel fear of the Creator, through the many trials and sufferings our exile from the spiritual brings us.

But in the end, we merit the reception of complete and devoted faith and fear before His greatness. It is written of this state: "He remembered His mercy and His allegiance toward the house of Israel, and all the worthless creatures of the earth witnessed the help and deliverance at the Creator's hands" (*Tehilim*, 98:3).

This is because at the end of days, the Creator will remember us in His mercy, and will give us the strength to receive complete and devout faith in Him. Thus, Jerusalem (the capital of altruism) will be rebuilt on the ruins of Tzur (the capital of egoism), for all the Light, which *Malchut* of the impure force was robbing of us throughout our exile from the spiritual, will return to us when we acquire complete and devout faith, and will shine within us with all its might.

All the worthless creatures of the earth (manifestations of egoism) will then see with their own eyes how our Creator saves (corrects) them. For all the nations of the world (within us) will see that they have always possessed this Light until the very last moment before their correction so as to give it back to us at the appropriate time. And all shall see that "one man's rule over another is to the detriment of the ruler!" (*Kohelet*, 8:9).

The burden of our slavery and the impure force's rule over us (over holiness) harms only the impure force, for it thereby compels us to attain complete and devoted faith in the Creator even faster! And the prophet speaks of this time,

"Who would not fear the King of the nations of the world?" for it has now been revealed that He is the King of the nations of the world, who persecutes and dominates those nations. It previously seemed to them (our egoistic intentions) that they persecuted us (our altruistic intentions), but now the opposite has been revealed to them—that they were merely blind enactors of the Creator's will, our servants and our slaves, whose purpose is to bring us to perfection.

It seemed to us that they were beating us. Now it turns out that they were beating themselves, for thanks to these blows (suffering from unrealized egoistic desires and constant frustration), they have accelerated our deliverance and attainment of perfection (our realization of the need to choose the path of faith above reason). Thus, they have also accelerated their own demise (their own correction).

And wherever it seemed to us (our reason) that they rebelled against the Creator (argued that the Creator is not the source of all reality) and acted (supposedly) however they pleased so as to humiliate us and satiate their base egoistic desires, and it appeared that there was no (Supernal) judge and no law (the advancement of creation toward its goal), it has now been revealed that they have always been fulfilling the Creator's will, to bring us (all our desires, them included) to perfection.

The same applies to every person in the world—whether he wants to or not, at all times and in every way, he fulfills only the Creator's will. Why then is he not called the Creator's servant? Because he acts unconsciously, not of his own will. To compel man to fulfill His will, the Creator gives him some alien desire to enjoy, which forces him to carry out an action, but he does so as a slave of his desire, and not as someone who fulfills the Creator's will.

For example, the Creator may give man an alien desire to make money, thereby compelling him to open a restaurant so as to carry out altruistic actions as a slave of his egoistic desire.

In other words, to compel us to do what is necessary, the Creator created within us an egoistic desire to receive pleasure, thus obliging us to do His will by enabling us to find pleasure in the actions and objects on which He wants us to work. This is why we live in constant chase of pleasures, whereas in truth we are constantly and unconsciously fulfilling the Creator's will. This resembles a situation in which children are given many toys to play with, but as they play, they also carry out work.

The entire world is doing the Creator's will, but our goal, the purpose of our development is to do it consciously. We must attain and realize His will; we must ascend so high that we will want to do it wholeheartedly and on our own, rather than as we do it now—unconsciously and coercively. We must achieve a state when our desires fully coincide with those of the Creator, which designates complete and conscious union with Him.

Thus, it becomes clear that the King of the nations of the world is the same Creator that rules over them and compels them to fulfill all His desires, as a King does with his slaves. And now fear before the Creator is revealed to all the nations of the world. The phrase, "all the nations of the world" alludes to the angels that rule over those nations, such as Afriron, Kastimon, Aza, Azael and others, from whom the sages of the nations of the world (our egoism and reason) receive their wisdom, and with whose help they oppress Israel (our altruistic desires).

IN THEIR KINGDOMS refers to the four existing Kingdoms, which govern the seventy nations of the world (ZON = seven *Sefirot*, each of which containing ten sub-*Sefirot*: in all seventy *Sefirot*) and over us (altruistic aspirations) in our four exiles, which correspond to the impure *Sefirot H-B-ZA-M* (described as Nebuchadnezzar). As the prophet writes: "Here is that idol, its head made of pure gold (the first Kingdom), its breast and its arms of silver (the second Kingdom), its belly and its thighs of brass (the third Kingdom), its shins of iron, its feet part iron and part clay (the fourth Kingdom)" (*Daniel*, 2:32-33).

There is not one among them who can make even the smallest action of their own, but only what You bid them. However, this will only be revealed at the end of correction, and all will know that all of our misfortunes and suffering that had the power to separate us from the Creator were but loyal executors of the Creator's aspiration to draw us closer to Him. Moreover, these cruel forces did nothing else but obey His orders.

And the sole purpose of all that transpired was to bring us to a state where we can receive all the perfection and infinite goodness that He intended to bestow upon us from the very beginning in His plan of creation. The Creator must lead us to complete and devout faith, the result of which will be, as the prophet said: "Then, at once, the iron, the clay, the brass, the silver, and the gold all crumbled to pieces and became like the chaff on summer threshing-floors; and the wind carried them away, and no trace was left of them; and the stone that smote their image became a great mountain, and filled the whole earth" (*Daniel*, 2:35).

Absolute faith is called "unbreakable (non-crumbling) stone." After one merits absolute faith, the impure force (his inner egoistic desires and thoughts) disappears as though it had never existed. And all the worthless creatures (reason, logic, philosophy, and common sense), which inhabit the earth, witness deliverance at the hands of the Creator, as the prophet said: "They shall not do evil nor destroy in all My holy mountain; for the earth shall be full of the knowledge of the Lord, as the waters fill the sea" (*Yeshayahu*, 11:9).

167. Yet, among all the sages of the nations of the world and in all their kingdoms, I have found in the ancient books that even though the Heavenly hosts and legions fully obeyed their given orders and each would receive precise instructions to be carried out, but who among them can do it if not You, who will do it better than You? For You excel over them all in both properties and deeds. Hence, it is written: "There is none like You."

The Creator Himself carries out all the creatures' actions with His Light, and leads them to His goal. Man's sole task is the realization of all creation and governance, to wholeheartedly agree with all of the Creator's actions, and take an active part in the process of spiritual creation.

168. Rabbi Shimon said to his friends: "This wedding must be a wedding for all of you, and each of you should bring a gift (his own part in the common *Malchut*) to the Bride." He said to Rabbi Elazar, his son: "Present the Bride with a gift, for on the following day *Zeir Anpin* will look as he enters the wedding canopy at the sound of these songs and praises of the sons of the wedding canopy, who stand before the Creator."

# Who Is This?

169. Rabbi Elazar opened and said, "Who is this coming up from the wasteland?" (*Shir HaShirim*, 3:6). MI ZOT—who is this—is the common ground of the two questions, the two worlds, **Bina** and **Malchut**, which are bound together. COMING UP—coming up to become the "Holy of Holies." For **MI** is **Bina**, called the Holy of Holies. And she joins with **ZOT** (**Malchut**), so that **Malchut** could come up FROM THE WASTELAND, for she inherits THIS from the wasteland, to become a bride and enter the bridal canopy.

*The Zohar* explains the following passage: "Who is this coming up from the wasteland, leaning upon her beloved!?" (*Shir HaShirim*, 8:5). It describes a state at the end of correction, when the bride enters the wedding canopy. MI ZOT: MI is *Bina* and ZOT is *Malchut*. At the end of correction, *Bina* and *Malchut* unite, and both are called "holy." But until the end of correction only *Bina* is called holy, while *Malchut* ascends to *Bina* and receives holiness from her.

Nevertheless, at the end of correction, *Malchut* becomes like *Bina*, and they both become holy. *Malchut* completely unites with *Bina* through equivalence of form, and fully merges with the source of life, for a screen (the restriction imposed on reception of Light within *Malchut*) creates the Reflected Light that combines all *Sefirot* into one.

The Creator's *Ohr Hochma* can be received precisely in this Reflected Light. As a result, *Malchut* ends with the letter *Yod* and becomes forever similar to *Bina*. Hence, it is written that *Malchut* and *Bina* unite by equalizing their desires to form a single whole.

Similarly, the Light of *Malchut* will be forever connected to the Light of *Bina*, for *Malchut* herself ascends to the level of the "Holy of Holies," thus becoming exactly like *Bina*. SHE COMES UP just like a sacrifice, which is the "Holy of Holies," for MI (AVI, *Bina* or the "Holy of Holies") joins ZOT (*Malchut*), so

*Malchut* would ascend and become the "Holy of Holies." Sacrifice is the part of *Malchut* (man's animal egoism) that ascends with its properties to *Bina*.

And when *MI* (*Bina*) joins *ZOT* (*Malchut*), and *ZOT* becomes the "Holy of Holies," there is no longer a diminution of *Malchut's* state, for this diminution occurred only because of the deterioration of *Malchut's* properties, when new egoistic desires emerge within her.

Now that *Malchut* has become as holy (altruistic) in her properties as *Bina*, death disappears, and the fall of *Malchut* into her egoistic desires is impossible, for she has been fully corrected and has attained the properties of *Bina*, which are referred to as holy. Through *Malchut's* acquisition of these properties, the Upper Light (life) enters her. *Malchut* emerges from the wasteland (the sensation of life's absence for want of altruistic properties) and enters her wedding canopy.

This occurs thanks to man's efforts, called "those who keep the Torah" (item 124). These efforts are the foremost part of creation, for they create the Torah and bring *Malchut* to the great *Zivug* at the end of her correction, to her complete fulfillment with the Light. This great *Zivug* on the entire corrected *Malchut* (including *Malchut de Malchut*) can be achieved by precisely this sensation (by man) of the spiritual wasteland.

**170. She comes up from the wasteland of the soft utterance of lips, as it is written, "And your mouth is comely" (*Shir HaShirim*, 4:3). This is because the Hebrew word *Midbar* (desert/wasteland) is derived from *Dibur* (speech). It is written of the mighty forces, that these mighty forces strike Egypt with all the plagues of the wasteland, for all that the Creator did to them was not in the wasteland, but in settlements. And the phrase "in the wasteland" means "by the power of speech, of spoken word." This comes up from articulation, from the mouth (*Malchut*) as she ascends and comes under the wings of *Ima* (mother, *Bina*). Then, through speech, she descends upon the entire holy nation (the difference between speech and articulation is that articulation is an action that forms speech).**

Before the end of correction, when *Malchut* is still called the "Tree of Good and Evil," all corrections occur through *MAN* (prayers or requests), through which the righteous (those who wish to become similar to the Creator in their properties) elevate *Malchut* to *Bina*. Consequently, *Malchut* receives *Bina*'s properties for as long as *Malchut* remains there, for spiritual ascent signifies an attainment of properties. *Malchut* becomes as holy (altruistic) as *Bina*.

*MAN* is a silent prayer in the heart of man, for *Malchut* signifies "speech." Yet, until the end of correction, good words cannot exist without bad ones. That is, this will not happen until both voice and speech come from *Bina* herself, when *Malchut* becomes like *Bina*, which designates the unity of voice and speech—the *Zivug* of ZON in their corrected state of *Gadlut*.

ZA receives the voice from *Ima* and passes it in his speech to *Malchut*. Hence, this speech is completely good, devoid of any evil. Thus, *Malchut* receives from *Bina* the Light of holiness, *Hassadim*. Unless it is corrected by the completely good, altruistic voice of *Bina*, *Malchut's* voice will always consist of both good and evil. This is why impure, egoistic forces cling to her, and *Malchut* cannot receive anything from holiness (*Bina*).

Hence, MAN that the righteous raise in their prayers is like a soft murmur of lips, a voiceless speech, as the prophet says: "Only the lips move, but the voice cannot be heard" (*Shmuel I*, 1:13). This is because there is no connection between MAN and the impure force, and *Malchut* can be elevated to *Bina* so she can receive her voice from *Bina*.

As a result, a holy edifice of *Malchut* is erected, and she receives the Light from a *Zivug* between voice and speech, and the holiness of her speech descends upon the heads of the righteous that raised MAN and thereby revived *Malchut*.

This is why it is written that SHE COMES UP FROM THE WASTELAND, for the bride (*Malchut*) is now invited to a great *Zivug* under the wedding canopy. This occurs thanks to the raising of MAN by the righteous, who thereby united *Bina* (voice, *Ima*) with *Malchut* (speech). As a result, *Malchut's* speech became as beautiful as that of *Bina*.

All of these individual *Zivugim* made by the various righteous (each of whom constitutes a small part of the common *Malchut*) during the 6,000 years, now connect all of *Malchut's* parts (souls of the righteous) together in one great *Zivug*, as the bride (*Malchut*) enters her wedding canopy.

In other words, it is precisely this soft prayer, the raising of MAN during the 6,000 years by a voiceless speech (seeing as good is still mixed with evil in the voice of *Malchut*), that creates the conditions for the great *Zivug* of *Malchut* with ZA, of man with the Creator.

And since *Malchut* received the voice of *Bina* (from *Ima*-Mother) thanks to the help of the righteous (all the good deeds performed by the righteous during the 6,000 years), everything is now combined into the great Supernal *Zivug* under the wedding canopy. This is because *Malchut* becomes completely good without a hint of evil—the "Holy of Holies," just like *Ima*.

Silent speech is defined as the movement of lips without the participation of the palate, larynx, tongue, and teeth. This is how *MAN* is raised when *Malchut* ascends between the wings of *Bina*, i.e., receives the voice of the wings of *Ima* in her speech. Afterwards, having acquired the speech, she descends upon the heads of the holy nation. For after the reception of voice through *Ima's* property of mercy, *Malchut* becomes as holy as *Bina* herself, and her holiness descends upon those who corrected her. Consequently, they are called the "holy nation," for now the speech of *Malchut* is as holy as that of *Ima-Bina*.

There is "voice" and there is "speech." "Voice" is the inner part, whereas "speech" is its outward appearance. This appearance is based on exhaling (the silent letter *Hey*). ZA is called "voice," and *Malchut* is called "speech." Letters are sung according to the note signs (*Taamim*), followed by the letters with their punctuation marks.

The level of *Ohr Haya* (called *Kol*—voice) emerges on the screen in the *Peh* of the third degree of thickness, known as "teeth." From this Light ZA receives *Ohr Hochma*, and his voice is then heard outside (begets the souls of the lower ones).

Yet, the voice of ZA is not heard below the level of *Neshama*, for his screen is not strong enough to receive *Ohr Hochma*. The level of *Ohr Yechida* in ZA, called *Dibur* (speech), emerges on the screen in the *Peh* of the fourth degree of thickness. This screen is the most powerful, as it reveals all of the Light, and is called "lips."

The Light of *NRNHY* reveals the inner, Supernal and concealed wisdom, *Hochma*, the concealed thought, the inner Light of *Bina*, which cannot shine to the lower ones, that is, in ZA, because ZON cannot receive from *Peh de AA*. Nevertheless, the two levels of the Light—*Haya* and *Yechida*—that descend from AA are converted into voice and speech with *Bina's* help, even though it is the Light of thought, wisdom and reason.

Voice is formed in ZA, and speech in *Malchut*. If a righteous one raises his prayers (*MAN*) to *Malchut*, thereby causing ZON to ascend to AVI, who are in constant union, to provide Light for the lower ones, ZON receive this Light from AVI, which is called "voice and speech." The property of the righteous is to create the pure and destroy the impure with their voice. In the beginning, there was only one language (one speech) in the world, *Lashon HaKodesh*—the holy language. In Hebrew (as in English) the same word (*Lashon*) means "tongue" (both as a body part and as a means of communication).

**171. He asks: "How does *Malchut* ascend in speech?" And he replies: "When man first awakens in the morning and opens his eyes, he must bless his Creator and Master. How is he to bless Him? The way it was done by the first**

*Hassidim*: they would prepare a vessel of water beside them, so that when they woke at night, they would wash their hands at once, and, having blessed the Torah, would rise to study it. When the rooster crowed, precisely heralding midnight, the Creator was with the righteous in the Garden of Eden. And it is forbidden to perform a blessing in the morning with unclean hands."

He asks: since it is written that the beginning of *Malchut's* correction must be expressed in a quiet murmur of lips, how can he who wakes up (spiritually) immediately pronounce a blessing at the top of his voice? After all, the blessing must also be uttered in whisper so as to first receive a voice from *Ima*, and with this voice (by the force of *Ima-Bina*) elevate *Malchut* to *Bina*, and impart onto her altruistic properties.

*The Zohar* replies: The first *Hassidim* have corrected this. As man falls asleep (falls to the level of the Light in his *Partzuf* called "sleep"), his holy soul (the Light that was in his spiritual *Partzuf*) ascends, and only the impure spirit of the primordial serpent (egoistic properties) remains in him, for sleep constitutes the 60th part of death (Talmud, *Berachot*, 57:2).

Since death is an impure property of the primordial serpent, the impure spirit (egoistic desires) does not leave man completely as he wakes up (receives a new Light from Above), but remains on man's fingertips (not all of man's desires change under the influence of the Light received from Above, called "the Light of morning" or "the Light of awakening").

And the greater holiness and Light that was present in man before he fell asleep (before he fell into a diminished spiritual state, called "sleep"), the more the impure (egoistic) force clings to these desires when the altruistic intentions exit them during sleep.

Fingertips constitute the purest place (desires) of the entire body (all desires), man's most spiritual desires, for they can be filled with *Ohr Hochma* (*Ohr Hochma* enters these desires during a *Zivug*, with the help of a screen). Therefore, even after awakening (at the beginning of the spiritual ascent), the impure (egoistic) force does not leave this place, wishing to receive at least some of that great Light, which can fill these most altruistic human desires.

Hence, hands must be washed in order to remove the residual egoistic desires. For this to happen, two vessels need to be prepared: the Upper One (cup) and the lower one that will accept the removed impurity.

The Upper Vessel designates *Bina*, whose Light drives the impure force away. Hence, washing the fingertips with water (the forces or desires of *Bina*) expels the impure force (man's egoistic desires) from them. Thus, *Malchut* rids herself of her evil (egoism) and becomes holy and good. Afterwards, one can study the Torah and bless the Creator for it, for washing hands is similar to raising MAN in a whispered prayer to the wings of Ima.

And when the rooster crows (this is a special spiritual sign of the angel Gavriel), it is precisely midnight, as it is written: "The greater star to rule the day and the lesser star to rule the night" (Beresheet, 1:16). For the lesser star, the holy Shechina-Malchut grew smaller, clothed in impure forces and "her feet descend to death" (Mishley, 5:5).

This is so because during the 6,000 years, up to her final correction, Malchut constitutes the Tree (foundations) of Good and Evil: if one is worthy, she becomes good for him and purifies him, if not—she turns evil. Accordingly, the rule of night is also divided into two parts: the first refers to a state called "unworthy–evil," and the second refers to a state called "worthy–good."

The first correction of Malchut's good part is made exactly at midnight (in a state so called "midnight"), for it is then that Malchut receives the voice of Bina. Put differently, Malchut ascends to Malchut de Ima-Bina and corrects herself within it. As a result, the strictness and judgment in Malchut become holy and good, completely devoid of evil. This means that strictness and judgment fall onto the impure forces, but for Israel, they turn into mercy.

Yitzchak signifies restriction, the property of Malchut within Bina. The Hebrew word for a "rooster" is Tarnegol, and also Gever (man) and designates the angel Gavriel, who attends to Malchut, the lesser star. The strictness of Bina pierces the wings of the rooster (Gavriel), and through it Malchut receives the voice of Bina.

And when Gavriel passes the voice of Bina to Malchut, his call reaches all the roosters of this world, the property of judgment in the spiritual void. Such a state is called "this world" or Malchut de Malchut. Everyone speaks only in this voice, which was corrected by Bina's property of mercy.

Therefore, the voice of Malchut (her judgment) no longer dominates the second half of the night, and the voice of Bina claims this place. This is what the "rooster of this world" heralds—the property of judgment in Malchut de Malchut.

Hence, a rooster's crow (change of properties) is heard precisely at midnight (when states change), for this crow means that Malchut has already been corrected by the voice of Bina, and that this voice is already within Malchut. This is defined as the moment of midnight, which marks the beginning of the second half—absolute goodness, devoid of evil.

After *Malchut* receives the voice of *Bina*, the righteous (man's properties in the worlds of *BYA*) raise MAN with the help of their study of Torah after (in the state of) midnight. They keep raising MAN to the "cheerful strictness" in *Ima*, of which it is written: "She rises also while it is yet night" (*Mishley*, 31:15), for it is precisely at night that the Supernal *Malchut* reveals herself in all her splendor.

And the actual revelation of *Malchut* takes place in the Garden of Eden, i.e., she is meant for those righteous who have corrected her with their work and studies (in the state) after midnight. The Creator rejoices with them (merriment signifies fulfillment with *Ohr Hochma*) in the Garden of Eden, for the corrected *Malchut* is called "the Holy *Shechina*" or "the Garden of Eden," for she receives *Hochma* and rejoices with the righteous that constitute MAN within her.

And the phrase that describes how impurity (egoistic desires) is washed away (corrected to altruistic properties) from man's fingers (his most exalted desires) is true not only with regard to nighttime. Man ascends from the lower degree of "sleep" onto a higher degree of "awakening," the difference between the two states being that previously, he was receiving only the vital *Ohr Hassadim*, called "sleep," while "awakening" signifies reception of *Ohr Hochma*. This is because the impure force constantly clings to man's fingertips (precisely for man to correct it and thus attain greater spiritual heights), and he is obliged to wash his hands (make his desires and intentions "for the Creator's sake") before uttering a blessing (appealing to the Creator for reception).

172. For when man is asleep, his soul (spirit) leaves him. And as soon as his soul departs from him, the impure spirit replaces it at once, and it fills his hands and defiles them, and it is forbidden to utter a blessing without washing one's hands. And should you object that when man is awake and his soul does not leave him, the impure force does not descend upon him, then, if he enters a washroom, he is forbidden from reading even a single word of the Torah until he washes his hands. And if you say that it is because his hands are soiled, this is not true, for how are they soiled?

173. But woe unto those who do not beware and do not guard the Creator's honor and do not know the foundation of this world. There is a certain spirit that dwells in every cesspool of the world, a spirit that relishes depravity and excrement, and it immediately settles on the fingers of man's hands.

Just like Rabbi Y. Ashlag, I refrain from commenting on items 172 and 173 of *The Zohar*, and he who merits it—will understand this text himself.

# HE WHO REJOICES ON HOLIDAYS

**174. Rabbi Shimon opened and said: "He who rejoices on holidays and does not give a part to the Creator, the evil eye hates and slanders him, removes him from this world, and brings him many miseries."**

We have already said (item 68) that the impure forces (egoistic spiritual forces within man that know of and hence desire the pleasures hidden in the Creator's Light) consist of male and female parts. The male part brings less harm than the female. It leads man to transgressions such as lying in the name of the Creator, as though it inspires man to observe the *Mitzvot*, but not in complete purity (with the sole purpose of pleasing the Creator). Instead, it causes man to also add a touch of personal benefit and selfish enjoyment, as it is written: "Eat not the bread of an ill-willer, nor desire his treats; for as one reckons within himself, such is he: 'Eat and drink,' he shall say to you; but his heart is not with you" (*Mishley*, 23:6-7).

Since the male impure force has absolutely no intentions to bestow, the commandment remains devoid of fear and love (without a heart). Yet, since the male impure force has already caught man in its net, it gains power to make a *Zivug* with its female half (the impure *Nukva*), which is a bitter and evil impure force that lies in the name of the Creator, and, upon seducing man, captures his entire soul.

Hence, *The Zohar* says that the evil eye hates and slanders man, and removes him from this world by provoking him to fail to observe the commandment of rejoicing on a holiday (the reception of *Ohr Hochma*, joy on a higher degree)—so that this joy would not be for the sake of the Creator. It is as though he eats alone and does not share his food with the needy, which leads to the male impure force making a *Zivug* with *Nukva* and capturing man's soul.

**175. The Creator's role is to cheer the poor, according to His ability. For the Creator appears on the holidays so as to look at His broken *Kelim*. He comes to them, and He sees that there is nothing to rejoice in, and He weeps for them, and ascends Above to destroy the world.**

To understand this passage and the angels' objections, one must first understand the words of the sages (*Midrash Raba*, 86): "When creating the world, the Creator asked the angels: 'Shall we create man in our image (*Tzelem*) and likeness?' And the four angels (forces, properties) of creation gave their answers:

Mercy said, LET US CREATE, for he creates *Hassadim*, mercy. Truth said, LET US NOT CREATE, for he is all falsehood. Justice said, LET US CREATE, for he dispenses justice. Peace said, LET US NOT CREATE, for he is all enmity."

What did the Creator do? He took truth and concealed it in the ground, as it is written: "cast down truth to the ground" (*Daniel*, 8:12). Our entire purpose in the study of the Torah and *Mitzvot* lies in that, thanks to them, as the Talmud says (*Psachim*, 50, 2): "From *Lo Lishma* (intentions for oneself) man comes to *Lishma* (intentions for the Creator's sake)."

And since man is born with such insignificant desires and powers, he is unable to immediately engage in the Creator's *Mitzvot* for the sake of pleasing the Giver of these *Mitzvot*, for as it is said: "Man is born akin to a wild ass" (*Iyov*, 11:12). Due to his egoistic nature, he is unable to make any inner movement or action if it is not for his own benefit.

Therefore, the Creator allows man to begin observing the *Mitzvot* solely for his own sake, seeking personal benefit. Yet, in spite of this, his actions attract spiritual Light to him. And then, with the help of the received Light, he comes to observe the *Mitzvot* for the Creator's sake, in order to please Him.

This is exactly what Truth presented when it objected to man's creation and said that he is all falsehood. After all, how can man be created to study the Torah and observe *Mitzvot* in a state of absolute falsehood, i.e., "for oneself?"

However, Mercy said, "Let us create," for man performs merciful deeds. Although the *Mitzvot* of mercy, which man observes (even if mechanically) initially "for his own sake," are mere external actions without the intention of bestowal, with their help he gradually corrects his intentions until he becomes capable of observing all the *Mitzvot* "for the Creator's sake." Hence, there exists an absolute certainty and guarantee that through his efforts, man will achieve the goal—altruistic actions "for the Creator's sake." And that it is okay to create man.

Peace also asserted that man is all "enmity;" hence, he can observe the *Mitzvot* "for the Creator's sake" only if it also brings him personal benefit. However, due to such mixed intentions and actions, man exists in constant conflict with the Creator, for it seems to him that he is great and righteous, and he utterly fails to see his shortcomings. In other words, he is completely unaware that all his work in the Torah and *Mitzvot* is exclusively for his own benefit.

And because he feels this way, he fills up with anger and resentment towards the Creator: why does the Creator not treat him as it befits one so perfectly righteous? It follows that he alternates between states of peace and conflict with the Creator. That is why Peace objected to the creation of man.

However, Justice said that man should be created, for he dispenses justice. By observing the *Mitzva* (singular for *Mitzvot*) of giving charity to the poor, even with the intention "for oneself," he gradually acquires the property of "bestowal," learns to act "for the Creator's sake," and merits eternal peace with Him.

After the Creator heard these opinions, He agreed with the angels of Mercy and Justice, and cast down Truth to the "ground." By this, He allowed man to begin observing the *Mitzvot* with the intention "for oneself," despite its falsehood.

It follows that the Creator cast Truth down to the ground because He had accepted the claims of Mercy and Justice, that thanks to the *Mitzva* of giving charity to the poor, man will ultimately come to Truth, i.e., work for the Creator's sake, and Truth will rise from the ground.

The only creation created by the Creator is *Malchut de Malchut*, egoism, and it can only be corrected by "instilling" the Creator's properties of *Bina* or mercy into it. Yet, if these properties are opposite, how can such a thing be accomplished? After all, in the spiritual world, distance is proportionate to the difference in properties. So how can *Malchut* be united with *Bina*?

To this end, the *Kli* was broken: the spiritual, altruistic desire lost its screen and became egoistic. Yet, it retained sparks of the Light, and these sparks exist within egoistic desires. This is why egoistic desires have power over us.

These sparks of the Upper Light are the source of various pleasures and love, for Light is pleasure. And since these particles of Light are clothed in impure garments and exist under the rule of the impure forces, man starts perceiving these feelings of love and delight as being inherent in the impure forces, as though these egoistic garments contain pleasures, and such is their property. And he associates the properties of love and pleasure with the impure forces, failing to understand that the impure forces draw him solely with the spiritual spark that has fallen into them.

However, as the impure force is very appealing, it lures man into all kinds of transgressions, such as theft, robbery, and murder. At the same time, it gives us the desire to observe the Torah and Mitzvot for our own sake. Even if we start observing them not "for the Creator's sake," but "for ourselves," (for our own benefit, to fulfill our base aspirations, according to the desires of the broken, egoistic Kelim-vessels), we gradually come to the intention "for the Creator's sake," and merit the goal of creation—to receive all the pleasure that was prepared for us back in the Thought of Creation—"to delight man." Thus, the impure forces destroy themselves, but that is exactly the purpose for which the Creator conceived and created them.

The Zohar says that the Creator appears on these holidays to look at all the broken Kelim. On holidays, when man observes the Mitzva of rejoicing because of the great Light that he receives from the Creator, the Creator appears to look at His broken vessels, by which man is given an opportunity to observe the Mitzvot not "for the Creator's sake." The Creator comes and looks at how well these broken vessels have fulfilled their mission to bring man to observance of the Mitzvot with the intention "for the Creator's sake."

However, the Creator comes to them and sees that there is nothing to rejoice in. He weeps over them, for He sees that nothing spiritual (altruistic) was created from the broken vessels, that man has yet to correct even a single broken vessel (egoistic desire). In other words, there's not one vessel that was intentionally broken by the Creator that has brought man to the intention "for the Creator's sake," and he rejoices on holidays solely for his own pleasure.

So the Creator weeps and regrets breaking the vessels, for He broke them and cast Truth to the ground only for man's sake, to give him an opportunity to start working in falsehood (in the intention "for oneself") and gradually come to Truth, to the intention "for the Creator's sake." Yet, when He sees that man has not changed at all in his aspirations for selfish pleasure, it is as though the vessels were broken in vain, and so He weeps for them.

And He rises Above, to destroy the world—meaning, He ascends so as to stop the Light's descent and thereby destroy the world. The world and creatures can exist only if they receive the Creator's Light (even if unconsciously). However, if man's state and selfish actions cannot lead him to the intention "for the Creator's sake," the Light itself becomes detrimental to him, for in pursuit of this Light, man sinks ever deeper into egoistic desires (impure forces) and growing dependency on egoism. Therefore, it is more desirable and beneficial for man to stop feeling pleasure in his impure desires, so that it would not destroy him completely and prevent him from sinking into such powerful egoistic desires that, having become a slave to their pleasures, he would never be able escape them and attain the spiritual.

**176. The members of the assembly then appear before the Creator and say: "Master of the world, You are called merciful and forgiving, send Your mercy upon Your sons." He answers them: "Have I not done so, when I created the world based on mercy? As it is written, 'The world is built by mercy' and the world is established upon it. However, if they do not show mercy to the poor, the world will be destroyed." The Heavenly angels then say to Him: "Master of the world, here is a man who had eaten and drunk to his heart's content, and could have been merciful to the poor, but did not do anything." The prosecutor appears, receives permission, and persecutes that man.**

The exalted souls, called "the members (or the sons) of the assembly" begin praying for the lower ones, so the Creator would have mercy on His sons and not discontinue the flow of Light descending onto them. They do everything within their power to justify man's state of being, and say that as long as he observes his *Mitzvot* in faith, he is called "the Creator's son," and hence deserves the Creator's mercy, as a son deserves the mercy of his father.

The Creator replies to them that He created the world by the property of mercy, and the world stands on this property alone. In other words, man will not be corrected by the Creator's Light as long as he disdains the poor, for the world's creation was the result of the Creator's agreement with the angel of Mercy, which states that due to man's merciful deeds, the world will be able to exist and will gradually come to the intention "for the Creator's sake." But now, since people are not showing mercy, there will be no correction.

Then the Supernal angels said, "Master of the universe, here is a man who had eaten and drunk, and had his fill, and could have been merciful to the poor, but did not give them anything." In this case, the angels begin to accuse man, instead of defending him, even the angels of Mercy and Justice. And all those who did not wish to create an egoistic man with desires "for oneself," but agreed to it only because they assumed that by deeds of mercy and justice he would escape his egoism "for one's own sake" and achieve the altruistic property "for the Creator's sake." Now, they, too, turn against man.

And if man is unable to acquire the intention "for the Creator's sake," the angels repent and regret at having agreed to his creation, and they now accuse him before the Creator. And after it becomes clear that man will not achieve the altruistic property "for the Creator's sake" by observing the *Mitzvot*, he is passed into the hands of the prosecutor.

177. There are none greater in our world than Avraham, who acted with mercy toward all creatures. It is written of the day that he prepared a feast: "The child grew and was weaned, and Avraham made a great feast on the day that Yitzchak was weaned." So Avraham prepared a feast and invited all the leaders of that generation. It is well known that at every feast, the supreme prosecutor is about, watching. And if there are any poor people in the house, he leaves that house and does not return there. However, if the prosecutor enters a house and sees rejoicing without the poor—without having first shown mercy to the poor—he ascends Above and brings accusations against the host of that feast.

178. Because Avraham was the leader of his generation, the prosecutor descended from Heavens and stood at the door of his house, disguised as a poor man. And nobody so much as looked at him. Avraham was attending to kings and ministers, and Sarah was feeding all of their children, for they did not believe that she had born a child, but rather claimed that Yitzchak was a foundling, whom they had bought at the marketplace. This is why they brought their children with them, and Sarah nursed them in front of all. And the prosecutor stands at the door. Sarah said: "The Creator has made laughter for me" ("For anyone who hears will laugh on account of me" (*Beresheet*, 21:6). The prosecutor ascended at once and stood before the Creator, and said to Him, "O Master of the world, You have said that You love Avraham, and here he had prepared a feast, but had not given anything to You nor to the poor, had not sacrificed even a single pigeon for Your sake. And Sarah says that You have laughed at her."

Until the end of correction, it is impossible to fully rid oneself of the impure forces. Hence, however hard even the most exalted righteous may try to observe the Creator's *Mitzvot* in purity of their altruistic intentions, without any touch of personal benefit, the impure forces can nonetheless accuse them and find faults in their observance of the *Mitzvot*.

Therefore, the Creator prepared another opportunity for the righteous to silence the prosecutor—by bribing him with a certain portion of holiness and purity, thus silencing him. This way, the prosecutor is reluctant to accuse a righteous one and does not want him to disappear, for then the prosecutor, too, will be deprived of his part of holiness, the Light that he receives as the righteous one observes each *Mitzvot*.

Hence, the need for external hair in *Tefillin* (phylacteries), scapegoat rite, red heifer, and so forth. (*The Zohar, Emor,* p. 88). From this we see how extraordinary, multifaceted, and complex this world is created, how impossible it is to judge human deeds and the Upper Governance by external manifestations, as they are seen by us, and how "entangled" and inseparably intertwined all the connections between the pure and impure forces really are.

Even when we look at our great leaders-Kabbalists, we see how much they've suffered, how they were forced to submit to the will of petty rulers or ignorant masses, and how persecuted they were—those who were closest to the Creator! Everyone feels these obstacles, even those who are just beginning on their spiritual journey.

But here, in the example of Avraham, *The Zohar* does not speak about an ordinary prosecutor, for Avraham had surely given food to all the poor, as he had always done even before he invited his distinguished guests to his table. But this prosecutor demanded his share of holiness, of the Light. However, Avraham did not wish to give anything of holiness to impurity. Rather, he wanted to overcome its power and push it away from himself completely. This is why the prosecutor ascended Above and accused Avraham.

*The Zohar* tells us that the prosecutor was not really poor, but only disguised himself as such, and demanded to be treated at Avraham's festive table. Avraham felt that this was an impure force that assumed the image of a poor man; hence, he refused to give it anything.

This is why it is written: "He did not sacrifice even a single pigeon," for in accordance to the sacrificial rites (rejection of egoistic parts, of man's "I"), only two pigeons are offered, which symbolize the two combined points in *Malchut*: the property of *Malchut* that was corrected by the property of mercy, *Bina*. This common point contains both the properties of restriction and mercy, but the property of restriction is concealed, whereas the property of mercy is revealed (item 122).

Without this combination of *Malchut*'s properties with those of *Bina*, called the "mitigation" or "sweetening" of *Malchut*, the world (*Malchut*) cannot exist, i.e., receive the Creator's Light. Therefore, it is necessary to offer precisely two baby pigeons. One of them was sent by Noah from his Ark, never to return (*Beresheet*, 8), for one pigeon designates the property of restriction in *Malchut* that is unmitigated by *Bina*'s property of mercy. And since Noah could not correct anything in her, the pigeon never returned to him (*The Zohar Shlach*, p. 52).

The prosecutor's claims and complaints concerning Avraham's feast on the day when Yitzchak was weaned stem from his demand to receive his share, the corrections of the part of *Malchut* that cannot be corrected until *Gmar Tikkun* (the end of correction). And this is the property of the restriction within *Malchut*, with which the world cannot exist; hence, it must be concealed. This property is the pigeon that did not return to Noah.

Man was not entrusted with the task of correcting his Creator-given primordial egoism, for it is impossible to alter what the Creator had made. However, man can hide his *Malchut*, his egoism (refrain from using it), and instead act by receiving his desires from *Bina*. This is why a combination of the properties of *Malchut* (egoism) and *Bina* (altruism) was formed in man—to let him make the effort and conceal the properties of *Malchut*, and act only according to the properties of *Bina*.

When one is able to completely reject the use of his egoism and is guided only by the properties of *Bina*, he will achieve a state called "the end of his correction." Correction is made during the 6,000 years, i.e., along the degrees of the 6,000 consecutive actions.

Then, man's *Mashiach* (Messiah/savior), the Upper Light, comes to him and transforms all of man's egoism (the primordial nature that he was rejecting during the 6,000 years) into altruism. Then, one's egoistic properties serve for the reception of the Light of pleasure for the Creator's sake, and he no longer needs to refrain from using them.

The property of *Malchut*, with which man cannot work for the Creator's sake until his final correction, is referred to as "restriction." Using the properties of *Malchut* herself remains forbidden until she is completely corrected through gradual purification by the properties of *Bina* during the 6,000 years. Alternatively, *Malchut* is called "strictness" or "judgment," for this restriction is also the source of all punishments and prohibitions.

Avraham could not correct this property of restriction in *Malchut*, i.e., receive the Light and fill *Malchut* entirely. Hence, he received nothing in this part, and that is exactly the way he treated the prosecutor, who ascended at once and began to accuse Avraham before the Creator, claiming that Avraham failed to correct anything in *Malchut*'s property of restriction with his feast. This property of restriction is called "poor," for it does not receive Light; hence, it constitutes the essence of *Malchut*, her egoism.

Since the Creator mitigated the restrictive property of *Malchut* with the property of mercy, and mixed *Malchut* with *Bina* for the sole purpose of giving the world an opportunity to exist, the Light that is received thanks to the property of mercy is defined as the part of Light belonging to all the world's inhabitants. This part helps *Malchut* become corrected. Since the Creator created *Malchut* in order to personally fill her with Light, she is regarded as His personal part.

As a result of a miracle of nursing the babies that were brought to Sarah, Avraham received all the Light that exists in the property of mercy, and began to doubt his ability to correct the poor part of *Malchut*. This part receives nothing (for it cannot be used during the 6,000 years) and constitutes the Creator's personal part.

Therefore, the prosecutor ascended, accusing Avraham of not giving to the poor, i.e., not giving to the part of the Creator, *Malchut de Malchut* herself, which no man can correct by himself, as even Noah was unable to do so. And he gave nothing to You nor to the poor, and sacrificed not even a single pigeon for Your sake.

And Sarah says that You have laughed at her. Sarah is the part of *Bina* that shines in *Malchut*. With the words: "Any who hears will laugh on account of me" (*Beresheet*, 21:6), Sarah-*Bina* gave *Malchut* such powerful *Ohr Hassadim* that *Malchut* stopped feeling her egoistic desires, felt the perfection of altruism, and temporarily acquired the properties of *Bina*, while under the influence of *Ohr Hassadim*.

However, there emerges fear that due to such a sense of perfection and absence of suffering from unfulfilled desires, the absence of the feeling of deficiency, *Malchut* would remain uncorrected. Such a state is similar to the following description of Adam's state in the Torah (*Beresheet*, 3:22): "Lest he put forth his hand, and take also of the Tree of Life, and eat, and live forever." In other words, he must not stop feeling his own nature nor forget the fact that he is obliged to correct his defect in the "Tree of Knowledge." And that is why Adam was cast down into a place that is suitable for correction, the lowest possible egoistic place, called our world.

**179. The Creator said to him: "Who in the world is like Avraham?" And the prosecutor did not leave from there until he had consumed the entire fare. So the Creator decreed that Yitzchak is to be sacrificed. And He said that Sarah shall die from grief for her son. The cause of this grief is that he did not give anything to the poor.**

Yitzchak's sacrifice was aimed at the correction of *Malchut*, to compensate for what Avraham could not correct at his great feast in honor of Yitzchak's weaning. Sarah's death was the result of the great Light that she passed to

*Malchut*, saying: "The Creator has made laughter for me," alluding to the Light that obstructs the correction of *Malchut*.

Therefore, the Light that descends to *Malchut* and gives her the sensation of perfection prevents her from correcting herself. Hence, the Creator stopped it. This is the significance of Sarah's death, for Sarah constitutes the Light of *Bina* that enters *Malchut*. Thus, all that the Torah speaks of is but the essence of the process of *Malchut's* correction, until her correction is completed.

# THE TORAH AND PRAYER

**180.** Rabbi Shimon opened and said: "It is written that Hizkiyahu (Hezekiah) turned his face to the wall and prayed to the Creator." Let us see how great and potent the power of the Torah is, and how high it rises above all. He who engages in the Torah has no fear of those Above or below, nor of any hardships or illnesses of this world, for he is connected to the Tree of Life and learns from it each day.

**181.** For the Torah teaches man how to walk a path of truth; it teaches him how to return to his Master and cancel what is predestined for him. And even if man is shown that what is predestined for him cannot be cancelled, it is nonetheless completely cancelled and annulled, then disappears at once and does not prevail over him in this world. Hence, man should study the Torah day and night, and never abandon it, as it is written: "Contemplate Him day and night." Whomever abandons the Torah, it is as though he abandons the Tree of Life.

"Contemplate Him day and night"—"Him" implies the Creator! In another place in *The Zohar*, it is said that Hizkiyahu's prayer was accepted by the Creator, for nothing (no egoistic desires) separated him from the wall (the *Shechina*, the sensation of the Creator, akin to the Wailing Wall).

This was the advice that he received from the Torah, when, through his efforts in the Torah, he realized how to achieve complete return to the Creator, whereby nothing would separate him from the Creator (from the wall, the *Shechina*, the sensation of the Creator). As a result, the decree of his death (the Light's exit from the *Partzuf*) was revoked. So great is the power of the Torah.

**182.** Come and see—such is the advice given to man. When he goes to bed at night, he must accept the Creator's governance from Above, and wholeheartedly entrust his soul with Him. Thus, man is immediately spared all the illnesses, slander, and evil eyes, and they will no longer have power over him.

Here we come to a precise understanding of certain definitions from the Torah, which are quite different from the notions that we are accustomed to. Daylight signifies the sensation of unity with the Creator. It is called "Light," for this is how man defines his good feelings. Therefore, daylight is when man feels closeness of the Creator and the greatness of spirituality.

Darkness coincides with nighttime in our world. Accordingly, with regard to man's spiritual states, darkness designates the absence of the sensation of the Creator, of the Upper Light, due to the actions of the impure, egoistic forces that separate man from the Creator. At night in our world, we sleep. The spiritual *Partzuf* is filled with the minimal amount of Light in an unconscious state called "sleep." The amount of Light within the *Partzuf* is so little that it is defined as one sixtieth—6 (*Sefirot* of ZA) x 10 (in each part)—of death or complete absence of spiritual Light, for the impure forces rule here.

Due to these two forces that govern and control us, we cannot completely and permanently merge with the Creator. As the result of our sensation of the state of night, the impure forces that rule at night impede us in our efforts, for their power over us keeps returning, thus creating gaps in our unity with the Creator and in our work for His sake.

To correct this, Rabbi Shimon gives us his advice: every "night" (a feeling of separation from the spiritual), when man goes to "sleep" (sinks deeper into the sensations of this world), he must wholeheartedly accept the Creator's governance, entrust himself completely under His rule. For if the night (the sensation of night) is corrected as in the act of creation, when day follows night, as it is said, "And there was evening and there was morning, one day," both night and day become as a single whole.

And the night, called "the rule of *Malchut*," shall not mix with any impure force, and shall not attack man because of the disappearance of the sensation of the Creator on account of egoistic desires and obstacles of "reason." For first, man has realized the necessity of the night for the attainment of the next day (greater sensation of the Creator, a bigger altruistic desire), and perceives these two states as a single whole and as an advancement, despite the fact that in his sensations, a night designates remoteness from spirituality.

In the language of spiritual work, this means that if man feels remoteness from the Creator, and is therefore without joy, despite all the possible pleasures, for him this state is called "night." It is precisely in such a state of complete absence of sensation and lack of faith in the Creator that man can, through his own effort, without feeling any taste in the Torah, yield before the Creator's rule. That is, he closes his eyes (as one who goes to sleep) and says: "I bring myself under the Creator's rule and submit to His will." This state is called "descent for the sake of a subsequent ascent," and serves as a springboard, by which man attains an even brighter "day."

However, to this end man must completely accept the Supernal Kingdom's rule, so that nothing will separate him from the Creator. In other words, he must submit to the Supernal Rule unconditionally, whether it brings life or death, so that no force in the world will be able to stop him from uniting with the Supernal Ruler, as it is written, "Love your Creator with all your heart, with all your soul and with all your might" (*Devarim*, 6:5).

If man accepts everything that the Creator sends him with all his heart, he is certain that nothing will separate him from the Creator. This determines the fulfillment of the condition of entrusting one's soul with the Creator. For he gives himself into the Creator's hands in advance, by deciding to fulfill all His desires (commandments) to the fullest, right up to self-sacrifice.

Hence, as man sleeps, when his soul (the sensation of the Creator), the Light that previously filled him, leaves his body (desires), he does not feel the taste of the sixtieth part of death, for the impure (egoistic) forces have no power over him. In other words, they do not separate him from the Creator. Rather, he merely fails to feel the Creator temporarily.

Thus, the impure forces cannot interrupt his spiritual work even in the state called "night," for his evening and morning are already as one day—the Creator's Light. The night becomes a part of the day, for it is precisely because of the night that he recognizes his future merit of receiving an even greater Light.

This is because his night stems not from the rule of the impure forces. Instead, he understands that the Creator intentionally sends him such states. Thus, even in such sensations as darkness and lack of feeling, absence of aspiration and taste for the spiritual, he sees an opportunity to merge with the Creator. And this means that nothing stands between him and the wall.

**183. And in the morning, when he rises from his bed, he must bless the Creator, enter His house, and bow before Him in fear and trepidation, and only then should he pray. He should take advice of his holy Patriarchs, as it is written, "By Your great mercy shall I come into Your house, to bow in fear of Your holy greatness."**

Thanks to Your great kindness, I can now bless You for being merciful to me, for ending my spiritual descent, and for letting me come into Your house once more, for allowing me to feel You. However, I am happy not because my suffering gave way to pleasure, but because now I can thank You. I come to Your house so as to kneel in awe before Your holy greatness, which I now attain more than ever before.

The prayer in our heart is the correction within *Malchut* (the *Shechina*, the sensation of the Creator, or the common soul of Israel), and the fulfillment of this common soul with the Upper Light (the sensation of the Creator), in accordance with all of its corrected desires. Hence, all our pleas are expressed in plural form, for we pray not for our own soul, but for the common soul of Israel. Naturally, all that is present in the *Shechina* is subsequently present in every soul of Israel, and vice versa, all that the common soul of Israel lacks is also absent in each soul.

Therefore, before we start praying, we need to understand (feel) what is lacking in *Malchut* (the *Shechina*), to know what we need to correct in her and how we can fulfill her. Our heart, the center of our desires, is a part of this *Malchut* (the *Shechina*). All the generations of Israel are included in the common soul—the *Shechina*. However, we need not correct what has already been corrected by previous generations, but only what is left after those generations of souls.

Our Patriarchs, the spiritual *Partzufim* called "Avraham, Yitzchak and Yaakov," also known as the *Sefirot Hesed*, *Gevura*, and *Tifferet* of *Partzuf ZA de Atzilut*, include the entire community of Israel, all the properties that subsequently manifest in the corrected *Malchut*, who, in her corrected state, is called "Israel." The Patriarchs designate the three spiritual roots of the 600,000 souls of Israel in all the generations. In other words, these are the three sources of desires born within man's part of *Malchut* for the purpose of his correction.

All the good deeds, the reception and bestowal of Light carried out by the "community of Israel" (by Kabbalists) in all the generations, first trigger reception of the Upper Light by our holy Patriarchs (*Sefirot de ZA*), for all the Upper Light descends through them from Above downwards. From them, this Upper Light descends onto the "community of Israel," the righteous of that generation who exist with their properties in the worlds of *BYA*, and evoke the descent of this Light with their prayers.

Such is the order of spiritual degrees: each branch can receive only through its root (the preceding, Higher Degree), but never independently. The main Light remains in the root, and only an insignificant part of it descends to the branch that evokes it. Therefore, all the corrections completed in the community of Israel (the *Shechina*, the common soul) are stored and preserved in the souls of our holy Patriarchs.

(The Light received in the corrected *Kelim* remains forever within them. Our description of the Light's exit and descent should be understood as a metaphor, for the *Partzuf* receives new empty desires that require correction, and the sensation of emptiness from the received empty desires is perceived as the Light's departure. Nevertheless, upon correcting these newly received desires, in them the *Partzuf* will receive an even greater Light than before).

Therefore, the essence of our prayer lies in supplementing the *Shechina* with whatever it needs to achieve complete correction, after all the previous corrections that were performed in it by the past generations of Kabbalists. Hence, he who spiritually ascends must first make all the corrections that have already been performed in the *Shechina*, and only then will he be able to recognize what is left for him to correct.

This is why it is written that one cannot enter the *Beit Knesset* (synagogue, but in Hebrew it means "the house of assembly" or "the house of prayer," from the word *Kones*—"to assemble") before he assembles his prayer and asks the holy Patriarchs for guidance, for he needs to know what has already been corrected and what still needs to be corrected. This is possible only after he receives everything that the Patriarchs have corrected through the *Shechina*. Only then will he come to know what is left for him to correct in the *Shechina*.

The Patriarchs have corrected the prayer in the *Shechina*. Prayer and the *Shechina* are one and the same, for prayer is a request, a raising of MAN, a *Kli*, the corrected *Malchut* or the desire for the Creator's sake. The correction performed by Avraham is called *Shacharit* (the morning prayer), by Yitzchak—*Mincha* (the afternoon prayer), and by Yaakov—*Arvit* (the evening prayer). Therefore, one must first repeat in his prayer everything that was already corrected by them, and then he will discover how to construct his personal plea, and what other imperfections are left that only he can, and consequently, must correct.

**184. Man cannot enter the *Beit Knesset* (synagogue, house of prayer) unless he first receives permission from Avraham, Yitzchak and Yaakov, for they have corrected the prayer to the Creator. It is therefore written, "And in Your great mercy shall I enter into Your house" (*Tehilim*, 5:8). The aforesaid refers to Avraham, for his property is mercy, the *Sefira Hesed*. "I will bow before Your holy chamber" refers to Yitzchak, for thanks to him *Malchut* is called *Heichal*—chamber, the *Sefira Gevura*. "In fear and trepidation" refers to**

Yaakov, for his property is the *Sefira Tifferet*, called "fear." And man must first enter into these properties, and only then enter the *Beit Knesset* to raise his prayers. Such a state is described by the verse, "Here is My slave, Israel, by whom I am adorned."

Here *The Zohar* analyzes the first three main corrections, made by the Patriarchs in the *Shechina*. Avraham corrected the property called *Bait* (house, permanent dwelling), which allows man to merge with it and to always exist in the Creator's properties and sensations, just as he can always dwell in his house.

Yitzchak complemented the correction and corrected *Malchut* in the property called the "holy temple," so that the King Himself would always dwell in it, as a king always dwells in his chambers. Yaakov added to the correction by the property of fear, which corresponds to a gate in front of a house, and designates the condition that (if met) allows man to enter *Malchut*, Avraham's house, and into Yitzchak's holy temple that are both within her.

Upon including within him all three corrections of the Patriarchs in full perfection, he attains what has already been corrected in the holy *Shechina*, and then proceeds to correct what has not been corrected.

Avraham is the source of the property of mercy in the souls of Israel. Therefore, he corrected the holy *Shechina* in such a way that it could receive *Ohr Hassadim*, the Light of Mercy. And the *Shechina* received this Light in its entirety for all the souls of Israel. Had it remained this way, all the souls of Israel would have been in complete and eternal unity with the Creator, and the *Shechina* would have been filled with Light (pleasure). Thus, no man would ever wish to part with the *Shechina* (the sensation of the Creator) even for a single moment.

Yet, Avraham's entire correction consisted in the creation of a perfect, bestowing *Kli*, which consisted only of *Ohr Hassadim*. There was no way of corrupting its properties or introducing imperfection within it, for, just like Avraham's property of mercy (*Hesed*), this *Kli* (desire) consisted only of the will to bestow upon, and please the Creator, as it is written: "Mine is yours and yours is yours designates the property of mercy" (*Avot*, 85). By imparting creation with his property, Avraham completely separated the impure forces (thoughts and desires) from the *Shechina*, and made it completely holy and pure.

However, the Thought of Creation does not end here, for it lies in fulfilling the souls with delight. And the extent of pleasure depends on the aspiration to enjoy, on the degree of hunger. Only the extent of preliminary hunger, the will to receive pleasure, determines the extent of the subsequent reception of pleasure.

The *Shechina* (*Malchut de Atzilut*, the sum of the souls) received its correction from Avraham—the Supernal force of *Hassadim*, the *Sefira Hesed* of ZA *de Atzilut*—and acquired the property of mercy from it. This property is completely free from any selfish will to receive, that is, its desire to receive something from the Creator has completely disappeared, and only the will to bestow upon Him remains. This desire is called "bestowal for the sake of bestowal." However, this brought no correction to the souls (parts of the *Shechina*), for their role is to receive the pleasure prepared for them by the Creator. To that end, they must first have the "will to receive." After all, pleasure is felt only when preceded by an aspiration or desire for it, and is determined by the extent of this desire.

It is hence written that Avraham fathered Yitzchak: Yitzchak found the *Shechina* in absolute spiritual perfection, in the property of pure selfless bestowal, filled with *Ohr Hassadim* because of all the corrections made by Avraham. However, in accordance with his properties, Yitzchak (the left spiritual force) felt imperfection in this state of the *Shechina*—that it was not yet corrected to "receive" *all* that was conceived in the Thought of Creation.

Therefore, he corrected it by turning it into a *Kli* (vessel) of reception, by supplementing it with the will "to receive," so that it could receive all the perfection prepared for it. Yitzchak evoked in the *Shechina* the will to receive pleasure from the Creator, albeit in the form of "reception for the Creator's sake"—with the intention of receiving pleasure in order to delight Him.

The reception for the Creator's sake means that although man fervently wishes to receive pleasure, he receives not because he wishes to enjoy, but only because the bestowing Creator wishes for him to receive it. And had the Creator not wished it so, man would have no desire to receive from Him.

Reception for the Creator's sake is equivalent to selfless bestowal. Thus, the egoistic, impure force, cannot cling to such a desire.

Hence, Yitzchak corrected the *Shechina* and brought it to complete perfection, for now it can receive all that the Creator conceived to bestow upon it, as this is the purpose of His creation.

Thus, after being corrected by Yitzchak, the state of *Malchut-Shechina* is called *Heichal* (the Creator's chambers), for now He can fill it with Himself, His Light, which means that He dwells in its halls.

Yet, Avraham's correction, called "house," did not yet allow the *Shechina* to be filled and worthy of the Creator's presence. Hence, Yitzchak is considered to have corrected all the *Gevurot* (willpower and resistance to egoism in the souls of Israel). This means that he mitigated all the laws and restrictions in the

Creator's governance. This is because all restrictions and punishments come into this world for the sole purpose of correcting the souls' will to receive, to make them suitable for reception of the infinite goodness contained in the Thought of Creation. And since Yitzchak corrected the *Shechina* to complete perfection, all its restrictions and forces have been corrected, and all of its properties have attained the desired goal.

However, his correction, too, did not retain this form in the *Shechina*, and became corrupted, for the world was still unprepared for the end of correction. Hence, Yitzchak fathered a sinner, Esav, who, being unable to resist the temptation to receive for himself, corrupted Yitzchak's correction in the *Shechina*. Unlike Yitzchak, he could not resist the selfish reception. This means that even when it became clear to him that the bestowing Creator did not wish for him to receive, he wanted to receive nonetheless, for such was his desire of self-gratification.

Therefore, the impure force (*Klipot*-shells, the husk, or rind surrounding the pure forces) clung to the *Shechina*. Thus, the legs (*Sefirot NHYM*) of *Partzuf Malchut de Atzilut* descended to the place of the *Klipot* below *Parsa*, where egoistic desires dominate the desires of *NHYM*.

Yet, the *Rosh* and the Upper Part of the *Guf* down to the *Tabur* of *Partzuf Malchut* remained above the rule of the impure forces. Hence, his head (*Rosh*) understands how he should act (hence, Yitzchak's head is buried together with the bodies of Avraham and Yaakov in the *Machpela* cave), but the body (*Guf*) still wants to receive pleasure for its own sake.

And since Yaakov saw the damage caused by Esav, he corrected the *Shechina* by adding his property of fear to it, as it is written: "His hand had hold on Esav's heel" (The Torah, *Beresheet*, 25:26). Because Yaakov realized what imperfection Esav had caused in *Shechina* (in the created souls), he corrected himself in fear to such an extent that he raised the holy *Shechina* as a crown-adornment. By this he also retained the corrections made by Avraham and Yitzchak.

However, Yaakov's correction was not final, for this fear is more similar to the fear of transgression than the selfless fear that comes from within. For this fear of his is born in him from Esav's hip, even though he had not transgressed by receiving, as did Esav. But the end of correction will bring a different state: Esav's hip will be annulled, as it is written: "Death will forever vanish from the world," and fear will remain only because the Creator is almighty and great.

Yaakov attained this genuine fear by himself. However, the entire "community of Israel," all the souls that form the *Shechina*, still need to correct themselves in all the generations, from the first to the last, to the end of correction. (Only

Moshe attained the property of true fear—one out of greatness and love—only he, and no one else. Hence, as the Talmud says, description of fear out of love for the Creator doesn't even exist.)

*The Zohar* cites the words of the Psalm (5:8): "By Your great mercy I shall come into Your house," since Avraham corrected the *Shechina* up to the property of a "house" that is filled with goodness, i.e., with *Ohr Hassadim*. The words, "So as to bow before Your holy chamber," refer to Yitzchak, who corrected the *Shechina* from a "house" to a "chamber" that befits the Creator. The words, "in fear" refer to Yaakov, who corrected the *Shechina* with his property of fear, whereupon he made it a *Kli* (vessel) of reception that includes all the corrections made by Avraham and Yitzchak.

Yet, how did he find out what else needed correction in the *Shechina*? Only by correcting and including himself in these three corrections performed by the holy Patriarchs before him. This means that, just as they did, Yaakov can act according to the conditions of these corrections. In other words, Yaakov merged with their properties, thereby ascending to their level.

Thus, man must first attain these properties and correct them within him. Only after he assumes the properties of these three corrections into himself can he start correcting them from where our Patriarch Yaakov left off, i.e., elevating fear to the extent of the Creator's greatness and omnipotence, and drawing the Upper Light with his prayer, with his awe of the Creator's greatness. And the Upper Light will bring with it the fulfillment of the *Shechina* and the end of its correction. Hence, man's prayer must include two objectives: to obtain fear of the Creator's true greatness, and with this attainment, to achieve the final correction of his egoism.

# Rabbi Shimon's Departure from the Cave

185. Rabbi Pinchas stood before Rabbi Rachuma on the shore of Lake Kinneret. He was wise, old, and almost blind. He said to Rabbi Pinchas: "I have heard that our friend Shimon Bar-Yochai has a jewel, a son. I have looked upon the Light from that jewel, and it shines like the light of the sun, and illuminates the entire world."

A fully corrected *Malchut* is called a jewel (usually a pearl). Rabbi Nachum tells Rabbi Pinchas that Rabbi Shimon has already merited complete correction, for a "son" designates the next state, the next *Partzuf* that emerges or is born from the preceding one. And Rabbi Pinchas sees this while looking (with his spiritual sight, called *Ruach HaKodesh*—the Holy Spirit) at the Light of this pearl, which shines like the sun emerging from its hiding (*Nartik*—sheath). This means that after the future correction of *Malchut* (the moon), her Light will become like that of the sun, and will illuminate the entire world.

And when the Light of the moon becomes like that of the sun, it will rise to the zenith and illuminate the whole world with a pillar of Light, from Heaven to earth. And it will shine until Rabbi Shimon completes the correction of *Atik*. This speaks to the fact that he has already merited attaining the degrees of the Creator's two revelations, i.e., the end of correction.

186. And that Light extends from the Heavens down to the earth and illuminates the whole world until *Atik-Keter* appears and sits upon its throne, which occurs at the end of correction. And that Light abides entirely in your household (for the daughter of Rabbi Pinchas was wife to Rabbi Shimon, and Rabbi Elazar was therefore his grandson). And a tiny ray of Light (called "the son of the household," Rabbi Elazar) separates from the Light that fills the household, comes forth and shines upon the whole world. Happy are those

who merit such a destiny! Come out, my son, come out! Go after that jewel, which illuminates the world, for it is a good time to do so!

Since the daughter of Rabbi Pinchas was the wife of Rabbi Shimon (Rabbi Shimon and his wife designate two spiritual *Partzufim* that are below Rabbi Pinchas), Rabbi Shimon (together with his wife) belonged to the household (was included in the *Partzuf*) of Rabbi Pinchas. This refers to Rabbi Elazar, the *Partzuf* that emerged from the Light and illuminated the world, which filled the household (ten *Sefirot*) of Rabbi Pinchas, i.e., came out of the *Partzuf* called "Rabbi Shimon and his wife."

187. He came out before him and stood waiting to board a ship. Two women were with him. He saw two birds soaring over the water. He raised his voice and said, "Birds, you soar over the sea; have you seen the place where one could find Bar-Yochai?" He waited some and said, "Birds, O birds, fly away." They flew away and disappeared into the sea.

Rabbi Shimon fled from the authorities that condemned him to death, and hid in a cave with his son. And no one knew where he was. Therefore, Rabbi Pinchas set out to look for him.

Although everything described here is historically true, it is nonetheless essential for us to understand the words of *The Zohar* as the actions of Supernal spiritual causes, whose consequences determine all that transpires on earth. The egoistic authorities (forces) of a *Partzuf* as exalted as Rabbi Shimon's try to overcome his own altruistic aspirations and deprive him of the Light, that is, to kill him. And he hides from them in a cave, i.e., assumes a small state (*Katnut*) and shines with the Light of Mercy. This is referred to as "hides in a cave"—becomes invisible to egoistic forces, for they desire *Ohr Hochma* and cannot see *Ohr Hassadim*.

188. Before he boarded the ship, the birds approached again, and in the beak of one of them was a letter. It read that Rabbi Shimon, the son of Yochai, had left the cave together with his son, Rabbi Elazar. Rabbi Pinchas went to them and found them completely changed: their bodies were covered with sores (like holes in the ground—see the Talmud, *Bava Batra*, 19:2) from staying in the cave for so long. He wept and said, "Woe that I have seen you so!" Rabbi Shimon replied: "O how happy is my lot that you have seen me so, for had you not seen me so, I would not have been what I am!" Rabbi Shimon opened about the *Mitzvot* of the Torah and said, "The *Mitzvot* of the Torah that the Creator gave to Israel are all described in a general form."

While staying in the cave (in *Ohr Hassadim*) for many years (degrees), Rabbi Shimon had no choice but to sit in the sand (the external garment—*Levush* covering the *Partzuf* with a particular property, called "earth") in order to cover his naked body (desires) so he could study the Torah (receive the Upper Light in his *Partzuf* with the intention for the Creator's sake). As a result of being covered with sand, his entire "body" was covered with "rust and sores" (but these were necessary corrections).

And not only did the *Partzuf* called Rabbi Shimon need the correction of concealment in *Hassadim* (cave) and the cover of an external garment (Reflected Light), but his next state, fathered by him, called his son, Rabbi Elazar (a lower *Partzuf*), also needed these corrections to attain all of the Creator's Light.

He wept and said: "Woe that I have seen you so!" Rabbi Shimon replied: "O how happy is my lot that you have seen me so, for had you not seen me so, I would not have been what I am!" In other words, if I would not look as I do, I would not have merited all the secrets of the Torah, for all that I have attained, I have attained during those thirteen years (thirteen successive corrections) of hiding in the cave.

Rabbi Shimon opened. It is written of the *Mitzvot* of the Torah: "The *Mitzvot* of the Torah that the Creator gave to Israel are all described in a general form." All of the *Mitzvot* of the Torah are described in the passage from the Torah, starting with "In the beginning the Creator created" and ending with "Let there be Light." These are the *Mitzvot* of fear and punishment, which include all the *Mitzvot* of the Torah. This is why they are called "in general."

# THE FIRST COMMANDMENT

**189. *BERESHEET BARAH ELOKIM* (In the beginning the Creator created)
is the first *Mitzva* (commandment), the root and foundation of everything.
And it is called "fear of the Creator" or *Resheet* (beginning), as it is written:
"Fear of the Creator is the beginning of wisdom." Fear of the Creator is the
beginning of wisdom, for this fear is called "the beginning." And it is the gate
that leads to faith. And the whole world is based on this *Mitzva*.**

It is difficult to understand why fear is called "the beginning," and why it
precedes wisdom and faith. *The Zohar* answers: it is because fear is the beginning
of every *Sefira*, and it is impossible to attain any *Sefira* (property) without first
attaining the property of fear. Yet, this implies that fear is merely a means of
attaining other qualities or properties. But then, if it is only a means, then why
is it included in the list of *Mitzvot* (plural for *Mitzva*) as the first *Mitzva*? Can it
be that fear is a kind of prerequisite?

Therefore, *The Zohar* says that it is impossible to attain perfect, selfless faith
in any way other than through fear of the Creator. And the extent of fear will
determine the extent of faith. Hence, the whole world is based on the *Mitzva*
of fear, for the whole world exists only thanks to the Torah and *Mitzvot*, as
the prophet said: "If not for My union with day and night, I would not have
appointed the ordinances of Heaven and earth" (*Yirmiyahu*, 33:25).

And since fear is the beginning and the gate to the other *Mitzvot* (for fear
is also the gate to faith), the whole world is based on this property of fear. It
is hence written that the *Mitzva* of fear includes all of the other *Mitzvot* of the
Torah; and were it not for fear, the Creator would not have created anything.

**190. There are three types of fear, two of which have no real basis, but one
does. If man fears that his children may die, or fears illness or bodily suffering,
or fears for his material well-being, this kind of fear (even if constant) is not
the basis or root, for only desirable consequences constitute the cause of fear.**

This is called "the fear of punishment in this world." But there is also another type of fear: the fear of punishment in the world to come, in hell. These two types of fear—the fear of punishment in this world and in the world to come—do not constitute real basis and root.

191. The real fear is the fear of the Creator, for He is great and almighty, for He is the Source of everything, and all else is nothing compared to Him. Man should concentrate all his attention on attaining this kind of fear.

There are three kinds of fear before the Creator, but only one of them is considered true fear. If one is afraid of the Creator, and observes His *Mitzvot* so he and his children will be well and prosperous, this constitutes the first kind, the fear of the various punishments in this world. If he observes the Creator's *Mitzvot* because he fears punishments in hell, this is the second kind of fear. *The Zohar* says that neither of these two kinds is true, for man observes the *Mitzvot* only out of fear of punishment, for the sake of his own benefit, and not because these are the Creator's *Mitzvot*.

In this case, his personal wellbeing is the cause of his observance, and his fear is merely a consequence of his will to receive pleasure. Rather, true fear must stem from the Creator's greatness and omnipotence, for He rules over all and is the source of everything. All the worlds emerge from Him, and His deeds testify to His greatness. And all that He created is nothing compared to Him, for it adds nothing to Him.

Thus, we can plainly see that there is no difference in action: one observes out of the first or second kinds of fear, while the other observes out of the third kind. To an onlooker, they perform the same actions, the Creator's *Mitzvot*. But the enormous difference between them lies only in their *intention*, their motivation—why they observe the Creator's decree!

Hence, it is impossible to discern man's spiritual degree by his external observance of the *Mitzvot*, which is visible to all. Moreover, those who observe them in order to receive an immediate reward from others usually do so with the utmost outward zeal. But one whose intentions and thoughts are directed inwardly, who seeks true observance, as a rule, does not stand out amidst the masses in any way.

One must constantly seek to perfect and complement his intentions only by observing the *Mitzvot* at an increasingly deeper level, while focusing on inner contemplation and direction of his thoughts. In no way should he engage in excessive "mechanical observance," on which there is a clear prohibition: "Do not exaggerate in the *Mitzvot*."

On the contrary, one must devote all his attention to the attainment of true fear, as the Creator's first *Mitzva* decrees. As Rabbi Baruch Ashlag said, "Fear of the Creator is the constant, selfless desire that is expressed in the thought: 'Have I done everything I could for the Creator, or is there anything more that I can do for Him?'"

**192. Rabbi Shimon started to weep, wailing, "Woe if I reveal and woe if I do not reveal. If I say, the sinners will know how to work for the Creator's sake, and if I do not say, it will not reach my friends." Wherever there is true fear, opposite it and correspondingly below stands an evil fear, which strikes and prosecutes. It is the scourge that whips the sinners (punishing them for their sins). This is why he is afraid to reveal it, for the sinners may learn how to avoid punishment, and punishment constitutes their correction!**

Here Rabbi Shimon warns that he cannot reveal everything in its entirety (this refers to *Avoda Lishma*—work "for the Creator's sake"), for he fears it may harm the sinners. Here he wishes to reveal how one can draw nearer and merge with the Tree of Life, and therewith refrain from touching the Tree of Death. However, this refers only to those who have already corrected themselves with regard to the Tree of Knowledge of Good and Evil.

Nevertheless, the sinners (those who have yet to correct their transgressions in the Tree of Knowledge of Good and Evil) are not entitled to know this, for they still need to toil in all the required tasks until they correct themselves in the Tree of Knowledge of Good and Evil. Thus we see that the Torah defines a sinner as one who is yet to correct the Tree of Knowledge in his soul.

The prohibition on revealing the true essence of the work for the Creator's sake is based on the words of the Torah: "Behold, Adam has become as one of us in knowledge of good and evil; and now, lest he put forth his hand, and take also of the Tree of Life, and eat, and live forever" (*Beresheet*, 3:22).

After Adam's sin in the Tree of Knowledge, the Creator banished him from the Garden of Eden to prevent Adam from connecting to the Tree of Life and gaining eternal life. This is because then, what he corrupted in the Tree of Knowledge would remain uncorrected. Therefore, to let only the righteous know this wisdom, Rabbi Shimon reveals it by way of allusion.

**193. But he who fears the punishment by whippings, the true fear of the Creator cannot descend upon him. Instead, evil fear overtakes him in the form of fearing punishment by whipping.**

**194. Therefore, the place that is named "fear of the Creator" is called the beginning of knowledge. This is why this *Mitzva* is included here. And it is the foundation and source of all the other *Mitzvot* of the Torah. And whoever observes the *Mitzva* of fear of the Creator, thereby observes all the others. But he who does not observe the *Mitzva* of fear of the Creator, does not observe the other *Mitzvot* of the Torah, for this *Mitzva* constitutes the foundation for all the others.**

Here *The Zohar* repeats that in one place it is written, "Fear of the Creator is the beginning of wisdom," while in another it says, "Fear of the Creator is the beginning of knowledge." And *The Zohar* explains that where the property of fear ends, another evil fear begins, one that slanders and whips. In this regard, it is said in Kabbalah that the legs of a pure *Partzuf Malchut* descend to a place of impure forces.

However, he who observes the *Mitzva* of fear because the Creator is great and almighty unites with Him (becomes equal to the Creator in his properties), so as to not feel shame in receiving from Him. Besides this correction, no other work exists for the creatures.

This is called "fear of the Creator for the sake of life," for as a result of merging with the Creator, creatures are filled with life. Otherwise, they fall under the power of the restriction, as *Tzimtzum Aleph* (first restriction) restricted the reception of Light in egoistic desires. Such a *Kli* (desire) becomes a cause of death, for it is an empty place (devoid of Light). Hence, creatures must fear failing to make the corrections that they were entrusted with.

However, those who observe the *Mitzvot* out of fear, rather than out of realization of the Creator's greatness and His decree, are ruled and whipped by the fear of an empty *Malchut*. And since the end of fear lies in the evil scourge, true fear is called "The beginning of knowledge of the fear of the Creator," which indicates the necessity to aspire only to this kind of fear, and beware of the evil kind. Because of this, Adam's sin is corrected.

**195. Therefore, it is written, IN THE BEGINNING (signifying fear) THE CREATOR CREATED THE HEAVENS AND THE EARTH. For whoever transgresses here, transgresses all of the Torah *Mitzvot*. And his punishment is the evil scourge, i.e., the evil fear that whips him. The words, AND THE EARTH WAS UNFORMED AND CHAOTIC, AND DARKNESS WAS UPON THE FACE OF THE DEEP, AND THE SPIRIT OF THE CREATOR refer to the four punishments of the wicked.**

**196. WITHOUT FORM refers to strangulation. CHAOTIC refers to stoning, i.e., the stones that fall into the great deep to punish the sinners. DARKNESS signifies burning, the fire that falls upon the heads of the wicked to burn them down. THE SPIRIT OF THE CREATOR refers to beheading.**

Those who observe the *Mitzva* of fear before the Creator not because such is His decree, but because they are afraid of punishment, fall into the impure force's trap, called "without form." As a result, they are lost, having no understanding of the Creator's thoughts and deeds. And this impure force is defined as a rope on man's neck, blocking the inflow of pure (holy) air to his soul and preventing him from gaining life. And to the extent of man's ignorance, the impure force strangulates him!

And when he is caught in the impure force's noose, tightening around his neck, it has the power to control man at its will: to stone, burn, or behead him. Stoning means that impure thoughts befall his head with desired pleasures, thus pulling him down into the deep. There they punish him with darkness (burning), and the impure force turns him on fierce fire until it burns all the pure life-force out of him.

**197. The spirit of the Creator means beheading, for the scorching wind (*Ruach Se'ara*) is a flaming sword—punishment for whoever does not observe the Torah and *Mitzvot* that are mentioned after the *Mitzva* of fear, called "foundation," as it includes all the *Mitzvot*. This is because after the word BERESHEET (BEGINNING), which signifies fear, it is written WITHOUT FORM, CHAOS, DARKNESS and SPIRIT—in all, the four penalties of death. And then follow the rest of the Torah and *Mitzvot*.**

Following the first sentence of the Torah, the remaining part of the Torah refers to the rest of the *Mitzvot*, which are particular with regard to the general and all-inclusive *Mitzva* of fear.

# The Second Commandment

**198.** The second *Mitzva* (commandment) is inseparably connected with the *Mitzva* of fear, and it is the *Mitzva* of love—for man to love his Creator with perfect love. What is perfect love? It is a great love, as it is written, "He walks before the Creator in complete sincerity and perfection" (*Beresheet*, 17:1), which signifies perfection in love. Thus, it is written, "And the Creator said, 'Let there be Light'" (*Beresheet*, 1:3)—this is perfect love, called "great love." This is precisely how man should love his Creator.

There exists conditional love, which appears as a result of all the goodness received from the Creator ("Introduction to The Study of Ten Sefirot," items 66-74), as a result of which man merges with the Creator with all his heart and soul. Yet, although he merges with the Creator in complete perfection, this love is considered imperfect. It is similar to Noah's love (*Beresheet Raba*, 30), who constantly needed to reinforce his feeling—to see that the Creator sends him only goodness.

Avraham, however, needed nothing to reinforce his love for the Creator, as it is written: "He walks before the Creator in complete perfection." For the words "walks before" mean that he needs nothing to reinforce his feeling of love for the Creator. And even if he does not receive anything from Him, his love remains constant and perfect, and he wishes to merge with the Creator with his heart and soul.

**199.** Rabbi Elazar said, "I have heard what perfect love means." He was told, "Tell this to Rabbi Pinchas, as he truly exists on that degree." Rabbi Elazar said, "Perfect love means that it is perfect on both sides; if it does not include both sides, such a love is imperfect."

He was told to turn to Rabbi Pinchas, for Rabbi Pinchas had already attained the degree of perfect love and will be able understand him correctly.

The words "on both sides" refer to both the good side and the evil side. In other words, if the Creator gives him not only goodness, but restrictions, too (which he perceives as unpleasant), and even if He takes his soul away, still man's love for the Creator remains perfect, as though he receives from Him nothing but the very best in the world.

**200. Therefore, there is he who loves the Creator in order to gain riches, live a long life, have many healthy children, and rule over his enemies—he receives everything he wants, and this is why he loves the Creator. However, should he receive the opposite, should the Creator lead him through a wheel of suffering, he will come to hate the Creator, and will feel no love toward Him whatsoever. Therefore, such a love is baseless.**

Since his love depends on what he receives from the Creator, when reception stops, so does his love. Clearly, man can love only one or the other—himself or the Creator!

**201. Love is considered perfect if it exists on both sides—on the side of judgment and the side of mercy (success in life). As we already mentioned, when one loves the Creator, even if He were to take away his soul, this love would remain perfect on both sides: mercy and judgment. Therefore, the Light of the First Act of Creation was revealed and then concealed. And because of this concealment, strict judgment appeared in the world, and both sides, mercy and judgment, united to form perfection. And this is the desired love.**

The Light that was created on the first day of creation (in the verse "Let there be Light") was later concealed, as it is written, for the righteous in the world to come. It was concealed so as to let strict judgment appear in this world.

This leads to the unification of the two sides (mercy and judgment) into one, for man receives an opportunity to reveal the perfection of love even when the Creator takes his soul away, and he is given an opportunity to supplement and perfect his love. And had the Light not been concealed, strict judgment would not have been revealed, and the GREAT LOVE would have been concealed from the righteous, and there would be no way of revealing it.

**202. Rabbi Shimon kissed him. Rabbi Pinchas approached, kissed and blessed him. He said, "It is clear that the Creator has sent me here. This is the tiny ray of Light that was said to be shining in my house, and would later light up the whole world" (item 186). Rabbi Elazar said that fear must certainly not be forgotten from all the *Mitzvot*; especially in this *Mitzva*, the *Mitzva* of love, fear must be attached to this *Mitzva* at all times. How is it attached? Love is**

good when it brings goodness, health, sustenance, and life from the Beloved One. And it is here that fear of sinning must be revived, so that the wheel does not turn against him, as it is written, "Happy is the man who always fears," for his fear is contained in his love.

203. This is how fear should be evoked from the perspective of strict judgment, for once man realizes that strict judgment hovers over him, he must evoke within him fear of his Master. Thus, his heart will not be hardened, of which it is written, "He that hardens his heart shall fall into evil," into the other side. This is called evil. Therefore, fear unites with both sides—with goodness and love, as well as with strict judgment, and consists of both. And if fear is united with the good side and love, as well as with the strictness of judgment, such a love is perfect.

The *Mitzva* of fear includes all the *Mitzvot* of the Torah; it is the gateway to faith in the Creator—to the extent of his fear, man acquires faith in the Creator's governance. Hence, he must not forget fear in observing every *Mitzva*, especially the *Mitzva* of love, at which time fear needs to be roused even more, for fear must constantly be present in the *Mitzva* of love. Therefore, man must evoke fear within him in the two states of love: in love from the good side, when he receives good sensations from the Creator, and in love from the evil side, when the Creator sends him harsh restrictions, according to judgment.

However, it would be incorrect to think that perfect love means a state where one receives bad feelings from the Creator, to the extent of feeling one's soul being taken away. It is incorrect to think that one should not fear the Creator's judgment and strictness, and, despite his feelings to cling unto Him with love, fearlessly and wholeheartedly.

First, one must rouse fear within him lest his love for the Creator will weaken. Thus, he combines love and fear. Second, from the other side of love, from the side of feeling the strictness, he must rouse within him fear before the Creator, and not let his heart harden, so it would not stop heeding the unpleasant sensations of punishment. Thus, here, too, he includes fear and love, and if he acts so in both sides of love, his love remains forever connected to fear, thus becoming perfect.

It is written about the good side's inclusion of fear into love: "Happy is the man who always fears." The word "always" indicates that although man always receives only goodness from the Creator, he fears Him nonetheless, for he fears that he may sin.

And it is written about the evil side's inclusion of fear into love, when man feels punishments and strictness of judgment: "He who lets his heart be hardened shall fall into awe." This means that one should in no way and under no circumstances let his heart be hardened under the judgment's influence. Otherwise, he will fall into the impure forces, called "evil." In such a case, he must rouse within him even more fear of the Creator, and mingle his fear into the love.

However, neither kind is fear for oneself, for one's own well-being. Rather, they both refer to man's fear of diminishing his intentions and actions for the Creator's sake, and his attempts to direct them all towards pleasing Him.

Thus, we have clarified the first two *Mitzvot* of the Torah—the *Mitzvot* of fear and love. The *Mitzva* of fear is the basis for all the other *Mitzvot* and of the entire Torah. It is contained in the first word of the Torah, BERESHEET (IN THE BEGINNING), and in its first sentence, IN THE BEGINNING THE CREATOR CREATED THE HEAVENS AND THE EARTH. Fear is called BEGINNING, from which THE HEAVENS and THE EARTH are born, meaning ZON and their descendants, the worlds of BYA. And the second sentence in the Torah refers to punishment in the form of four kinds of spiritual death: WITHOUT FORM means strangulation, CHAOTIC means stoning, DARKNESS means burning, and SPIRIT means beheading. The *Mitzva* of love is described in the Torah in the verse: AND THE CREATOR SAID, 'LET THERE BE LIGHT.'

There are two sides to this *Mitzva*, which are called "kindness and longevity" and "with all one's soul." This implies that man should feel love even under the worst kinds of circumstances, i.e., when the Creator takes his soul away, just as he feels it when everything is well.

Just to reveal this perfect love, the Light of creation was concealed. Fear must also be included in both sides of love: in the part where man must fear to commit a sin, thereby reducing his love for the Creator, and in the part where he must fear because of the concealment and the Creator's judgment. Yet, to understand these spiritual categories, we must clarify them in a slightly different manner.

Calls for love are used repeatedly in the Torah: "Love thy neighbor...," "Do not do what you hate to another," and so on. But the basis of all this is love between man and the Creator; this is where our requests are directed: "Draw us nearer with love...," "He who chooses Israel with love..."

The revelation of the Creator is the revelation of His love for man. However, altruistic love is completely different from our understanding of love. Our love always relies on egoistic reasons. And should the reasons suddenly disappear, love disappears at once.

We can take as an example the natural love between father and son. Parents naturally love their only son more than anything in the world. Accordingly, the son should hold the same kind of love for his parents. Yet, we see that this is not so: if the son feels unconditional love from his parents, then, in accordance with nature's law and regardless of himself, his love for them will decrease.

This is so because the father's love for his son is natural; and just as the father wants his son to love him, his son wants to be loved by his father. This reciprocal desire gives rise to fear in both their hearts: the father is afraid that the son may hate him (even a little), and the son fears the same.

This constant fear begets good deeds between them: each of them aspires to show his love to the other, so as to promote reciprocity. Yet, when their love reaches peaks, and there is nothing else that can be added to it, the beloved son discovers absolute and unconditional love in the heart of his loving father.

The loved one immediately stops fearing that he will be loved less; neither can he hope that the love for him will grow. And this leads to a situation where the son grows lazy and stops expressing his love with good deeds. And as they lessen, his love lessens, too, until it is reversed into its opposite—hatred, for he deems everything his father does as worthless and insufficient in comparison with what the father's actions out of "absolute" love should be. Therefore, the union of love and fear within man brings him to the state of perfection.

The four letters *HaVaYaH* (*Yod* + *Hey* + *Vav* + *Hey*) correspond to *Sefirot* *H-B-ZA-M*. *The Zohar* calls them, FEAR, LOVE, TORAH, COMMANDMENT, respectively.

| YOD | – | HOCHMA | – | FEAR |
|-----|---|--------|---|------|
| HEY | – | BINA | – | LOVE |
| VAV | – | ZA | – | TORAH |
| HEY | – | MALCHUT | – | COMMANDMENT |

*Partzuf AA* is the main *Partzuf*, and includes the entire world of *Atzilut*. It shines upon all the other worlds through its garments, called *AVI*, *YESHSUT* and *ZON*, where *AVI* and *YESHSUT* clothe *AA* from its *Peh* to *Tabur*, while *ZON* clothe *AA* from *Tabur* down to its *Sium Raglaim* (end of legs) that stand on *Parsa*.

*AA* is called "the concealed *Hochma*," as its *Ohr Hochma* is concealed in its *Rosh* and does not shine upon the other *Partzufim* and worlds, and only its *Bina* shines below. Thus, it is *Bina* (and not *AA*) that is called BERESHEET—BEGINNING, for she is the foundation and the source of all the worlds.

And she is also called FEAR OF THE CREATOR, i.e., fear of His greatness, "for He is the only Master and the root of all, and all that exists is as nothing compared to Him." And ZON (called HEAVEN AND EARTH) emerge from *Bina*. It is therefore written in the Torah, IN THE BEGINNING (with fear) *AVI*, THE CREATOR CREATED HEAVEN (ZA) AND EARTH (*Malchut*).

Hence, it is said: "Fear of the Creator is the beginning of wisdom (*Hochma*)" and "Fear of the Creator is the beginning of knowledge (*Daat*)." *Ohr Hochma* stems not from the *Sefira Hochma de AA*, but from *Bina de AA* alone. For when *Bina de AA* ascends to *Rosh de AA*, it turns to the *Sefira Hochma* and then passes the Light downward. It follows that the *Sefira Bina*, fear of the Creator, is the source of *Ohr Hochma*; hence, it is said, "Fear of the Creator is the beginning of *Hochma*."

Also, fear is the beginning of knowledge, for the *Sefira Daat* is the beginning of ZON: ZON raise their request to *Rosh de AA* in order to receive *Hochma*. And this request of ZON regarding reception of *Ohr Hochma*, which is received and felt by AA, is called *Daat*, knowledge. This is why it is written: "Fear of the Creator is the beginning of knowledge (*Daat*)."

*The Zohar* also tells us that afterwards fear and love unite so as never to part again, for *Hochma* is called "love." Indeed, the letter *Yod* of the name *HaVaYaH* is *Bina*, i.e., GAR *de Bina* (AVI) that wants only *Ohr Hassadim*, whereas *Ohr Hochma* is concealed within it.

And the place of revelation of *Ohr Hochma* is ZAT *de Bina*, called YESHSUT, the first letter *Hey* of the name *HaVaYaH*. Therefore, this place is called love, and it is the second *Mitzva* that follows the first *Mitzva* of fear, which shines in ZON, for this *Ohr Hochma* does not stem from *Hochma de AVI*, but from *Bina*, and *Bina* is known as fear.

And *The Zohar* says that fear unites with love so as to never let it go. This means that *Bina* forever unites with *Hochma* and does not part with it. And wherever there is *Bina*, *Hochma* is there alongside her. And although it seems to write that one *Mitzva* is fear and another is love (that these are separate *Mitzvot*), they are nonetheless always together and are never apart: just as the first *Mitzva* includes the first, so the first includes the second.

The reason they have separate names is that we distinguish them by their dominance: in the first *Mitzva*, it is AVI, GAR *de Bina*, *Bina* herself along with her property. Hence, it is called "fear." However, in the second *Mitzva* it is *Hochma* that is dominant; hence, it is called "love."

Therefore, the words of the Torah, IN THE BEGINNING THE CREATOR CREATED constitute concealment, and the revelation of these words begins with the words LET THERE BE LIGHT, designating the ascent of *Bina* (BEGINNING) to *Rosh de AA*, where *Bina* becomes like *Hochma*.

The combination of *Hochma* and *Bina* is then called GREAT LOVE. This is the meaning of the words, LET THERE BE LIGHT, for *Bina* ascends to *AA* and passes the Light to all the lower worlds with GREAT LOVE, i.e., by means of two Lights: *Hassadim* and *Hochma*.

This is why it is said that the CREATOR'S LOVE IS CLARIFIED FROM TWO SIDES, as it is written: LET THERE BE LIGHT IN THIS WORLD AND IN THE WORLD TO COME. Because the Creator saw that this world cannot receive the Light, He concealed His Light and raised it above *Parsa de AA*, called (according to its corrected properties) "the world to come," above *Chazeh de AA*, where *AVI* or *GAR de Bina* reside.

*Parsa* is located below *Chazeh de AA*, and it separates the Supernal Waters (*AVI*) from the lower waters (*YESHSUT* + *ZON*). Since *Ohr Hochma* does not shine below *Chazeh de AA*, it is said that the Light is concealed from *Partzufim YESHSUT* and *ZON*.

Thus, we see that *Bina* is divided into two parts: *GAR de Bina* (*AVI*), located above the *Chazeh* (*Parsa de AA* or the Supernal Waters), upon whom the Upper Light shines, meaning that secrets are revealed within them. He who ascends to this degree receives its Light, thereby meriting "wealth (*Hochma*) and longevity (*Hassadim*). His sons (his future corrections) are like olive sprouts (olive oil symbolizes *Hochma*), they gather round his table (*Hassadim*), and he rules over his enemies (impure forces), and whatever his wish may be, he succeeds in it (for *Ohr Hochma* is clothed in *Ohr Hassadim*)." *ZAT de Bina* are the lower waters, located below *Chazeh de AA*. The Light is concealed from them, and those who receive from them must love the Creator with the kind of love called "even if He takes away his soul."

These are the two degrees of love for the Creator. That is to say, love for the Creator is not the desire and decision of man alone. Rather, like any of our other desires, it appears only by attaining a particular degree: if one attains the degree of *YESHSUT*, it allows him to love the Creator "even if He takes away his soul." However, an even more perfect love emerges within him who reaches the degree of *AVI*: he receives such Light from it that his love for the Creator becomes perfect on both sides.

Yet, fear must be included in both kinds of love. For at the degree of *AVI*, one needs fear so as to not sin while in a state of spiritual ascent in *AVI*. And while at the degree of *YESHSUT*, one must fear lest his heart be hardened, for *Hochma* and *Bina* correspond to love and fear in a state of eternal unity. Therefore, one must include the properties of *Bina* (fear) into GAR *de Bina* (AVI), as well as into ZAT *de Bina* (YESHSUT).

Only then will love be perfect on both sides, in both forms: GAR and ZAT *de Bina*. Love cannot possibly be perfect only on one side, but only if fear exists on both sides, for *Hochma* (love) cannot exist without *Bina* (fear).

It follows that conditional love is the degree of AVI, whereas unconditional (perfect) love is the degree of YESHSUT. Yet, YESHSUT is below AVI. The thing is that man first receives Higher *Sefirot* of his emerging *Partzuf*, in the order KHB-ZA-M, but the Light enters them in the reverse order of NRNHY: first, he receives the *Sefira Keter* with the Light of *Nefesh*, and in the end he receives the *Sefira Malchut*, though the Light of *Yechida* enters *Keter*. Therefore, if we measure according to the *Sefirot* (*Kelim*), the degree of AVI = GE = K-H (conditional love) is smaller than the degree of YESHSUT = AHP = B-ZA-M (unconditional love).

# THE THIRD COMMANDMENT

**204.** The third *Mitzva* is to know that there is an Almighty Lord who governs the world, to unite this every day in the six Supernal limbs: *HGT NHY* of *Zeir Anpin*, and to unify them in the six words of the prayer "Hear O Israel," and with it to direct our desires upwards. Therefore, we must prolong the word "one" in the six words: "Hear, O Israel, the Lord is our Creator, the Lord is one."

In correspondence with the instruction to prolong the word "one," he who utters this verse should pronounce this word lengthily, as ooone. However, *The Zohar* obviously alludes not to a simple utterance of one's mouth, but rather to our true heartfelt intentions.

What is indicated here is that one needs to *know* and make a *union*. First, one must know the two sides of love, *AVI* and *YESHSUT*. *AVI* are called the "big and great ones in *Hassadim*," whereas *YESHSUT* is called "the Master of the World," for it contains judgment and restriction.

After man has attained both degrees of love and merited perfect love, he needs to know that there is a great Master who governs the entire world, and to unite this knowledge every day by using the six Supernal limbs, sides, that is, to raise *MAN* to *ZON de Atzilut*, and *ZON* will raise their *MAN* to *YESHSUT*. As a result, *ZON* and *YESHSUT* will ascend and unite with *Partzuf AVI*. This common *Partzuf* has six Supernal sides-limbs, for they all clothe *VAK*, the six lower *Sefirot* of *AA*.

Because of this unity, *YESHSUT* ascends above *Parsa de AA*, to the place from the *Peh* down to the *Chazeh*, the place of the Supernal Waters. This is the permanent place of *AVI*, and the place where Light is revealed. When *YESHSUT* is filled with this Light, it passes it to *ZON*, which pass it on to the lower worlds, leading to the revelation of *Ohr Hassadim* in all the worlds. This is the secret of the union of "Hear, O Israel."

393

The six words: "**Hear**, O **Israel**, the **Lord** is **our** Creator, the **Lord** is **One**" constitute the six sides of ZON, which need to be united so as to unite them with the six Supernal sides, that is, AVI and YESHSUT. And man must direct his intentions and NRN upwards, so they, too, would unite with Supernal unity, just as MAN.

To achieve unity in VAK *de* ZA, in its six sides, the word "one" must be prolonged, meaning to receive *Ohr Hochma* within it, for *Ohr Hochma* descends from *Ein Sof* (infinity) to Supernal VAK, i.e., to AVI and YESHSUT, and unites VAK *de* ZA with the Light of *Ein Sof*. This is because the *Gematria* (numerical value) of the Hebrew word *Echad* (one) is *Aleph* + *Chet* + *Dalet* = 1 + 8 + 4 = 13, which indicates reception of *Ohr Hochma*.

Hence, while pronouncing the word "one," one should intend to draw *Ohr Hochma* to VAK *de* ZA. However, this unity lacks the intention to receive the Light of GAR in ZA, but only to enlarge its VAK through unity with the Supernal VAK, and to receive VAK *de Gadlut*.

**205. It is therefore written, "Let the waters under the Heavens be gathered together onto one place." This means that all the degrees under the Heavens will gather onto one place, to become perfect in the six ends. Therewith, fear must be attached to the unity of the words: "Hear, O Israel," which is done by prolonging the pronunciation of the letter *Dalet* in the word *Echad*. This is why the letter *Dalet* in the word *Echad* is written larger than the other letters. It is written, "Let the dry land appear," to let the letter *Dalet* (designating dry land) be attached to that unity.**

As was already explained, the unity contained in the words "Hear, O Israel" refers to the reception of *Gadlut* by VAK. This is because "one place" signifies the Supernal VAK, where the Light of *Ein Sof* shines within *Ohr Hochma*, under the Heavens (*Bina*), with regard to the earth (ZA). The words "onto one place" imply the unification of all the six Upper and lower sides, so the lower *Partzufim* will receive *Ohr Hochma* and unite with VAK *de* ZA, but only as VAK *de Gadlut*.

As we have already clarified, there are two kinds of fear and two kinds of love: the Upper fear and love are called AVI, whereas the lower fear and love are called YESHSUT. However, perfection is attained only by attaining both degrees together. Hence, the Light is concealed in YESHSUT, so the lower kind of love ("even if He takes away the soul") will be revealed. But even in this case, fear must cling to love and prevent the hardening of the heart; only then does one reveal perfect love, merges with AVI and YESHSUT, and receives the complete Creator's goodness.

In the unity of "Hear, O Israel," and after ZON ascend and unite with their properties in the six Upper sides to receive within them the "Great Love" in the word "one," they receive the Light that was made on the first day of creation, of which it is written: "And the Creator said, 'Let there be Light'" (*Beresheet*, 1:3).

And to all of this unity one must attach fear, since he needs to reveal and receive the Light that is deliberately concealed in *YESHSUT*, so as to unite the lower love and fear, for they still cannot be considered perfect.

Therefore, it is said that one should prolong the pronunciation of the *Dalet* in the word *Echad* (one) when reciting the prayer, *Shema Israel, Adonay Eloheinu, Adonay EchaD-D-D!* (Hear, O Israel, the Lord is our Creator, the Lord is One). In this case, the letter *Dalet* is written in large font. This is because big letters refer to *Tvuna*, and the big *Dalet* in the word *Echad* indicates that its place is in *Tvuna*, and that the Light is concealed there. By attracting it, not by utterance, of course, but by the spiritual action, man unites its concealment with the lower fear and love.

AND THE DRY LAND APPEARED means that there is no perfection in the Upper fear and love, expressed in the six words of the prayer "Hear, O Israel" with the help of the word "one." These words correspond to "Let there be Light," until the unity of fear and love is achieved below. This unity is revealed in the Light that is concealed in *Tvuna*, designated by the letter *Dalet* (D) in the word *Echad.*

Therefore, after the WATERS GATHERED TOGETHER ONTO ONE PLACE, signifying the descent of *Ohr Hochma* into the six parts of ZA, DRY LAND APPEARED. It denotes the letter *Dalet* in the word *Echad*, which should be pronounced with (spiritual) prolongation, with the aim to turn it into land through the concealment of the Light.

All of this is essential in order to unite the D, *Tvuna*, with *AVI*, resulting in the descent of the Light to *VAK de* ZON, so that love could be made perfect.

**206. After *Malchut* unites with ZA Above (in VAK de ZON), they must now be united below, in the masses, i.e., in all six sides of *Malchut*, in the words, BARUCH SHEM KVOD MALCHUTO LEOLAM VAED (Blessed be the great name of His kingdom for ever and ever), which contain six other words of unity. And then, what was dry land will become fertile soil, yielding fruit and plant.**

After the Supernal union is achieved, when the letter *Dalet* in the word *Echad* becomes whole Above, in *AVI*, it is essential to unite the *Dalet* in the word *Echad* below, in *VAK*, in the six aspects of *Nukva de* ZA (Rachel), who stands from *Chazeh de* ZA and below. All 600,000 souls of Israel, called "the inhabitants of *Nukva*," are included in Rachel.

After ZA unites in the Light of *AVI*, and the concealment of *Tvuna* (in the words DRY LAND APPEARED or in the letter *Dalet*) is revealed in him, *Nukva* must be filled with these two revelations. This is designated by the six words, *BARUCH SHEM KVOD MALCHUTO LEOLAM VAED*, corresponding to the six *Sefirot HGT NHY* of *Nukva*.

It was already explained that the Light was concealed in order to reveal both sides of love—good and evil. Yet, neither side of love, good or evil, can be revealed through concealment, but only through revelation of judgment. Before judgment was revealed, the letter *Dalet* in the word *Echad* was DRY LAND—utterly useless. This is because it emerged from the Light due to the concealment. Even fear to unite in the lower fear and love, which supplement the Upper fear and love was absent from it, for the judgment that reveals the lower fear and love was not yet revealed.

Strictness and judgment are located in the legs of *Partzuf* Leah, which are included in the *Rosh* of *Partzuf* Rachel. ZA has two *Nukvaot* (plural for *Nukva*): Leah (above his *Chazeh*) and Rachel (below his *Chazeh*). Leah's legs end at the *Chazeh de* ZA and touch Rachel's *Rosh*.

**World of Atzilut**

| | | |
|---|---|---|
| Atik | | |
| AA | | |
| AVI | | |
| YESHSUT | | |
| Nukvaot of ZA | | ZA |
| Leah: | Head | Head |
| | Body | Mouth |
| | Legs | Chest |
| Rachel: | Head | Chest |
| | Body | Legs |
| | Legs | Feet |

— — — — — — — — — Parsa
Worlds of BYA
— — — — — — — — — Machsom
Our World

Since strictness and judgment are located at the end of the legs of *Partzuf* Leah, this affects only *Partzuf* Rachel, as each spiritual property acts only from the place of its manifestation and below. Therefore, the concealment in the lower love and fear manifests only in the place in Rachel where the force of strictness and judgment is manifested.

Prior to the revelation of judgment, the letter *Dalet* in the word *Echad* was dry land, a place that is unfit for living. Now, however, after the descent of *Partzuf* Rachel into *VAK*, below *Chazeh de* ZA, the dry land became fertile, suitable for settlement and cultivation of fruits. In other words, the lower love and fear were revealed in it in completion and perfection. And they complement the Upper love and fear, so that all are perfect on both sides, for that is when all the goodness is revealed in *AVI*.

It is therefore said, THE CREATOR CALLED THE DRY LAND EARTH-ERETZ (the word *Eretz* is derived from *Ratzon*—desire), for it is the property of the letter *Dalet* in the word *Echad* in the six *Sefirot* (sides) of *Nukva de* ZA (where the property of strictness and judgment is already revealed). The letter *Dalet* that was in DRY LAND and made its property inanimate and unfit to live on turns into EARTH in *Nukva de* ZA (as a result of a *Zivug* with ZA), can now be settled and cultivated; hence, the Creator called it "earth."

**207. It is written, AND THE CREATOR CALLED THE DRY LAND EARTH. This refers to the same unity below, by the words, BLESSED BE HIS GREAT NAME FOR EVER AND EVER, when the earth, called "desire," became what it should be. For the word "earth" (*Eretz*) means desire (*Ratzon*). Hence, the expression IT WAS GOOD appears twice on the third day of creation: once for the Upper unity and once for the lower. For *Malchut* merges with both sides of ZA—with *VAK de* ZA and with her own *VAK*. Henceforth, the earth brings forth grass, for it has been corrected to yield fruit.**

The Upper unity (described by the words, WATERS GATHERED TOGETHER ONTO ONE PLACE) passes the Light that was created on the first day of creation from Above downwards, from the six Upper sides of *AVI* to *VAK de* ZA. This is called by the first word, IT WAS GOOD, uttered by the Creator on the third day of creation.

And then occurs the lower unity, designated by the verse, BLESSED BE HIS GREAT NAME FOR EVER AND EVER. This means that the letter *Dalet* in the word *Echad* attains perfection only from the six sides of *Nukva*, as described by the verses, AND THE CREATOR CALLED THE DRY LAND EARTH and

THE EARTH SHALL BRING FORTH GRASS, for in *VAK de Nukva*, DRY LAND turned to EARTH, yielding fruits.

With regard to this unity of *VAK de Nukva*, the Creator said, IT WAS GOOD, for the second time on the third day of creation. It follows that when IT WAS GOOD is said for the first time, it refers to the Upper unity. And the second time refers to the lower. Because of the lower unity, both sides of love achieve perfection, and the Light of *AVI* descends to *VAK de Nukva*, and bears fruit for the 600,000 souls of Israel that inhabit her.

# THE FOURTH COMMANDMENT

**208.** The fourth *Mitzva* is to know that *HaVaYaH* (the Creator) is *Elokim* (Lord), as it is written: KNOW THIS DAY AND LAY IT IN YOUR HEART THAT *HaVaYaH*-CREATOR IS *ELOKIM*—LORD. That is, the name *Elokim* is included in the name of the *HaVaYaH*, and there is no distinction between them.

*HaVaYaH* is ZA, and *Elokim* is *Nukva de* ZA. It is essential to unite ZA with *Nukva* by making their properties similar, so there is no distinction between them. Thus, the name *Elokim* of *Nukva* will be included in the name *HaVaYaH* of ZA, so that *Nukva* herself will become as *HaVaYaH*.

This union signifies the reception of *Ohr Hochma* (GAR) in ZON, for the union implied by the words HEAR, O ISRAEL is the reception of the Light of VAK from AVI in ZON. The unity in question here is the reception from AVI in ZON of the Light of GAR (*Hochma*). One can never receive an entire degree in one go: first VAK is received, and only then GAR.

**209.** Hence, it is written, "Let the stars in Heaven shine upon the earth." This means that both names, *HaVaYaH* and *ELOKIM*, are as one. This way, *Malchut* (*Elokim*) should merge with the name *HaVaYaH* (ZA). The black Light (*Malchut*) with the white Light (ZA), as one, without distinction. The white cloud by day (ZA) with the pillar of fire by night (*Malchut*); the property of day (ZA) merged with the property of night (*Malchut*), so they shine as one star.

*Nukva* is called "a small star." Initially, there were two stars, ZA and *Malchut*, and both were the same size. But the moon (*Malchut*) complained that two stars cannot use one crown (source of Light). The Creator reply to *Malchut* was, "Go and diminish yourself" (Talmud, *Hulin*, 60:2).

As a result, the nine lower *Sefirot* of *Malchut* descended below the *Parsa* to the world of *Beria*, and only one *Sefira*, *Keter de Malchut*, remained in the world of *Atzilut*. The task of the righteous is to elevate the nine lower *Sefirot* of *Malchut* from the world of *Beria* to the level of ZA, to correct her distinction from ZA, i.e., to grow and make her equal to ZA once more, so she will make a *Zivug* with ZA face to face. Thus, they shall correct the detachment of *Malchut* from ZA that was born of the moon's complaint.

The moon complained because it was unable to receive the Light directly from *Ima*, but only via ZA. Hence, the Creator gave it His advice: diminish yourself to a point (the *Sefira Keter*) and lower the nine *Sefirot* from *Hochma* to *Malchut* below the *Parsa*. Then, through the unity of "Hear, O Israel," rebuild *Malchut* in VAK, in the lower unity of "Blessed be His great name for ever and ever," for the power of judgment within it corrects the letter *Dalet* in the word *Echad*, turning the DRY LAND into the fruit-yielding EARTH.

Therefore, the now black point of *Malchut* that caused its fall became as important as Light, for it is precisely the strictness of judgment that builds the letter *Dalet* in the word *Echad* and makes it fruit-bearing. And if *Malchut* had not had this power of judgment, the letter *Dalet* in the word *Echad* (*Tvuna*) would have remained DRY LAND. Hence, when the Light spreads inside her, the power of judgment and restriction becomes more important than Light itself, for it becomes the cause, the source of the Light of VAK, *Ohr Hassadim*.

Thus, it is now possible to receive *Ohr Hochma* in VAK *de Malchut*, while elevating ZON to AVI. For now, just like ZA, *Nukva* can unite with AVI in her properties. This was the basis of her previous complaint, for the Light-restricting power within her turned into the cause of the Light's diffusion. Hence, ZA and *Malchut* are considered a single whole: each of them constitutes the source of Light for the other, whereas previously, *Malchut* was completely dependent on ZA, and therefore felt humiliated.

As a result of the union between ZA and *Nukva* in AVI, ZA connects to *Aba*, and *Nukva* to *Ima*. ZA turns into white clouds in the daylight and *Nukva* turns into a pillar of fire in the Light of night, i.e., the properties of day and night merge into one property, as it is written: AND THERE WAS EVENING AND THERE WAS MORNING, ONE DAY. Together they illuminate the earth and those who inhabit *Nukva* in the worlds of BYA.

**210. This is the sin of the primeval serpent that unites below but separates Above; hence, it caused what it caused to the world. What should be united Above, should be separated below. The black light, which is *Malchut*, should be united Above with ZA into a single whole and then separate it from the "evil side."**

The union and fulfillment of ZON with *Ohr Hochma* occurs only when they ascend to *AVI*, above *Chazeh de AA*, where ZA merges with *Aba* and *Nukva* merges with *Ima*. As a result, they unite, and ZA passes *Ohr Hochma* to *Malchut*. However, in the permanent place of ZON, below *Chazeh de AA*, they cannot form a union and allow *Nukva* to receive *Ohr Hochma*.

This is exactly what provoked Adam's sin and allowed the Serpent to bring death into the world (cause the disappearance of *Ohr Hochma* from *Malchut*), by compelling Adam and Chava (Eve) to make a *Zivug* (union) in the permanent place of ZON, below *Chazeh de AA*. As a result, the Upper *Zivug* stopped in *AVI*, as ZA started passing *Ohr Hochma* from *AVI* down to *Malchut*.

Thus, all the parts (souls) of *Malchut* existing in the world stopped receiving *Ohr Hochma* from *AVI*. This is regarded as death, for as soon as the impure forces approach ZON to draw their *Ohr Hochma*, *AVI* immediately terminate their *Zivug* for the sake of ZON, to prevent the impure force from clinging to ZON. And as soon as *Ohr Hochma* departs from ZON, the impure force leaves them at once, for it approaches ZON with the sole purpose of feeding on *Ohr Hochma*.

However, after being in *Ima* and receiving *Ohr Hochma*, *Malchut* descends to her permanent place and passes this Light to the souls of the righteous, called the "inhabitants of *Malchut*." She unites with them via equivalence of their properties, for in the absence of unity with ZA below, *Malchut* draws far from the evil side and the impure forces cannot receive from her.

**211. Nevertheless, one should know that *Elokim* and *HaVaYaH* are one, without distinction. *HaVaYaH* is *Elokim*. If man knows that all is one and does not cause any separation, then even the opposite, impure forces disappear from the world, instead of descending below.**

Although there is fear that a *Zivug* will occur in ZON in their place below, this is no cause to stop aspiring for a *Zivug* Above, in *AVI*. Moreover, one must attain that *HaVaYaH* is *Elokim*, which is achieved by uniting ZA with *Nukva*. And if man raises his MAN, thereby causing ZON to ascend to *AVI* and unite there, the impure forces are completely rejected by the Light, weaken and finally disappear from the world.

**212. The secret behind the word *Me'orot*, which consists of the words *Mavet* (death) and *Ohr* (Light), is that the impure forces follow knowledge, understanding, and thought. And this is Light, which is the opposite from death—*Mavet*, for the Light (*Ohr*) is inside death—*Mavet* (spelled as *Me'ot*) in**

the word ME'ohrOT. This alludes to the fact that Light separates death, but when Light disappears, the letters unite and form the word "death."

The impure forces follow reason (knowledge, understanding, and thought). Reason signifies "Light," and the impure force is "death," where Light connects the letters, while death separates them.

Here is the explanation of this: the power of restriction in *Malchut* is the source of the emergence of the impure forces. Because ZON united with AVI so as to receive the Light of VAK and GAR, the power of restriction in *Malchut* turned into Light by receiving the Light of VAK in the union below. Then, it ascended to AVI once more, and *Malchut* merged with ZA at the degree of AVI.

This union Above is designated by the word *Me'orot* = *Ohr* + *Mavet*. As a result of the Light of VAK and GAR descending to *Nukva* in the union with ZA at the level of AVI, the power of restriction in *Malchut* turns into Light, and all the impure forces that were created by this restriction disappear, for their root turns to Light. Consequently, the letters of the word *Mavet* of the impure forces disappear, and the words *Me'ohrot Ohr* appear instead.

213. Chava started with these letters, and brought evil into the world. As it is written, the woman SAW that it was good to bring the letters of the word *Me'ohrot* back. From there she took the letters *Vav-Tav-Reish-Aleph*, leaving only the letters Mem and Vav. And they took with them the letter Tav, thus forming the word Mem-Vav-Tav (*Mavet*—death). And they brought death into the world.

Thanks to the unity of the letters in the word *Me'ohrot*, designating the reception of *Ohr Hochma* in ZON, in the unity of ZON Above, the received Light separates the letters of *Mavet* in AVI, for it shines within them and forms a new combination of the letters *Me'ohrot*. And if ZON make a union below, at their permanent place, the Light disappears from the combination of letters *Me'ohrot*, and the word *Mavet* (death) remains.

AND THE WOMAN SAW THAT THE TREE WAS GOOD (*Beresheet*, 3:6). The Hebrew equivalent for the words "and saw" is *Vetir'e* = *Vav-Tav-Reish-Aleph*. These are the letters that depart from the word *Me'ohrot* (stars), leaving only *Mem-Vav*. They attach the letter *Tav* (*Nukva* of the impure forces) and form the word *Mavet*—the name for *Klipot*.

Chava drew these letters from the word *Me'ohrot*, meaning she followed the serpent's advice to unite ZON at their place below. In doing so, she violated the holy union of the letters in the word *Me'ohrot*, for the union of ZON below immediately causes the separation of *AVI* and the word *Me'ohrot* into *Ohr* (Light) and *Mavet* (death).

The impure forces, called "death," contain a male part, called "Sam," and a female part, called "Lilit." The letter *Mem* is the male part of the word *MaveT*, called "Sam," and the letter *Tav* is its female part, called "Lilit." Thus, there was a *Zivug* between the male and female parts, the letters *Mem*, *Tav* and *Yesod* (*Vav*), forming the word *MaVeT*, as the name of the impure force.

This signifies the appearance of the serpent before Chava, and the transference of impurity from it to her. As she followed its advice, the letter *Tav* entered her, splitting the word *Ohr* (Light) and combining the letters into the word *Vetir'e* (AND SAW). Then, the male part of the impure force (*Mem-Vav*) appeared and made a *Zivug* with *Tav*, which was already present in Chava; thus, death (*MaVeT*) appeared in the world.

**214. And look: said Rabbi Elazar: "My father, I have learned that after Chava had removed the letters *VeTiR'E* from the word *Me'ohrot*, the letters *Mem* and *Vav* did not remain. Only the letter *Mem* remained, for the letter *Vav*, which is the letter of life, turned into death. This occurred because it attached the letter *Tav* to itself, thus forming the word *MaVeT*." He replied: "Blessed are you, my son!"**

Rabbi Elazar answered that the letter *Mem* remained alone, without the letter *Vav*, for *Vav* designates *Yesod*, whereas Sam (the male part of the impure forces) lacks *Yesod*; hence, it is written that it is unable to procreate offspring, akin to a castrated man. The letter *Vav* designates *Yesod*, the place of a *Zivug*, the union of the male and female parts of ZON. The letter *Vav* always designates life, *Yesod* of the pure forces, whose *Zivug* bears fruit, for it is made on the screen that stands in *Yesod*.

Here, the pure letter *Vav* became impure and turned into *Yesod* of the impure force, *MaVeT*. After *Vav* received from *Yesod* of the pure forces, it united in a *Zivug* with *Tav*, and the word *MaVeT* was formed. This was precisely the sin of Adam, which defiled the pure *Vav*.

# THE FIFTH COMMANDMENT

**215. The fifth *Mitzva*.** It is written: LET THE WATERS SWARM WITH SWARMS OF LIVING CREATURES (*Beresheet,* 1:20). This verse contains three *Mitzvot*. The first is to study the Torah, the second is to procreate and multiply, and the third is to remove the foreskin on the eighth day. And it is necessary to study the Torah on all the days, at all times, in order to correct one's soul and spirit.

The four previous *Mitzvot* originate in the first four days of creation, and are intended for the correction of the degrees *H-B-ZA-M* of the world of *Atzilut*.

The **First Mitzva** originates from the word BERESHEET (*Bina*, fear of the Great and Mighty Creator, who rules over all), referring only to *GAR de Bina* that is located in *AVI*. The position of *AVI* is from *Peh* to *Chazeh de AA*, *Yod* of the name *HaVaYaH*.

The **Second Mitzva** originates from the words LET THERE BE LIGHT, and is meant for the correction of *ZAT de Bina* (called *YESHSUT*), located from *Chazeh* to *Tabur de AA*, i.e., below its *Parsa*. However, when it is said, LET THERE BE LIGHT, this means that *YESHSUT* ascended and united with *AVI*, forming one *Partzuf* above *Chazeh de AA*. And from there they ascended to *Rosh de AA*.

Such a state (degree) is called "Great love," designated by the first letter (*Hey*) of the name *HaVaYaH*: *Yod-Hey-Vav-Hey*, and the Light passes from it to *ZON*. However, *ZON* cannot receive *Ohr Hochma* from *AVI*, for they are *GAR de Bina* and will always remain only with *Ohr Hassadim*, unwilling to receive, hence their name, "fear."

*ZON*, however, receive *Ohr Hochma* from *ZAT de Bina* (*YESHSUT*), which ascended above *Parsa de AA*, called "Great love." However, *YESHSUT*, which stand below *Parsa de AA*, cannot pass *Ohr Hochma* to *ZA*, for *Ohr Hochma* is concealed within them. Also, their *Tvuna* is called DRY LAND.

The **Third Mitzva** originates from the two stars that were created on the third day of creation, of which it is written: LET THE WATERS UNDER THE HEAVENS BE GATHERED TOGETHER ONTO ONE PLACE, AND LET THE DRY LAND APPEAR... and LET THE EARTH BRING FORTH GRASS. This Mitzva is intended for the correction of VAK de ZON, whose union Above stems from the verse, LET THE WATERS, referring to ZA, whereas the union below stems from the verse, LET THE EARTH PUT FORTH GRASS, and refers to VAK de Nukva.

The **Fourth Mitzva** originates from the verse, LET THE STARS, and is meant for the correction of GAR in ZA and Malchut. Thus, all the corrections necessary for AVI, YESHSUT and ZON de Atzilut have already taken place in the first four days of creation. ZON received GAR (Ohr Hochma), and, being of equal height, can now make a Zivug face to face. Therefore, the rest of the Mitzvot are intended for this Zivug of ZON.

The **Fifth Mitzva** is LET THE WATERS SWARM WITH SWARMS OF LIVING CREATURES. Now there is a need to bring ZON to a perfect face-to-face Zivug, i.e., (i) to receive Ohr Neshama onto this Zivug, so that Adam, too, will receive this Light and make a holy and pure Zivug, which is attained by man's efforts in the study of the Torah; (ii) to give birth to holy souls; and (iii) to correct the holy covenant by circumcision and rejection.

Man's efforts lie in that he studies the Torah, although he realizes that he does not attain it (receives nothing in his corrected desires, called Guf, body). He merely utters its words with his "mouth" (not yet able to receive the Light (Torah) in his body for the Creator's sake), but as a result, he attains Ohr Nefesh.

Man's efforts should correspond to his readiness to do everything in his power to attain and understand the Torah, which causes him to attain Ohr Ruach. However, he must not limit himself to such attainments, but rather multiply his efforts so as to attain Ohr Neshama. Thus, every day he must aspire to correct his Nefesh and Ruach, and by increasing them, attain Neshama.

**216. Because man labors in the study of the Torah, he corrects the other holy soul, as it is written, SWARMS OF LIVING CREATURES, referring to the life-giving holy soul, Malchut. For when man does not study the Torah, he lacks the holy soul and the holiness that descends from Above. Yet, when he does study the Torah, he merits its Light, just like holy angels.**

Nukva de ZA that makes a face-to-face Zivug with ZA in the state of Gadlut is called "living," for ZA is then called the "Tree of Life." Consequently, Nukva is called "Life." By raising MAN during the study of Torah for the Creator's sake, man causes ZON to make a *Zivug* and receives *Ohr Nefesh* from it. And if he does not study the Torah for the Creator's sake, he cannot even attain *Ohr Nefesh*, for he fails to bring about the Creator's *Zivug* with the *Shechina*. And a *Zivug* can be attained only by raising MAN.

It is therefore written: LET THE WATERS SWARM WITH SWARMS OF LIVING CREATURES, for the Torah is called "water." If man raises MAN with the help of the Torah, he merits *Ohr Nefesh* (holy spirit) from *Ohr Haya* (Life). Moreover, he merges with the Creator only after he attains *Nefesh*, *Ruach*, and *Neshama* from HAYA (Supernal holy life). He unites *Ohr Nefesh* with *Ohr Ruach*, *Ohr Ruach* with *Ohr Neshama*, and *Ohr Neshama* with the Creator.

**217. It is written, "Angels of the Creator shall bless Him." This refers to those who study the Torah, as they are called His angels on earth. It is also written, BIRDS SOARING OVER THE EARTH. This refers to this world. However, in the world to come, as it is said, the Creator will make them wings like those of an eagle so they may soar in the whole world.**

Why does *The Zohar* mention angels? Because angels are spiritual forces—mechanical enactors of the Creator's will. They were repeatedly compared to animals in our world (e.g., a horse) that fulfill man's will. Angels are spiritual forces without freedom or egoism; hence, they never sin and have no need for the Torah, which is why they are spiritually inanimate, motionless—they do not grow spiritually.

Man is created in such a way that before he carries out any task, he needs to realize what he is supposed to do. But angels carry out their assignments even before they hear and understand what the Creator wants from them, for His desire rules over them. Hence, nothing prevents them from instant fulfillment of His will. They always follow the Creator, just like man's shadow follows him. This is why they are believed to act before they even hear.

Man can therefore act like an angel (even though his desires are of egoistic nature) if his desires become like those of angels, whose actions precede their understanding (hearing). Just like an angel, such a person fulfills all the Creator's desires before he realizes, hears and understands them, for he follows the Creator as a shadow follows man.

This can be illustrated by the following example: when a strong wind throws dust in one's eyes, he quickly shuts them, even before his brain and thoughts feel and realize the need to do so: the action (shutting the eyes) precedes the actual realization of the thought of dust.

Although the physical body of such a person exists together with us in this world, his spiritual body (desires) becomes angel-like, and his actions precede his hearing. He does not need to hear in order to fulfill the Creator's will, but observes any Mitzva even before his brain realizes what he is doing. Therefore, he is regarded as an angel.

Hence, The Zohar says that in the future the Creator will provide him with wings to enable him to soar over the whole world. For until man attains the holy soul (Ohr Nefesh—the smallest spiritual Light), the impure force rules over him, as the prophet said: "The souls of your enemies, them shall he sling out, as from the hollow of a sling" (Shmuel I, 25:29).

Hence, one cannot merge with the Creator and observe His desires (Mitzvot) until he has acquired faith in the Creator's names and knows that He is absolutely good to all and bestows only goodness. And if one has not yet attained the holy soul, and the impure force still rules over him, when his thoughts soar above the world, it seems to him as though the Creator's rule is not quite as good as it should be according to His names. This feeling of his brings corruption to the Creator's holy names, and he cannot find a quiet place for himself, cannot have faith in His names and draw closer to Him.

Therefore, he stains himself with such impurity that it leads him toward lack of faith in the Creator and in His names. However, nothing of this affects the spiritual; it occurs simply because man has not yet attained the spiritual realm, and is making no effort to do so.

But as soon as he receives the holy soul (Ohr Nefesh), his body (desires and thoughts) instantly becomes angel-like: his actions precede realization. It is written about such a person: "And the birds shall soar above the earth," for in the future, the Creator will give him wings, and he will soar above the whole world.

For he soars mentally above the whole world and sees how the Creator governs all. Yet, not only does he not err when seeing the manifestation of this governance, he receives the strength to raise MAN to increase his spiritual anti-egoistic powers. By looking upon all the forms of the Creator's rule over this world and, seeing the harshness of the external manifestations of this rule, such a person is given an opportunity to ask for the strengthening of his faith. And owing to his faith in the Creator's unity and absolute kindness of His rule, he raises MAN and receives increasingly greater Light for the Creator's sake.

**218. It is written in this regard: LET BIRDS SOAR OVER THE EARTH, for the Torah, called THE WATERS, will SWARM WITH SWARMS OF LIVING CREATURES from its place of life, Malchut, and all will descend**

down below. This is what King David referred to, when he said, **THE CREATOR CREATED IN ME A PURE HEART** to study The Torah, and **A HOLY SPIRIT WAS RENEWED WITHIN ME.**

So as to continue to explain the aforementioned text, *The Zohar* compares the Torah to water—just as living creatures emerged from water, in the same way the Light of life descends from *Malchut* (called "life") upon the entire world. This is the Light for which King David asked the Creator. He begged for a pure heart in order to study the Torah and raise *MAN*, for this would lead him to the reception of the holy spirit of renewal—the strength to merge with the Creator even more.

# THE SIXTH COMMANDMENT

**219. The sixth *Mitzva* is to procreate and multiply, for he who does so turns the stream, called *Yesod de ZA*, into an inexhaustible fountain. And the sea, *Malchut*, shall be filled from all directions, and new souls shall come forth from that tree, and a multitude of forces shall appear together with those souls, to guard them. Hence, it is written: LET THE WATERS SWARM WITH SWARMS OF LIVING CREATURES. This is the mark of the holy Covenant. The stream grows stronger, turns into a river, and thus brings more and more new souls to life.**

An awakening from below causes an awakening from Above: raising MAN, the prayers and requests of the lower ones to receive strength so they can perform spiritual, altruistic actions, stimulate a *Zivug* Above between the Creator and the *Shechina*. As a result, the stream, *Yesod de ZA*, fills with water and descends to *Nukva de ZA*, filling her on all sides, wishing to both revive all the worlds (to bestow *Ohr Hassadim*) and bear new souls (pass *Ohr Hochma* downward, for birth is possible only in *Ohr Hochma*).

There are two kinds of *Zivugim de ZON*: (i) a "*Zivug* of existence" on *Ohr Hassadim*, from which *Ohr Hassadim* descends to provide the lower souls with what they need for their existence. This *Zivug* on *Ohr Hassadim* also gives birth to angels. (ii) A "*Zivug* of birth" on *Ohr Hochma*, which leads to the creation of new *Partzufim*, new human souls.

These new souls emerge from the Tree (ZA). However, although they are called new, the genuinely new souls originate in the world of *Ein Sof* (Infinity), whereas these souls were already within Adam, and fell into the impure forces as a result of his sin. Now they are revived with the help of the Tree of Life (ZA); hence, they are called "new souls." A multitude of other forces, called Heavenly hosts or armies, descends along with them. But completely new souls descend to the world only after the correction of Adam's sin has been completed.

*Yesod de ZA* is called a "covenant," because we (*Malchut*, souls) feel and receive from it all the Light of our life. It constitutes the source of our life, descending to us from the Tree of Life (ZA). ZA ascends to *AVI* (called "garden") in order to take the waters from them and fill *Malchut*, his *Nukva*. A *Zivug* on VAK (*Hassadim*) is called WATERS SWARM, and a *Zivug* on GAR (*Hochma*) is called LIVING CREATURES.

**220. A number of birds (angels) that soar above the whole world enter *Malchut* along with those souls. When a soul comes into this world, the bird that came from that tree along with that soul accompanies it. How many angels leave with each soul? Two: one on the right, and one on the left. If one so merits, they guard him, as it is written: FOR HE WILL GIVE HIS ANGELS CHARGE OVER YOU. Yet, if he does not merit, they report and accuse him. Rabbi Pinchas said: "There are three angels that guard man, if he so merits, as it is written, IF THERE BE AN ANGEL OVER HIM, A DEFENDER, ONE AMONG A THOUSAND THAT WARNS MAN. If there be an ANGEL—is the first; A DEFENDER—is the second; one among a thousand THAT WARNS man—is the third."**

**221. Rabbi Shimon said: "In all, there are five angels, for the verse continues: 'there is one after the giver and two more, so in all there are five.'" He replied: "This is not so. 'The giver' refers solely to the Creator Himself, and not to an angel, for only the Creator is permitted to give, but no one else."**

A number of angels come forth together with the begotten souls. These angels are called "soaring" or "flying." They help the souls to sentence to the scale of merit, or, conversely, complain to the Creator about these souls, and push them toward the scale of sin, which entails punishments. These angels soar above the world, see how the Creator rules over all, and report all this to the soul. If the soul so merits, it sentences itself and the entire world to the scale of merit; if not, it sentences itself and the entire world to the scale of sin.

Therefore, Rabbi Pinchas does not dispute Rabbi Shimon when he says that only two angels are born with a soul. Rather, he says that as long as there are only two angels in man, he cannot sentence to the scale of merit completely, and keeps moving between the scales of sin (punishment) and merit (reward). However, through one's good deeds, the third angel is born within him, which enables man to sentence everything to the scale of merit. Hence, only with the help of the three angels can he achieve his correction.

222. And he who abstains from procreating and multiplying belittles (so to speak) the form that includes all other forms, the form of man, causes that stream, *Yesod* of **ZA**, to dry out, and harms the holy Covenant (*Yesod* of **ZA**) from all sides. It is written of such a man, "Go forth and look upon the corpses of those that have transgressed against the Creator." Of course, those who transgress against Me. This is said about the body, as the soul never even enters the screen, i.e., the Creator's domain. And such a man shall be banished from the world.

*Malchut* is called a "form," a "property" that contains all of the other properties, for all the forms of *NRN* of the righteous and of the angels in the three worlds of *BYA* originate from her. They constitute all the hosts and armies. And those that do not procreate and multiply thereby diminish the form of *Malchut* and prevent her from using all of her hosts and armies. For with the help of *MAN* that the lower ones raise, the Light descends from Above and stimulates a *Zivug* between the Creator and the *Shechina*. This *Zivug* creates *NRN*—the souls of the righteous and the angels in the worlds of *BYA*.

And those that impede this *Zivug* cause the stream (*Yesod* of *ZA*) to dry out and stop the flow of its male waters into the holy *Shechina*, *Malchut*. In doing so, they harm the holy covenant in all of its properties, for they delay the two parts of the *Zivug*: *VAK* (on *Ohr Hassadim*) and *GAR* (on *Ohr Hochma*).

This is because the *Mitzva* of procreation and multiplication constantly develops the soul. As a result, man defeats his body forever, so it can rise again during the resurrection from the dead. And he who abstains from procreating and multiplying turns his body into a corpse, of which it is written: GO FORTH AND LOOK UPON THE CORPSES OF THE PEOPLE, for his soul will not be able to enter the Creator's domain and merge with Him. Thus, he is rejected from the world to come.

# THE SEVENTH COMMANDMENT

**223. The seventh *Mitzva* is to perform circumcision on the eighth day, and thus remove the impurity of the foreskin, for *Malchut* constitutes the eighth degree of all the degrees, beginning with *Bina*. And the soul that soars from her must appear before her on the eighth day; hence, she constitutes the eighth degree.**

*Nukva de ZA* is called *Haya* if she rises and clothes *Ima-Bina*, the eighth degree from *Malchut* (provided that you count all ten *Sefirot* from below upwards). *Malchut* is hence called "the eighth," for she ascended eight degrees, from her own place to that of *Bina*. And when she reaches *Bina*, she receives the name *Haya*, just like *Bina*.

Therefore, man's soul, which is born in *Malchut* (that ascended to *Bina*), must appear before *Malchut* in all the appropriate corrections of circumcision, removal of the foreskin and the rolling up of its remains, on the eighth day from its birth in *Malchut*. This is because then it becomes clear that it is a soul that was born from none other than the holy degree of *Haya*.

Because of the force of circumcision and rolling up, man's soul sloughs the impure force, and the soul can receive the perfection of *Ohr Haya*. LET THE WATERS SWARM—thus *Malchut* receives the Supernal male waters from ZON, and is filled with them.

**224. It then becomes clear that the type of this soul is *Haya*. That is, belonging to that holy degree of *Haya* (*Malchut*), and not to any other degree. And this is implied by, LET THE WATERS SWARM, as is explained in the book of Hanoch, the waters of the holy seed merge in the properties of the soul of *Haya*. And it is the property of the letter *Yod*, marked on the sacred flesh, more than any other mark that exists in the world.**

Because of the circumcision, the Supernal male waters fill man's soul the way they were received in *Nukva* (called "the soul of *Haya*"). The Upper World, called *Bina*, is designated by the letter *Yod*, and the lower world, *Malchut*, is designated by the letter *Hey*—its property. However, as *Malchut* ascends to *Bina*, the letter *Hey* disappears from her, and, just like *Bina*, turns into *Yod*.

Similarly, through man's observance of the *Mitzva* of spiritual circumcision, the letter *Hey* disappears, and just like in the *Nukva* that ascended to *Bina*, the property of the letter *Yod* appears in him instead. And if man's body acquires the property of *Yod*, he can receive the soul of *Haya* from *Nukva*.

**225. The verse, LET BIRDS SOAR OVER THE EARTH, refers to Eliyahu, who flies across the whole world in four flights in order to be present in the place, where the Holy Covenant is made. And a chair must be prepared for him, and it must be said out loud, THIS IS THE CHAIR OF ELIYAHU. For this is not done so, he will not appear in that place.**

Angels originate from *AVI*; hence, they remain exclusively in the sky and consist of *HGT NHY*. Therefore, when they appear in this world to fulfill their tasks, they are said to make six flights, for they clothe in six *Sefirot*.

However, Eliyahu stems from *Malchut* (not from *AVI*). Hence, he is constantly connected to the earth. And since *Malchut* contains only four *Sefirot* of ZA, for her position is parallel to the *Sefirot TNHY* (*Tifferet-Netzah-Hod-Yesod*, pronounced, Tanhi) from *Chazeh de* ZA downward, it is written that Eliyahu flies on four flights, i.e., by clothing in *Sefirot TNHY*.

Under no circumstances should one interpret the words about Eliyahu's presence at every rite of circumcision literally. Yet, if he is obliged to be there, why should he be invited?

*The Zohar* explains this in another place (*Shlach*, 18): there are four impure forces, called "Stormy Wind," "Great Cloud," "Blazing Flame," and *Noga*. The lowest of them, Stormy Wind, is at the center, as though clothed by Great Cloud, which is in turn clothed by Blazing Flame. And they are all clothed from the outside by *Noga*.

All the worlds, forces, and everything that was ever created exists within man. And these are our spiritual forces, by which we can attain the goal of creation. The first three impure forces are completely impure (egoistic). Whereas *Noga* is half good and half evil. But how is that possible if the spiritual is always true? How can it be half good (altruistic) and half evil (egoistic) at the same time?

In fact, this is impossible. *Noga* is a neutral force that can be used by the pure force (then *Noga* is considered good) or by the impure force (and then it is considered evil). Hence, *Noga* is called "half good and half evil" although neutral in itself. It may be attached to either pure or impure forces, and this depends entirely on man.

### MAN'S SPIRITUAL FORCES

| | |
|---|---|
| Pure | - altruistic |
| Noga | - neutral |
| Blazing Flame | - egoistic |
| Great Cloud | - egoistic |
| Stormy Wind | - egoistic |

These four impure forces are located at the end of each spiritual *Partzuf*, in its *Sefira Yesod*. The *Sefira Yesod* has two layers of skin, one atop of the other. One layer is called *Orla*, and contains the three impure forces. The other is called *Preia*, and this is *Noga*.

The first man, Adam, was born circumcised, meaning that he did not have the three impure forces at all—he was completely unaware of his egoistic desires. In other words, they could not cling to him. *Noga* prevailed in him, in his sensations. Yet, since it was separated from the three impure forces and attached to the pure force (Adam's altruistic desires), *Noga* itself was considered completely good.

The three impure forces are collectively called the Serpent. These three impure desires were roused in Adam and tempted him to use them. In so doing, Adam attracted the *Orla* to himself, as it is described in the Talmud (*Sanhedrin,* 38:2). As soon as he attached *Orla* to himself, his pure soul (the Light of the world of *Atzilut*) immediately disappeared, for his desires became egoistic, and he fell with his properties (desires) to the world of *Assiya*, to its lowest degree, called "this world," and was condemned to death (disappearance of the Supernal spiritual Light).

Therefore, it is written about him that since he violated the prohibition of not eating the fruits of the Tree of Knowledge, he attached the *Orla* to himself. Consequently, the impure desires acquired both layers of skin on the *Sefira Yesod* of *Partzuf* Adam, and *Preia*, called *Noga*, became impure, too, because of its contact with the *Orla*, with the three impure forces. However, there is a distinction between them, which lies in the fact that prior to Adam's sin, *Preia* was pure, and all of its impurity stems from its contact with the *Orla*.

Accordingly, there are two types of correction: circumcision and rolling up of the remaining skin. The *Orla* must be cut off and cast in the dust, since only thus can man free himself from these egoistic desires. *Preia*, however, can be left attached to *Yesod*. But the skin around the *Sefira Yesod* must be rolled up. This is a special spiritual action that frees the *Preia* from the impure forces remaining in it. Hence, this action causes the Light to return to the *Partzuf*. This Light previously disappeared because of the egoistic desires that ruled in the *Partzuf* before the spiritual circumcision took place.

However, this is still insufficient for the fulfillment of the spiritual *Partzuf*, Adam, with the Light, as it was before he sinned, i.e. used the Serpent's impure forces and tasted the forbidden fruit from the Tree of Knowledge (received *Ohr Hochma* in egoistic desires). For now, after Adam's sin and fall, a special angel by the name of SAM makes accusations and complaints against man.

To neutralize the power of SAM, Eliyahu took upon himself his role of a prosecutor, and was thereby granted an opportunity to defend Israel (one who aspires to the Creator) when he circumcises himself (his egoistic desires).

Hence, it is said that Eliyahu must be present at each rite of circumcision (Hebrew, *Brit Mila*—the Covenant with the Creator). For since it is he, rather than SAM, who complains to the Creator about Israel's neglect of their Covenant, he can also testify that when Israel aspires to the Creator, it is loyal to the covenant. As a result, the Light returns to the *Partzuf*.

This is why, besides the chair occupied by the man who holds the baby (*Sandak*–godfather), one more chair must be prepared for the prophet Eliyahu. For the chair designates the beginning of correction, the influence of the Upper One on the lower one. The first chair, on which the *Sandak* sits, belongs to the Creator, for the filling of Light as the result of the circumcision and the rolling up of the impure forces. The second chair is saved for Eliyahu, so he can neutralize the impure forces' complaints to the Creator against man, so they would not be able to accuse man.

However, to make Eliyahu appear, one must say out loud: THIS IS THE CHAIR OF ELIYAHU. The thing is that a male baby is circumcised on the eighth day after *Shabbat* (*Malchut* with the Light of AVI, called "holy") has passed over him. Since the sloughed desires (*Orla*) are cast away, the impure force sees that it is given a part of the Creator's Covenant. Because of this gift, it stops complaining and accusing man. On the contrary, it begins to advocate him before the Creator.

The spiritual desires (objects) pass their properties from one to another. Since the *Orla* was attached to *Yesod*, after the circumcision (separation from *Yesod*) it takes part of the pure desires with it. And since we throw it to the dust, to the impure forces, they draw from it that weak Light, which they can receive from the circumcision and the rolling up.

This is why the impure forces stop complaining against Israel, and no longer wish to destroy this Light, for in so doing they will lose the part that they draw from it. Thus, they become defenders of the pure forces, to allow the pure forces to be filled with Light.

Yet, Eliyahu cannot bear this correction, for although the *Klipa* stops impeding and slandering Israel, it takes part of the Light for itself in return. To correct this, Eliyahu takes upon himself all the accusations against Israel, and refuses to give anything from the pure to the impure forces.

Thus, although the impure force stopped complaining against Israel, and actually became its defender, Eliyahu himself continues to accuse in order to wrest all the power from the impure forces and fully separate them from the pure. Hence, a chair must be prepared for Eliyahu, for it is he who fully separates the impure forces from the pure ones.

One must therefore verbalize the words: THIS IS THE CHAIR OF ELIYAHU. For after the circumcision, part of the Light still remains in the impure forces, and the mention of Eliyahu completely deprives them of any contact with the Light.

Thus, if man does not express his desire to detach himself completely from the impure forces, through his own effort (by the screen positioned in *Peh*), it does not happen, even though the first chair belongs to the Creator. This is because the Creator starts the process of creation (makes His foundation in the form of a chair), and man continues and corrects his nature by performing altruistic deeds.

**226. And the Creator created great Leviathans. They were two: *Orla* and *Preia*, male and female forces, and all living creatures. This is the mark of the Holy Covenant, the soul of the holy *Ohr Haya*, as it is written, LET THE WATERS SWARM, the Supernal Waters that descend to this Covenant.**

Leviathan and his wife designate that which is opposite from *Orla* and *Preia*. They are also called *Nachash* (Serpent) and Alcaton (his wife). *Orla* is the Serpent, and *Nachash* is the male part that must be cut off and committed to dust. *Preia* is the correction, liberation from the Serpent's female part, Alcaton. Through these corrections, *Ohr Haya* of AVI descends from Above.

**227. The reason why Israel below is marked in the holy form, similar to its form from Above, is to separate the pure part from the impure, to distinguish**

between the holiness of Israel and the other nations that originate from the other side. And just as Israel was marked, so were the animals and birds—to determine which of them belong to Israel, and which belong to the nations of the world. Happy is the lot of Israel!

Man's attitude toward all the living creatures in our world is similar to the attitude of the general spiritual creation, called "man," toward his parts. This is because Adam includes absolutely everything within his spiritual body. And there is nothing except for this spiritual *Partzuf*, called "man" or "Adam."

All spiritual objects, angels, souls, both pure and impure forces are parts of Adam's body. All that is described in Kabbalah speaks only of the spiritual world, of one creature called "man," Adam. Adam's various parts, his various desires—are called "Israel," "nations of the world," "pure animals," "impure animals," and so forth.

All that man must do in our world (for every one of us was created in the image of Adam, recreating Adam's entire *Partzuf* within him) is build a pure, altruistic *Partzuf* within him. This is done by cutting off all of the egoistic desires in his heart, and separating the pure from the impure in all his desires, on all the levels of his soul.

# THE EIGHTH COMMANDMENT

**228. The eighth *Mitzva* is to love an outsider from another nation, who desires to come under the wings of the *Shechina, Malchut,* who takes under her wings those who separate themselves from the other, impure side, and draw near her, as it is written: LET THE EARTH BRING FORTH A LIVING SOUL AFTER ITS KIND.**

*Malchut, Nukva de ZA,* is called the *Shechina,* for she does not distance from us even when our properties are distant from her, as it is said: WHEREVER YOU ARE BANISHED, THE *SHECHINA* WILL BE WITH YOU, and ABIDES IN THEM, IN THEIR IMPURITY. ZA is called *Shochen* (dweller) and *Nukva* is called *Shechina.*

The revelation of the Creator in *Malchut,* of the *Shochen* in the *Shechina,* of ZA in *Malchut* of the world of *Atzilut* is possible only by a face-to-face *Zivug* of ZON in *Gadlut.* This is because the Light of this *Zivug* is so great that it reveals unity even in the most remote and concealed places, in the most opposite and uncorrected desires.

However, the creation of *Gadlut de ZON* occurs gradually: first, a *Partzuf* of ZON in *Katnut* is created with the Light of VAK, and only then does it grow to reach *Gadlut.* Moreover, this process takes place in each state of ZON. Furthermore, even as ZON in *Gadlut* make a *Zivug* and receive *Ohr Hochma,* the Light from their previous state of *Katnut* does not disappear, but facilitates a *Zivug* in *Gadlut.* And this Light of *Katnut* is called the "Wings of *Shechina.*"

Hence, it is written in the Torah: "And the cherubim shall spread out their wings on High, screening the ark-cover with their wings" (*Shemot,* 25:20). For the main thing is to cover the Light of the great *Zivug* with their wings, so that even the most distant ones would receive the Light, and, at the same time, keep it out of the reach of the impure forces.

This is so because those who have yet to completely purify their egoistic desires are rejected by the Light for fear that the Light may fall to the impure forces. But now the wings guard the Light so vigilantly that even the closest ones will not err and let the Light through to the impure forces.

Therefore, an outsider is one who decides to join the people of Israel (to correct his egoistic desires and make them altruistic), and to be circumcised (reject his egoistic desires), for his body (collection of desires) still retains the properties of the *Orla*, as his ancestors (previous spiritual states) did not stand at the foot of Mount Sinai (did not receive the Light, called the Torah, and were not corrected by it), i.e., have not yet rid themselves of the serpent's impurity (have neither revealed all the impure egoistic desires within them nor recognized them as evil). Nevertheless, other altruistic desires have the power to elevate him to the level of Supernal purity.

This occurs through raising MAN, by evoking the great *Zivug* of ZON (where the Wings of *Shechina* rule and cover the Light of this *Zivug*). We can also elevate the outsider's soul (his yet uncorrected desires) to that level and sanctify it in the Light of this *Zivug*.

And although this soul is not yet completely pure, it can receive the Light from this *Zivug*, for the wings protect it and do not allow its Light through to the impure forces (desires), even though they are very close to it. And it is said, UNDER THE WINGS OF *SHECHINA*, for this soul can receive the Light only from the wings of *Malchut-Shechina*, i.e., receive only the small, outer Light of *Malchut*. This is not the Light in the body of *Malchut* (*Shechina*) herself, let alone that of ZA (the Creator, *Shochen*). Rather, it is merely the Light of the Wings of *Shechina*.

The outsider's soul (his egoistic desires) can be corrected (made altruistic) only during the great *Zivug*, for only then is the Light protected by the Wings of *Shechina*. Hence, we (altruistic desires) must first raise MAN for the great *Zivug*, and receive its Light in our souls (desires corrected by the screen). Then, the *Shechina* spreads her wings, protects this *Zivug*, and takes the outsider's soul under them. It follows that initially, we elevate the outsider's soul with the help of our MAN, and then the *Shechina* takes it under her wings.

**229. One might say that the soul of *Haya* exists in Israel and is ready for anything. He specified, "After its kind," which refers to both Israel and to an outsider. Like chambers and passages between them, the same exists in the land called *Haya*, under the wings.**

Here *The Zohar* tells us that although the new soul (the corrected properties called the "outsider") receives the Light, just like the properties called "Israel," Israel receives from the inner Light, whereas the outsider receives from the outer. It was already mentioned that wings designate the Light of *VAK*, received during the great *Zivug*, but from the previous state of *Katnut*, so as to cover the Light of the great *Zivug*.

This *VAK* includes *Sefirot HGT NHY*, where *HGT* are called "chambers," in which one can abide and sit (sitting means *Katnut* as opposed to standing, which is *Gadlut*). The *Sefirot NHY* are called "passages," entrances to the chambers, and it is impossible to sit there; their only role is to allow access to the chambers.

The reason for this lies in the property of *Tifferet*, the main *Sefira* in *HGT*. *Tifferet* is their middle line, a complete *Kli* for the reception of *Ohr Hassadim*. And the main *Sefira* in *NHY* is *Yesod*, which constitutes their middle line. It contains no property of the receiving *Kli*, and is used only for passing the Light onto *Malchut*, for the creation of the Reflected Light. Hence, *NHY* are called "entrances."

As for the outsiders (to purify from egoistic desires) from the seventy nations of the world (seventy egoistic properties), the chambers in *HGT* of the wings, as well as the passages in *NHY* of the wings are prepared for them. They receive *Ohr Nefesh* from the passages (*NHY*) and *Ohr Ruach* from the chambers (*HGT*).

**230. The right wing of Malchut has two passages, which are split from this wing in two so as to let in two nations that are close to Israel. And under the left wing there are two additional passages, called Amon and Moav. And they are all called the souls of Haya.**

Previously, *The Zohar* mentioned that there are many entrances-passages, yet now it speaks of only two. This is because it speaks in general: there are two entrances for the nations belonging to the right line, and two entrances for the nations belonging to the left line. There are also two nations in all of the right line, which include all the nations of the right side, and there are two nations of the left line, which include all the nations of the left side.

The nations of the right side refer to the two general passages in the right wing. And *The Zohar* does not reveal what these nations are. And as for the nations of the left side, generally called "Amon and Moav," there are two passages in the left wing that are meant for them.

All the souls of the outsiders that come from all the nations are collectively called *Nefesh Haya*, for they can receive only from the great *Zivug* of *ZON* when

ZON are inside AVI. Thus, *Malchut* is called *Nefesh Haya*, for she receives *Ohr Haya* from AVI. And since the souls (*Nefashot*) of the outsiders receive from the wings of *Nefesh Haya*, they are named after the received Light.

231. **Each wing contains a multitude of closed chambers and halls. From them, spirits emerge and are divided among all the outsiders, called *Nefesh Haya*, but each "after his kind." And they all come under the wings of the Shechina, but no further.**

Each wing includes *VAK* (*HGT NHY*), called "passages" and "chambers." Each nation has its own chamber in *HGT* and its own passage in *NHY*. Each receives *Nefesh* in the passages and *Ruach* in the chambers. It is written that the chambers are closed, since *HGT de VAK* have only *Ohr Hassadim* without any *Ohr Hochma*; hence, they are called "closed."

232. **However, the soul of Israel stems from the body of that tree (ZA), and from there the souls fly off to this land (*Malchut*). Therefore, Israel is the darling son of Malchut, and is sustained by her womb, and not by the wings that are on the outside of the body. Moreover, the outsiders have no part in the Holy Tree (ZA), especially not in its body. They refer only to the wings of Malchut, and no further. The outsider's place is under the wings of the Shechina, and no further. The righteous among the outsiders also refer to the outer side, and not to the inner. It is hence written: LET THE EARTH BRING FORTH A LIVING SOUL (*Nefesh Haya*) AFTER ITS KIND. All receive Nefesh from that Haya, but each according to its kind.**

ZA is referred to as the "Tree of Life" and his *Nukva* is called the "Land of Life." For in the state of *Gadlut*, they both ascend and clothe *AVI*, who have *Ohr Haya* (the Light of Life). Therefore, it is said that the soul of Israel stems from the body of that tree, meaning from ZA himself.

And the souls from that tree fly off to the Land of Life: as a result of a *Zivug* between the tree (ZA) and the land (*Malchut*), ZA gives the souls of Israel into *Nukva*, and Israel receives these souls from her, as opposed to the outsiders, who receive their souls from the wings of *Malchut*, but not from *Malchut* herself, not from what ZA passed to *Malchut*.

The reason for this is that *Nukva* has three *Partzufim*, which clothe one another. They are called *Ibur* (embryo), *Yenika* (nursing), and *Mochin* (adulthood, *Gadlut*). The big (*Mochin*) *Partzuf* is the innermost of the three, and is clothed by *Partzuf Yenika*, which is in turn clothed by *Ibur*.

Israel receives from the innermost *Partzuf* (*Gadlut* of *Nukva*); hence, it is called the "darling son," for it stems from the inner part of *Malchut*, and not from her outer part (wings).

*NHY de Malchut* are called "womb," for it is the place where the souls of Israel are conceived and grown. However, this does not refer to the *NHY* of the two outer *Partzufim*, called *Ibur* and *Yenika*, as they are the wings of the *Shechina-Malchut*. Here *The Zohar* refers to the *NHY* of the *Partzuf* in *Gadlut*, the innermost *Partzuf* (the womb of *Malchut*).

This is what the words of the prophet refer to: "Is Ephraim a darling son unto Me? Is he a child that is dandled? For as often as I speak of him, I do earnestly remember him still; therefore, My heart yearns for him, I will surely have compassion upon him" (*Yirmiyahu*, 31:19). Because the souls of Israel stem from the inner part of *Malchut*, *The Zohar* says that they appeared from *Malchut*'s womb, from *NHY* of the *Partzuf* in *Gadlut*, and not from *NHY* of the two outer *Partzufim*, called "wings."

The outsiders (desires for correction) have no part in the Supernal Tree, especially not in its body. Their place is under the wings of the *Shechina*, and no further. The outsiders that come (to correct themselves) are called righteous, for the *Shechina* is also called the "righteous one." They come under her wings and unite within her. Yet, they have no place above the *Shechina*, and receive from *Nefesh Haya*, from a *Zivug* of *Malchut* with ZA in *Gadlut*. But they only receive the portion of the Light called "wings"; hence, they are said to be under the wings of the *Shechina*, where each receives according to his properties.

# THE NINTH COMMANDMENT

233. The ninth *Mitzva* is to show mercy to the needy and supply them with food, as it is written: LET US MAKE MAN IN OUR IMAGE, AFTER OUR LIKENESS, and this man will consist of two parts, male and female. IN OUR IMAGE refers to the rich; AFTER OUR LIKENESS refers to the poor.

234. For from the male side, they are rich, but from the female side, they are poor. And as they are united together, merciful to each other, and help each other, so below should the rich and the poor be united as one, and should share with each other, and show mercy to one another.

235. We see this in the book of King Shlomo (Solomon): he who shows mercy to the poor with all his heart, his image never differs from that of Adam, the first man. And since he was created in the image of Adam, he therefore governs all the creatures on earth by his image, as it is written: "And the fear of you and the dread of you shall be upon every beast of the earth" (*Beresheet*, 9:2), all fear that image, existing in him. For this *Mitzva*, to show mercy to the poor, is the most important of all the *Mitzvot* for elevating man to the image of Adam.

236. How do we know this? From Nebuchadnezzar. Even though he dreamt a dream, as long as he had mercy upon the poor, that dream did not come true. However, as soon as he started looking badly upon the poor, his image changed at once, and he distanced from people. Hence, it is written, LET US MAKE MAN. It is said in the form as it was said of charity in another verse. Therefore, MAKE—is the same as charity.

The rich and the poor correspond to the male and the female principles, to ZA and his *Nukva*. However, there is nothing here that hints at the obligation of the rich to be merciful to the poor and provide for his needs. But this instruction differs from the rest in that in all the others, the Creator's command is separated

427

from the action that follows it, as it is written, AND THE CREATOR SAID: 'LET THERE BE LIGHT. AND THERE WAS LIGHT;' and also, AND THE CREATOR SAID: 'LET THE WATERS BE GATHERED...' AND IT WAS SO; and so on in all the *Mitzvot*.

And none of the other *Mitzvot* contain the Creator's instruction mixed with action. This is so because the entire creation originated from *AVI*, where *Aba* spoke and *Ima* acted—*Aba* gave the Light to *Ima*, and after he gave it to her, he started acting on it himself. For only with the property of *Aba* could creation not have manifested in action, as there are no boundaries in creation, in which actions could be revealed.

Hence, *Aba* issues a command that designates the passage of Light from him to *Ima*. However, since this is merely a command, and not an action (like a force instead of an action), the future tense is used. The same language is used in the description of man's creation: AND THE CREATOR SAID, "LET US CREATE MAN." Note that the plural form is used: LET US CREATE.

Before the creation of the world of *Atzilut* (called the world of correction), an action known as *Shevirat HaKelim* (the breaking of the vessels in the world of *Nekudim*) took place in the spiritual worlds. It is written: "The Creator kept creating and destroying worlds, until He created this world (*Atzilut*), and He told it to stop spreading below the boundaries in which it was created" (*Beresheet Raba*, 3:7).

The breaking of the vessels was essential, for it was the only opportunity to mix the egoistic properties (desires) with the altruistic ones; after all, distance in the spiritual is determined by the disparity of properties (desires). And that is why egoism and altruism are infinitely remote from each other. Yet, if this is so, how can egoism possibly be corrected? How can such properties or even notions of the existence of altruistic desires be introduced to man?

So then, to allow egoistic desires to be corrected, the Creator performed the breaking of the vessels—the striking impact between opposite desires, egoistic and altruistic. It is called "striking," for it is impossible to unite these desires by any means other than an "explosion."

As a result of this explosion, the altruistic, pure *Kelim* (desires) penetrated the egoistic, impure ones, and gave man an opportunity for free will and self-correction. After the destruction of the pure *Kli* and the descent of its parts into impurity, the world of *Atzilut* was formed.

Out of all the mixed desires, the world of *Atzilut* selected only altruistic ones, attached them to itself, corrected them and filled them with Light. Out of these corrected parts, it made the worlds *BYA* with everything that exists within them.

These corrections of the broken and mixed *Kelim* by the world of *Atzilut* are depicted in the first chapter of the Torah, which speaks of creation. It uses the instructions of exposing and separating the egoistic *Kelim* from the altruistic ones, as, for instance, in the following verses: AND THE CREATOR DIVIDED LIGHT FROM DARKNESS; THE CREATOR DIVIDED WATERS FROM DRY LAND; THE CREATOR DIVIDED DAY FROM NIGHT, and so forth. All these examples speak of the separation of the pure forces from the impure ones, of good from evil. And all that diverged became part of the pure system.

Therefore, the entire act of creation is contained in the depiction of the first day of creation, in the words, LET THERE BE LIGHT, as this is when Light was separated from darkness. This is because, on the whole, purity is called "Light" and impurity is called "darkness." And all the other definitions of purity and impurity are only particular names designating their various manifestations.

The world of *Atzilut* made only a partial correction: it only separated altruistic desires from egoistic desires, Light from darkness, and thus created the system of creation, described in the beginning of the Torah. However, this does not complete the correction, as darkness and impurity are simply detached from participating in creation, but remain utterly uncorrected. They are simply separated as an entirely unnecessary part, and this completely defies the perfection of the Creator, who created everything (including darkness) for His final goal. Moreover, correction ends specifically with the correction of darkness, as it is said: "Night shines as day; darkness as Light." (*Tehilim*, 139:12).

To correct this, man was created containing everything, and consisting of all the properties of creation: from the absolute goodness to total evil. This enables man to execute the correction and achieve complete perfection. In other words, he must turn evil to good, bitter to sweet, and darkness to Light. As a result, death will disappear forever, and the Creator will manifest as the King of all creation.

Hence, there is a great difference between the description of man's creation and that of all the other creatures and parts of creation. Here, the action itself was mixed with the instructions, for the instructions, descriptions come from *Ima*, not from *Aba*, who said, LET US CREATE MAN—together with *Malchut* of the world of *Atzilut*.

The reason for this is that *Malchut* includes everything, for she also gives the Light of sustenance to the impure forces to keep them from disappearing from the world, as, like all the other elements of creation, the impure forces cannot exist without Light, and immediately disappear. It is written in this regard: HER FEET DESCEND TO DEATH, for the impure forces receive a tiny spark of Light to sustain their existence.

This is why *Malchut* is called *Assiya* (action), for she spreads and rules in the whole of creation. She is also called "darkness," for she shines with a spark of Light, to sustain the darkness and evil.

Hence, when *Ima* unites with *Malchut* and their properties mix, she receives the properties of darkness, of which it is said: LET US CREATE MAN IN OUR IMAGE, AFTER OUR LIKENESS, for Light is called "image," and darkness is called "likeness." Indeed, after *Ima* mixes with *Malchut*, these two forces, IMAGE and LIKENESS, appear in her as well. As a result, man, who was created by her, contains these two forces—IMAGE and LIKENESS, too.

From the phrase, LET US MAKE, it follows that *Ima* consists of two parts, male and female. Although *Ima* is a male part (giving is a male property), she is connected to *Malchut*. Besides, the male property suggests the presence of Light, while the property of *Nukva* (the female part) is poverty and darkness.

And since *Ima* accepted *Malchut* as her partner with the purpose of creating man (accepted the properties of *Malchut*), she is now filled with poverty and darkness. It follows that man consists of the properties of *Ima* (wealth and Light), as well as of the properties of *Malchut* (poverty and darkness).

And it is this precise combination of the properties of *Ima* and *Malchut* that enables man to correct *Malchut*, fill her with Light, and spread spiritual purity and holiness throughout the entire earth (*Malchut*). It is written that at the end of correction, "the Creator and His Name shall be one," for the darkness in *Malchut* will be transformed into Light, as in the male part, *HaVaYaH*. Everything will be as one in the male property, as it is said, "There will be no poor in your nation."

This *Mitzva* says that as *Ima* united with *Malchut* so as to correct her, which is why *Ima* includes Image and Likeness, man needs to correct his qualities in order to correct the parts of darkness within him. To this end, he must diminish his properties, just like *Ima*, and give his part (charity) to the poor *Malchut*, who is deprived of Light. He must show mercy to the LIKENESS (poverty) within him, and provide it with everything it needs.

By observing this *Mitzva*, man receives IMAGE and LIKENESS from *Ima*, the Upper Light that was received by Adam, created in IMAGE and LIKENESS. This is why he has the power to rule over all the animals in the world (all of his animal desires) to such an extent that no impure force (desire) remains within him, which he cannot defeat and correct.

*The Zohar* gives the example of Navuchadnetzar (Nebuchadnezzar): although the Supreme verdict with regard to him was reached, his dream did not come true as long as he was merciful to the poor. However, as soon as he allowed his evil eye to look badly upon the poor, the sentence was immediately executed, and his image changed (those who are interested can turn to *The Book of Daniel*). Thus we see that this *Mitzva* is greater than all the others, and that it can overrule the Supreme verdict made against man.

"Charity" signifies the union of *Bina* and *Malchut*. Similarly, the story about the marriage of Rut (Ruth) the Moavite, King David's grandmother (*Malchut*), and Boaz, who was merciful to her (this marriage started Israel's Royal Dynasty), describes the correction of *Malchut* by *Bina* (See *Megilat Rut— The Book of Ruth*).

# The Tenth Commandment

**237.** The tenth *Mitzva* obliges man to put on *Tefillin* and to attain the Supernal properties, as it is written, THE CREATOR CREATED MAN IN HIS OWN IMAGE. He opened and said, "Your head upon you is like the Carmel." This text refers to the Supernal head—the *Tefillin* worn on the head of the Holy, Supernal King *HaVaYaH*, written in separate letters. Each letter in the holy name *HaVaYaH* corresponds to a certain paragraph in the *Tefillin*. Thus, the Holy, Supernal Name is written in the scrolls of *Tefillin*, in the secrets of the letters. For THE NAME OF THE CREATOR IS UPON YOU, AND THEY SHALL BE AFRAID OF YOU refers to the head *Tefillin*, which contains the Holy Name *HaVaYaH*.

By being merciful to the poor, one merely begins to receive the Creator's Supernal image. *Bina* absorbs the properties of *Malchut*, described by the verse, LET US CREATE MAN IN OUR IMAGE, AFTER OUR LIKENESS. By unifying *Bina*'s properties with those of *Malchut*, *AHP de Bina* (the letters *ELEH*) fell to *ZON*, and only the letters *MI* (*GE*) remained in *Ima*. *AHP de Bina* that fell to *ZON* consist of *Aba* and *Ima*: *Aba* assumes the properties of *ZA*, and *Ima* assumes the properties of *Nukva*.

Since *AVI* descended to the place of *ZON*, they became like *ZON*. And from them *ZON* receive the state of *Katnut*, called *TZELEM Elokim*, likeness to *Bina* (*VAK*), for *Ima* lost the *GAR* of her own state, that is, since her *AHP* fell to *ZON*, she lost the Light of *GAR* (see diagram on next page).

Therefore, only the letters *MI* = *GE* = *K-H* remained in *Ima*, whereas her *B-ZA-M* = *AHP* = *ELEH* fell to *ZON*. Thus, of the five Lights *NRNHY* that were inside *Ima*, she retained only *Ohr Ruach* in *Keter* and *Ohr Nefesh* in *Hochma*. Thus, *Ima* can only give *ZON* the Light of *VAK* = *Ruach* + *Nefesh*, but not the Light of *GAR* = *NRNHY*. Also, *ZON* are considered to have acquired likeness to

433

the Upper One only upon receiving the Lights *NRNHY*. And this is achieved by the fulfillment of the *Mitzva* of *Tefillin*.

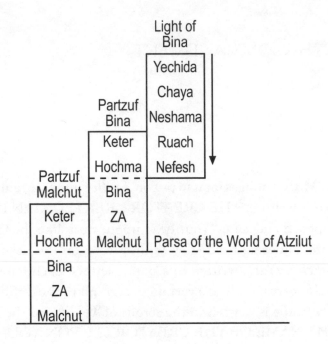

Yet, a question arises: we have already learned that to create the *Partzuf* of lower man out of ZON, ZON must ascend to *AVI* and receive the Light of *GAR*, for a small *Partzuf* without *Ohr Hochma* cannot beget. So why is it said that *Ima* is in a state of *Katnut*?

When ZON attain reception of the Light of *AVI*, they thereby ascend to *AVI* and become similar to *AVI* in their properties, for each lower one that ascends to the Upper One becomes like it. Indeed, only the magnitude of the screen distinguishes between spiritual objects, as only the magnitude of the screen determines all of the object's properties.

Thus, upon ascending and clothing *AVI*, ZON become like *AVI*, and all the properties of *AVI* are now naturally adopted by ZON. Just as *AVI* create ZON, ZON in *AVI* beget and pass the Light into the *Partzuf* of lower man. Hence, there is no need to even change names, for everything occurs at the degree of *AVI*. And upon ascending there, ZON are already called *AVI*, and the Light that they pass to man is regarded as the Light intended for ZON.

It is written: THE CREATOR CREATED MAN IN HIS OWN IMAGE. The Hebrew word "image" that is used in the Torah is *TzeLeM*, and is formed by three letters: *Tzadi-Lamed-Mem*. In item 2, we said that there are no *Kelim* for *Ohr*

*Haya* and *Yechida*; rather, there are only *Kelim Bina-ZA-Malchut* for the Lights NRN: *Nefesh-Ruach-Neshama*.

So even when we say that there is a *Kli* called *Keter*, we imply that the count starts with *Bina de Keter*, not with *Keter de Keter*. *Bina* and ZON, the *Kelim* that remained in the *Partzuf*, are divided into three lines: the line of *Bina—HBD*, the line of *ZA—HGT*, and the line of *Malchut—NHYM*. This is characteristic of *Ohr Hassadim*.

Bina - Hochma

Daat ———— Bina

Gevura - Hesed

Tifferet ———— ZA

Hod - Netzah

Yesod

Malchut ———— Malchut

However, when *Ohr Hochma* is transferred, *Partzuf Bina* divides into two *Partzufim*: AVI and YESHSUT. These constitute HBD = three and HGT = three. Along with ZAT = seven *Sefirot*, from *Hesed* to *Malchut*, and form the *Gematria* of thirteen (3 + 3 + 7) of the word *Echad*, which alludes to the complete name, state, and attainment.

The thing is that *Sefirot Keter* and *Hochma* are concealed in AA, and only its *Sefira Bina* sends her Light down. This *Sefira Bina de AA* is divided into two *Partzufim*, AVI and YESHSUT: her GAR shines in AVI and her ZAT shines in YESHSUT. These two parts of *Bina* are called M (*Mem*) and L (*Lamed*) of the word *TzeLeM*:

1. AVI are called M of the word *TzeLeM*, as they form a closed ring guarding *Ohr Hochma*, preventing it from reaching the other, lower *Partzufim*. This *Ohr Hochma* is referred to as "concealed" (from all the *Partzufim* of the world of *Atzilut*), and only *Ohr Hassadim*, *Ohr Ruach*, descends from them to all the *Partzufim* of the world of *Atzilut* during the 6,000 years until the end of correction.

2. YESHSUT is called L of the word *TzeLeM*, as it bows its head (GAR) and resembles a tower. It is written about this tower: "The Tower of Oz (strength) of the Creator's name." This is because YESHSUT is

called a "tower," and ZA is known as the "righteous one." After all, YESHSUT is ZAT *de Bina*, the properties of ZON that are included in *Bina*; hence, it passes its *Ohr Hochma* to ZON.

If ZON in *Katnut* are filled with *Ohr Hassadim* (*Ruach* called *Avir*—air), then during the reception of *Ohr Hochma* from YESHSUT, the letter *Yod* in the word *Avir* exits, and *Avir* turns into *Ohr* (Light). Hence, YESHSUT is called a "tower," i.e., a *Partzuf* in *Gadlut* that contains *Hochma*, soaring in the air (*Avir*).

However, this state in ZON is inconstant. YESHSUT intermittently returns to *Katnut* and to *Gadlut*; therefore, such a state is called "soaring." ZA is called *Tz* (*Tzadi*) of the word *TzeLeM*, for such is his property inside this tower. Thus:

- AVI—M (*Mem*)—*Hochma* that is concealed inside a ring.

- YESHSUT—L (*Lamed*)—*Bina*, though as she ascends to AA, she becomes *Hochma* (tower) and passes *Ohr Hochma* down.

- ZON—*Tz* (*Tzadi*)—*Daat*, receives the Light from YESHSUT.

However, one should not confuse the three letters *Tz-L-M* with the three lines called *HBD*: *TzeLeM* consists of three *Partzufim*, one inside the other. *Partzuf Hochma* (M of the *TzeLeM*, AVI) is the innermost *Partzuf*; *Partzuf Bina* (YESHSUT, L of the *TzeLeM*) clothes it from *Chazeh de AVI* downward; and from *Chazeh de YESHSUT* downwards, *Partzuf Bina* is clothed by *Partzuf Daat*, ZA, *Tz* of the word *TzeLeM*.

The words, THE CREATOR CREATED MAN IN HIS OWN IMAGE (*TzeLeM*), mean that with the help of the spiritual observance of the *Mitzva* of *Tefillin*, *Ohr Hochma* is received in accordance with the ascending order of the letters *Tz-L-M*. This is the Light that Adam received after his creation, whereas we first stimulate the reception of this Light in ZON, and from ZON we stimulate its reception into ourselves.

THE HEAD *TEFILLIN* CONTAINS THE NAME OF THE HOLY KING, INSCRIBED IN THE LETTERS *HaVaYaH*—the head *Tefillin* is the name of the Supernal King, inscribed in the letters *HaVaYaH*. The *Tefillin* are called the Carmel (*Car Maleh*—all goodness), as it is written: YOUR HEAD UPON YOU IS LIKE THE CARMEL. This is because when the heads of ZA and *Malchut* put on the head *Tefillin* (the Upper Light of *TzeLeM*), they become like the Carmel (*Car Maleh*—all goodness).

This Light is called "The name of the Supernal, Holy King," the four letters of *HaVaYaH*, where each letter is written separately: *Yod-Hey-Vav-Hey*. And the reason why man feels that the letters are written separately is that each

*Partzuf* contains the four letters of *HaVaYaH*, and each of them designates an independent *Partzuf*.

Every letter constitutes a separate passage on the parchment (in the *Tefillin*); four separate passages correspond to the four letters of *HaVaYaH*. A passage (Hebrew—*Parashah*) represents a separate and complete *Partzuf*, and its corresponding letter in *HaVaYaH* symbolizes the Light in this *Partzuf*. The order of *Partzufim* corresponds to the order of the letters of *HaVaYaH*: *Yod-Hey-Vav-Hey*. Such a *Tefillin* is called the *Tefillin* of *Rashi*.

However, there is a *Tefillin* with the order of passages (*Partzufim*) *Yod-Hey-Hey-Vav*, called *Tefillin Rabeinu Tam*. The passages that are written on fragments of parchment are identical, but the order of putting them into the boxes of *Tefillin Rabeinu Tam* is different: *Yod-Hey-Hey-Vav*.

**238. The first passage in the *Tefillin* corresponds to the letter Yod of the name *HaVaYaH* (Hochma) and refers to the Mitzva, "Sanctify to Me all the firstborn." This is because *Hochma* is the firstborn of all the Supernal Ones. It opens the place of conception for the future firstborn with the help of a thin line of Light that emanates from Yod, which opens the womb and impregnates it.**

*AVI* are designated by the letter *Yod* of the name *HaVaYaH*, where *Yod* signifies *Aba* and the filling of *Yod* (according to its pronunciation: *Yod* = *Yod* + *Vav* + *Dalet*), i.e., *Vav* + *Dalet* constitutes *Ima*. *Partzuf AVI* is called "holy" and "first born," for *Partzufim YESHSUT* and *ZON* are called holy only when they receive holiness (*Ohr Hochma*) from *AVI*. All the holiness in the world of *Atzilut* comes from *AVI*.

This is so because *Ohr Hochma* is called "holiness" and *AVI* is *Mem* of the word *TzeLeM* (*Hochma de Atzilut*), for the Supernal *Hochma* of the world of *Atzilut* is concealed within them. *AVI* themselves are defined as *Bina* in the property of *Hassadim*, as *Hochma* is concealed within *Rosh de AA*, and the lower ones can receive it only if *Bina* ascends to *Hochma*, to *Rosh de AA*, where *Bina* unites with *Hochma* of *Rosh de AA* and assumes the name *Hochma*. However, she is not the ordinary *Hochma*; she is called "*Hochma* of the thirty-two paths" of descending *Ohr Hochma*, and only this *Hochma* bestows *Ohr Hochma* upon all the *Partzufim* of the world of *Atzilut*.

This is why *The Zohar* says that this thin ray of Light, called the "path of Light," opens the womb and conceives the future offspring. *Yod* consists of three parts: (i) the upper "spike" of the letter *Yod*, a small line above the point, which is called *Rosh* and designates *Partzuf AA* that is concealed in *AVI*; (ii) the body of the *Yod*, which forms *Partzuf AVI*; and (iii) the lower "spike" of the letter, which designates *Yesod*, the end of *Partzuf AVI*.

Through the continuous *Zivug* between *Yesod de Aba* and *Yesod de Ima*, the great waters descend onto all the lower worlds with all that inhabits them. This *Zivug* on *Ohr Hassadim* is called a "*Zivug* that revives the worlds." *Yesod de Ima* is also called *Rechem* (womb), for all *Rachamim* (mercy) stems from this part of Its *Partzuf*. Yet, if *AVI* do not make a *Zivug*, this part of *Ima* is closed, and mercy does not descend below. Only *Yesod de Aba* can open *Yesod de Ima*, whereupon *Ima* passes her great waters to the lower ones.

**239. The second passage in the *Tefillin*, WHEN YOU COME, corresponds to the first letter Hey of the name HaVaYaH, the hall (Bina) that opens up under the influence of the letter Yod (Aba) in fifty entrances, passages, and chambers concealed within it. The revelation that Yod made in that hall was done so as to hear the voice of the Shofar (a ram's horn), Bina. The Shofar is closed on all sides, but the letter Yod came and opened it so that its sound could be heard. And since it opened the Shofar and derived sound from it, Yod led all to freedom.**

The letter *Hey* of the name *HaVaYaH* is *YESHSUT*, *L* in the word *TzeLeM*. It is called a "tower soaring in the air," a hall with fifty entrances, for the concealed *AVI* are designated by the *M* of *TzeLeM*, by the ring that surrounds *Ohr Hochma* and prevents it from shining outside. And they shine only with *Ohr Hassadim*.

However, by rising to *Rosh de AA*, where *Bina* turns into *Hochma*, *YESHSUT* can pass *Ohr Hochma* to *ZON*. *Bina*, who turns into *Hochma* in order to receive *Hochma* for *ZON*, is called the "fifty gates of *Bina*," for she consists of five *Sefirot KHB-ZA-M*, ten in each. Each of these fifty *Sefirot* consists of a chamber and an entrance: *HGT* are called a "chamber" and *NHY* are called an "entrance," a "passage," implying the absence of a *Kli* for reception. Instead, it serves for transferring the Light into, or out of the chamber.

Therefore, the second passage used in the *Tefillin*: AND WHEN YOU COME designates the letter *Hey* in the name *HaVaYaH*, *YESHSUT* of the world of *Atzilut*, which ascends to accept *Ohr Hochma* and pass it on to *ZON* below.

*Yod* opened this hall so as to hear the voice that comes from the ram's horn, for this horn is closed on all sides. As was already mentioned, *YESHSUT* (*Bina*) united with *Malchut* by lowering her three *Sefirot ELEH* (*Bina* and *ZON*) to *ZON*, while *YESHSUT* remained with only two *Sefirot K-H*, *MI*.

Then, as a result of raising *MAN*, *Malchut* descends from the *Eynaim* (eyes), the *Eynaim* of *YESHSUT* open up, *Malchut* descends to her own place in the *Peh*, and the three letters *ELEH* reunite with *MI* to form the name *ELOKIM*. *GE* = *K-H de ZON* ascend to *Bina* along with these *ELEH*. However, although *ELEH* ascended and joined *MI*, the name *ELOKIM* is still considered closed, for it has only *Ohr Hochma*, and *Ohr Hochma* cannot shine in *ELEH* without *Ohr Hassadim*.

These three letters *ELEH* are therefore defined as a horn (*Shofar*), and *ZON* that ascended to *Bina* along with *ELEH* are concealed within them. And these *ZON* in *ELEH* are referred to as a "voice." This voice sounds in the hall with the help of the letter *Yod*, for *Yod* designates *AVI* that bestow the Light from Above, which facilitates the lowering of *Malchut* from *Nikvey Eynaim de YESHSUT* to her place in the *Peh*, and raising *ELEH* back to *Bina*. Hence, *Yod* opens up the hall of Light in *YESHSUT* in order to pass this Light to *ZON* from the *Shofar* (the ascended letters *ELEH*).

*ZON*, too, ascend to *Bina* along with *ELEH* and there receive *Hochma*. This great Light in *ZA* is called a "voice," and its reception is known as "listening to the voice." However, this horn is closed on all sides, on the sides of *Hochma* and *Hassadim*, for the letters *ELEH* (called a "horn") fall to *ZON*, where they remain closed and inaccessible both to *Ohr Hochma* and to *Ohr Hassadim*.

Consequently, two corrections are needed: (i) to elevate and unite them with *Bina*, enabling them to once more attain their *Ohr Hochma*; (ii) to provide them with *Ohr Hassadim* so it can serve as a garment for *Ohr Hochma*.

First, *Yod* (*AVI*) pass the Light to *Hey* (*YESHSUT*), whereupon *ELEH* rise above *Malchut*, to *Bina*, together with *ZON*, and there receive *Ohr Hochma*. However, this *Ohr Hochma* is called concealed or closed, for it cannot shine without being clothed in *Ohr Hassadim*. This means that the voice has not yet emerged—*ZA* has not yet been born.

After that, *Yod* enters into the word Light = *Ohr*; hence, it turns into *Avir* = air (*Ohr Hassadim*). And since the horn (the letters *ELEH*) received air (*Ohr Hassadim*), they can beget *ZA* (the voice of the *Shofar*), for being clothed in *Ohr Hassadim*, *Ohr Hochma* can enter *ZA*.

The general Light that *ZA* receives is called "voice." And this voice frees all the slaves that were enslaved by the egoistic desires in all the worlds, for *ZA* shines down on all the lower ones. Thus, the sons of Israel (man's spiritual aspirations) merit the Light of deliverance (defeat the earthly, egoistic ones).

**240. At the sounds of the *Shofar*, the sons of Israel were delivered from Egypt. And so shall the *Shofar* be blown in the future, the next time at the end of days. And all deliverance originates from this *Shofar*, which is *Bina*. This is why the deliverance from Egypt is mentioned in this chapter of the Torah, for**

this *Shofar* stems from the force of the letter **Yod**, which opens the womb and delivers the captives to freedom. And this is the letter **Hey**, the second letter of the name *HaVaYaH*.

All of the Light in ZON comes from the horn (*ELEH*), including the great Light that delivers Israel from Egypt, and the Light that is destined to be revealed in the future, at the end of days (complete deliverance from egoism). This is why the *Tefillin* contain a passage that refers to the exodus from Egypt, for the Light delivering from Egypt comes from the horn, which is inside *YESHSUT*. This is done by the power of *AVI*, called *Yod de HaVaYaH*, which open the womb of *YESHSUT* (*ELEH*) and free the voice (ZA) from its captivity.

This Light has sufficient power to deliver Israel from slavery. Only after the attainment of this Light (*Ohr Haya*), and not a degree lower, can ZA and *Nukva* be called "voice" and "speech." All deliverance comes only from *Ohr Haya* (only upon ascending the spiritual degree of *Ohr Haya* can man liberate himself from egoism and become free).

**241. The third passage in the *Tefillin* is the secret of the Unity in "Hear O Israel," the letter Vav in *HaVaYaH*, which includes all and designates ZA, who contains the unity of all. Everything merges in unity within him, and he receives all. The fourth passage that reads, "You shall hear," includes two sides, Hesed and Gevura, which unite with the Assembly of Israel, called the lower Gevura or Malchut. And this is the last letter Hey of the name *HaVaYaH*, which takes and includes them all.**

The third passage in the *Tefillin* (Hear O Israel) is *Partzuf* ZA, the letter *Vav* in *HaVaYaH*, which includes all four passages contained in the *Tefillin*. Although the first two passages (*AVI* and *YESHSUT*) represent *Hochma* and *Bina*, they do not really constitute *Hochma* and *Bina* themselves, but rather, their part, which clothes in *Rosh de ZON*, called M and L of *TZeLeM de ZA*.

Similarly, the fourth passage, *Malchut* of ZA, does not imply that this is *Malchut* herself. Rather, it refers to her part that is included in ZA and is called *Mochin* (brain) *de Gevura*. There are three parts of *Mochin* in ZA: *Hochma*, *Bina*, and *Daat*, which are accordingly called M, L and *Tz* of *TzeLeM de ZA*. They are the same H-B-ZA-M as in *Mochin de ZA*. This is because *Daat* (*Tz*) includes *Hesed and Gevura*. And this *Hesed* in *Daat* is defined as ZA himself, and *Gevura* is defined as the inclusion (of the properties) of *Nukva* in ZA. And these H-B-ZA-M constitute the four passages contained in the *Tefillin*.

This is why ZA, the letter *Vav* in the name *HaVaYaH*, includes all four passages. And all the unions that come from *AVI* and *YESHSUT* are done within him, i.e., for his sake. For all the Higher *Partzufim* that precede ZA are united (with the Creator), and need no MAN from the lower ones to reach the state of unity. Whereas all the MAN raised by the lower ones to the Upper *Partzufim* are meant solely for the unification of ZA, and in no way affect the constant unity of the Higher *Partzufim* with the Creator.

The unification of *Hochma* with *Bina*, as a result of which *Bina* becomes like *Hochma*, occurs only on account of ZA being raised to *Bina* in the form of MAN. For when ZA is raised to *Bina* as MAN, *Bina* ascends to *Rosh de AA* and there receives *Hochma* for ZA. Since *Bina* aspires only to mercy (*Ohr Hassadim*), she never receives *Ohr Hochma* for the Creator's sake, but only if the lower ones are in need of it. Her role, her properties are only to bestow, and not to receive. (Note that in the spiritual, "reception" is always for the Creator's sake.)

Hence, *Bina* ascends to *Rosh de AA* only for the sake of ZON. And it is ZA alone that ascends to *Bina* and stimulates her to ascend to *Rosh de AA*, where she makes a *Zivug* with *Hochma* and passes this Light to him. It is therefore said that ZA receives all, as *Bina* passes everything that she receives in *Rosh de AA* to him. And *Ohr Hochma* is revealed only in the place of ZA (not *Bina*), as he descends back to his place below *Chazeh de ZA*.

The prayer "Hear O Israel" designates ZA, the letter *Vav* of the name *HaVaYaH*, the Supernal unity (item 207) that reveals love only from the good side. And since it refers only to "Love your Creator...," it contains no restrictions or strictness of judgment.

However, in the fourth passage, "You shall hear," the last *Hey* of the name *HaVaYaH*, *Nukva de ZA* that is included in him, *Gevura* in *Rosh de ZA*, reveals both sides of love—good, as well as evil (item 206), reflected in the words of this passage. It ends with the words: "Blessed be His great name for ever and ever," which corresponds to the inclusion and unity of *Nukva* in ZA, meaning not *Nukva* herself, but her part in ZA, i.e., *Mochin de Daat*.

*Gevura* in *Daat* is the second *Hey* in *HaVaYaH*. It accepts all the Light of the Supernal unity contained in "Hear O Israel," and includes all. And since it contains all the perfection of unity, it reveals all the Light and both sides of love, for the property of judgment that complements love to perfection exists only within it, and not Above.

It is therefore written: "Your head upon you is like the Carmel," designating the head *Tefillin*. Indeed, after ZA is clothed in all four Lights, designated by the four paragraphs of the *Tefillin*, which are the three letters *Tz*, *L*, and *M* of the word *TzeLeM*, his head is defined as the Carmel (*Car Maleh*—completely filled with goodness).

**242. *Tefillin* are the letters of the holy name. Therefore, "Your head upon you is like the Carmel" refers to the head *Tefillin*. The letter *Dalet* refers to the hand *Tefillin*, *Malchut*, who is depleted of Light, compared to the head *Tefillin*, *ZA*, but she contains the perfection of the Upper One.**

The hand *Tefillin* designates *Malchut*. And she is poor in comparison with *Bina*, the Upper World. Yet, she has her own perfection, for she now receives it from *Bina* thanks to the unity between *Nukva* and *ZA* in "Blessed be His great name for ever and ever."

And since she is not the *Nukva* that is included in *ZA* (his body), but a separate *Nukva* of *ZA*, she takes all four passages from him, *H-B-ZA-M* of *ZA*, for she has a separate, complete *Partzuf*. However, these four passages of the Torah are in the same place; they are not separated from each other by partitions, as in the *Tefillin* of *ZA*.

The reason for this is that a passage of the Torah is the Light, and the place where it dwells is a *Kli* (the *Tefillin* in our world is a box made of a "pure" animal's skin, into which four parchment scrolls are placed, and the corresponding passages from the Torah are written on each). As we know, every *Zivug* emanates Light. Since *ZA* receives four Lights *H-B-H-G* in four *Kelim*, as a result of four *Zivugim*, he contains four compartments for four passages, each compartment containing a particular passage from the Torah.

However, no *Zivug* is made on *Malchut* herself. Everything that *Malchut* has, she receives from *ZA*. *Malchut* receives all four Lights (four passages from the Torah that result from one *Zivug* with *ZA*); hence, she has only one place for all four passages (Lights).

**243. "The King is held captive in the tubs" means that he is tied down and held in those four compartments of the *Tefillin* for the purpose of being properly united with that holy name. And he who makes this correction, exists in image and likeness, TZELEM, with the Creator. Just as the holy name is united in the Creator, the holy name is united in him. "Male and female he created them" refers to the head and the hand *Tefillin*. And it is one.**

"The King is held captive in the tubs" signifies *ZA*, who is bound and unified in those compartments of the *Tefillin*. The compartments of the *Tefillin*, which contain the passages from the Torah, are called "tubs" or "troughs," just like the tubs from which sheep drink water, for the waters of *Ohr Hochma* and

*Ohr Hassadim* are bound and restricted by these *Kelim*, the compartments of the *Tefillin*. And it is the Creator who is bound tight and held in these *Kelim*, so as to be unified in the holy name.

The compartments of the *Tefillin* are the TNHY of *Tvuna*, the lower part of YESHSUT (*Israel-Saba* and *Tvuna*, where *Israel-Saba* is the male part and *Tvuna* is the female). This part of *Tvuna* is called the big letter *Dalet* of the word *Echad* (one) in the verse, "Hear O Israel, our Creator is one." It is written about this letter: "Let the dry land appear."

As was already mentioned in the third *Mitzva*, because this "dry land" was revealed in ZA, he can pass the Light to *Malchut*. Thus, were it not for these four places in ZA, the dry land within him, he would have been unable to give the Light to *Nukva*. Hence, it is said that ZA "is tied down and held in those places" that stem from dry land so as to enable him to unite and pass the revelation of the Creator's Light into the holy name, *Nukva*. As a result, the dry land becomes fertile and produces fruit.

Therefore, he who has completed the corrections of these four passages from the Torah acquires the image and likeness (*TzeLeM*) of the Creator. In other words, when man "below" (below the world of *Atzilut*, in the worlds BYA) "puts on" the *Tefillin* (attains the level of this degree), he receives the Light of H-B-H-G from ZA. This Light is called *TzeLeM*, since *Hochma* and *Bina* are called M and L, whereas *Hesed* and *Gevura* are called *Tz*. And just like *Elokim*, *Bina* unites with the holy name of *Malchut*, thereby uniting the holy name within man, for man is a part of *Malchut*.

There are two parts—male and female—in the Light of *Hochma* and *Bina* (called *TzeLeM*): *TzeLeM* of ZA and *TzeLeM* of *Nukva*, the head *Tefillin* and the hand *Tefillin*. Hence, it is said that the Creator created a man and a woman, referring to the head *Tefillin* and the hand *Tefillin*.

# THE ELEVENTH COMMANDMENT

**244.** The eleventh *Mitzva* is to give a tithe of the fruits of the earth. Here there are two *Mitzvot*: to separate a tithe of the fruits of the earth, and to bring the first fruits of the trees, as it is written, "Behold, I have given you every herb-yielding seed, which is upon the face of all the earth" (*Beresheet*, 1:29). Here it is written, I HAVE GIVEN YOU. Elsewhere it is written, "And to the children of Levi, behold, I have given all the tithe in Israel" (*Bamidbar*, 18:21). It is also written, "And all the tithe of the land, whether of the seed of the land or of the fruit of the tree, is the Creator's" (*Vayikra*, 27:30).

These verses say that the Creator gave everything to Adam. Yet, why does that oblige us to separate a tithe, to bring the first fruits of the earth, and why are we forbidden from eating them? After all, this contradicts the aforesaid.

The thing is that the process of (spiritual) nourishment includes exposure, selection, and separation of the holy sparks of the Light from the impure forces. In the process of feeding (reception of Light), the sparks of the Light (*Nitzotzin*) that are contained in the food unite with man's soul, with his very flesh, and the waste, except for the sparks, leaves the body. This continues throughout man's life (6,000 degrees of ascent); he gradually accumulates within him all the holy sparks, with which he complements his soul. Without them, the soul cannot attain completeness and perfection.

I think that the reader already understands that *The Zohar* in no way speaks about the process of feeding, digestion, and secretion of our physical body. As the whole of the Torah, *The Zohar* speaks only of the goal of creation and the ways of its attainment. Therefore, I call upon the reader (in defiance of what his mind suggests to him after the first reading) to realize that these texts are written in the language of branches, when spiritual objects are described in the language of our world; yet, despite the corporeal language, the objects remain spiritual!

It is written in the weekly portion *Lech Lecha* that Adam was forbidden to eat meat: "I have given you every herb..." (*Beresheet*, 1:29). However, since Adam sinned, and egoism, impurity entered his body, it was said to Noah: "Every moving thing that lives shall be for food for you; as the green herb have I given you all" (*Beresheet*, 9:3), that is, including meat.

Since Adam was created in absolute perfection, everything was sorted and corrected within him, which corresponds to the animate part of creation, as it is written (*Beresheet*, 2:19): "Out of the ground the Creator formed every beast of the field," and also, "whatsoever the man would call every living creature, that was to be the name thereof." This means that Adam attained every name (spiritual level) of the animal souls, for the pure forces were already separated from the impure ones.

Hence, Adam was not given the task of exposing, sorting, and correcting animals by eating them, for even before the creation of man, the Creator corrected this in the world of *Atzilut*. And only the inanimate and vegetative (parts of the soul) remained uncorrected, containing both pure and impure forces. Therefore, Adam was instructed to expose the sparks that his soul lacked in the inanimate and vegetative food.

However, as a result of Adam's sin, pure and impure desires (forces) were mixed once more. And as Adam's soul was shattered into many parts, all of which fell into the impure forces, all the animals (animate desires) were corrupted along with him (with the human level of desire). Thus appeared the need to expose, sort, and correct them. Therefore, after the sin the Creator ordered Adam and the subsequent generations to eat animals, and thus extract the sparks from impurity.

It is said that Adam was created IN THE IMAGE AND AFTER LIKENESS, i.e., with the help of the *TzeLeM Elokim*, the Light of *Bina*, by the four passages from the Torah in the *Tefillin*. And this is his soul. However, after he was born with this holy soul, thanks to his good deeds, he merited raising MAN and receiving *Ohr Haya*, and then, on *Shabbat*, attaining *Ohr Yechida* as well.

Therefore, Adam was left to correct the creation with the help of only a tithe and offerings. And by feeding on tithe and offerings, he attained the revelation of his desires and raised MAN to the level of *Ohr Haya* and *Yechida*. Yet, after he sinned, all of his corrections and everything that had filled his soul was corrupted, mixed, and egoism took over the body.

Due to our egoism, tithe and offerings are forbidden for us, for fear that we will desire Supernal purity. Instead, we are obliged to extract and pass them on to the *Cohanim* and *Levi'im* (parts of the soul). And if we observe this Creator's *Mitzva* of spiritually separating a tithe of the fruits of the earth and the offerings (as He commanded), we will receive the strength to raise MAN and receive *Ohr Haya* on *Shabbat* (the ascent of the worlds is called *Shabbat*) in the same way that Adam attained this state while feeding on tithe and offerings.

Thus, after man receives *Ohr Neshama* by putting on the *Tefillin*, he can raise MAN with the help of the two *Mitzvot* (tithe and offerings) in order to receive *Ohr Haya*. As it is explained, Adam was receiving *Ohr Haya* by feeding on tithe and offerings. However, we are forbidden to feed on them (to try to receive this Light for the Creator's sake) because of the egoism that acts in our body (desires). Instead, we are bid to give a tithe and the offerings to the *Cohanim* and the *Levi'im*. As a result, we receive the strength to receive this Light.

# The Twelfth Commandment

**245.** The twelfth *Mitzva* is to bring the first fruits of the trees as an offering, as it is written, "And every tree in which is the fruit of a tree yielding seed" (*Beresheet*, 1:29). All that is worthy of Me shall not be eaten by you. I have given you My permission and I have given you all the tithe and offerings of the trees. "To you," and not to the subsequent generations.

From the aforesaid, it becomes clear that we, the subsequent generations, are forbidden to feed on tithe and offerings. The Light called "tithe" and "offerings" is so great that until all the *Kelim* (desires) of Adam's soul have been corrected, it is impossible to receive it for the Creator's sake.

Hence, it is forbidden to even try, lest we sin, as it happened to Adam. There is a *Mitzva* to not receive this Light, which refers to *Malchut de Malchut*. Every time the sparks are revealed, it is sufficient to let this Light be, to refrain from receiving it during the 6,000 years. Herein lies its actual correction until, at the end of correction, the Creator's great Light, called *Mashiach* (Messiah), manifests and gives us the strength to receive tithe and offerings for the Creator's sake.

# THE THIRTEENTH COMMANDMENT

**246.** The thirteenth *Mitzva* is to perform the redemption of a first-born son so as to strengthen him in life. For there are two appointed angels in charge—one over life and one over death. And they both rule over man from Above. And when man redeems his son, he redeems him from the angel in charge of death, so that the angel can no longer govern the first-born son. Hence, it is written, AND THE CREATOR SAW EVERYTHING THAT HE HAD MADE—this is in general, AND, BEHOLD, IT WAS... VERY GOOD alludes to the angel of life, while the word VERY alludes to the angel of death. Therefore, by this act of redemption, the angel of life is strengthened and the angel of death is weakened. Life is purchased by this redemption, for the evil side leaves him be and clings to him no more.

The ascent of the worlds occurred on the sixth day of creation: ZA ascended to the place of AA, *Malchut* ascended to AVI, and Adam attained *Ohr Haya*. As a result, the angel of death (egoism) lost his power completely. On the contrary, he became very good, for upon being corrected, egoism becomes a great and holy *Kli*, the one *Kli* that can receive the greatest Light.

Such a state will come at the end of the general correction, when, due to the revelation of this great Light, death (egoism) will disappear forever. This is the meaning of the verse: "when the Creator saw EVERYTHING that He had made (i.e., at the end of all creation), He saw that it was very good."

However, since Adam's sin, the worlds can no longer ascend as high. This is why we need special *Mitzvot* in order to perform special preparations and actions for the reception of *Ohr Haya*, at least in a state called *Shabbat*. This is precisely the *Mitzva* to redeem one's first-born son, when we weaken the powers of the angel of death and strengthen the angel of life, much like what the Creator did to Adam by the preliminary ascents of all the worlds, for during such an ascent, called *Shabbat*, the angel of death becomes very good. Such is the power of that *Mitzva*.

Yet, it is not observed as fully as previously, when the angel of death lost all of his power. Now, by observing the *Mitzva* of redemption of the first-born son, we merely distance from the angel of death without actually destroying the impure forces, and they no longer cling to him. And after preventing the impure forces from clinging, accomplished with the help of this *Mitzva*, he can receive life, i.e., *Ohr Haya* of the state of *Shabbat*.

# THE FOURTEENTH COMMANDMENT

**247. The fourteenth *Mitzva* is to observe *Shabbat*, which is a day of rest from all the actions of creation. There are two *Mitzvot* here: to observe the day of *Shabbat* and to adorn its holiness, namely to receive *Ohr Hochma,* called "holiness;" and to observe *Shabbat* as a day of rest for all the worlds, in which all actions are multiplied and realized even before this day is sanctified.**

*Shabbat* is a state of the spiritual worlds where the Light descending from Above elevates ZA to AA, *Nukva* to AVI, the worlds of BYA to YESHSUT, and ZON of the world of *Atzilut*. As a result, man's NRN (whoever has it, whoever is spiritually present in the worlds of BYA) also ascends to *Atzilut* with the worlds of BYA, and there receives *Ohr Haya*.

```
              Atik
ZA -    AA
M -     AVI
BYA -   YESHSUT + ZON
        ——————————————————— Parsa of the World of Atzilut
```

It follows that there are two *Mitzvot*: to refrain from working and carrying things from one household to another. This is so because when all the worlds are completely freed from the impure forces, we must guard against the impure forces, so they do not return and mingle with the holiness of *Shabbat*. And he who works causes the impure forces to mingle with the pure ones.

The second *Mitzva* is to adorn the day of *Shabbat*: through the pleasures of *Shabbat* (the ascent of the worlds of ABYA), man receives (in his spiritual desires existing in the world of BYA) the Light of the world of *Atzilut* from Above. This Light of *Atzilut* is called "holiness" (*Hochma*); hence, man becomes sanctified by it.

All purifications and corrections take place only in our work and struggle with the impure forces, preventing us from drawing nearer and merging with the Creator in our properties. It is precisely in the wars with the impure forces that we extract the sparks of the Light that they swallowed up, and each extraction of a spark of the Light from the impure forces and its ascent to the world of *Atzilut* is defined as independent, individual work.

In the beginning, these sparks were sorted and extracted from the impure forces by the Creator Himself. This is described in His actions in the six days of creation. And when all the extractions of the Light sparks ended, the work was considered finished, and the corrected state, called *Shabbat*, arrives; and it is the day of rest, for there is nothing else to correct.

Hence, *Shabbat* is the day (the state when the Light shines in the worlds) when all the correction work in all the worlds ceases. For every *Shabbat* (the state of ascent in the spiritual worlds to the level of correction of all the impure forces), the same state of the perfection of creation's first *Shabbat* returns and brings rest to all the worlds of ABYA. All the impure forces become detached, remote, and return to their place (*Tehom Raba*—great abyss), and all the worlds ascend to the world of *Atzilut*, defined as perfect unity. And we are destined to receive this holiness, the Light of the world of *Atzilut*; it descends upon us through our observance of the two *Mitzvot*: REMEMBER AND GUARD THE DAY OF *SHABBAT*.

**248. Because that day was sanctified, the creation of bodiless spirits was to be completed. Asks: "Was the Creator unable to delay the sanctification of that day until the bodies for those spirits were created?" And answers: "The Tree of Knowledge of Good and Evil contained an evil side that wanted to govern the world. And many spirits separated and went forth, armed, to clothe in the bodies of this world."**

Because that day was sanctified, the creation of bodies for the spirits was to be completed. This means that the day had been sanctified before the Creator had time to create bodies for those spirits. It is written about this on the first *Shabbat* of creation: "And on the seventh day the Creator finished His work, which He has made; and He rested on the seventh day from all His work, which He has made."

This passage from the Torah is unclear. For if the Creator completely finished all His work by Himself, then He left nothing for us to do. After all, He finished everything Himself. However, the Creator sorted the Light sparks and separated the pure forces from the impure ones precisely to enable us *to do*, i.e., to complete this work by making our own efforts in the observance of the Torah and *Mitzvot*.

And the rest that is mentioned here refers only to what the Creator Himself had to do. Therefore, the Torah says that the Creator finished His work, for He has completed all the preparations for us, and nothing else is required of Him, for the rest HE HAS MADE for us to do. This enables us to do and to complete creation.

Hence, it is written that the Creator did not have time to create bodies for the spirits before the arrival of *Shabbat*. These bodiless spirits constitute all of our impure and evil forces that drive man to transgressions. And the Creator intentionally left them this way, for it is precisely because they are present within us that we have freedom of will in our work with the Torah and *Mitzvot*.

As a result of Adam's sin in *Malchut*, called "The Tree of Knowledge of Good and Evil," pure and impure forces were mixed. At that, the impure forces wished to rule over the forces of good in the world, so the forces of good would never prevail over them. Thus, a number of armed spirits went forth, intending to attack the bodies, capture them, and clothe in them.

Two points merged in *Malchut*: one was corrected by receiving the properties of *Bina*, mercy, and the other is the strictness of judgment, the result of restrictions within *Malchut* herself. When *Malchut* is united with the pure forces, her property of restriction is concealed, and the point of mercy is revealed (item 123). Then man is said to merit only goodness.

However, if man transgresses, he attacks the good point and thereby reveals the point of restriction in *Malchut*. Thus, the forces that wish to harm and destroy the corrected part and to rule over man become revealed, and this is evil.

However, if he merits for the point of mercy to reveal itself and dominate, he can elevate *Malchut* to *Bina*, thereby causing Supernal mercy and Light to descend. However, if he does not merit, and the point of restriction is revealed in *Malchut*, not only does he thereby harm *Malchut*, but he also harms the point of *Bina* that unites with *Malchut*. Thus, this point turns from good to evil, from mercy to judgment, as restriction is revealed in *Malchut* herself, and every revealed property dominates.

This is why the point of judgment was revealed in *Malchut* after Adam's sin. By this, Adam damaged the point (property) of *Bina* that united with *Malchut*, too, turning it from mercy to strictness, judgment. Yet, the correction of *Malchut* is possible only with the help of this point, for it is called "goodness." And when this point of *Bina* is revealed within her, *Malchut* is called "goodness," too.

But now that the very point of *Bina* in *Malchut* was damaged and turned from good to evil, the impure force thought that the time has come for it to dominate the world and clothe human bodies, meaning Adam and his sons (spiritual *Partzufim*). In other words, the body (desires) of the impure force inherits the place of Adam's body. Thus, the correction of *Malchut* from the good point becomes impossible, for no more goodness comes to *Malchut* from *Bina*, and this property has become evil, strictness, and judgment, due to the restricted reception in *Malchut*.

And many armed and destructive impure forces went forth to attack so as to clothe human bodies (desires) in this world, and rule over them. For the impure force thought that nothing could protect and save the pure forces from it because of the harm that Adam's sin brought to the system of governance and the point of mercy in *Malchut*.

**249. However, as the Creator saw this, He roused the wind from within the Tree of Life, ZA, and struck the other Tree, *Malchut*. And the other, good side was awakened, and the day was sanctified. For the creation of bodies and the awakening of spirits on that night of *Shabbat* stem from the good side, and not from the evil one.**

Since the Creator saw the strengthening of the power of judgment and the impure forces, their ability to clothe the bodies in this world (completely excluding the possibility of correcting the world in the future), He roused the wind within the Tree of Life and struck the other Tree (made a *Zivug* with it), *Malchut*. Due to this *Zivug*, the Tree of Life passed the spirit of life to the other Tree, *Malchut*, thus enabling *Malchut* to tear away from the impure forces.

As a result, the good side reappeared in *Malchut*, as it was prior to Adam's sin, and the sanctity of *Shabbat* descended to the world. That is, although the impure forces had the strength to clothe in bodies, and were more powerful than the pure forces, and, according to the law, they were supposed to prevail, at that moment the Creator intervened, disregarding the destruction caused by Adam's sin.

Consequently, ZON (the Tree of Life and the Tree of Knowledge of Good) united in a *Zivug*, as before Adam's sin, and the Light of sanctity of *Shabbat* descended into the world. This action of the Creator caused *Shabbat* (the Light of *Shabbat*) to descend into the world, and the impure forces lost the opportunity to clothe in human bodies in this world. The impure force remained as a bodiless spirit, which enables man to draw closer to the Creator (with his properties). This is referred to as his return (*Teshuva*).

The creation of bodies and the arousal of spirits on that night of *Shabbat* stems from the good side, and not from the side of the impure forces, for the Creator's action remains in creation forever. Just as on the first *Shabbat* of creation, the Creator completely disregarded the damage of Adam's sin, instead compelling ZON to make a *Zivug*, and the day was sanctified as before the sin, for He destroyed all the power of the impure forces, despite the fact that they had the strength to rule.

The same applies to all *Shabbatot* (plural for *Shabbat*)—the spiritual ascents for those who exist in the worlds of BYA—during the 6,000 years. Although man is still full of impurity, for he has yet to correct the sins of the Tree of Knowledge, when he makes a *Zivug* (of the Light with a screen) on the night of *Shabbat* (in a spiritual state of that name), the impure forces (of man) have no power over him (his altruistic desires). In this *Zivug*, man assumes the body and spirit of a newborn, as though he was unharmed by Adam's sin, as though he himself corrected the Tree of Knowledge.

And despite the fact that man has yet to merit liberation from his egoism, the impure forces have no power over him on that night. Thus, he can receive the bodies and spirits in his *Zivug* on the side of the Tree of Good, but not from the impure forces.

250. **And had he hastened on that night to put forward the other side, before the good side came forward, he would not have been able to withstand it for even an instant. But the Creator provided the remedy in advance. And He sanctified the day beforehand. And He warned to appear before the other side. And the world exists. And that the opposite side thought to rule in the world, i.e., in defiance of it, the good side was created and strengthened on that night. And the good, holy bodies and spirits were created on that night from the good side. Therefore, the delight of sages who know this spans from** *Shabbat* **to** *Shabbat*.

251. **However, when the other (impure) side saw that what it had planned to do was already done by the holy side, it started to check its own forces and properties, and saw all those who perform a** *Zivug* **naked and in the candlelight. Therefore, all of the sons born from that** *Zivug* **are enslaved by the spirit of the other side. And these naked spirits of the wicked are called "harming," and they are ruled and killed by Lilit.**

252. **And since the day was sanctified, and holiness rules in the world, the other side diminishes itself and hides on each** *Shabbat* **day and on each** *Shabbat* **night. With the exception of Asimon and his group, who walk secretly in the**

Candlelight, to observe the naked *Zivug*. And then they hide inside the cave, called *Tehom Raba* (the great abyss). And as soon as *Shabbat* ends, many hosts fly and prowl in the world. As a result, everything is corrected by the song of the sufferers, "He who dwells in concealment," to prevent impurity from governing holiness.

According to the law, the impure force was supposed to rule in the world, for it was stronger than the pure one, and it was to clothe in human bodies. But then, the earth would have been given over to the wicked, and all the generations in the world originating from man would have stemmed from the side of the impure forces. And there would have been no chance of correction, for impurity would have dominated over all the generations to such an extent that there would have been no opportunity to get hold of the good side even for a moment.

However, the Creator provided a remedy, thereby forestalling the defect, for He elevated *Shabbat* and removed the impure forces, which caused the Light of peace and rest to be revealed in all the worlds. And all the impure forces were thrown into *Tehom Raba* (the great abyss). Thus, the world was revived, as this enabled the creation of bodies and spirits from the pure side in a *Zivug* of the *Shabbat* night, and the world advances toward the desired goal.

So what does it mean to forestall the defect via a remedy? The whole of creation is based on a cause and effect sequence, and all that transpires not according to the worlds' development is called "forestalling" (skipping several degrees, bypassing some of the causes and effects in this chain).

And since the sanctity of *Shabbat* came as an awakening from Above, from the Creator's desire, without any desire or request from below, for Adam had yet to make any corrections and draw closer to the Creator in order to merit *Shabbat* (when the Creator Himself prevented the defect by providing a remedy for the correction of the world), this action on the Creator's behalf is called "forestalling."

Just as the impure force planned to assume power over the world, the good side forestalled its actions on that night. For this night that followed the sin in the Tree of Knowledge was given entirely to the impure forces. Hence, they thought that they would obviously rule over the world. However, the opposite had happened—sanctity took their place: pure bodies and spirits were created on that night by the good side. This is because such a preparation took place that all the *Zivugim* on that night created bodies and spirits from the good side, without any participation of the impure force. In other words, what transpired was exactly the opposite of the impure force's expectations.

Therefore, the time of sages who know this spans from *Shabbat* to *Shabbat*— for at this time, bodies and spirits are created from the pure, good side. And when the impure force sees that what it wanted to create was created by the opposite side, it collects its evil powers and searches through the whole world, and sees all those who make a *Zivug* in the candlelight, exposing their naked bodies. And ill sons are made from this *Zivug*. The impure side sends these sons its evil spirits of the wicked, called "wreckers." As a result, they are ruled and killed by Lilit. Garments refer to *Ohr Hassadim*, the garments of *Ima*, the intention "for the sake of the Creator."

When the sanctity of *Shabbat* comes into the world, and *Shabbat* rules in the world, the power of the impure force dwindles and hides on the night and on the day of *Shabbat*. Hence, this is the time of sages.

And only the wreckers, called "Asimon and his group," walk secretly in the candlelight, to observe those who expose their *Zivug*. Afterward, they hide in the *Nukva* of *Tehom Raba*. Thus, although Asimon has the power to see the *Zivug* in the candlelight and on *Shabbat*, he cannot do harm on *Shabbat*, but must immediately return to the *Nukva* of *Tehom Raba*. Only after *Shabbat* is over can he resume causing harm.

Rabbi Shimon felt the difficulty of explaining the words regarding *Shabbat* being the time of sages. For each day (not only on *Shabbat* night), starting at midnight, the Creator walks around the Garden of Eden and makes *Zivugim* with the sages. *The Zohar* asks the same question (*Veyikahel*, item 194), and answers that there is a difference between a *Zivug* on a week night and one that is made in the candlelight on *Shabbat*. On weekdays, the impure force has the power to inflict maladies on the newborns, and Lilit has the power to kill them.

However, on *Shabbat* nights, although the wrecker Asimon and his group are present, he has not the power to harm, but only after *Shabbat* is over. However, opposite his opportunity to cause harm after *Shabbat* there exists a correction, called *Havdalah*, the separation of *Shabbat* from the weekdays through a blessing, a prayer, and a cup of wine, which completely annul the power of this wrecker. Hence, there is a significant difference between a *Zivug* on a week night and a *Zivug* on the night of *Shabbat*.

The thing is that there is a source of Light, ZA, Supernal unity, and a source of fire, *Malchut*, lower unity (item 209). Also, there are three details in the candle flame (this refers to a spiritual candle, designated in corporeality by a wick floating in olive oil):

- White Upper flame;
- Lower flame;
- The coarse part—wick and oil, supporting the lower flame.

This lower flame is called "devouring flame." It designates judgment, the power of restriction in the candle. Thus, it devours everything below it, the wick *and* the oil. And the Upper white flame signifies mercy contained in the candle, for white means mercy.

And he who makes a *Zivug* in the candlelight will see his children damaged, and Lilit will be able to kill them, for the candle contains the strictness of judgment, and the impure forces can therefore cling to such a *Zivug*. Due to the strictness of judgment, their bodies (the impurities contained in the bodies that participate in a *Zivug*, each of which finds what suits them) become revealed.

Therefore, a *Zivug* is permitted only at midnight, i.e., only in the darkness, when there is absolutely no Light, when *Malchut* is said to "awaken at night," and mercy is revealed. However, if there is some candlelight, it reveals the impurity in the bodies, and the impure forces cling to them.

In the candlelight, the impure force sees impurity in the bodies of those making a *Zivug*, and it informs on them and clings to their bodies. However, all the restrictions of strictness and judgment disappear on the night of *Shabbat*, and the coarse lower flame becomes like the white Upper flame. This means that even candlelight is permitted. Moreover, under the influence of the sanctity of *Shabbat*, all the impurity disappears from man's body, hence there is no fear to reveal the body in the candlelight.

Yet, even on *Shabbat*, when the coarse flame turns white and the judgment of restrictions disappears, the white flame of the candle nonetheless requires the light's coarse part, so it would act as foundation. And the coarse foundation designates an indispensable presence of judgment and restrictions, for coarseness constitutes restriction.

Nevertheless, these restrictions do not appear on *Shabbat*. This resembles a coin without any image, so its denomination is unknown. Therefore, the wrecker, this coarse, detrimental part of the candle that supports the white flame, is called Asimon (Hebrew, *Token*), signifying a coin without image.

The coarse part of the candle secretly ascends along with the white candlelight, as the candle cannot burn without it. Hence, this coarse part sees the exposed *Zivug* and can therefore do harm after the end of *Shabbat*. Although the revelation (exposure) of bodies does no harm on the night of *Shabbat* (the impurity of the body remains concealed during *Shabbat*), as soon as *Shabbat* is over, the impure force can reveal itself and harm.

And since, after *Shabbat*, Asimon and his group return to their forms (properties) and rise up from the Great Abyss (*Tehom Raba*) to the place of settlement, they soar above the world and can cause harm. There is a song: "He who sits in the shadow of the Supernal One," for man saves himself from harmful forces by praying and returning to the Creator:

"He who sits in the shadow of the Supernal One (dwells under the shelter of the Supernal One) dwells in the shadow of the Almighty. I will say to the Lord: 'my refuge and my fortress, my God, in whom I trust.' Surely he will save you from the fowler's snare and from the deadly pestilence. He will cover you with his feathers, and under his wings will you find refuge; his faithfulness will be your shield and rampart. You will not fear the terror of night, nor the arrow that flies by day, nor the pestilence that stalks in the darkness, nor the plague that destroys at midday. A thousand may fall at your side, ten thousand at your right hand, but it will not come near you. You will only observe with your eyes and see the punishment of the wicked..." (*Tehilim*, 91:1-8).

**253. What places do they visit on the night of the end of *Shabbat*? When they come out in haste and wish to govern the holy nation, they see it standing in prayer and singing this song: "He who sits in the shadow (concealment) of the Supernal One," first separating *Shabbat* from the weekdays in his prayer, and then over a cup of wine, these forces flee thence and fly away to the desert. May the Merciful One save us from them and from the evil side.**

Here the question concerns only the night of the end of *Shabbat*, but not the night of weekdays, as the night of the end of *Shabbat* still contains some force of the sanctity of *Shabbat*. Hence, although the impure forces rise from *Tehom Raba* and fly to conquer Israel, when they see Israel's actions in song of prayer and in the blessing over a cup of wine, they fly away to the wasteland, an unpopulated place. Thus, people escape their reach.

It follows that impure forces dwell in three places:

- On *Shabbat*, they dwell in *Nukva* of *Tehom Raba* and have no power to cause harm;
- When *Shabbat* is over, they are kept in the wasteland with the help of prayer, *Havdalah*, separation of *Shabbat* from weekdays, and the blessing over a cup of wine. They have the power to cause harm, but can't, as they are in an unpopulated place;
- On other nights they are also present in populated places.

**254. The three that cause evil to themselves: a) he who curses himself; b) he who throws away bread or bread crumbs bigger than an olive; c) he who lights the candle at the end of *Shabbat* before Israel attains sanctity in the prayer, "And You are holy." And the light from that candle ignites hellfire.**

**255. There is a place in hell for those who transgress *Shabbat*. And as they are punished in hell, they curse him who lit the candle before its time, and they say to him, "Behold: the Creator will thrust you about with a mighty throw, and He will seize you firmly. He will violently roll and toss you like a ball into a large land; there shall you die" (*Yeshayahu*, 22:17-18).**

One wrecker is called the "evil eye." And he loves cursing, as it is said; "Yea, he loved cursing, and it came unto him; and he delighted not in blessing, and it is far from him" (*Tehilim*, 109:17). When man curses himself, he thereby empowers the evil eye to love cursing, and it rules over him—thus, man brings harm to himself.

There is nothing in this world that does not have an Upper Root Above. Especially bread, on which man's life depends, has its own special root Above. Therefore, he who neglects his bread brings harm to the root of his life Above. Everyone understands this, but only to the extent of the portion that satiates him, giving him life.

However, if a piece of bread and crumbs are smaller than an olive, there are those who neglect and throw them away, as such amount cannot satiate man. Yet, the sages instructed us to bless as a meal even an olive-sized amount of bread, obliging us to treat such portion as satiating, so we have no right to neglect such an amount. And he who neglects it brings harms to himself.

The reason for this is explained in the Talmud: "They asked the Creator: Master of the world, it is said in your Torah that one should not turn his face and accept bribes. Yet, You turn Your face to Israel..." The Creator replied: "How can I help turning my face to Israel if they observe the law 'down to the size of an olive...'" (*Berachot*, 20:2). In other words, by accepting an olive-sized bread crumb as a satiating meal, we merit revealing the Creator's face, even though we are unworthy of it. Therefore, those who neglect the amount of bread the size of an olive and do not consider it a satiating meal do not merit revealing the Creator's face; hence, they bring harm to themselves.

He who lights the candle at the end of *Shabbat* before Israel has reached sanctity in the blessing, thereby ignites hellfire. This is because prior to that moment, it was *Shabbat*; its sanctity prevailed, and hellfire has no power on *Shabbat*. Hence, he who transgresses *Shabbat* and lights the candle prematurely, Ignites hellfire and brings harm to himself, for the transgression of *Shabbat* is regarded as the gravest transgression. Hence, there is a special place in hell for those who transgress *Shabbat*. And they who are punished in hell curse the sinner for igniting hellfire prematurely.

**256.** For he should not light the candle at the end of *Shabbat* before Israel separates *Shabbat* from the weekdays in their prayer and over a cup of wine, as until that time, it is still *Shabbat*, and the sanctity of *Shabbat* still rules over us. And during the separation by means of blessing over a cup, all those hosts and legions that the rulers appointed to govern the weekdays return each to their place to resume the work for which they are responsible.

The main prohibition remains in effect only until the blessing in the prayer. Nevertheless, one should beware of lighting a candle before the actual separation of *Shabbat* from the weekdays in the blessings over a cup, as it is still *Shabbat*. Of course, one can light a candle for the actual separation of *Shabbat* from the weekdays, i.e., for the blessing over a lit candle.

**257.** As soon as *Shabbat* starts and the day is sanctified, holiness awakens and rules over the world; the power of weekdays disappears and returns only when *Shabbat* ends. However, although *Shabbat* is over, other forces do not regain their power until Israel says the prayer, "He who separates holiness from the weekdays." Only then does holiness disappear, and the legions that govern the weekdays awaken and return to their places, each to its above-appointed post.

**258.** Nevertheless, the impure forces do not assume control until the flame of the candle is lit, for they all come from the root (element) of fire, from which everything originates, and they descend to rule over the lower world. All this happens if one lights the candle before Israel has finished the blessing in the prayer.

*Malchut* is called the "pillar of fire" (item 209), and the forces that exist in the candlelight are the restrictions in *Malchut*. It is impossible to use these forces before the candle is lit.

**259.** Yet, if he waits until they complete the blessing, the wicked in hell justify the Creator's justice over them, and they bring upon him all the blessings, recited by the congregation: "Therefore, the Creator gives you of the dew of Heaven," "Blessed shall you be in your town," and "Blessed shall you be in the field."

By reciting the blessings, we evoke the descent of the great Light, and its power saves us from hell. And since the wicked in hell see this, they regret committing their sins and justify the Creator's judgment brought upon them by seeing their punishment. And since man evoked such justification of the Creator's judgment, all the blessings, recited at the end of *Shabbat* by the congregation become fulfilled in him.

260. "Blessed is he who considers the poor; the Creator will deliver him in the day of disaster" (*Tehilim*, 41:2). What do the words "in the day of disaster" mean? This refers to the day when evil gains power and wants to take his soul away from him. The word "poor" alludes to someone very sick. "He who considers" refers to one who realizes the need to be cured from transgressions before the Creator. Another explanation is that this is the Day of Judgment in the world. "He who considers" signifies one who knows how to save himself from it, as it is written: "The Creator will deliver him in the day of disaster," meaning that on the day when the judgment against man dominates the world, the Creator will deliver him.

"The day of disaster" is a state when the impure forces, called "evil," govern man and take his soul away. "He who considers the poor" is one who tells the sick to return to the Creator to correct himself. It is him who the Creator delivers from the rule of the impure forces.

*The Zohar* continues by saying that there are three sources of evil for the soul of a man that attracts it onto himself. Hence, it advises one who considers and is compassionate to the poor, to appeal to the sick man's heart (he who feels sick in his own evil, egoism) to return to the Creator. Then the Creator will cure him. And on this day of disaster, which man caused to his soul, the Creator will deliver him through this reward.

Even if judgment dominates the world, the Creator will deliver him, for he taught the sick to return to the Creator and explained to them the need for correction. And the difference in the explanations is that the first refers to an individual who discovers evil within himself, and the second refers to the evil of the entire world. And here, the Creator, too, will deliver man as a reward for fulfilling this *Mitzva*.

# The Intention in the Prayer

It is written in *The Zohar* (*Veyikahel*, pp. 32-52): "Each day a voice calls upon all people in the world, 'This depends on you. Separate a part of yourself and devote it to the Creator.'" At some point in life, thoughts and desires to draw closer to the spiritual come to every person, and it depends on us whether or not we heed that inner call. The voice reassures man that by casting aside his needless, transient, and earthly desires, by ceasing his endless chase for their appeasement, he will attain true and eternal happiness.

From this we can understand the secret meaning of prayer: he who fears the Creator and directs his heart and desires in his prayer, carries out great and exalted corrections. If one wishes to enter the spiritual realm and feel the Creator, the only thing he must do is pray, i.e., ask the Creator to correct his nature, to transform it from the nature of our world (egoistic) into the nature of the spiritual realm (altruistic). He will then enter eternity and transcend the boundaries of our world. Being completely enslaved by his egoism, man is unable to change himself on his own.

To correct himself, man needs to receive the strength that exists outside of him, beyond the bounds of his egoism. He must ask to receive this strength; hence, the only thing man must do is pray.

However, prayer is not uttered by one's mouth. Rather, it is the desire in our heart, for the Creator reads the desires in our hearts. Therefore, man's only task is to transform his heart's desires—for his heart to wish to change its own desires. Yet, even this man is unable to do it by himself; he must ask the Creator for it.

Thus, everything boils down to exalting the Creator's rule, faith in Him, in His singularity, His power, His ability and desire to help. All of man's efforts aim to create the only true desire within him—to feel the Creator! Here, *The Zohar*, as well as all the other books of Kabbalah and the Torah, speak of those who

465

have already attained the spiritual worlds with their desires and properties, and, while being in our world, perceive and exist in the two worlds simultaneously. The prayer the book refers to here constitutes the spiritual actions of one who has already acquired spiritual instruments, and can utilize them in exactly the same way we use our hands and auxiliary means in our world.

First, in the songs and hymns of the Supernal angels, and according to the order of chants sung by the sons of Israel below, *Malchut* adorns and corrects herself as a wife who adorns herself for her husband. The sons of Israel are those who wish to become *Yashar* (straight) and *El* (Creator), i.e., to draw closer to, or go straight to the Creator. Such people, who exist in the Upper Worlds with their spiritual (altruistic) instruments (desires), can change the states of Higher *Sefirot* and worlds by their spiritual actions.

Our prayer-book was compiled by the sages of the Great Assembly twenty centuries ago. Before that, everyone addressed the Creator in accordance with what he or she felt. About twenty centuries ago, coarser souls began descending to our world, which needed orderly prayers. Hence, the members of the Great Assembly (great Kabbalists) created the prayer book that we still use today.

In an orderly fashion, the prayer book expounds all the consecutive degrees of man's correction. Behind the words of the prayer book, one who understands sees the spiritual actions that he needs to perform. This information is conveyed in letters, in their forms and combinations, as well as in the sequence of sentences and parts of the whole prayer.

According to the order of the prayer, correction of the worlds comes first by the morning blessings (See *Tefilat Kol Peh*) up to the prayer of *Shmone Esreh*, correction in a sitting position. Then, when they reach the words *Emet ve Yatziv* that conclude *Kriyat Shema*, all the worlds achieve correction. And as they reach the words *Gaal Israel*, all the corrections are to take their places; hence, they continue reciting the *Shmone Esreh* prayer while standing.

In spirituality (and, consequently, in corporeality) a person can be in one of three states: lying, sitting, or standing. A newborn infant in our world and a spiritually newborn person develop in the same order. Lying means that the position of the head, the legs, and the body are at the same level. In the spiritual, this corresponds to the embryonic state, when all that exists in the ten *Sefirot* is the same. This is the lowest spiritual state.

Sitting means that the head is above the body, and the body is above the legs, but one cannot use his legs. Such a state is called *Katnut* (smallness) or *VAK*. Standing implies absolute distinction between the levels of the head, body, and legs. It is called *Gadlut* (big state) or *GAR*. Thus, according to one's ability to ask for correction, he gradually receives strength from the Creator and grows.

Therefore, when he reaches the words *Emet ve Yatziv*, everything has already been corrected: all of the worlds bear *Malchut* in them, while *Malchut* herself bears the Supernal King. When man reaches the words, *Gaal Israel*, the Supernal King advances along the degrees, along the three lines, and comes forward to receive *Malchut*.

The Supernal King (the Creator), with regard to all created beings, constitutes ZA of the world of *Atzilut*, for *Malchut de Atzilut* is the sum of all creations. Everything that was ever created, including us and all the worlds with all that inhabit them, is a part of *Malchut*.

In our initial state, we are the parts of *Malchut* that receive the smallest portion of the Creator's Light, *Ner Dakik* (tiny candle). As we draw closer to the Creator in our properties (making them similar to His), we receive increasingly greater Light, in proportion to our advancement, which we feel as infinite bliss, peace, delight, eternity, and as a life-force.

The degrees of our closeness to the Creator (our "I" and Him, *Malchut* and ZA) are described in Kabbalah using a special language: the nearing of properties is considered a transition from the state of "back to back" between ZA and *Malchut* to the state of "face to face." The souls' union with the Creator is described as a *Zivug*–sexual act between ZA and *Malchut*, whereupon ZA passes the Light to *Malchut*, and each soul, in proportion to its correction, can thereby receive this Light.

Naturally, the Creator remains in a state of absolute rest, and all His alleged movements are felt with regard to *Malchut*, depending on the changes in her properties. At times she feels Him more and at times less, and she perceives this as His movement toward her.

We must stand in humility and awe before the Supernal King, each in his place, for He extends His right hand to *Malchut* in *Magen Avraham*, the first blessing in the *Shmone Esreh* prayer, designating the right line. Then He puts His left hand under the head of *Malchut*, as it is written: "Let his left hand be under my head, and his right hand embrace me" (*Shir HaShirim*, 2:6) in the blessing *Ata Gibor*, the second blessing in the *Shmone Esreh* prayer, designating the left line.

The entire magnificent *Shir HaShirim* (Song of Songs) speaks of the Supernal merging of all the creatures with the Creator. Since our world is created as a reflection of the spiritual world, spiritual merging can only be described with the corresponding words of our world. Because our world is egoistic, the spiritual, altruistic actions, directed toward the merging of properties and desires, are described in the words of our world as *Malchut* (man's soul) drawing closer to the Creator in her properties, followed by their gradual unification. First, it manifests in the form of an embrace, followed by a kiss, then a coition, when the soul is sufficiently corrected to receive the Light (*Ohr Hochma*) from the Creator.

Afterward, ZA and *Malchut* embrace and unite in a kiss of the blessing *HaEl HaKadosh*, designating the middle line. From this state and higher on, everything transpires in the state of a kiss, up to the last three blessings in the *Shmone Esreh* prayer. This is the spiritual, true meaning of the first three blessings of the *Shmone Esreh* prayer.

In other words, if one is able to make a spiritual action that corresponds to the conditions described in these blessings, he attains unity with the Creator that it is called "embrace" and "kiss." The detailed explanation of the spiritual actions is given in *The Study of the Ten Sefirot* by Rabbi Ashlag. The language of *The Zohar* and the Torah describes these actions with words of our world.

The language of Kabbalah describes them by using the names of *Sefirot*, *Partzufim*, and Lights. The most complete and precise language for the description of spiritual actions is the language of *Sefirot*. Therefore, this was the language chosen by Kabbalists for their inner work and for explaining to us the practice and method of spiritual ascent.

Man must aspire to the Creator in his heart and desires in order to acquire the intentions that bring him to correction in all the spiritual states described in this prayer—for his mouth and his heart (desires) to become a single whole, so his lips will not speak against the wishes of his heart. The Creator awaits only the sincerity of our desires so as to fulfill them at once and bring us closer to Him:

> *Beloved of the soul, Compassionate Father!*
> *Draw Your servant to Your will.*
> *Your servant will hurry like a hart, will bow before Your majesty.*
> *To him Your friendship will be sweeter*
> *Than the dripping of the honeycomb and any taste.*
>
> *Majestic, Beautiful Radiance of the universe!*
> *My soul pines for Your love.*
> *Please O God, heal her now showing her the pleasantness of Your radiance.*
> *Then she will be strengthened and healed*
> *And eternal gladness will be hers.*

*All-worthy One, may Your mercy be aroused*
*And please take pity on the son of Your beloved.*
*Because it is so very long that I have yearned intensely to see the splendor of strength.*
*These my heart desires, and please take pity and do not conceal Yourself.*

*Please be revealed and spread upon me, my Beloved, the shelter of Your peace.*
*Illuminate the land with Your glory, we shall rejoice and be glad in You.*
*Make haste, do love, for the time has come, and pardon us as in days of old.*

*(Song Yedid Nefesh)*

When the Creator and *Malchut* merge in a kiss, he who needs advice and assistance can ask for it, for this state is called the "time of desire." And since man appealed before the King and Queen in the twelve intermediate blessings of the *Shmone Esreh* prayer, he thereby corrected and prepared his heart's desires for the last three blessings. He aroused the Creator's desire for him, for thanks to these last three blessings, he merges with the Creator in Supernal Unity.

The "time of desire" is an appropriate state for making requests and receiving the answer—the strength for self-correction. The King and Queen are ZA and *Malchut*. Each blessing constitutes a sequence of individual corrections of man's soul. Consequently, man ascends to a Higher spiritual level. Thus, he gradually attains Supernal Unity with the Creator.

Then, he must fall on his face, and when *Malchut* holds the souls within her, submit his soul to the Creator's absolute power, as this is the appropriate time (state) to entrust one's soul amongst all the other souls, for *Malchut* is the source of life.

To fall on one's face and entrust one's soul means that man has but a single desire—to completely rid himself of his egoistic desires, and receive the Creator's altruistic desires in their stead. Upon receiving the Creator's desires, man becomes similar to Him, and to the extent of his similarity, he merges with the Creator. By merging with the Creator, man acquires all that the Creator has: immortality, complete knowledge of all creation, might, and perfection.

The secret of the Light is available only to the chosen ones: when *Malchut* holds human souls by her single desire to merge with the Creator (because the same desire fills man's heart), he submits himself entirely to the aspiration for this merging, so as to include his soul in the collective merging between *Malchut* and the Creator. And if his soul is received by the Creator, man instantly merges with Him and enters the source of life (*Tzror HaChaim*), both in this world and in the world to come.

Although Kabbalah is considered a secret teaching, it holds no secrets. It is perceived as secret only by those who are yet unable to create the spiritual organs within themselves with which to perceive their surroundings. We are the only ones who conceal our surroundings from ourselves in default of the corresponding sensory organs.

The King (Creator, ZA) and Queen (*Malchut*) must be connected to the souls on all sides, Above and below, and be adorned with the souls of the righteous (those who wish to merge with the Creator, entrust their souls to Him). And if man directs all the intentions of his heart (desires) to this goal and completely submits his soul to the Creator's will, the Creator makes peace and a covenant with him (both in the Upper Covenant, called *Yesod*, and in the lower covenant). He blesses *Malchut* by this peace and covenant, and surrounds her on all sides.

Unity on all sides means that the souls attain similarity with the Creator in all their properties. The righteous are those who want to merge with the Creator, attain the entire creation, and as a result, discover the righteousness of the Creator, who created and thus governs them. Those who wish to justify all the Creator's actions are called "righteous."

Although they have not yet reached this state and are only en route to it, even if only at the very beginning of their path, and they are yet to correct even a single desire and only feel the smallest aspiration to draw closer to the Creator, they are already called "righteous," after this desire. The Creator surrounds *Malchut* on all sides, and *Malchut* feels Him with all of her corrected properties, sensations.

Thus, man also receives the name *Shalom* (peace), for he has made a covenant with *Malchut* below, similar to the covenant of the *Sefira Yesod* Above. And when such a man leaves our world, his soul rises through all the Heavens and none stand in its way, and the Creator calls for it and says: "Let Peace come." The soul reveals the thirteen elevations of the holy peach and no one stands in its way. Hence, happy is he who makes an offering to the Creator.

As soon as the soul tears itself from egoism altogether, it completely merges with the Creator and is no longer obliged to descend into this world, clothe in a physical body, and receive an additional portion of egoistic desires. An offering to the Creator signifies rejection of the body's egoistic desires; it is called a "sacrifice," for our body is no different from that of an animal.

Therefore, the aspiration to rid oneself of the animate body and its desires is called an "offering." Depending on the kind of desires man is already able to wish to rid himself of, his offering takes the form of a bird (one part of his desires) or cattle (another part). Certain parts of *The Zohar* and some of the ARI's compositions discuss this matter in great detail.

Rabbi Chiya raised his voice: "Oh, Rabbi Shimon, you are alive, and I was already mourning over you! Yet, it is not you that I mourn for, but for all my friends and for the whole world that will remain orphans after you." Rabbi Shimon is like a torchlight, shining both Above and below. With this Light below, he illuminates the whole world. Woe unto this world when this Light will leave it and rise up Above. Who will shine in this world with the Light of the Torah? Rabbi Aba rose, kissed Rabbi Chiya, and said, "If such words are within you, I thank the Creator for sending me to you, so that I could be closer to you. How happy I am with my lot!"

All of the characters described in *The Zohar* are spiritual objects, *Partzufim*. As does the whole Torah, *The Zohar* speaks only of things that exist in the spiritual worlds, rather than in our world. Therefore, all of the objects, animals, plants, and people described in *The Book of Zohar* constitute spiritual degrees, desires, and *Partzufim*.

The Creator deliberately sends into our world special souls that are close to Him, to help all the others to attain the spiritual in this lifetime, while they are still in this world. These great Kabbalists serve as guides for those who have realized that they lack spiritual sight, and are hence ready to follow them blindly.

Rabbi Yehudah said after him: When the Creator told Moshe to choose among the people those who are wise and understanding, Moshe looked at the people and could not find any. Then he was instructed to pick the heads of the tribes who were known for their wisdom. The word "understanding" is not used here, for the degree of the understanding is higher than that of the wise. What is the difference between one who is wise and one who understands? Wise is one who learns from a *Rav* (Teacher) and wants to attain wisdom. Wise is one who knows all that he has to know.

He who understands consists of several levels-degrees, for he sees into every thing and knows for himself and for others. The mark of him who understands is formulated in the phrase: "The righteous one knows his animal soul." The righteous one signifies *Yesod* that passes the Light to *Malchut* (animal), for the *Gematria* of *HaVaYaH* of *Malchut* is fifty-two = *BON* = *BeHeMaH* (beast) = *Bet-Hey-Mem-Hey* = $2 + 5 + 40 + 5 = 52$.

*Malchut* constitutes the level called "wise at heart," as wisdom is found within the heart. But he who understands, sees Above and below, for himself and for others. He who is wise designates *Malchut*, for it is *Malchut* that reveals wisdom. He who understands is *Yesod* that stands above *Malchut*. *Ohr Hochma* in *Malchut* shines only from below upwards. It is impossible to receive the Light from Above downwards, as it would surely enter egoistic desires. Therefore, it is said that the wise (*Hacham*) sees only for himself, from himself upwards, and cannot pass the Light to others below.

It is hence said that wisdom is found within the heart, as the heart receives from below upwards; whereas he who understands (the *Sefira Yesod*, *Tzadik*, the righteous one) shines with the Light of Mercy, *Ohr Hassadim*, from Above downwards. He sees that he receives for himself, and shines upon the others, i.e., shines upon *Malchut*, as it is written: "The righteous knows his animal soul."

# RAISING A PRAYER

Here *The Zohar* speaks about the prayer, which every man offers his Creator (*Veyikahel*, pp. 32-52). This inner action of man constitutes his greatest and most valuable work in his efforts for the Creator's sake.

The Creator made man at the farthest, completely opposite spiritual level to His: with only the egoistic will to enjoy. And since man has no other properties-desires but the egoistic will to receive pleasure, not only is he unable to change himself, he cannot even wish for the desire to change.

We can change only under the influence of the Creator's Light, by receiving His properties from Him. Hence our only task is to cultivate a desire to change. As soon as this true desire appears within man, the Creator will immediately give him the strength needed for its realization. So the problem is not how to realize a prayer; it is, rather, how to attain it, how to formulate one's request for the strength to become like the Creator!

A prayer is a sensation, a desire in one's heart. Man does not realize it completely and cannot describe it, for the sensation in one's heart *is not subject to any control and conscious correction*—it cannot be "created" by one's own will. The sensations in one's heart constitute the consequence of man's mental and spiritual condition, the result of the current degree of his spiritual development.

Thus, the desire to change is also in the Creator's hands. However, He gave us the opportunity to stimulate this process and to determine our own spiritual advancement:

- He allows Kabbalists to write books, and when we read them, we develop the desire to draw closer to Him;

- He allows some of the true Kabbalists to be revealed to a wide circle of those who desire spiritual development;

473

- Indiscernibly, He transforms our desires (modifies our souls) so we suddenly take an interest in spirituality;

- He changes our desires with regard to this world, helping us realize its insignificance and transience through sensations of disappointment and suffering.

By creating man a worthless egoist, i.e., by making a worthless creation that is seemingly so unbefitting Him, the Creator allowed man to create himself and elevate himself to an equal degree to that of the Creator Himself—to attain His level of perfection. Thus, the Creator reveals the perfection of His creation: although He created man a worthless creature, He thereby enables him to make a "Creator" of himself (in his properties).

Man cannot claim that although he is created with only one desire, he is unable to induce the reception of an altruistic desire instead of his natural, egoistic one. The Torah, Kabbalah, teachers, and suffering are all prepared to accelerate his advancement toward the goal of creation by the path of the Torah, or otherwise, the path of suffering.

However, the path of suffering is not only undesirable for man, whose life on earth makes him feel as though he is caught between the millstones of a tirelessly revolving mill. Ruthlessly and methodically, it pulverizes him both mentally and physically, to the very last day of his life. But this painful path is equally undesirable in the eyes of the Creator. After all, His goal is to delight man, which is in accord with the path of the Torah—a quick and painless way to transform our desires from egoistic into altruistic.

Since only the Creator can accomplish this (and He will, either painfully or painlessly, in accord with our conscious request), the development of such a request toward Him is all that man must do in his life. It is hence written: "Let him pray all day long!" Yet, we now understand that this phrase does not speak of sitting over a prayer-book, but refers to man's inner work on himself.

There are various forms of work that man must do in action, with his body, as in the case of physically observing the *Mitzvot*. And then there is man's inner, most important work, when observance of the *Mitzvot* depends on the words and desires of the heart.

Never does Kabbalah allude to or even mention our physical body, for it is no different from the body of an animal—it is born, functions, and dies as an animal. And all the various forms of work that the body performs are mere mechanical actions utterly unconnected to man's inner intention, and can even be outright opposite to it.

Therefore, the body's actions are completely disregarded in Kabbalah. Instead, man's *desire* is taken into account and is regarded as an action. In itself, when stripped off the physical body (in which it presently exists), it constitutes man's inner spiritual action.

The spiritual world is a world of incorporeal desires that have no volume, size, movement, or time. Just as in our imagination, where our desires are fulfilled instantly by the power of thought, everything in the spiritual world is determined only by our desires-thoughts, and not by physical actions.

Nevertheless, since in this world we temporarily exist in a physiological body, our task is to observe the Creator's *Mitzvot* both physically (with our body) and spiritually. Physically, we can observe them, as a person usually does—because of his upbringing or for a reward in this world (money, health, luck, peace, and so forth) or in the world to come (the best that he can imagine). Alternatively, he performs these actions because he was taught from childhood to do so mechanically, so he cannot avoid doing them in view of the acquired desire (instinct)—if he does not do them, he suffers.

This feeling of suffering is exactly what compels him to carry out the mechanical actions of the *Mitzvot*. It is not even the desire to receive a reward in this world or in the world to come: in this case, the reward is instantaneous—man feels no discomfort, since he does what he is accustomed to do.

Hence, it seems to such a man, who observes the *Mitzvot* because of the acquired nature (habit), that he demands no reward for his actions either in this world or in the world to come. After all, he truly does not think about any reward, as his habit, which became his second nature, compels him to perform these actions. If he feels this way, he is absolutely positive that he acts "for the Creator's sake." The fact that his habit, his second nature, compels him to perform the *Mitzvot* mechanically, escapes his awareness.

However, since our body is no more than an animal, the mechanical fulfillment of the *Mitzvot* by force of habit or for a reward is quite sufficient for him. There is a difference between those who observe because of upbringing or habit, and those who do it for a reward: the former do not even care whether or not the Creator actually exists; they perform purely mechanical actions that they cannot help performing, for they immediately begin to suffer for lack of habitual actions.

Yet, one who observes the *Mitzvot* because he has faith in reward and punishment believes in the Creator, His Torah, and His governance, but simply uses it for his own benefit. By observing the *Mitzvot* with such an intention and remaining in it all of his life, he, naturally, does not grow spiritually. And he who does not grow in our world is called "still" (inanimate), as we divide all nature into the following levels: still, vegetative, animate, and speaking (human). Therefore, such people are regarded as spiritually still (*Domem de Kedusha*), but they are already "spiritually" still, as opposed to those who observe mechanically, by force of habit.

In Kabbalah, the word "body" implies desire. A desire or a body can be egoistic or spiritual (altruistic). The gradual passing of the egoistic body and its replacement with the altruistic one is called man's "spiritual birth."

Man's spiritual growth is designated by an increasingly growing intention to observe the *Mitzvot* only because such is the Creator's desire. Man observes it only for His sake, completely selflessly, as if no reward of any kind will ever be given to him in return, not even in the form of his own self-content. It is as though the Creator does not know who fulfills His desire, as though man himself is uncertain of whether or not he observes the *Mitzvot*. Yet, he does it anyway, for such is the Creator's will.

So then, the notion of "body" in Kabbalah alludes to man's corrected desires, whereas uncorrected desires, without a screen, cannot be used. It is as though they are not considered body parts, existing beyond the body. Hence, they are considered foreign forces or desires—*Klipot* (shells).

The only existing creation besides the Creator is the egoistic will to enjoy Him that was created by Him. This desire can be either egoistic (corrupted) or altruistic (corrected), spiritually pure or impure. All the spiritual forces: angels, *Klipot*, etc., constitute our uncorrected or corrected desires (the will to bestow delight upon the Creator). Nothing else exists in the universe!

There are twelve parts in the spiritual body that perform spiritual actions: two arms and two legs, each consisting of three parts, in all 4 x 3 = 12. These parts of our spiritual body (our desires that were corrected by the screen) observe the positive *Mitzvot*.

Just like the body of a spiritual object (*Partzuf*), man's body is his altruistic desires, in which he can receive the Creator's Light according to his intentions (screen). Man's desires are determined by his intentions.

All the work with the intention "for the Creator's sake" is performed by the external body parts: the twelve parts of arms and legs, and by the twelve internal body parts: brain, heart, liver, mouth, tongue, five parts of the lungs, and two kidneys. These inner corrections of the body are meant for reception of the Supernal spirit, Light, inside the body, and represent man's most important work with regard to the Creator.

These inner actions are called *Mitzvot*. They depend on speech, such as a prayer—supplications, blessings, and praises. And he who comes to know this work is happy in all things. Man does not realize that his prayer permeates all the Heavens, rising up to the very pinnacle of the universe and reaching the Creator Himself.

As was repeatedly mentioned, not a single word in the Torah speaks of our world, especially not of our body. All the words in the Torah are the Creator's sacred names—the various sensations of the Creator felt by those who attain Him. As we have explained, the attainment and sensation of the Creator is impossible without a screen, an altruistic intention, meaning that all that man desires is to please his Creator. Only the sensations in the heart (the essence of man) can perform this work, and never the physiological organs of our animate body, which is no different from that of an animal.

When the morning Light begins to shine, separating Light from darkness, a call pierces through all the Heavens: *prepare for the opening of entrances and chambers, and each go to your position.* For the ones that serve at night are not the ones that serve in the daytime. And when the night comes, the daytime servants are once more replaced by the nighttime ones.

When the morning Light begins to shine—when man begins to realize that his egoistic desires are death and darkness, whereas altruism and spirituality are life and Light, the Light within man thereby separates from darkness, and he begins to analyze and realize his states, to feel spiritual ascents and descents—he feels his proximity to the Creator as Light, while remoteness from Him and descents into his egoistic desires feel like darkness.

However, one can feel it only if he feels the Creator (even if only a little, even if indistinctly). To start feeling the shame of receiving from the Creator and the insignificance of one's nature (the sensation of darkness), one must first feel the Creator. Only His Light contains all that man needs: strength for correction, desires, life. Hence, the main thing to which man must aspire is the sensation of the Creator, but not for pleasure, for correction.

The forces that serve in the daytime are called the "rulers, the government of the day," and the forces that serve at night are called the "rulers, the government of the night." As soon as the morning call is heard, they all take their positions,

*Malchut* and Israel descend and enter the *Beit-Knesset* (the House of Assembly— a place, where all of man's wishes are collected; hence, it is called the house of prayer) to exalt the Creator and begin their singing and blessings.

It is written: "We shall praise Your mercy in the morning and Your faith at night." Feeling the Creator's Light descending upon him, man perceives it as morning that comes after the darkness, and upon feeling such a state, he praises the Creator in his heart. All alien thoughts retreat before the influence of the Creator's Light, and all impure desires become restrained.

After man has corrected himself in the positive *Mitzvot* (in the first part, in the corrections of *Tzitzit* and *Tefillin*), he must unite all of his heart's desires in inner work (in the second part), and wholeheartedly dedicate himself to the work of praises, since speech rises upwards.

It is impossible to offer a brief explanation of the *Mitzvot* of *Tefillin* and *Tzitzit*, observed only by those who spiritually attained the level of *Partzuf* ZA.

These servants, who stood in their places in the air, are appointed to rule over the four sides of the world. Gazaria soars in the air to govern the East, and all the others that are appointed are together with him, and await the words of the prayer that rises on that side from below. And this ruler takes the prayer.

If the words of a prayer are proper, then all these rulers absorb them and rise with them to the firmament, where the other rulers stand. Upon absorbing these words, they proclaim, "Blessed be Israel. Blessed be the lips that utter these words!"

The letters that were hanging in the air then fly up and form the holy name that rules in the air and consists of twelve letters. This is the name by which Eliyahu flew before rising up to the sky. The letters fly up in the air, and the ruler, who holds the keys to the air in his hand, rises to Heaven along with all the other rulers, and pass the letters into the hands of another ruler for further ascent.

After *Malchut* had been separated from ZA, ZA filled himself with only *Ohr Hassadim* and became the right line, whereas *Malchut* formed the left line. These two lines are in conflict with one another, just as the right and the left lines of *Bina* oppose one another. This continues until ZA ascends to *Bina* as the middle line, balances the right and the left lines, and makes peace between them by uniting them in a single, middle line.

Similarly, ZA and *Malchut*, the two opposite lines, need a middle line to balance them, to bring them balance and peace, and to unite them. This occurs with the help of MAN (*Mei Nukvin*), the prayers of the righteous, for they offer up the desires from this world. Also, the screen that they raise is called the *Masach* (screen) *de* (of) *Hirik*—the middle line—causing the left and the right lines to unite, and *Malchut* to unite with ZA.

Thus, a prayer becomes a request, MAN, and the middle line that leads to peace and unity between ZA and *Malchut*. Just like *Yesod* Above (the middle line) unites the Creator with the *Shechina-Malchut* by gathering all the created souls, man's prayer creates the middle line and unites all by its ascent—bringing peace and unity between the Creator and the *Shechina* (His creatures), the unity of souls with their Creator.

Hence, just like the *Sefira Yesod* Above, man, too, is called *Shalom* (peace). Moreover, the world below precedes and determines the world Above, for the awakening from below (requests of the lower ones) precedes and evokes the awakening from Above.

> The spiritual world is a world of desires. There are only two desires:
>
> 1. The Creator's desire to bestow perfect delight upon His creation, i.e., upon man;
>
> 2. The will to receive pleasure for oneself, created by the Creator, called creation, or man's essence.
>
> Nothing else exists except for these two desires! Everything we can possibly imagine derives only from these two spiritual forces. Man's desire is called a "prayer," for intentionally or unintentionally, this desire appeals to the One who created man, to the Creator. Spiritually, man develops in accordance with his prayer.
>
> However, one's true prayer is his request for spiritual correction and elevation. Such a prayer, a desire in the heart, can be achieved only by consistent study of Kabbalistic sources, which affect man's egoistic desire with their concealed inner Light, and evoke him to ascend spiritually ("Introduction to The Study of Ten Sefirot," item 155).
>
> A soul is none other than man's corrected, altruistic desire, his spiritual *Partzuf*, his desire to receive the Creator's Light with the screen (intention) "for the Creator's sake."

Man's speech in a prayer is none other than parts of his soul (the soul itself) clothed in a body. A prayer is man's soul in this world, *VAK de Nefesh* of *Malchut de Malchut* within *Malchut de Assiya*.

World of AK
World of Atzilut
World of Beria
World of Yetzira
World of Assiya:     Keter

Hochma

Bina

ZA

Malchut = K + H + B + ZA + M

K + H + B + ZA + M

GAR + VAK = Soul of Man

Yet, how can one's prayer, his desire, rise through all the degrees of all the worlds of *BYA* and reach *Malchut de Atzilut* so as to become *MAN* and the middle line, uniting *Malchut* with ZA? After all, it is well known that no degree can rise above itself, let alone make such an incredible leap from the lowest degree of the spiritual ladder (our world) to the world of *Atzilut*.

To understand that, we must first thoroughly understand the meaning of *Malchut's* ascent to *Bina*. As a result of this ascent, each degree splits into two parts: *Keter* and *Hochma* of each degree remain within it, while *Bina*, ZA, and *Malchut* fall to a lower degree. This occurs because *Malchut* ascended to *Bina* and thereby created in *Bina* a new *Sof* (end) of the degree. This is because *Malchut* exists under the prohibition of the first restriction, and hence cannot receive the Light. Due to the second restriction, *Bina*, ZA, and *Malchut* are located below the new *Sof* of the degree. Thus, being below *Malchut* that ascended to *Bina*, they are defined as a lower degree.

| | | |
|---|---|---|
| Keter | = Galgalta | |
| Hochma | = Eynaim | Together they are called GE (Galgalta-Eynaim) |
| Parsa = Ascended Malchut | | |
| Bina | = Awzen | |
| ZA | = Hotem | Together they are called AHP (Awzen-Hotem-Peh) |
| Malchut | = Peh | |

Afterward, through the MAN raised by the lower ones, the Light AB-SAG descends and gives strength to *Malchut*, which stands in *Bina*, to descend to her own place: *Malchut* descends from *Bina* to her own place, thereby returning all the *Sefirot* to their places and uniting them all into one degree, consisting of ten whole *Sefirot*. Consequently, *Bina* and ZON, which were below each degree, return to their degree, to their previous level. Thus, each degree restores itself back to ten *Sefirot*.

However, although *Malchut*, who stood in *Bina* as the new *Sof* (end) of the degree, returns from *Bina* to her own place at the end of every ten *Sefirot*, this new *Sof* that she created in *Bina* does not entirely vanish from *Bina*. As a result, *Bina* and ZON do not descend to their place. Instead, they must rise above the new *Sof* and there create the left line with regard to *Keter* and *Hochma*, which never fell from their degree and constitute the right line.

This is why the new *Sof* remains in its place in all the degrees even after *Malchut's* descent from *Bina*. And this *Sof* is called the "firmament," while *Bina* and ZON, which fell from their degree, but now have returned to it, are called "air." For each lower degree is defined as VAK (called *Avir*—air) with regard to the Upper One.

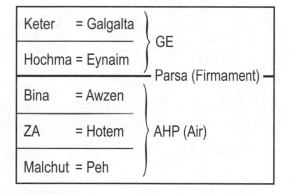

Since *Bina* and ZON fell from their degree, they became as VAK (air) with regard to it, as the entire lower degree with regard to the Upper. And after the descent of *Malchut* from *Bina*, the air (*Bina* and ZON) that was under the firmament rises above it and becomes the left line.

When *Bina* and ZON ascend above the firmament, they take with them the lower degree, where they existed when they were below, and elevate it along with them above the firmament. It is so because unlike our world, there are no ascents and descents in the spiritual; a descent constitutes the deterioration of one's properties from one spiritual level to a lower one.

Hence, being equivalent in properties with the lower degree, when *Bina* and ZON ascend together, they take the entire lower degree along with them. For after being together once, and having become similar, they receive help, ascend, and never part again.

Ultimately, *Malchut's* ascent to *Bina* forms an entrance, an opening, a gate for the lower degree, through which it can ascend to the Upper One. Hence, when *Malchut* descends from *Bina*, thus allowing the lower part, *AHP de Bina*, to ascend, the lower degree can rise along with the ascending *AHP de Bina*.

| | | | |
|---|---|---|---|
| K | | **GE of the Upper One** | |
| H | | Firmament | |
| B | | **AHP of the Upper One** (Air) | |
| ZA | K | **& GE of the Lower One** | |
| M | H | Land or Earth of the Upper One | |
| B | | | |
| ZA | | **AHP of the Lower One** | |
| M | | | |

The entire level ascends

Thus, as a result of *Malchut's* ascent to *Bina* and her subsequent descent due to the influence of *Ohr AB-SAG*, three parts were formed in each degree:

- Air, *Bina* and ZON that fell down;

- The firmaments, the new ends of degrees that appeared through *Malchut's* ascent to *Bina*. These never disappear, even if *Malchut* returns to her place;

- The entrances for the lower degrees that were formed through *Malchut's* ascent to *Bina*, when the lower degree ascends along with her. Without it, the lower degree can never reach the Upper One, for no degree can ascend above itself.

This process is described in the Chassidic tales as the mission of a righteous one (the Upper Degree) in our world: to descend to the most vile and corrupt people (the lower degree). In other words, while essentially remaining itself, the Upper Degree should corrupt its properties so as to equalize with the lower degree. Thus, it shows to the lower ones that in its desires, thoughts, and actions, it is the same as them.

Then, when he completely unites with them, and they fully trust him, when he becomes "one of them" (designating the union of *AHP* of the Upper One with *GE* of the lower one), he gradually, inconspicuously or openly, begins to correct them—by his own example, he propagates his thoughts to them. These thoughts cannot be perceived from an outsider, but only from "one of their own." That is, the Upper One receives additional Light (strength) in its *GE* so as to be able to raise its own *AHP*, correct its desires of reception, start working with them for the Creator's sake, and elevate them to its own level.

And since there is no distinction between the desires of *AHP* of the Upper One and *GE* of the lower one, into which *AHP* of the Upper One fell, they both rise together. This way, the Upper One elevates, i.e., improves, corrects a certain part of the lower one's properties (*GE*), and elevates them to its true level.

Therefore, the most important thing in our state is to come to feel *AHP* of the Upper Degree, located at the very center of our heart, and to become equal with it in our properties so as to afterwards rise together with it.

This process is described in the book *Attaining the Worlds Beyond*, which provides a more personal perspective of this spiritual process:

Inside the internal sensations of the Kabbalist exists a part of the Higher Level, of the future state (*AHP*). One who perceives a Higher Spiritual Level as an unattractive vacuum, rather than a state full of Light, does not receive from the Higher level.

Even though the Higher Level is full of Light, the lower level perceives the Higher only to the degree that the lower qualities permit one to do so. Since the present qualities are not sufficient to receive the Higher Light, the individual does not perceive it.

We can perceive the Upper Level because all the spiritual steps are arranged sequentially from lowest to highest. Moreover, the subsequent states overlap with one another; the lower half of the Higher state is situated within the Upper half of the lower state (*AHP* of Upper falls into *GE* of lower).

Thus, the lowest part of our Upper State is always present within us, but is usually not felt by us. The Upper State above us is referred to as "the Creator" because it functions as the Creator for us.

It gives birth to us and it gives us life and guidance. Since we do not have a perception of this Higher State, we often insist that the Creator does not exist.

*But if we are in a state in which we clearly see the Creator's Upper Domain over all the creations in this world, then we lose the possibility to choose freely.*

We can see only One Truth, only One Force, and only One Will that operates in everything and in everyone.

Since the Will of the Creator is to grant each human being a free will, then the concealment of the Creator from His creations is necessary. Only if He is hidden can we argue that we can aspire *of our free will* to attach ourselves to the Creator—to act for His sake, without any trace of self-interest.

The entire process of self-correction is possible only when the Creator is concealed from us. As soon as He reveals Himself to us we immediately become His servants and fall into the control of His thought, grandeur and power.

At that point, it is impossible to determine what our true thoughts are. Thus, in order to allow us to act freely, the Creator has to conceal Himself.

On the other hand, to give us a chance to break free from the blind slavery of egoism, the Creator must reveal Himself. This is so because a human being obeys only two forces in this world: the force of egoism—the body—and the force of the Creator—altruism.

It follows, then, that alternating the two states is necessary. These states are the concealment of the Creator from us when we perceive only ourselves and the egoistic forces governing us, and the revelation of the Creator when we feel the power of the spiritual forces.

In order for one who is still under the influence of egoism to perceive the closest Upper Object (the Creator), the Creator must equalize some of His qualities with those of the lower being—the person seeking a connection with the Creator.

He will endow some of His altruistic qualities with egoistic attributes, and can then come into balance with the person seeking connection with Him.

The Upper Part elevates the *Malchut-Midat HaDin* to the level of His *Galgalta ve Eynaim*. As a result, His *AHP* acquires egoistic qualities. In this manner, His *AHP* "descends" to the lower part (the spiritual level of the seeker) and comes into a state of equivalence with the qualities of the lower part.

Initially the lower part was not able to perceive the Upper Spiritual State. However, because the Creator hid His highest altruistic qualities behind egoistic ones, He was able to descend to the level of the person so that the person was able to perceive Him.

Because we perceive higher qualities as being egoistic, we are unable to truly grasp their essence. It appears that there is nothing positive in the spiritual that may bring pleasure, inspiration, confidence, or tranquility.

It is precisely at this point that we have an opportunity to exercise our willpower. We may, instead, declare that the absence of pleasure and taste in the spiritual and in Kabbalah is because of the Creator's deliberate concealment for our own sake. Because we do not yet possess the necessary spiritual qualities, it is therefore impossible for us to perceive the Upper spiritual pleasures; rather, all our earthly desires are governed by egoism.

***It is crucial for beginners to understand that they are given descents in order to overcome them.***

They may direct their pleas for relief to the Creator, they may study, or they may do good deeds. The fact that such people do not experience pleasure or vitality from spiritual aspirations is directed from Above.

This gives them the free will to conclude that their lack of pleasure comes from a lack of appropriate altruistic qualities in themselves. Hence, the Upper One must hide His true qualities from them.

Therefore, we must remember that the first stage of perceiving the spiritual is the feeling of spiritual deprivation. If the lower part is capable of realizing that the Upper One is concealing Himself because of their incongruity of qualities, and if that lower part asks for help to correct its own egoism by raising a prayer (*MAN*), then the Upper Part partially reveals Himself (lifts His *AHP*) and displays His true qualities, which prior to this moment, were disguised beneath egoism.

As a result, spiritual pleasure also becomes apparent. Thus, the lower part begins to experience the grandeur and the spiritual pleasure felt by the Higher Being, Who possesses spiritual altruistic qualities.

Because the Upper Part elevated His altruistic qualities in the eyes of the individual, He thus elevated the individual to the middle of His State (He lifted *GE* of the lower together with His own *AHP*).

This spiritual state is known as a person's "lesser spiritual level" (*Katnut*). The Upper Part, in a way, elevates the lower part to His own spiritual level by revealing both His grandeur and the grandeur of altruistic qualities. By seeing the magnificence of the spiritual and comparing it to the material, we may spiritually rise above our world.

When we perceive the spiritual, regardless of our will, our egoistic qualities are changed into altruistic ones, that is, into the qualities of the Creator. In order to allow the lower part to take complete possession of the Higher first level, the Upper Part wholly reveals Himself and all His qualities to that lower part; meaning He reveals his Grandeur, makes *Gadlut*.

At this point, the person perceives the Upper Part as the One and Only Absolute Sovereign of everything in the universe. At the same time, the lower part grasps the highest knowledge of the purpose of creation and of the Upper's dominion.

It becomes clear to the lower part that there is no other way to conduct oneself than in the way prescribed by Kabbalah. Thus, the lower part's reason now requires proper action. As a result of this clear awareness of the Creator, one must deal with the contradiction between faith and knowledge, between the right and the left lines.

Now, having acquired altruistic qualities (*Katnut*), the lower part prefers to proceed only by means of faith in the strength of the Creator. This serves as an indication of the seeker's sincere desire to come closer to the Creator.

However, the Creator's revelation of His grandeur (*Gadlut*) now obstructs one from advancing by faith. Consequently, the individual must willingly dispense with the acquired knowledge.

When one pleads to proceed blindly, relying only on one's faith in the magnificence of the Creator, rather than by realizing His power and grandeur, and only by using reason in proportion to one's faith, the Creator is compelled to limit His disclosure. When such an action compels the Creator to diminish His disclosure of His general dominion, His omnipotence, and His Light (*Ohr Hochma*), this is called "the screen of *Hirik*."

Through this screen, we are able to diminish the revelation of the Upper reason (the left line) to the point at which this revelation can be balanced with faith, the right line. The correct correlation between faith and knowledge is called a "spiritual balance," or the middle line.

We, as individuals, determine the state we desire to be in. Once the correct correlation of faith and knowledge is in place, we can then attain perfection. This is known as "the middle line."

The part of revealed knowledge (the left line) that we can use in proportion to our faith (the right line), by proceeding by faith above reason (the middle line), is added onto those spiritual qualities that we possessed before, in the state of *Katnut*. The newly acquired spiritual level is known as *Gadlut*, meaning big and complete.

After the first complete spiritual level has been attained, we will become equal in qualities to the very first (the lowest) state of the spiritual ladder. As was mentioned earlier, all the states, or steps of the ladder, overlap with each other.

Having reached the first level, we may discover the presence of a higher level within us. Using the same principle as when advancing to the first level, we can proceed step by step to the goal of creation—complete unification with the Creator on the Highest level.

An essential part of our spiritual ascent is a special process that requires that, on discovering a greater evil within us, we ask the Creator to grant us the strength to overcome that evil. We then receive strength in the form of a greater spiritual Light.

This continues until we actually reach the original level and size of our souls: at that point, our egoism is completely corrected and filled with Light.

When we are distracted by outside thoughts, we feel that thoughts obstruct us from ascertaining the spiritual, because our strength and minds are wasted on extraneous concerns, while our hearts become filled with petty desires. At times like this, we lose faith in the fact that only the Kabbalah contains the true life.

Once we overcome this condition, we come out of our state and move into the Light, receiving a Higher Light that helps us ascend further. In this manner, our extraneous thoughts work to help us in our spiritual advancement.

We can overcome obstacles only with the help of the Creator. We can only work on something if we perceive some personal benefit in the task. However, our bodies, hearts and intellects do not understand what benefits can result from altruism.

Therefore, as soon as we try to make even the slightest altruistic move, we lose all strength of the mind, heart and body. We are left with nothing else but to turn to the Creator and ask Him for help. In this way, unwillingly and without any free choice, we advance toward the Creator until we merge with Him completely.

The lower half of the Higher spiritual object is found within the Upper half of the lower spiritual object. In the lower object, the screen (*Masach*) is found in the eye area. This is known as "spiritual blindness," because in such a state only the lower half of the Higher object is visible to us, since the screen of the lower spiritual object conceals part of the Higher spiritual object.

The Higher spiritual object drops its screen to the lower one, then reveals itself to the lower object, which in turn begins to view the Higher object as the Higher One views itself. As a result, the lower object receives the state of fullness (*Gadlut*).

The lower object, then, sees that the Higher One is in a "great" state, and realizes that the Higher object's prior concealment and apparent manifestation as the "small" state (*Katnut*), was done exclusively for the benefit of the lower one. In this way, the lower object could become aware of the importance of the Higher One.

A person in the right line (*Kav Yamin*) is happy with his lot (*Chafetz Hesed*). This is called a "small spiritual state" (*Katnut*), because a person feels no need for the Torah. He does not feel evil, egoism within himself, and without the need for self-correction, he needs no Torah.

Hence, he needs the left line (*Kav Smol*). He has to critically appraise his state (*Heshbon Nefesh*), decide what he wants from the Creator and from himself, and whether he understands the Torah and advances toward the goal of creation. Here he sees his genuine state and is obliged to integrate it in the right line. In other words, he has to be content with what he has and be pleased with his state, as if he has everything that he wishes.

In the left line, which brings about suffering as a result of the absence of the desired, a need is awakened for the help of the Creator, which comes in the form of Light of the soul.

In the right line, in a state when a person desires nothing for the self, there exists only the Light of Mercy (*Ohr Hassadim*), the joy from the similarity in spiritual qualities. But this state is not perfect, because it lacks knowledge and the understanding of the inner meaning. In the left line there is no perfection because the Light of Wisdom can illuminate only if there is congruence in qualities between the Light received and the recipient of the Light.

The congruence results in *Ohr Hassadim*, which is found in the right line. Spiritual gains can be made only by having a desire. But the right line has no desire for anything. All the desires are concentrated in the left line. However, the desired cannot be received into the egoistic desires.

Thus, it is necessary to unite these two qualities so that the Light of knowledge and pleasure of the left line can enter the Light of altruistic qualities of the right line, and the Light of the middle line will illuminate the created being. Without the Light of the right line, the Light of the left is not revealed and is perceived only as darkness.

The ascent from our world, in which we do not consciously perceive *AHP* of the Upper One, occurs in the following way:

All of one's thoughts about the Creator and spirituality constitute his contact with *AHP* of the Upper One. How can this Upper *Partzuf* descend to him? Only by equalizing one's desires (properties) with it. All of man's thoughts and desires (or lack thereof), with regard to the spiritual, constitute his contact with the Upper One. When man feels a lack of desire for spirituality, it means that the Upper *Partzuf* descended and entered him, equalized itself with him; hence, man feels spiritual emptiness.

It is precisely in this state of not being drawn to the spiritual that man should tell himself that it only seems to him this way, whereas in truth, by faith above reason, he desires and acts for the sake of nearing the spiritual. In other words, if, in the state when the Upper One "falls" (spiritual values lose their significance) in his eyes, one can nonetheless aspire to spirituality, he thereby binds, connects himself to *AHP* of the Upper One. This is because *AHP* of the Upper One deliberately degraded its properties and assumed an outward form similar to the properties (desires) of man.

Therefore, as soon as one can establish contact with *AHP* of the Upper One (even if it appears to him absolutely unattractive, precisely because it lowers its properties to man's level), this *AHP* of the Upper One immediately elevates man to its GE. Thus, man ascends to a Higher Degree.

"Piercing through the air" means that the air boundary, consisting of *Bina* and ZON of the Upper Degree, created as a result of *Malchut's* ascent to *Bina*, is pierced by *Malchut's* descent from *Bina* to her place, for then the air rises above the firmament and reaches GAR (GE) of the degree.

Thus occurs the piercing of the firmaments. For the firmaments constitute the borders of new ends, which appeared because the air (*Bina* and ZON) was pushed off from its own degree to a lower one, and was not allowed to return to its degree. Hence, the firmament is pierced from *Malchut's* descent, and no longer prevents *Bina* and ZON from ascending and joining that degree.

| K<br>H | | **GE of the Upper one** |
|---|---|---|
| B | | - - - - Firmament - - - - - - - - - - - - - |
| ZA | K | **AHP of Upper one (Air) + GE of Lower one** |
| M | H | |
| | B | |
| | ZA | **AHP of of the Lower one** |
| | M | |

1. *Malchut* ascended to *Bina* = firmament.

2. *Malchut* descends back. This creates a passage for *AHP* to its *GE*. Thus, the entrances for the lower degree are opened: due to *Malchut's* descent to her place and the piercing through the firmaments, *Bina* and *ZON* ascend to a Higher Degree above the firmament together with the lower degree that they were with during their descent.

In other words, the Upper One deliberately opened up the entrances to enable the lower degree to ascend to a Higher Degree, and not for *Bina* and *ZON* (*AHP* of the Upper One), who simply return to their place.

The Light that lowers *Malchut* from *Bina* to her own place at the end of the ten *Sefirot* stems from *Partzufim AB-SAG*. These are the *Partzufim Hochma* and *Bina* of the world of *AK*. Although the second restriction—*Malchut's* ascent to *Bina*—occurred in *Partzuf Bina* of the world of *AK*, the *Partzufim Bina* (*SAG*) and *Hochma* (*AB*) of the world of *AK* were unaffected by it, and *Malchut* remains in her place at the end of the ten *Sefirot*.

Only the Creator Himself, meaning the properties of the Light, can correct and transform man's egoistic properties to altruistic. Indeed, man is simply unable to pull himself out of his current state "by his own hair," as from birth he has absolutely no spiritual strength (desires). Hence, only the Upper Light can correct him. And it can only be *Ohr Hochma*, for this is the Light that the Creator emanates. *Ohr Hochma*, unrestricted by *Tzimtzum Bet*, is located in *Partzuf AB* of the world of *AK*. *Partzuf SAG de AK* is a *Partzuf* of *Bina*.

Therefore, when one raises his *MAN* (prayer), it reaches the Highest *Partzufim* of the world of *Atzilut*, which turn to *SAG-Bina-Ima* (mother), who in turn appeals to *AB-Hochma-Aba* (father), receives *Ohr Hochma* from him and passes it to her children—the souls of the righteous, those who wish to become righteous and to ascend spiritually.

Hence, when *Hochma-AB* unites with *Bina-SAG* in the world of *AK*, this Light (*Ohr AB-SAG*) descends from *Partzuf Bina de AK* to *Partzuf Bina de Atzilut*, called *EKYEH* = *Aleph-Hey-Yod-Hey*. *Partzuf Bina de Atzilut* sends the Light to all the degrees of the worlds of *ABYA*. Upon attaining a particular *Partzuf*, this Light lowers the *Malchut* of each degree (that ascended to *Bina*) from the degree of *Bina* to her previous place.

Starting with *AVI*, all the *Partzufim* are in the state of *Katnut*: *AHP* of the Upper *Partzuf* is inside *GE* of the lower one. The received *Ohr Hochma* descends to him who raised *MAN*, thus evoking *Gadlut* in all the *Partzufim*, through which the Light descends to him. The Light descends to each *Partzuf* along his personal path, which is precisely what connects everyone, each soul, to the Creator.

## World of AK
Keter - Galgalta
Hochma - AB
Bina - SAG

ZA - MA Elyon  --------

Malchut - BON Elyon

These Partzufim channel the Light of AB-SAG from SAG of AK down to AVI de Atzilut

## World of Atzilut
Keter - Atik

Hochma - AA  --------

Bina - AVI = EKYEH

ZA

Malchut

## World of Beria

## World of Yetzira

## World of Assiya

## Our World

This is why the name *EKYEH* is referred to as the ruler of air that moves the boundary of air because of *Malchut's* descent from *Bina* to her previous place. Each degree and each world consists of four *Sefirot H-B-ZA-M*, each of which Consists of its own individual ten *Sefirot*, where, as a result of *Malchut's* ascent to *Bina* in each degree, *Bina-ZA-Malchut* of each degree fell to a lower degree.

Thus, there are four kinds of airspace in each world that are governed by the three names of *EKYEH*: *EKYEH* in the air of *Hesed*, *EKYEH* in the air of *Gevura*, and *EKYEH* in the air of *Tifferet*. *Malchut* receives from them, and all three names govern in her air together.

The triple name, *EKYEH*, comprises twelve letters. This twelve-letter name rules in the air by lowering *Malchut* from *Bina* to her previous place, returning *Bina* and ZON (called "air"), who fell to a lower degree, back to the degree above the firmament. For *Malchut's* ascent to *Bina* created an entrance, to enable the lower one rise to the Upper Degree as soon as it opens, i.e., during *Malchut's* return to her place.

Hence, when the prophet Eliyahu (a particular spiritual degree) wished to soar to the sky, *Malchut* of each degree ascended to *Bina* of the corresponding degree, while *Bina* and ZON of this degree fell to the lower degree, and a firmament was formed between them. It turned out that each degree doubled: now it contained its own degree, as well as *Bina* and ZON of the Upper Degree, who fell and clothed the lower degree.

This occurred at each degree of the worlds of ABYA, down to the lowest one: *Bina* and ZON of the *Sefira Malchut* of the world of *Assiya* fell and emerged in our world below *Malchut*. *Malchut de Assiya* ends at its firmament, which is a new end, in *Bina*. Also, this degree doubled, as *Bina* and ZON of the *Sefira Yesod* of the world of *Assiya* fell and clothed in its degree.

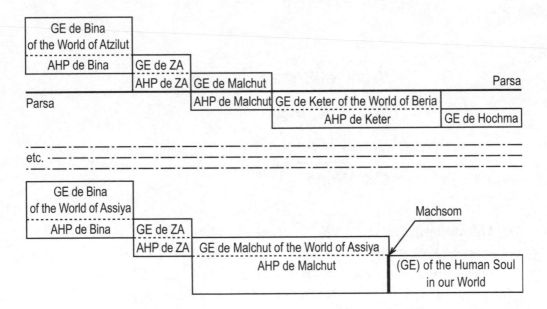

In the diagram, GE of man in our world are put in brackets, for he who exists (spiritually, not with his body) at the degree of our world has no desires of bestowal. Hence, it is said that he who exists with his properties in this world, in egoism, has only a point in his heart, from which he can start his spiritual development.

Similarly, the *Sefira Yesod* of the world of *Assiya* also ends with its firmament and contains *Bina* and ZON of the *Sefira Hod de Assiya*. The *Sefira Netzah de Assiya* also doubled, and so on up to *Bina de Atzilut*. This is why the prophet Eliyahu rose up and united with *Bina* and ZON, who fell from *Malchut de Assiya* to this world. He equalized with them and clothed in them, whereupon they became like him—reached his degree.

Not all ten *Sefirot* of the world of *Assiya* are shown in the above diagram, but as it was previously mentioned, each degree is divided into its own *GE* and *AHP*. Man's task is to find *AHP* of the Upper One within him, and connect to it, merge with it in all of his sensations and desires.

Subsequently, the twelve-letter name exerted its influence (thanks to the Light *AB-SAG*), causing *Malchut de Assiya* to descend from *Bina* of *Malchut de Assiya* to its place, *Malchut de Malchut*, the end of the ten *Sefirot*. And as before, *Bina* and *ZON* ascended to their degree above the firmament of *Malchut*. And since Eliyahu's properties were already merged with this air (with the ascending *Bina* and *ZON*), he rose together with them above the firmament of *Malchut*, as he was similar to them.

| GE de Hochma of the World of Assiya | | | | Sefira Yesod of the World of Assiya |
|---|---|---|---|---|
| AHP | GE de Bina | | | |
| | AHP de Bina | GE de ZA | | Sefira Malchut of the World of Assiya |
| | | AHP de ZA | GE de Malchut | |
| | | | AHP de Malchut | (GE) of the Human Soul in our World |

And since he rose above the firmament of *Malchut de Assiya*, he entered the air (*AHP*) of *Yesod de Assiya*, i.e., *Bina* and *ZON* of *Yesod* that fell down there. Then he merged in his desires with this air and is considered to have clothed in it, for they were previously at the same degree. Then the influence of the twelve-letter name lowered *Malchut* from *Bina* of *Yesod de Assiya* to her place at the end of the ten individual *Sefirot* of *Yesod de Assiya*.

After that, *Bina* and *ZON* (the air of *Yesod*) ascended above the firmament of *Yesod*. And since Eliyahu had already merged with this air, he (man's soul, his desire) too ascended above the firmament of *Yesod de Assiya*, due to his concord with them.

And because he rose above the firmament of *Yesod de Assiya*, he met with the air (*AHP*) of *Hod de Assiya*, i.e., *Bina* and *ZON* of *Hod de Assiya* that fell down there. Subsequently, he merged in his desires with this air and clothed it, for they were previously at the same place (spiritually similar to one another).

As soon as man merges in his properties with *AHP* of the Upper One, the influence of the twelve-letter name (the descent of the Light of *AB-SAG* from Above) brings *Malchut* back (gives strength to the screen) to the end of the ten individual *Sefirot* of *Hod de Assiya*. And the air, its *Bina* and *ZON*, returned to their place above the firmament of *Hod de Assiya*. They took Eliyahu (man's soul, his desires) with them, for he had merged with them, and they elevated him to the firmament of *Hod de Assiya* in view of his similarity with them.

And when he was already in the firmament of *Hod de Assiya*, he met with the air (*AHP*) of *Netzah de Assiya* and merged with it in his properties. When the influence of the twelve-letter name (the Light of correction, *AB-SAG*, that was sent by the Creator) brought *Malchut* back to her place (*Malchut* descended from *Bina* to *Malchut* of this *Sefira*, because she received strength from the Light to resist the egoistic desires of *AHP* and make them altruistic), the air of *Netzah* ascended above the firmament, and being merged with Eliyahu (man's soul), took him with it. Being already in the firmament of *Netzah*, he met with the air of *Tifferet* and so on, until he ascended with this air above the firmament of *Tifferet de Assiya*.

In the same way, the air (*AHP*) of each degree rose higher, up to the Highest Degree of the world of *Assiya*. From there, it rose to *Malchut de Yetzira*, and from there—one step at a time—along all the degrees of the world of *Yetzira* and the world of *Beria*, up to the Heavens (*ZA*) of the world of *Atzilut*.

It is therefore said about the prophet Eliyahu that the Creator's spirit (the Light *AB-SAG*) elevated him (merged with *AHP* of the Upper One) to the Heavens: spirit means *Ruach*, *Sefirot Bina* and *ZON* of the Upper Degree, called "air," that fell down to the lower degree. And this air (spirit) elevates one from a lower degree to a Higher One through all the individual degrees, from the lowest degree (*Sof de Assiya*) up to the world of *Atzilut*.

An Upper Degree is regarded as the Creator of the lower degree: it creates it, vitalizes it with Light, and governs it. At each degree, man considers the next Highest spiritual degree with regard to him as the Creator. As Rabbi Zushe said: "Every day I have a new Creator." In other words, as man ascends to a Higher Degree (which he calls "day" or "Light"), he thereby reveals a new property of the Creator in this Higher Degree.

The air of each of the four sides of the world (in *Sefirot Hesed-Gevura-Tifferet-Malchut*) has its own rulers, who hold the keys to the activation of the twelve-letter name so as to lower *Malchut* from *Bina* to her own place. The ascending order of these four kinds of air is as follows: West-*Malchut*, East-*Tifferet* (including *NHY*), North-*Gevura*, and South-*Hesed*.

Hesed     –     SOUTH

Gevura     –     NORTH

ZA        –     EAST

Malchut    –     WEST

It is not the rulers that raise a prayer (the desire that man feels in the very depths of his heart) from air to air, and then from firmament to firmament. The air raises a prayer from the firmament, each air to its firmament: first, the prayer ascends to the air of the *Sefira Malchut de Assiya*, i.e., to *Bina* and ZON (*AHP*) that fell from *Malchut de Assiya* down to our world. They resemble the prayer itself, for this air (*AHP*) is similar to a prayer (the Upper One lowered itself deliberately to equalize its properties with the lower one); hence, they merge as one degree.

Then the one that rules there, Zvuliel (Zebuliel), activates the twelve-letter name, which lowers *Malchut* from *Bina de Assiya* to her place. This causes the air to return to its degree and rise above the firmament of the world of *Assiya*. And since the air became similar to the degree of the actual prayer, it also takes the prayer along with it, raising it above the firmament of the *Sefira Malchut de Assiya*. This is similar to the ascent of Prophet Eliyahu.

And since the prayer ascended to the firmament of the world of *Assiya*, it meets the air of *Yesod de Assiya* that fell there, as in the case of Eliyahu. It also encounters the ruler of the air of the East, Gazaria (Gazardiel), because East designates the *Sefira Tifferet* (ZA is often called *Tifferet*, as the properties of this *Sefira* dominate and determine all the properties of ZA), which includes the *Sefira Yesod*, for *Tifferet* includes *Sefirot NHY*.

This ruler activates the twelve-letter name and lowers *Malchut* from *Bina de Yesod* to her place, which causes the air of *Yesod* to ascend to its degree, the firmament of *Yesod*. By merging with the prayer into one degree via equivalence of form, he takes it with him and raises it above the firmament of *Yesod*. Then, a similar action occurs in the air and firmament of *Sefirot Netzah*, *Hod*, and *Tifferet*.

Since the prayer ascended to the firmament of *Tifferet*, it encounters the Northern air, i.e., *Bina* and ZON of *Gevura de Assiya* that fell there. There it unites with this air into one degree. Then the ruler of the North, Petachia (Petahyah), activates the twelve-letter name and lowers *Malchut* from *Bina* to her place. Consequently, the air returns, ascends to the firmament of *Gevura* and takes with it the prayer, which merged with it into one degree during its fall.

Since the prayer has already reached the firmament of *Gevura*, it meets with the Southern air, *Bina* and ZON of *Hesed de Assiya* that fell there, and merges with this air. Then the ruler of the Southern air, named Pisgania (Pesagniyah), *Hesed de Assiya*, activates the twelve-letter name and lowers *Malchut* from *Bina* of *Hesed de Assiya* to her place. The Southern air returns and ascends to its degree in the sixth firmament, *Hesed de Assiya*, called "south."

Since the prayer has reached the sixth firmament, it encounters the air that fell from the seventh firmament, which is *Bina* that includes GAR, and the prayer merges with this air into one degree. When the twelve-letter name lowers *Malchut* from *Bina* (the seventh firmament) to her place, the air returns to its degree (the seventh firmament) and takes the prayer with it, as they merge during its fall.

Since the prayer has reached the seventh firmament, it encounters the air that fell from *Malchut de Yetzira*, and merges with it. Next, the general ruler, Sandalphon, who governs the entire world of *Assiya*, takes it and activates the twelve-letter name, which lowers *Malchut* from *Malchut de Yetzira* to her place. And the air ascends and returns to its degree, the firmament of *Malchut de Yetzira*, takes the prayer with it, and elevates it to the firmament of *Malchut de Yetzira*.

In exactly the same way, the prayer ascends through all seven *Heichalot* (halls) of the worlds *Yetzira* and *Beria* up to the world of *Atzilut*. This clarifies the question posed in the beginning: how can a prayer ascend from the very lowest degree of the world of *Assiya* to the world of *Atzilut*, for no degree can ascend above itself? From the aforesaid, it follows that since the prayer merges with the first air that fell from *Malchut de Assiya* to our world, it is exactly this air that elevated them to the firmament of *Malchut*, whereas the air of *Yesod de Assiya* was elevated to the firmament of *Yesod*, and so forth. In other words, the air with which the prayer merges and ascends elevates it to *Malchut* of the world of *Atzilut*.

He who falls from *Malchut de Assiya* to our world descends from the spiritual degree called *Malchut de Assiya* to the spiritual degree called our world. Of course, this in no way refers to the physical existence in our world. *AHP* of the Upper Degree are considered fallen when one feels in his heart (in the center of all of his desires) the desire to attain the spiritual, merge with it, and annul his egoistic properties because they harm and impede his advancement.

One should not think that the fall of *Bina* and ZON to our world from the world of *Assiya* can be experienced by anyone. And only he who felt this way and was then able to make a sufficient amount of quantitative and qualitative efforts, merits being elevated above our world by *AHP* of the Upper One.

On the Southern side (*Hesed*), there is he who governs the air of that side, and his assistants. His name is Pisgania, and he holds the keys to the air of this side. All those who suffer pray to their Creator from the depths of their broken hearts (the very sensation of suffering constitutes a prayer, and requires no words). If their speech (desires) is worthy, it ascends to the air of this side, and the ruler accepts and kisses it ("embrace," "kiss," and *Zivug* are forms of spiritual union of *Partzufim*), and then declares: "The Creator will be merciful and will spare you in His mercy."

All of the holy rulers (*Ohr Hochma* is called holy) and their assistants of that side rise together with him. The letters of the Creator's holy name, of the twelve-letter name *EKYEH* soar: four letters *Aleph-Hey-Yod-Hey* on each side, which rule the corresponding sides of air. They ascend on this side of the air to the Southern firmament, *Hesed* (the sixth firmament), to the ruler of the firmament of the Southern side, named Anafiel.

On the Northern side (*Gevura*) there is Petachia, who governs the air with his assistants. If he who prays for his enemies and haters, i.e., for those who make him suffer is righteous, then as the speech of his prayer rises to the air of that side, the ruler accepts his heart's speech and kisses it (unites it with his properties so as to raise it higher).

The air that comes from the North stirs and calls upon all the firmaments, and they all take this speech, raise it to the Northern, fifth firmament, kiss it and say: "The Lord will cast your enemies down and take them away from your face." This occurs in the following order: after the governor of the air had accepted the prayer and kissed it, which means that it merged with the degree of the air and the ruler, the air stirs on the Northern side (the new end that *Malchut* made as she ascended to *Bina*, called *Techum*—space, from the word *Tohu*—chaos), and the twelve-letter name lowers *Malchut* from *Bina* of *Gevura de Assiya* back to her place.

The air that fell into the restrictions (*Dinim*) of this space is aroused by the desire to rise to the firmament of *Gevura*. Also, all the degrees that merged with it during its fall rise along with it to the firmament of *Gevura* due to their similarity to it. Similarly, the prayer that was merged with it during its fall ascends along with it to the fifth firmament.

The order of the ascent (offering up of a prayer) starts from here: it ascends and pierces through the air (*AHP*), which fell from *Malchut de Assiya* to our world, and ascends with it to the first firmament, the firmament of *Malchut de Assiya*. The prayer ascends and approaches the ruler (in its properties), who was appointed to control the Western side, *Malchut*. There are nine entrances where the assistants to the ruler, Zvuliel stand.

The ten *Sefirot* of *Malchut* herself have nine (not ten) entrances, for a restriction to receive the Light is imposed on *Malchut* of the *Sefira Malchut*, and it is connected to *Yesod de Malchut*. Hence, *Yesod* and *Malchut* of *Malchut* share the same entrance.

However, a question arises: "Why do all the parts of the air have one ruler for the air and a separate ruler for the firmament? For example, on the Eastern side Gazaria controls the Eastern air and Shimshiel controls the Eastern firmament (*Tifferet*, the fourth firmament). Similarly, Pisgania controls the Southern air on the Southern side, and Anafiel controls the Southern firmament. And on the Northern side, the ruler Petachia governs the Northern air, and Gadriel is in charge of the Northern firmament. So why does only *Malchut* have one general ruler, called Zvuliel, who governs both the air and the firmament?"

The reason is that due to *Malchut's* ascent to *Bina*, *Bina* and ZON of each degree fall to a lower degree, the degree of air. However, only the lower part of *Bina* (ZAT or *VAK de Bina*) falls, whereas *Keter*, *Hochma*, and the Upper half of *Bina* (GAR *de Bina*) remain at the same degree. Only the lower half of *Bina*, ZAT *de Bina* (ZA and *Malchut*) fell from this degree and became air.

| Keter | GE |
|---|---|
| Hochma | |
| Bina — GAR of Bina / ZAT of Bina | — Parsa = Malchut — |
| ZA | AHP |
| Malchut | |

Therefore, two separate rulers were needed: one for the Upper Degree remaining above the firmament, and the other—for the lower half of the degree that fell and turned into air. The degree (ten *Sefirot*) of *Malchut*, from whom all nine lower *Sefirot* fell to the lower degree during *Malchut's* ascent to *Bina*, retained only one *Sefira Keter de Malchut*, which remained as a point below *Yesod de ZA*.

Nevertheless, even this point refers more to the *Sefira Yesod*, which is superior to *Malchut*, because its properties are more similar to *Yesod*. And since all of

*Malchut* refers to the properties of air (except for her individual *Keter*), she has only one ruler.

The ruler wishes to act in the firmament in the daylight, but does not receive permission until the moon rises, i.e., until nightfall, when all the rulers and forces emerge. And when the day breaks (the Upper Light starts shining), they all ascend (the spiritual properties become corrected and improve under the Light's influence) to the Highest of the nine entrances, the point of *Keter de Malchut*, which remained at its degree above the firmament (*Parsa*).

And when the prayer ascends, it enters through this Upper entrance, and all the rulers with their assistants emerge from it, led by their Supreme ruler, Zvuliel, the only ruler of the air of this Upper entrance, who is above the firmament of *Malchut de Assiya*. They all emerge, kiss the prayer, and accompany it up the second firmament of *Yesod de Assiya*.

*Malchut* constitutes the left line—*Hochma* without *Hassadim*. Therefore, when she dominates, the Light does not shine and darkness prevails. *Hochma* cannot shine without *Hassadim*, which means that when *Malchut* rules, it is nighttime (not daylight). Indeed, all nine of her lower *Sefirot*, from which all the rulers (of man) and forces (man's desires) of the left side originate, rule at night.

This is why it is said that *Malchut* descends from *Bina* to her place, although her nine lower *Sefirot* remained untouched by the impure force, for *Malchut* descended from the firmament, which transformed her into air. Even so, they (nine *Sefirot*) have no power in her place, and must rise above the firmament to the Upper entrance, *Keter de Malchut*. There they enter the right side (*Hassadim*), and the prayer ascends with them because of their similarity (in desires, properties), achieved while they were below the firmament (in the state called "our world").

And since the prayer (MAN) rose above the firmament of *Malchut* (to GE of the Upper One), it encounters the air (AHP of the still Higher One) that fell there from the second firmament. After the descent of *Malchut* from *Bina* of *Yesod de Assiya* to her place, this air ascends to the firmament of *Yesod*, and takes with it all the rulers, their assistants, and the prayer, which were merged with it during its fall, and elevates all of them to the firmament of *Yesod de Assiya*.

And when the prayer ascends to this firmament (*Yesod*), the twelve gates of this firmament open up. A special ruler, Ana'el (Anahel), who is in charge of many forces, stands at the twelfth entrance, and when the prayer ascends, proclaims to all the entrances: "Open the gates." And all the entrances open up, and the prayer enters through them.

This happens because *Tifferet* has twelve borders of the diagonal, defined by the *Sefirot H-G-T-M*, each of which contains three lines of *HGT*, twelve in all. And all that exists in *Tifferet* is also present in *Yesod*, but there these twelve borders are called "twelve gates," through which the prayer enters.

And then awakens a very old ruler, who stands at the Southern side. His name is Azriel-Saba, sometimes referred to as Machaniel, for he is responsible for 600,000 groups (camps—*Machanot*). All the groups have wings and eyes; they stand and listen to all those who are quietly praying, to the prayers that come from the depths of the heart and are directed only to the Creator. Only such prayers are heard by those who have ears.

There is a special opening in the *Sefira Yesod de Hesed* (Supernal mercy) that descends from the right line of *Bina*. Hence, the ruler of this mercy is called Azriel-Saba. He is called *Saba* (grandfather), because *Hochma* and *Bina* are called "old men." And he is appointed to rule over 600,000 groups (camps), because $600 = 6 \times 100$, where $6 = HGT\ NHY$ *Sefirot* in *Bina*. And since each *Sefira* in *Bina* is designated by 100, $6 \times 100 = 600$. And the thousands stem from *Ohr Hochma*, which shines in each of these *Sefirot*. Hence, $600 \times 1,000 = 600,000$ groups.

*GAR de Tvuna*, the lower part (*ZAT*) of *Bina*, are called "ears." Only *Ohr Hassadim* shines in them, without *Hochma*. *VAK de Tvuna* are called "eyes," and *Ohr Hochma* shines in them.

*Malchut* and *Bina* constitute two kinds of air, West and North, which unite and intermix, and form a diagonal, a combination of judgment and mercy that mitigates strictness and judgment. Hence, they hear good words from one who merits it, i.e., they accept one's prayer to the extent of the mercy in the diagonal. Alternatively, they hear bad things about one who does not merit, accepting one's prayer to the extent of the judgment in the diagonal.

If man's ears hear the prayer (which means that he speaks not from the depths of his heart, but with his mouth, so outwardly that his ears hear it, but not his heart), no one will accept it Above. Therefore, man must be watchful: no one should hear his prayer, for the speech of the prayer unites in the Upper World, in ZA, and the speech of the Upper World must not be heard.

Consider how the Torah is read: one reads and the others keep silent. However, if they all read it out loud, they lessen the faith Above, for the voice and speech of one mingle with the voice and speech of the others, and undermine faith, i.e., *Malchut*. The voice and speech (ZA is called "voice" and *Malchut* is called "speech") of one must be similar to the voice and speech of the other.

Two reasons are mentioned above as to why a prayer must be speech without voice, unheard by man's ear. The first is that *Malchut*, who begets people, consists of two points: the Light cannot be received from *Malchut* with a measure of judgment, whereas the Light can be received from *Malchut* that is corrected in *Bina* with a measure of mercy.

Similarly, man consists of a combination of these two points. If he merits, the measure of judgment becomes concealed, the measure of mercy is revealed, and he merits receiving the Upper Light. However, if he does not merit, the measure of judgment becomes revealed and the Light disappears from him.

Therefore, the Upper ear has an inclined form so as to be able to receive the prayer of man-righteous one, him who merits the concealment of the measure of judgment, so that the listening ear would not arouse judgment, concealed in the speech of the prayer. Hence, if an outsider hears the prayer before it ascends, he evokes the judgment concealed in the speech of the prayer, and it cannot be heard Above.

There is another reason for this: the speech of the prayer constitutes parts of *Malchut*. And he who prays must be a part of *Malchut*. Hence, the prayer must ascend and be included in the Supernal *Malchut*, called "speech." Then *Malchut* unites with ZA (voice) and the prayer is accepted, i.e., the Light is accepted from ZA.

Therefore, one must not raise his voice during prayer so as to allow the Supernal voice, the Light of ZA, to descend to the praying person. The speech ascends to *Malchut*, merges with ZA with the help of *Malchut*, and receives a completely corrected voice from ZA. As a result, the prayer can receive the Light. It is therefore said that the words of a prayer pronounced by man's voice must not be heard.

He who reads the Torah must also be a part of ZA, called "Torah." And the voice of one who reads Torah must be instead of the voice of ZA. Hence, it is forbidden to hear someone else's voice, for it will be the voice of one who exists under judgment, and not under mercy.

Thus, the voice of an outsider harms the voice of one who reads the Torah, and *Malchut* is unable to receive the Light from ZA. Yet, if this is the voice and speech of one man, then the voice, called ZA, and speech, called *Malchut*, merge into one combination. But if voice and speech of an outsider join the reader's, it will harm him.

With regard to everything mentioned above, one can say that only he who approaches the described state can understand what *The Zohar* narrates.

Spiritual actions are understood in one's heart, his desires, his properties. If they do not correspond to those that are described above, no explanation of any kind will help. An "outsider" designates man's "foreign" (distant from spiritual aspirations) thoughts and desires.

When a quiet, concealed, and secret prayer ascends, the governor Azriel-Saba himself and all of his assistants, who are in charge of the 600,000 groups (camps), and all those who have eyes and ears emerge and kiss the ascending word of the prayer.

This is said in the verse: "The Creator's eyes and ears are upon them." The Creator's eyes rest upon the righteous. The Creator's eyes refer to those below who have eyes, meaning the angels that exist in the firmament of *Yesod de Assiya*. They exist Above, at the degree of GAR, for eyes signify the property of *Hochma*. However, these eyes are the eyes of the *Sefira Yesod*, as it is written: "The Creator's eyes rest upon the righteous," as *Yesod* is called the "righteous one."

The third firmament is the *Sefirot Netzah* and *Hod de Assiya*. The prayer ascends to this firmament. The ruler Gadria, who controls this firmament with his assistants, acts three times a day during the ascent of the three lines to the world of *Atzilut*, when the luminous scepter of Light ascends and descends, but does not stay in one place, for *Ohr Hochma* of the left line (called the "scepter of Light") wants to shine.

The word "scepter" (Hebrew, *Sharvit*) signifies eyesight, and *Ohr Hochma* is called the Light of eyesight. The scepter moves three times and conceals itself, because *Hochma* reveals itself only when the three lines move in the three points: *Holam* (the dot above the letters), *Shuruk* (the dot inside the letters), and *Hirik* (the dot below the letters).

When the prayer, which is the middle line, ascends and carries the screen of *Hirik*, the scepter (the Light of the left line) descends and bows its head before the prayer, designating the concealment of GAR, called "head." This is because the middle line reduces the left line with the help of the screen of *Hirik*. This third firmament of *Sefirot Netzah* and *Hod de Assiya* is called the "firmament of the scepter," for the scepter of Light acts within it.

When the prayer ascends, the ruler bows his head before it (diminishes his level) and then strikes the iridescent rock with his scepter. The rock stands at the center (the middle line) of the firmament, and 365 hosts emerge from the rock, which were concealed within it since the Torah descended to the earth. Because they objected to this descent, the Creator reproached them, and they concealed themselves in the rock.

Here, by analogy with the aforesaid and in accordance with the definitions of such notions as a "scepter," a "rock," "hosts," "Light," "concealment," "to bow," the reader is offered an opportunity to translate from the language of legends into the language of spiritual actions. And when the reader attains what is written, he will feel it within him!

And they do not emerge from there, except for when the prayer ascends. Then they praise the Creator, saying: "Our Creator, how great is Your name upon the earth!" This prayer is called "Great," because it ascends to all these firmaments, and they bow before it.

This occurs because the angels that opposed the descent of the Torah (see the article "Heaven and Earth"), i.e., the middle line, to the earth (*Malchut* and the worlds of *BYA*), emerge from the left line. And they wanted the left line to dominate in *Malchut* and in the worlds of *BYA*, but not the middle one, called the "Torah," which reduces the *GAR* of the Light of the left line.

*Malchut*, called "earth," includes all the worlds of *BYA*. However, the Creator (middle line) reproached and compelled her to receive the Light of the middle line and conceal herself in the rock, in the forces of judgment, which exist in the middle line that stands at the center of the firmament.

However, the prayer can ascend only by activating the left line, namely *Bina* and *ZON* that fell to the lower degree, then ascended once more above the firmament, and became the left line. They take the prayer that existed with them during their descent to the lower degree.

This is why the ruler receives the scepter, the Light of the left line, for during the ascent of the prayer, the left line shines in his domain. The 365 hosts then awaken and receive the Light of the left line from the scepter. Hence, they exclaim: "The Creator, Our Lord, how great is Your name upon the earth!" for the prayer ascends to this firmament, called "Great," and includes the screen of *Hirik* of the left line, from the *GAR*. Thus, they bow their heads, i.e., do not use the *GAR* of *Ohr Hochma*, but only *VAK*.

Afterward, the prayer clothes in the Supernal adornments and rises to the fourth firmament, *Tifferet*. Then the sun (*Tifferet*) emerges at its level, the Supreme ruler Shimshiel, and the 365 hosts ascend to this firmament along with him. They are called "the days of the sun," for these levels stem from the sun, *Tifferet*. And they all clothe and adorn *Malchut* in the Heavens of the Garden of Eden.

The prayer pauses there to merge with the air of *Gevura* of those degrees, because it was not supposed to pause at the previous firmament, *NHY*, as they are included in *Tifferet*. And the prayer remains there until all the hosts have risen with it to the fifth firmament (*Gevura*), where Gadriel rules; he is in charge of all the hosts of the other nations, for *Gevura* constitutes the left line, which the other nations hold on to.

And when the prayer ascends, carrying within the screen of the middle line (which reduces the left line from *GAR* to *VAK*), it shakes him and all of his hosts, and they lose all their strength, emerge and bow their heads, i.e., *GAR*, and adorn this prayer.

They ascend with it to the sixth firmament, *Hesed*, and the legions and hosts come forth and accept the prayer until they reach the seventy gates, *HGT NHYM*, each of which consists of ten, as *Hesed* includes all seven lower *Sefirot*. The Supreme ruler, Anafiel, stands there and adorns the prayer with seventy adornments.

And since the prayer was adorned, all the legions and hosts of all the firmaments that accompanied the prayer from firmament to firmament unite and raise the prayer to the seventh firmament, *Bina*, which includes *GAR*.

The prayer enters the seventh firmament, and the Supreme ruler Sandalphon, who is in charge of all the guards at the entrances, ushers the prayer into the seven halls of the world of *Yetzira*. These are the seven halls of the King, the seven halls of *Malchut de Atzilut*, where ZA rules.

When the prayer, adorned with all of these adornments, ascends there, it unites ZA with *Malchut*, for everything grows with similarity to everything else. And the Creator's name, i.e., *Malchut* is adorned from Above and from below, and on all sides, as *Malchut* merges with ZA into one. And then *Yesod* (the righteous one) fills *Malchut* with its blessings.

Happy is the lot of him who can put his prayer in proper order, so the Creator will clothe in this prayer. He waits until all the prayers of Israel finish ascending and unite into a complete and perfect prayer, whereupon everything will become perfect both Above and below.

Besides the prayer, there are the *Mitzvot* of the Torah that depend on speech and action. There are six *Mitzvot* that depend on speech:

1. To fear the Great and Mighty Creator;
2. To love the Creator;
3. To bless the Creator;
4. To proclaim the Creator's unity;
5. To bless the nation, which is incumbent on *Cohanim* (priests);
6. To entrust one's soul with the Creator.

Out of the six above-mentioned *Mitzvot*, the first finds its place in the blessings that King David sang during his offerings in the Torah, where man must fear his Master, for these songs stand in a place called "fear" or *Malchut*. And all of these written blessings constitute the essence of fear of the Creator, *Malchut*. And man must sing these songs with his desires in fear.

Man must achieve a level of spiritual development where his desires will coincide with what is said in the texts of these blessings. It is impossible to force someone to wish something; all our feelings are the product, the result of our spiritual level. The Light of that degree influences one's egoism and corrects it with the power of that degree. Therefore, man can only ask for correction, but it will come from Above, from the Light, from the Creator.

Here we have a list of degrees that man must gradually go through in his correction. These degrees are usually called *Mitzvot*, and in all there are 620 of them between us and the Creator: 613 *Mitzvot* of the Torah for Israel (altruism) and seven *Mitzvot* of the Torah for all the nations (egoism). Here they are expounded in a different way: since the most important is to ask for correction (and if the request is genuine, the answer in the form of Light immediately descends to it), all of man's work on himself, all of his efforts in the study, work and actions are aimed only at the creation of a true request, MAN. Hence, the stages of man's spiritual development are described as his path in prayer; as if he stands and prays, although this process continues within him throughout his life on earth.

The second *Mitzva*: to love the Creator (as it was repeatedly stated, this feeling is the result of correction; see "Introduction to the Study of Ten Sefirot," item 45–the four degrees of sensation of governance, from darkness to love), when in his prayer one reaches *Ahavat Olam* (great love) and *Le El* (for the Creator). These two blessings precede the appeal, *Shema Israel* (Hear, O Israel) and *Ve Ahavta Et* (and love the Creator), the blessing of the Creator for one's love for Him that follows the appeal *Shema Israel*. And this is the secret of love for the Creator.

The third *Mitzva*: since man reaches a place in the prayer that is called *Lehishtabe'ach* (blessed is the Creator), he must attain praises and blessings of the Creator in his desire, as in parts of the prayer *Yotzer Ohr* (He who creates Light) and *Yotzer HaMeohrot* (maker of the stars).

The fourth *Mitzva* is to proclaim the Creator's unity, i.e., *Shema Israel* (Hear, O Israel, our Creator is one!). From this point (degree) on, one must express the secret of the Creator's unity (in all His manifestations to man) in his heart's desire (one's heart must be filled only with the sensation of the One, Upper Force). Afterward, the *Mitzva* to remember and remind others of the exodus from Egypt (egoism) is observed, as it is written: "Remember how you were a slave in Egypt."

The fifth *Mitzva* is for a *Cohen* to bless the people (the Light's descent to the *Partzuf*), so that Israel will be included when the prayer (the *Cohanim*'s blessing) ascends, for at this time (state), *Knesset Israel* (all those who correct themselves by aspiring to the Creator and constitute a part of *Malchut de Atzilut*), i.e., *Malchut*, receives a blessing (Light).

The sixth *Mitzva* and the desired time (state, spiritual level when man wishes only to give all of his desires, i.e., his soul, to the Creator, meaning that he can act for the Creator's sake in all of his desires) is to entrust one's soul with the Creator with complete desire in one's heart. When one falls (willingly accepts the small state) on his face (*Hochma*) and proclaims (raises MAN): "I entrust my soul with You, O Creator." The intentions and desires of his heart are to give his soul completely to the Creator (this desire is the consequence of this spiritual degree and comes naturally to those who attain it).

These six *Mitzvot* of the prayer correspond to the 600 *Mitzvot* of the Torah. And the remaining thirteen *Mitzvot* are required in order to attract the thirteen properties of mercy (thirteen *Midot HaRachamim*), which include all the rest. The prayer is adorned with 600 *Mitzvot*, which corresponds to *HGT NHY*, to what the prayer, *Malchut*, receives from ZA.

Happy is he who heeded and focused his desire on this (who was able to raise a proper request for his correction), who completed all that was required each day (in the Creator's daylight), and directed his heart's intentions and desires to fulfill this *Mitzva*, which depends on the word.

THE END

# Appendix One
# Further Reading

To help you determine which book you would like to read next, we have divided the books into five categories—Beginners, Intermediate, Advanced, All Around, and Textbooks. The first three categories are divided by the level of prior knowledge readers are required to have. The Beginners Category requires no prior knowledge. The Intermediate Category requires reading one or two beginners' books first; and the Advanced level requires one or two books of each of the previous categories. The fourth category, All Around, includes books you can always enjoy, whether you are a complete novice or well versed in Kabbalah.

The fifth category—textbooks—includes translations of authentic source materials from earlier Kabbalists, such as the Ari, Rav Yehuda Ashlag (Baal HaSulam) and his son and successor, Rav Baruch Ashlag (the Rabash).

Additional translated material that has not yet been published can be found at *www.kabbalah.info*. All materials on this site, including e-versions of published books, can be downloaded free of charge.

## BEGINNERS

### *Kabbalah for Beginners*

*Kabbalah for Beginners* is a book for all those seeking answers to life's essential questions. We all want to know why we are here, why there is pain, and how we can make life more enjoyable. The four parts of this book provide us with reliable answers to these questions, as well as clear explanations of the gist of Kabbalah and its practical implementations.

Part One discusses the discovery of the wisdom of Kabbalah, and how it was developed, and finally concealed until our time. Part Two introduces the gist of the wisdom of Kabbalah, using ten easy drawings to help us understand the structure of the spiritual worlds, and how they relate to our world. Part Three reveals Kabbalistic concepts that are largely unknown to the public, and Part Four elaborates on practical means you and I can take, to make our lives better and more enjoyable for us and for our children.

## Kabbalah Revealed

This is a clearly written, reader-friendly guide to making sense of the surrounding world. Each of its six chapters focuses on a different aspect of the wisdom of Kabbalah, illuminating the teachings and explaining them using various examples from our day-to-day lives.

The first three chapters in *Kabbalah Revealed* explain why the world is in a state of crisis, how our growing desires promote progress as well as alienation, and why the biggest deterrent to achieving positive change is rooted in our own spirits. Chapters Four through Six offer a prescription for positive change. In these chapters, we learn how we can use our spirits to build a personally peaceful life in harmony with all of Creation.

## Wondrous Wisdom

This book offers an initial course on Kabbalah. Like all the books presented here, *Wondrous Wisdom* is based solely on authentic teachings passed down from Kabbalist teacher to student over thousands of years. At the heart of the book is a sequence of lessons revealing the nature of Kabbalah's wisdom and explaining how to attain it. For every person questioning "Who am I really?" and "Why am I on this planet?" this book is a must.

## Awakening to Kabbalah

A distinctive, personal, and awe-filled introduction to an ancient wisdom tradition. In this book, Rav Laitman offers a deeper understanding of the fundamental teachings of Kabbalah, and how you can use its wisdom to clarify your relationship with others and the world around you.

Using language both scientific and poetic, he probes the most profound questions of spirituality and existence. This provocative, unique guide will inspire and invigorate you to see beyond the world as it is and the limitations of your everyday life, become closer to the Creator, and reach new depths of the soul.

## Kabbalah, Science, and the Meaning of Life

Science explains the mechanisms that sustain life; Kabbalah explains why life exists. In *Kabbalah, Science, and the Meaning of Life*, Rav Laitman combines science and spirituality in a captivating dialogue that reveals life's meaning.

For thousands of years Kabbalists have been writing that the world is a single entity divided into separate beings. Today the cutting-edge science of quantum physics states a very similar idea: that at the most fundamental level of matter, we are all literally one.

Science proves that reality is affected by the observer who examines it; and so does Kabbalah. But Kabbalah makes an even bolder statement: even the Creator, the Maker of reality, is within the observer. In other words, God is inside of us; He doesn't exist anywhere else. When we pass away, so does He.

These earthshaking concepts and more are eloquently introduced so that even readers new to Kabbalah or science will easily understand them. Therefore, if you're just a little curious about why you are here, what life means, and what you can do to enjoy it more, this book is for you.

## From Chaos to Harmony

Many researchers and scientists agree that the ego is the reason behind the perilous state our world is in today. Laitman's groundbreaking book not only demonstrates that ego has been the basis for all suffering throughout human history, but also shows how we can turn our plight to pleasure.

The book contains a clear analysis of the human soul and its problems, and provides a "roadmap" of what we need to do to once again be happy. *From Chaos to Harmony* explains how we can rise to a new level of existence on personal, social, national, and international levels.

## INTERMEDIATE

## The Kabbalah Experience

The depth of the wisdom revealed in the questions and answers within this book will inspire readers to reflect and contemplate. This is not a book to race through, but rather one that should be read thoughtfully and carefully. With this approach, readers will begin to experience a growing sense of enlightenment while simply absorbing the answers to the questions every Kabbalah student asks along the way.

The Kabbalah Experience is a guide from the past to the future, revealing situations that all students of Kabbalah will experience at some point along their journeys. For those who cherish every moment in life, this book offers unparalleled insights into the timeless wisdom of Kabbalah.

### The Path of Kabbalah

This unique book combines beginners' material with more advanced concepts and teachings. If you have read a book or two of Laitman's, you will find this book very easy to relate to.

While touching upon basic concepts such as perception of reality and Freedom of Choice, The Path of Kabbalah goes deeper and expands beyond the scope of beginners' books. The structure of the worlds, for example, is explained in greater detail here than in the "pure" beginners' books. Also described is the spiritual root of mundane matters such as the Hebrew calendar and the holidays.

## • ADVANCED

### The Science of Kabbalah

Kabbalist and scientist Rav Michael Laitman, PhD, designed this book to introduce readers to the special language and terms of the authentic wisdom of Kabbalah. Here, Rav Laitman reveals authentic Kabbalah in a manner both rational and mature. Readers are gradually led to understand the logical design of the Universe and the life that exists in it.

The Science of Kabbalah, a revolutionary work unmatched in its clarity, depth, and appeal to the intellect, will enable readers to approach the more technical works of Baal HaSulam (Rabbi Yehuda Ashlag), such as The Study of the Ten Sefirot and The Book of Zohar. Readers of this book will enjoy the satisfying answers to the riddles of life that only authentic Kabbalah provides. Travel through the pages and prepare for an astonishing journey into the Upper Worlds.

### Introduction to the Book of Zohar

This volume, along with The Science of Kabbalah, is a required preparation for those who wish to understand the hidden message of The Book of Zohar. Among the many helpful topics dealt with in this text is an introduction to the "language of roots and branches," without which the stories in The Zohar are mere fable and legend. Introduction to the Book of Zohar will provide readers with the necessary tools to understand authentic Kabbalah as it was originally meant to be, as a means to attain the Upper Worlds.

## The Zohar

*The Book of Zohar (The Book of Radiance)* is an ageless source of wisdom and the basis for all Kabbalistic literature. Since its appearance nearly 2,000 years ago, it has been the primary, and often only, source used by Kabbalists.

For centuries, Kabbalah was hidden from the public, which was deemed not yet ready to receive it. However, our generation has been designated by Kabbalists as the first generation that *is* ready to grasp the concepts in *The Zohar*. Now, we can put these principles into practice in our lives.

Written in a unique and metaphorical language, *The Book of Zohar* enriches our understanding of reality and widens our worldview. Although the text deals with one subject only—how to relate to the Creator—it approaches it from different angles. This allows each of us to find the particular phrase or word that will carry us into the depths of this profound and timeless wisdom.

## ALL AROUND

### Attaining the Worlds Beyond

From the introduction to *Attaining the Worlds Beyond*: "...Not feeling well on the Jewish New Year in September 1991, my teacher called me to his bedside and handed me his notebook, saying, 'Take it and learn from it.' The following morning, my teacher perished in my arms, leaving me and many of his other disciples without guidance in this world.

"He used to say, 'I want to teach you to turn to the Creator, rather than to me, because He is the only strength, the only Source of all that exists, the only One who can really help you, and He awaits your prayers for help. When you seek help in your search for freedom from the bondage of this world, help in elevating yourself above this world, help in finding the self, and help in determining your purpose in life, you must turn to the Creator, who sends you all those aspirations in order to compel you to turn to Him.'"

*Attaining the Worlds Beyond* holds within it the content of that notebook, as well as other inspiring texts. This book reaches out to all those seekers who want to find a logical, reliable way to understand the world's phenomena. This fascinating introduction to the wisdom of Kabbalah will enlighten the mind, invigorate the heart, and move readers to the depths of their souls.

### Basic Concepts in Kabbalah

This is a book to help readers cultivate an *approach to the concepts* of Kabbalah, to spiritual objects, and to spiritual terms. By reading and re-reading in this book, one develops internal observations, senses, and approaches that did not previously exist within. These newly acquired observations are like sensors that "feel" the space around us that is hidden from our ordinary senses.

Hence, *Basic Concepts in Kabbalah* is intended to foster the contemplation of spiritual terms. Once we are integrated with these terms, we can begin to see, with our inner vision, the unveiling of the spiritual structure that surrounds us, almost as if a mist has been lifted.

Again, this book is not aimed at the study of facts. Instead, it is a book for those who wish to awaken the deepest and subtlest sensations they can possess.

### Together Forever

On the surface, *Together Forever* is a children's story. But like all good children's stories, it transcends boundaries of age, culture, and upbringing.

In *Together Forever*, the author tells us that if we are patient and endure the trials we encounter along our life's path, we will become stronger, braver, and wiser. Instead of growing weaker, we will learn to create our own magic and our own wonders as only a magician can.

In this warm, tender tale, Michael Laitman shares with children and parents alike some of the gems and charms of the spiritual world. The wisdom of Kabbalah is filled with spellbinding stories. *Together Forever* is yet another gift from this ageless source of wisdom, whose lessons make our lives richer, easier, and far more fulfilling.


## TEXTBOOKS

### Shamati

Rav Michael Laitman's words on the book: Among all the texts and notes that were used by my teacher, Rabbi Baruch Shalom Halevi Ashlag (the Rabash), there was one special notebook he always carried. This notebook contained the transcripts of his conversations with his father, Rabbi Yehuda Leib Halevi Ashlag (Baal HaSulam), author of the *Sulam* (Ladder) commentary on *The Book of Zohar, The Study of the Ten Sefirot* (a commentary on the texts of the Kabbalist, Ari), and of many other works on Kabbalah.

Not feeling well on the Jewish New Year in September 1991, the Rabash summoned me to his bedside and handed me a notebook, whose cover contained only one word, *Shamati* (I Heard). As he handed the notebook, he said, "Take it and learn from it." The following morning, my teacher perished in my arms, leaving me and many of his other disciples without guidance in this world.

Committed to Rabash's legacy to disseminate the wisdom of Kabbalah, I published the notebook just as it was written, thus retaining the text's transforming powers. Among all the books of Kabbalah, *Shamati* is a unique and compelling creation.

# APPENDIX TWO
# ABOUT BNEI BARUCH

B nei Baruch is a group of Kabbalists in Israel, sharing the wisdom of Kabbalah with the entire world. Study materials in over 20 languages are based on authentic Kabbalah texts that were passed down from generation to generation.

## HISTORY AND ORIGIN

In 1991, following the passing of his teacher, Rabbi Baruch Shalom HaLevi Ashlag (The Rabash), Rav Michael Laitman, Professor of Ontology and the Theory of Knowledge, PhD in Philosophy and Kabbalah, and MSc in Medical Bio-Cybernetics, established a Kabbalah study group called "Bnei Baruch." He called it Bnei Baruch (Sons of Baruch) to commemorate the memory of his mentor, whose side he never left in the final twelve years of his life, from 1979 to 1991. Rav Laitman had been Ashlag's prime student and personal assistant, and is recognized as the successor to Rabash's teaching method.

The Rabash was the firstborn son and successor of Rabbi Yehuda Leib HaLevi Ashlag, the greatest Kabbalist of the 20th century. Rabbi Ashlag authored the most authoritative and comprehensive commentary on *The Book of Zohar*, titled *The Sulam Commentary (The Ladder Commentary)*. He was the first to reveal the complete method for spiritual ascent, and thus was known as Baal HaSulam (Owner of the Ladder).

Today, Bnei Baruch bases its entire study method on the path paved by these two great spiritual leaders.

## THE STUDY METHOD

The unique study method developed by Baal HaSulam and his son, the Rabash, is taught and applied on a daily basis by Bnei Baruch. This method relies on authentic Kabbalah sources such as *The Book of Zohar*, by Rabbi Shimon Bar-Yochai, *The Tree of Life*, by the Holy Ari, and *The Study of the Ten Sefirot*, by Baal HaSulam.

While the study relies on authentic Kabbalah sources, it is carried out in simple language and uses a scientific, contemporary approach. Developing this approach has made Bnei Baruch an internationally respected organization, both in Israel and in the world at large.

The unique combination of an academic study method and personal experiences broadens the students' perspective and awards them a new perception of the reality they live in. Those on the spiritual path are thus given the necessary tools to research themselves and their surrounding reality.

## THE MESSAGE

Bnei Baruch is a diverse movement of many thousands of students worldwide. Students can choose their own paths and the personal intensity of their studies, according to their unique conditions and abilities. The essence of the message disseminated by Bnei Baruch is universal: unity of the people, unity of nations and love of man.

For millennia, Kabbalists have been teaching that love of man should be the foundation of all human relations. This love prevailed in the days of Abraham, Moses, and the group of Kabbalists that they established. If we make room for these seasoned, yet contemporary values, we will discover that we possess the power to put differences aside and unite.

The wisdom of Kabbalah, hidden for millennia, has been waiting for the time when we would be sufficiently developed and ready to implement its message. Now, it is emerging as a solution that can unite diverse factions everywhere, better enabling us, as individuals and as a society, to meet today's challenges.

## ACTIVITIES

Bnei Baruch was established on the premise that "only by expansion of the wisdom of Kabbalah to the public can we be awarded complete redemption" (Baal HaSulam).

Therefore, Bnei Baruch offers a variety of ways for people to explore and discover the purpose of their lives, providing careful guidance for the beginners and the advanced students alike.

### Kabbalah Today

*Kabbalah Today* is a free monthly paper produced and disseminated by Bnei Baruch. It is apolitical, non-commercial, and written in a clear, contemporary style. Its purpose is to expose the vast body of knowledge hidden in the wisdom of Kabbalah at no cost and in a clear, engaging format and style for readers everywhere.

*Kabbalah Today* is distributed for free in every major U.S. city, as well as in Toronto, Canada, London, England, and Sydney, Australia. It is printed in English, Hebrew, and Russian, and is also available on the Internet, at *www.kabtoday.com.*

Additionally, a hard copy of the paper is sent to subscribers at delivery cost only.

### Internet Website

Bnei Baruch's homepage, *www.kabbalah.info,* presents the authentic wisdom of Kabbalah using essays, books, and original texts. It is the largest Kabbalah website on the net, and contains a unique, extensive library for readers to thoroughly explore the wisdom of Kabbalah. Additionally, there is a media archive, *www.kabbalahmedia.info,* containing more than 5,000 media items, downloadable books, and a vast reservoir of texts, video and audio files in many languages. All of this material is available for free download.

### Kabbalah Television

Bnei Baruch established a production company, ARI Films (*www.arifilms.tv*) specializing in production of educational TV programs throughout the world, and in many languages.

In Israel, Bnei Baruch broadcasts are aired live through cable and satellite on Channel 98 Sunday through Friday. All broadcasts on these channels are free of charge. The programs are adapted specifically for beginners, and do not require prior knowledge of the material. This convenient learning process is complemented by programs featuring Rav Laitman's meetings with publicly known figures in Israel and throughout the world.

Additionally, ARI Films produces educational series and documentaries on DVDs, as well as other visual teaching aids.

### Kabbalah Books

Rav Laitman writes his books in a clear, contemporary style based on the key concepts of Baal HaSulam. These books serve as a vital link between today's readers and the original texts. All of Rav Laitman's books are available for sale, as well as for free download. Rav Laitman has thus far written thirty books, translated into ten languages.

### Kabbalah Lessons

As Kabbalists have been doing for centuries, Rav Laitman gives a daily lesson at the Bnei Baruch center in Israel between 3:15-6:00 a.m. Israel time. The lessons are simultaneously translated into six languages: English, Russian, Spanish, German, Italian, and Turkish. In the near future, broadcasts will also be translated into French, Greek, Polish, and Portuguese. As with everything else, the live broadcast is provided gratis to thousands of students worldwide.

### Funding

Bnei Baruch is a non-profit organization for teaching and sharing the wisdom of Kabbalah. To maintain its independence and purity of intentions, Bnei Baruch is not supported, funded, or otherwise tied to any government or political organization.

Since the bulk of its activity is provided free of charge, the prime source of funding for the group's activities is donations, tithing—contributed by students on a voluntary basis—and Rav Laitman's books, which are sold at cost.

# HOW TO CONTACT BNEI BARUCH

1057 Steeles Avenue West, Suite 532
Toronto, ON, M2R 3X1
Canada

Bnei Baruch USA,
2009 85th street, #51,
Brooklyn, New York, 11214
USA

E-mail: info@kabbalah.info
Web site: www.kabbalah.info

Toll free in USA and Canada:
1-866-LAITMAN
Fax: 1-905 886 9697